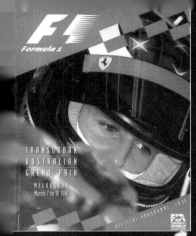

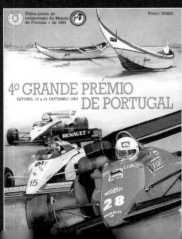

GRAND PRIX BATTLEGROUNDS

© Christopher Hilton, 2010

All rights reserved. No part of this publication may be reproduced, stored in a retrieval system or transmitted, in any form or by any means, electronic, mechanical, photocopying, recording or otherwise, without prior permission in writing from Haynes Publishing.

First published in June 2010

A catalogue record for this book is available from the British Library

ISBN 978 1 84425 694 5
Library of Congress control no. 2010921623

Published by Haynes Publishing, Sparkford, Yeovil, Somerset BA22 7JJ, UK
Tel: 01963 442030 Fax: 01963 440001
Int. tel: +44 1963 442030 Int. fax: +44 1963 440001
E-mail: sales@haynes.co.uk
Website: www.haynes.co.uk

Haynes North America Inc.
861 Lawrence Drive, Newbury Park,
California 91320, USA

Printed in USA

GRAND PRIX BATTLEGROUNDS

A comprehensive guide to all Formula 1 circuits since 1950

Christopher Hilton

Haynes Publishing

CONTENTS

Man, machine, confined space: Heikki Kovalainen, Monaco 2008. (Peter J. Fox)

CIRCUIT LOCATIONS

Note: The circuits are numbered 1 to 66 according to the alphabetical order of countries and circuits appearing in the following pages.

ARGENTINA
1   Buenos Aires

AUSTRALIA
2   Adelaide
3   Melbourne

AUSTRIA
4   A1-Ring (Formerly Österreichring)
5   Zeltweg

BAHRAIN
6   Sakhir

BELGIUM
7   Nivelles-Baulers
8   Spa-Francorchamps
9   Zolder

BRAZIL
10   Interlagos
11   Rio De Janeiro

CANADA
12   Mont-Tremblant
13   Montréal
14   Mosport Park

CHINA
15   Shanghai

FRANCE
16   Bugatti Au Mans
17   Clermont-Ferrand
18   Dijon-Prenois
19   Magny-Cours
20   Paul Ricard
21   Reims-Gueux
22   Rouen-Les-Essarts

GERMANY
23   Avus
24   Hockenheim
25   Nürburgring

GREAT BRITAIN
26   Aintree
27   Brands Hatch
28   Donington
29   Silverstone

HUNGARY
30   Hungaroring

ITALY
31   Imola
32   Monza
33   Pescara

JAPAN
34   Aida
35   Fuji
36   Suzuka

MALAYSIA
37   Sepang

MEXICO
38   Mexico City

MONACO
39   Monte Carlo

MOROCCO
40   Âin-Diab

NETHERLANDS
41   Zandvoort

PORTUGAL
42   Estoril
43   Monsanto Park
44   Porto

SINGAPORE
45   Singapore

SOUTH AFRICA
46   East London
47   Kyalami

SPAIN
48   Jarama
49   Jerez De La Frontera
50   Montjuïc Park
51   Montmeló (Barcelona)
52   Pedralbes
53   Valencia

SWEDEN
54   Anderstorp

SWITZERLAND
55   Bremgarten

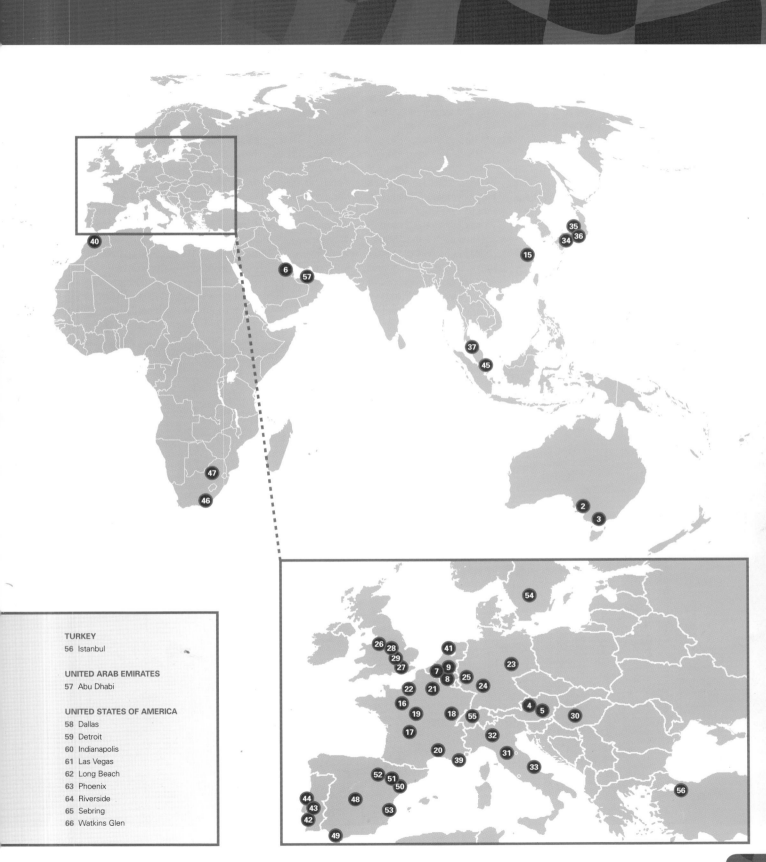

INTRODUCTION

On 13 May 1950, 21 cars set off under a plain wooden bridge with gently-angled stairways at either side and an advertisement for a motoring magazine draped over it. The bridge connected a field in England's green and pleasant land with rudimentary pits.

On 1 November 2009, 20 cars set off under a white-painted bridge shaped like a spaceship, the centre sculptured in glass so that anyone wandering across it could see the cars directly beneath. The bridge connected one part of a luxurious hotel to another. The parts resembled cliff-faces

Watkins Glen, USA, 1974, the day after.
(Courtesy Linda Carlson)

of curvature, immense in their sloping symmetry, and dwarfed the cars which scurried far beneath them. Unimaginable oil wealth had superimposed itself on the desert.

It's been a long, dangerous, wonderful – and sometimes bizarre – journey from there to here, from Silverstone and the very first World Championship Grand Prix to Abu Dhabi which, as I write these words, is the 820th and most recent – if you include 11 Indy 500s which were regarded as part of the Championship from 1950 to 1960, although nothing really to do with it. I prefer to exclude them, leaving 809 Grands Prix.

The journey travels five continents, 28 countries, and 64 other circuits. In many

important aspects it *is* the core history of the Championship because it all happened *here.*

The character of the circuits reflects the Championship's evolution from there to here. Between 1950 and 1970 the cars went annually to Spa in deepest Belgium, a circuit which measured 8.7 miles (14.0 km) on ordinary roads with stone walls, houses, farms, trees, and ditches decorating it. The drivers were offered minimal protection, and that made Spa a lethal place. In 1950, Giuseppe Farina set fastest lap in an Alfa Romeo, averaging 115.2mph (185.4kph), and when was the last time you did 115 on an ordinary road for more than two and a half hours? In 1970, Chris Amon set fastest lap in a

March, averaging 152.0mph (244.7kph), and I'm assuming you've never done 152 anywhere, never mind a Belgian country road. Now think about *averaging* it.

The old Spa was replaced by a truncated version in 1983, incorporating some of the original – especially the dangerous, wonderful and bizarre downhill-uphill Eau Rouge with its blind crest – and it accorded with the modern concept of safety at a place small enough to allow *complete* television coverage.

That's evolution in action, and it reached to Abu Dhabi, custom-built at fantastical expense (we shall see) on an island in the Middle East for many reasons, only some of them having to do with motor racing. What had begun under the bridge at Silverstone was now a desirable international status symbol luring in governments, especially ones with liquid gold – oil – beneath them.

During this evolution a problem arose. To satisfy safety and television demands the new circuits all became 'technical', which is another way of saying that they all looked the same. They were mostly designed by the same man, the German Hermann Tilke (only four circuit designers are recognised by the FIA), and they were open to the criticism that they were tedious in their repetition. Some drivers will be expressing pungent views on the new Hockenheim, for example – and Tilke will be defending it (see Hockenheim).

However, a former Grand Prix driver, Anthony Davidson, has said: 'He understands the demands of the modern cars. You see very wide circuits with a lot of space; he gives us run-off

Jacarepaguá, Brazil, 1983.
(Courtesy Brian Hart)

East London, South Africa, 2009.
(Courtesy Neville Fisher)

Indianapolis, USA, 2007.
(Courtesy David Corbishley)

areas and it's all well thought out. They are enjoyable to race on because they suit modern Formula 1 cars. At a track like Silverstone you do not get as much overtaking because it was designed for cars that were slower and did not depend on downforce for speed. But the circuits designed in recent years have a long straight and bigger braking zone.'

Tilke explains that 'one of the very first things we do is to sit down with Mr Ecclestone, who has a very good understanding and talent for design and has a feel for what is necessary for a venue to be a success.'

Tilke has his critics, but *MotorSport* says: 'Supporters of his work argue that he does a fine job considering he has to observe FIA safety guidelines and work to a brief and a budget laid down by local authorities or race organisers.'

You see the result on your television

screens, because he's designed every new circuit for ten years.

John Watson, who drove in 152 Grand Prix races between 1973 and 1985, points out that the contemporary car would be totally unsuitable for the circuits he drove because he'd been drifting through corners which, now, wouldn't really be corners at all: contemporary cars have so much grip that they could be taken flat out, as if they were a straight.

Sir Stirling Moss, who drove 66 Grand Prix races between 1951 and 1961, says: 'Yes, technology – but that's what's wrong with it!' Moss points out that the cars *he* drove were intended for road racing and built accordingly. If a team was quartered some distance from the circuit, mechanics drove the racing cars there along ordinary roads quite naturally. Moss's eyes sparkle with delight when he explains that the circuits might present you with cobblestones, tram lines, kerbstones, straw bales and manhole covers as well as Belgian *farmhouses*. 'You have a manhole cover and you don't

want to go over it so you steer round it,' he says impishly. 'Some circuits were lined with straw bales – useless! – and of course you missed them. You were a *racing driver*.'

I want to tell you that both Moss and Watson were, in their different ways, expressing delight at the circuits which allowed them to explore the ultimate of what a man can make a machine do. Watson became positively *adolescent* when he spoke about Watkins Glen in upstate New York. Two corners there 'gave you a real feeling of what driving a Grand Prix car, or what being a Grand Prix driver, was about.'

It is an experience denied to most human beings and very precious to the ones it is not denied to. This book is, I hope, many things, but above all a celebration of that. The modern drivers give you the same message, however different are the circuits which they inhabit. It is the same message because Moss, Watson and, say, Jenson Button must work within the specific

contexts of their eras as they explore the limits of circuit, car – and themselves. There is, therefore, a common thread running through the book and it unites the differences.

If you'll allow me poetic licence, the journey from there to here will take you to within sight of the Indian Ocean, you'll peer through the morning mists of The Glen, you'll taste poverty in Mexico City, you'll get soaked (almost annually) at Spa, you'll come to know Adelaide's streets intimately, you'll still be mystified at having a race round Monaco at all, you'll taste *bratwurst* in Austria, hotdogs in Phoenix and burgers at Silverstone, you'll be burnished in Buenos Aires, terrified at the old Nürburgring (and very relaxed about the new one), you'll run along Detroit's shoreline, turn-turn-turn in a Las Vegas car park, you'll have the Riviera sun full on your forehead and hear the tribal chanting as it echoes like rolling thunder round the royal parkland which cloaks Monza…

Ah, Monza.

Perhaps is better to go there any mid-week day when no cars are going round. Admission is five Euros and you're free to wander, explore, *feel*. Monza becomes

Monaco, 2009. (Author)

Monza, Italy, 1983. (Courtesy Brian Hart)

Bremgarten, Switzerland, 1952.
(Courtesy Thomas Horat)

Bremgarten, Switzerland, 2009. (Author)

personal to you then, a living museum of your memory and imagination.

Stand motionless and you can hear the silence.

A Grand Prix circuit, especially one with lineage direct to the 1920s, is not an inanimate object even on those days when, physically, there is nothing to animate it. You *feel* yourself in the presence of something enormous that lives by fractions of a second and yet remains timeless.

You can see the evolution, too. Come with me. We're past the main gigantic pits complex and paddock, past some modern offices and shops, and we're walking down a narrow road under – not that it matters – a low stone bridge. We're in woodland with a pathway to the left. The place we reach is a small clearing shaded by the canopy of the trees. A metal fence cuts across it, screening a grandstand of tubular metal and constructed so that you can see underneath it to what looks like a light-coloured concrete wall just beyond. You have to get closer to see that the wall is not a wall but banking. It rears at you, tall, steep, angular, somehow almost angry. Rusted Armco runs along its top lip. Here, once upon a time, a soft-spoken American called Phil Hill took his Ferrari round averaging 138mph/223kph, the sections of banking hammering at him and the surface capable of tearing his tyres to shreds. As you stand motionless here, your imagination is being forced to work very hard.

The grandstand of tubular steel stands at a junction. It gives a panoramic view past the banking to the familiar geography of today: the first chicane that the modern driver has to navigate among a shoal of other cars as he reaches it from the grid in the Italian Grand Prix.

In your direct line of vision you have the 1950s and the 2000s, all at the same moment and all in the same place. The banked circuit, of such terrible memory, runs from the new circuit like an umbilical cord. They are no longer physically connected, of course, but that doesn't matter.

You *can* hear the silence from both.

All sports divide into those with variable playing terrains and those without. The Monza circuit has its own unique features, and makes its own unique demands, but any football pitch around the town of Monza, or anywhere else on earth, doesn't. A pitch is a pitch. Many good men and true have written books about the football stadiums but none can write one about the pitches.

However, someone once put it to Patrick Tambay, a vastly experienced driver, that footballers spoke in awe of *stadiums*. Was it the same sort of thing for the driver? 'When you were on your own at Hockenheim on those long straights for almost one and a half minutes, or in Monaco just a few feet from the spectators – so close they are almost inside the cockpit – the atmosphere and the pressures are completely different. You have to adapt to circuits depending on the conditions of the day and the technical conditions. You have to be constantly adapting to circumstances and it depends on your technique. Some drivers may be more at home at Monaco than Spa or Zeltweg (the panoramic Austrian circuit). We know

Nürburgring, Germany, 2008.
(Courtesy Filipp Gorelik)

the *environments* of the circuit by heart and the experienced driver will find the engine's peak performance in a couple of laps.'

The variable terrain gives unending fascination to golf tournaments, some

Avus, Berlin, 2009. (Courtesy Birgit Kubisch)

OPPOSITE TOP: Brands Hatch, Britain, 1972.
(Courtesy David Corbishley)

OPPOSITE BOTTOM: Dallas, USA, 1984.
(Courtesy David Corbishley)

RIGHT: The Österreichring, Austria, 1973.
(Courtesy Gareth Rees)

horse races, ski racing, the tennis Grand Slam, cricket (the pitches) and all forms of motor sport, although, and it's a reasonable argument, none except motor sport have had the extremes of – to stay with Tambay – Hockenheim and Monaco, never mind the Las Vegas car park and wild, wild Watkins Glen.

Football, rugby, athletics, gymnastics, boxing, and swimming have a reverse attraction. Because their terrain is constant, direct comparisons can be made. But these comparisons are difficult in motor sport because technology constantly renders yesterday a long time ago, just as the absence of technology makes film of a football match in the 1930s familiar and, in its essentials, close.

The circuits have had to reflect the technology or dictate it – at one point, 'skirts' down the sides of the cars gave so much downforce that they were making the circuits obsolete, and since changing circuits is a bigger undertaking than changing cars, the skirts went.

This book is a celebration of 66 different approaches to the same thing: creating a narrow strip of track on which brave men and brilliant engineers can make fast cars go as fast as possible within the confines each of the 66 circuits imposes.

In this book the circuits are arranged alphabetically under their countries, which are also arranged alphabetically, so we reach Argentina first and the United States last.

Telephone and fax numbers, addresses, and websites are given only for those circuits in current use.

Each circuit carries a date for its construction, although this is problematical for a place like Monaco, which, using normal roads, isn't by definition really constructed at all. For uniformity, I have left it as Constructed throughout, but in places like Monaco read First Used.

Each circuit is self-contained, so all the information you need is there. You can dip into the book wherever you like, selecting an individual circuit or country, or read it from beginning to end.

Each circuit has five sections:

Text covering its history.

COCKPIT VIEW – a driver's impression.
EYEWITNESS – someone (a non-official) giving their personalised impression. These are drawn from a wide variety of sources, mainly first person, and many are frankly (and delightfully) quirky. The witnesses were invited to say whatever they wanted, and they did.
MEMORIES AND MILESTONES – a self-contained paragraph on every Grand Prix at the circuit, giving pole, major incidents, winner, winning margin, and who he beat. Cumulatively these paragraphs constitute a complete history of the World Championship since its inception. The first reference to a driver always includes his first name no matter how many other times he appears in the book. (Note: Schumacher is always Michael Schumacher; whenever it's his brother Ralf, that is signified.) The car he was driving is always given, even if he appears in successive paragraphs – years – and the car is the same. It's just easier that way on the eye, the brain and the memory.

The Fastest Lap is given at the end of each paragraph with, in brackets, whether and by how much it is faster or slower than the year before. This is to capture the authentic pace of Grand Prix racing, invariably increasing and increasing everywhere all the time.

Major changes to a track are given in italic paragraphs when the changes took place. Because the Fastest Laps are intended to be exact year-on-year comparisons, when a track does change the Fastest Laps begin afresh from the change. Wet races are not included in the comparisons.

BELOW: Anderstorp, Sweden, 1976.
(Courtesy Scandinavian Raceway Nostalgia.)

Spa, Belgium, 2009.
(Courtesy Tom Bellingham)

FACTS OF THE MATTER – quick-reference, set-out statistics giving the race winners, each change in circuit length, and the progressive pole and fastest laps reflecting the changes. Where the changes in circuit length are minimal, the poles and fastest laps don't change to reflect that – for example, at Adelaide: 2.348m/3.778km in 1985; 2.348/3.779km in 1986; 2.349m/3.780km from 1987 to 1995. Note that the abbreviation 'm' in this section stands for miles, of course, not metres.

All statistics are to the end of the 2009 season.

Note: the statistics which are given to one decimal point – fastest laps and pole positions – have been rounded from three decimal points, something else which is easier on the eye and the brain.

I owe a great debt to the statistician David Hayhoe, who provided a wealth of statistics – especially all the fastest laps –

especially for this book and allowed me to use his published work too. I leant heavily on his *Grand Prix Data Book* (with David Holland), published by Haynes, and have followed it in recording the revisions to circuits.

Thanks also, in no particular order, to: Sir Stirling Moss, John Surtees, John Watson, Johnny Herbert, Derek Warwick, Johnny Herbert, Brian Hart, Mónika Déri, Erika Schneider; Roger McCleery and Neville Fisher in South Africa; Juan Carlos Ferrigno, Ann Bradshaw, Linda and Gary Carlson, David Fern (who was Donington's Press Officer), David Corbishley, Martyn Pass of Audi UK, Steven Tee of LAT Photographic and his wife Cynthia, Greg Wesson; Matthias Persson, Thyrone 'Ticko' Persson and Anette Claesson; Gareth Rees, Roger Chapman, Ted Tofield, Tom Bellingham and Katy Peach, Tony Bagnall, Rob Semmeling, Charles Reisen, Theo Bertschi, Monica Meroni, E.L. Gordon, Bernard Beaumesnil, Patrice Besqueut (for an interview and sending his *Charade: 'Le plus beau circuit du monde'*), Gabriella Strauss (for patrolling

German and Austrian websites), Birgit Kubisch (for gallant service in Berlin), Andy Shaw and Vanessa Harwood, Amandio de Franca of the *New Mexico* restaurant, Sawbridgeworth (for instant translation – across the bar!), Inge Donnell (for translation), Alfred Brumsch, Stefan Kienzl, Paul Kooyman, Kris Heber, Michel Bonte, Martin Pfunder, and Rob Semmeling.

I have been touched by how many people have sent their precious photographs, and thanks to Damian Smith, Editor of *Motor Sport*, for carrying a letter that opened the way. I am grateful to the following for their photographs: Linda Carlson, Brian Hart, Neville Fisher, David Corbishley, Thomas Horat, Filipp Gorelik, Birgit Kubisch, Gareth Rees, Scandinavian Raceway Nostalgia, Tom Bellingham, Vodafone, LAT Photographic, Juan Carlos Ferrigno, Tony Watson, Peugeot, ICN U.K. Bureau, Mark Young, Fred Lewis Photos, Martin Hadwen's National Motor Racing Archive, Paul Kooyman, Camel, Jeroen Saeijs, Chris Puddy, Julian Nowell, Arthur Willmer, Les Willox, Erika Schneider, Autodromo Nationale Monza,

Hockenheim-Ring GmbH, Marlboro, Greg Wesson, Bill Wagenblatt, Braun, Sebastien Carter, Dan Diaz, David Yeang, Andrew Clegg, Norman Hickel and the Julian Nowell Archive.

For permission to quote I am grateful to: Peter Higham, Publishing Director, *Autosport*; Damien Smith of *MotorSport*; Steve Small, Publisher, *Autocourse*; Tony Bagnall and Paul Lawrence of *tfm* for *The Unfulfilled Dream;* Roger Hart and David Bull Publishing for *Postcards From Detroit*; Matt Bishop, Group Head of Communications and Public Relations, McLaren Marketing; and Nicola Armstrong, Brawn GP. I offer special thanks to Keith Collantine of www. f1fanatic.co.uk, who very kindly set up a mechanism so that his readers could contact me. They did, from far and wide. You'll see.

Equally, I offer my thanks to a wide variety of publications and books I have consulted: *Motoring News, Autocar, MotorSport, The Los Angeles Times, The Times* (London), *Le Soir* (Brussels), *Corriera della Serra* (Milan), the *Marlboro Grand Prix Guide 1950–2004*, The *Guinness Guide to International Motor Racing* by Peter Higham, The *Grand Prix Who's Why* by Steve Small, and *The Motor Yearbook* 1954 and 1955.

Melbourne, Australia, 2008. (Vodafone/LAT)

Abu Dhabi, United Arab Emirates, 2009. (Vodafone/ LAT)

ARGENTINA
BUENOS AIRES

Location: Southern outskirts of Buenos Aires.
Constructed: 1952.
World Championship Grands Prix: 20.

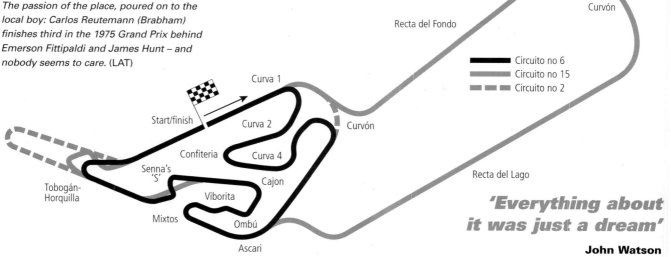

The passion of the place, poured on to the local boy: Carlos Reutemann (Brabham) finishes third in the 1975 Grand Prix behind Emerson Fittipaldi and James Hunt – and nobody seems to care. (LAT)

Curvón

Recta del Fondo

Curva 1

—— Circuito no 6
—— Circuito no 15
- - - Circuito no 2

Start/finish

Curva 2

Confiteria   Curva 4

Curvón

Senna's 'S'

Tobogán-Horquilla

Cajon

Viborita

Recta del Lago

Mixtos

Ombú

'Everything about it was just a dream'

Ascari

John Watson

The Argentine Grand Prix was the plaything of a dictator, a slaughterhouse, and an inferno, which evolved into a motor race like (more or less) others.

The dictator, Juan Peron, was the country's President (yes, *that* song was about his wife Evita), who decreed that a circuit be built on swampland near Buenos Aires, the first proper one in South America. The circuit could accommodate 12 different layouts, each numbered. Initially they raced on No 2.

The races between 1953 and 1960 remain period pieces illustrating how rough and ready Grand Prix racing was. The races were literally lethal, but this in no way prevented their continuation. Motor racing was dangerous and life was dangerous too.

Peron had gone into exile in 1955 but the country found stability elusive and the currency collapsed. A measure of stability was introduced by the military government in the mid-1960s but the Grand Prix did not return until 1972, using circuit No 9 – essentially the same as before except for an alteration to Toboggan hairpin.

From 1974 the race settled at Circuit No15 for seven years, establishing itself as the starting point for each new season, although 1976 fell victim to those familiar maladies, politics and

lack of finance. They almost claimed the 1977 race too.

Politics and finance *did* claim it after 1982 and the invasion of the Falkland Islands.[1] With Carlos Reutemann – an enigmatic Argentinean who'd been in Formula 1 since 1972 – poised to retire, the Grand Prix moved into limbo. Reutemann had taken pole at the circuit in his first Grand Prix, for Brabham in 1972, and his presence always attracted thousands.

A private consortium bought the circuit in 1991 and produced layout

Part of the circuit was a killing ground, part a stately run in the country with no passion evident at all. Giuseppe Farina wrestles the Ferrari in 1955 while Karl Kling tried, and will fail, to keep the Mercedes with him. (LAT)

No 6 – the long circuit had had a power station built on it. Instead, a tighter, more technical track emerged for the 1995 Grand Prix.

The race lasted until 1998, when financial difficulties consumed it again.

COCKPIT VIEW

John Watson, who drove in the race seven times between 1974 and 1981:
'The biggest surprise about Buenos Aires was getting off the aeroplane and finding an interlocking between venue and racetrack. It was a combination of the venue – the city – and a proper racetrack. It's a great shame the original circuit is no longer available because of housing development.

'Before I first went, I had only *heard*

The Esses known as Tobogan and a Williams doing demonstration laps, 2007. Tony Watson explains: 'The Tobogan is fast downhill Esses which have always been part of the circuit. When the Formula 1 cars came back I remember the FIA thought they needed slowing down there so the Senna Esse was created.' On this day, however, the Williams was using Tobogan, bypassing the Senna Esse. (Courtesy Tony Watson)

about Argentina, I had never realised what a fantastic country it was. It's very passionate, being Latin, although not passionate Latin in the sense that Brazil is, because Argentina is predominantly made up of Spanish, Italian, British, and German stock. There's not a lot of the indigenous South Americans integrated into the Argentinean population, certainly in Buenos Aires.

'You got to the hotel, you went out to the pool and you were gobsmacked at these unbelievable-looking females. The city reminded me of somewhere like Madrid, big, grand boulevards, magnificent buildings – although pockmarked form various revolutions – and fantastic restaurants.

'Everything about it was just a dream.

'Then you went to this wonderful racetrack, dominated ultimately by the two main straights and the 180° corner, *Curvón*. The challenge was to try and take it flat out: go into it flat, flat all the way round, come out flat. It was an exceptionally long corner and getting the

'This is a painting I made about MY RACE, the first international I ever saw. I was ten years old and it made me fall in love with motor racing forever. Derek Bell won driving the great Porsche 917.' Juan Carlos Ferrigno on 10 January 1971, the day Bell and Jo Siffert beat Pedro Rodriguez and Jackie Oliver (in another 917).

entry right was difficult because you had to put your balls in your mouth to do it.

'The exit was much longer than the entrance and you were getting a lot of *slip*, scrubbing speed off. It was more psychological whether it was flat out or not. You'd get back and say, *Cor, I went flat through there.*

'Turns 1 and 2, with the ground effect car, became almost flat out and horrendously quick, a massive series of corners. Just to bring things into the contemporary, we moan about modern tracks, but they are dictated to by the technological level that Formula 1 is attaining.

'In a lot of areas, circuits like this one at Buenos Aires wouldn't reflect the cars in the same way that they did with our cars. Our cars looked fantastic on it because the slip angle was so great, the car was sliding and you could see the drivers working on the wheel. A modern car would go straight through.'

EYEWITNESS

Juan Carlos Ferrigno, native of Buenos Aires and leading motor sport artist:

'I always called the circuit *El Autódromo*, because when I was a child it was unthinkable to ever get to know any other circuit, so for me only this one existed. Motor racing has always been popular in Argentina, second behind football, and it was always like this.

'I've got fantastic memories of

moments I lived in the circuit since my first international race (the 1971 Buenos Aires 1,000km) when I fell in love with motor racing forever. I was just ten years old. A year later I went to my first Grand Prix and I met Ronnie Peterson, my favourite driver since that day. I remember the beautiful sound of the Ferrari engine and, even better, the Matra V12.

'The circuit always seemed full of people.

'When I was about 15 I began to go to as many races as possible, but the problem was that I didn't have the money to pay for the bus to the circuit *and* an entry ticket. A group of us used to go very early in the morning, or even at night, to be there before anybody else, including the police, arrived. All around the exterior fences were holes in places we knew…

'Once we'd got in we had to wait for *hours* until other people did arrive and we could sit in the grandstand pretending we'd paid. Sounds very easy now, but I tell you there were big dogs patrolling the fence.

'In the 1970s the Grand Prix was the first of the season. In January or February – summer in Argentina – the heat was terrible. The gates were opened at 8:00 in the morning but the race started around 4:00 in the afternoon. When the gates opened people *ran* to get seats as near the top of the grandstand as possible. In 30 minutes the grandstand was almost full with more than seven hours to the race! Crazy…

'So many hours in the sun was hard, but normally everybody wore hats, took cold drinks, sunbathing cream, some even umbrellas.

'Carlos Reutemann came to test his Lotus before the 1979 season. The circuit was guarded by police but we knew the holes better than they did and slipped in again. We were in the pit lane and got on very well with the Lotus mechanics, who were laughing about our "science" of the holes. Reutemann was going out but stalled that marvellous black Lotus in front of us. Lole [Carlos] moved his arm, asking for someone to push the car, so we ran-pushed until the Cosworth came alive again. I remember the exhausts burning my legs and the Lotus guys applauding us because they hadn't had to run the length of the pit lane to do the push. We couldn't believe we'd pushed Reutemann's car – we didn't want to wash our hands!

'Little by little we all became older, started going out with girls, earned money and we could go to the circuit later in the morning and buy a ticket.

'I'll never forget the great fighting in 1973 between Stewart and Fittipaldi … the day when all the circuit suddenly went *dumb* after Reutemann's retirement in the final laps in 1974, after having been cheering all the race in the lead … the big Gilles Villeneuve's shunt in 1980, and the ovation when we saw he was unhurt, walking and waving to the crowd, who loved him.

'Many years later (1998), when I was living in Spain, I was invited by the Formula 1 Paddock Club to be in *El Autódromo* to exhibit my work and spend the weekend painting. Arriving there by car with one of my old racing friends, we were honoured with a red carpet. A man with white gloves opened my door and said "Good morning, sir!" Later we both laughed that times had changed so much and those little boys who'd slipped through the holes were now welcomed in luxury…

'I think all enthusiasts have a story to tell. This is mine.'

MEMORIES AND MILESTONES

1953 Alberto Ascari (Ferrari) took pole. Mike Hawthorn's first race for Ferrari and he'd never forget the heat and the massive crowd, who'd been subjected to day after day of publicity for the race from loudspeakers all over Buenos Aires. The crowd was uncontrollable inside the circuit and Hawthorn compared it to a tidal wave.[2] From the grid the drivers were confronted by an overspill of people eight or ten deep. There was trouble in the grandstands, Hawthorn noted, with ticket holders being driven out by the crowd, which stuck lighted cigarettes into them. Ascari led but a Cooper went into the crowd, injuring several people, and a small boy sprinted in front of Giuseppe Farina's Ferrari which slewed into the crowd, killing 15. Ascari finished a lap ahead of Luigi Villoresi in another Ferrari. Fastest lap: Ascari 80.7mph/129.9kph.

1954 The municipal authorities decided the race would be run anticlockwise. Juan Manuel Fangio (Maserati) – a great Argentinean hero – felt 'it made the whole thing much more dangerous because when we were going flat out we practically had to go under the roof of the

pits in order to take the following bend to the right.'[3] Giuseppe Farina (Ferrari) took pole but, in a downpour, Fangio beat him by 1 minute 19 seconds. Fastest lap: F. González 80.9mph (+0.2)/130.2kph (+0.3).

1955 The race remains perplexing because the temperature reached 100°F in the shade and 123°F on the track (36°C and 51°C). That made it the hottest championship race, although Dallas in 1984 and Bahrain in 2005 were reportedly as hot. It was scheduled for 96 laps – three hours. Froilan González (Ferrari) took pole and the race melted into a surreal sequence of drivers handing over to team-mates. The sequence of car No 12: González to Farina to Maurice Trintignant to González who then spun off, regained the track, pitted, and gave the car back to Farina, who brought it home 1 minute 30 seconds after the winner, Fangio (Mercedes). Fangio remembered it was so hot he thought his car had caught fire. Fastest lap: Fangio 80.8mph (-0.1)/130.0kph (-0.2).

1956 Fangio (Ferrari), pole, shared a drive with Luigi Musso and they beat Jean Behra (Maserati) by 24.4 seconds, but Maserati protested that Fangio had been push-started after a spin. Nobody in Argentina was going to take the race off Fangio, and nobody did. Fastest lap: Fangio 83.1mph (+2.3)/133.7kph (+3.7).

1957 Stirling Moss (Maserati), pole, remembered[4] 'the start was chaotic, as it so often is, and before the parade the crowd invaded the circuit intent on mobbing their idol, Fangio' – who beat Behra (they were both in Maseratis) by 18.3 seconds. Fastest lap: Moss 83.6mph (+0.5)/134.5kph (+0.8).

The passion did endure down the years although John Watson insists not as much as Brazil. Make your own mind up.
(ICN U.K. Bureau)

1958 Fangio (Maserati) took pole but the race had four leaders, Moss winning in a Cooper-Climax, the first rear-engined car to do this in the Championship. He beat Luigi Musso (Ferrari) by 2.7 seconds. Fastest lap: Fangio 86.0mph (+2.4)/138.3kph (+3.8).

The race wasn't held in 1959.

1960 Moss (Cooper) took pole. Jack Brabham would remember seeing what Hawthorn had seen, the crowd uncontrollable and spilling on to the circuit, especially one photographer at the first corner who sprang out on the opening lap to get a picture of Brabham coming at him. Brabham braked to miss him (the photographer didn't move) and passed so close he thought he may even have brushed the photographer's trousers.[5] Bruce McLaren (Cooper) beat Cliff Allison (Ferrari) by 26.3 seconds. Fastest lap: Moss (Cooper) 88.5mph (+2.5)/142.4kph (+4.1).

Speed increase 1953–60: 7.8mph/12.5kph.

Like 1971, the No 9 circuit would be used for 1972 but only after substantial changes, not least Armco, wide run-off areas, and a chicane by the new garage complex and pits. A toilet block and air-conditioned restaurant were considered the height of modernity. Autocourse described how the circuit was too 'Mickey Mouse' for the Grand Prix cars of the day. The only real overtaking place was at the end of the pit straight. The driver in front could block you everywhere else.

1972 A new generation of drivers found, in their turn, the heat overpowering. Carlos Reutemann (Brabham) – another Argentinean hero – took pole, but Jackie Stewart (Tyrrell) beat Denny Hulme (McLaren) by 25.9 seconds. Fastest lap: Stewart 101.6mph/163.5kph.

1973 Emerson Fittipaldi (Lotus) was having his first race after his 1972 championship. There were[6] 'at least 10,000 of my Brazilian countrymen in Buenos Aires for the race and, anyway, the whole subcontinent wanted a South American victory in a field which included Europe's finest drivers. I felt all these pressures on me.' Clay Regazzoni (BRM) took pole, but Fittipaldi beat François Cevert (Tyrrell) by 4.6 seconds. Fastest lap: Fittipaldi 105.1mph/169.1kph.

Speed increase 1972–73: 3.5mph/5.6kph.

The race moved to No 15, the long circuit and new to Grands Prix. This gave more overtaking opportunities. Autocourse described it in detail. 'From what had been the very fast long right-handed first turn the circuit bent back left making a thrilling fourth-gear esses. Following 10 or 12 seconds' worth of straight, another very long, very fast bend … brought the lap back along another straight and to a right-left-right esses on to the former circuit. This was substantially the last opportunity

Luca Badoer rolled his Forti Ford after 24 laps of the 1996 race, and emerged unscathed. (ICN U.K. Bureau)

of overtaking before the very tight stop-and-go of the infield section which was unaltered from last year. Generally smooth, level and wide, having bumps only in a few slower places and one fairly stimulating heave in the first-turn esses, the … circuit was thought to be quite safe and not especially difficult.'

1974 Ronnie Peterson (Lotus) took pole, but Reutemann (Brabham) led from laps 3 to 51 until his airbox worked loose, then a plug lead came loose, then he ran out of fuel. Hulme (McLaren) went by to beat Niki Lauda (Ferrari) by 9.2 seconds. Fastest lap: Regazzoni (Ferrari) 119.1mph/191.7kph.

1975 Jean-Pierre Jarier (Shadow) took pole but, doing a practice start, the car failed. The race had three leaders, Reutemann (Brabham), James Hunt (Hesketh), and Fittipaldi (McLaren), who beat Hunt by 5.9 seconds. Fastest lap: Hunt 120.4mph (+1.3)/193.7kph (+2.0).

The 1976 race was cancelled for financial and political reasons.

1977 Hunt (McLaren) took pole. The start was moved to 4:00 to miss the hottest part of the day, but even so Carlos Pace (a Brazilian in a Brabham) almost passed out. On lap 48 of the 54 Jody Scheckter (Wolf) went past him to win it by 43.2 seconds. Fastest lap: Hunt 120.2mph (-0.2)/193.5kph (-0.2).

1978 Mario Andretti (Lotus) led every lap from pole and beat Lauda (Brabham) by 13.2 seconds. Fastest lap: Gilles Villeneuve (Ferrari) 121.6mph (+1.4)/195.7kph (+2.2).

1979 The accent was heavily French. Jacques Laffite (Ligier) taking pole, team-mate Patrick Depailler leading, then Laffite beating Reutemann (Lotus) by 14.9 seconds. Fastest lap: Laffite 124.9mph (+3.3)/201.0kph (+5.3).

1980 Alain Prost (McLaren) made his Grand Prix debut. 'It was high summer in the southern hemisphere and the cockpit temperatures were unbearable. Worse still, you could actually see the asphalt starting to melt. The circuit had been patched and re-patched – all to no avail. After practice, the foundation blocks of the circuit were showing through, particularly in the corners, where wear-and-tear was at its most pronounced. I vividly recall a painful scene during the pre-race briefing. Fangio – the great Juan Manuel Fangio, for me a living legend – suggested, although perhaps not in so many words, that we make a special effort to keep our speed down in the early laps.'[7] Alan Jones (Williams), pole, beat Nelson Piquet (Brabham) by 24.6 seconds, and 15 cars retired. Fastest lap: Jones 120.9mph (-4.0)/194.5kph (-6.5).

1981 Piquet (Brabham, and *Brazilian*) took pole and won, but his team-mate Hector Rebaque (a *Mexican*) actually overtook Reutemann (an *Argentine*, of course) for second place before an engine problem halted him. Piquet beat Reutemann by 26.6 seconds. Fastest lap: Piquet 126.8mph (+5.9)/204.1kph (+9.6).

Speed increase 1974–81: 7.7mph/12.4kph.

The race returned, but to circuit No 6, bumpy, slow and requiring high downforce. It was mostly second and third gear corners – four of the former, five of the latter. David Coulthard (Williams) said 'You don't get to a point where you are hard on the power or hard on the brakes, you sort of have a little bit of power and then another corner, a little bit of brake – there are so many slow corners it is quite amazing.' It was a common sentiment: the circuit could have been anywhere and that downbeat expression 'technical' was used about it. The week of the race, by a great irony, John Hughenholtz died and many were moved to compare this circuit with some of his masterpieces, like Suzuka, Hockenheim and Spa.

1995 Coulthard took pole. Williams team-mate Damon Hill beat Jean Alesi (Ferrari) by 6.4 seconds. Fastest

FACTS OF THE MATTER

Circuit No2: 2.431m/3.912km

Year	Winner
1953	A. Ascari (Ferrari)
1954	J.M. Fangio (Maserati)
1955	J.M. Fangio (Mercedes)
1956	L. Musso/J.M. Fangio (Ferrari)
1957	J.M. Fangio (Maserati)
1958	S. Moss (Cooper)
1960	B. McLaren (Cooper)
Fastest pole	S. Moss (Cooper) 1960 (90.3mph/145.3kph)
Fastest lap	S. Moss 1960 (88.5mph/142.4kph)

Circuit No9: 2.078m/3.345km

1972	J. Stewart (Tyrrell)
1973	E. Fittipaldi (Lotus)
Fastest pole	C. Regazzoni (BRM) 1973 (106.1mph/170.7kph)
Fastest lap	E. Fittipaldi (Lotus) 1973 (105.1mph/169.1kph)

Circuit No15: 3.708m/5.968km

1974	D. Hulme (McLaren)
1975	E. Fittipaldi (McLaren)
1977	J. Scheckter (Wolf)
1978	M. Andretti (Lotus)
1979	J. Laffite (Ligier)
1980	A. Jones (Williams)
1981	N. Piquet (Brabham)
Fastest pole	N. Piquet 1981 (130.0mph/209.3kph)
Fastest lap	N. Piquet 1981 (126.8mph/204.1kph)

Circuit No6: 2.646m/4.259km

1995	D. Hill (Williams)
1996	D. Hill (Williams)
1997	J. Villeneuve (Williams)
1998	M. Schumacher (Ferrari)
Fastest pole	J. Villeneuve (Williams) 1997 (112.8mph/181.5kph)
Fastest lap	G. Berger (Ferrari) 1997 (108.3mph/174.3kph)

1 The straight in 1995. Tony Watson, who provided the photograph, says: 'The grandstands are the same ones which adorned the circuit when it was officially opened on 9 March 1952. They're all concrete and still there nowadays.'

2 The way the circuit was in 1964. *(Courtesy Tony Watson).*

3 A serious matter in Argentina: President Carlos Menem presents Damon Hill with the trophy for pole position, 1996. *(ICN U.K. Bureau)*

lap: Michael Schumacher (Benetton) 105.2mph/169.4kph.

1996 Hill (Williams) took pole. He resisted pressure from Schumacher (Ferrari) and both Benettons to beat team-mate Jacques Villeneuve by 12.1 seconds. Fastest lap: Jean Alesi (Benetton) 106.6mph (+1.4)/171.5kph (+2.1).

1997 The 600th Championship race. Villeneuve (Williams) took pole and found himself under sustained pressure from Eddie Irvine (Ferrari) but resisted it and

won by 0.9 of a second. Fastest lap: Gerhard Berger (Benetton) 108.3mph (+1.7)/174.3kph (+2.8).

1998 Coulthard (McLaren) took pole. It did not prevent Schumacher (Ferrari) dealing roughly with him – brushing him aside – and then going past Mika Häkkinen in the other McLaren, exploiting the fact that he – Schumacher – was on a two-stop strategy, Häkkinen only one. Schumacher needed to gain time and did. He beat Häkkinen by 22.8 seconds.

Fastest lap: Alexander Wurz (Benetton) 108.0mph (-0.3)/173.9kph (-0.4).

Speed increase 1995–98: 2.8mph/4.5kph.

Footnotes
[1]Argentina had long claimed the Falkland Islands from the British and invaded in 1982, overwhelming the small British garrison. Britain responded with a full-scale task force, which reclaimed the Islands. There was an undercurrent, because traditionally the Argentines and Britain had enjoyed such good relations that Argentina was regarded as an honorary member of the British Empire. [2]*Challenge Me the Race*, Hawthorn. [3]*My Racing Life*, Fangio. [4]*A Turn at the Wheel*, Moss. [5]*When the Flag Drops*, Brabham. [6]*My Greatest Race*, edited by Adrian Ball. [7]*Life in the Fast Lane*, Prost.

AUSTRALIA
ADELAIDE

Location: Adelaide city centre.
Constructed: 1985.
World Championship Grands Prix: 11.

'You don't have to fight the car and the corners in the same way as Monaco'

Mika Häkkinen

Wakefield Corner

Flinders Street

Hutt Street

East Terrace

Wakefield Road

Senna Chicane

Rundle Road/ Jones Straight

Start/finish

Malthouse Corner

Foster's Corner/ Adelaide Hairpin

Dequetteville Terrace/ Brabham Straight

No drought in Australia in 1989, when Ayrton Senna and Alain Prost, McLaren team-mates, set off on the single lap before the race was stopped. (LAT)

Dequetteville Hairpin

Grand Prix racing discovered Australia 215 years after Captain Cook and proceeded to make up for lost time by falling in love with it (or as near as Formula 1 is capable of doing such a thing). Alain Prost even spoke of moving to live there, and years later engine manufacturer Brian Hart, on a flying visit, was having a superb lunch overlooking the ocean, washed down by fine local wine. His companion said 'and to think the first settlers had to be forced to come here…'

Mika Häkkinen said (a year before he had a terrible accident in qualifying): 'I like Australia and I like Adelaide. There is an end-of-year party atmosphere about the place.' That summed it up neatly and nicely.

The idea of the race was a familiar one, to promote a city which had the reputation of being sleepy and promoting the area around it. Hugh Johnson's *World Wine Atlas*[1] says: 'The southern suburbs of Adelaide shade on to the northern limits of McLaren Vale … now a wine region with a proud sense of its own identity.'

It was all well worth promoting.

Because the circuit was to run though parklands there were environmental concerns, although these were overcome. The track included part of Victoria Park racecourse (the pit straight was inside it) and amazingly felt like a permanent circuit, although the pits and grandstands were erected each year and taken down again after the race.

In the build-up to the first race the *Beatrice FISA Official Media Guide* said rather charmingly: 'A new country and circuit, on the World Championship schedule for the first time. Financed by the South Australian Government, the circuit will be constructed within the centre of the city. The streets are said to be wide and the pits area will be in a park giving extra space. The Australians are very experienced at running race meetings at permanent circuits and the preparations and promotion of the race have been first class.

'Hotels: rather limited in Adelaide and at the time of going to press are full. Arrangements being made for lodging in private homes.

'Clothes: it should be pleasantly hot at this time of year without being oppressive.'

Actually, Adelaide fell in love with the Grand Prix, too, and when they lost it to Melbourne some citizens were moved to say some very salty things about Mr Bernie Ecclestone, the man who decides where the races go.

The Adelaide race was always the last of the season, which meant the Championship might well be decided before it, and usually was, except twice. That those two (1986 and 1994) were classics of suspense and controversy, accompanied by some old-fashioned biffing and bashing, could be regarded as consolation, but Adelaide didn't need that. The love affair was already too strong.

COCKPIT VIEW

Mika Häkkinen, who drove there from 1991 to 1994 and was seriously injured practising in 1995:

'Adelaide bears no relation to Monaco. The difference is mainly in the downforce that we use. At Monaco you have maximum downforce but in Adelaide you use a lot less, and you don't have to fight the car and the corners the same way. Adelaide is a flat track without the climbs and descents of Monaco.

'Like all temporary circuits the track takes a while to get up to speed. There is a lot of dirt and dust at first and not enough rubber to improve the grip. If it rains, which it does quite often here, one problem with it being a street track is that the road markings – the white lines – are really treacherous and slippery in the rain.

'After the first corner you head for the first tight 90° right-hander [*Wakefield*] which used to be very bumpy under braking – so bumpy it is not easy to see where you are going. Hit the kerb on the left-hand side and you lose control immediately. You can brake very late but it is tricky.

'The left-hander is again very bumpy and it is easy to lose the back end. It is particularly difficult as there is very little grip at the entry to the turn. Then you accelerate hard for the next right-hander [on to Hutt Street], and again you are always searching for the grip level of the car: the track is bumpy and it is hard to get the car balanced. It is also difficult to get a rhythm in your driving with these tight right-hand corners.

'The chicane before coming to Rundle Road is extremely fast and adverse camber. The run-off areas are poor so if you lose it here you are in big trouble. It is what I call a confidence corner. Then you come to the Rundle Road right-hander under braking, a tricky corner with no grip throughout the whole weekend and a lot of cars going off there. The kerb at the exit is very high so you can't risk using it to slow you down.

'Then we come to *Flying Finn Corner*, the very fast right-hander. It is taken in fifth, very quickly, and it is quite frightening. The road is very wide at this point but they have narrowed it with the

Ayrton Senna gave his lap and gear changes before the 1987 race. His estimate that the Lotus would do 310kph (192mph) is quite something on a street. (Courtesy Camel)

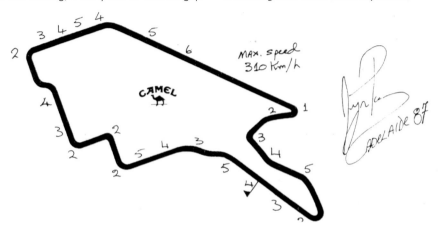

kerbs, so you are looking at the kerbs and checking where your wheels are. The walls are a long way off but if you touch a kerb, like I did last year, it sucks the car up and off you go and you fly really high. I was lucky not to touch anything.

'Fly down Dequetteville Terrace straight to the hairpin where you use second or first depending on your engine, accelerate hard with a bit of wheelspin as you head for the double left-hander, which is a third or fourth gear corner. It is not an easy corner because again it is adverse camber. Then it's flat out all the way through the next corners until the hairpin before the pit straight. I like those last few turns because they are so quick but with several changes of direction.'

EYEWITNESS

Ann Bradshaw, PR expert:
'Not only hadn't we ever been to Australia, none of us knew where Adelaide was. We'd barely heard of it, but when we got there it was stunning. The people were the nicest you could wish to meet. Mal Hemmerling [Executive Director], the guy who was running it, and John Bannon, who was the South Australian Premier, really were just amazing: they had one thing in mind, to make sure it was the best Grand Prix – and it was.

'Remember, we were coming from

Adelaide had a certain grace about it which didn't stop combative Keke Rosberg (Williams) winning handsomely in 1985. (LAT)

South Africa [the Grand Prix two weeks before] and there were an awful lot of dramas about getting us into Australia because in those days apartheid was still in place. There was talk of blockades because we were coming from South Africa. You couldn't fly direct. There was a direct flight for the cargo but they had to publish the wrong landing times because the unions were going to blockade it to prevent the cars being unloaded.

'I had to go by Zimbabwe, and now you'd do it the other way round: go to South Africa, avoid Zimbabwe. I remember sitting at the airport at Harare for several hours waiting for the Qantas flight.

'The circuit wasn't a straightforward street circuit. It went round a park and was a bit like Melbourne in a way, but a mixture: a street circuit and a park circuit with a racecourse for horses in the middle. The Media Centre was where they used to run the tote. It was wonderful!

'When I got there, the PR agency dealing with it were girls and the excitement rose the day the first flight came in with the mechanics. All the girls were there and they were saying "Look at these lovely men, they look so smart". You'd look round one way and there were all the Australian men with badly-fitting jeans, look the other way and there were the Ferrari mechanics all wearing their red uniforms, styled in Milan no doubt.

'It was party after party, and in the restaurants and the hotels everything was to do with the Grand Prix. Wherever you went the first thing they said was "Are you here for the Grand Prix? How

are you doing? Lovely to see you." Every shop window was full of Grand Prix stuff. They were closing Rundle Street [see the circuit map] off for parties and we'd never seen anything like it.

'We'd been to Long Beach but you didn't feel that everybody wanted you there and the Americans didn't understand us. By contrast Adelaide was open-armed. I don't like Melbourne (in terms of the Grand Prix) because I don't feel it has the heart that Adelaide had: Adelaide *was* the race and the race *was* Adelaide. There wasn't a great deal else there apart from churches!'

MEMORIES AND MILESTONES

1985 Ayrton Senna (Lotus) took pole at this, Niki Lauda's 171st and final Grand Prix. He made his debut in 1971. John Surtees was on that grid and *he* made his debut in 1960. Stirling Moss was on that grid and *he* made his debut in 1951. It meant that the lineage from virtually the start of the World Championship was maintained by only three men. Lauda (McLaren) retired after 57 laps (brakes/accident) and Keke Rosberg (Williams) beat Jacques Laffite (Ligier) by 46.1 seconds. Fastest lap: Rosberg 100.9mph/162.4kph.
1986 Nigel Mansell (Williams), pole, looked favourite for the Championship until a tyre exploded at big speed on Dequetteville Straight, leaving him fighting for his life and providing some unforgettable television images. Alain Prost (McLaren) beat Nelson Piquet (Williams) by 4.2 seconds to take the Championship. Fastest lap: Piquet 104.6mph (+3.7)/168.4kph (+6.0).
1987 Gerhard Berger's day. He put the Ferrari on pole but Piquet (Williams) made the better start from the second row and led. Berger muscled him aside, led every lap and beat team-mate Michele Alboreto by 1 minute 07.8 seconds. Fastest lap: Berger 105.1mph (+0.5)/169.2kph (+0.8).
1988 Senna (McLaren) took pole in this, the last race when turbo engines were permitted and, the Championship already settled, Berger (Ferrari) announced he intended to ignore fuel consumption and go for it – which involved going past Prost (McLaren), who was quite happy. He was watching his fuel. Berger had an accident and Prost beat Senna by 36.7 seconds. Fastest lap: Prost 104.1mph (-1.0)/167.6kph (-1.6).

The amazing start-finish straight for a street circuit. This is 1995, the Williamses of Damon Hill and David Coulthard already pulling clear. (ICN U.K. Bureau)

1989 A wet race, Senna (McLaren) leading from pole and travelling into the spray fast, but Martin Brundle (Brabham) lurked in that spray and the McLaren struck him a savage blow. Thierry Boutsen (Williams) beat Sandro Nannini (Benetton) by 28.6 seconds Fastest lap: Satoru Nakajima (Lotus) 85.9mph/138.2kph (no comparison).
1990 The 500th World Championship race produced a strong duel between Senna (McLaren), pole, and Mansell

(Ferrari), which ended when Mansell went down an escape road and Senna tapped a tyre barrier, letting Piquet (Benetton) win it from Mansell by 3.1 seconds. Fastest lap: Mansell 108.1mph (+4.0)/174.0kph (+6.4).
1991 Another wet race, stopped after 14 laps, to become the shortest in Formula 1 history (24m 34.8s, next Spain 1975 at 42m 53.7s). Senna (McLaren), pole, beat Mansell (Williams) by 1.2 seconds. Fastest lap: Berger (McLaren) 83.6mph/134.5kph (no comparison).
1992 Another strong duel involved the same combatants – Mansell (Williams), pole, Senna (McLaren) – which ended when Senna went into the back of the Williams. Mansell, who was going

to IndyCar racing, accused Senna of ramming and said he was glad to be going. Berger (McLaren) beat Michael Schumacher (Benetton) by 0.7 of a second. Fastest lap: Schumacher 111.1mph (+3.0)/178.9kph (+4.9).
1993 The race of farewells: Senna's last for McLaren, and from pole he won his last victory. It was Prost's last race too. His Williams finished 9.2 seconds behind Senna. Fastest lap: Hill (Williams) 112.2mph (+1.1)/180.5kph (+1.6).
1994 The Championship decider, although Mansell (Williams), not involved in that, took pole. Schumacher (Benetton) crashed and then controversially struck Damon Hill's Williams on lap 35. Both retired, giving Schumacher the Championship. Mansell won the race, beating Berger (Ferrari) by 2.5 seconds. Fastest lap: Schumacher 109.6mph (-2.6)/176.4kph (-4.1).
1995 Mika Häkkinen crashed during free practice – a tyre failed on his McLaren at Malthouse Corner (known as Brewery Bend). Two doctors carried out a tracheotomy at the site, opening his throat so that he could breathe. Hill (Williams), pole, beat Olivier Panis (Ligier) by two *laps,* equalling Jackie Stewart in Spain in 1969. Fastest lap: Hill 108.5mph (-1.1)/174.6kph (-1.8).

Speed increase 1985–95: 7.6mph/12.2kph.

Footnote
[1] Published by Mitchell Beazley, 5th edition.

FACTS OF THE MATTER

2.348m/3.778km circuit 1985;
2.348m/3779km 1986; 2.349m/3.780km 1987–95

Year	Winner
1985	K. Rosberg (Williams)
1986	A. Prost (McLaren)
1987	G. Berger (Ferrari)
1988	A. Prost (McLaren)
1989	T. Boutsen (Williams)
1990	N. Piquet (Benetton)
1991	A. Senna (McLaren)
1992	G. Berger (McLaren)
1993	A. Senna (McLaren)
1994	N. Mansell (Williams)
1995	D. Hill (Williams)
Fastest pole	A. Senna (McLaren) 1993 (115.2mph/185.5kph)
Fastest lap	D. Hill (Williams) 1993 (112.2mph/180.5kph)

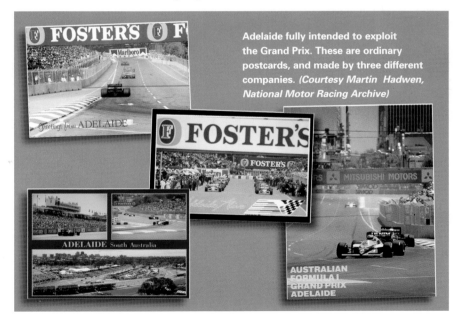

Adelaide fully intended to exploit the Grand Prix. These are ordinary postcards, and made by three different companies. *(Courtesy Martin Hadwen, National Motor Racing Archive)*

AUSTRALIA
MELBOURNE

Location: Albert Park, inner suburb.
Constructed: 1953.
World Championship Grands Prix: 14.

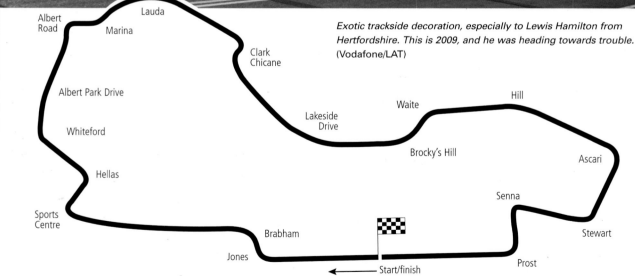

Exotic trackside decoration, especially to Lewis Hamilton from Hertfordshire. This is 2009, and he was heading towards trouble. (Vodafone/LAT)

Albert Road
Lauda
Marina
Clark Chicane
Albert Park Drive
Waite
Hill
Lakeside Drive
Whiteford
Brocky's Hill
Ascari
Hellas
Senna
Sports Centre
Brabham
Stewart
Jones
Prost
Start/finish

'If your car is prone to rear-locking you have to be careful'

Rubens Barrichello

The Australian Grand Prix moved from Adelaide to Melbourne in circumstances of acrimony, confusion, and mystery. Bernie Ecclestone claimed it was because of endless media criticism of how much the race cost. That seemed to be borne out by the *Adelaide Advertiser*, which claimed the race had lost the equivalent of £14.15 million during its 11 years although, of course, that had to be balanced against how much the race generated for the area every year.

In 1993 a prominent Melbourne businessman and former lord mayor, Ron Walker, started work on securing the Grand Prix for the city. Walker became Chairman of the Australian Grand Prix Corporation.

Melbourne had a history of motor racing because non-Championship Grands Prix were run at Albert Park, situated in the inner southern suburbs, in 1953, and again in 1956 when Stirling Moss won in a Maserati at 95mph.

'The race was arranged in conjunction with Melbourne's role as host city to that year's Olympic Games. With few exceptions, previous Australian Grands Prix had featured predominantly Australian drivers, and only the 1953 event had been held so close to a major city … The real coup, though, was the announcement that Stirling Moss and Jean Behra would be travelling to Melbourne to compete in the event.

'The spectacle of Moss hurling his Maserati 250F around the (small man-made) lake would ensure that the crowd would be treated to something never seen in Australia before. Like the Formula 1 Grands Prix that would return to the park in the mid-1990s, the 1956 race was one that people would travel vast distances to experience as something more than a mere date on the sporting calendar.'[1]

Not everyone was delighted in 1996, particularly environmentalists, and a group campaigned to 'Save Albert Park.' The wildlife – black swans, magpie larks, rainbow lorikeets[2] – didn't seem to mind either way.

The circuit used the ordinary road round the lake but it was reworked for smoothness before the first Grand Prix.

Because it is in a park, the necessary infrastructure – including grandstands – is temporary. The infrastructure is completed a few weeks before each race and dismantled within a few weeks of it, as at Adelaide.

Because the corners have a consistency to them – in other words, no real surprises – drivers learn it fast and drive it fast. What they don't have is much of a choice of overtaking places, which puts real pressure on the hard right Turn 1 at the start, where places can be gained and races ended. Jenson Button emphasises how much precision is demanded: you brake a *foot* late and it can cost a lot of time.

Timo Glock of Toyota describes the circuit as 'very picturesque but not the most challenging on the calendar for a driver. It's quite unusual because it is only used for the Australian Grand Prix – there are no other motor sport meetings there during the year. This means that every time we go there it is a green track, so there is no grip at all to start with, and that makes it sometimes quite difficult to find the right direction in terms of the set-up.' Button says 'you need a car that dances on its toes', while confirming how difficult passing is.

Reportedly Bernie Ecclestone wanted a night race to make it more suitable for the European audience but a compromise took it to 5:00pm locally and early breakfast time in Europe.

Like Montréal, the television cameras never show how near the circuit is to water. (LAT)

COCKPIT VIEW

Rubens Barrichello, Brawn, 2009:
'The Albert Park circuit is quite technical and the relatively high top speeds for a street circuit mean that you need to run a high level of downforce, which in turn compromises your grip through the slower second-gear corners.

'The lap has some very quick changes of direction and you can gain a lot of time through the quick chicane at Turns 11 and 12 if you get it hooked up well. You need a car with a good front-end to make the most of these corners.

'Because the circuit uses public roads there are a lot of bumps under braking and if your car is prone to rear-locking you have to be careful that these don't unsettle it enough to throw you off the circuit.

'It's reasonably difficult to overtake around the circuit with Turns 3 and 13 offering the best opportunities.'[3]

EYEWITNESS

Gareth Rees, motor sport enthusiast:
'I was lucky to be able to combine a business trip with a visit to the 2003 Australian Grand Prix, where I experienced the other side of life as a corporate guest in the Paddock Club above the pits: excellent catering, all you can drink, a view directly down on the pit road and a simulator in the hospitality unit.

'This was almost for my personal use during the whole of qualifying day because most of the other guests were only coming to the race. Anyway, I could try to learn to drive the circuit from the cockpit of Rubens Barrichello's Ferrari. I felt quite guilty when I looked across to the real race fans who had paid for their tickets and were out there enduring the elements – the weather was being very British.

'The win for all-round good-guy David Coulthard was a pleasure to see but a couple of things stick in my mind about that weekend.

'The first was the ease of getting to the circuit. I stayed in a small hotel in the centre of Melbourne and on both qualifying and race days I just wandered out to the end of the street around 8:00am and got on a tram with the other race fans, simple as that. It was the same for the journey back: no hassle, no queues, no traffic jams, and without that all-too-familiar Silverstone feeling of *will I, won't I, make it on time to see the race?*

LEFT: *Damon Hill explores Albert Park in the Williams in practice. On race day there will be advertisements on those bare green walls.* (ICN U.K. Bureau)

ABOVE: *Eddie Irvine (Ferrari) couldn't get near the Williamses of Hill and Jacques Villeneuve, and anyway Hill beat Villeneuve by 38.0 seconds.* (ICN U.K. Bureau)

'The other thing was the incredible value for money that the Aussie fans got that weekend, with countless multiple supporting races for V8 Supercars, Aussie GTs, Formula Ford, Historic single-seaters, karting, and they all had separate races on both days. Bernie, why can't it be like that everywhere?'

MEMORIES AND MILESTONES

1996 An extraordinary debut race for Melbourne because Jacques Villeneuve put the Williams on pole on *his* debut, only the third driver ever to do that (discounting Giuseppe Farina in 1950, because somebody *had* to do it at the first Championship race; Mario Andretti, USA 1968, and Carlos Reutemann, Argentina 1972, were the others). At Turn 3 at the start of the race Martin Brundle (Jordan) found himself trapped by two other cars, was launched, and landed in the sand trap upside down. He was unhurt. Villeneuve got to within five laps of winning when he had an engine problem. Team-mate Damon Hill beat him by 38.0 seconds. Fastest lap: Villeneuve 127.0mph/204.3kph.
1997 The race was now established as the first of the season and Villeneuve took pole again, but Eddie Irvine (Ferrari) tried inside and punted Villeneuve (and Johnny Herbert's Sauber) off. David Coulthard (McLaren) beat Michael Schumacher (Ferrari) by 20.0 seconds. Fastest lap: Heinz-Harald Frentzen (Williams) 130.9mph (+3.9)/210.7kph (+6.4).
1998 The McLarens announced that they

were a class apart but their drivers – Mika Häkkinen (pole) and Coulthard – and the team reached an agreement: whoever took Turn 1 first would win. Coulthard honoured it, handing Häkkinen the race with two laps left. Formula 1 was not pleased, despite the winning margin of only 0.7 of a second. Fastest lap: Häkkinen 129.4mph (-1.5)/208.3kph (-2.4).
1999 Häkkinen (McLaren) took pole. Schumacher's Ferrari had an electrical problem and he started from the back, freeing Irvine to win for the first time in his 34th race for the team. He beat Frentzen (Jordan) by 1.0 second. Fastest lap: Schumacher 128.8mph/ (-0.6)/207.3kph (-1.0).
2000 If the era of Schumacher and Ferrari dominance had a specific beginning it was here. Häkkinen (McLaren) took pole but Schumacher beat new team-mate Rubens Barrichello by 11.4 seconds, the first of nine wins for him that season. Fastest lap: Barricello 129.7mph (+0.9)/208.7kph (+1.4).
2001 Schumacher (Ferrari) took pole. On the fifth lap Villeneuve (BAR) ran into the back of Ralf Schumacher's Williams and was airborne. A wheel, torn clean off, passed through a gap in the barrier and killed a volunteer official, Graham Beveridge. Michael Schumacher beat Coulthard (McLaren) by 1.7 seconds. Fastest lap: Schumacher 134.5mph (+4.8)/216.4kph (+7.7).
2002 Barrichello (Ferrari) took pole but suffered a horror at Turn 1. Ralf Schumacher (Williams) rode up the

back of the Ferrari and flew like a plane. Coulthard (McLaren) had a gearbox problem and Michael Schumacher (Ferrari) inherited the win, beating Juan-Pablo Montoya (Williams) by 18.6 seconds. Fastest lap: Kimi Räikkönen (McLaren) 134.0mph (-0.5)/215.6kph (-0.8).

2003 Schumacher (Ferrari) took pole. In changing conditions, Coulthard (McLaren) pitted early – lap 2 – for dry tyres, would stop only once more, and by lap 29 was second. He made his other stop (fifth) and leader Montoya (Williams) spun. It was all that Coulthard, 1.2 seconds behind, needed, and he beat Montoya by 8.6 seconds. Fastest lap: Räikkönen 135.2mph (+1.2)/217.6kph (+2.0).

2004 Schumacher (Ferrari) went fastest in all practice sessions, took pole, and led every lap (including his three pit stops) to beat team-mate Barrichello by 13.6 seconds. Fastest lap: Schumacher 141.0mph (+5.8)/226.9kph (+9.3).

2005 Giancarlo Fisichella, newly signed by Renault from Sauber, took pole and scored the second victory of his 141-race career in a Championship-winning car (as team-mate Fernando Alonso would prove). Fisichella beat Barrichello (Ferrari) by 5.5 seconds. Fastest lap: Alonso 138.4mph (-2.6)/222.8kph (-4.1).

2006 The race moved to the third round on the calendar. Jenson Button

(Honda) took pole but Alonso showed that the Renault was good enough for a second Championship, beating Räikkönen (McLaren) by almost two seconds. Fastest lap: Räikkönen 137.9mph (-0.5)/221.9kph (-0.9).

2007 The race returned to Round 1 and Räikkönen, now with Ferrari, suggested the team might not miss Schumacher too much by taking pole and leading every lap except the pit stops. He beat Alonso (McLaren) by 7.2 seconds. Alonso's team-mate Lewis Hamilton, making his debut, qualified fourth and finished third. Fastest lap: Räikkönen 139.2mph (+1.3)/224.0kph (+2.1).

2008 Hamilton (McLaren) took pole. Five cars went out at Turn 2, which surprised nobody because traction control had been banned, but Hamilton remained very much still in the race. He beat Nick Heidfeld (BMW) by 5.4 seconds. Neither Ferrari finished. Fastest lap: Heikki Kovalainen (McLaren) 135.7mph (-3.5)/218.4kph (-5.6).

2009 The race which shook up the whole of Formula 1. The Brawn team (Honda reborn, but with a Mercedes engine) gave Jenson Button all he needed for pole and the win, team-mate Barrichello second on the grid and second in the race. Button beat Barrichello by 0.8 of a second. Ross Brawn was so moved that on the way to the podium he could

not speak. Fastest lap: Nico Rosberg (Williams) 135.3mph (-0.4)/217.7kph (-0.7).

Speed increase 1996–2009: 8.3mph/13.4kph.

Footnotes
[1] atlasf1.autosport.com/2001/feb07/glendenning.html.
[2] *Autocourse*, 2008–9. Lorikeets are small to medium-sized parrots. [3] Courtesy Brawn GP.

FACTS OF THE MATTER

3.295m/5.302km circuit	
Year	*Winner*
1996	D. Hill (Williams)
1997	D. Coulthard (McLaren)

3.295m/5.303km circuit	
1998	M. Häkkinen (McLaren)
1999	E. Irvine (Ferrari)
2000	M. Schumacher (Ferrari)
2001	M. Schumacher (Ferrari)
2002	M. Schumacher (Ferrari)
2003	D. Coulthard (McLaren)
2004	M. Schumacher (Ferrari)
2005	G. Fisichella (Renault)
2006	F. Alonso (Renault)
2007	K. Räikkönen (Ferrari)
2008	L. Hamilton (McLaren)
2009	J. Button (Brawn)
Fastest pole	M. Schumacher (Ferrari) 2004 (140.5mph/226.2kph)
Fastest lap	M. Schumacher (Ferrari) 2004 (141.0mph/226.9kph)

Above: No, it's not Monza although an Italian, Giancarlo Fisichella, has just won the 2005 Grand Prix in a Renault. *(Courtesy Mark Young)*

Left: No, it's not Monza although a photographer hurries to get a picture of Rubens Barrichello's Ferrari, which finished second in 2005. *(Courtesy Mark Young)*

Above: The safety fence doesn't stop spectators from having an almost intimate view of the pit lane entrance. *(Courtesy Mark Young)*

A1-RING (FORMERLY ÖSTERREICHRING)

Location: 4 miles (6km) from Knittlefeld.
Constructed: 1969.
World Championship Grands Prix: 25.

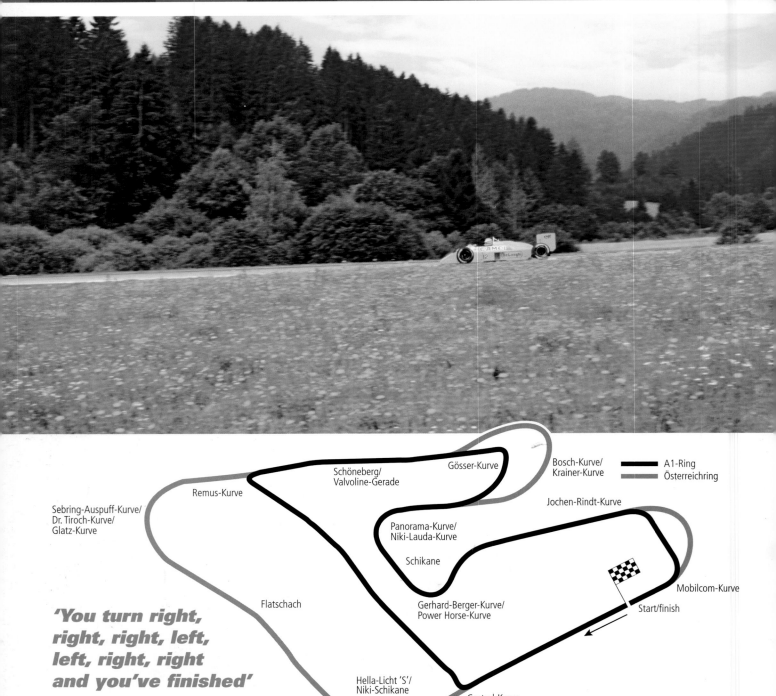

Sebring-Auspuff-Kurve/
Dr. Tiroch-Kurve/
Glatz-Kurve

Remus-Kurve

Schöneberg/
Valvoline-Gerade

Gösser-Kurve

Bosch-Kurve/
Krainer-Kurve

■ A1-Ring
■ Österreichring

Jochen-Rindt-Kurve

Panorama-Kurve/
Niki-Lauda-Kurve

Schikane

Gerhard-Berger-Kurve/
Power Horse-Kurve

Mobilcom-Kurve

Start/finish

Flatschach

Hella-Licht 'S'/
Niki-Schikane

Castrol-Kurve

Vöest-Hügel

'You turn right, right, right, left, left, right, right and you've finished'

Jacques Villeneuve

ABOVE: Ayrton Senna in 1987, when he'd be fifth, the Lotus almost a psychedelic vision against the foreground. (LAT)

OPPOSITE: Heartland Austria in 1974, all eyes on Niki Lauda's Ferrari – but a faulty valve halted him. (Courtesy Gareth Rees)

The Österreichring demanded awe and annually received it. Like Spa and the Nürburgring, it also reflected the two eras of Grand Prix racing: the first, when men were men and fed on raw meat, the second when men were still men but dining on pasta, bananas, and vitamin-rich drinks. There are precise dates for this: 1970–87 and then 1997–2003. The awe died with the first and did not return with the second, a truncated version of the original conforming to modern safety standards and ease of television coverage rather like … Spa and the Nürburgring.

The Zeltweg airfield (see next entry) had served its purpose in giving Austria a Grand Prix and promoted sustained interest in the sport but was plainly unsuitable for more. Zeltweg was flat. Its successor demanded mechanised mountaineering and that was part of the awe. Set in the foothills of the Styrian mountains, the track rose and descended in a sequence of great loops through pastureland and trees as if it had been laid on to a great, rolling, roiling panorama.

It was immediately fast. At the first Grand Prix, in 1970, Jochen Rindt took pole in a Lotus with a lap of 133.2mph/214.4kph – 21mph faster than his pole at Brands Hatch, for example.

Most of the drivers were reportedly enthusiastic about the circuit although (and this would become a familiar complaint in years to come) the facilities were basic. One report[1] suggested the protective fencing for spectators was 'completely inadequate'.

This was deepest Austria, and *felt* like deepest Austria too. You'd see whole campsites on the far side of the circuit. A surprising number of spectators wore lederhosen and hats with feathers. The smell of barbecued sausages hung in the air or was borne on the breeze, and a great deal of beer was drunk.

The circuit also reflected Austria as a European crossroads. Huge numbers of Italians flooded over the border for a bonus opportunity to see the Ferraris, and Germans came in numbers to mingle with the Austrians. In time the Hungarians (who were, incidentally, entitled to passports even before Communism collapsed) would come across the Iron Curtain for a taste of ultimate capitalism. They liked it.

COCKPIT VIEW –
OLD CIRCUIT
Ayrton Senna, Lotus, 1987:
'It's one of the fastest circuits, with long, flat corners and high-speed straight lines. The aerodynamics play a very important part in the car's performance. It's so important to have good power from the engine. You have a low downforce set-up due to the high-speed corners and it's quite hard on tyres.'

Patrick Tambay, who drove in eight Grands Prix there:
'This was a particularly big circuit. The right-left-right chicane at the top of the start/finish straight was the slowest part and then you accelerate hard up to the long curves taken at 260kph (160mph), maybe up to 300kph. In the *Sebring* you slow a bit, go down a gear and accelerate to 260kph – a wonderful experience – then you're on a long straight line rising. You reach maximum speed before the long right-hand bend (*Bosch-Kurve*), which is slightly banked. You leave it very, very fast, and very close to the Armco on the left, at close to 265kph. You come up to two long left-hander curves (*Texaco Schikane*) and then you are flat out towards the *Rindt-Kurve*, another long bend. The car is very light and you have to anticipate your acceleration. You need the right speed coming out and you need

The start with the fearsome final corner behind and minimal protection for anybody. (Courtesy www.fredlewisphotos.com)

to use that momentum to attack the long start/finish before braking for the right-left-right chicane into the next lap.'

COCKPIT VIEW –
NEW CIRCUIT
Jacques Villeneuve, Williams, 1997:
'It's very easy to learn. You turn right, right, right, left, left, right, right and you've finished the lap. The rhythm is good because you have corner, straight line, corner, straight line. The two first corners feel like they've cut the straight line and put a bend in.

'*Gösser-Kurve* [see the circuit map] is interesting. You brake going downhill and you start turning in. It's not very fast, but it's not an easy corner.

'The last corner is really strange. You turn in and it drops away. At the apex the track goes flat but the car gets light and then heavy again.'[2]

EYEWITNESS
Gareth Rees, motor sport enthusiast:
'While Spa and the (real) Nürburgring had much more history, the Österreichring was in my opinion another true classic Formula 1 circuit and I had the good fortune to go there three times in the early years of the race.

'As a teenager I loved the country and, with its regular position in the middle of August, the Austrian Grand Prix became the obvious target of my summer hitchhiking trips. I've no idea if schoolboys can hitchhike across Europe so easily these days, but in 1973–74 it was great fun and never a problem. In 1970 I had

even persuaded my parents to make far-away Zeltweg the ultimate destination of our family's first overseas camping holiday.

'This was the first Grand Prix on the new circuit, and also, for me, the first race I ever saw outside England. With many fans making the short trip from Italy, the atmosphere was terrific: Ferraris running one-two all race, as Clay Regazzoni shadowed Jacky Ickx all the way, with another of my favourites, Jean-Pierre Beltoise's Matra, an early challenger.

'Of course the locals were all there to see their Championship-leader, Jochen Rindt, continue his winning streak, but he retired at less than half-distance and I remember watching in amazement as most of the locals seemed to be leaving the circuit with so much of the race still to go.

'The Österreichring was an amateur photographer's dream. The weather was normally good, and the scenery, with its flowery meadows and mountains, simply idyllic. All this formed a magnificent backdrop to some spectacular views of the track: in my case, either from the hillside in the middle of the circuit – perfect for following the race, as you could see more than half the action – or close up on the open terraces around the outside of the spectacular *Bosch-Kurve*.

'In 1973, most of all, the sight of Ronnie Peterson's drifting Lotus 72 was unforgettable. Paying spectators at Grands Prix these days cannot begin to imagine what it was like to witness oversteering Formula 1 cars on the limit in long fast corners like that and at such close quarters.

'In 1970 my long-suffering Mum and Dad, with no particular interest in the racing, stayed all day in the campsite. When I think of that first visit, it's my mother's description of the symphony of sound from the Formula 1 race echoing in the valley which really gives me goose pimples, and part of me wishes I'd been in the campsite too. Those hills were certainly alive with the sound of music.'

MEMORIES AND MILESTONES
1970 A crowd of 100,000 came to the race, Jochen Rindt (Lotus) on pole and Clay Regazzoni (Ferrari) alongside him. That guaranteed the locals would come and the Italians too. Regazzoni waved team-mate Jacky Ickx through on lap 2 (Ickx had more points in the Championship) and Rindt's engine

failed after 22 laps, leaving Ickx to beat Regazzoni by 0.6 of a second. Fastest lap: Ickx and Regazzoni 131.7mph/211.9kph.

1971 Jo Siffert (BRM) took pole. The Tyrrells of Jackie Stewart and François Cevert suffered mechanical problems, opening the way for Siffert to win despite nursing a puncture for two laps at the end. He beat Emerson Fittipaldi (Lotus) by 4.1 seconds. Fastest lap: Siffert 134.3mph (+2.6)/216.1kph (+4.2).

1972 Fittipaldi (Lotus) took pole and held off a long, sustained attack by Denny Hulme (McLaren) to win by 1.18 seconds. Fastest lap: Hulme 134.5mph (+0.2)/216.4kph (+0.3).

1973 After Roger Williams' death at Zandvoort three weeks before (see Zandvoort), when the racers had been passing the burning wreck at speed, a Safety Car experiment was carried out during practice. Fittipaldi (Lotus) took pole. His lap of 139.2mph/224.0kph made the circuit the fastest on the calendar (Monza nearest, 136.2mph/219.3kph). Ronnie Peterson (Lotus) won a straightforward race, beating Stewart's Tyrrell by 9.04 seconds. Fastest lap: Carlos Pace (Surtees) 135.9mph (+1.4)/218.7kph (+2.3).

1974 Lauda on pole in the Ferrari brought 150,000 Austrians and Italians to the race but his engine failed on lap 17. Carlos Reutemann (Brabham) beat Hulme (McLaren) by 42.9 seconds. Fastest lap: Regazzoni (Ferrari) 136.0mph (+0.1)/218.9kph (+0.2).

Speed increase 1970–74: 4.3mph/7.0kph.

1975 Lauda on pole in the Ferrari again and that brought the 150,000 back, but in Sunday morning warm-up American driver Mark Donohue had a tyre fail on his March and ploughed into catch-fencing at the first corner, *Vöest-Hügel*, then it 'collected two marshals and a scaffolding pole from a nearby advertising hoarding before eventually coming to rest in a wrecked heap with the driver unconscious.'[3] One of the marshals was killed and Donohue died in hospital two days later. Vittorio Brambilla (March) beat James Hunt (Hesketh) in a wet race by 24.0 seconds. Fastest lap: Brambilla 116.1mph/186.8kph (no comparison).

After Donohue's death, the circuit was modified. The first corner's inside edge was brought in approximately 6ft (2m), meaning the drivers could comfortably take it flat out. The resurfacing produced what were described as vicious bumps, but a bigger run-off area on the outside compensated for them. This run-off area was improved by the removal of catch-fencing so that a driver went on to grass before he reached the triple-height Armco, topped by debris fencing. Similar Armco fencing was installed on the outside of other corners.

1976 Hunt (McLaren) took pole but John Watson (Penske) won, beating Jacques Laffite (Ligier) by 10.7 seconds. Fastest lap: Hunt 137.8mph/221.8kph.

Turn 1 had now become a chicane, Hella-Licht – *although it was termed an S: over the top of the hill from the start/finish straight it curled left then right as the track moved out into the majestic scenery.*

1977 Lauda (Ferrari) took pole, bringing the 150,000 back yet again. On the Saturday night a big crowd was already there, drinking, setting off fireworks and chanting *N-i-k-i L-a-u-d-a* on and on against the mighty sound of a Wurlitzer from the fairground. Young Australian Alan Jones won and would remember the whole context for a career. 'A season with Shadow kept me in play. Either at the end of the year Shadow would get a new competitive car or somebody would spot me and ask me to drive for a better team. Around the business, people know when it's your car that's at fault and not you. I think I was rated at Shadow by what I could do within the limitations of the machinery at my disposal.'[4] Jones beat Lauda by 20.1 seconds. Fastest lap: Watson (Brabham) 131.7mph/211.9kph.

1978 Ronnie Peterson (Lotus) took pole. A damp start, all the cars on slick tyres and some driving more adventurously than others. The rain hardened, cars spun, and the race was stopped. After the restart the track dried and everyone pitted for slick tyres. Peterson beat Patrick Depailler (Tyrrell) by 38.0 seconds. Fastest lap: Peterson 128.9mph (-2.8)/207.4kph (-4.5).

1979 René Arnoux (Renault) took pole. Jones (Williams) attacked Gilles Villeneuve (Ferrari) for the first three laps for the lead. Jones powered past the pits and beat Villeneuve into the chicane, the decisive move of the race. Jones beat him by 36.0 seconds. Fastest lap: Arnoux 138.8mph (+9.9)/223.4kph (+16.0).

1980 Arnoux (Renault) took pole but did not figure in a tremendous finish, with Jones (Williams) reeling in Jean-Pierre Jabouille's Renault and failing by 0.82 of a second at the line. Fastest lap: Arnoux 143.6mph (+4.8)/231.2kph (+7.8).

1981 'Turmoil' had engulfed the Ligier team from the beginning of the season. The local band welcomed them to the hotel in a village called Obdach they'd used for years. The team decided to join the band. Owner Guy Ligier played the bass drum, Patrick Tambay played the cymbals, and Jacques Laffite fooled around with the conductor's baton. 'The team may have undergone political change, switched engines, swapped drivers and, more recently, fired their team manager,

In 1997 David Coulthard took the McLaren to second place – and the crowds were still coming. Many must have remembered the old circuit. (ICN U.K. Bureau)

There were vantage points on the new circuit where you'd swear you were still looking at the old one. This is 1997 and Jarno Trulli (Prost) who'd have an engine failure. (ICN U.K. Bureau)

but it scarcely showed in Austria.'[5] Arnoux (Renault) took pole but heroically Laffite beat him by 5.17 seconds. Fastest lap: Laffite 136.2mph (-7.4)/219.1kph (-12.1).

1982 Nelson Piquet (Brabham) took pole. An even more tremendous finish with Elio de Angelis (Lotus) holding his nerve and Keke Rosberg (Williams) launching a final lunge to the line which failed by 0.05 of a second. This was Colin Chapman's final win at Lotus. Fastest lap: Piquet 141.9mph (+5.7)/228.3kph (+9.2).

1983 Tambay (Ferrari) took pole. Although Alain Prost (Renault) and Piquet (Brabham) banged wheels at the chicane Prost won from Arnoux (Ferrari) by 6.8 seconds. Fastest lap: Prost 141.5mph (-0.4)/227.7kph (-0.6).

1984 The 400th Championship race. Piquet (Brabham) took pole. By now the circuit was showing its age but Lauda (McLaren), going for the Championship, could still draw a crowd. He led the race but towards the end the differential

LEFT: An ordinary postcard depicting several aspects of an extraordinary place. (Courtesy Martin Hadwen, National Motor Racing Archive)

BELOW: The race of 1971, and note the mighty backdrop: Denny Hulme (9, McLaren) had an engine failure, Jackie Stewart (11, Tyrrell) lost a wheel and Tim Schenken (8, Brabham) finished third. Fred Lewis, who took the pictures, says: 'What a gorgeous setting for a race – or anything else. That's my favourite place in the world. There was nothing between me and the track except for the spectator tunnel. Those were the days.' (Courtesy www.fredlewisphotos.com)

failed, leaving him prey for Piquet. 'In that kind of situation it is hard to think logically,' Lauda would remember. 'You are so attuned to driving at the limit that you can't improvise once you leave the realm of super-fast instincts and reflexes and enter a much more banal world.' However, after he kept the car going 'it flashes through my head, of course, Nelson knows the way I drive, he knows that I throttle back in the final stages and don't give a damn how much lead I have when I cross the line. He probably thinks I'm deliberately driving more slowly, that I'm driving a tactical race, and that there is no point at all putting me under pressure because I'll only respond immediately and put my foot down again.' Piquet's rear tyres were finished and Lauda duly won it, by 23.5 seconds.[6] Fastest lap: Lauda 143.1mph (+1.6)/230.3kph (+2.6).

1985 Lauda called a press conference and, approached by the Marlboro publicity lady about what he was going to say, riposted: 'Maybe I'm going to tell them I'm pregnant.' He wasn't. He was retiring. Prost (McLaren) took pole and beat Ayrton Senna (Lotus) by 30.0 seconds. Fastest lap: Prost 148.9mph (+5.8)/239.7kph (+9.4).

1986 A Benetton front row (Teo Fabi pole from Gerhard Berger) but a decisive win for Prost in the McLaren, beating Michele Alboreto (Ferrari) by a lap. Fastest lap: Berger 148.6mph (-0.3)/239.2kph (-0.5).

1987 Piquet (Williams) took pole. The narrow pit straight – pit lane to one side, Armco to the other – finally ended Grand Prix racing at the circuit. Half a dozen cars blocked the track after a multiple crash from the start. At the restart Nigel Mansell's clutch failed on the Williams, there was a collision between Riccardo Patrese's Brabham and Eddie Cheever's Arrows, and then chaos behind. At the third restart – at 4:10 – Senna stalled, was push-started, and six cars came from the pit lane. Mansell beat team-mate Piquet by 55.7 seconds. Fastest lap: Mansell 150.5mph (+1.9)/242.2kph (+3.0).

Speed increase 1977–87: 18.8mph/30.3kph.

The circuit fell from prominence but was redesigned by Hermann Tilke to modern conceptions and standards. The scenery could not be neutered but the circuit certainly was, using only part of the old layout. Berger caught the mood when he said that the old had been the best in the world, the new one fitted Formula 1's

new world, especially in terms of safety.
1997 Jacques Villeneuve (Williams) took pole. The first corner had become a right-right-hander ripe for chaos after the start, but they all got through. Michael Schumacher (Ferrari) took the lead from ninth and made his only pit stop but had a ten-second stop'n'go for overtaking under yellow flags and finished sixth. Villeneuve beat David Coulthard (McLaren) by 2.9 seconds. Fastest lap: Villeneuve 134.7mph/216.7kph.

1998 Giancarlo Fisichella (Benetton) took pole. In Turn 1, from the start, four cars crashed; then Schumacher (Ferrari), trying to take Mika Häkkinen's McLaren, ran off at the final corner and had to limp all the way round to the pits, resuming last. Häkkinen beat team-mate Coulthard by 5.2 seconds. Fastest lap: Coulthard 132.6mph (-2.1)/213.3kph (-3.4).

1999 Häkkinen (McLaren) took pole but he and team-mate Coulthard touched when Coulthard tried to take him. They both kept on. Neither could overhaul Eddie Irvine (Ferrari), who beat Coulthard by 0.3 of a second. Fastest lap: Häkkinen 134.0mph (+1.4)/215.6kph (+2.3).

2000 Häkkinen (McLaren) took pole. In Turn 1, from the start, the BAR of Ricardo Zonta punted Schumacher's Ferrari as five cars scattered to miss them. Schumacher tried to get the Ferrari back on – to have the race stopped and get into the spare? It wasn't stopped. Häkkinen beat team-mate Coulthard by 12.5 seconds. Fastest lap: Coulthard 134.8mph (+0.8)/217.0kph (+1.4).

2001 Schumacher (Ferrari) took pole. Coulthard created victory over the Ferraris by making his final pit stop later and using those laps to build a cushion. He beat Schumacher by 2.1 seconds. Fastest lap: Coulthard 136.6mph (+1.8)/219.8kph (+2.8).

2002 Rubens Barrichello (Ferrari) took pole, leading to a notorious race. Ferrari ordered him to slow at the end and gift the victory to Schumacher, which he did, holding Grand Prix racing up to ridicule and earning a torrent of abuse from the crowd. Schumacher's winning margin was 0.182. Fastest lap: Schumacher 139.6mph (+3.0)/224.7kph (+4.9).

2003 Schumacher (Ferrari) took pole and won with a two-stop strategy, even after his Ferrari caught fire at the first of them. He was not, he insisted, tempted to jump out. He beat Kimi Räikkönen (McLaren) by 3.3 seconds. Fastest lap: Schumacher 141.6mph (+2.0)/227.9kph (+3.2).

FACTS OF THE MATTER

3.673m/5.911km circuit

Year	Winner
1970	J. Ickx (Ferrari)
1971	J. Siffert (BRM)
1972	E. Fittipaldi (Lotus)
1973	R. Peterson (Lotus)
1974	C. Reutemann (Brabham)
1975	V. Brambilla (March)
Fastest pole	N. Lauda (Ferrari) 1975 (139.4mph/224.3kph)
Fastest lap	C. Regazzoni (Ferrari) 1974 (136.0mph/218.9kph)

3.672m/5.910km circuit

1976	J. Watson (Penske)
Fastest pole	J. Hunt (McLaren) (139.1mph/223.9kph)
Fastest lap	J. Hunt (137.8kph/221.8kph)

3.692m/5.942km circuit

1977	A. Jones (Shadow)
1978	R. Peterson (Lotus)
1979	A. Jones (Williams)
1980	J.-P. Jabouille (Renault)
1981	J. Laffite (Ligier)
1982	E. de Angelis (Lotus)
1983	A. Prost (Renault)
1984	N. Lauda (McLaren)
1985	A. Prost (McLaren)
1986	A. Prost (McLaren)
1987	N. Mansell (Williams)
Fastest pole	N. Piquet (Williams) 1987 (159.5mph/256.6kph)
Fastest lap	N. Mansell (Williams) 1987 (150.5mph/242.2kph)

2.686m/4.323km circuit 1997, 2.684m/4.319km 1998–9, 2.688m/4.326km 2000–3

1997	J. Villeneuve (Williams)
1998	M. Häkkinen (McLaren)
1999	E. Irvine (Ferrari)
2000	M. Häkkinen (McLaren)
2001	D. Coulthard (McLaren)
2002	M. Schumacher (Ferrari)
2003	M. Schumacher (Ferrari)
Fastest pole	R. Barrichello (Ferrari) 2002 (142.1mph/228.7kph)
Fastest lap	M. Schumacher (Ferrari) 2003 (141.6mph/227.9kph)

Speed increase 1997–2003: 6.9mph/11.2kph.

Footnotes
[1] *Autocourse.* [2] *Autosport.* [3] *Grand Prix!,* Lang. [4] *Driving Ambition,* Jones. [5] *Autocourse.* [6] *To Hell and Back,* Lauda.

AUSTRIA

ZELTWEG

Location: 4 miles (6km) from Knittlefeld.
Constructed: 1958.
World Championship Grands Prix: 1.

Hangar-Kurve

Inner-Kurve

Südenburg-Kurve

Flatschacher-Kurve

Start/finish

Zeltweg, the aerodrome that looked like an aerodrome. Tony Maggs (19) in the BRM leads Lorenzo Bandini (Ferrari), who'd go on to win. (LAT)

'I wasn't sorry that we didn't return'

John Surtees

The circuit, sometimes called Zeltweg and sometimes Aspern, looked exactly like an aerodrome because that's what it was. It had been an airbase and some enthusiasts from Zeltweg, the town nearby, asked if they could use it for races, marking the circuit out with bales and cones. In 1959 a Formula 2 race was held over the 3.2km and a Briton, Tony Marsh, won it in a Cooper. A year later Stirling Moss won in a Porsche.

After two non-Championship races in 1961 and 1963, the circuit was finally given a Grand Prix for 1964.

The Zeltweg airfield was chosen because circuit races were very popular in Austria at the time. There'd been small races on public roads before, even going through cities or villages, but with the Grand Prix cars you couldn't go there.

Apart from Zeltweg there had been

airfield races at Tulln-Langenlebarn (Lower Austria) and Aspern in Vienna. Airbases were the best places for hosting races because there was no permanent racetrack in Austria and hill-climbs were another kind of racing altogether.

Airfields offered the space and run-off areas you wouldn't have on public roads.

COCKPIT VIEW

John Surtees, Ferrari:

'Not the best of circuits by any means, as it used the runways and perimeter roads of an operational military airfield, the surface of which was hardly up to normal Grand Prix standards.

'The facility was only available to the organisers for a few days each year, allowing the absolute minimum of time to get the circuit organised.

'Under the circumstances, I think the local automobile club did a very fine job to stage the race at all, although I wasn't sorry that we didn't return because of all the suspension breakages that its bumpy surface produced.'[1]

EYEWITNESS

Alfred Brumsch, spectator:

'It's a race I remember very well: Austria's first Championship race, and all top stars like Bandini or von Trips at the airbase circuit, as well as our rising star Jochen Rindt, who debuted in Grand Prix racing that day.

'The track itself had two quite long straights, only separated by bales of straw functioning as "guardrails" and, considering the speeds they were going on the straights, we were lucky that no major accidents happened. Compare this to safety requirements nowadays!

'From the start/finish line drivers would accelerate along the straight and then pass into a medium-fast corner which was followed by a kink. Out of that kink you could see the drivers going sideways and working very hard indeed at the steering wheel. Maybe this was the best place to get an impression of the speed and precision of racing – from outside a car.

'That kink was followed by a short straight and, because it was just a communication road from the runway to

the hangar, it was very bumpy there, as well as in the braking zone for the hairpin in front of the hangar where the paddock was situated.

'This was the first good overtaking opportunity, although just the bravest amongst the drivers tried some out-braking there. It was also the area where you could see the largest amount of spectators.

'After that hairpin Bandini & Co fired their cars into a long left-hander, which opened at the exit where they'd join the runway again. It was very important to get that corner right because afterwards there was a long straight leading up to the final corner (another hairpin).

'Of course, as always at the end of a straight, this was a superb place to overtake, although the very bumpy surface and some dust off the line did not favour late brakers. Constant wind meant there'd always be some dust from the quite dry and short-mown grasslands surrounding the track. After that hairpin the cars returned to the start/finish straight.'

MEMORIES AND A MILESTONE

1964 Graham Hill had crashed during testing at Snetterton and chipped a bone in his neck. He found being in a car, whether driving or a passenger, such agony that he bought what he described as an inflatable rubber collar in

order to support his neck. This was just before Zeltweg, which he swore (double entendre intended) was the bumpiest surface he or any of the others had been on. He estimated that the airfield dated to the war, was therefore elderly and as a result 'the surface had a bad ripple'.

That would bring him further agony and after a couple of exploratory laps he couldn't tolerate the pain. He pitted and took codeine tablets, waited for them to take effect and ventured out again. The pain was now bearable and he devised a technique for the corners, holding the steering wheel with one hand and supporting his head with the other. Using this he took pole.[2]

During practice car after car broke because of the battering they were taking. The steering arm on Jim Clark's Lotus broke on both practice days and Dan Gurney (Brabham) had a suspension upright snap. Of the 20 starters 11 did not finish, including Hill (five laps, distributor) and Surtees (nine laps, rear suspension). For a time towards the middle of the race there was a real possibility that *no* car would finish. Lorenzo Bandini (Ferrari) beat Richie Ginther (BRM) by 6.2 seconds.

This was Austria's first championship Grand Prix, Jochen Rindt's first (in a Brabham), and the aerodrome's last.

Footnote
[1] *World Champion*, Surtees. [2] *Life at the Limit*, Hill.

FACTS OF THE MATTER

1.988m/3.200km circuit

Year	Winner
1964	L. Bandini (Ferrari)
Pole	G. Hill (BRM) (102.5mph/164.9kph)
Fastest lap	D. Gurney (Brabham) (101.4mph/163.2kph)

SAKHIR

Location: 20 miles (30km) west of Manama, capital and largest city.
Constructed: 2004.
World Championship Grands Prix: 6.

The modern face of the racing circuit, all clean lines and custom built. This is 2009 and the Toyotas of Timo Glock and Jarno Trulli lead into the first corner. (LAT)

'Confidence under braking is the key to a quick lap'

Jenson Button

Start/finish

'This is a new world, which is why I have been trying to get here for a long time. We are a world championship and we will service the world.' The words are Bernie Ecclestone's, and he spoke them after the inaugural Grand Prix in April 2004.

The motive was to make Bahrain the centre of motor sport in the Persian Gulf (literally overtaking Kuwait) and make it the host to a Grand Prix, which Egypt, the Lebanon, and the United Arab Emirates also coveted.

The 5.4km track – and the six possible configurations it comprised, including a 2.5km oval – was designed by Hermann Tilke and work began in 2002. It was intended to house 70,000 spectators with 10,000 in the main grandstand.

When it opened it ran a variety of events from drag racing to Formula 3 and the Australian V8 series. The Grand Prix came in 2004, and came to the desert – plus an oasis section – where a magnificent complex awaited them, as well as the sand. The grass round the pits and paddock was heavily watered. Jean Todt of Ferrari commented: 'The circuit is more reminiscent of a rally than a Grand Prix.'

Revealingly, *Autosport* magazine wrote: 'Leading drivers (as well as Ecclestone) also praised the venue, which proved both challenging and even allowed several overtaking opportunities.'

This was (subconsciously) presented as something almost revolutionary – surely a commentary on modern tracks and modern racing? The 15 corners were linked by four straights with overtaking opportunities at Turns 1 (a 39mph hairpin), 4 (68mph adverse camber), 10 (39mph, constantly tightening), and 14 (179mph and bringing understeer) – the corners where outbraking was possible, again in the modern way.[1] The track had extensive run-off areas.

The circuit proved hard on brakes,

Lewis Hamilton alone in a lonely landscape as he moves to fourth place in 2009. (Vodafone/LAT)

which didn't get the time to cool: a Grand Prix car was covering the 3.3 miles and 15 corners in a minute and a half.

In 2007 it became the first track to get the FIA's Institute Centre of Excellence award for every aspect of the circuit. Incidentally, although alcohol is not illegal in Bahrain the champagne on the podium was replaced with rosewater.

COCKPIT VIEW

Jenson Button, Brawn, 2009:

'I'm a big fan of Bahrain as a country and I also really enjoy the circuit: there are some great fast-flowing sections which really suit my driving style and allow you to push the car to its limits.

'It's a good circuit for overtaking, particularly at Turn 1 after the long straight, where you brake very hard from over 300kph in seventh gear down to first gear. People tend to brake surprisingly early here so you can make up crucial ground if you are brave.

'Confidence under braking is the key to a quick lap. You have to believe in the car's performance and have full confidence that you can stop effectively.

The colours of Formula 1 in 2009 – unashamedly exotic. (Vodafone/LAT)

The shape of Formula 1 in 2009, custom built and unashamedly exotic. (Vodafone/LAT)

'The sand blowing onto the tarmac can be a challenge as you never know how the grip levels will change.'[2]

EYEWITNESS

Steven Tee, LAT Photographic:
'Bahrain the circuit I like. It's the complete opposite to, say, China. I don't like Bahrain as a place. They rip you off in the hotels and there's not really anywhere decent to go out in the evenings, but what they have done at the circuit is really good.

'It's a really friendly paddock with a nice *vibe* about it. Bahrain would be a great place to have the first Grand Prix of the season regularly, because the drivers are very visible there. The hospitality area is on a raised level, so whereas normally Ferrari would have a reserved area and you feel you couldn't go in if you weren't invited, you can very easily see and photograph people as they are sitting there. It's a little bit like the Australian paddock, which is very sociable.

'The track itself is not bad but very one-dimensional, because basically you have racing cars racing through the desert, which is where you are.

'They had some palm trees there the first year and they were taken down. I asked why – because they were nice and gave a bit of foreground– and I was told the Crown Prince has this vision of the paddock being the oasis and the racetrack being the desert so he didn't want the trees to intrude.

'One thing they did add for the last race, which was really good, was to put some Arabic writing in red and orange script on the run-off areas so photographically you do get some nice pictures there.'

MEMORIES AND MILESTONES

2004 Michael Schumacher (Ferrari) took pole. He recorded his initial impression as 'the track layout is very demanding'. He won because, he said, 'someone dashed back to the hotel to get my wife's lucky charm for me'. He beat team-mate Rubens Barrichello by 1.3 seconds. Fastest lap: Schumacher 134.3mph/216.1kph.

Truly, new horizons for Formula 1 in 2004 although the marshals keep their eye on the track – just like everywhere else. (LAT)

FACTS OF THE MATTER

3.366m/5.417km circuit

Year	Winner
2004	M. Schumacher (Ferrari)
Pole	M. Schumacher (134.4mph/216.3kph)
Fastest lap	M. Schumacher (134.3mph/216.1mh)

Turn 4 eased, 3.363m/5.412km circuit

2005	F. Alonso (Renault)
2006	F. Alonso (Renault)
2007	F. Massa (Ferrari)
2008	F. Massa (Ferrari)
2009	J. Button (Brawn)
Fastest pole	F. Alonso (Renault) 2005 (134.1mph/214.2kph)*
Fastest lap	P. de la Rosa (McLaren) 2005 (132.4mph/213.1kph)

* The grid was decided by the aggregate of two sessions. Alonso did 3m 01.9s, with a first session time of 1m 29.8s.

2005 Fernando Alonso (Renault) had pole from Schumacher and, into Turn 1 from the lights, Schumacher briefly contemplated a move down the inside. He didn't do it. Alonso led every lap (except the pit stops) and beat Jarno Trulli (Toyota) by 13.4 seconds. Fastest lap: Pedro de la Rosa (McLaren) 132.4mph (-1.9)/213.1kph (-3.0).

2006 If Bahrain was a new world, Robert Kubica, BMW's Polish test driver, brought a new country into it -- Poland – by going fastest in Friday's free practice. Schumacher (Ferrari) took pole but Alonso (Renault) beat him by 1.2 seconds. Fastest lap: Nico Rosberg (Williams) 131.0mph (-1.4)/210.8kph (-2.3).

2007 Newcomer Lewis Hamilton (McLaren) outlined the difficulties of the circuit after qualifying. 'Turn 13 was a little bit hectic and the wind is always changing here, coming across in different ways so you always have a tail wind or a crosswind. It's quite tough to put the car on the limit and anticipate what's going to happen.' He put the car on the front row, but Felipe Massa (Ferrari) had pole and beat Hamilton by 2.3 seconds. Fastest lap: Massa 128.7mph (-2.3)/207.1kph (-3.7).

2008 Kubica (BMW) took pole from Massa (Ferrari). Hamilton (McLaren) on the second row eyed a major move into Turn 1 but on the grid he didn't press the right engine mapping button. Massa led every lap (except the pit stops) and beat Ferrari team-mate Kimi Räikkönen by 3.3 seconds.

Fastest lap: Heikki Kovalainen (McLaren) 129.9mph (+1.2)/209.1kph (+2.0).

2009 Jarno Trulli (Toyota) took pole. Jenson Button of the 'new' Brawn team slipstreamed Hamilton into Turn 1 on the second lap and went through, opening the way to victory. He beat Sebastian Vettel (Red Bull) by 7.1 seconds. Fastest lap: Trulli 128.0mph (-1.9)/206.0kph (-3.1).

Speed decrease 2004–9: 6.3mph/10.1kph.

Footnotes
[1] Button's figures taken from *Autosport*, April 2009.
[2] Courtesy of Brawn GP.

Reinforcing the modern face of the racing circuit, comprehensive and constantly updated websites.

BELGIUM

NIVELLES-BAULERS

Location: 20 miles (30km) south of Brussels.
Constructed: 1971.
World Championship Grands Prix: 2.

'This was what I would call the forerunner of the modern circuit layout'

John Watson

Start/finish

On the Friday in 1974 it rained and Fittipaldi (McLaren) was one of only two drivers in the 1m 17s bracket. (Courtesy Paul Kooyman)

'It's gone, completely gone. You won't find anything.'

A long sloping road in the country, houses, shops, and businesses strung along either side: they look specifically Belgian in a way which is difficult to define. It's a village called Baulers.

Light traffic ebbs by. Spring 2009 and I've stopped to ask directions because there is no sense of a Grand Prix circuit being anywhere near or, frankly, anything else being near. The man giving the directions was wrong, though. You have to go just outside Baulers, to a very modern industrial estate, and look carefully – actually behind a police training academy – to find one wide strip of what was clearly a straight, being used as a car park; look carefully a little further on, through the wire of a closed gate forbidding entry, to see another straight stretching into the distant trees. Nature is trying to reclaim it and no doubt will if the industrial estate doesn't expand there first.

Trespassers (not me, of course) may find a curve with coarse grass advancing on it and dogged moss eating into the track surface, may find little sections of kerbing, may even find discarded, rusting artefacts.

Nobody, it seems, mourns this. Baulers is part of the larger commune of Nivelles (hence the circuit's name) and known *only* for the circuit. It was constructed under the Belgian political imperative of alternating their Grand Prix between the Walloon and Flemish parts of the country. By 1972, the old road circuit at Spa (Walloon) was simply too dangerous to survive and Zolder, in use since 1965, would in Grand Prix terms cover the Flemish part of the country from 1973. Baulers replaced Spa as the Walloon race and in fact became the first Belgian Grand Prix not to be run at Spa.

It was flat, it was unpopular among drivers and disliked by spectators because for safety reasons they were kept a long way from the track. The drivers were protected by guardrails, catch-fencing, and run-off areas.

The last race on the circuit was held in 1979 and the conversion to an industrial estate began in 2002.

COCKPIT VIEW

John Watson:

'This was what I would call the forerunner of the modern circuit layout. It was purpose-built, flat, and would go into the Anderstorp category [see Sweden]. It didn't have a lot of atmosphere or character about it – in truth I can hardly remember doing a lap on it.

'It was shaped like a hockey stick and it was bland. One of the races was on a dullish, damp day and I didn't have any great success there so maybe that's why I can't remember.

'The paradox is that Belgium had two circuits which I enjoyed, Spa and Zolder. I only raced in Formula 1 at Spa once and that was 1983. Nivelles was just not on the same radar.'

EYEWITNESSES

Special Envoy, *Le Soir*, Brussels, 6 June 1972:

'Fit-ti-pal, Fit-it-pal-di!

'Waving their national flags dominated by green, the Brazilian supporters let their joy explode once they'd got across the security barriers.

'How many were they, these "*tifosi* of Sao Paulo"? Twenty or thirty, more or less, but never unnoticed.

'Very confident about the possibilities of their idol, they arrived early in the morning in order to reserve seats in the grandstand just above the Lotus pit. Each time the black single-seater number 32 passed, they expressed their joy.

'When the Brazilian crossed the line to win it was delirium, and the mechanics had a lot of trouble protecting the driver and the car from the enthusiasm of the supporters.'

Paul Kooyman, a Belgian who worked as a camshaft grinder:

'I always was (and still am) a racing fanatic – I saw my first race at Zolder and I've been hooked ever since. I became an amateur photographer and I have always tried to make a picture archive of the races I've been to and capture some atmosphere shots.

'I never became a pro because I did not have the right equipment, and I wanted to go to races of my own choice, rather than being told where to go to. I have a wife and two children, and the weekends were for them too!

'My first Formula 1 experience was Zandvoort 1969 but in 1970 and 1971 I was in the army, so my next chance to be there was Nivelles 1972. I simply jumped in my car and went.

Working conditions were traditional. This is Tim Schenken's Surtees. (Courtesy Paul Kooyman)

'The circuit was a very modern complex in those days. There were decent pits where the cars and mechanics could work inside a small garage, out of the rain – not like Zolder where there was not even a place for this team and they had to work at the end of the pit lane.

'There was the famous catch-fencing and an enormous distance between the main straight and the pits so the pitboard guys had to run a marathon. Only a few had radio contact with the timekeepers inside the pits.

'I remember sneaking into the 1972 paddock by "helping" to push a car from the parking through the paddock gate, and then it was trying not to be caught, although the Friday practice was always a low tension affair. The real business started on Saturday.

'In 1974 I was so early at the paddock entry there was not even a marshal. I walked through the opened gate as if it was St Peter's in Heaven!

'The lady was some sort of scrutineering official. She walked from car to car to check if they had a decent number, seat belts and a fire extinguisher, and that was it! Again I was trying not to get thrown out but it was cold and rainy and nobody paid attention to an early bird with a camera so I had plenty of time for my pit lane walk. When the action began I simply walked out and stood between the professional photographers and took some very nice shots.

'The track layout was rather simple: the straight slightly uphill, the first right-hander a fast kink and not really flat (surely not in the rain) then a 90° right, then a fast downhill right-left combination, a short straight, again an even faster right-left towards the hairpin, coming on to the uphill straight again. They even planned an extension to the left before the hairpin to bring it to a decent length, but it never materialised.

'After the drivers refused to race on the old Spa, they were going to Zolder, but the Walloons wanted it to alternate north-south, Flemish-French, so they built an interim track and the Walloons had their Grand Prix after all.

'Then Gilles died at Zolder. The track-owners built an entire new paddock and pit complex but to no avail. The new Spa was almost ready, and Nivelles as well as Zolder were doomed.

'The Nivelles track is still there, although not as it was in the 1970s. The police trained their drivers there but most of the place is broken up and you can't do a lap any more.'

MEMORIES AND MILESTONES

1972 Unpopular? According to Elizabeth Hayward,[1] Emerson Fittipaldi (Lotus), pole, 'obviously enjoyed' the circuit. He very soon got the measure of it, as a new track. He said: 'It is very easy to learn, but not so easy to go quickly to the limit.' He beat François Cevert (Tyrrell) by 26.6 seconds. Fastest lap: Chris Amon (Matra) 115.5mph/185.9kph.
1974 The race seems to have been surrounded by mild chaos. The number of pit passes was restricted but not

Mike Hailwood (Surtees) would finish fourth in 1972. Nivelles was not only flat, it had an open feel about it. (Courtesy Paul Kooyman)

FACTS OF THE MATTER

2.314m/3.724km circuit

Year	Winner
1972	E. Fittipaldi (Lotus)
1974	E. Fittipaldi (McLaren)
Fastest pole	C. Regazzoni (Ferrari) 1m 9.8s (119.3mph/192.0kph), 1974 (see text)
Fastest lap	D. Hulme (McLaren) 1m 11.3s (116.8mph/188.0kph), 1974

Nivelles really was flatland, as Ronnie Peterson (March) discovers. He'd finish ninth. (Courtesy Paul Kooyman)

the number of people in the pits; some accredited journalists were turned away when they tried to reach the pits, while children played there; non-accredited photographers wandered the circuit and put themselves in dangerous positions – like between catch-fences.[2] Marshals 'lounged' against the guardrails and their use of flags was 'ludicrous'. The published qualifying times were 'generally regarded as a wild fantasy', according to *Autocourse*, while 'no one believed Clay Regazzoni's pole position time … not even the Ferrari team.'[3] Despite all this, Fittipaldi (McLaren) still obviously enjoyed the circuit because he beat Niki Lauda (Ferrari) by 0.35 of a second. Fastest lap: Denny Hulme (McLaren) 116.8mph/188.0kph.

Speed increase 1972–74: 1.3mph/2.1kph.

Footnotes
[1] *Flying on the Ground*, Fittipaldi and Hayward.
[2] *Autocourse*, 1974–5. [3] *Grand Prix!*, Lang.

The Grand Prix was big news wherever it was held in Belgium. The main headline in Le Soir of Brussels says: Fittipaldi has taken out an option on the World Championship by imposing himself at Nivelles!

On the Friday in 1974 it rained and this is how they coped: Hans Stuck (March) only went out in the morning, Jochen Mass (Surtees) was solid in the morning and afternoon sessions. *(Courtesy Paul Kooyman)*

SPA-FRANCORCHAMPS

Location: 30 miles (50km) south-east of Liège.
Constructed: 1922.
World Championship Grands Prix: 41.

La Source hairpin looks very tight from here – and even tighter to Ayrton Senna (McLaren) on pole on the right. He won. (LAT)

La Source
Start/finish
Eau Rouge
Le Raidillon
Blanchimont
Kemmel
La Carrière
Haut de la Côte
Burnenville
Stavelot Holowell Masta Kink Masta Straight Malmédy

Start/finish
La Source
Bus Stop
Eau Rouge
Le Raidillon
Blanchimont
Kemmel
Le Pouhon
Stavelot
Les Fagnes
Pif-Paf
Les Combes
Rivage
Malmédy

'One's chance of survival was slight'

Jochen Rindt – original circuit

'It has a layout which gives you everything you could want as a driver'

Jenson Button – current circuit

Current Circuit
Original Circuit

There's a metal gate at *Les Combes* which is padlocked, although, because it's made like a grille, anyone standing on the inside can see out through it and anyone standing on the outside can see in through it. That's wonderfully apt. The gate is a demarcation line in time itself. Inside is a very modern circuit familiar to every televiewer – including the dramatic right-hander of *Les Combes* – and outside is a country road that no modern televiewer would imagine was ever a circuit.

Before 1979, the track did not turn right at *Les Combes* but continued through where the gate is. This was sometimes known as the *Virage du Haut de la Côte*, a blind left-hander, the road tightening. The cars were out into the pleasant pasturelands of Belgium, flanked at first by neat, detached houses.

The track descended in a great left curve through an unnamed bend and another blind left taken flat out. That brought the cars to the *Virage de Burnenville* – two right-hand bends flowing round the village of Burnenville (which the drivers naughtily called Bournville after the British chocolate bar). It was taken as one continuous corner, the cars drifting in the first part at some 115mph/185kph. It was a place where time could be gained or lost.

They hugged the inside kerb to position themselves for the burst to the left-right *Virage de Malmédy*, done flat out until 'about the second telegraph pole' (according to Paul Frère, driver and journalist). That cut the speed to some 105mph/170kph and was 'tricky', because it had a blind entrance and slight adverse camber. On race days a flagpole was erected inside the right-handed exit, giving drivers an aiming point.

They went on the *Masta Straight* travelling towards the *Masta Kink*, a left-right taken at 120mph/193kph. Through that they descended to the *Virage Holowell* and, just beyond it, the *Virage de Stavelot*. They formed a curving right-hander, entered at some 118mph/190kph, braking to 105mph/169kph as the corner tightened. It was bumpy here and drivers tried to mitigate that by staying to the inside.

The track rose from Stavelot,

running between fields to one side (and a drop) and tall trees on the other. The cars went flat out through two gentle left-handers and almost flat out through a right-hander to the right-handed *Virage de la Carrière* – a 90mph/145kph corner, turning in at the apex 'almost exactly where the telegraph pole stands. There is little margin if the corner is misjudged … the ditch being very close to the outside of the road.'

After a short straight, these days you reach another metal gate.

This is a second demarcation line, fenced off: here the old circuit and the new would be joined, because they followed the same original shape round *Blanchimont* to *La Source* hairpin, went down to and up from *Eau Rouge* like the big dipper on a fairground, then fled along the straight to *Les Combes*.

The old circuit, first used for the Belgian bike Grand Prix in 1922, was conceived as a way of attracting tourists to the area. It measured 14.8km (9.2 miles) and was very, very dangerous, especially in changeable weather. That meant one part of the circuit could be dry and another have standing water on it. It was also very, very fast. Antonio Ascari, whose son Alberto would dominate the race in

the early 1950s (see winners), won the first car Grand Prix in 1925, averaging 74.8mph – more than the British speed limit 85 years later. The organisers fully intended the circuit to be the fastest in Europe and the Malmédy kink was eased in 1934. A hairpin just after *Eau Rouge* was abandoned in 1939, enabling big speeds to be maintained and creating the contour of the *Eau Rouge* that would become familiar to generations. That year, 1939, Briton Dick Seaman crashed his Mercedes fatally. Without the hairpin, Spa measured 14.5km (9.0 miles).

Grand Prix racing resumed in 1947.

Because of its nature, the track became a barometer recording the evolution of safety (or absence of it), until after 1970 the Grand Prix didn't return. In 1973 Henri Pescarolo, driving a Matra sports car, averaged 163mph/262kph to establish an outright lap record which, of course, will stand forever since the old, full road circuit has been abandoned and won't be used again.

Nivelles staged the race in 1972, Zolder in 1973, Nivelles again in 1974,

The full majesty of the circuit looking towards the pits and paddock.
(Courtesy Tom Bellingham)

then Zolder from 1975 to 1982 when the new Spa – built in 1979 – hosted the race again in 1983 to general rejoicing, not least that *Eau Rouge* was back.

As John Watson, who was in that race, says: 'Every circuit is about confidence but none more so than Spa. Today *Eau Rouge* is a shadow of its former self, a straight run through. In 1983 it was a distinct turn left, turn right up the hill and that transition up the hill made you go *oh-oh-oh-oh*. Even in a Cosworth-powered car it was a big corner.'

The new track incorporated the Bus Stop chicane, an actual bus stop – normal traffic used most of the circuit as public roads until 2000. The starting grid, traditionally on the slope to *Eau Rouge*, was moved back beyond *La Source*.

The circuit still used public roads but felt and looked much more like a track. (This did allow everyday motorists to take on *Eau Rouge* any day of the year except when there was racing. It really was steeper than it looked on television.)

The circuit is completely enclosed now. That's what the gate and fencing are doing: guarding the present from the past.

1 The corner at Stavelot originally went left to a hairpin but was by-passed, direction Blanchimont, curving to the right. *(Author)*

2 The point where the old circuit meets the new, the gate separating them. *(Author)*

3 The Masta Kink. No more than a gentle curve for law-abiding Belgian motorists but something else in a racing car. *(Author)*

4 The barn where Jackie Stewart was carried at the Masta has gone. This stands on the site today. *(Author)*

5 This picture was taken a moment or two before 6am by Jeroen Saeijs, who says: 'We had already been there since 5.30. We slept in the back of the car, parked on the side of the road close to the Blanchimont entrance. When we woke (still dark, 5 degrees C) there was already a big stream of people. I'll never forget it: a great atmosphere.' *(Courtesy Jeroen Saeijs)*

COCKPIT VIEW –
OLD CIRCUIT
Jochen Rindt, 1970:

Rindt took journalist Heinz Prüller round in a saloon car for a television programme. 'Up to a year ago the safety precautions around this track were virtually non-existent. If something went wrong with the car, if there was oil on the track or anything else happened, one was bound to hit the embankment or finish up in the woods. One's chance of survival was slight. That's why the GPDA[1] insisted on crash barriers being erected, and that's why we won't drive if it rains. Regrettably they only completed 70% of the work we had asked for. In any case Spa will never be safe, except when we move to another circuit.'

Prüller pointed out that eight of the more important corners can be 'taken in fifth gear at 160 to 190mph.'

Burnenville: 170mph – 'They have guard rails on the outside, but if you spin off on the infield, you dive down a steep cutting.'

Masta straight: 200mph-plus – 'Telegraph poles with only six- to nine-foot long rails in front of them. Whether I hit the guard rails or the poles at 180mph, or

BELOW: Looking up from Eau Rouge, the pits up on the left and no protection anywhere except the stone wall, right. (Courtesy Thomas Horat)

BELOW RIGHT: Eau Rouge exercises powerful images – so powerful you have to experience it yourself, even if that's just on foot. (Courtesy Filipp Gorelik)

ABOVE: Imagine a lap of the old Spa... this is Eau Rouge from the pits in 1952. (Courtesy Thomas Horat)

BELOW: Senna's lap of Spa, 1987, in the Lotus. (Courtesy Camel)

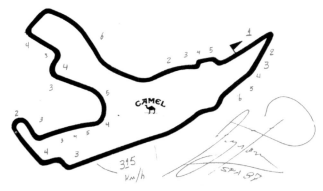

whether the car is split open by the rails, it all amounts to much the same.'

Masta kink: 180mph.

Stavelot: 150mph – 'Guardrails outside, on the inside just a wall, at right-angles to the track.'

COCKPIT VIEW –
NEW CIRCUIT
Nelson Piquet, 1988:

'Spa is a very challenging track. It goes up and down, has difficult corners but also long straights. It's good for turbos but not

for atmos (normally aspirated engines) – they are very tired.

'The track and surroundings are very pretty, and especially when the sun is shining it is a good place to be. Often it rains and then the track can be very dangerous but exhilarating.'

Jenson Button, 2009:

'Spa is one of my favourite circuits and has a layout which gives everything you could want as a driver. It's one of the fastest and most challenging circuits in the world with hills, fast corners and long straights which combine to give you a real buzz to drive, just like Suzuka and Silverstone.

'It's also a very beautiful circuit with the forest setting, although the weather can be unpredictable. It can play a big part in the race weekend, even in the summer, so you have to be ready to react – but that unpredictability is part of the thrill of racing at Spa.

'*Eau Rouge* is still a legendary

First lap duelling up Eau Rouge, 2009 – Lewis Hamilton (McLaren) trying to hold off Rubens Barrichello in the Brawn. (LAT)

corner, although it is usually easy flat for us in the dry, but the feeling when you hit the bottom of the hill, touch the ground and shoot straight back up again is … amazing.'[2]

EYEWITNESSES

Gareth Rees, motor sport enthusiast:

'Nowadays Spa, perhaps with Monza, is the last remaining classic Grand Prix circuit. Even today's shortened and necessarily sanitised version is still in a class of its own.

'I was a bit too young to get to see Formula 1 in its full glory on the old circuit, though I was lucky to make it to a couple of other races, including the Spa 1,000km in 1973 when Henri Pescarolo took his Matra 670 sports car round at an average of 163mph!

'In 1989 I made the pilgrimage to *Eau Rouge* and even on an otherwise grey day the stunning neon-like colours and sounds of the first cars to leave the pit road in practice made my world feel perfect as they eased their way, engine barely on more than tick-over, up the hill at *Le Raidillon*.

'A lap later, when the same cars came through at racing speed, it reminded me

all over again why we love this sport. Right there before my very eyes were the world's best drivers in the best cars in the best corner of the world's best circuit.

'They accelerated on the downhill approach, then just the tiniest lift at the bottom of the dip, then back full on the gas, then up the deceptively steep hill, then over the blind left brow at the top, continually gathering speed until they were out of earshot – or the next car came and the sequence started again.

'Inwardly, I was also pleased with myself. I was there watching it, loving it, but also *enjoying* it again. I've watched races all my life but the previous two times at *Eau Rouge* had, in fact, scared me a bit, because this bit of road is special and demands respect.

'When I think of Spa, it's all about *Eau Rouge* and the incomparable sense of anticipation: you'd hear the field approaching the end of each lap down there in the forest, flat out through *Blanchimont* towards the pits and *La Source*, knowing that soon they would be heading down the hill to conquer *Eau Rouge* just one more time.

'In 1982 I was there for a Formula 2 race held in torrential rain. Even in those

conditions ground effect made those cars look like they could do anything. Clearly many of the drivers thought so too. Each lap I was thinking *this time he won't make it*. Local Belgian hero Thierry Tassin in his Toleman was bravely putting his life on the line every time. It was Russian Roulette and it couldn't last. Around lap 10, he turned left at the bottom, still a hero, then tried to turn right up the hill but his car was already heading the other way – straight into the wall and a fierce impact.

'The race continued and in the next ten or so laps three more *kamikaze* heroes followed him at full speed: quick pirouette and wham, into the wall. Under black clouds, it was like a horror movie.

'In 1985, this time in pleasant weather, I was watching practice for the Spa 1000km, having myself driven in the day's Formula Ford race. The Group C cars were fast and furious and I had this feeling that it couldn't last without somebody having a huge *off* sooner or later.

'My mates were heading home that Saturday evening and I was wondering whether to stay alone for the race on Sunday. I decided I'd go home and, I swear, one of the factors playing on my mind was that I didn't want to see someone get killed there the next day. I've never felt that way at a racetrack before or since.

'When I got to work on Monday morning, a colleague came to ask me if I'd seen the accident. It was the weekend when Stefan Bellof died at the same wall at *Eau Rouge*.'

Tom Bellingham and Katy Peach, enthusiasts:

'We went to Spa in summer 2009 and it was an amazing experience, our favourite holiday ever. The circuit is set in the most beautiful surroundings and this allows for some great views, because if you stand on the high ground you can see so much of the track.

'For fans that can't pay the huge ticket prices for a grandstand seat at the famous *Eau Rouge*, you can see the top of the corner from the Formula 1 village, a truly breathtaking experience. The area seems to have its own microclimate and the weather is constantly changing: it can go from warm and sunny to overcast and raining within minutes. This meant we

experienced the Formula 1 cars in the wet and dry.

'On the Thursday of the race weekend we got to meet some of the drivers during the pit lane signing session, a rare chance to see them in person.

'Throughout the weekend we were amazed by the amount of fanatical fans that must get there at 7:00am to get the best views. They sit in their folding chairs with thick coats, blankets and flasks to keep warm.

'We were lucky enough to be stood right where Kimi Räikkönen overtook Giancarlo Fisichella for the race lead and the *tifosi* standing next to us were going crazy. The atmosphere there is incredible. Everyone we met was friendly and talkative, and these fans have a clear love for the sport.

'After the race we were able to walk the track. You could still smell and see the rubber the cars had left just minutes before. In our opinion, the best circuit in Formula 1.'

MEMORIES AND MILESTONES

1950 For the fourth round of the new World Championship the track had been resurfaced and in places made wider, reducing the length to 14.1km (8.7 miles). Giuseppe Farina (Alfa Romeo) took pole but Juan Manuel Fangio (Alfa Romeo) won at an average speed of 110mph/177kph, beating Luigi Fagioli in another Alfa by 14.0 seconds. Fastest lap: Farina 115.2mph/185.5kph.

1951 Only 13 entries, centred round Ferrari and Alfa Romeo. Fangio in an Alfa took pole and three cars led – a Ferrari, and two Alfa Romeos. The one driven by Farina beat Alberto Ascari (Ferrari) by 3.0 seconds. Fastest lap: Fangio 120.5mph (+5.3)/193.9kph (+8.4).

1952 Ascari (Ferrari) took pole. The race was run in heavy rain and Piero Taruffi (Ferrari) and Jean Behra (Gordini) crashed, both ending in a ditch. Ascari beat Farina in another Ferrari by 1 minute 55.2 seconds. Fastest lap: Ascari 107.1mph/172.3kph (no comparison).

1953 Fangio (Maserati) took pole. Hot weather (for once) and mechanical problems for the leading runners opened the race to Ascari, who took the lead on lap 14 and beat Luigi Villoresi (in another Ferrari) by 2 minutes 48.1 seconds. Fastest lap: Froilan González (Maserati) 115.3mph (-5.2)/185.5kph (-8.4).

1954 The world waited for the return of Mercedes-Benz but it happened at Reims the race after. Fangio (Maserati) took pole and beat Maurice Trintignant (Ferrari) by 24.0 seconds, before becoming a Mercedes driver. Fastest lap: Fangio 119.0mph (+3.7)/191.5kph (+6.0).

1955 Mercedes were too strong for the other ten starters. Eugenio Castellotti (Lancia) took pole but Fangio led every lap to beat team-mate Stirling Moss by 8.0 seconds. Fastest lap: Fangio 121.2mph (+2.2)/195.1kph (+3.6).

1956 The Mercedes were gone, withdrawn in the wake of the Le Mans disaster, and Moss had a Maserati. Fangio (Ferrari) took pole. Moss led but up *Eau Rouge* a wheel came off. He ran back to the pits and took over the Maserati of Cesare Perdisa and recovered to finish third. Peter Collins beat Paul Frère in another Ferrari by 1 minute 51.0 seconds. Fastest lap: Moss 124.0mph (+2.8)/199.6kph (+4.5).

1957 Cancelled through financial problems.

Speed increase 1950–6: 8.8mph/14.1kph.

Corners were eased.

1958 The dangers were emphasised when Archie Scott Brown crashed a Lister in a sports car race and died. Jim Clark was in that race and wrote:[3] 'I had never seen Spa before and had only heard that it was fast. Actually if I had known the kind of track it was I'd never have gone.' Clark's mounting apprehension – which reached naked fear – wasn't helped when Jack Fairman, an occasional driver, drove Clark round to show him the circuit, pointing out where people had been killed. Mike Hawthorn (Ferrari) took pole but Tony Brooks (Vanwall) beat him by 20.7 seconds. Fastest lap: Hawthorn 132.4mph/213.0kph.

1960 The dark race. During practice Moss (Lotus) was doing some 140mph through *Burnenville* corner when he struck a bump in the road and the left rear wheel came off. He went into a bank backwards at just less than 100mph. 'I next remember coming round, realising I was out of the car, crouching on my hands and knees, gasping for breath. The car was lying right-side up at the end of a long smear of … debris laid across the road. I felt terribly alone. I simply could not breathe. I remembered passing Bruce McLaren earlier on that lap and I couldn't think why he was taking so long to arrive. In fact he stopped immediately and ran to me. I begged him to give me artificial respiration but he rightly refused in case I had broken ribs. Others drivers arrived, parked their cars, switched off and came to help. Then eventually marshals and an ambulance appeared.'[4]

Michael Taylor in another Lotus was about halfway along the back from *Stavelot* when his steering column broke and he was pitched into the trees. He was injured and, like Moss, lucky to be alive. Jack Brabham (Cooper) took pole.

On lap 19 of the race Chris Bristow lost control of his Cooper at *Burnenville*. He'd been duelling with Willy Mairesse in a Ferrari. The Cooper thrashed and rolled, and Taylor was flung out. He almost certainly died instantaneously.

Five laps later, Alan Stacey (who amazingly had an artificial leg) lost control of his Lotus at *Malmédy* after, it seems, he'd been struck in the face by a bird. The Lotus rode a bank, flipped, caught fire, and Stacey was flung to his death.

Brabham beat McLaren (Cooper) by 1 minute 03.3 seconds. Fastest lap: Phil Hill (Ferrari)/Brabham/Innes Ireland (Lotus) 136.0mph (+3.6)/218.9kph (+5.9).

1961 The race continued quite normally despite 1960. As practice began Cliff Allison (in a Lotus) crashed at *Blanchimont*. The car left the track and overturned in a field, throwing him out. He suffered serious damage to his legs. Phil Hill (Ferrari) took pole and beat team-mate Wolfgang von Trips by 0.7 of a second. Fastest lap: Richie Ginther (Ferrari) 131.5mph (-4.5)/211.7kph (-7.2).

1962 Graham Hill (BRM) took pole. Trevor Taylor and Mairesse duelled. The Lotus came out of gear at *Blanchimont*, touched the Ferrari and both cars went off the road. The Ferrari flipped, burst into flames, and Mairesse was thrown out. The Lotus struck a telegraph pole and Taylor was thrown out. They were both injured but alive. Clark beat Hill by 43.9 seconds. Fastest lap: Clark 133.9mph (+2.4)/215.5kph (+3.8).

1963 The rear of Taylor's Lotus failed during practice and he struck a hut. Graham Hill (BRM) took pole but Clark beat McLaren (Cooper) by slightly under five *minutes*. Fastest lap: Clark 132.4mph (-1.5)/213.1kph (-2.4).

1964 Dan Gurney (Brabham) took pole and led to lap 28 with Clark (Lotus) and

Graham Hill (BRM) duelling behind, sometimes side by side. Gurney was running out of fuel. McLaren (Cooper) passed Clark – pitting, engine overheating – and now passed Gurney. Graham Hill led but the fuel pump malfunctioned. Into *La Source* on the final lap McLaren's engine died and Clark beat him to the line by 2.6 seconds. Fastest lap: Gurney 137.6mph (+5.2)/221.5kph (+8.4).

1965 Graham Hill (BRM) took pole. Heavy rain left the track awash and Hill found the BRM almost impossible to control. Clark (Lotus) led and at one point only Jackie Stewart (also BRM) was on the same lap. Clark had clutch problems and slowed, beating Stewart by 44.8 seconds. Fastest lap: Clark 124.7mph/200.7kph (no comparison).

1966 John Surtees (Ferrari) took pole. The race began in the dry but a downpour soaked *Burnenville* and four cars spun off at *Malmédy*. One hung over a farm wall. Towards the *Masta* kink Jochen Rindt's Cooper launched into a wild sequence of spins but he regained control. Moments later, and at the same place, Bob Bondurant's BRM went off into a ditch upside down, Stewart's BRM went into a post sideways trapping him, and Graham Hill (in a third BRM) found himself going backwards at tremendous speed. He got the car to the side of the road and while trying to restart it noticed Stewart 'in the ditch beside me but on the other side of some railings. Jackie was still in the car and obviously in some sort of pain; he looked terribly helpless.'[5] Hill eventually levered him out and, in a barn, took his petrol-soaked overalls off. Some nuns arrived and did not approve of that. The ambulance taking Stewart to hospital got lost. Surtees beat Jochen Rindt (Cooper) by 42.1 seconds. Fastest lap: Surtees 121.9mph/196.2kph (no comparison).

1967 The second race for the Ford Cosworth engine and Clark (Lotus) put it on pole. He led but had plug failures, and now Stewart (BRM) led – but Gurney (Eagle) overtook on lap 21 of the 28, beating Stewart by 1 minute 03.0 seconds. Fastest lap: Gurney 148.8mph (+11.2)/239.5kph (+18.0).

1968 Chris Amon (Ferrari) took pole. Five leaders, culminating in Bruce McLaren (McLaren) beating Pedro Rodríguez (BRM) by 12.1 seconds. Brian Redman (Cooper) went off after six laps when the

suspension failed, striking parked cars and bursting into flames. A marshal got him out. Fastest lap: Surtees (Honda) 149.8mph (+1.0)/241.1kph (+1.6).

1969 The campaign for safety in motor racing began after Stewart's crash in 1966 and had gathered such momentum by 1969 that the Grand Prix Drivers' Association was demanding a flexible start time for the race to mitigate changes in the weather, something refused by the organisers because of television coverage. Stewart claimed[6] that the organisers said royalty might be coming (and would presumably need a specific time) and 'the commissionaires and the marshals and the spectators in Belgium were accustomed to a three-hour break for lunch and would not like their lunch interrupted if it was suddenly decided to run the motor race.'

Stewart went to Spa in advance and reported back to the drivers, who unanimously agreed the circuit was too dangerous, and the more so because the organisers 'would not make any concessions on safety *at all*.'

The Belgian government were insisting on what Stewart describes as 'unlimited cover' for spectators at all sports events in the country and the insurers wouldn't cover the Grand Prix. The race was off.

1970 The race returned. A chicane had been built at *Malmédy* and a lot of Armco put in place. Stewart (March) took pole. Rodríguez (BRM) beat Chris Amon (March) by 1.1 seconds. The impetus for safety continued to gather: the governing body (the CSI) banned open-wheel racing at the circuit until a raft of improvements had been implemented. It was in fact the end of Spa as the motor racing world had known it. Fastest lap: Amon 152.1mph (+2.3)/244.7kph (+3.6).

Speed increase 1958–70: 19.7mph/31.7kph.

The new circuit, incorporating the old. It received a broad welcome from the drivers although the transporters and motorhomes had difficulty manoeuvring into their berths – the area wasn't big – and the distance from the pits to the paddock caused problems for Goodyear, Michelin, and Pirelli tyre people.

Graham Hill leads BRM team-mate Jackie Stewart up Eau Rouge in 1965. Richie Ginther in the white Honda follows. (LAT)

1983 Alain Prost (Renault) took pole and drove consummately to beat Patrick Tambay (Ferrari) by 23.1 seconds. Fastest lap: Andrea de Cesaris (Alfa Romeo) 121.9mph/196.2kph.

Circuit length recalculated.

1985 The race ought to have been held on 2 June but the track, recently resurfaced, broke up. It was postponed to 15 September, when Prost (McLaren) took pole and Ayrton Senna (Lotus), exploiting the wet-dry conditions, beat Nigel Mansell (Williams) by 28.4 seconds. Fastest lap: Prost 127.5mph/205.2kph.

Spa staged a 24-hour endurance race from 1924 (a year after the first Le Mans) and a World Sports Car 1000km from

Nigel Mansell coming round in the Williams.

1966 to 1990. It was in this, in 1985, that Stefan Bellof, an outstanding young German driver, died when his Porsche touched another car, crashed, and caught fire.

1986 Elio de Angelis had been killed a few days before testing a Brabham at the Paul Ricard circuit in the south of France and former Lotus team-mate Mansell (Williams) was visibly sombre. Team-mate Nelson Piquet (Williams) took pole but Mansell beat Senna (Lotus) by 19.8 seconds. Fastest lap: Prost (McLaren) 130.1mph (+2.6)/209.5kph (+4.3).

1987: Mansell (Williams) took pole. He and Senna (Lotus) crashed on the opening lap and in the pits Mansell sought Senna out to explain, physically, the facts of life. Prost, meanwhile, undemonstratively beat McLaren team-mate Stefan Johansson

by 24.7 seconds. Fastest lap: Prost 132.5mph (+2.4)/213.3kph (+3.8).

1988 The Championship was entirely between the McLarens of Prost and Senna, and from pole Senna won an overpoweringly psychological victory, beating Prost by 30.4 seconds. Fastest lap: Gerhard Berger (Ferrari) 128.5mph (-4.0)/206.9kph (-6.4).

1989 Typical Spa, drowning in rooster tails of spray but through them came Senna (McLaren), leading every lap from pole and beating Prost in the other McLaren by 1.3 seconds. Fastest lap: Prost 118.0mph/189.9kph (no comparison).

1990 Senna led every lap from pole again and beat Prost (Ferrari) by 3.5 seconds to lead the Championship 63–50. Fastest lap: Prost 134.9mph (+6.4)/217.1kph (+10.2).

1991 Senna (McLaren) pole. Mansell (Williams) took the lead from him but an electrical failure halted him. Jean Alesi (Ferrari) inherited the lead but had an engine problem and Senna beat Gerhard Berger in the other McLaren by 1.9 seconds. Fastest lap: Roberto Moreno (Benetton) 134.8mph (-0.1)/216.9kph (-0.2).

Speed increase 1985–91: 7.3mph/11.7kph.

Minor revisions to the circuit.

1992 Mansell (Williams), imperious in his strength – he'd already won the Championship the race before – took pole from Senna (McLaren) but, in a tactic which would become familiar, Michael Schumacher (Benetton) stayed out longer at the late pit stops and gained enough time to beat Mansell by 36.5 seconds. Fastest lap: Schumacher 137.1mph/220.6kph.

1993 Prost (Williams) took pole. Damon Hill won only the second Grand Prix of his career when he held off pressure from team-mate Prost and then Schumacher (Benetton). He beat Schumacher by 3.6 seconds. Fastest lap: Prost 140.4mph/226.0kph.

Speed increase 1992–3: 3.3mph/5.3kph.

Chicane at Eau Rouge.

1994 Rubens Barrichello (Jordan) took a joyous pole, aided by the weather. Schumacher beat Hill (Williams) by 12.5 seconds and was then disqualified because his Benetton had an illegal undertray, something which kept the whole Championship alive

(Schumacher 76, Hill 55). Fastest lap: Hill 133.7mph/215.2kph.

1995 Gerhard Berger (Ferrari) took pole in the very height of the Schumacher/Hill struggle. In the wet Schumacher used his Benetton very robustly on slicks to try and keep Hill's Williams at bay. The Stewards banned him for one race for that after he'd beaten Hill by 19.4 seconds. A fire, when Eddie Irvine pitted his Jordan, produced some of motor racing's most astonishing photographs – the car, driver, and mechanics engulfed by a vast sheet of molten flame. All three survived largely unburnt. Fastest lap: David Coulthard (Williams) 137.6mph/221.4kph.

Speed increase 1994–5: 3.9mph/6.2kph.

La Source eased.

1996 Jacques Villeneuve (Williams) took pole. Astonishingly Hill was leading the Championship and Williams were planning to replace him the following season. It could not give him peace of mind and he finished fifth. Michael Schumacher (Ferrari) helped Hill's Championship by beating his rival Villeneuve by 5.6 seconds. Fastest lap: Berger (Benetton) 137.9mph/221.9kph.

1997 Villeneuve (Williams) took pole. In wet weather, Schumacher left his decision – race car or spare, set up differently? – until he'd done a lap to have a look. He chose the spare, a medium setting, and after a start behind the Safety Car cut past leader Villeneuve (Williams) and beat Giancarlo Fisichella (Jordan) by 26.7 seconds. That tightened the Championship to Schumacher 66, Villeneuve 55. Fastest lap: Villeneuve 138.3mph (+0.4)/222.6kph (+0.7).

1998 Mika Häkkinen (McLaren) took pole. In more wet weather an extraordinary multiple crash down towards *Eau Rouge* from the start made the track into, literally, an extensive scrapyard. From the restart Hill (Jordan) led, then Schumacher (Ferrari) took the lead and in the murk ran into Coulthard's McLaren. Schumacher descended into a volcanic rage and Hill beat team-mate Ralf Schumacher by 0.9 of a second to give the Jordan team their first victory after 127 races. Fastest lap: Schumacher 125.9mph/202.7kph (no comparison).

1999 Häkkinen (McLaren) took pole but team-mate Coulthard beat him by 10.4 seconds, although this was drowned by complaints from Williams Technical Director Patrick Head accusing Ferrari of ordering their driver Mika Salo to block Ralf Schumacher of Williams. Fastest lap: Häkkinen 136.8mph (-1.5)/220.1kph (-2.5).

2000 Häkkinen (McLaren) took pole. With three laps left, and approaching *Les Combes* flat out, Häkkinen thrust his McLaren inside back-marker Ricardo Zonta (BAR), who was letting Schumacher's Ferrari through on his outside. It was an overtaking move which, momentarily, defied credulity and gave the race to Häkkinen by 1.1 seconds. Fastest lap: Rubens Barrichello (Ferrari) 137.0mph (+0.2)/220.4kph (+0.3).

2001 Juan-Pablo Montoya (Williams) took pole and Schumacher (Ferrari) took his 52nd victory. He beat Coulthard (McLaren) by 10.0 seconds and beat Prost's record of 51 victories. Luciano Burti (Prost) crashed at *Blanchimont* at 175mph but was not seriously hurt, although he was taken to hospital. Fastest lap: Schumacher 142.0mph (+5.0)/228.5kph (+8.1).

Speed increase 1996–2001: 4.1mph/6.6kph.

La Source and the Bus Stop reprofiled.

2002 Schumacher (Ferrari), pole, was shattering records now, and when he beat team-mate Barrichello by 1.9 seconds he had his tenth win of the season out of 14 rounds (and his four 'failures' were a third and three second places). Fastest lap: Schumacher 145.3mph/233.9kph.

2003 No race – it fell victim to Belgium's tobacco advertising laws.

From Blanchimont to the Bus Stop the track was opened out and provided with more extensive run-off areas. Blanchimont was now taken flat, even in the wet. Former Grand Prix driver Mika Salo said: 'Before, when you exited Blanchimont, you could stay on the right side of the track ready for Bus Stop. Now you have to go sharp left, because you have the line for breaking into the new chicane. It's hard and bumpy.' The Bus Stop itself had been reprofiled, removing it as an overtaking opportunity. Eau Rouge, too, had been softened with the Armco moved back and the gravel traps asphalted over. Coulthard (McLaren) still enthused over Eau Rouge, however, and quantified it citing the example of a newcomer trying to take it flat out for the first time. 'The challenge is purely yourself, it's not the car. It's whether you can do it. That's the sort of challenge that a driver thrives on.'

2004 Jarno Trulli (Renault) took pole in the very first single-lap qualifying. Seven cars had accidents, or eight if you include Kimi Räikkönen (McLaren), who was tapped by the Ferrari of Felipe Massa but continued and outdrove Schumacher in the other Ferrari by 3.1 seconds. Fastest lap: Räikkönen 148.5mph (+3.2)/238.9kph (+5.0).

2005 Montoya (McLaren) took pole. Fernando Alonso (Renault) could have become the youngest champion but Räikkönen (McLaren) led the last 12 laps to beat him by 28.3 seconds. Alonso would have to wait another two weeks, until Brazil. Fastest lap: Ralf Schumacher (Toyota) 140.0mph/225.3kph.

Speed decrease 2004–5: 8.5mph/13.6kph.

2006 No race – the organisers went bankrupt in 2005 and improvements to the track could not be made in time.

The Bus Stop was completely reconfigured into a right-left, making the track 4.5 miles (7.0km).

2007 Ferrari rampant, Räikkönen leading every lap from pole and Felipe Massa running second (except for pit stops) while Alonso was very robust with McLaren team-mate Lewis Hamilton, much to Hamilton's displeasure. Räikkönen beat Massa by 4.6 seconds. Fastest lap: Massa 145.0mph/233.3kph.

2008 Hamilton (McLaren), pole, made a brave move to take Räikkönen (Ferrari) at the chicane but cut across it, ceded the place to Räikkönen then immediately afterwards overtook him into *La Source*. The Stewards gave Hamilton a post-race 25-second penalty, so Massa (Ferrari) beat Nick Heidfeld (BMW) by 9.3 seconds. Fastest lap: Räikkönen 145.2mph (+0.2)/233.6kph (+0.3).

2009 Giancarlo Fisichella (Force India) took a genuinely amazing pole for a small team. Four cars were out on the first lap, including Jenson Button (Brawn) and Hamilton (McLaren). Räikkönen (Ferrari) beat Fisichella, who might even have won the race at one point, by 0.9 of a second. Fastest lap: Sebastian Vettel (Red Bull) 146.1mph (+0.9)/235.1kph (+1.5).

Speed increase 2007–9: 1.1mph/1.7kph.

Footnotes
[1] GPDA, the Grand Prix Drivers' Association. [2] Courtesy Brawn GP. [3] *At the Wheel*, Clark. [4] *My Cars, My Career*, Moss. [5] *Life at the Limit*, Hill. [6] *World Champion*, Stewart.

3 *Paddock people*

bonjour de
groeten uit

greetings from
grüsse aus

S P A

5

FORMULA 1
WORLD
CHAMPIONSHIP

CHAMPION
BELGIAN
GRAND PRIX

SPA-FRANCORCHAMPS
25-26-27 AUGUST 1989

BARCLAY

Tactel

OFFICIAL SPONSOR   CHAMPION

PROGRAMME

VENDREDI
8.00—9.00: Préqualification Formule 1
10.00—11.30: Essais Formule 1
13.00—14.00: Qualifications Formule 1
A partir de 14.30: Qualifications des courses annexes.

SAMEDI
10.00—11.30: Essais Formule 1
13.00—14.00: Qualifications Formule 1
A partir de 14.30: Qualifications des courses annexes.

DIMANCHE
10.00—10.30: Warm-up Formule 1
11.00: GM Lotus Euroseries
14.30: CHAMPION GRAND PRIX DE BELGIQUE.
16.30: Groupe N.

Des manifestations supplémentaires peuvent être ajoutées à ce programme.

VRIJDAG
8.00—9.00: Prekqualificatie Formule 1
10.00—11.30: Oefenritten Formule 1
13.00—14.00: Kwalifikatie Formule 1
Vanaf 14.30: Kwalifikatie omlijstende wedstrijden.

ZATERDAG
10.00—11.30: Oefenritten Formule 1
13.00—14.00: Kwalifikatie Formule 1
Vanaf 14.30: Kwalifikatie omlijstende wedstrijden.

ZONDAG
10.00—10.30: Opwarming Formule 1
11.00: GM Lotus Euroseries
14.30: CHAMPION GROTE PRIJS VAN BELGIË.
16.30: Groepe N.

Bijkomende manifestaties kunnen aan dit programma toegevoegd worden.

FRIDAY
8.00—9.00: Prequalification Formula 1
10.00—11.30: Untimed Practice Formula 1
13.00—14.00: Qualifying Formula 1
From 14.30: Qualifying for supporting rac

SATURDAY
10.00—10.30: Untimed pratice Formula 1
13.00—14.00: Qualifying Formula 1
From 14.30: Qualifying for supporting rac

SUNDAY
10.00—10.30: Warm-up Formula 1
11.00: GM Lotus Euroseries
14.30: CHAMPION BELGIAN GRANE PRIX.
16.30: Group N.

Additional events may be added to this programme.

6 FORMATION

1. Les billets du vendredi et samedi seront disponibles uniquement au circuits les 25, 26, août 1989.

2. Tarif réduit pour les tickets week-end achetés avant le 21 août 1989.

3. Le prix des billets tribune comprend aussi l'accès à l'enceinte générale.

4. Pour les enfants de moins de 12 ans, des tickets week-end au prix de BFR 975 sont en vente, permettant l'accès à toutes les tribunes, excepté la tribune couverte.

5. Tous les billets seront envoyés au plus tard quinze jours avant la course.

6. Tribune Raidillon disponible uniquement au circuit les 25, 26, 27 août.

1. Tickets voor vrijdag en zaterdag zijn slechts beschikbaar op het circuit van 25 en 26 augustus 1989.

2. Speciale tarief voor Week-End tickets gekocht voor de 21 augustus 1989.

3. In de tribuneprijzen is de algemene ingang inbegrepen.

4. Voor Kinderen jonger dan 12 jaar zijn weekend-tickets te verkrijgen tegen 975 BF. Deze geven toegang tot alle tribunes met uitzondering van de overdekte tribune.

5. Alle tickets zullen u ten laatste 2 weken voor de race toegezonden worden.

6. De tribune „Raidillon" is slechts toegankelijk van 25 tot 27 augustus.

1. Friday and Saturday tickets will only be available at the circuit on the 25th and 26th of August.

2. Special rate for Week-End tickets purchased before the 21st August 1989.

3. Grandstand ticket prices include General Admission.

4. For children under 12 years of age, weekend tickets for the price of BFR 975 are available, valid for all the grandstands, except covered grandstand.

5. All the tickets will be mailed to you at the latest 2 weeks before the event.

6. Grandstand Raidillon only available from 25th to 27th of august.

TICKET PRICES

Tous les prix en francs belges Alle prijzen in belgische frank		Vendredi Vrijdag	Samedi Zaterdag	Dimanche Zondag	Weekend 21.08.89	Weekend
Enceinte générale Algemene omheining		500	1000	2000	2000	3000
Tribune Francorchamps		1200	3000	4000	5000	6500
Tribune couverte Overdekte tribune		—	—	5500	6000	7000
Tribune Spa		1200	3000	4000	5000	6500
Tribune Raidillon		1200	3000	4000	—	6500
Tribune Chicane		1200	3000	4000	5000	6500

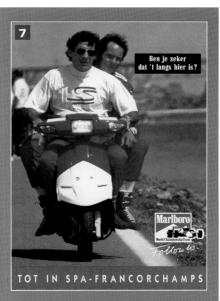

Ben je zeker
dat 't langs hier is?

TOT IN SPA-FRANCORCHAMPS

1 The crowd at the chicane. *(Courtesy Jeroen Saeijs)*

2 You need an aerial view to understand just how much the circuit is surrounded by woodland. *(Courtesy Martin Hadwen, National Motor Racing Archive)*

3 The official programme liked celebrities. *(Courtesy Martin Hadwen, National Motor Racing Archive)*

4 Spa is the most genteel place, as this postcard shows. The circuit of course isn't there – it's at Francorchamps. *(Courtesy Martin Hadwen, National Motor Racing Archive)*

5 and 6 The ticket brochure from 1989 gives details of the programme, with GM Lotus Euroseries and Group N saloon supporting races, and ticket prices – 2,000 Belgian francs (equivalent to around £40 in 2010) in advance for general enclosure weekend admission, a bargain by today's standards.

7 These were the days when Marlboro were major players in motor racing, and understandably exploiting it. Ayrton Senna gives Gerhard Berger a lift, and Berger contemplates what seems to be an absence of track action.

FACTS OF THE MATTER

8.774m/14.120km circuit

Year	Winner
1950	J.M. Fangio (Alfa Romeo)
1951	G. Farina (Alfa Romeo)
1952	A. Ascari (Ferrari)
1953	A. Ascari (Ferrari)
1954	J.M Fangio (Maserati)
1955	J.M. Fangio (Mercedes)
1956	P. Collins (Ferrari)
Fastest pole	J.M. Fangio (Lancia Ferrari) 1956 (126.4mph/203.5kph)
Fastest lap	S. Moss (Maserati) 1956 (124.0mhp/199.6kph)

8.761m/14.100km circuit

1958	T. Brooks (Vanwall)
1960	J. Brabham (Cooper)
1961	P. Hill (Ferrari)
1962	J. Clark (Lotus)
1963	J. Clark (Lotus)
1964	J. Clark (Lotus)
1965	J. Clark (Lotus)
1966	J. Surtees (Ferrari)
1967	D. Gurney (Eagle)
1968	B. McLaren (McLaren)
1970	P. Rodríguez (BRM)
Fastest pole	J. Stewart (March) 1970 (151.6mph/244.0kph)
Fastest lap	C. Amon (March) 1970 (152.1mph/244.7kph)

4.318m/6.949km circuit

1983	A. Prost (Renault)
Pole	A. Prost (124.7mph/200.7kph)
Fastest lap	A. de Cesaris (Alfa Romeo) (121.9mph/196.2kph)

Recalculated, 4.312m/6.940km circuit

1985	A. Senna (Lotus)
1986	N. Mansell (Williams)
1987	A. Prost (McLaren)
1988	A. Senna (McLaren)
1989	A. Senna (McLaren)
1990	A. Senna (McLaren)
1991	A. Senna (McLaren)
Fastest pole	A. Senna (McLaren) 1991 (144.0mph/231.7kph)
Fastest lap	A. Prost (Ferrari) 1990 (134.9mph/217.1kph)

4.333m/6.974km circuit

1992	M. Schumacher (Benetton)
1993	D. Hill (Williams)
1994	D. Hill (Williams)

(Note: in 1994 Eau Rouge was slightly altered, making the circuit 4.350m/7001km but returned to its former length in 1995.)

1995	M. Schumacher (Benetton)
Fastest pole	A. Prost (Williams) 1993 (145.0mph/233.4kph)
Fastest lap	A. Prost 1993 (140.4mph/226.0kph)

La Source eased, 4.330m/6.969km circuit

1996	M. Schumacher (Ferrari)
1997	M. Schumacher (Ferrari)
1998	D. Hill (Jordan)
1999	D. Coulthard (McLaren)
2000	M. Häkkinen (McLaren)
2001	M. Schumacher (Ferrari)
Fastest pole	M. Häkkinen (McLaren) 1998 (143.4mph/230.8kph)
Fastest lap	M. Schumacher 2001 (142.0mph/228.5kph)

La Source and Bus Stop reprofiled, 4.327m/6.963km circuit

2002	M. Schumacher (Ferrari)
Pole	M. Schumacher (150.2mph/241.7kph)
Fastest lap	M. Schumacher (145.3mph/233.9kph)

Bus Stop reprofiled, 4.335m/6.976km circuit

2004	K. Räikkönen (McLaren)
2005	K. Räikkönen (McLaren)
Fastest pole	J.-P. Montoya (McLaren) 2005 (146.7mph/236.0kph)
Fastest lap	K. Räikkönen 2004 (148.5mph/238.9kph)

Bus Stop removed, 4.532m/7.004km circuit

2007	K. Räikkönen (Ferrari)
2008	F. Massa (Ferrari)
2009	K. Räikkönen (Ferrari)
Fastest pole	K. Räikkönen (Ferrari) 2007 (147.8mph/237.9kph)
Fastest lap	S. Vettel (Red Bull) 2009 (146.1mph/235.1kph)

ZOLDER

Location: 10 miles (6km) from the town of Hasselt, which is 48 miles (77km) from Brussels.
Constructed: 1961, converted for Grands Prix 1973.
World Championship Grands Prix: 10.

The atmosphere of Zolder, flatland dominated by trees. This is the grandstand opposite the pits. (Courtesy Filipp Gorelik)

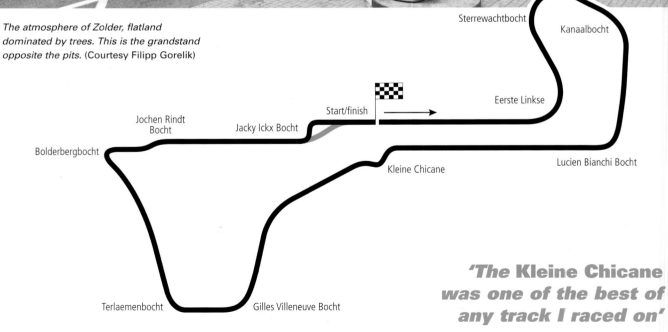

Sterrewachtbocht
Kanaalbocht
Eerste Linkse
Start/finish
Jochen Rindt Bocht
Jacky Ickx Bocht
Bolderbergbocht
Lucien Bianchi Bocht
Kleine Chicane
Terlaemenbocht
Gilles Villeneuve Bocht

'The Kleine Chicane was one of the best of any track I raced on'

John Watson

Zolder feels anonymous, which is always difficult to quantify. Perhaps it's to do with the approach through anonymous suburbs, perhaps it's to do with so many trees everywhere, perhaps it's to do with being pancake flat, and anyone going there will surely be making a comparison, even subconsciously, with Spa.

The feeling may not be entirely fair because Zolder – frequently derided as a purpose-built circuit – didn't come from nowhere and does have a history. Once upon a time, enthusiasts used the town square as their temporary playground but decided they wanted something more fitting. They had a circuit by 1961 and extended it in 1963. It hosted a variety of events. In a festival in March 1964 Jacky Ickx drove in touring cars, Denny Hulme won a Formula 2 race from Lucien Bianchi, and Peter Arundell set the very first lap record in a Formula Junior Lotus (92.6mph/149.1kph).

In 1966 the Formula 2 race (grandly called the *Grand Prix de Limburg*) attracted Hulme, Jack Brabham, Jochen Rindt, and Graham Hill. A year later John Surtees beat Jim Clark, Jean-Pierre Beltoise third, Brabham fourth, and Bruce McLaren fifth.

The first Formula Ford event to be held outside Britain was at Zolder in 1968, while in 1970 Peter Gethin (McLaren) won a Formula 5000 race from Mike Hailwood. Eventually Roland Bruyseraede became Clerk of the Course.

Once Spa had been declared too dangerous, and the Belgian politics of equality between the Walloon and Flemish communities came to bear (see Nivelles), Zolder found itself in a special kind of race: to be ready for the 1973 Belgian Grand Prix in May.

Autocourse reported: 'The freshly redecorated old Zolder circuit is not actually too bad a place. A bit tight, dull in some places, it does have a couple of more stimulating sections. There is a startlingly fast left-right swerve on to the pits straight which some Fl cars could not quite take flat-out, and right behind the pits where everybody can watch is a newly-built chicane not unlike the famous one at Thruxton. Three times per lap the brakes are taxed very heavily, which, as at Barcelona, caused nearly everyone some grief. The miles of newly-sunk guardrail and catch-fencing, the adequate pits, paddock and official facilities, and the acres of advertising boards and banners, many of which proclaimed Marlboro's heavy investment in the well-being of the *GP d'Europe*, created quite a serious up-to-date atmosphere.'

By 1982 as experienced a driver as Patrick Tambay felt that Formula 1 had outgrown it. The track was too narrow and times were not particularly fast.

The Grand Prix returned to Spa in 1983, leaving only 1984 for Zolder before it settled permanently at Spa.

Within the anonymity and the melancholy, Zolder would be lamented and unlamented forever.

COCKPIT VIEW

John Watson, who won in 1982:

'It was a circuit I enjoyed racing on. I suppose it's Belgium's version of Brands Hatch, similar length, good corners on it, a circuit you could get a good feel for. The corners following the pits were good corners. The worst part was the chicane they had had to install some years earlier before the start/finish – the other chicane, *Kleine Chicane*, was one of the best of any track I raced on. Then you climbed uphill. The car wasn't taking off but it was getting slightly light. Over the top the road dropped away from you and went to the left doing 145, maybe 150 miles an hour. *Terlaemanbocht* was quite a quick corner, actually – the two right-handers on that loop were quick, third, maybe fourth gear just depending on your ratio. On the straight you'd reach 160 miles an hour.'[1]

EYEWITNESSES

Gareth Rees, motor sport enthusiast:

'Partly blamed on the fact that it could never replace Spa, Zolder always seemed

Jean-Pierre Beltoise digs a dust storm in the BRM in 1973 – and the engine failed.
(Courtesy Paul Kooyman)

a bit dull. For me, it was also down to a combination of the typical grey weather, the colourless flat pine forest, and the trackside sand where you would like to have seen green grass.

'My first visit was by overnight ferry and coach from the UK in 1975. I remember particularly the innumerable catch-fencing poles, which seemed to dominate all my photos. It was another Niki Lauda win, with an exciting early battle at the front with the likes of Carlos Pace and Vittorio Brambilla. It seemed to typify the way that, in those days, apart

TOP: The Kleine Chicane behind the paddock. (Author)

CENTRE: The approach to the Eerste Linkse. (Courtesy Filipp Gorelik)

BOTTOM: Into the Eerste Linkse. (Courtesy Filipp Gorelik)

from Lauda, you just never knew who would be competitive at each next race.

'In 1981 and 1982, my next visits were gloomy for more reasons than just the location. In 1981 I had managed to get a pit pass, but it was the year when Carlos Reutemann knocked down an Osella team mechanic during practice in that crazily small pit road.

'Showing just how single-minded a Formula 1 driver can be, this tragedy didn't stop him from taking pole and dominating the race. At the start there was that mad incident when an Arrows mechanic jumped on to the grid to help start one car and got hit by the other when the flag dropped. I remember watching the race and waiting for the next disaster. It was a relief when the weekend was over.

'In 1982 it got worse. I'll never forget the deathly silence that suddenly fell over Zolder in final qualifying and then hearing the commentator talk of a massive crash for one of the Ferraris. To this day, I have always felt slightly ashamed of the fact that, confronted with the choice, I was hoping it would be Didier Pironi.

'Minutes later, when Pironi (the recent villain of Imola, remember) drove slowly past, helmet off and very emotional, this and the commentator's lack of further information confirmed my worst fears. Difficult to imagine these days, but the next day it was business as usual: a good race and a great win from behind for Wattie (John Watson), who looked after his tyres better than Keke Rosberg.

'On the bright side, Zolder was where I was able to witness, at first hand, the real arrival in Formula 1 of two budding British stars. I'd seen them race in Britain many times in lower formulae but was not yet convinced of their ability to hack it in Formula 1. They were Tony Brise, who ran well in his first drive for the Embassy-Hill team in 1975, and Nigel Mansell, who was impressive when taking a totally deserved third place in 1981.'

Paul Kooyman, intrepid fanatic:

'1973...

'Friday practice and brand new asphalt was laid. The cars had to wait until it was laid!

'The tarmac would break up badly over the weekend. A new layer was ready just before the start of the race but it did not hold, so there were lots of accidents. [See 'Memories and Milestones', 1973.] Maybe that's why the race went to Nivelles the year after.

'1976...

'This time I could only spend a few moments in the pits, because I got caught and thrown out. I sneaked back in, got kicked out again, and then it was securely locked. Anyway, I photographed a designer measuring a DFV engine and a pile of small Tyrrell front wheels.

'1978...

'I did Friday practice *and* the Sunday Grand Prix. Seconds after the start we lost three world champions when Hunt and Lauda collided, and Fittipaldi was victim of the melee.

'1980...

'I was there for the supporting race – the Belgian Touring Car championship – with our Ford Escort RS2000, so I had a real paddock pass, but the pit lane was locked solid for anyone without a decent Formula 1 pit pass. Damn.

'In the paddock stood some oil drums used as dustbins, and what is better than a turned-over oil drum to stand on if you want to peep over the fence at the chicane? No one bothered me because it was raining like hell, so that lunatic photographer on his drum took some nice pics!

'1981...

'I went for the Sunday Grand Prix and tried the paddock without a pass. I thought *oh well, I'll give it a go*, and walked straight through the paddock gate. The guy there was on his own and couldn't get after me without leaving his post so I was in. I had a few seconds in the pit lane, and in the paddock there was not much to see. The cars were, of course, in front of the pits.

'I did the warm-up at the first right-hander behind the hill and prepared to install myself for the race, only they'd raised the fences so I could take no pictures this time. Wait a minute, there's a crane to remove crashed cars at the Bianchi corner. What if I ask very nicely

if I can climb on top of it to take a few pictures? Bingo. And then Alan Jones crashes very politely in front of me…

'1984...

'Two weeks before the Grand Prix there was a midweek tyre test and of course I just had to go. In the early morning there was a small ceremony at the new Gilles Villeneuve Memorial. The wreath of red roses had an Enzo Ferrari ribbon.

'The paddock was for free this time so I could stroll the whole day in and out of the pits, which was closest to Heaven as ever can be. It was a first for me to see that other great driver, Ayrton Senna. In 1975 I met Rory Byrne while he was doing Formula Fords, and now he was here with the Formula 1 Toleman and Ayrton. Great!

'I also paid attention to a "new" Gilles in Stefan Bellof, and what he was doing with that Tyrrell go-kart in relation to the turbo missiles was amazing!

'Alain Prost was driving with Lauda's helmet because his own was stolen the day before, so in pictures the McLaren driver is Prost.

'I was there again for the Grand Prix because the ticket prices were for normal mortals those days. I tried the trick of sneaking into the paddock: I was a member of an amateur photographers' club which was itself a member of the *Fédération Internationale des Amateurs Fotografes*. The capitals read "FIAF" and showing my card simply opened the paddock gate. The old fox did it again!

'Again I went to the inside of the Bianchi corner, turned an oil drum upside

down and I was ready. Apart from a BMW blow-up in the morning warm-up nothing really happened this time – just a nice, warm, sunny day at the races.'

MEMORIES AND MILESTONES

1973 Internal Grand Prix politics came to bear with, as one account puts it, 'various factions trying to assert their control over the "sport".' Work enlarging and transforming the circuit only finished on the week of the Grand Prix meeting. Two practice sessions were scheduled for the Friday but during the first of them the track surface began to break up and five cars went off in one place. *Autocourse* reported that 'at many points merely the pressure of a shoe was enough to make it shift and squirm'. (See 'Eyewitnesses', Paul Kooyman.)

The second session was cancelled and more politics came to bear on the Saturday. The track had been patched but the drivers (through the GPDA) made demands about financial indemnity if they themselves called the race off.

The drivers met on the Saturday but at 1:35, while the meeting was still going on, Jacky Ickx, not a GPDA member and of course Belgian, went out in his Ferrari followed by Nanni Galli (Iso Marlboro). The marshals stirred, the tannoys played

The era when safety fencing seemed to offer … safety. Jacques Laffite (Ligier) on his way to third in the 1976 race.
(Courtesy Paul Kooyman)

The race of 1975, Niki Lauda (Ferrari) leading Vittorio Brambilla (March) and Carlos Pace (Brabham) through the new chicane on to the start/finish straight. (Courtesy Gareth Rees)

loud music and you might have thought a real practice session was going on. People seriously wondered if a Grand Prix could be run with only two cars. Ronnie Peterson (Lotus) eventually took pole.

They all raced and Jackie Stewart (Tyrrell) beat team-mate François Cevert by 31.8 seconds. Fastest lap: Cevert 110.5mph/177.9kph.

The double kink into the start/finish straight had been tightened, making it into a chicane dedicated to Ickx because, so the legend goes, he'd been instrumental in breaking the deadlock in 1973 when he went out with Galli. It required hard braking at a circuit already notorious for hard braking.

1975 Niki Lauda (Ferrari), pole, beat Jody Scheckter (Tyrrell) by 19.2 seconds although Vittorio Brambilla (Beta Team March) had been in his usual feisty form at the start, muscling past Lauda and

Carlos Pace (Brabham) to lead until Lauda re-took him on lap 6. Fastest lap: Clay Regazzoni (Ferrari) 109.9mph/176.8kph.
1976 Lauda took pole from Ferrari team-mate Regazzoni and led every lap, beating Regazzoni by 3.4 seconds. Fastest lap: Lauda 110.9mph (+1.0)/178.5kph (+1.7).
1977 Mario Andretti (Lotus) took pole. After a wet, treacherous race Gunnar Nilsson (Lotus) beat Lauda (Ferrari) by 14.1 seconds. It was Nilsson's only win. Fastest lap: Nilsson 108.9mph (-2.0)/175.3kph (-3.2).
1978 The track had been completely resurfaced, and in pre-qualifying three drivers went faster than Andretti's pole time of the previous year. Andretti (Lotus), pole again, beating team-mate Peterson by 9.9 seconds. Fastest lap: Peterson 114.7mph (+5.8)/184.6kph (+9.3).
1979 Jacques Laffite (Ligier)a took pole in a wet session but the weather turned hot for the race which, as one account said, embraced four leaders, five crashes, a new lap record, many tyre and brake problems, and an extraordinary drive by Gilles Villeneuve (Ferrari), who was

one of the five crashes, rose from last to third, and ran out of fuel. Villeneuve's team-mate Scheckter beat Laffite by 15.3 seconds. Fastest lap: Villeneuve 114.7mph/184.6kph (no change).
1980 Didier Pironi (Ligier) led every lap and beat Alan Jones (Williams), pole, by 47.3 seconds. Fastest lap: Jacques Laffite (Ligier) 117.9mph (+3.2)/189.7kph (+5.0).
1981 In Friday qualifying an Osella mechanic, Giovanni Amadeo, slipped from the signalling ledge and fell just as Carlos Reutemann (Williams) was travelling slowly by. The car's rear wheels threw Amadeo against the pit lane wall. He died three days later in hospital. Reutemann took pole.

The 'race' brought chaos and near tragedy too. The GPDA had been involved in a technical dispute over the number of cars for qualifying (30) because Patrick Tambay (Theodore) made 31. The drivers wanted a special pre-qualifying session on the Saturday morning but the organisers refused. The drivers waited until just before the race, when live television coverage had begun, to make their feelings known. The mechanics, unhappy about their working conditions, the cramped pit lane, and even more unhappy about what had happened to Amadeo, made *their* feelings known.

The drivers who were *not* protesting went away on their parade lap and the whole thing became a 'jumble' of cars. On the grid Reutemann waved his arms – his water temperature giving alarming readings – and Riccardo Patrese (Arrows) waved his arms because he'd stalled. Another parade lap seemed inevitable – and necessary – but instead the red lights came on. That was followed by the green, and by then a mechanic, Dave Luckett, had reached Patrese's car to fire it up. He was struck heavily, broke his leg and was left lying on the track. Reutemann won a shortened race – rain – beating Laffite (Ligier) by 36.0 seconds. Fastest lap: Reutemann 114.5mph (-3.4)/184.2kph (-5.5).

1982 The pit complex had been completely rebuilt but the sense of anonymity would be overlaid by

melancholy. Deep into second qualifying Gilles Villeneuve, on an 'in' lap but driving his Ferrari at maximum speed, came upon the March of Jochen Mass through the left kink before the run to *Terlaemenbocht*. Mass saw Villeneuve and moved right to get out of the way but Villeneuve was on him. What happened next was, as someone has observed, an aeroplane crash. Villeneuve died that night in hospital. Alain Prost (Renault) took pole. John Watson (McLaren) beat Keke Rosberg (Williams) by 7.2 seconds. Fastest lap: Watson 118.9mph (+4.4)/191.3kph (+7.1).

1984 Michele Alboreto (Ferrari) took pole, led every lap, and beat Derek Warwick (Renault) by 42.3 seconds. Fastest lap: René Arnoux (Ferrari) 120.2mph (+1.3)/193.5kph (+2.2).

Speed increase 1975–84: 10.3mph/16.7kph.

Footnote
[1] *1982*, Hilton.

FACTS OF THE MATTER

4.220m/2.622km circuit

Year	Winner
1973	J. Stewart (Tyrrell)
Pole	R. Peterson (Lotus)
	(114.5mph/184.2kph)
Fastest lap	F. Cevert (Tyrrell)
	(110.5mph/177.9kph)

4.262m/2.648km circuit

Year	Winner
1975	N. Lauda (Ferrari)
1976	N. Lauda (Ferrari)
1977	G. Nilsson (Lotus)
1978	M. Andretti (Lotus)
1979	J. Scheckter (Ferrari)
1980	D. Pironi (Ligier)
1981	C. Reutemann (Williams)
1982	J. Watson (McLaren)
1984	M. Alboreto (Ferrari)
Fastest pole	M. Alboreto (Ferrari) 1984
	(127.4mph/205.0kph)
Fastest lap	R. Arnoux (Ferrari) 1984
	(120.2mph/193.5kph)

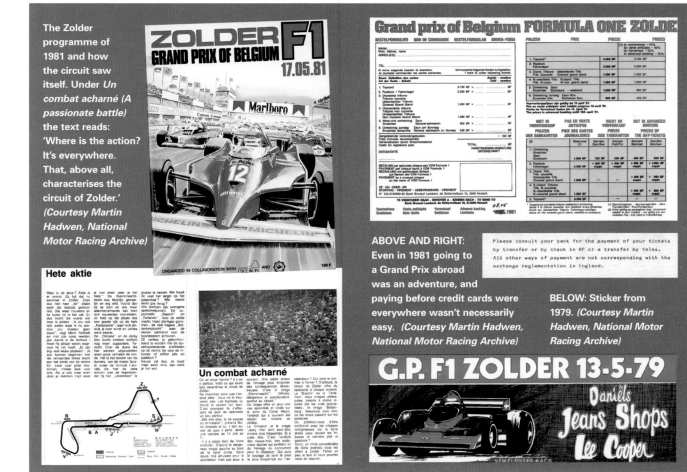

The Zolder programme of 1981 and how the circuit saw itself. Under *Un combat acharné (A passionate battle)* the text reads: 'Where is the action? It's everywhere. That, above all, characterises the circuit of Zolder.' *(Courtesy Martin Hadwen, National Motor Racing Archive)*

ABOVE AND RIGHT: Even in 1981 going to a Grand Prix abroad was an adventure, and paying before credit cards were everywhere wasn't necessarily easy. *(Courtesy Martin Hadwen, National Motor Racing Archive)*

BELOW: Sticker from 1979. *(Courtesy Martin Hadwen, National Motor Racing Archive)*

BRAZIL
INTERLAGOS

Location: 10 miles (16km) south of São Paulo city centre.
Constructed: 1940.
World Championship Grands Prix: 26.

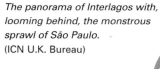

The panorama of Interlagos with, looming behind, the monstrous sprawl of São Paulo.
(ICN U.K. Bureau)

Retao

Reta Oposta

Curva 2

Curva do Sol

Descida do Lago

Senna's 'S'

Curva 3

Sargento

Estacionamento

Curva 1/
Descida do Sol

Junçáo

Ferradura

Pinheirinho

Mergulho

Subida
dos Boxes

Curva do Laranjinha

Start/finish

Cotovêlo/Bico de Pato

Arquibancadas

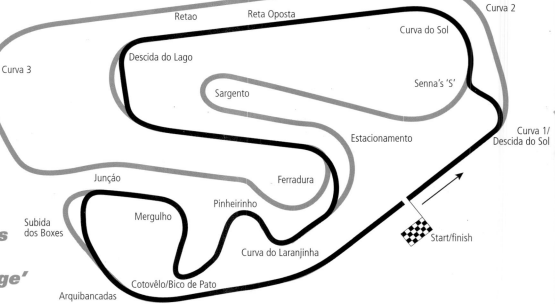

'The high-speed left-hand corners add an extra physical challenge'

Jenson Button

Racing at São Paulo, Brazil's second city, began in 1936. It was a genteel, semi-rural place then. Two years later property developers bought land south of the city with a view to a housing project but some of the land wasn't suitable for that. They built a circuit there instead.

The lie of that land – a panoramic, undulating bowl originally between two lakes – gave it a name: *Between Lakes*. This bestowed (an appropriate word, actually) a tremendous advantage on it, because spectators in the grandstands could see almost all of it. This was aided by the fact that the circuit was tightly packed into the area

available, constantly doubling back on itself.

First used in May 1940, it had by 1972 – when a non-Championship race was run as a rehearsal – a rustic, slightly worn feel to it. The facilities in the paddock were described as crude. The circuit was no longer rural, however, because the suburbs and industry had crawled out and surrounded it.

It hosted Brazil's first Grand Prix a year later, as recognition of the country's interest in motor sport *and* the fact that three of the 20 drivers were Brazilian: Emerson and Wilson Fittipaldi (from São Paulo), and Luiz Bueno. Emerson was defending World

Champion. It was all a toxic mix designed to pack the circuit, and it did.

The Grand Prix fraternity was impressed by Brazil's vitality, what someone called its 'youthful zest'.

The track measured 4.9 miles (7.9km), but in a relatively compact area. The distance was achieved by using loops all crammed in so that an aerial view resembled spaghetti. It began with two left-hand looping curves which could be taken flat out as one corner and featured other corners – the ones feeding on to the straights – which could also be taken fast. The track surface was extremely bumpy, which made teams fear for their chassis.

COCKPIT VIEWS

**Rubens Barrichello,
Brawn, 2009:**

'The circuit has become almost like a second home to me over the years but it still retains a real sense of challenge. You need to have full confidence in your set-up to maximise the quick corners, the tight infield section, and the bumpy surface.

'Interlagos has some great corners, such as the *Curva do Laranjinha*. There are real overtaking opportunities into the *S do Senna* at the start of the lap and under braking for *Descida do Lago* at the end of the back straight.'[1]

Jenson Button, Brawn, 2009:

'Interlagos is quite an unusual circuit and it's an enjoyable challenge for the drivers.

The anticlockwise direction, changes in elevation, and bumpy surface all keep your attention fully focused and the high-speed left-hand corners add an extra physical challenge.'[2]

Emerson Fittipaldi leads in the Lotus in 1973 as he will on every lap – and set fastest lap. (LAT)

EYEWITNESS

Ann Bradshaw, PR expert:

'There is no other place where you can stand on the grid and have such atmosphere, because the crowd is right *there,* they can touch you. Ayrton could go and wave to them and they could see the guys on the grid. Absolutely electric, one of the most electric grids. It's even more electric than Monza, oh yes, much more. The *tifosi* are very excitable but this was a passion: it was Ayrton's race because that was where he came from, and Rubens Barrichello came from there too, and Ayrton is buried in Morumbi just down the road.

'The first year we went they'd devalued their currency and suddenly you couldn't spend your money. In the past we'd been at Rio and people were trying to buy your dollars. You took dollars and that was brilliant.

'At São Paulo nobody wanted your dollars because everybody's bank accounts were frozen and they couldn't get the money to buy them. The hotels would only offer you a rate per day. We stayed in the Hilton in the centre, you couldn't go out anywhere, it was horrendous – and we didn't have Copacabana Beach...

'Over the years there were quite frightening moments with people being held up and that sort of thing. I find it quite intimidating now because before they were thieves, now they mean you harm because they have guns.

'Elf used to do a party in a private house – I don't know where they found these houses – and we'd have the carnival dancers. Amazing! However, where you'd expect to see amazing girls with skimpy bikinis on the grid holding up the driver boards they have men.

'The other amazing thing was that the circuit dips and dives and you see São Paulo all around you.

'It's a *great* circuit and it has produced great races.'

MEMORIES AND MILESTONES

1973 Brazil was politically a nervous, unstable place. Armoured vehicles patrolled the circuit and the crowd controllers were armed. The weather was so hot that the fire brigade sprayed the crowd. Ronnie Peterson (Lotus) took pole but team-mate Emerson Fittipaldi beat

Jackie Stewart (Tyrrell) by 13.5 seconds. Fastest lap: Fittipaldi and Denny Hulme (McLaren) 114.9mph/184.9kph.
1974 Fittipaldi (McLaren), pole, was leading at lap 30 of the 40 when drizzle began, soon deepening into torrential rain. He gestured for the race to be stopped and it was. The Brazilians liked that even more than the cool water sprays the year before. He beat Clay Regazzoni (Ferrari) by 13.5 seconds. Fastest lap: Regazzoni 114.1mph (-0.8)/183.6kph (-1.3).
1975 The grandstands were full from early morning and the crowd amused itself by throwing things on to the track, delaying the untimed session while it was cleared. Jean-Pierre Jarier (Shadow) took pole. The race climaxed with Carlos Pace (Brabham) – from São Paulo – leading but being caught by Fittipaldi (McLaren). Pace held on and won by 5.7 seconds, his first and only Grand Prix victory. Fastest lap: Jarier 115.5mph (+1.4)/185.9kph (-2.3).
1976 Argentina was cancelled and Interlagos became the first race of the season. James Hunt (McLaren) took pole from Niki Lauda's Ferrari, giving a template for the whole season. Hunt, however, had mechanical problems and Lauda won, beating Patrick Depailler (Tyrrell) by 21.4 seconds. Fastest lap: Jarier (Shadow) 114.8mph (-0.7)/ 184.8kph (-1.1).
1977 Hunt (McLaren) took pole but Pace (Brabham) jumped the start from the third row and led. However, on lap 7, with the track breaking up on the long curving left-hander after the pits – it had been resurfaced – Pace struggled to control the car and Hunt struck him. Pace retired on lap 34 after another accident and Carlos Reutemann (Ferrari) beat Hunt by 10.7 seconds. Two months later Pace died in a light aeroplane accident near São Paulo. The Interlagos circuit was renamed in his memory. Fastest lap: Hunt 115.2mph (+0.4)/185.4kph (+0.6).
    Speed increase 1973–7: 0.3mph/0.5kph.

An estimated $2 million was spent on new pits, grandstand, and safety improvements. Corners had been eased although the circuit, notorious for bumps, resembled a patchwork where it had been resurfaced. Autocourse noted that when cars were travelling fast they jumped around 'in violent jerks of protest, as if trying to rid themselves of their tormentors'.

1979 In 1978 the Brazilian GP went to Rio, but it now returned. Jacques Laffite (Ligier), pole, beat team-mate Depailler by 5.2 seconds, but only after Depailler had pressured him for most of the race. Fastest lap: Laffite 118.4mph/190.6kph.
1980 This race ought to have gone to Rio but the circuit there was found to be sinking into the sandbed it stood on. The drivers were not happy and said in Argentina, two weeks before, that a boycott was possible because Interlagos was too bumpy – even the FISA said it should be resurfaced before hosting another Grand Prix. They raced with a full grid of 24. Jean-Pierre Jabouille (Renault) took pole and team-mate René Arnoux beat Elio de Angelis (Lotus) by 21.8 seconds. Fastest lap: Arnoux 119.6mph (+1.2)/192.4kph (+1.8).

The race was run at Rio from 1981 but by the late 1980s that circuit was considered unsuitable for Formula 1 cars. A shorter circuit, incorporating part of the old, was built quickly, but Brazil was engulfed by a financial crisis so bad that reportedly teams could not exchange money to buy food. (See 'Eyewitness'.)
1990 The president of the FISA, Jean-Marie Balestre, locked into a verbal dispute with Ayrton Senna, visited the circuit and needed bodyguards. Senna (McLaren) took pole. Alain Prost (Ferrari) beat Gerhard Berger in the other McLaren by 13.5 seconds. Fastest lap: Berger 121.1mph/194.9kph.
1991 Senna's race in the McLaren. From pole he led, although the Williamses of Nigel Mansell and Riccardo Patrese pushed him. Towards the end Senna's gearbox began to fail and he was so exhausted when he'd won that he had to be lifted from the car. He beat Patrese by 2.9 seconds. Fastest lap: Mansell 120.3mph (-0.8)/193.6kph (-1.3).
1992 Perry McCarthy, due to drive for the tiny Andrea Moda team – his long desired entry to Formula 1 – arrived at Interlagos sure that his Superlicence (enabling him to drive) was waiting for him. FISA seemed confused and he was refused it. Mansell (Williams), pole, beat team-mate Patrese by 29.3 seconds. Fastest lap: Patrese 121.7mph (+1.4)/195.9kph (+2.3).
1993 McLaren lost Honda engines and replaced them, on a customer basis, with Fords. Senna exploited a cloudburst to slice past Damon Hill (Williams) for

the lead – Prost in the other Williams, pole, had already floated off the track. Senna beat Hill by 16.6 seconds. Fastest lap: Michael Schumacher (Benetton) 120.9mph (-0.8)/194.6kph (-1.3).

1994 Interlagos was the first race of the season and opened the Schumacher era. Senna (Williams) took pole and he and Schumacher exchanged the lead before Senna spun off trying to catch him on lap 56. Schumacher beat Hill (Williams) by a lap. Fastest lap: Schumacher 123.3mph (+2.4)/198.5kph (+3.9).

1995 In Friday qualifying Schumacher's Benetton snapped away from him – a

steering problem, carrying nightmare memories of Senna at Imola the year before. Schumacher was involved in a weight controversy: he was 8kg heavier than the year before and people wondered where that had come from. Hill (Williams) took pole. Schumacher won the race but the Benetton was disqualified for a fuel irregularity, then stripped only of points towards the Constructors' championship. Schumacher beat Coulthard by 8.0 seconds. Fastest lap: Schumacher 119.6mph (-3.7)/192.4kph (-6.1).

1996 Hill (Williams) took pole. The race

started in heavy rain but, decisively, Hill got to the first corner before team-mate Jacques Villeneuve and almost majestically led every lap except his pit stops to beat Jean Alesi (Benetton) by 17.9 seconds. Fastest lap: Hill 118.6mph (-1.0)/190.9kph (-1.5).

1997 Villeneuve (Williams), pole, won but was lucky because, trying to stay with Schumacher's Ferrari in the first corner, he journeyed across the gravel trap, the race seemingly lost. However, a stalled car brought out red flags to stop the race. At the restart Schumacher led again but Villeneuve went by on the

1 Jacques Villeneuve (Williams) explores the depth of the kerbing in the days when it was painted yellow and white, not today's red and white.

2 The start in 1996: Damon Hill (Williams) leads. This is the famous Senna S, scene of overtaking and mayhem down the years.

3 Interlagos was unforgiving in the wet, as David Coulthard (McLaren) discovered.

4 Damon Hill (Williams) mastered it and beat Jean Alesi (Benetton) comfortably. *(All ICN U.K. Bureau)*

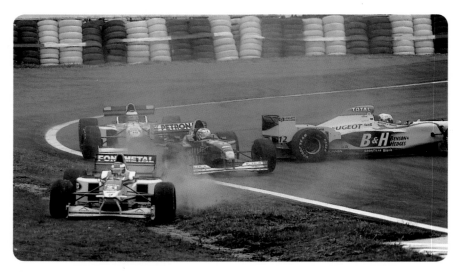

Explosive start in 1997, confirming that Interlagos invariably produced some kind of drama. Giancarlo Fisichella (Jordan) is on the right, Jarno Trulli (Minardi) coming across the grass towards the camera. (ICN U.K. Bureau)

opening lap and beat Berger (Benetton) by 4.1 seconds. Fastest lap: Villeneuve 122.5mph (+3.9)/197.1kph (+6.2).

1998 The McLarens of Mika Häkkinen, pole, and Coulthard, front row, dominated, running every lap 1-2 – but they had to disconnect a secondary braking system under protest from Ferrari. Häkkinen beat Coulthard by 1.1 seconds. Fastest lap: Häkkinen 121.0mph (-1.5)/194.8kph (-2.3).

1999 Now Häkkinen (McLaren), pole, dominated although he had a gearbox problem after four laps, letting Rubens Barrichello (Stewart) into the lead and convulsing the circuit in the way Pace, Fittipaldi, and Senna had done. He held the lead to lap 26 and was down to third when his engine failed on lap 43. Häkkinen beat Schumacher (Ferrari) by 4.9 seconds. Fastest lap: Häkkinen 122.4mph (+1.4)/197.0kph (+2.2).

2000 Häkkinen (McLaren) took pole but Schumacher's time at Ferrari had come. He'd won Australia massively two weeks before and now did it again, aided by the fact that Coulthard (McLaren), who finished four seconds behind, was disqualified for an illegal front wing – so Schumacher beat Giancarlo Fisichella (Benetton) by 39.8 seconds. Fastest lap: Schumacher 128.9mph (+6.5)/207.5kph (+10.5).

2001 Juan-Pablo Montoya (Williams), the Colombian with the big reputation from racing in the United States, announced himself with a power-play to go past Schumacher (Ferrari), pole, prompting some to wonder if he wasn't The Second Coming, after Senna. He had a crash and Coulthard (McLaren) beat Schumacher by 16.1 seconds. Fastest lap: Ralf Schumacher (Williams) 127.3mph (-1.6)/204.9kph (-2.6).

2002 Montoya (Williams) took pole. This was the third race of the season and Ferrari had taken the previous year's car to the first two races. Schumacher won Australia and was third in Malaysia. What would the new car do? Whatever Schumacher demanded of it – and for the rest of the season, too. He beat brother Ralf (Williams) by 0.5 of a second. Fastest lap: Montoya 126.7mph (-0.6)/203.9kph (-1.0).

2003 The 700th Championship race. Fisichella (Jordan) won his first Grand Prix. Barrichello (Ferrari) took pole. Heavy rain caused chaos with, finally, three different leaders on the last three laps. It took the FIA to confirm – in Paris the following Friday – that Fisichella had beaten Kimi Räikkönen (McLaren) by 0.9 of a second. Fastest lap: Barrichello 117.5mph/189.1kph (no comparison).

2004 The race moved to the other end of the calendar and when Barrichello put the Ferrari on pole he packed Interlagos – Schumacher 18th in the other Ferrari crashed in Saturday practice. Montoya, strong in the Williams, ran fifth at the end of lap 1 but led by lap 19 and didn't let go, beating Räikkönen (McLaren) by 1.0 second. Fastest lap: Montoya 134.9mph (+8.2)/217.0kph (+13.1).

2005 Fernando Alonso (Renault), pole, came to the race saying he wanted to take the Championship by winning it but instead, after leading for two laps, couldn't hold Montoya (McLaren). Alonso settled behind Montoya and Räikkönen (McLaren) and in the end that was all he needed to become the youngest champion. Montoya beat Räikkönen by 2.5 seconds. Fastest lap: Räikkönen 133.4mph (-1.5)/214.7kph (-2.3).

2006 Michael Schumacher's 249th and last race before his retirement (his first retirement, anyway) but he qualified only tenth. Alonso, looking for his second Championship, was on the second row. Felipe Massa (Ferrari), yet another native of São Paulo, took pole and led throughout (except for his first pit stop) with Alonso (Renault) following – and Schumacher, last at lap 9 with a shredded tyre, powering his way to fourth at the end. Massa beat Alonso by 18.6 seconds. Fastest lap: Schumacher 133.6mph (+0.2)/215.0kph (+0.3).

2007 A three-way for the Championship: Lewis Hamilton (McLaren) 107, Alonso (Mercedes) 103, Räikkönen (Ferrari) 100. Massa, pole again, led for two-thirds of the race before Räikkönen took it from him, Alonso trapped in third and Hamilton at one stage 18th after a gear selection problem. Räikkönen beat Massa by 1.4 seconds. Fastest lap: Räikkönen 133.1mph (-0.5)/214.1kph (-0.9).

2008 The great Hamilton finale when, on the last lap and in rain, he took the vital fifth place from Timo Glock (Toyota), marooned on dry tyres. Massa won (from his third consecutive pole at the circuit) and for a moment thought he had the Championship – until, with two corners left, Hamilton was past Glock. Massa beat Alonso (Renault) by 13.2 seconds. Fastest lap: Massa 130.7mph (-2.4)/210.4kph (-3.7).

2009 Jenson Button (Brawn) qualified fourteenth and had a 14-point Championship lead but team-mate Barrichello, pole, and Sebastian Vettel (Red Bull) were strong. Button heroically worked his way up to fifth and it was enough. Mark Webber (Red Bull) beat Robert Kubica (BMW) by 7.6 seconds. Fastest lap: Webber 130.7mph/210.4kph (no change).

Speed increase 1990–2009: 9.6mph/15.5kph.

Footnotes
[1] Courtesy Brawn GP. [2] Courtesy Brawn GP.

Nobody could ever replace Senna at São Paulo but the mantle fell on Rubens Barrichello, who had to try. *(Courtesy Martin Hadwen, National Motor Racing Archive)*

FACTS OF THE MATTER

4.964m/7.960km circuit

Year	Winner
1973	E. Fittipaldi (Lotus)
1974	E. Fittipaldi (McLaren)
1975	C. Pace (Brabham)
1976	N. Lauda (Ferrari)
1977	C. Reutemann (Ferrari)
Fastest pole	J.-P. Jarier (Shadow) 1975 (118.8mph/191.2kph)
Fastest lap	J.-P. Jarier 1975 (115.5mph/185.8kph)

Corners eased, 4.893m/7.874km circuit

1979	J. Laffite (Ligier)
1980	R. Arnoux (Renault)
Fastest lap	J.-P. Jabouille (Renault) 1980 (124.6mph/200.5kph)
Fastest lap	R. Arnoux (Renault) 1980 (119.5mph/192.4kph)

2.687m/4.325km circuit

1990	A. Prost (Ferrari)
1991	A. Senna (McLaren)
1992	N. Mansell (Williams)
1993	A. Senna (McLaren)
1994	M. Schumacher (Benetton)
1995	M. Schumacher (Benetton)
1996	D. Hill (Williams)
Fastest pole	N. Mansell (Williams) 1992 (127.8mph/205.7kph)
Fastest lap	M. Schumacher (Benetton) 1994 (123.3mph/198.4kph)

2.667m/4.292km circuit

1997	J. Villeneuve (Williams)
1998	M. Häkkinen (McLaren)
1999	M. Häkkinen (McLaren)
Fastest pole	J. Villeneuve (Williams) 1997 (126.3mph/203.3kph)
Fastest lap	J. Villeneuve 1997 (122.4mph/197.0kph)

2.677m/4.309km circuit

2000	M. Schumacher (Ferrari)
2001	D. Coulthard (McLaren)
2002	M. Schumacher (Ferrari)
2003	G. Fisichella (Jordan)
2004	J.-P. Montoya (Williams)
2005	J.-P. Montoya (McLaren)
2006	F. Massa (Ferrari)
2007	K. Räikkönen (Ferrari)
2008	F. Massa (Ferrari)
2009	M. Webber (Red Bull)
Fastest pole	R. Barrichello (Ferrari) 2004 (136.4mph/219.6kph)
Fastest lap	J.-P. Montoya (Williams) 2004 (134.8mph/217.0kph)

RIO DE JANEIRO

Location: 19 miles (30km) south-west of city centre.
Constructed: 1972.
World Championship Grands Prix: 10.

ABOVE: The mountains always dwarfed the doings of mere men: 8 Andrea de Cesaris (McLaren), 7 John Watson (McLaren), 6 Hector Rebaque (Brabham), 22 Mario Andretti (Alfa Romeo) meet at the start, 1981. (LAT)

'It's difficult to finish in good shape because of the high temperature'

Nelson Piquet

OPPOSITE: Ayrton Senna's lap in 1987, Nelson Piquet's lap in 1988 – and there are differences. (Courtesy Camel)

Lagoa

Carlos Pace

Morette

Cheirinho

Girao

Box

Molykote

Vitoria

Nonato

Norte

Start/finish

Sul

Junçáo

The circuit, known as Jacarepaguá from the nearby town and now called the Autodromo Nelson Piquet, was constructed in 1978 some 30km from Rio on reclaimed marshland. By definition that made it absolutely flat.

It was also bumpy and offered long corners of constant radius. It was no place, *Autocourse* complained, for driver enjoyment or spectator enjoyment – you could hardly overtake anywhere round it.

Then there was the heat, at 100°F on a normal day. The first year, to combat this, cars were ventilated to get as much cool air to the driver as was possible – so ventilated that someone remarked in the event of a downpour they'd drown before they could reach the pits. James Hunt had a cold water system pumping through a special suit under his overalls. Emerson Fittipaldi (in a Fittipaldi) did too, but his was supposed to be fed by cold air from a duct. It didn't work.

The crowd was sometimes cooled by fire hoses, which seems to have been thoroughly enjoyed.

The circuit did have one stunning feature: a backdrop of luxuriant green mountains, and it did become an annual haunt for the pre-season tyre testing.

Apart from ten Grands Prix the circuit hosted CART races from 1996 to 2000 on a linked oval, and the Brazilian bike Grand Prix.

Brazil was casting covetous eyes on the 2016 Olympic Games for Rio and in 2008 an announcement suggested the track might be demolished to make way for an Olympic Training Centre.

COCKPIT VIEW
Ayrton Senna, Lotus, 1987:
'Quite bumpy with long radial corners, hard physically, specially on the neck. The circuit is mainly anticlockwise. The first race is like the start of a new term and after the winter it's always difficult and of course it is *Brasil*!

'Normal wing set-up, and reasonably stiff car for the long corners. You have to look after the consumption and look after the tyres on a very abrasive surface. You need good cooling and a cool head!'

Nelson Piquet, Lotus, 1988:
'It's very important to have a good balance to save the tyres. Another important point is to keep the temperature down when you are following another car. You need maximum downforce and it's a very easy circuit on brakes. It's difficult to finish in good shape because of the high temperature.'

EYEWITNESSES
David Corbishley, New Jersey:
Besides being a Formula 1 fan, what brought me to Rio de Janeiro in 1988 was that my youngest brother and fellow fan lived there. At that time inflation was out of control in Brazil. With no exaggeration, if you were a Brazilian with money you spent half of each day looking at what bank to place it in overnight. For the poor it meant you could not save money to improve your situation and had to spend the money you received that same day to avoid losing buying power. In 1988 the rate of inflation was 629%!

'The money dropped in value so fast they had to rubber stamp more zeros on to the bills to keep up. The meter in a cab was just an index and new conversion charts were pasted to the windows weekly. I mention all this to explain the background against which this race was run.

'When we arrived at the circuit race day we found our grandstand filled with local citizens who had been there for some time taking care of their thirst. When any attractive woman came in, the competing sections would send an "emissary" to suggest she sit in their area. The unsuccessful sections would then pelt her with pieces of wet newspaper. Our guest was a former Benetton model so plenty of wet newspaper came our way. The Uzi-armed police found this very amusing and kept their distance.

'In some of the pictures you can see the tall wall that surrounded the racetrack with a swamp in the middle. The terrain was uneven and patrolled by police on horseback and with rifles. People had set up a small community in this area and literally lived in wooden shipping crates. One family had a second crate to garage their taxi and another had one converted into a walk-up tavern. Electricity was

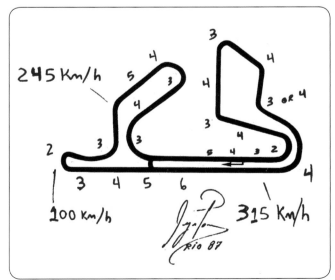

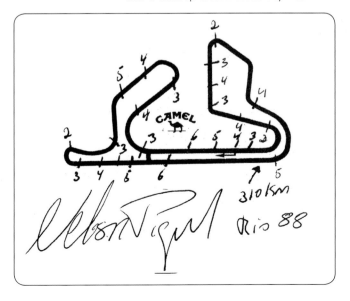

David Corbishley's ticket.

The hills were alive with the sound of engines, too, in 1989: Riccardo Patrese (Williams) leads Ayrton Senna (McLaren) with nimble Gerhard Berger nipping the Ferrari down the inside. (LAT)

provided by a hot and cold line running between home-made overhead power poles and was stolen from the lines going into the circuit.

'Oh yeah, the race. The start was waved off on the first try and Ayrton Senna's McLaren had a gear selector failure, so he took the restart from the pits in the spare car. He worked his way up to second before being disqualified on lap 31 for restarting with the backup car. Nelson Piquet finished third so not all was lost for the locals after their disappointment with Ayrton.'

Ann Bradshaw, PR expert:
'You had to go into your garage each morning to make sure there were no snakes in there. You were quite near a nasty bit of wetland so the mosquitoes were around. The insulation in the Press Office – to keep the noise out – was egg cartons stapled to the wall. It was very primitive.

'In Rio, there were two hotels near each other, the Intercontinental and I think the Sheraton, just before you get on to Ipanema beach, and these were the ones

we stayed at. You looked out of your hotel window and you saw *favelas*[1] hanging to the side of the road next to you. The people seemed happy because there was the sun and the sea.

'In those days people didn't complain about circuits the way they do these days, because the circuits still had some characteristics of their own. They weren't all done by a man from Germany.'

MEMORIES AND MILESTONES

1978 Ronnie Peterson (Lotus) took pole. To have *their* race won by Carlos Reutemann (Ferrari) from Argentina was only softened for the Brazilians because Emerson Fittipaldi (Copersucar) came second 47.1 seconds behind. Fastest lap: Reutemann 109.2mph/175.7kph.

Rio ought to have hosted the race in 1979, but it had to be moved to Interlagos when tests discovered the circuit was sinking (see Interlagos).

1981 Reutemann (Williams) dominated again, particularly after Nelson Piquet (Brabham), pole, gambled on dry tyres for a wet race. He completed the opening lap

15th, while Reutemann would lead every lap until the two-hour limit was reached and the race stopped. He beat Alan Jones (Williams) by 4.4 seconds. Fastest lap: Marc Surer (Ensign) 98.5mph/158.5kph (no comparison).

1982 Piquet (Brabham) beat Keke Rosberg (Williams), with Alain Prost (Renault), pole, third, but Renault protested that the Brabham and Williams had used illegal 'disposable ballast' – filling large water tanks to help cool the brakes. Piquet and Rosberg were disqualified. Prost beat John Watson (McLaren) by 3.0 seconds. Fastest lap: Alain Prost (Renault) 116.0mph (+6.8)/186.7kph (+11.0).

1983 Rosberg (Williams) took pole and started with half tanks, but so did Piquet and by lap 7 Piquet was in the lead. Rosberg made his pit stop on lap 28 but a flash fire flared and Rosberg was out of the cockpit in some of the fastest human movements ever seen. He got back in and finished second to Piquet but was disqualified because he'd had a push start in the pits. Piquet beat Niki Lauda (McLaren) by 51.8 seconds. Fastest lap: Piquet 112.7mph (-3.3)/181.4kph (-5.3).

1984 Elio de Angelis (Lotus) took pole. Prost had left Renault for McLaren. 'I set off cautiously, trying to get the measure of the car on that particular circuit – trying it on for size, you might say. Alboreto's Ferrari, Lauda in the other McLaren and Warwick's Renault held the top three positions for lap after lap, and I didn't squeeze past them until we were on the 51st lap. I had to keep one eye permanently on my fuel gauge – this would soon become second nature to us all, but Brazil was the first time we had ever raced under the new fuel restrictions. However, I eased home quite comfortably.'[2] He beat Rosberg (Williams) by 40.5 seconds. Fastest lap: Prost 116.6mph (+3.9)/187.7kph (-6.3).

1985 Prost qualified sixth and Lauda ninth, Michele Alboreto's Ferrari on pole so that if 1984 had been entirely about McLaren, 1985 might not be. Prost took 18 laps to get into the lead and beat Alboreto by 3.2 seconds. Amazingly Rosberg was not disqualified. Fastest lap: Prost 116.4mph (-0.2)/187.3kph (-0.4).

1986 Ayrton Senna put the Lotus on pole, Piquet's Williams alongside him. It might have been explosive because neither man liked the other, and each represented one of Brazil's twin pillars,

Rio and São Paulo. In the event the Williams was clearly superior and by lap 3 Piquet had the lead, and the race. He beat Senna by 34.8 seconds. Fastest lap: Piquet 120.3mph (+3.9)/193.6kph (+6.3).

1987 Nigel Mansell (Williams) took pole but team-mate Piquet led. Senna took that from him but wasn't happy with the Lotus's handling and Prost sailed by, never to be seen again. He beat Piquet by 40.5 seconds. Fastest lap: Piquet 119.9mph (-0.4)/193.0kph (-0.6).

1988 Senna's debut for McLaren but, from pole, his car was jammed in first gear. He raised his arm, aborting the start, and headed for the spare. Because the race had been delayed, not stopped and restarted, he was disqualified. Prost in the other McLaren beat Gerhard Berger

(Ferrari) by 9.8 seconds. It gave him 28 wins, beating Jackie Stewart's record of 27. Fastest lap: Berger 121.1mph (+1.2)/194.9kph (+1.9).

1989 Senna (McLaren) took pole. Mansell was making his debut for Ferrari in a car that was never going to last 61 laps. It did. He beat Prost (McLaren) by 7.8 seconds and at Maranello the church bells rang. Without knowing it they were sounding the death knell of Grand Prix racing at Rio. Fastest lap: Riccardo Patrese (Williams) 121.7mph (+0.6)/195.8kph (+0.9).

Speed increase 1978–89: 12.5mph/20.1kph.

Footnotes
[1] *Favela*, a Brazilian Portuguese word for a slum. [2] *Life in the Fast Lane*, Prost.

FACTS OF THE MATTER

3.126m/5.031km circuit

Year	Winner
1978	C. Reutemann (Ferrari)
1981	C. Reutemann (Williams)
1982	A. Prost (Renault)
1983	N. Piquet (Brabham)
1984	A. Prost (McLaren)
1985	A. Prost (McLaren)
1986	N. Piquet (Williams)
1987	A. Prost (McLaren)
1988	A. Prost (McLaren)
1989	N. Mansell (Ferrari)
Fastest pole	A. Senna (McLaren) 1989 (131.9mph/212.3kph)
Fastest lap	R. Patrese (Williams) 1989 (121.6mph/195.7kph)

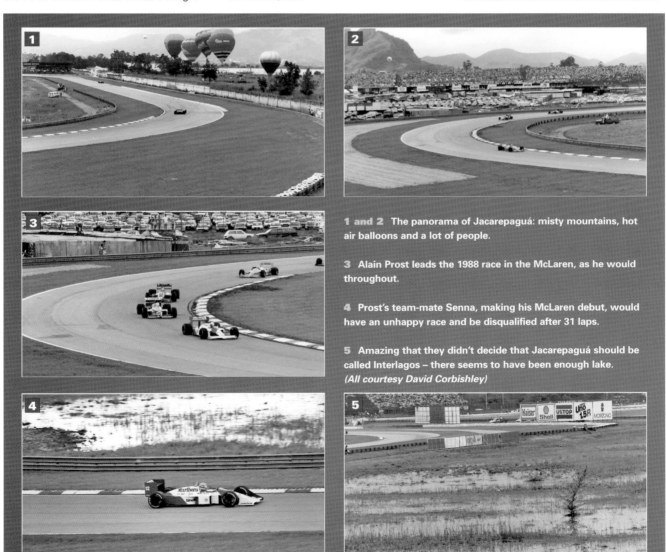

1 and 2 The panorama of Jacarepaguá: misty mountains, hot air balloons and a lot of people.

3 Alain Prost leads the 1988 race in the McLaren, as he would throughout.

4 Prost's team-mate Senna, making his McLaren debut, would have an unhappy race and be disqualified after 31 laps.

5 Amazing that they didn't decide that Jacarepaguá should be called Interlagos – there seems to have been enough lake. *(All courtesy David Corbishley)*

MONT-TREMBLANT

Location: 90 miles (145km) north-west of Montréal. Sometimes known as St Jovite.
Constructed: 1964.
World Championship Grands Prix: 2.

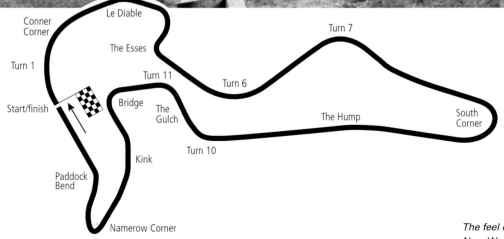

Conner Corner

Le Diable

Turn 7

The Esses

Turn 1

Turn 11

Turn 6

Start/finish

Bridge

The Gulch

The Hump

South Corner

Turn 10

Kink

Paddock Bend

Namerow Corner

'The secret here, really, is in the braking'

Jackie Stewart

The feel of the place, idyllic, enthusiastic and New World. Dan Gurney leads Denny Hulme in 1968, both driving McLarens. Hulme won from Bruce McLaren – in another McLaren. (LAT)

A powerful name, Trembling Mountain, and a track that would have a powerful effect on the Grand Prix cars – by destroying them. As Graham Hill said, it was 'very tight and bumpy', and it played 'hell with the transmission'.

It also played hell with gearboxes and of the 20 cars which began the 1968 Grand Prix 13 didn't finish (six with transmission failure). Compounding that, of the seven which did finish only two were running properly: the remainder limped.

The undulating track has attracted adjectives like 'picturesque' as well as 'challenging'.

In his authoritative history of the Canadian Grand Prix[1] Gerry Donaldson has written: 'After the success of the first Grand Prix of Canada held at Mosport in 1967, it was decided to share the wealth between Ontario and Quebec, with the Formula 1 circus visiting the Mont-Tremblant venue on alternate years. To facilitate travel arrangements, the event was scheduled two weeks before the traditional fall date of the United States Grand Prix at Watkins Glen, which meant the Laurentians were ablaze in

their autumn finery. The Grand Prix establishment was very impressed with the location within reach of Montréal, calling it one of the most beautiful settings in the world for a motor racing circuit (although they said that about Montréal, too.) They also appreciated the luxurious accommodations at the nearby resorts, where they could relax, fish, swim, golf or play tennis after taking on the difficult track.

'The 15-corner course had been carved out of the rugged terrain of the Pre-Cambrian Shield in the shadow of Mont Tremblant. Surrounded by spring-fed lakes, rushing streams and high rocky promontories, the course afforded spectators many excellent viewing points and the circus a spectacular backdrop to go about the business of motor racing in the grand manner.'

Gordon Kirby, a seigneur of American motor racing journalism, 'commented that turn one at Mont-Tremblant – a fifth-gear right-hander over a brow leading into a steep dive into a valley – used to be hands-down the finest place to watch race cars at speed in North America.'[2]

It opened in September 1964 near the town of St Jovite, a ski and tourist destination. Soon after opening the track was lengthened to 2.6 miles (4.2km) so that in 1966 it was able to stage a CanAm race, then IndyCars and the Grand Prix.

After the two Grands Prix the circuit continued to be used. Gilles Villeneuve had a tremendous crash in Formula Atlantic testing in 1976. Villeneuve was found 'trudging up the hill just past the pit straight, apparently none the worse for wear, though his car lay in ruins at the bottom of a ditch.'[3] A year later British driver Brian Redman crashed heavily in CanAm.

The circuit wasn't used for a long time but in 1999 a Montréal businessman bought it and it has been rebuilt to conform to modern safety requirements.

Scenic? Yes. Plenty of woodlands? Yes. And in there, there's a racing circuit, too. (Courtesy Julian Nowell Archive. Nowell explains: 'From a seaplane excursion ... take-off and landing on nearby lake!')

COCKPIT VIEW

Jackie Stewart, 1970 practice, Tyrrell:
'I could probably have gone faster, picking up a tenth here and then a tenth there over the course's 14 corners, but usually I need five or six laps to really hit a good one, a super good one, and this afternoon I didn't have the time. On the first two or three laps I was braking fairly hard, but as I went on I was easing the car into the corners rather than diving in, trying to keep it smooth, and the secret here, really, is in the braking.

'I was driving well, but I still don't feel I've mastered St Jovite. This isn't false modesty speaking, I'm still a bit untidy. I haven't been hitting my apexes well. Some of this is the car, but some of it is also me. I'm not doing anything drastic, it's just the difference between everything being tied perfectly together and things not clicking into place, and there's nothing I can do about it. It's a matter of touch, not mood. Tomorrow I might have it, but then again, I might not.'[4]

EYEWITNESS

Denis Jenkinson, *MotorSport*, November 1970:
'The Canadian Grand Prix is only four years old, twice being held at Mosport and twice at St Jovite, and judging by the small crowd that attended the 1970 race the word has not really got through that the European Circus was coming to town. Fortunately the financial loss was made good by the Imperial Tobacco Company, and more fortunate is the fact that people do not heed the dire warnings of the medical profession, and continue to smoke Player's cigarettes in sufficient numbers to allow the profits to be spent

RIGHT: A circuit with a view, 1968, and the hillclimbers are watching Dan Gurney lead Denny Hulme and Bruce Mclaren, all in McLarens. (LAT)

on supporting money-losing motor races. I am told this is called sponsorship, which sounds like a cover-up for a business failure. It is a nice little circuit, carved out of forest land and undulates in quite a spectacular manner in places, and is 2.65 miles to the lap, being something of a cross between Oulton Park and Brands Hatch, and is run on very European lines.'

MEMORIES AND MILESTONES

1968 The Grand Prix Drivers' Association, now becoming safety conscious, demanded run-off areas, Armco, and the removal of earth banks. This was done. Jochen Rindt (Brabham) took pole. Denny Hulme (McLaren) beat team-mate Bruce McLaren by a lap. Fastest lap: Jo Siffert (Lotus) 78.1mph/125.8kph.

1970 The drivers were unhappy about the track surface and Mauro Forghieri of Ferrari described it as a shock absorber test rig. The surface was rippled, particularly in the braking areas, so that the tyres left broken black lines of rubber rather than continuous ones. Jackie Stewart (Tyrrell) took pole. Jacky Ickx (Ferrari) won, beating team-mate Clay Regazzoni by 14.8 seconds, which created a terrible dilemma within him because, depending on the final two races, he could still take the Championship from Rindt, something he had no wish to do after Rindt's death at Monza the race before. Fastest lap: Regazzoni 103.4mph/166.5kph.

Speed increase 1968–70: 25.3mph/40.71kph.

Footnotes
[1] *The Grand Prix of Canada*, Donaldson.
[2] www.nationalspeedsportnews.com/columns/john-oreovicz/canada2019s-mont-tremblant-2018seeps-with-history2019. [3] *Villeneuve*, Donaldson. [4] *Faster!*, Stewart.

FACTS OF THE MATTER

2.650m/4.265km circuit

Year	Winner
1968	D. Hulme (McLaren)
1970	J. Ickx (Ferrari)
Fastest pole	J. Stewart (Tyrrell) 1970 (104.3mph/167.8kph)
Fastest lap	C. Regazzoni (Ferrari) 1970 (103.4mph/166.5kph)

CANADA
MONTRÉAL

Location: East of city centre.
Constructed: 1978.
World Championship Grands Prix: 30.

The panorama with two dimensions, the circuit and lake in the foreground, Montreal skyline in the background. (Courtesy Linda Carlson)

Pits Hairpin/
Épingle

Original Startline
until 1986

Droit du Casino

Start/finish

Senna

Island Hairpin/
Épingle de l'Ile

'It was almost as if you were driving on a semi-frozen surface'

John Watson

The idea that you could catch a metro in the normal way and find yourself a short walk from a Grand Prix circuit was amazing in the proper sense of that word, especially if you have grown visibly older in immense traffic queues every other place you went. In Montréal, simply go in the direction *Longueuil-Université-de-Sherbrooks* and get off at the station before that, *Jean Drapeau*. Walk across the bridge and you'll be facing the famous (and infamous) hairpin where reputations have been made and come to grief. You'll recognise it immediately and feel at home.

You might find the rest less familiar because, naturally, television cameras follow the track rather than the hinterland. I guess you won't have realised how much of an island the circuit is on, or how close to the water it goes. You won't have appreciated how verdant it all is, giving it a specific charm. Some called it the most beautiful circuit in the world when it was first built.

Mosport had become outdated in the way of the Nürburgring and Spa. Safety, allied to modernity, was becoming the new direction and it pointed to a new circuit on the Île Notre-Dame at Montréal. Roger Peart, former driver and mechanic who lived in Montréal, designed it. Work began on 20 June 1978 and was completed in time for an introductory race two weeks before the Grand Prix.[1]

The weather can be damnably hot or damnably cold but somehow Canadian human warmth takes care of both. The looming artefacts from Expo 1967 won't surprise you at all because at least two generations of Formula 1 photographers have been unable to resist the temptation to frame them in the background as the cars go by. The curiously round-shaped one will be like meeting an old friend.

Eddie Cheever, American but raised in Italy, captured it all nicely: 'To me, Montréal is halfway between the States and Europe – which is like me.'

COCKPIT VIEW

John Watson, who drove in six Canadian Grands Prix at Montréal between 1978 and 1983:

'I liked it. It was a funny surface, always relatively low grip, which made it difficult to get tyre temperatures up and you were sliding quite a lot. It was almost as if you were driving on a semi-frozen surface.

'You couldn't say it was a great circuit in the way that some of the other circuits in the World Championship were. The key to it was that it was a part of the town of Montréal. It had that atmosphere of being within the town – you could get there on the tube and see the skyscrapers. In fact, the atmosphere was something like Adelaide or Melbourne.

'Formula 1 has sometimes lost its proximity. I don't think today it's reasonable for people to have to travel substantial distances to get to a venue, then have to pay a fortune to watch it.

'What Montréal did was provide a natural audience of large numbers, plus whatever came over the border from the United States. It was a great event – Montréal was about an event, not about a race.

'The pits used to be way further back but as Formula 1 grew they had to develop them and they didn't have enough room there. What they were using was old wood, basically. Where the new pits are there used to be sweeping corners, very fast.

'The hairpin was actually much further down the road than it is today because the run-off that is required means that the circuit has had to bring it forward. We'd have continued 30m further on. The hairpin was on the one hand the easiest place to overtake, but on the other it was easily defended.

'If you had a good run out of the previous sequence, Turns 11 and 12, and a run down to the hairpin bend – we had a longer run down in our day – therefore if you had the momentum, you could get alongside somebody and get by on the inside. Equally, for all the good overtaking moves there you have all the fluffed ones.'

EYEWITNESS

Vanessa Harwood of Toronto, a former principal ballerina at the National Ballet of Canada, interviewed by Andy Shaw:

'I saw my first Montréal Grand Prix watching on television from Vancouver in 1982, when Riccardo Paletti died in a crash right at the beginning. [This did not deter her from attending almost every Montréal Grand Prix race since.]

'I was born in Cheltenham, England, and my father told me I saw my first Grand Prix race when I was a one-year-old at Silverstone. After we emigrated and I was growing up in Canada we went regularly as a family to stock car races at the old Pinecrest Speedway in north Toronto, and also up to what was then the new formula racing circuit at Mosport.'

Harwood married leading Canadian heart surgeon Dr Hugh Scully, also a life-long motor sport enthusiast, who served as Medical Director for the Montréal Grand Prix from 1978 to 1992.

'Safety conditions weren't nearly as stringent back then, so I was just sitting on a flatbed truck behind the fence at the first corner after the cars came out of the pits. I think it was Stefan Johansson in a red Ferrari who had just driven out of the pit but didn't see another car coming. So he veered off and there was a Ferrari zooming full speed straight at me. I leapt off the truck and ran. He spun out and hit the fence. But for a moment I thought, this could be *it*.

'One of the unique features of the race is that you can get to it by boat – and I remember seeing this daring racer Gilles Villeneuve cruising about very happily on the little motor scooters they gave the racers to help them get around.'

The Scullys' regular attendance at Montréal and other Grands Prix has led to lasting relationships. They count Nigel Mansell and his wife Roseanne as well as Professor Sid Watkins, the neurosurgeon who headed up the Formula 1 medical team, and his wife Susan, among their good friends.

'We made and renewed a lot of lasting acquaintances, especially, of course, in Karl-Heinz Zimmerman's trailer every year in Montréal. It was like belonging to a family. He lives in Austria but went to every race, running the hospitality trailer for Bernie Ecclestone. It's not connected to any particular team and so Sid Watkins would hang out there at the end of a race. That's where drivers could come and find him if they had any concerns.

'In fact Hugh had a long conversation with George Harrison in that trailer.

The artefacts of Expo 1967 (with, here, David Coulthard in front of one, 1995) and the majesty of the Montréal skyline (with, here, Damon Hill in 1994, Coulthard in 1996 and Hill in 1995) proved irresistible to a generation of photographers. *(All ICN U.K. Bureau)*

George was an avid fan and very low key, a very personable guy. I would be sitting in the trailer beside drivers as they came and went.

'[Now, with the Grand Prix returning] it's like having Christmas in June, because it's not just the race, it's all the other events and activities associated with it throughout the city. It's a very uplifting, joyous time in Montréal.'

MEMORIES AND MILESTONES

1978 The Friday session was run in heavy rain with cars veering off all over the place while Hans Stuck (Shadow), a master in the wet, was 'catching fearsome-looking power slides at the last moment on the slippery surface with his superb reflexes.'[2] On Saturday morning more rain fell but it dried for qualifying. Jean-Pierre Jarier (Lotus) took pole. Gilles Villeneuve put his Ferrari on the second row, helping to attract 72,632 spectators for the race. Villeneuve took the lead on lap 50 and won, convulsing the whole circuit. Fastest lap: Alan Jones (Williams) 102.6mph/165.2kph.

The circuit was modified, some corners eased and the chicane at the end of the pit straight becoming a fast left-right kink.

1979 Niki Lauda (Brabham) suddenly decided to retire on the Friday and walked away from Grand Prix racing, as he thought forever. This was almost forgotten as Villeneuve (Ferrari) and Alan Jones (Williams), pole, engaged in a titanic battle, Jones winning by 1.0 second. Fastest lap: Jones 108.1mph/173.9kph.

1980 Nelson Piquet (Brabham) took pole. A sequence of crashes at the start claimed ten cars and created a bizarre situation. Mike Thackwell, then, at 19 years 5 months and 29 days, the youngest driver ever to start a Grand Prix, hadn't been involved but his car was given to Jean-Pierre Jarier for the restart – giving Thackwell the shortest ever debut. Jones (Williams) beat Carlos Reutemann (Williams) by 15.5 seconds to take the World Championship. Fastest lap: Didier Pironi (Ligier) 111.1mph (+3.0)/178.8kph (+4.9).

1981 Piquet (Brabham) took pole. Run in torrential rain, only 11 of the 24 starters finished. Jacques Laffite (Ligier) beat John Watson (McLaren) by 6.2 seconds.

Fastest lap: Watson 90.1mph/145.0kph (no comparison).

1982 The race of terrible images in a country mourning Villeneuve, killed at Zolder the month before. The circuit was now named after him. Didier Pironi (Ferrari) took pole but stalled on the grid and Riccardo Paletti (Osella), from the second last row, struck it at great speed. The Osella caught fire and Paletti died in hospital. Piquet (Brabham) won the restart, beating team-mate Riccardo Patrese by 13.7 seconds. Fastest lap: Pironi 111.7mph (+0.6)/179.7kph (+0.9).

1983 Turbo power now, and on anything but cramped circuits this power could not be resisted, although Keke Rosberg, in qualifying, made the non-turbo Williams into a missile in the kink after the pits. René Arnoux (Ferrari) took pole and won from Eddie Cheever (Renault) by 42.0 seconds. Fastest lap: Patrick Tambay (Ferrari) 108.6mph (-3.1)/174.7kph (-5.0).

1984 Piquet (Brabham) took pole. The race turned on lap 44 when Lauda (who had come back) overtook McLaren team-mate Alain Prost and set out to do the same to leader Piquet – but Piquet responded and held him off to win by 2.6 seconds. Fastest lap: Piquet 111.1mph (+2.5)/178.9kph (+4.2).

1985 Two Lotuses on the front row, Elio de Angelis pole from Ayrton Senna, but the race belonged to Michele Alboreto and Stefan Johansson. They gave Ferrari its first 1-2 since 1983, Alboreto winning by 1.9 seconds. Fastest lap: Senna 112.8mph (+1.7)/181.6kph (+2.7).

1986 Nigel Mansell took the Williams to a crushing victory from pole, leading every lap and beating Prost's McLaren by 20.6 seconds. It was only the fourth win of Mansell's career. Fastest lap: Piquet (Williams) 115.5mph (+2.7)/185.8kph (+4.2).

Speed increase 1979–86: 7.4mph/11.9kph.

New pits and garages (bland but satisfactory, as one reporter phrased it) had been built much further down the circuit than the old ones, but drivers complained that the entry and exit were both dangerous: the former requiring a driver to slow on the racing line and use the equivalent of an escape road, the latter feeding cars out into a left-hander. Nelson Piquet was publicly critical.

1988 The year McLaren and Honda produced an unbeatable car and gave it

The tragedy at the start in 1982. The smoke is from the fire engulfing Riccardo Paletti's Osella. (Courtesy Linda Carlson)

to the two outstanding drivers, Senna and Prost, who hogged the front row (Senna pole) and ran in the first two places throughout – Senna overtaking Prost at the hairpin on lap 19 to win by 5.9 seconds. Fastest lap: Senna 115.6mph/186.0kph.

1989 Prost (McLaren) took pole. A wretchedly wet race, Senna in the other McLaren leading but the Honda engine let him down three laps from home and Thierry Boutsen (Williams) won for the first time, beating team-mate Patrese by 30.0 seconds. Of the 26 starters only seven were running at the end. Fastest lap: Jonathan Palmer (Tyrrell) 106.8mph/171.9kph (no comparison).

1990 A drying track and this time the Honda did not fail Senna, pole, although Gerhard Berger in the other McLaren finished in front of him. He was penalised a minute, however, for jumping the start, relegating him to fourth. Fastest lap: Berger 119.6mph (+4.0)/192.6kph (+6.6).

Speed increase 1988–90: 4.0mph/6.6kph.

The track had been resurfaced, eliminating most of the bumps. The final corner had been tightened into a dog-leg, giving a slower pit lane entry. It would become a favourite overtaking place and claim its victims (see 1992).

1991 Patrese (Williams) took pole but team-mate Mansell had the race won on the final lap and was waving to the crowd when, mysteriously, the revs on his Williams dropped at the hairpin and the engine cut out, marooning him. Piquet

(Benetton) beat Stefano Modena (Tyrrell) by 31.8 seconds. Fastest lap: Mansell 120.3mph/193.6kph.

1992 Senna (McLaren) took pole. Mansell (Williams) tried to take Senna in the dog-leg, ploughing across the run-off area. Senna was hobbled by a gearchange problem, leaving team-mate Berger with the broadest grin in Canada. He beat Schumacher (Benetton) by 12.4 seconds. Fastest lap: Berger 120.4mph (+0.1)/193.7kph (+0.1).

1993 Prost (Williams) took pole, team-mate Damon Hill led, then Prost led again while Schumacher brought the Benetton up to second, 14.5 seconds away. Fastest lap: Schumacher 121.6mph (+1.2)/195.7kph (+2.0).

Speed increase 1991–3: 1.3mph/2.1kph.

In the shadow of Senna's death at Imola, a first-gear chicane was added after the old pits to slow the cars.

1994 The 1993 pole speed of 125.4mph/201.9kph became 115.5mph/185.8kph, set by Schumacher (Benetton), who led all 69 laps and beat Hill (Williams) by 39.6 seconds. Fastest lap: Schumacher 111.9mph/180.1kph.

1995 Schumacher (Benetton) took pole. Jean Alesi's career at Ferrari had been, since 1991, a catalogue of frustrations and bad luck. That changed

The start was always a compression of acceleration into a tight space. Coulthard leads Hill in the Williamses – but, in 1994, Michael Schumacher (Benetton) would win. (ICN U.K. Bureau)

so dramatically that when he realised victory finally beckoned he had to use his willpower to control his emotions. If he burst into tears, he reasoned, he wouldn't be able to see where he was going. He beat Rubens Barrichello (Jordan) by 31.4 seconds. Fastest lap: Schumacher 111.1mph/178.8kph.

Speed decrease 1994–5: 0.8mph/1.3kph.

The esse just beyond the old pits had been removed, creating a straight that led to the dog-leg, enhancing the opportunity when drivers got there.

1996 Hill took an important step towards the World Championship by leading every lap from pole except during his first pit stop, when Williams team-mate Jacques Villeneuve led. Hill beat him by 4.1 seconds. Fastest lap: Villeneuve 120.7mph/194.3kph.

1997 Schumacher (Ferrari) took pole. Olivier Panis lost control of his Prost at some 145mph and it smashed its front against the Armco, breaking both his legs. For a long time it looked much, much worse than that. The race was stopped 15 laps short, Schumacher a clean winner by 2.5 seconds from Alesi (Benetton). Fastest lap: David Coulthard (McLaren) 124.2mph (+3.5)/199.9kph (+5.6).

1998 David Coulthard (McLaren) took pole. The left-right after the grid had come to resemble the first chicane at Monza: a twisting funnel which annually challenged all the cars to get safely through from the start. Alexander Wurz (Benetton) was in contact with the Sauber of Jean Alesi and barrel-rolled off. At the restart Jarno Trulli (Prost) rode up and on to Alesi. Meanwhile after the race Frank Williams lodged a protest against Schumacher's driving, describing it as 'out of order' – at one point he pushed Heinz-Harald Frentzen (Williams) off. Schumacher beat Giancarlo Fisichella (Benetton) by

Gilles was mythology by 1996 and a great weight was falling on his son Jacques. (Courtesy Martin Hadwen, National Motor Racing Archive)

The luxury of proximity: take the Metro to the circuit and walk in. The Montreal streets always caught the mood of the race, too. (Courtesy Chris Puddy)

16.6 seconds. Fastest lap: Schumacher 124.6mph (+0.4)/200.5kph (+0.6).

1999 Schumacher, pole, battered his Ferrari against the wall opposite the pits when he was leading (Villeneuve in the BAR did the same five laps later) and Mika Häkkinen (McLaren) won to lead the World Championship (34 points, Schumacher 30). Fastest lap: Eddie Irvine (Ferrari) 123.0mph (-1.6)/198.0kph (-2.5).

2000 Schumacher (Ferrari) took pole. Coulthard (McLaren) stalled on the grid and was given a ten-second stop'n'go penalty because the mechanics worked on the car on the grid. Schumacher helped himself, beating team-mate Barrichello by 0.1 of a second. Fastest lap: Häkkinen (McLaren) 125.1mph (+2.1)/201.3kph (+3.3).

2001 The Schumacher brothers made history by finishing first and second – Michael (Ferrari) pole but Ralf (Williams) beating him by 20.2 seconds. Fastest lap: Ralf Schumacher 128.1mph (+3.0)/206.1kph (+4.8).

Speed increase 1996–2001: 7.4mph/11.8kph.

Variation, including chicane.

2002 Juan-Pablo Montoya (Williams) took pole. Michael Schumacher held off a determined late assault by Coulthard (McLaren) to win by 1.1 seconds and lead the Championship by *42* points after this, only Round Eight. Fastest lap: Montoya 128.4mph/206.7kph.

2003 The Schumacher brothers again, this time Michael (Ferrari) leading and Ralf (Williams), pole, chasing all through the race. Michael beat him by 0.7 of a second. Fastest lap: Fernando Alonso (Renault) 128.3mph (-0.1)/206.5kph (-0.2).

2004 And again: Ralf (Williams) took pole, Michael (Ferrari) on the third row but in the lead by lap 17 during the first pit stops. He was fuelled long and, when Ralf made a second stop, resumed in the lead. Ralf chased him home but was disqualified for a brake duct irregularity so that Michael beat team-mate Rubens Barrichello by 5.1 seconds. Fastest lap: Barrichello 132.5mph (+4.2)/213.2kph (+6.7).

2005 Jenson Button (BAR) took pole. The story of the race is told by the lap leaders: Fisichella (Renault, 1–32, hydraulics), Fernando Alonso (Renault, 33–38, accident), Montoya (McLaren, 39–48, disqualified for pit lane offence), Kimi Räikkönen (McLaren) winning it

---

FACTS OF THE MATTER

2.796m/4.500km circuit

Year	Winner
1978	G. Villeneuve (Ferrari)
Pole	J.-P. Jarier (Lotus)
(102.7mph/165.3kph)	
Fastest lap	A. Jones (102.6mph/165.2kph)

Corners eased, 2.740m/4.410km circuit

Year	Winner
1979	A. Jones (Williams)
1980	A. Jones (Williams)
1981	J. Laffite (Ligier)
1982	N. Piquet (Brabham)
1983	R. Arnoux (Ferrari)
1984	N. Piquet (Brabham)
1985	M. Alboreto (Ferrari)
1986	N. Mansell (Williams)
Fastest pole	Mansell 1986 (117.3mph/188.7kph)
Fastest lap	N. Piquet (Williams) 1986 (115.5mph/185.8kph)

Pits, corner change, 2.738m/4.390km circuit

Year	Winner
1988	A. Senna (McLaren)
1989	T. Boutsen (Williams)
1990	A. Senna (McLaren)
Fastest pole	A. Senna 1990 (122.1mph/196.6kph)
Fastest lap	G. Berger (McLaren) 1990 (119.6mph/192.6kph)

New corner before pits, 2.753m/4.430km circuit

Year	Winner
1991	N. Piquet (Benetton)
1992	G. Berger (McLaren)
1993	A. Prost (Williams)

Temporary chicane, 2.765m/4.450km circuit

Year	Winner
1994	M. Schumacher (Benetton)
Pole	M. Schumacher (115.5mph/185.9kph)
Fastest lap	M. Schumacher (111.9mph/180.1kph)

Reverted to 2.753m/4.430km circuit

Year	Winner
1995	J. Alesi (Ferrari)
Fastest pole	A. Prost (Williams) 1993 (125.5mph/201.9kph)
Fastest lap	M. Schumacher (Benetton) 1993 (121.6mph/195.7kph)

Chicane alteration, 2.747m/4.421km circuit

Year	Winner
1996	D. Hill (Williams)
1997	M. Schumacher (Ferrari)
1998	M. Schumacher (Ferrari)
1999	M. Häkkinen (McLaren)
2000	M. Schumacher (Ferrari)
2001	R. Schumacher (Williams)
Fastest pole	M. Schumacher (Ferrari) 2001 (130.5mph/210.0kph)
Fastest lap	R. Schumacher (Williams) 2001 (128.1mph/206.1kph)

Hairpin changes, 2.710m/4.361km circuit

Year	Winner
2002	M. Schumacher (Ferrari)
2003	M. Schumacher (Ferrari)
2004	M. Schumacher (Ferrari)
2005	K. Räikkönen (McLaren)
2006	F. Alonso (Renault)
2007	L. Hamilton (McLaren)
2008	R. Kubica (BMW)
Fastest pole	R. Schumacher (Williams) 2004 (135.0mph/217.2kph)
Fastest lap	R. Barrichello (Ferrari) 2004 (132.5mph/213.2kph)

---

from Michael Schumacher (Ferrari) by 1.1 seconds. Fastest lap: Räikkönen 131.1mph (-1.4)/211.1kph (-2.1).

2006 Everyone passed through the first corner safely, Alonso (Renault), pole, leading, as he would for all but the pit stops. He beat Schumacher (Ferrari) by 2.1 seconds. Fastest lap: Räikkönen (McLaren) 128.6mph (-2.5)/207.0kph (-4.1).

2007 Lewis Hamilton (McLaren) took pole. Robert Kubica (BMW Sauber) was approaching the hairpin at about 184 miles an hour when he lost control. The car struck the central Armco and barrel-rolled, threshing wildly, to the hairpin itself. The television images were stunning and frightening, the car coming to rest

completely savaged. Kubica was fine. Hamilton beat Nick Heidfeld (BMW) by 4.3 seconds. Fastest lap: Alonso (McLaren) 127.7mph (-0.9)/205.6kph (-1.4).

2008 And guess who won? Robert Kubica. Hamilton (McLaren), pole, rammed Kimi Räikkönen's Ferrari, stationary at the pit lane end under a red light, an amazing sight and still inexplicable. Seven drivers led, Kubica taking it on lap 42 – and keeping it to beat BMW team-mate Heidfeld by 16.4 seconds. Fastest lap: Räikkönen 126.1mph (-1.6)/202.9kph (-2.7).

Speed decrease 2002–8: 2.3mph/3.8kph.

Footnotes
[1] *Grand Prix of Canada*, Donaldson. [2] *Ibid.*

MOSPORT PARK

Location: 60 miles (100km) north-east of Toronto. Now known as Mosport International Raceway.
Constructed: 1961.
World Championship Grands Prix: 8.

'It was a super layout but a difficult circuit to pass on'

John Watson

Turn 3

Turn 1

Start/finish

Turn 2

Turn 4

Moss Corner
(Turn 5)

Turn 5C

White's Corner
(Turn 10)

Turn 9

Turn 6

The Esses
(Turn 8)

Mario Andretti Straightaway

Turn 7

ABOVE AND OPPOSITE: Season of mists and mellow fruitfulness, Mosport, 24 September 1972. This is the formation lap, the fog so bad the race was almost postponed to the following day. Jacky Ickx (Ferrari) would be twelfth after losing power and suffering a puncture. (Courtesy Linda Carlson)

In 1958 the British Empire Motor Club[1] began searching for land to build a circuit and they found a 450-acre site near Bowmanville, Ontario. It was a farm on a hill, pastoral and with a lot of trees. The Club realised that developing it into a circuit was beyond their means. Instead they formed Mosport Limited to do it – Mosport is (wait for it, wait for it) a contraction of motor sport. It would be only the second road-race course in Canada built specifically to be such,[2] and succeeded three Ontario airport circuits: Edenvale, Green Acres, and Harewood Acres.

By 1960 extensive work was in progress to accommodate the 'sweeping bends that rose and fell over the contours of the site'. A great deal of earth had to be moved, including a hillside.[3]

That summer Stirling Moss visited the circuit and thereby hangs a lovely anecdote. Moss said that Turn 5 would be better as two corners rather than a hairpin and, when this had been done, the corner was named after him. It also produced confusion because people thought the circuit, which they mistook as 'Mossport', had been named after him.

Mosport opened in 1961 with a clubman's race and in June hosted an international event, the Player's 200 sports car race, which Moss (Lotus) won in front of a crowd of 40,000.

The circuit is Canada's biggest motor sport complex and multi-track: the 2.4-mile (3.9km) ten-corner road course, entirely resurfaced in the early 2000s to comply with FIA specifications, making it 42ft (12.8m) wide, with an oval measuring half a mile; a 2.4km advanced driver and racing driver training facility plus skid pad; and a kart track. Significantly, when the resurfacing was being done drivers were consulted in order to maintain the track's character.

Mosport grew through sports car races (naughtily called the Canadian

Grand Prix), which were very popular but, because it was a driver's circuit, the dangers were inherent. In September 1965, John Surtees was practising for a CanAm race: 'I remember climbing into the car, but recall nothing more until about four days later. It was later pieced together that, accelerating past the pits, heading towards the downhill right-hander, I lost a front wheel. The car ploughed into a barrier, somersaulted over it and landed on top of me …

The car was fitted with a harness, but whether the mountings pulled out of the chassis or not I just don't know. All I do know is that one of the marshals who pulled me out of the wreck came to see me in hospital and explained that their biggest worry was fire. I was doused in petrol from head to toe. Mercifully, it didn't catch fire.'[4]

The big crowds and Can-Am races opened the way for a real Grand Prix in Canada's centennial year.

COCKPIT VIEW

John Watson, who drove in the 1973, 1976, and 1977 races:

'Another great North American racetrack, like Watkins Glen, although inadequate now because it is almost exactly the same as it was when I last raced there in 1977. It was in a beautiful location, good elevation changes, good challenging corners.

'Turns 1 and 2 were big, big challenges for the cars we were racing because we didn't have the levels of grip, so the speed and the corner layouts brought it in many respects very close to Watkins Glen in terms of driver fulfilment.

'It was a super layout but a difficult circuit to pass on because you'd got a sequence of corners, one blending into the other. Then you had the long drag uphill, which was a series of steps going in a very gentle curve. A good-feel racetrack.

'It was one of those places that didn't have sex appeal, which Watkins Glen did have for a variety of reasons – maybe because it was much more cosmopolitan.

'Canada was always the penultimate and Watkins Glen the final race of the season. Watkins Glen was like going into Andy Warhol's factory[5] but the circumstances of Mosport weren't quite like that. People were dispersed around the venue and if you were a high roller you might even have stayed in Toronto, so it didn't have that buzz.'

EYEWITNESS

Linda Carlson and husband Gary, New York State:
'We were happy enough to carve out another long weekend for a second Grand Prix [Watkins Glen the first] fairly close to home. The ability to drive there and back in one day qualified it as such, although we only tried that once. In 1972 we made our first visit to Mosport and the Canadian Grand Prix. It was an enjoyable weekend, bad weather and all, and we returned every year through the last Grand Prix in 1977.

'We have many memories, mostly good ones, but one in 1972 stands out above all the rest. Camping, we awoke on race morning to find thick fog surrounding the track. The fog hung on through the day and the race start was delayed. It was finally decided to send each race car out, one at a time, on a reconnaissance lap.

'Conditions seemed to be improving a bit but it was still fog-shrouded when Jackie Stewart was sent out first. We had placed ourselves along the spectator fence at Turn 5, also known as Moss Corner. It was a natural bowl-like spectator area great for picture taking, and the large crowd gathered there could see the cars as they approached the Turn, follow them around it and on up the hill and away.

'I don't remember the exact order but I believe the third car around was Chris Amon in the Matra. Visibility was virtually nil. We heard the car coming long before it was seen. The Matra was famous for its memorable and distinct sound, like a banshee screaming. So you *could* hear it coming and, because the visibility was so poor, Amon seemed to be holding it in a lower gear when he normally would be advancing through the gears, which made the sound even more pronounced.

'As the seemingly invisible car came toward us through the mist the sound grew and all eyes strained to catch sight of its approach. It was just *shrieking* as it came into the turn, suddenly popping out of the mist, revealed. It passed by making the sharp turn to the right and then the power was on again and the engine wailed away.

'The track bore to the left and the car disappeared out of view but the sound was coming back at us as if amplified. The noise finally died out and there was a hushed silence all around Turn 5. The crowd seemed to be holding its collective breath. No one seemed to move. Breaking the silence, I heard a guy behind me exclaim, "That was almost as good as sex!" There were a few titters and then another voice, louder, "*Almost?*"'

MEMORIES AND MILESTONES

1967 Clark (Lotus) took pole while team-mate Graham Hill spun in the wet and tried to push-start it on a flat piece of track. It was not, he reported, easy. Race day was wet too. Hill would remember that 'with water running across the track one or two drivers spun out on the warming-up lap. Everyone regarded it as a most uncomfortable race. It rained, then stopped, the track would begin to dry, and then it would rain again; conditions were never the same one lap to the next. It turned out to be quite a tiring race.'[6] Jack Brabham (Brabham) beat team-mate Denny Hulme by 1 minute 01.9 seconds. Fastest lap: Clark 106.5mph/171.4kph.
1969 Guardrails and Armco had been added but curiously the track surface was not as even as it had been. Jacky Ickx (Brabham), pole, beat Brabham (in the other Brabham) by 46.2 seconds. Fastest lap: Ickx and Brabham 113.3mph (+6.8)/182.4kph (+11.0).
1971 The race-day warm-up was delayed an hour because of a fatal accident in a Formula Ford race, and then run in heavy rain, cars spinning and crashing. Jackie Stewart (Tyrrell), pole, led the first lap by three seconds, the others lost in the ball of spray. Stewart beat Ronnie Peterson (March) by 38.3 seconds. Fastest lap: Denny Hulme (McLaren) 85.5mph/137.6kph (no comparison).
1972 It ought to have been at Mont-Tremblant but that suddenly closed. Mosport offered yet more Armco but the track hadn't been resurfaced. 'There were new installations of guardrail, sections of the track were bordered by low, ribbed anti-dust curbings and a permanent machine shop was erected in the paddock.'[7]

Peter Revson (McLaren) took pole. It rained again. Emerson Fittipaldi would

The Tyrrell mechanics go skateboarding at Turn 1, but the man on the board hasn't found the racing line round it. Well, he is a mechanic.

The grid waiting for the starting procedures to begin, 1977.
(Both courtesy Linda Carlson)

1 Niki Lauda practising in the Ferrari. He'd qualify fifth. *(Courtesy Peter Dick)*

2 Clay Regazzoni practising in the other Ferrari, Canada's wide open spaces spreading beyond. *(Courtesy Linda Carlson)*

3 The start of the 1976 race, Peterson storming into the lead from James Hunt (McLaren) then Patrick Depailler's Tyrrell (4). *(Courtesy Bill Wagenblatt)*

4 The lonely splendour of Lauda. He'd finish fourth, an important result for the Championship because Hunt spun off. *(Courtesy Bill Wagenblatt)*

remember asking Colin Chapman to change the Lotus and 'he didn't allow it. It was a big mistake. My car was undrivable in the wet. I went out on the warm-up laps, and I just could not put on the power in top gear, I was spinning wheels and sliding all over the place … I was driving quite hard. It was raining very hard at the start of the race, and then it became foggy as the rain stopped a bit. It seemed such a long race. In the end the organisers stopped it.'[8] Stewart (Tyrrell) beat Peter Revson (McLaren) by 48.2 seconds. Fastest lap: Stewart 116.9mph/188.2kph (no comparison).

1973 Fog descended on the Saturday practice and the organisers said drivers could go out one at a time and do no more than four laps – then the fog lifted. Peterson (Lotus) took pole. The race day warm-up was wet too, and a host of cars – one report says eight – spun off. During the race a pace car came on for the first time in a Grand Prix. As the track dried cars pitted for new tyres and created great confusion. Revson (McLaren) beat Fittipaldi (Lotus) by 32.7 seconds. Fastest lap: Fittipaldi 117.3mph (+4.0)/188.7kph (+6.3).

1974 'With its sandy subsoil and severe winters, the track surface at Mosport was prone to frost heaves in the spring. The annual visit of the sensitive Formula 1 cars, which saw them skittering and swerving around these undulations, was great fun to watch, but rather dangerous and very hard on suspension systems. This year some of the circuit's bumps

had been flattened and the first third of a lap, down to Corner 3, had been repaved. But the smoother surface was offset by the lack of grip of the tires on the new asphalt in the cool weather. The net result was no loss in spectacle with full-blooded power slides and stimulating back-end breakaways available at every turn.'[9] Fittipaldi (McLaren), pole, beat Clay Regazzoni (Ferrari) by 13.0 seconds. Fastest lap: Niki Lauda (Ferrari) 120.2mph (+2.9)/193.4kph (+4.7).

1976 The weather behaved and so did James Hunt (McLaren), pole, who won, but many eyes were on Niki Lauda (Ferrari), eighth in only his second race after his fiery crash at the Nürburgring. Hunt beat Patrick Depailler (Tyrrell) by 6.3 seconds. Fastest lap: Depailler 119.9mph (-0.3)/193.0kph (-0.4).

1977 The track was regarded as unacceptably bumpy by the drivers and there was talk of a boycott. In practice, Ian Ashley's Hesketh took off 'as it crested the brow of the hill towards the end of the lap, somersaulted, jumped the guard-rail and then landed heavily against a high television tower, wrecking itself and causing serious injuries to its unlucky driver … he lay trapped in the wreckage and subsequent rescue operations, assisted by Jochen Mass, were to take some 40 minutes to free him and even then there was a similar wait before a helicopter arrived.'[10] Mario Andretti (Lotus) took pole. Jody Scheckter (Wolf) beat Depailler (Tyrrell) by 6.7 seconds. Fastest

lap: Mario Andretti (Lotus) 120.8mph (+0.9)/194.4kph (+1.4).

Speed increase 1967–77: 14.3mph/23.0kph.

Grand Prix racing had outgrown the circuit and never went back, but there is a sad final memory. Manfred Winkelhock, a Grand Prix driver, was killed in 1985 during a Group C sports car race. His Porsche struck a concrete wall.

Footnotes
[1] The British Empire Motor Club was created in 1928 to promote British motorbikes in Canada. [2] The circuit was the second purpose-built road-race course in Canada after Westwood Motorsport Park in Coquitlam, British Columbia. [3] www.mosport.com/history.htm. [4] *World Champion*, Surtees. [5] For younger readers, Andy Warhol (1928–87) was a bohemian artist who became iconic although, as I remember, nobody was quite sure what. If I tell you he painted soup cans and Coca Cola bottles you might begin to understand. [6] *Life at the Limit*, Hill. [7] *Grand Prix of Canada*, Donaldson. [8] *Flying On The Ground*, Fittipaldi. [9] Donaldson, *op cit.* [10] *Grand Prix!*, Lang.

FACTS OF THE MATTER

2.459m/3.957km circuit

Year	Winner
1967	J. Brabham (Brabham)
1969	J. Ickx (Brabham)
1971	J. Stewart (Tyrrell)
1972	J. Stewart (Tyrrell)
1973	P. Revson (USA)
1974	E. Fittipaldi (McLaren)
1976	J. Hunt (McLaren)
1977	J. Scheckter (Wolf)
Fastest pole	M. Andretti (Lotus) 1977 (124.0mph/199.6kph)
Fastest lap	M. Andretti 1977 (120.8mph/194.4kph)

SHANGHAI

Location: 16 miles (25km) north of Shanghai.
Constructed: 2002.
World Championship Grands Prix: 6.

The 2009 race was run in a rainstorm and the Safety Car controlled the first eight laps. As we look, Sebastian Vettel (Red Bull) has pole from (left) Fernando Alonso (Renault). Jenson Button (Brawn), the Championship leader, is two cars behind Vettel. (LAT)

Start/finish

'It's a real challenge for the drivers and the engineers'

Heikki Kovalainen

The Chinese Grand Prix was the direct descendant of the Hungarian. Both were communist countries eager to sample Formula 1, which can fairly be described as ultimate capitalism, and both were happy to use this symbolism to demonstrate that they were outward-looking. A round of the World Championship, globally the third biggest sporting event on television, did that nicely.

When it was awarded the Grand Prix in October 2002, Shanghai was poised to host the ATP Tennis Masters tournament, and Beijing had the 2008 Olympic Games of course.

The circuit was designed by Hermann Tilke and cost $240 million. It was built in a year and a half on marshland, using a reported 40,000 polystyrene blocks for stability.

Its shape resembles the Chinese character *shang*, which evidently bears a close resemblance to the first character in Shanghai. Tilke didn't know this so it's a simple coincidence.

Initial reaction was entirely favourable, as reflected in what Ferrari had to say when they reached it for the first Grand Prix, in 2004:

Jean Todt: 'This has been an historic day for Formula 1, making its first appearance in the world's most heavily populated country which for the past

few years has been experiencing a period of amazing economic growth. As we were able to ascertain in June at its official opening, the circuit is a grandiose facility with some amazing avant-garde buildings.'

Rubens Barrichello: 'I like the track very much and think it's amazing. The number of corners and different lines into the corners make it interesting. It will be tough physically and I think there will be some good overtaking opportunities.'

Almost an alien landscape in China. It would become familiar to Formula 1. (Vodafone/LAT)

Michael Schumacher: 'Several corners have a blind apex and generally it is a very challenging circuit.'

Turns 1 and 2 tightened like a tourniquet and offered the chance to gain time while Turn 14, according to Jenson Button, was the favourite overtaking place even if it wasn't the only one.

COCKPIT VIEW

Heikki Kovalainen, McLaren, 2009:
'The best corners are Turns 6 and 7 – the fast, sweeping left-and right-handers. The left is almost flat in sixth before you shift down a gear and change direction at very high speed.

'It's difficult to find the ideal set-up because of the variety of different corners: there's some heavy braking, fast esses, and high-speed changes of direction, which require a good aero package, and some slower corners where mechanical grip is important.

'It's all about compromise – it's a real challenge for the drivers and the engineers. But at least you can overtake – mainly into Turns 4, 10 and 13.'[1]

EYEWITNESS

Steven Tee, LAT Photographic:
'I had been to China before – Shanghai. I went to do a Mika Häkkinen photo

shoot when he was on a tour as World Champion. I remember the place being absolutely full of bikes and the airport being tiny. We came back for the Grand Prix and since then they had built this enormous great airport and everybody was driving cars in the worst traffic jams in the world.

'China is one of my least favourite races, not because of Shanghai – I'm a big city person, so I love big cities – but because where they've stuck the circuit means you've got at least an hour if not an hour and a half to get back each night in solid, solid traffic.

'You don't want to stay at the track because there are no decent hotels there.

'The circuit is not very good – the complete opposite to Singapore, for example. Everything is way too big. The paddock takes you 20 minutes to walk across and, if you are like us and work

for teams, you can never find anyone because there are four different places they could be at any one time.

'You get out on to the circuit and it all looks exactly the same. There is nothing that tells you that you are in China at all.'

MEMORIES AND MILESTONES

2004 Max Mosley said Shanghai had redefined circuit standards and all other tracks would be judged against it. The inaugural Grand Prix brought the best of racing too, with three leaders before Rubens Barrichello (Ferrari), pole, beat Jenson Button (BAR) by 1.0 second. Fastest lap: Michael Schumacher (Ferrari) 132.2mph/212.7kph.
2005 The 750th Championship race. Fernando Alonso (Renault), pole, had taken the championship two races before (Brazil) and now drove like a

champion, leading every lap from pole and beating Kimi Räikkönen (McLaren) by 4.0 seconds. Fastest lap: Räikkönen 130.8mph (-1.4)/210.5kph (-2.2).
2006 Michael's Schumacher's 91st career victory (next Prost 51, then Senna 41). He got his tactics for a cloudy, rainy, drying day just right – and his choice of tyres just right after Alonso (Renault),

pole, led. Schumacher beat him by 3.1 seconds. Fastest lap: Alonso 125.0mph/ 201.1kph (no comparison).
2007 Although the race – in light rain – was Round 16 of the Championship, Lewis Hamilton (McLaren), pole, made his first real mistake of the season when he stayed out too long and, tyres worn, slithered off in the pit lane entrance never

to return. By then Räikkönen (Ferrari) was in the lead. He beat Alonso (McLaren) by 9.8 seconds, the Championship alive with only Brazil left: Hamilton 107 points, Alonso 103, Räikkönen 100. Fastest lap: Felipe Massa (Ferrari) 125.1mph/201.4kph (no comparison).
2008 Hamilton (McLaren), pole, beat Massa (Ferrari) by 14.9 seconds, so that

Spectator Norman Harrera took these photographs during a 2007 practice session. He says: 'I was on the topmost seat on Grandstand B. Unfortunately, my camera has no panoramic features so I just took four shots to get the total view from that particular seat. If there's one word to describe this circuit it's MASSIVE: good clean facilities, good views from the grandstand, good climate and a great circuit to watch a Formula 1 race.'

they went to the decisive last round in Brazil 94–87. Fastest lap: Hamilton 126.6mph (-4.2)/203.7kph (-6.8).

2009 The Grand Prix was the third of the season and Jenson Button (Brawn) had won the first two. Sebastian Vettel (Red Bull) took pole. In wet conditions Red Bull announced themselves as a major force when Vettel beat team-mate Mark Webber by 10.9 seconds. It set up the whole season. Fastest lap: Rubens Barrichello (Brawn) 108.3mph/174.3kph (no comparison).

Speed decrease 2004–9: 5.6mph/9.0kph.

Footnote
[1] Courtesy of McLaren.

FACTS OF THE MATTER

3.387m/5.451km circuit

Year	Winner
2004	R. Barrichello (Ferrari)
2005	F. Alonso (Renault)
2006	M. Schumacher (Ferrari)
2007	K. Räikkönen (Ferrari)
2008	L. Hamilton (McLaren)
2009	S. Vettel (Red Bull)
Fastest pole	R. Barrichello (Ferrari) 2004 (129.7mph/208.7kph)
Fastest lap	M. Schumacher (Ferrari) 2004 (132.2mph/212.7kph)

The photograph which proves China was just like any other track which had ever been: it rained there. Here Hamilton (McLaren) duels with Kimi Räikkönen in the Ferrari. (Vodafone/LAT)

The pits and paddock didn't resemble this anywhere else in the world. (LAT)

BUGATTI AU MANS

Location: At the Le Mans circuit, Le Mans.
Constructed: 1966.
World Championship Grands Prix: 1.

The Grand Prix had almost none of the feel of the 24 Hour sports car race. Denny Hulme (Brabham) is running in second place. (LAT)

Garage Vert

La Chapelle

'S' du Chemin aux Boeufs

Le Musée

'S' du Garage Bleu

'A real Mickey Mouse type of circuit'

Graham Hill

Dunlop

Virage du Raccordement

Start/finish

Le Mans. The name itself is impossibly evocative, adding a new layer each year since 1923 to make the 24-hour race a monumental thing. Le Mans is one of the central pillars of world motor sport, *so* evocative that a whole American series has been named after it.

The very first Grand Prix was run in the countryside around Le Mans in 1906, the same countryside from which emerged on a summer's evening in 1955 an Austin-Healey, a Jaguar, and a Mercedes, to create the worst crash in motor racing history. That remains evocative, too, in scope, savagery, and consequences.

The events of July 1967 stand in astonishing contrast. For 'financial and political pressures,'[1] the Grand Prix was brought to a very unsatisfactory bastardised circuit, called Bugatti after the celebrated car-maker. (See 'Eyewitnesses'.)

You can argue that right from the beginning the Grand Prix had been itinerant, passing through Dieppe (1907–12), Amiens (1913), Strasbourg (1922), Tours (1923), Lyons (1924), Montlhéry (intermittently from 1925 to 1937), Comminges (1928), Pau (1930), Reims (intermittently from 1932 to 1966), Lyons (1947), Rouen (intermittently from 1952 to 1964), and Clermont-Ferrand (1965). Why not pass through Le Mans? You can further argue that, remembering 1906, the Grand Prix was simply coming home.

The reality *was* very unsatisfactory.

COCKPIT VIEW

Graham Hill, Lotus:

'It uses the pits and the Dunlop Bridge corner of the … 24-hour circuit and then branches off into the parking area, where they had made a real Mickey Mouse type of circuit going backwards and forwards with 180° corners and then joining the main circuit again just at the beginning of the pits.

'It wasn't a particularly imaginative sort of circuit, but we had to make the best of it.

'It was rather a shame, because the Grand Prix cars don't show up too well on this sort of thing – they were coming past the pits accelerating away from a second-gear corner whereas everyone was used to seeing the cars coming out of White House Corner at 120mph and getting up to about 160 by the time they reached the pits. The Grand Prix cars tended to look slower and rather lost on this large circuit.'[2]

EYEWITNESSES

Bernard Beaumesnil, spectator and car constructor for Le Mans:

'I went to Le Mans from 1949. Normally the French Grand Prix was at Reims or Rouen, but the problem was that Reims was no longer viable and Le Mans was a circuit which could be adapted to Grand Prix cars. And it was available.

'There had been a Formula 2 race at the circuit the year before (with seven drivers in it who would also be in the Grand Prix) – Clark, Brabham, Rindt, people like that.

'There is an extraordinary story. Guy Ligier, Jim Clark, and Graham Hill were behind the pits signing the T-shirts of the circuit publicity girls. They amused themselves signing them and Graham Hill did his on a girl's chest…

'It was another era.

'Me, I have an equally extraordinary image. I still remember Jack Brabham in his car without the bodywork on it and he appeared to be sitting in a bath of petrol because the petrol tank went round his seat and was made of transparent polyester. That made a strong impression.

'For the Grand Prix there was a crowd because Le Mans is not far from Paris and other big towns and people came from there to watch, so it was seen by a lot of people. The locals went out of curiosity because they wanted to see what a Grand Prix looked like in comparison to the 24 Hours. One impression was how short the Grand Prix was compared to the 24 Hours. The Grand Prix lasted just over two hours – in that time the 24 Hours was just beginning.

'The speeds in the Grand Prix were big. I remember that later on the Bugatti, Jackie Stewart – privately testing a Matra – did a lap of 1m 21s [compare Hill's fastest lap in the Grand Prix].'

Gregor Grant, *Autosport*, 7 July 1967:

'For Friday's practice the entry was reduced to an unlucky 13 by a little Hitler at Dieppe, who kept the two Lotuses so long in the customs that they were unable to reach Le Mans in time. This left Jimmy Clark and Graham Hill the unenviable task of learning all about the appallingly difficult Bugatti Circuit in the 90 minutes of Saturday's practice, although they had both driven F2s there last year.

'The heat during the first day's practice was intense. The drivers complained that the road appeared to be covered in ball bearings, no doubt due to the sand which blows everywhere at La Mans. There was also some oil on the course.

'Everybody was gearing very low, as there is no real straight. As tyre changes are extremely rare in grand prix racing, the majority of the cars had bolt-on wheels, with six studs for the Eagles but only four for the Coopers. However, a centre-locking wheel can be equally light, especially when the hub caps have no ears, as on the Lotus. Each BRM had a spanner taped to its steering wheel spokes, for easy removal of the wheel in case of accident.'

MEMORIES AND A MILESTONE

1967 The race only attracted 20,000 spectators, although one report puts that at 30,000. Graham Hill (Lotus) took pole in weather so hot fuel began to vaporise, and led then team-mate Jim Clark, but both had mechanical problems and Jack Brabham (Brabham) beat team-mate Denny Hulme by 49.5 seconds. Hill set fastest lap (102mph/164.4kph) and at Reims the year before it had been 141.4mph/227.6kph by Lorenzo Bandini (Ferrari). That's a big, big difference. The race never returned. Le Mans meant, and would always mean, something else altogether. By a paradox, the full 24 Hour circuit faced major alterations to slow the sports cars to 60mph as they passed the pits…

Footnotes
[1] *Grand Prix!*, Lang. [2] *Life at the Limit*, Hill.

FACTS OF THE MATTER

2.748m/4.422km circuit

Year	Winner
1967	J. Brabham (Brabham)
Pole	G. Hill (Lotus) (102.8mph/165.5kph)
Fastest lap	G. Hill (102.2mph/164.6kph)

CLERMONT-FERRAND

Location: 6 miles (10km) south-west of Clermont-Ferrand, central France.
Constructed: 1958.
World Championship Grands Prix: 4.

Jo Bonnier (Brabham) explores verdant France and its extinct volcanoes, 1965 – before the alternator drive failed. (LAT)

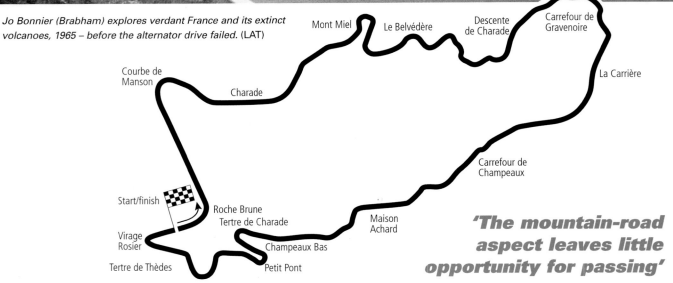

Mont Miel
Le Belvédère
Descente de Charade
Carrefour de Gravenoire
La Carrière
Courbe de Manson
Charade
Carrefour de Champeaux
Maison Achard
Start/finish
Roche Brune
Tertre de Charade
Virage Rosier
Champeaux Bas
Tertre de Thèdes
Petit Pont

'The mountain-road aspect leaves little opportunity for passing'

Jackie Stewart

This is a strange place. One report assures us that the circuit was 'built in 1958 around the sides of an extinct volcano', as if they might have chosen an active volcano instead but couldn't find one. In his study of the history of the French Grand Prix, David Hodges wrote that the circuit is 'largely built round two hills, the *Puy de Charade* and *Puy de Gravenoire* (the former just tops 900 metres, neither would require that a mountaineer ascending them exercise his climbing skills, therefore technically they are not mountains).'[1]

Some say the circuit, developed from public roads with 2km of new track linking them, was the most beautiful in the world. Others insisted that because of its contours – dipping and rising – it was the Nürburgring on a smaller scale (see 'Eyewitness').

In 1908 there were moves to create a 30-mile (48km) circuit round the *Puy-de-Dôme*, a volcano (presumably extinct too) 10km from Clermont-Ferrand, but nothing happened. After the Second World War the president of the local motor sports association and Louis Rosier, a noted Grand Prix driver who also had a major Renault dealership in Clermont-Ferrand, promoted the idea of a circuit near the town. They had designs drawn for a circuit of between 4km and 6km in the hills. Again nothing happened, because the 1955 crash at Le Mans, which killed at least 80 people, essentially halted all motor racing in France.

The project was revived as a dedicated racetrack, was approved, and work began in May 1957, but by then Rosier was dead, killed at the Montlhéry circuit near Paris a year before when his Ferrari crashed.

When the circuit at Clermont-Ferrand was opened in 1958 it was named after him, although sometimes it is also called Charade after the mountain.

John Surtees, who drove a Ferrari in the first Grand Prix there, remembered it as 'tortuous and undulating' but a 'real drivers' circuit.' The only 'real problem was that, lying in the foothills of heavily wooded mountains, it tended to attract quite a lot of mist, something which we learned all about during the practice sessions.'[2]

They also had to learn its 51 corners with, here and there, rock faces at the exits. Graham Hill (BRM) found out all about that. He described it as 'a very twisty, pretty circuit high above the town'.[3] He also recounted how during practice his throttle stuck open and the car rammed a rock face...

The track received general approval, despite this, although Hodges complained that 'the amenities – particularly the pits, which are squeezed on to the side of a hill – are primitive and hardly of an adequate standard' for a Grand Prix.

A year later John Frankenheimer used the track for his film *Grand Prix* with, reportedly, 3,000 locals posing as the crowd.

COCKPIT VIEW

Jackie Stewart, driving a March, 1970:
'It is probably one of the four most difficult tracks in the world. Clermont is different. You can read all the corners with much more accuracy than the Nürburgring because you can get to know them all better.

'It is a winding course, climbing and swooping round two volcanic "*puys*" (peaks) high above the industrial city centre. I know several Grand Prix drivers who have suffered from car sickness there during the race, probably due to a combination of the fatiguing nature of the circuit and the humidity in the Auvergne area in July.

'The surface at Clermont is good. There are two very similar places on the circuit, two corners where the scenery is alike and you have to think out every lap which one you are approaching. Confusion would not be dangerous. You would be unlikely to have an accident through mistaking one for the other, but you could be slower.

'The mountain-road aspect leaves little opportunity for passing – that's one of the most frustrating things about Clermont-Ferrand – but the driver who does get out in front can show his virtuosity to the fullest. The seemingly endless succession of corners demands that you do each one exactly right or your line is ruined for the next and you break the important "rhythm" of the track.'

EYEWITNESS

Patrice Besqueut, *Directeur de l'Automobile Club de l'Auvergne*:
'I was born in 1949 in Clermont-Ferrand so I was a young man when Jim Clark won the first Grand Prix. I was passionate about motor sport.

'Clermont-Ferrand is a mountain circuit, the younger brother of the Nürburgring: the same style. The drivers knew it was a bit risky. The drivers paid attention to what they were doing.

'I can still remember that first Grand Prix. The atmosphere was extraordinary and I say that because *everybody* wanted to be there. There were a lot, a lot of people, and they came from Paris, they came from everywhere, because it was a Grand Prix of France.

'I went to all four Grands Prix and each was different. Clark was alone from beginning to end but that was just Jim Clark in the Lotus. The first victory of Jackie Stewart and the Matra (in France) *was* extraordinary because in effect there were two races. You had the victory of Stewart but above all the French public were passionate about the second place. You had an amazing struggle between Jean-Pierre Beltoise in the other Matra and Jacky Ickx with the Brabham. They were passing and re-passing in each corner, the sort of spectacle you don't see today. It was happening three, four, five times during a lap and the nature of the circuit permitted that.

'In 1970 all the spectators hoped that there would be a French victory with Beltoise with the Matra. He was on the first row [Ickx, Ferrari, pole], but Beltoise took the lead and it looked as if the French dreams would be coming true and then he had a puncture. It was a terrible moment for the spectators because at that instant the race was lost. It was almost a moment of despair. The public liked Rindt [the winner] but certainly they wanted Beltoise!

'Something happened which is little known. There was a driver due to make his debut: Jean-Luc Salomon, but he was killed in a race at Rouen the week before in a Formula 3 race [see Rouen]. He was a great French hope and he would have been driving a Lotus. Rouen was very dangerous.

1 Photographer Julian Nowell says: 'This is the fast Esses at one of the highest points of the track (taken 1982). The reason I have taken pictures of tracks is because it was a chance to see first hand how and where the Grands Prix took place that, sadly, I was too young to visit in my youth in the 1950s – not that we could have afforded European travel anyway in those immediate post-war years. This, however, is what created my interest in the sport and captured my imagination.'

2 The nature of the beast: you can understand how Jochen Rindt didn't feel well. *(Author)*

3 and 4 The reception, offices and entrance today. *(Author)*

'The last Grand Prix was 1972 and, firstly, there was something else extraordinary: the Matra, with Chris Amon on pole. I remember the noise the Matra made, an amazing noise which echoed far down the valley – unique. Everybody had eyes for Amon because they hoped he'd win a race at last and it would be the Grand Prix of France. He was very popular and when we did a Grand Prix Retro in 1989 with Fangio, Brabham and so on I had a special word for him because he set the fastest lap at Charade [see 'Facts of the Matter']. He was an outstanding driver but he had something more than that because he set the fastest pole and then the fastest lap in the race. The two. Extraordinary.

'Charade lost the Grands Prix because it was a circuit which was badly adapted to the modern era and to host a race today there must be the political will, which is what happened at Magny-Cours with President Mitterand, who had decided that there would be a race there.

'I have another memory, which isn't exactly Formula 1 but nearly. It was the making of the film *Grand Prix* at Charade. Some of the scenes were shot there. They put a Formula 1 monocoque, mounted on a big wheel, on top of a Grand Prix car. The monocoque, with its onboard camera, could swivel left or right to simulate 180° spins while the car underneath continued straight ahead. Amon was driving that car.'

MEMORIES AND MILESTONES

1965 Wet on race morning but drying, and Clark (Lotus) led every lap from pole to beat Jackie Stewart (BRM) by 26.3 seconds. Fastest lap: Clark 90.6mph/145.8kph.

1969 Jochen Rindt (Lotus) complained of 'motion sickness' and during practice changed from a fully enclosed crash helmet to an open one. A car ahead threw a stone back 'the size of a fist.'[4] It struck Rindt on the cheek and might have been much worse if it had hit elsewhere. Alex Soler-Roig, the son of a Barcelona surgeon and an aspiring driver, had a look at Rindt, took him to the Mobile Grand Prix Hospital and sewed four stitches. Stewart (Matra) took pole and beat Jean-Pierre Beltoise (also Matra) by 57.1 seconds. Fastest lap: Stewart 98.6mph (+8.0)/158.7kph (+12.9).

1970 The French Grand Prix should have been at Albi but financial problems ruled that out and 23 entries came for the 20 places. That meant qualifying. Jacky Ickx put the Ferrari on pole after a long wait for the transporter to arrive. Ickx had a transmission failure and lost the lead to Beltoise (Matra) but he had a fuel pressure problem and Rindt (Lotus) beat Chris Amon (March) by 7.6 seconds. Fastest lap: Jack Brabham (Brabham) 99.7mph (+1.1)/160.4kph (1.7).

1972 Drivers were using the full width of the track and more, churning mud and stones. Emerson Fittipaldi's Lotus threw one back and it struck Helmut Marko (BRM) in the face, piercing his left eye and ending his career. Amon (Matra) took pole. Stewart (Tyrrell) beat Fittipaldi (Lotus) by 27.7 seconds. Fastest lap: Amon 103.6mph (+3.9)/166.8kph (+6.4).

FACTS OF THE MATTER

5.005m/8.055km circuit

Year	Winner
1965	J. Clark (Lotus)
1969	J. Stewart (Matra)
1970	J. Rindt (Lotus)
1972	J. Stewart (Tyrrell)
Fastest pole	C. Amon (Matra) 1972 (103.9mph/167.2kph)
Fastest lap	C. Amon 1972 (103.6mph/166.8kph)

Footnotes
[1] *The French Grand Prix*, Hodges. [2] *World Champion*, Surtees.
[3] *Life At The Limit*, Hill. [4] *Jochen Rindt*, Prüller.

Jackie Stewart looking very relaxed in the era when pit and paddock were not fortresses. Stewart would finish second to Jim Clark. *(Courtesy Arthur Willmer)*

Many scenes in the film *Grand Prix* were shot at Clermont-Ferrand. Note at bottom left the swivelling car and next to that Yves Montand, one of the leading French actors of the day. At right Françoise Hardy, one of the leading French pop singers of the day, relaxes between takes.

Masterly British understatement in *The Times* for the first Grand Prix at Charade, 1965.

DIJON-PRENOIS

Location: 9 miles (15km) north-west of Dijon.
Constructed: 1972.
World Championship Grands Prix: 6.

The culmination of the most audacious and astonishing motor racing duel ever captured on film: Gilles Villeneuve (Ferrari) crosses the line 0.24 of a second in front of René Arnoux (Renault). (LAT)

Parabolique

Virage de la Combe

'S' des Sablières

La Bretelle

Courbe des Gorgeolles

Double-droite de Villeroy

Courbe de Pouas

Ligne Droite de la Fouine

Start/finish

'It was lethal, that place'

Keke Rosberg

Burgundy is a sensuous, sumptuous region of genuinely great wine and long, feast-like dinners. The stone villages with the world-famous names are so quaint that time itself seems to have stilled its hand, and the vine-dressed hillsides encased by dry stone walls provide a perfect backdrop, ever changing with the seasons.

If I tell you that publicity always claimed the circuit of Dijon-Prenois to be Burgundian – Nuits St Georges not far away and so on – you might even be seduced. Don't. The circuit was nondescript (unless you like sweeping corners, dips, and rises), the officials officious to a remarkable degree, the sanitation a disgrace even by French standards, and the owner (rumoured to be a former wrestler) – how shall I put this? – eccentric.

To compound all this, in 1982 the circuit hosted the Swiss Grand Prix. Switzerland is sort of near Dijon and, although not so close as Nuits St Georges, it had the same relevance: nil. In other words, with Alain Prost and René Arnoux World Championship contenders in the Renaults, it was a good excuse to give France a second Grand Prix.

When Formula 1 first ventured there in 1974 – the sixth different French circuit since 1965 – the track measured only 2.0 miles (3.2km), which meant the first 12 cars in qualifying covered it in less than a minute. (Comparison: Paul Ricard 3.6 miles/Clermont-Ferrand 5.0.) In a sense this made Dijon like Monaco: very crowded, so crowded that the entry of 30 would have to be pruned to 22. It was originally treated with derision because it was so short. Niki Lauda (Ferrari) took pole with a lap of 58.7 seconds and the race lasted only 1h 21m 55.0s.

The drivers discovered, however, a circuit that was described as essentially a continuous downhill right-hand corner and a straight reached by a bump so pronounced that drivers needed opposite lock. Perhaps not so nondescript after all…

COCKPIT VIEW

Keke Rosberg, driving a Williams, 1982:
'The track surface was always dirty, sandy, and not a very grippy place. It didn't deserve to be part of the Grand Prix calendar every year, no. The facilities were non-existent. You'd run a medium set-up and that was always the compromise there: how fast you got on to the straight. The corners at the back had no run-off areas: I mean none. It was lethal, that place.'[1]

EYEWITNESS

Gareth Rees, motor sport enthusiast:
'In 1974, I went to the first French Grand Prix held at the new Dijon-Prenois circuit. It was an against-the-odds win for Ronnie Peterson in the ageing Lotus 72, and that was special in itself, but strangely it is not the Formula 1 race that is my best memory of that weekend.

'There was an unusual supporting race for "Group 3" cars, basically road-going sports cars which all looked like they had been loaned out for the day from the various importers' showrooms.

'Gerard Larrousse was the easy winner in a Porsche 911 Carrera, but it was the sight of Derek Bell, a normally very tidy driver, in a standard BMW 2002 Turbo, that

Dijon wasn't flat but undulating. Ronnie Peterson (Lotus) goes into a dip lapping Patrick Depailler (Tyrrell).
(Courtesy Gareth Rees)

Ronnie Peterson (Lotus) moving past Jody Scheckter (Tyrrell) and going on to win in 1974. *(Courtesy Gareth Rees)*

Niki Lauda in the Ferrari will finish second but 20.3 seconds behind Peterson. *(Courtesy Gareth Rees)*

wowed the crowd that day as he came into view at the back of the circuit, lap after lap, totally sideways and with tyres smoking. He was running about eighth but that didn't

Here John Watson (Brabham) leads Mario Andretti (Lotus) through the undulations. Note the fencing to their left. (LAT)

matter, he was just wringing the neck of his car and providing huge entertainment. He got a real ovation as he came round one last time after the finish.

'Next day I got the chance to go back and walk around the circuit. On the face of it, it was a pretty unimaginative track, with a long straight and a succession of undulating curves running down the

opposite side. This was before the extra loop was added at the back and, to me, it seemed much too short and simple to be a real Grand Prix circuit.

'Nevertheless it had one big redeeming point: the long sweeping downhill-entry-uphill-exit curve at the end of the lap, essential for a good run on to the long straight, which was normally the only

place on the track where a car could overtake. Of course, a few years later somebody forgot to explain this to Gilles Villeneuve and René Arnoux… [See 1980]'

MEMORIES AND MILESTONES

1974 Niki Lauda (Ferrari) took pole. A start-line crash claimed James Hunt in the Hesketh and he stood shaking his fist when Emerson Fittipaldi (McLaren) came round. Because the circuit was so short the leaders began moving through slower cars from lap 22 of the 80 and by the end only six were on the same lap. Ronnie Peterson (Lotus) beat Lauda by 20.3 seconds. Fastest lap: Jody Scheckter (Tyrrell) 122.6mph/197.3kph.

A long loop, called the Parabolique, was added, making the circuit a more manageable 2.3 miles. The Parabolique was reached by 'an adverse camber downhill right-hander, there was a sharp left-hander where the road fell away steeply to the left. Then, separated by two uphill straights and situated at the apex of the loop, there was a right-hand hairpin, and finally … a seemingly never-ending left-hander leading back to the existing circuit'.[2]

1977 Mario Andretti (Lotus), pole, beat John Watson (Brabham) by 1.5 seconds. Fastest lap: Andretti 115.3mph/185.5kph.
1979 Jean-Pierre Jabouille was handling the Renault well enough to take pole (1m 07.1s) from team-mate René Arnoux. The race was historic: Jabouille became the first man to win a Grand Prix with a turbo car while, behind him, Arnoux and Gilles Villeneuve (Ferrari) indulged in the most sustained wheel-to-wheel combat ever seen. Villeneuve crossed the line 14.59 seconds after Jabouille, and Arnoux 0.24 of a second after Villeneuve. Fastest lap: Arnoux 122.9mph (+7.6)/197.8kph (+12.3).
1981 Arnoux (Renault) took pole. The race was stopped after 58 laps because of a downpour and the final 22 laps were run when the track had dried. Alain Prost (Renault) beat Watson (McLaren) by 2.2 seconds. Fastest lap: Prost 122.9mph/197.8kph (no change).
1982 Run as the Swiss Grand Prix, it produced one bizarre moment in qualifying when Derek Daly (Williams) got the entry to *Parabolique* wrong and used the escape road – in fact the old track which the *Parabolique* had replaced.

He waited for Watson (McLaren) to go by and followed him. When he reached the pits a senior Williams team member realised that nobody else would know and told Daly to keep his mouth shut. For the only time that year Daly out-qualified his team-mate Keke Rosberg, who beat Prost (Renault) in the race by 4.4 seconds and would win the World Championship without winning another race. Fastest lap: Prost 126.0mph (+3.1)/202.7kph (+4.8).
1984 Run as the French Grand Prix, the circuit seemed to suit the McLarens, and did. Patrick Tambay (Renault) led from pole but Niki Lauda was stalking him into second place by lap 18 and leading from lap 41. Pit stops reversed it but Lauda led again from lap 62 of the 79 and beat Tambay by 7.1 seconds. Fastest lap: Prost (McLaren) 133.2mph (+7.2)/214.4kph (+11.7).

Speed increase 1977–84: 17.9mph/28.9kph.

Footnotes
[1] *1982*, Hilton. [2] *Grand Prix!*, Lang.

How the magazine *Grand Prix International* caught the mood at Dijon.

MAGNY-COURS

Location: 7 miles (12km) south of Nevers, central France.
Constructed: 1960.
World Championship Grands Prix: 18.

The sweeping left just after the start could stretch the field straight away: this is 1994 and Michael Schumacher (Benetton) leads Damon Hill (Williams) – and they finished in that order. (ICN U.K. Bureau)

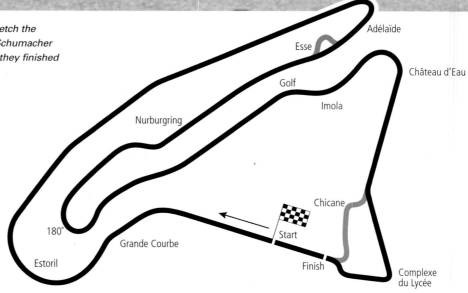

'Its characteristics change a lot, probably more than most other circuits'

Kimi Räikkönen

Magny-Cours is uncannily like Silverstone: set in rolling, verdant countryside, essentially flat, it could just as easily have been built somewhere else – in the next field, in fact. Significantly it was bought by the regional council of the *Département* (county) with the support of then French President François Mitterrand in 1988. The race survived until 2008, when the governing body, the *Fédération Française du Sport Automobile*, withdrew financial support. Magny-Cours left a stir of memories but little you could call nostalgia. It wasn't that kind of countryside, that kind of circuit, or that kind of track.

It was initially constructed in 1960 on the site of a hospital that had been used for American troops during the Second World War, which in turn had been replaced by a farm. The local mayor, seeking to promote the area, had the circuit built. It was named for Jean Behra, who had been killed the year before. The circuit measured only 2km but soon earned enough of a reputation for the leading French school for young drivers, Winfield, to be based there (as well as Paul Ricard). Patrick Depailler, Jean-Pierre Jarier, François Cevert, and Jacques Laffite were among the pupils.

In 1971 the mayor decided to extend the circuit to 3.85km and in 1978 it was hosting a round of the European Formula 3 championship (Dutchman Jan Lammers won, Alain Prost had

an engine failure after one lap). This continued until 1984 when the circuit began to deteriorate to the point where international events were no longer held.

In 1988 the circuit was reborn as part of an ambitious regeneration project for the area, embracing an industrial park, an 18-hole golf course, a motor museum, and an extension to the Nevers-Fourchambault airport. The Ligier Grand Prix team based itself at the circuit.[1]

When Grand Prix racing arrived in 1991 the drivers found a very modern facility with an extremely smooth track surface and fast chicanes with prominent kerbing, but with only one real overtaking place, the Adelaide hairpin. Nelson Piquet (Benetton) commented that it was 'similar to Monte Carlo and the Hungaroring. It will be very difficult to overtake during the race', while Riccardo Patrese (Williams) found perhaps the perfect word – 'nice' – while pointing out that, because of the overtaking problems, qualifying would be 'critical'.

The bon viveurs (the author among them) who accompanied Grand Prix racing found that Nevers was not a gastronomic centre.

The spectators who came to watch the cars found they could see a great deal if they could get in along the single access road. *Autocourse* reported that it was 'appallingly restricted ... In fact the circuit would become so frighteningly overcrowded

A photograph, seemingly ordinary, which distils the frustrations of Magny-Cours, one car following another all afternoon. This is Alesi (now Benetton) and team-mate Gerhard Berger. They ran the final twenty five laps like that. (ICN U.K. Bureau)

on race morning that the gates would be shut, effectively locking out thousands who had tickets but had not managed to battle their way through the clogged local roads in time to gain entry. Predictably, they would cut up rough with the local gendarmerie and some ugly episodes ensued.'

The race ran every year to 2008.

COCKPIT VIEW
Kimi Räikkönen, McLaren, 2006:
'Magny-Cours can be quite a challenging track to set up for, because its characteristics change a lot, probably more so than at most other circuits. However, I quite like driving here, it seems to suit my style.

'It is a slow track – and with low-speed corners, hairpins, and no major straights, a total contrast to the previous three circuits we have raced at [Indianapolis, Montréal, Silverstone].

'Magny-Cours has a smooth surface, with no bumps and less kerbs. As a result we can run with more front wing and a lower ride-height because the car is less upset by kerbs and bumps.

'You tend to generate high tyre temperatures here, so blistering can be a problem. This is because the track gets very hot during the day due to the blackness of the asphalt. The track has reasonable grip levels.'

EYEWITNESS
Ann Bradshaw, PR expert:
'I was quite lucky: when I worked with both Williams and Arrows I got private jets out, because Frank used to always let a group of us go back on his jet on the Sunday night and Tom Walkinshaw [of Arrows] the same.

'Rothmans would fly a group of us out of Luton to Nevers, too. You'd get to Nevers airport – it was round the back

by the trading estate – and there'd be Frank, there'd be Ron [Dennis], there'd be all the drivers – Gerhard Berger with his own plane. I remember the Schumachers there. It was like standing in a car park full of jets.

'That was its only saving grace. I could be back home by eight o'clock in the evening, well before the highlights of the race on television because in those days I lived in Oxford and we'd come into Kidlington.

'We all hated Magny-Cours on sight, but at the end of the day that was because it wasn't Paul Ricard. It never stood a chance. The drivers didn't get very excited about it, although there were some interesting races there. The hotels round were not nice and they were expensive. You could stay in a chateau but they were all shabby.

'To be honest the food wasn't that good considering it was near Sancerre and all those lovely wines.

'Where the Williams team stayed was a proper French country hotel. *Madame* ruled it with a rod of iron but she used to love Patrick Head and give him a big kiss whenever he appeared.

'Because there was nowhere to go in the evenings the paddock became quite a nice area to be in. I remember the Tyrrell guys used to get their guitars and we'd have parties in the paddock.'

MEMORIES AND MILESTONES

1991 Riccardo Patrese (Williams) took pole but team-mate Nigel Mansell duelled with Alain Prost (Ferrari) – both led twice (Prost laps 1–21, 32–54, Mansell 22–31, 55–72) – to win by 5.0 seconds. Fastest lap: Mansell 120.7mph/194.2kph.

The esse just after the Adelaide hairpin was straightened, giving a straight run to the Nürburgring kink.

1992 French truck drivers blockaded many of the country's roads (protesting against government regulations) but all the Grand Prix vehicles reached the circuit except the Andrea Moda transporter and

The sweeping left could act as a compression, as Ukyo Katayama (Tyrrell) and Taki Inoue (Footwork) discovered in 1995. (ICN U.K. Bureau)

the AGIP and Yamaha trucks. Mansell (Williams) took pole. Ayrton Senna (McLaren) and Schumacher (Benetton) crashed at the Adelaide hairpin. Mansell beat team-mate Patrese by 46.4 seconds. Fastest lap: Mansell 123.4mph/198.5kph.

1993 The Williams team had taken time to assert itself but now Prost and Damon Hill, pole, ran first and second throughout, Prost winning by 0.3 of a second. Fastest lap: M. Schumacher 120.0mph (-3.4)/193.0kph (-5.5).

1994 Mansell returned from exile in the United States and 'guested' for Williams but the transmission failed. Team-mate Hill took pole, but Schumacher (Benetton) beat him by 12.6 seconds. Fastest lap: Hill 119.3mph (-0.7)/192.0kph (-1.0).

1995 Hill (Williams) took pole but Schumacher accused him of lifting off when he was directly behind – their rivalry, central to the Championship, was deepening. Schumacher took the lead at the first pit stops and beat Hill by 31.3 seconds. Fastest lap: Schumacher 118.5mph (-0.8)/190.7kph (-1.3).

1996 Schumacher (Ferrari) took pole but the engine failed on the parade lap, opening the race to Hill (Williams), who beat team-mate Jacques Villeneuve by 8.1 seconds. Fastest lap: Villeneuve 120.9mph (+2.4)/194.6kph (+3.9).

1997 Even a late cloudburst could not prevent Schumacher (Ferrari), pole, winning comfortably enough. He led every lap (except the pit stops) and beat Heinz-Harald Frentzen (Williams) by 23.5 seconds. Fastest lap: Schumacher 122.0mph (+1.1)/196.4kph (+1.8).

1998 Mika Häkkinen (McLaren) took pole but the race was straight Ferrari: Schumacher led every lap (except one, at his first pit stop) with team-mate Eddie Irvine second – except laps 44 to 54 of the 71, and Ferrari had their first 1-2 for eight years. Schumacher beat Irvine by 19.5 seconds. Fastest lap: David Coulthard (McLaren) 122.6mph (+0.6)/197.4kph (+1.0).

1999 Rubens Barrichello (Stewart) pole. Torrential rain made the track treacherous and produced five leaders – Frentzen the last of them, to give Jordan their second Grand Prix victory. He beat Häkkinen (McLaren) by 11.0 seconds. Fastest lap: Coulthard (McLaren) 120.0mph (-2.6)/193.1kph (-4.3).

2000 Michael Schumacher (Ferrari) took pole, but Coulthard forced his McLaren past him at the Adelaide hairpin, their cars so close they rubbed wheels. Coulthard beat McLaren team-mate Häkkinen by 14.7 seconds. Fastest lap: Coulthard 119.6mph (-0.4)/192.5kph (-0.6).

2001 Ralf Schumacher (Williams) took pole from brother Michael (Ferrari), but Michael won the race, beating Ralf by 10.3 seconds. He now led the Championship 78–47 from Coulthard (McLaren) but insisted, with seven rounds left, nothing was settled. Fastest lap: Coulthard 125.0mph (+5.4)/201.1kph (+8.6).

2002 Juan-Pablo Montoya (Williams) took pole but Schumacher won his fifth World Championship, an extraordinary feat, by July. It had never been done (or imagined) at a French circuit before. Kimi Räikkönen (McLaren) seemed poised to take the race but slithered briefly on oil – at Adelaide hairpin, of course – and Schumacher was through, winning by 1.1 seconds. Fastest lap: Coulthard (McLaren) 126.7mph (+1.7)/203.9kph (+2.8).

Speed increase 1991–2002: 6.0mph/9.7kph.

The last corner and chicane, a corkscrew of a thing, were eased in an effort to make overtaking more possible. Juan-Pablo Montoya complained that before this was done the final corner was 'difficult because you come in hard and the kerb on the inside is really big. If you turn in a bit early it is going to throw you off.' Schumacher complained about the circuit's lack of grip: 'It is so slippery, especially with the heat, that it is not driving, it is sliding.'

RIGHT: The year before Alesi spun in the Esse on to the pit lane straight and collected Rubens Barrichello (Jordan). *(ICN U.K. Bureau)*

LEFT and ABOVE: Three weeks before, Jean Alesi had won the first Grand Prix of his career in Canada (1995) after years of bad luck. He celebrated and France did, too. *(Courtesy Martin Hadwen, National Motor Racing Archive)*

LEFT and BELOW: Autosport capturing the full span at Magny-Cours, from the problems of 1991 to the last moments there, 2008.

FACTS OF THE MATTER

2.654m/4.271km circuit

Year	Winner
1991	N. Mansell (Williams)
Pole	R. Patrese (Williams)
	(128.1mph/206.2kph)
Fastest lap	N. Mansell (120.7mph/194.2kph)

Straightening at esse, 2.641m/4.250km circuit

1992	N. Mansell (Williams)
1993	A. Prost (Williams)
1994	M. Schumacher (Benetton)
1995	M. Schumacher (Benetton)
1996	D. Hill (Williams)
1997	M. Schumacher (Ferrari)
1998	M. Schumacher (Ferrari)
1999	H.-H. Frentzen (Jordan)
2000	D. Coulthard (McLaren)
2001	M. Schumacher (Ferrari)
2002	M. Schumacher (Ferrari)
Fastest pole	J.-P. Montoya (Williams) 2002
	(132.1mph/212.6kph)
Fastest lap	D. Coulthard (McLaren) 2002
	(126.7mph/203.9kph)

Final corner reprofile, 2.741m/4.411km circuit

2003	R. Schumacher (Williams)
2004	M. Schumacher (Ferrari)
2005	F. Alonso (Renault)
2006	M. Schumacher (Ferrari)
2007	K. Räikkönen (Ferrari)
2008	F. Massa (Ferrari)
Fastest pole	F. Alonso (Renault) 2004
	(133.9mph/215.5kph)
Fastest lap	M. Schumacher (Ferrari) 2004
	(130.9mph/210.7kph)

2003 The BAR-Honda cars were impounded by the police over allegations about payments and a sponsorship. They were able to race, Jacques Villeneuve ninth but Jenson Button out of fuel after 21 laps. Ralf Schumacher, pole, beat Williams team-mate Montoya by 13.8 seconds. Fastest lap: Montoya 130.7mph/210.3kph.

2004 Michael Schumacher (Ferrari) forced Alonso (Renault), pole, into second place, beating him by 8.3 seconds, but the move of the race came from team-mate Rubens Barrichello, who forced his way past Jarno Trulli (Renault) at the end

of the final lap. Fastest lap: Schumacher 130.9mph (+0.2)/210.7kph (+0.4).

2005 Alonso (Renault) took a commanding step towards becoming the youngest champion by leading every lap from pole and beating Räikkönen (McLaren) by 11.8 seconds. Fastest lap: Räikkönen 129.1mph (-1.8)/207.8kph (-2.9).

2006 Schumacher, pole, won the race for the eighth time, a record made more astonishing because they had all been at Magny-Cours. He beat Alonso (Renault) by 10.1 seconds after leading every lap except pit stops. It was not

exactly exciting, perhaps even for him. Fastest lap: Schumacher 128.0mph (-1.1)/205.9kph (-1.9).

2007 Felipe Massa (Ferrari) took pole. Lewis Hamilton's consummate debut season continued with McLaren because, by finishing third, he had put himself on the podium for all of the eight rounds so far. Räikkönen beat Massa by 2.4 seconds. Fastest lap: Massa 129.7mph (+1.7)/208.7kph (+2.8).

2008 By now the future of the race was uncertain for financial reasons, which didn't disturb the Ferraris – Massa beat Räikkönen, pole, by 17.9 seconds, the rest spread far back. Fastest lap: Räikkönen 128.8mph (-0.9)/207.2kph (-1.5).

Footnote
[1] www.fanaticf1.com/formule1/114-France.html.

PAUL RICARD

Location: 21 miles (34km) east of Marseilles.
Constructed: 1969.
World Championship Grands Prix: 14.

Signes
L'Epingle
de Bendor
Ligne droite du Mistral
La Tour
'S' du Village
Virage de l'école
'S' de l'école
Double droite du Beausset
Virage de la Sainte-Beaume
La Bretelle
Virage du Pont
'S' de la
Verriere
Start/
finish

*Ricard wasn't just an arid moonscape. This
is Nelson Piquet who'd fail to catch Williams
team-mate Nigel Mansell in 1986. (LAT)*

'The whole thing was can you get through it flat?'

John Watson

To get the Paul Ricard circuit into any kind of proper focus is not easy, which is itself a strange thing to say about a circuit. It was portrayed as being part of the South of France experience, embracing (forgive me) Brigitte Bardot, St Tropez, starlets on topless beaches and all the rest. In reality it could have been positioned among any bleached hills in any hot country and the nearest to starlets you'd see were ladies of the night (operating in the day) from clearings on the winding journey up to it. Since the track was custom-built and almost completely clad in Armco, a visit to the ladies ought to have carried more risk than being a driver – until you remember Elio de Angelis.

The facilities, including an air-conditioned Press Room, were not just modern but almost modern art in 1971 when the Grands Prix came. Ricard *shimmered* with all that glass and everything was in the right place. However, the approach remained ordinary roads that clogged instantly on race day, like just about everywhere else on the calendar.

The pits complex certainly was futuristic with its hospitality suites, restaurants, conference facilities, and garages with enough space and equipment. Marshals 'operated coloured light signals suspended from gantries at various parts of the circuit'.[1]

The track escaped the curse of the custom-builders. It had its own character and demanded courage to take it on as well as skill, although some critics condemned it as bland or worse. Its backbone, the *Mistral* straight (named for the fierce wind which blows down the Rhône-Saone valley), measured a mile – 1,800km – and allowed cars to reach their absolute maximum speed. At the end, the *Signes* right-hander issued a stark invitation: *take me flat out*.

There were also tricky medium-speed corners and proper run-off areas, a novelty.

Everyone was happy (including presumably the ladies) except members of the public confronted by the access: it seemed as if the queue began in Marseilles 21 miles away, but that must have been a mirage in the heat haze – mustn't it?

The circuit brought a specific problem, as Mario Andretti, winner in 1978, explained: 'Paul Lauritzen of Goodyear drew our attention to the tyre temperatures we were getting. They were generally up on what we usually ran, which indicated perhaps we were sliding around too much. Like they say, Ricard is always a compromise, sacrificing a little here to gain a little there. You have to decide where the gain is most important. For straightaway speed, we'd been running very little rear wing, which had to account for us sliding more than usual. After the warm-up on race morning, we decided to go for more wing, a touch more at the front. That was done on the grid! I didn't have too many hopes for that race. We just hoped we were doing the right thing.'[2]

Paul Ricard, born in Marseilles, created an aniseed drink combining Syrian liquorice and Provencal herbs in 1932. It became a French institution and made him wealthy enough to build his own aerodrome in 1962. Then he had the idea of building a racing circuit next to it, and ten months later there it was. Henri Pescarolo and Jean-Pierre Beltoise, both experienced drivers, acted as technical consultants for the track.

It opened with a sports car 2-litre race which Britain's Brian Redman won. The inauguration proved so successful that the way opened for the circuit to become a settled home for the French Grand Prix. Between 1971 and 1990 it would be held there 14 times. It also became a favourite test track and a home to the Winfield racing school (the other at Magny-Cours), producing Prost, Patrick Tambay, Didier Pironi, Jean Alesi, and Olivier Panis. At one stage the Larousse team used the circuit as its base, while the leading French Formula 3000 team, ORECA, stayed longer.

Various factors, political and financial, took the 1991 French Grand Prix to Magny-Cours, where it settled. Ricard continued as a venue for bike racing, French national racing, and Formula 1 testing. Paul Ricard died in 1997 and two years later Bernie Ecclestone bought the circuit. It remained a Formula 1 test track.

COCKPIT VIEW

John Watson, who drove in 1982 and 1983:

'Ricard had an atmosphere and a number of challenges. It was sunny, it was warm, it was the Riviera, it was sexy. OK, dragging them in from the beach was not easy. The Provençales are swarthy-skinned, the women are dark-haired and very sexy. It didn't have the atmosphere of a Latin race – as you got in Italy and Spain – but it had a different atmosphere, which was *sort of* what we'd call a Latin race.

'It was also the definitive modern circuit amongst racetracks which were little more than they had always been. The Nürburgring was little different to 20 years earlier. Spa now had a shortened circuit but the actual pits were the originals.

'Ricard was, if you like, the Abu Dhabi of its time and it is still in many respects advanced, although it's been around for a long time now.

'We were racing on the full circuit with a lot of big challenges, namely the esses following the pit straight – which was quite a long pit straight – and that's where Elio lost his life. [See 'Memories and Milestones', 1986.]

'The whole thing was *can you get through it flat?* In 1975, when I first went there, doing it flat was just about impossible, and the last time I was there, 1983, you could just about squeak through flat out.

'Then on the return leg down that very long *Mistral* straight [Tambay in a Ferrari did 343kph/213mph in 1983] you had an incredible corner called *Signes* at the end. Again, it was a big-balls corner. The *Mistral* was long and it gave you time, too much time, to think. You just sat there. You might have tried to pick up somebody's slipstream.

'You had to make sure that coming at *Signes* you were positioned so that you were not committing without an escape route. If you wanted to be brave and go down the inside side-by-side, we didn't have downforce so you'd be doing that without it. I read recently that Jochen Mass interlocked his wheels, cartwheeled, and went into the barrier. I remember seeing it and thinking *that's a big shunt*.

'It was a single-car entry. You got

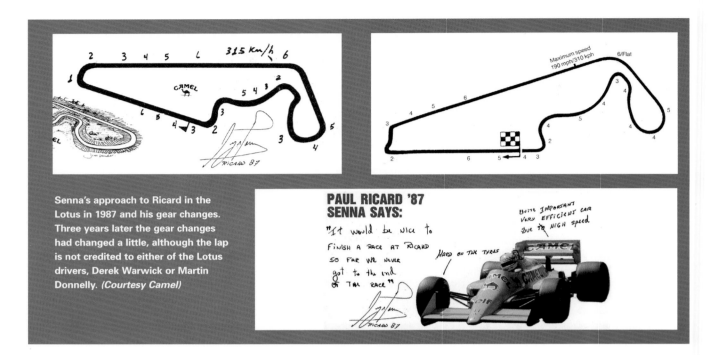

Senna's approach to Ricard in the Lotus in 1987 and his gear changes. Three years later the gear changes had changed a little, although the lap is not credited to either of the Lotus drivers, Derek Warwick or Martin Donnelly. *(Courtesy Camel)*

PAUL RICARD '87 SENNA SAYS:

"It would be nice to FINISH A RACE AT RICARD SO FAR WE NEVER got to the end of THE RACE"

QUITE IMPORTANT VERY EFFICIENT CAR due to HIGH speed

HARD ON THE TYRES

some idiots who thought they would be brave or whatever, so you never really wanted to be in a situation of vulnerability. It was another psychological corner where you'd say, *yeah, I've just taken it flat*, but in fact very often the quickest way through *Signes* was to come up to the corner and, if you weren't braking, *breathe* – take a breath. If you decided to go flat you might achieve it but scrub off too much speed. So being flat through it wasn't in fact always the quickest way, although you did want to come into the pits and say to someone like Niki [Lauda, Watson's team-mate], *I just went through Signes flat on a set of qualifying tyres.*

'Then you had a sequence of what I call purely technical corners – the corner following *Signes* was a long, long double apex, and important because you had to get the very last part of it right. You were then into a short burst.

'It's a bit like golf and Paul Ricard is like a golf course. You drive for show, you putt for dough.'

EYEWITNESS

Ann Bradshaw, PR expert:

'I shudder when I think what a beautiful place that was. Ricard was *lovely*. You were in the South of France in July, and where else would you have wanted to be at that time of the year? Food, wine, sunshine – and it fell halfway through the season. Everybody seemed quite happy there.

'It was always my birthday and we always got drunk. We'd go down to Cassis, we'd go to Bandol,[3] we'd drink Provence rosé, we'd eat lovely *bouillabaisse* [fish soup].

'The likes of Frank Williams and people like that could bring their private planes into there because there was a landing strip at the circuit. Executive jets could fly into there.

'And you'd get a good, knowledgeable crowd for the Grand Prix. It was just holiday time.'

MEMORIES AND MILESTONES

1971 Jackie Stewart (Tyrrell) took pole as the drivers explored the new circuit, took the lead, led every one of the 55 laps and beat team-mate François Cevert by 28.1 seconds. This was Stewart at his most clinical and overwhelming. Fastest lap: Stewart 113.9mph/183.3kph.

1973 Stewart (Tyrrell) took pole again but Jody Scheckter (McLaren) led to lap 41, when he collided with the Lotus of Emerson Fittipaldi. That passed the lead to Ronnie Peterson in the other Lotus, and he beat Cevert (Tyrrell) by 40.9 seconds. Fastest lap: Denny Hulme (McLaren) 117.1mph (+3.2)/ 188.4kph (+5.1).

1975 Niki Lauda (Ferrari) took pole from Scheckter (Tyrrell), led every lap and beat James Hunt (Hesketh) by 1.5 seconds.

This was Lauda at his most clinical and overwhelming. Fastest lap: Jochen Mass (McLaren) 117.5mph (+0.4)/189.1kph (+0.7).

1976 The Hunt-Lauda Championship struggle, although Lauda went into this eighth round with a lead of 35 points (or even more, depending on various appeals). Lauda led to lap 8 when the engine failed, and Hunt beat Patrick Depailler (Tyrrell) by 12.7 seconds. Fastest lap: Lauda 117.1mph (-0.4)/188.4kph (-0.7).

1978 John Watson (Brabham) took pole but Mario Andretti (Lotus), alongside him, led every lap and beat team-mate Peterson by 2.9 seconds. A pattern had formed over these first five races at Ricard: the nature of the circuit meant that, far from cut-and-thrust racing, the leader was difficult to overtake. The five had had only seven leaders. Fastest lap: Carlos Reutemann (Ferrari) 119.7mph (+2.6)/192.7kph (+4.3).

1980 Jacques Laffite (Ligier) took pole and led to lap 34 but his front tyres were wearing and Alan Jones (Williams) outbraked him at the chicane. Jones beat Didier Pironi in the other Ligier by 4.5 seconds. Fastest lap: Jones 128.1mph (+8.4)/206.2kph (+13.5).

1982 René Arnoux, pole, convulsed France by ignoring pit lane boards to slow down and let Renault team-mate Alain Prost through for the win – Prost having

Paul Ricard, lost among the barren hills and invariably sun-kissed. This is 1988, the McLarens (Alain Prost, Ayrton Senna) filling the front row, the Ferraris (Gerhard Berger, Jean Alesi) the second, the Benettons (Thierry Boutsen, Sandro Nannini) the third, the Lotuses (Nelson Piquet, Satoru Nakajima) the fourth.

a better chance at the Championship. Arnoux won by 17.3 seconds and remains unrepentant to this day. Jochen Mass (March) and Maudo Baldi (Arrows) crashed – Mass, airborne, almost reached a spectator area. Fastest lap: Riccardo Patrese (Brabham) 129.9mph (+1.8)/209.0kph (+2.8).

1983 Prost, still with Renault, took pole from team-mate Eddie Cheever and was so dominant he could afford a slow pit stop to beat Nelson Piquet (Brabham) by 29.7 seconds. Fastest lap: Prost 126.6mph (-3.3)/203.7kph (-5.3).

1985 Nigel Mansell (Williams) crashed during the Saturday morning untimed session when a tyre disintegrated at *Signes* at 210mph. He was taken from the car unconscious. At 210mph, Mansell would say,[4] 'it was more like a land speed record than a motor race.' Team-mate Piquet beat Keke Rosberg (Williams), pole, by 6.6 seconds. Fastest lap: Rosberg 130.1mph (+3.5)/ 209.3kph (+5.6).

Speed increase 1971–85: 16.2mph/26.0kph.

The circuit was truncated, turning sharp right just before Verriere *and joining the* Mistral *a third of the way down, in the wake of the accident to Elio de Angelis (see below). Mansell explained that if* Verriere *had remained as it was, taken at some 190mph, anything going wrong would have brought catastrophe. Prost*

described the new 'link' as 'not very interesting, no, but then nowhere at this circuit is very interesting, is it?'

1986 In March, after testing, Frank Williams was in a hire car which plunged off the road, leaving him paralysed. In May, during the second day of testing for the Grand Prix, de Angelis was out on the circuit alone in his Brabham. Through the second part of the *Verriere* S-bend the car snapped out of control and somersaulted for perhaps a hundred yards before vaulting the Armco. The rescue services proved chaotic but eventually de Angelis was taken by helicopter to hospital in Marseilles, where he died. At the Grand Prix, Ayrton Senna (Lotus) took pole but Mansell (Williams) won the race, beating Prost (McLaren) by 17.1 seconds. Fastest lap: Mansell 121.9mph/196.1kph.

1987 Mansell (Williams) took pole but team-mate Piquet gambled on a late pit stop for fresh tyres to overhaul Mansell and gambled wrong. Mansell beat him by 7.7 seconds. Fastest lap: Piquet 122.6mph (+0.7)/197.4kph (+1.3).

1988 Prost (McLaren) took pole and, locked into psychological warfare with McLaren team-mate Senna, abandoned his smooth style for attack. It worked. He seized the lead on lap 61 and won by 31.7 seconds. Fastest lap: Prost 118.9mph (-3.7)/191.3kph (-5.9).

1989 Prost (McLaren) took pole. At the start of the race Mauricio Gugelmin (Leyton House) went for a gap into the first corner, struck Mansell's Ferrari, and was pitched completely upside down – giving one of modern Grand Prix's more astonishing images. In mid-air Gugelmin had the presence of mind to switch off the electrics. Prost beat Mansell by 44.0 seconds. Fastest lap: Gugelmin 118.3mph (-0.6)/190.4kph (-0.9).

1990 Mansell (Ferrari) took pole and t he race had six leaders, Gerhard Berger and Senna in the McLarens, Mansell (Ferrari), Riccardo Patrese (Williams), Ivan Capelli (Leyton House), and Prost, who beat Capelli by 8.6 seconds. Fastest lap: Mansell 125.4mph (+7.1)/201.8kph (+11.4).

Speed increase 1986–90: 3.5mph/5.7kph.

Footnotes
[1] *Grand Prix!*, Lang. [2] *Mario Andretti World Champion*, Andretti.
[3] Cassis and Bandol were two favourite watering holes on the Mediterranean (if you see what I mean). [4] *My Autobiography*, Mansell.

FACTS OF THE MATTER

3.610m/5.810km circuit

Year	Winner
1971	J. Stewart (Tyrrell)
1973	R. Peterson (Lotus)
1975	N. Lauda (Ferrari)
1976	J. Hunt (McLaren)
1978	M. Andretti (Lotus)
1980	A. Jones (Williams)
1982	R. Arnoux (Renault)
1983	A. Prost (Renault)
1985	N. Piquet (Brabham)
Fastest pole	K. Rosberg (Williams) 1985 (140.6mph/226.2kph)
Fastest lap	K. Rosberg 1985 (130.1mph/209.3kph)

Sainte-Beaume section dropped, 2.369m/3.813km circuit

1986	N. Mansell (Williams)
1987	N. Mansell (Williams)
1988	A. Prost (McLaren)
1989	A. Prost (McLaren)
1990	A. Prost (Ferrari)
Fastest pole	N. Mansell (Ferrari) 1990 (132.4mph/213.1kph)
Fastest lap	Mansell 1990 (125.4mph/201.8kph)

Prost liked Provence. He learnt to kart on the coast, learnt to drive at the Winfield school at the circuit and won the Grand Prix in 1988, 1989 and 1990. This is 1989 and he's beating Nigel Mansell (Ferrari) by 44.0 seconds.

How Ricard saw itself and its many faces – on postcards. (Courtesy Martin Hadwen, National Motor Racing Archive)

REIMS-GUEUX

Location: 4 miles (7km) west of Reims, northern France.
Constructed: 1925.
World Championship Grands Prix: 11.

Simple French pleasures: a roadside inn, a road junction to negotiate and a fast car to do it. This is Jo Bonnier in the Brabham in 1968, although he wasn't classified. (LAT)

'This rather rough, rough circuit...'

Mike Hawthorn

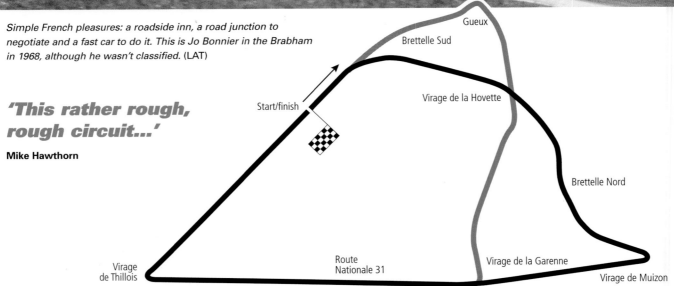

Gueux

Brettelle Sud

Start/finish

Virage de la Hovette

Brettelle Nord

Virage de Thillois

Route Nationale 31

Virage de la Garenne

Virage de Muizon

'It is a circuit with a most tremendous atmosphere, and yet one feels constantly that in many ways it is a barren, open space, devoid of attraction. Many will tell you that old theatres carry within their walls an atmosphere of past triumphs, and the cornfields of Reims certainly do the same. Even today there are few, who can remember 1939, able to stand near the great up-sweeping road before the grandstands without picturing in their mind's eye the silver white monsters of Hitler's motoring army thundering their way up and over the brow of the hill.'[1]

The circuit was created by Raymond Roche, known as Toto, secretary-general of the *Automobile Club Ardennais*, which became *AC de Champagne*. It was a very important body in the area and Roche, a flamboyant starter of races, evidently wanted to showcase Reims, which, although it already had several small car makers, was much better known for champagne. The area is nothing like as romantic as the drink – flat, largely featureless and, if you *are* a romantic, difficult to fall in love with. The circuit couldn't change that but it could bring its own dimension.

'The champagne growers liked the idea a lot and, in 1925, Roche organised a race called *Grand Prix de la Marne* on 22km of ordinary road nicely close to the city. *Route Nationale 31* gave the circuit a big, strong backbone, although it went on a smaller road through the village of Gueux.

'Here, where houses, walls and concrete posts crowded the road, it turned through a right angle by a grocery shop,' wrote Hodges.[2]

In 1925 some 8,000 spectators watched a wet race and seven years later the Grand Prix went there. Reims was by its nature fast, a triangle with three hairpins. On the eve of the Grand Prix, Charles Faroux – another legend of motor sport – persuaded the organisers to re-measure the track and found it was 7.8km rather than the claimed 8.0.

'A vast crowd gathered to watch, among others, the great Tazio Nuvolari in an Alfa-Romeo as part of a three-car factory assault. At the finish the team manager signalled Nuvolari to slow down so that the three cars could cross the line together but Nuvolari "did not understand the signal…"'[3]

Nuvolari covered the 461 miles at an average of 92.3mph/148.5kph.

By 1938, when the white (actually silver) monsters – Mercedes and Auto Union – came, the winner's speed had increased to 101.1mph/162.7kph, rising to 105.2mph/169.3kph the following year. Racing began again in 1947 with a variant on the *Grand Prix de la Marne* and in 1950 the circuit hosted the fifth round of the new World Championship.

The Championship races – 11 – spanned 1950 to 1966, when the circuit fell into disuse and was consumed by financial problems.

COCKPIT VIEWS

Mike Hawthorn, who drove in five Grands Prix there:

'This rather rough, rough circuit … is a car-circuit rather than a driver's one, calling for top speed, acceleration, and braking. In the 5.16 miles that it measures it is only the tremendously fast right-hander beyond the Dunlop Bridge at the end of the pit lane that calls for driving skill of a high order.

'… The car was going fine and was extremely fast. I was turning at 8,600rpm down the straight, a speed of 180mph. I asked Chiti the chief engineer whether it was all right to hold it there, and he said that it was, but to be on the safe side, eight thousand four or five would make him happier.

'[In the race] sometimes we would be hurtling along three abreast, at 160mph (255kph), down an ordinary French main road. It was a bit frightening to see the nose of one of the other cars come alongside, then drop back again as the driver decided he could not make it before the next corner.

'The cars were evenly matched and we could only get past each other by slip-streaming. The trick was to tuck in close behind the other man, get a tow from his slipstream, ease back the throttle as far as possible without losing position, and then suddenly tramp on the pedal and use the sudden surge of urge to nip out and pass him. Whereupon he would try to get into position to return the compliment.'[4]

John Fitch, an American who raced a Cunningham car in the 12 Hours of Reims sports car race, 1953:

'The course, about five and a half miles to the lap, was roughly a triangle with the hypotenuse snaking through four fast curves over the rolling farm country. The first of the curves [I didn't like] … The rest of the course was straight, the two shorter sides of the triangle rolling over the low hills to 30mph hairpins.

'The road climbed past the pits to the top of the hill where the Dunlop Bridge, shaped like half a tyre on end, crossed over it. The bridge was a marker of more than the hilltop. Before the bridge was the starting line – the tribunes, the timers, the lights, the pits, the social part of the race where friends and officials wandered between the paddock and the pits, greeting campaigners from other races and detouring by the bar regularly. This was the heart of the champagne country.

'Past the bridge was the curve. At night the bridge caught all the light from what we called Broadway. You could feel a slight compression as you popped through it into the deserted darkness. No lights and no parties here; just the approach to the fast curve, almost invisible after the bright lights. You went into it fast because you knew you had done it before, not because you could see it or know how you were going to do it again. That's how it was; before the bridge was Broadway, and past it was the fast curve where everyone was on his own in the dark – the kind of place where people talk to themselves seriously.'[5]

EYEWITNESS

Denis Jenkinson, *Motor Sport*, 1954:

'Once again the *Automobile Club du Champagne* organised a veritable feast of speed for a night and a day, and as last year the form was a 12-hour sports-car race, from midnight Saturday to midday Sunday, and after a lunch break the French Grand Prix for Formula I cars.

'Under the direction of Raymond Roche the club continued to improve the amenities of the circuit, providing more stands, restaurants, a row of shops and one of the best refuelling systems yet seen. This last addition was a welcome sight, because last year there was a great deal of nonsense over refuelling during the sports-car race, as the organisers left everything to the competitors.

'The new installation comprised a vast tank behind the pits, like a water tower, with pipelines running underground to each pit, where a flexible hose and quick-action nozzle was hung, there being a very efficient-looking filter and stop-valve in each pit. To avoid the danger of spilling when the hose was not in use each one had a box in front of the pit-counter into which the nozzle was inserted.'

MEMORIES AND MILESTONES

1950 Juan Manuel Fangio (Alfa Romeo) took pole, averaging 116mph/186kph, although Giuseppe Farina (in another Alfa Romeo) led to lap 16, when he had fuel starvation and his pit stop lasted seven minutes. Fangio swept to victory, beating Luigi Fagioli (in yet another Alfa Romeo) by 25.7 seconds. Fastest lap: Fangio 112.4mph/180.8kph.

1951 Fangio (Alfa Romeo) took pole, averaging 119mph/193kph, so the speeds were increasing. Alberto Ascari (Ferrari)

led the race but had a gearbox failure and Fangio suffered a misfire. He took over Fagioli's car and with it beat Ascari, now in Froilan González's car, by 52.2 seconds. Fastest lap: Fangio 118.3mph/190.4kph.

Speed increase 1950–1: 5.9mph/9.6kph.

The 1952 race went to Rouen and Reims changed radically. 'Once again [the organisers] altered their famous circuit in a matter of weeks. In 1952 the first phase of the plan bypassed Gueux. In 1953 the "by-pass" was carried on across the old Gueux-Garenne road, up the far hillside and

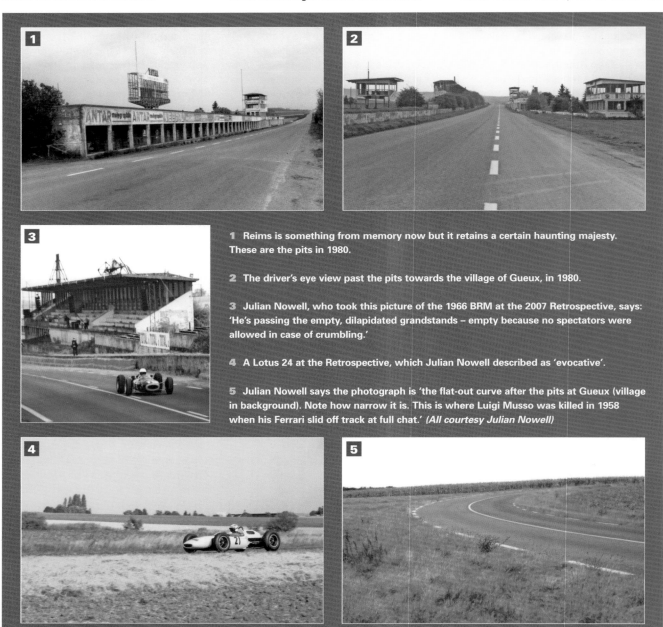

1 Reims is something from memory now but it retains a certain haunting majesty. These are the pits in 1980.

2 The driver's eye view past the pits towards the village of Gueux, in 1980.

3 Julian Nowell, who took this picture of the 1966 BRM at the 2007 Retrospective, says: 'He's passing the empty, dilapidated grandstands – empty because no spectators were allowed in case of crumbling.'

4 A Lotus 24 at the Retrospective, which Julian Nowell described as 'evocative'.

5 Julian Nowell says the photograph is 'the flat-out curve after the pits at Gueux (village in background). Note how narrow it is. This is where Luigi Musso was killed in 1958 when his Ferrari slid off track at full chat.' *(All courtesy Julian Nowell)*

joined the Soissons-Reims main road about half a mile higher up, lengthening the fast straight down to Thillois and adding a second hairpin at this new junction. [6]

1953 Ascari (Ferrari) took pole but the race developed into a great, historic duel between young Mike Hawthorn (in another Ferrari) and Fangio (Maserati). The lead changed 12 times and in a tremendous climax Hawthorn accelerated out of the final corner first to win by 1.0 second. Fastest lap: Fangio and Ascari 115.9mph/186.5kph.

The hairpin at Thillois had been eased, making the circuit an estimated two seconds faster.

1954 Mercedes returned after 20 years. Their team leader, Fangio, took pole and won by a tenth of a second from Karl Kling in another Mercedes. Fastest lap: Hans Herrmann (Mercedes) 121.5mph/195.5kph.

The 1955 race was abandoned after the tragedy at Le Mans.

1956 Fangio (Ferrari) took pole, averaging 129mph/208kph. Hawthorn's friend Peter Collins (Ferrari) won, beating Eugenio Castellotti (Ferrari) by 3.1 seconds. Fastest lap: Fangio 127.4mph (+5.9)/205.0kph (+9.5).

The 1957 race went to Rouen.

1958 Jack Brabham (Cooper) remembered 'it was so hot the road broke up, and great big pieces of asphalt were thrown back by other cars'.[7] Hawthorn (Ferrari) took pole. Luigi Musso, team-mate to Hawthorn, was struggling to stay with him as they moved into the right-hander beyond the Dunlop Bridge and plunged off into a cornfield. He was killed. Hawthorn beat Stirling Moss (Vanwall) by 24.6 seconds. Moss remembered: 'I would slipstream [Jean] Behra [BRM] and then pull out and pass him; then he would do the same to me; this was happening time and time again. I suppose we were doing it partly to keep amused on a rather dull track.'[8] Fastest lap: Hawthorn 128.2mph (+0.8)/206.3kph (+1.3).

1959 Tony Brooks (Ferrari) took the average pole speed to 133mph/214kph and led all 50 laps to beat Phil Hill in another Ferrari by 27.5 seconds. Fastest lap: Moss (BRM) 130.0mph (+1.8)/209.3kph (+3.0).

1960 Jack Brabham (Cooper) took pole to 135mph/218kph and engaged in an extraordinary duel with Phil Hill

(Ferrari) – the lead changed 13 times before Hill's transmission failed. Brabham beat Olivier Gendebien (Cooper) by 48.3 seconds. Fastest lap: Brabham 135.1mph (+5.1)/217.4kph (+8.1).

1961 Phil Hill (Ferrari) took pole. Italian Giancarlo Baghetti (in another Ferrari) won a desperate finish against Jo Bonnier and Dan Gurney in Porsches, so desperate that the respective teams were out waving frantically *Faster!* Baghetti became the only man to win the first World Championship Grand Prix he competed in (except, inevitably, Farina at Silverstone in 1950. *Somebody* had to win the first). Fastest lap: Phil Hill 126.2mph (-8.9)/203.2kph (-13.2).

The 1962 race went to Rouen.

1963 Jim Clark (Lotus) took pole and led all 53 laps while constant slipstreaming and overtaking went on behind him. Clark beat Tony Maggs (Cooper) by 1 minute 04.9 seconds. Fastest lap: Clark 131.2mph (+5.0)/211.1kph (+7.9).

1966 In 1966 Clark (Lotus) was hit in the eye by a bird during practice and withdrew, while Farina died when he crashed at Chambéry, France, on his way to watch. Lorenzo Bandini (Ferrari) took pole and led at half distance, but the throttle cable snapped. Using wire from a straw bale he made a hand-held throttle that got him back to the pits. Brabham (Brabham) beat Mike Parkes (Ferrari) by 9.5 seconds. Fastest lap: Bandini 141.4mph (+10.2)/227.6kph (+16.5).

Speed increase 1954–66: 19.9mph/32.1kph.

FACTS OF THE MATTER

4.857m/7.816km circuit

Year	Winner
1950	J.M. Fangio (Alfa Romeo)
1951	J.M. Fangio-L Fagioli (Alfa Romeo)
Fastest pole	J.M. Fangio 1951 (120.0mph/193.1kph)
Fastest lap	J.M. Fangio 1951 (118.3mph/190.4kph)

Gueux bypass, 5.187m/8.347km circuit

1953	M. Hawthorn (Ferrari)
Pole	A. Ascari (Ferrari) (115.8mph/186.4kph)
Fastest lap	J.M. Fangio (Maserati)/A. Ascari (115.9mph/186.5kph)

Thillois eased, 5.159m/8.302km circuit

1954	J.M. Fangio (Mercedes)
1956	P. Collins (Ferrari)
1958	M. Hawthorn (Ferrari)
1959	T. Brooks (Ferrari)
1960	J. Brabham (Cooper)
1961	G. Baghetti (Ferrari)
1963	J. Clark (Lotus)
1966	J. Brabham (Brabham)
Fastest pole	L. Bandini (Ferrari) 1966 (145.3mph/233.9kph)
Fastest lap	L. Bandini 1966 (141.4mph/227.6kph)

Footnotes
[1] *Motor Racing Circuits of Europe*, Frostick. [2] *The French Grand Prix*, Hodges. [3] *L'Auto Italiana*. [4] *Champion Year*, Hawthorn.
[5] *Omnibus of Speed*, Beaumont and Nolan. [5] *The Motor Year Book*, 1953. [6] *When the Flag Drops*, Brabham. [7] *A Turn at the Wheel*, Moss.

The spirit of Reims captured in the authoritative book *Circuit de Reims* which appeared in 2006, demonstrating the enduring interest in the circuit.

ROUEN-LES-ESSARTS

Location: 7 miles (12km) south-west of Rouen, northern France.
Constructed: 1950.
World Championship Grands Prix: 5.

'There was a truly dramatic intensity to going into the blind corner at 240kmh'

Jean-Pierre Jarier

Virage du Nouveau Monde

Virage des Six Frères

Virage Sanson

Virage de Beauval

Virage du Gresil

Virage de la Scierie

Virage de l'Etoile

Virage du Paradis

Start/finish

The tragic race for Honda in 1968. John Surtees finishes second but Jo Schlesser will pay the ultimate price. (LAT)

'This charming little circuit,' wrote Frostick[1] in 1958 – before Innes Ireland ended up in trees, a young Swede called Picko Troberg's Brabham punched a concrete milestone, the Portuguese Mario Cabral was seriously injured when his Brabham barrel-rolled and disintegrated, young Frenchman Jean-Claude Bernasconi lost control of his Gordini which rolled five times, throwing him out and killing him, Jo Schlesser was burnt to death in his Honda, Jean-Luc Salomon and Denis Dayan were killed in a Formula 3 race, Bob Wollek was seriously injured, and Gerry Birrell was killed.

That does not, of course, affect the topography of the circuit, which many likened to Spa because it was very rural, went through woods, and used public roads. Instead of *Stavelot*, it had a hairpin called *Virage du Nouveau Monde* which was partly cobbled. The roads were cut into chalk soil in places, giving spectators at the top a panoramic view of what was a wide track. It had modern pits and grandstands for the spectators who didn't want to stand high above. Les Essarts, incidentally, is a nearby village.

From the start-line the track went downhill through right- and left-hand curves taken at between 120 and 160mph to the first-gear *Nouveau Monde*, then climbed to a left, *Virage Sanson*. Just beyond this the 1951 track turned right but by 1957 it had been extended so the cars continued to the right-handed *Virage du Gresil*.

From *Nouveau Monde* they'd climbed 305ft (93m). Now they were on the only proper straight, measuring about a kilometre. At the end of it the cars turned right again at *Virage de la Scierie* on to another straight before a gentle right-hander and the start/finish line. Graham Hill, who drove it in 1962, 1964, and 1968, described it as 'very picturesque, and a real road circuit. It is fast; demands a certain amount of courage, a good car and very good roadholding.'[2]

The Automobile Club of Normandy conceived the idea of a circuit in 1950 and it was first used in 1951. The Grand Prix was run the following year and excited enormous interest because, a week before, France's own Jean Behra in a Gordini had beaten the works Ferraris in a race at Reims and might do it again.

The times were very different.

Mike Hawthorn was making his way into Grand Prix racing and had been invited to drive a Cooper in a non-Championship race at Reims before he went on to Rouen and the first Grand Prix there. The car needed repairs, which were carried out in Paris. 'They finished the car late in the afternoon and we had no lorry to get it to Rouen; I said: "Fair enough, I'll drive it there." So we started up the engine, it was getting on quite late by that time. I leapt into this single-seater racing car and drove off through Paris all the way to Rouen. It was a wonderful drive. Wherever we went the police held up the traffic immediately and waved us through and the people in the villages cheered us on. A wonderful sight. We eventually arrived in the dark, it was absolutely pitch black. We had no lights on the car, open exhausts, no mudguards, no lights, no insurance, no anything. Nobody seemed to give a damn over there.'[3]

After Schlesser's death in 1968 the track was used for Formula 2 and Formula 3. However, chicanes were added and extensive work done when the *Autoroute A 13* was built. The racing finally stopped in 1993 because the circuit was considered too dangerous even for Formula 3.

The French Circuits Commission refused to put Rouen on the 1994 race calendar, the finances were in a desperate state, and the organisers even tried to hold a race on the Bugatti circuit at Le Mans to maintain, even if in name only, a link with Normandy.

The circuit was essentially demolished. 'Of the circuit des Essarts, there remains *nothing*. They have reduced the "beast" to its bones with a sort of jubilation to eradicate even the smallest traces of anything that could bear witness to the past. Doubtless the sheet metal of the big grandstand, which might have been blown away, had become dangerous for the traffic and [the local authority] made a wise decision. But the control tower! On 3 October 1996 at midday the heart of the circuit ceased beating. A few days later the bulldozers attacked the grandstand at the *Nouveau Monde*, then the pits fell under the blows of the bulldozers' jaws and the wrecking balls.'[4]

The circuit was returned to the department for forestry, just as if nothing had ever happened there at all.

COCKPIT VIEW

Jean-Pierre Jarier:

'As a young driver my discovery of the Rouen-les-Essarts circuit was also my discovery that automobile sport is the strongest and most cruel. The very big speeds in the ultra-rapid curves, the driving technique on a circuit which did not forgive mistakes – I encountered all that.

'There was a truly dramatic intensity to going into the blind corner at 240kph just after the pits. My greatest victory in Formula 2, I owe to *les Essarts*.

'Certainly it would have been necessary to invest in and improve the circuit, making it permanent. Too many obstacles were in the way. This, perhaps, is not too bad because the circuit will keep forever an incomparable halo in the memories of the drivers.'[5]

EYEWITNESSES

Michael Frostick, author:

'If the circuit is for the most part without problems, the same regrettably cannot be said of the approaches to it, although let it be confessed that the jam on the way in is nothing to be compared with the jam on the way out. This is occasioned by the circuit's remote and delightful situation and is once more a reminder that the cake cannot be both had and eaten.

'It is not an especially fast circuit but really is a driver's circuit. The premium here is definitely on the conductor's ability to conduct. Of course if the car is not fast enough, no effort however superhuman will prevail, but racing at Rouen is a battle of man and machine as opposed to some circuits where it would be more fair to say it was only a battle for the machines.

'It is a circuit which has found much favour with the motorcycle brigade – especially before it was lengthened when it was, in fact, on the short side for Grand Prix racing.'[6]

Bernard Beaumesnil, spectator:
'I was at the old circuit on the descent to *Nouveau Monde*. In 1967 my best friend was killed in a Gordini Cup race and in 1968 I saw the smoke from Schlesser's crash, and among the people who went with me was a certain Jean Rondeau.[7] We were friends.

'Rouen was different to Le Mans in that you couldn't circulate round the circuit during a Grand Prix. Le Mans is a real circuit. At Rouen you bought a ticket and stayed where that admitted you. At Le Mans even during the Grand Prix it was easy to go where you wanted.'

MEMORIES AND MILESTONES

1952 Alberto Ascari (Ferrari) took pole and led every lap to beat Giuseppe Farina in another Ferrari by a lap. Hawthorn had an ignition problem after working his way up to fifth, while Jean Behra (Gordini) went into a ditch and lost time getting back to the pits. Fastest lap: Ascari 83.1mph/133.7kph.

The circuit extension had been completed, making it significantly longer and faster.

1957 Juan Manuel Fangio (Maserati), pole, faced the Ferraris of Luigi Musso, Hawthorn, and Peter Collins. Fangio's mastery of the downhill curves after the start – regarded as difficult to take at big speed – demonstrated his car control. Frostick said Fangio 'alternately slid and slithered down this section in a manner quite impossible to believe.'[8] Hodges spoke of a 'glorious slide cum drift sequence' which gave those who witnessed it 'the memory of an outstanding motor racing performance.'[9]

Fangio explained it. 'I made a bad start … and had to make up a lot of lost ground until finally I found an ace up my sleeve. I discovered that it was possible to come into the so-called New World corner [*Nouveau Monde*] at high speed, put my car slightly crosswise and hold it by progressively accelerating. Gaining precious time each lap I worked my way out in front. Only once did I skid a bit, scratching the nose of the Maserati; after that, all went well, although the track had become dangerous from spilt oil.'[10] Fangio beat Musso by 50.8 seconds. Fastest lap: Musso 102.8mph/165.4kph.

1962 Jim Clark took pole in the Lotus but his front suspension failed and American Dan Gurney gave Porsche their

Pedro Rodriguez (BRM) pits in 1968. Note that there is no protection between the circuit and the pits – the way it was. (LAT)

Looking towards the motorway, which passes below where the traffic is. Note the blue sign saying this was the racing circuit.

Just before the motorway the original circuit turned left on to what is now a tarmac track through the woods.

The authentic Rouen, still cradled by nature.

The *Nouveau Monde* hairpin in more peaceful times. *(All Author)*

FACTS OF THE MATTER

3.169m/5.100km circuit

Year	Winner
1952	A. Ascari (Ferrari)
Pole	A. Ascari (84.6mph/136.2kph)
Fastest lap	A. Ascari (83.1mhp/133.7kph)

Extended, 4.065m/6.542km circuit

1957	J.M. Fangio (Maserati)
1962	D. Gurney (Porsche)
1964	D. Gurney (Brabham)
1968	J. Ickx (Ferrari)
Fastest pole	J. Rindt (Brabham) 1968 (126.0mph/202.9kph)
Fastest lap	J. Brabham (Brabham) 1964 (111.3mph/179.1kph)

first victory after virtually every other car suffered mechanical problems. Gurney beat Tony Maggs (Cooper) by a lap. Fastest lap: Graham Hill (BRM) 106.9mph (+4.1)/172.0kph (+6.6).

1964 Jim Clark (inevitably) took pole in the Lotus and (inevitably) led, but after 32 laps his engine failed and Gurney (Brabham) inherited it with Graham Hill (BRM) and Jack Brabham (Brabham) behind. Gurney gave the Brabham team their first win, which Jack Brabham couldn't – he was third. Gurney beat Hill by 24.1 seconds. Fastest lap: Brabham 111.4mph (+4.5)/179.2kph (+7.2).

1968 Honda decided to race their new and untested RA302 car, built at John Surtees' factory. Surtees insisted the car was not ready but suddenly found it was gone. Honda France wanted to race it at Rouen and put a Frenchman, Jo Schlesser, in it. Jochen Rindt (Brabham) took pole. Rain fell and on lap three Schlesser lost control at the *Six Frères* curve. It struck a bank, flipped and burst into flames of such intensity that they covered the track and even reached some spectators. Schlesser died, and although the race was not stopped the Grand Prix never returned. Jacky Ickx (Ferrari) beat Surtees (Honda) by 1 minute 58.6 seconds. Fastest lap: Pedro Rodríguez 111.3mph (-0.1)/179.1kph (-0.1).

    Speed increase 1957–68: 8.5mph/13.7kph.

Footnotes
[1] *Motor Racing Circuits of Europe*, Frostick. [2] *Life at the Limit*, Hill. [3] *Challenge Me the Race*, Hawthorn. [4] *Rouen-les-Essarts*, Biot. [5] Jarier in *Rouen-les-Essarts*. [6] Frostick, *op cit.* [7] Jean Rondeau, driver and constructor, won Le Mans in 1980 in a Rondeau. [8] Frostick, *op cit.* [9] *The French Grand Prix*, Hodges. [10] *My 24 Years of Racing*, Fangio.

GERMANY

AVUS

Location: West of Berlin in woodland.
Constructed: Between 1914 and 1921.
World Championship Grands Prix: 1.

Tony Brooks (Ferrari)
leads Stirling Moss,
Masten Gregory, Jack
Brabham (all Cooper),
Jo Bonnier (BRM) and
Dan Gurney (Ferrari).
(LAT)

Südschleife

Start/finish

Nordschleife

*'Every time you went
round the banking you were glad
to get to the other end of it'*

Jack Brabham

Everything about the Avus (a contraction of the *Automobil Verkehrs und Ubungs-Strasse*) was, and remains, unreal, not least that it is still there but now an ordinary, unremarkable autobahn. It runs gun-barrel straight through woodland near the Wannsee lake where Berliners have always taken their leisure and, as a circuit, was in the form of twin dual carriageways 26ft (8m) wide and separated only by a grass strip. The carriageways were linked by the North Curve, a one-in-ten banked loop, and the South Curve, a one-in-nine banked loop so tight someone has called it a virtual hairpin.

It was conceived in 1907 by the German Automobile Club, who realised that car manufacturers would need a testing ground, but progress proved sporadic (during the First World War, Russian prisoners worked on it). It finally opened as a track and toll road in 1921. In time speed records were set on it and the Avus was a dangerous place.

The first German Grand Prix, in 1926, was open to sports cars and attracted an entry of 46 and an estimated 230,000 to watch them. During practice two cars crashed into each other in the South Curve, killing a riding mechanic and badly injuring a driver. Rudolf Caracciola, one of the most gifted drivers, remembered the mechanic 'sprawled out on his back, arms flung wide as if he were nailed to an invisible cross. His wide-open eyes reflected the sky. The rain fell in long skeins and ran over his face. Presently an ambulance man came with a piece of canvas and covered him. Only

The Avus is now an ordinary autobahn, although you go past the tower to get on to it if you're coming from Berlin. (Courtesy Birgit Kubisch)

the feet in the white canvas shoes protruded from the covering.'[1]

Rain fell during the race and one car went off the North Curve into the timekeeper's hut, killing two students there. A man in the hut died 12 hours later. Then a car went off the South Curve and somersaulted. Then a car floated off into a petrol lorry. Then a car lost control and came across from the other carriageway, just missing Caracciola…

The Nürburgring opened the following year, casting a long shadow over the flat and uninteresting Avus, even though the North Curve banking was increased to 43°.

Germany was partitioned after the Second World War and the South Curve fell close to the Soviet Zone. The circuit was shortened to 5.6 miles

(8.3km) but kept its configuration: the South Curve was moved halfway up.

The Grand Prix returned in 1959.

Two years later the Berlin wall was built. Transit from West Berlin across the Soviet Zone (later East Germany) remained possible on designated autobahns. One of the checkpoints, complete with Soviet tank on a vast plinth, stood just beyond the end of the old Avus. It gave the circuit an even more surreal atmosphere.

It continued to stage junior races and some national events but the touring cars did not return after 1995 when a Briton, Keith Odor, was killed.

COCKPIT VIEW

Jack Brabham, driving a Cooper, 1959:
'A shocking circuit. A lot of bricks had sunk and it was very, very rough. The banking wasn't really steep enough for the speeds that we were doing round there, and the G force, coupled with the bumps, was unbelievably bad.

'Every time you went round the banking you were glad to get to the other end of it; it was a tremendous relief to have got round each time without something breaking on the car or your crash hat coming down over your

eyes so that you couldn't see where you were going.'[2]

EYEWITNESS

Frankfurter Allegemeine Zeitung, Monday, 3 August 1959:
'The motor race for the Great Prize on the Avus in Berlin had a tragic beginning on Saturday in the sports car event. French master Jean Behra had a fatal accident when he crashed on a rain-soaked surface on the banking at the North Curve and his car broke apart against a flagpole. It was nearly cut into two pieces. Behra

was killed instantly. The doctors reported fractures to the base of the skull and neck. A number of further accidents at nearly the same place happened without drastic consequences.

'Jean Behra, 38 years old, son of Alsatian parents [from Alsace] was born in Nice. He leaves a wife, who was present at the race, and also an 18-year-old son. His racing career started almost 20 years ago. He had earned a good reputation as a motorbike rider and only six years ago did he move to cars. A glorious career opened and he was

1 The banking has long gone, but the grandstand remains – and how many passing motorists know what it signifies?

2 Everyday traffic on, now, an everyday autobahn.

3 Drivers approaching the banked North Curve saw this.

4 The Avus flowing into the countryside, and once it was ramrod straight.

5 This part of the circuit used to be the last petrol station before the Iron Curtain. *(All courtesy Birgit Kubisch)*

France's best driver. He was not only exceptionally well-liked in motor racing circles but worldwide. All sports deaths are tragic but the sorrow for Jean Behra is extraordinarily great and is based on how this great man behaved.'

MEMORIES AND A MILESTONE

1959 The move from Nürburgring, a road circuit, to the 'ninety per cent pure speed track of Avus had been dictated largely by finance; at the Ring spectators can watch the race for nothing, whereas Avus is enclosed and admission can be controlled and charged for,' Stirling Moss remembered.[3] 'It was not a popular decision with the drivers' because 'the track was a freak' with its 'parallel carriageways'.

He found the North Curve 'a steep

bank so curved that a car does not find a natural line round it, and, to make things worse, it is built of bricks, which become extremely dangerous if they get wet … I was getting 6,600rpm and coming off the banking at 140mph, but the suspension was still bottoming on the banking.'

The day before the Grand Prix, Jean Behra was killed in a supporting sports car race. In the wet he spun off and hit a flagpole. 'It had been raining and the surface was like an ice rink. The Porsche just lost adhesion and rode backwards up the banking and over the top.'[4]

Tony Brooks (Ferrari) took pole from Stirling Moss (Cooper).

The Grand Prix was decided over two heats because of fears over tyre wear. In the second, Hans Hermann (BRM) had a brake failure, left the track and was thrown clear. He skidded down

the track while the car somersaulted into the air.

Brabham remembered that none of the drivers 'wanted to go back to Avus – well, none of the sane ones anyway. There were quite a few sane ones.'

Brooks beat Dan Gurney (Ferrari) by 1.9s.

Footnotes
[1] *Racing Driver's World*, Caracciola. [2] *When the Flag Drops*, Brabham. [3] *A Turn at the Wheel*, Moss. [4] *Ibid.*

FACTS OF THE MATTER

5.157m/8.300km circuit

Year	Winner
1959	T. Brooks (Ferrari)
Pole	T. Brooks (147.5mph/237.3kph)
Fastest lap	T. Brooks (149.1mph/240.0kph)

How the respected newspaper *Frankfurter Allgemeine Zeitung* covered Behra's crash.

The official programme naturally highlighted the banking. *(Courtesy Martin Hadwen, National Motor Racing Archive)*

How Cyril Posthumus presented the slightly bizarre circuit in his definitive *The German Grand Prix*. Note that the tower at the end of the banking is still there – see page 121.

GERMANY

HOCKENHEIM

Location: 16 miles (25km) south-west of Heidelberg.
Constructed: 1932.
World Championship Grands Prix: 31.

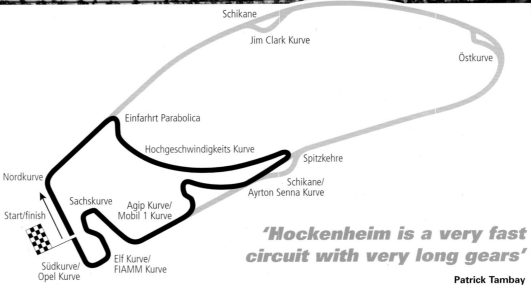

The old Hockenheim with the track stretching like two arms into the trees. The arm on the right was the electrically-fast approach to the Stadium.

(All pictures are courtesy of Hockenheim-Ring GmbH except where stated)

Schikane

Jim Clark Kurve

Östkurve

Einfahrht Parabolica

Hochgeschwindigkeits Kurve

Spitzkehre

Nordkurve

Schikane/
Ayrton Senna Kurve

Sachskurve

Agip Kurve/
Mobil 1 Kurve

Start/finish

Elf Kurve/
FIAMM Kurve

Südkurve/
Opel Kurve

'Hockenheim is a very fast circuit with very long gears'

Patrick Tambay

Bikes in 1932, sidecars in 1937, cars in 1938.

Hockenheim was fast. In 1991 Nigel Mansell (Williams) took pole with an average speed of 156.7mph/252kph, and even when two chicanes had been tightened in 2001 Montoya was taking the Williams round at 155.6mph. This is well over double the legal maximum speed on Britain's motorways, and when Montoya did it he had to thread through three chicanes and the contorting Stadium Complex.

Here are the pole speed averages in miles an hour for all the other circuits that season (and I'll spare you the decimal points): Australia 136, Malaysia 130, Brazil 130, San Marino 132, Spain 135, Austria 139, Monaco 97, Canada 130, Europe (Nürburgring) 135, France 130, Britain 142, Hungary 120, Belgium 137, Italy 157, USA (Indianapolis) 130, Japan 141. These statistics are interesting, not least because only Monza was quicker, and not by much.

Hockenheim belonged to another era and would be consigned to that in 2002 when a shortened version replaced it. There was a precedent not too far away,

the Nürburgring. The old Hockenheim had none of the majestic madness of the old Ring and wasn't intended to have because it had originally been built on forest roads as a replacement for a circuit at Karlsruhe that was no longer being used. Motorbikes raced there.

In 1936 the 'circuit' was updated into a test track to be used for Mercedes and Auto-Union racing cars, then poised to annihilate all opposition. The circuit measured some 8km and was made up of two straights with a corner in the forest and another at Hockenheim, a town with a population of 20,000.

This was in use until 1947 and was principally about bike racing, but a new autobahn which opened in 1965 bisected it. The revised circuit, complete with Stadium Complex, opened a year later and became notorious in 1968 when, during a Formula 2 race, Jim Clark suffered a puncture, lost control and was killed against a tree trunk. In the wake of that, two chicanes were added to slow the

The pre-war circuit.

The new circuit, and the arms are gone.

cars and Armco laid round the circuit. When Patrick Depailler was killed testing an Alfa Romeo in 1980 a third chicane was built, at the *Östkurve*.

Because the Nürburgring had not carried out safety work, the German Grand Prix went to Hockenheim in 1970 and, after Lauda's terrible crash at the Nürburgring in 1976 – condemning the old circuit forever in Grand Prix terms – Hockenheim became the race's new home.

It was a curious place, very Teutonic in feel because the grandstands flanking the Complex were vast edifices of characterless stone which accommodated more than 100,000, and virtually all the rest of the circuit was lost in tall, dense trees.

This ended in 2002 when the forest section was removed and the track became what they call technical – indistinguishable from many others – rather than unique.

The future of the race, centred round its subsidy by the local government, came into question and its future uncertain. One solution, to alternate the German Grand Prix with the Nürburgring, depended on finding finance because Hockenheim was loss-making.

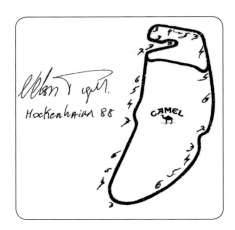

Nelson Piquet's lap in 1988 – notice how he builds up speed in four distinct sections. (Courtesy Camel)

COCKPIT VIEW – Old circuit

Patrick Tambay, Renault, 1984:

'The *Östkurve* is a long curve that hasn't been changed very much. It's a very difficult bend that you take almost flat out when your car is properly adjusted. Then you are braking for the so-called *Ayrton Senna Chicane* and it was exiting this chicane, with a lot of mist on the day, that Didier Pironi was catching Alain Prost and took off and ended up in the barrier on the right-hand side. On the long left-hander before the Stadium you always go up on the kerb a little bit before braking hard for the *Sachskurve*. The car drifts a little bit from the rear end.

'Hockenheim is a very fast circuit with very long gears.'

Nelson Piquet, Lotus, 1988:

'I like Germany and I enjoy Hockenheim, although fuel consumption can be a problem here. You need a compromise between downforce and speed for the set-up and the set-up is important because the car has to be good for the chicanes.'

COCKPIT VIEW – New circuit

Michael Schumacher, Ferrari, 2002:

'I like this new circuit and in my opinion it is a great success. Of course it requires a lot more aerodynamic downforce than the old Hockenheim and that means the Motodrom [Stadium] section has become more fun to drive. The new layout flows nicely and there are some overtaking opportunities. It is quite demanding.'

Pedro de la Rosa, Jaguar, 2002:

'From my point of view Hockenheim has lost all its personality. It was a different type of track, a low downforce set-up with long straights. The problem is you come here now and it is the same track as other places and I don't think it is good for Formula 1. The tracks have to be different from one another because otherwise it doesn't really matter where we go. During qualifying I was driving around and it was hard to tell where I was – the [new] Nürburgring, Hockenheim, or Malaysia. There is no personality and it is very boring.'[1]

EYEWITNESS

Steven Tee, LAT Photographic:

'It's a real shame they got rid of the old Hockenheim with the chicanes although I can understand why they did. You used to go out in the woods for that very early practice session on the Saturday morning and you could feel history, even though it is not the most historical place.

'What you could *really* feel was that you were at a racetrack. You could hear the cars coming down through the trees at ridiculous speeds, bouncing through those chicanes.

'The old circuit had its own unique challenge and funnily enough there were some really cracking races considering there were no corners. I remember the anticipation in the Stadium Complex for the cars to come round. There were big screens towards the end but in the early days they didn't have them so you just sat and waited. Nobody knew what had happened out at the chicanes.

'It's a bit of a mish-mash now and if you never had to go there again it wouldn't really bother you.'

MEMORIES AND MILESTONES

1970 Jacky Ickx took pole in the Ferrari with Jochen Rindt (Lotus) alongside – Rindt Austrian by nationality but German by birth (he was evacuated during the war). Ickx and Rindt exchanged the lead 13 times, and Clay Regazzoni in the other Ferrari led too. Rindt beat Ickx by 0.7 of a second. Fastest lap: Ickx 126.0mph/202.8kph.

The race went back to the Nürburgring for six years.

1977 Jody Scheckter (Wolf), pole, led to lap 12 then Niki Lauda (Ferrari) outbraked him and won the Grand Prix, which had all but cost him his life at the Nürburgring the year before. He beat Scheckter by 14.3 seconds. Fastest lap: Lauda 130.9mph (+4.9)/210.7kph (+7.9).

1978 Mario Andretti (Lotus), pole, would describe the *Östkurve* as the most important single corner on the circuit. 'That one's a character-builder, no question about it. You go through there flat, and it's vital to get it absolutely right so you're running wide open on to the straightaway.' In general, Andretti felt 'Hockenheim was not a race I was looking forward to at all. After the year with the [Lotus] 78, I'd gotten it into my head that Lotuses and straightaways just weren't meant to be. I knew the 79 had been good on the Ricard straight, but I just thought maybe that was a fluke. I hoped we'd do well at Hockenheim, but no way did I think we'd start from the front row and walk the race. No way. It was that race that made me a total believer in the car.'[2] He beat Scheckter (Wolf) by 15.1 seconds. Fastest lap: Ronnie Peterson (Lotus) 131.3mph (+0.4)/211.4kph (+0.7).

1979 The Williams team breakthrough. Regazzoni had given them their first victory in the British Grand Prix and now, two weeks later – although Jean-Pierre Jabouille (Renault) took pole – Alan Jones conquered Hockenheim, beating Regazzoni by 2.9 seconds. From this moment on, Williams would be a major team. Fastest lap: Gilles Villeneuve (Ferrari) 135.7mph (+4.4)/218.4kph (+7.0).

1980 Jones (Williams) took pole. Patrick Depailler had been killed only the week before. Alfa Romeo did, however, send one driver, Bruno Giacomelli, and he finished fifth. Jacques Laffite (Ligier) pitted for a broken valve spring – and still won, beating Carlos Reutemann (Williams) by 3.1 seconds. Fastest lap: Jones 140.0mph (+4.3)/225.3kph (+6.9).

1981 Alain Prost (Renault) took pole. Nelson Piquet (Brabham) passed Prost for the lead with seven laps to go. Prost's car wasn't revving properly and Piquet beat him by 11.5 seconds. Fastest lap: Jones (Williams) 135.1mph (-4.9)/217.4kph (-7.9).

Speed increase 1970–81: 9.1mph/14.6kph.

The Östkurve *was 'desecrated into a ludicrous chicane' (Autocourse).*

1982 Didier Pironi (Ferrari) crashed in heavy rain on Saturday morning, the car destroyed and Pironi crippled. Technically he had pole from the day before. A collision between Piquet and Eliseo Salazar (ATS) at the *Östkurve* towards the halfway point in the race produced some of the most bizarre television pictures, even by Grand Prix standards, as Piquet punched Salazar and tried to kick him in a delicate place. Patrick Tambay (Ferrari) beat René Arnoux (Renault) by 16.3 seconds. Fastest lap: Piquet 133.3mph/214.6kph.

1983 Arnoux agreed to give his (now) Ferrari team-mate Tambay priority because Tambay had a better chance for the championship. Tambay had pole, Arnoux outbraked him on lap 2 and won the race from there, beating Andrea de Cesaris (Alfa Romeo) by 1 minute 10.6 seconds. Fastest lap: Arnoux 133.4mph (+0.1)/214.8kph (+0.2).

1984 Prost (McLaren) took pole and, with team-mate Lauda, provided the only excitement: Prost leading, Lauda constantly trying to attack, Prost constantly countering to win by 3.1 seconds. Fastest lap: Prost 133.9mph (+0.5)/215.5kph (+0.7).

1986 Keke Rosberg (McLaren) took pole. Team-mate Prost ran out of fuel on the final lap and, to protest against the new 220-litre fuel maximum, tried to push the car to the finish, knowing the television cameras would feast on that. Piquet (Williams) beat Ayrton Senna (Lotus) by 15.4 seconds. Fastest lap: Gerhard Berger (Benetton) 142.6mph (+8.7)/229.5kph (+14.0).

1987 Nigel Mansell (Williams) took pole for a race of attrition with only six of the 26 starters running at the end. Prost (McLaren) seemed certain to win but his alternator drive belt failed and Piquet (Williams) beat Stefan Johansson in the other McLaren by 1 minute 39.5 seconds. Fastest lap: Mansell 143.8mph (+1.2)/231.5kph (+2.0).

1988 A wet race, and Senna, pole, spread his mastery while McLaren team-mate Prost, who hated the wet, came in 13.6 seconds behind. Fastest lap: Alessandro Nannini (Benetton) 123.6mph/198.9kph (no comparison).

1989 The Honda engine delivered awesome power, separating the McLarens from all the others in qualifying (Senna pole 1m 42.3s, Prost 1m 43.2s, Mansell's Ferrari next, 1m 44.0s). The race was more of the same and Senna beat Prost by 18.1s (and Mansell by 1m

23.2s). Fastest lap: Senna 143.6mph (-0.2)/231.1kph (-0.4).

Speed increase 1982–9: 10.3mph/16.5kph.

The Östkurve *was altered.*

1990 A tale of the unexpected. Senna (McLaren) led from pole, Nannini (Benetton), who'd qualified in the fifth row, running eighth. By the time Senna made a tyre stop on lap 18 Nannini went into the lead, didn't pit and held a very determined Senna off to lap 34, when a back-marker baulked him and Senna was through to win by 6.5 seconds. Fastest lap: Thierry Boutsen (Williams) 144.1mph/231.9kph.

1991 In second qualifying Mansell (Williams) was baulked by Erik Comas (Ligier) and remonstrated afterwards so vehemently that some reports say Comas was reduced to tears. Mansell, pole, beat Williams team-mate Riccardo Patrese by 13.7 seconds. Fastest lap: Patrese 146.9mph/236.4kph.

Speed increase 1990–1: 2.8mph/4.5kph.

Tighter Östkurve.

1992 A tale of the expected. Mansell had pole, Senna (McLaren) on the second row. Mansell pitted and hounded Senna so vehemently that in the *Östkurve* he went straight on, ran over a marker cone and rejoined just behind Senna – who waved him through. Did he do it because he thought Mansell might become too

vehement? After the race he didn't say. Mansell won by 4.5 seconds. Fastest lap: Patrese (Williams) 150.1mph/241.5kph.

1993 Prost (Williams) had pole and team-mate Damon Hill had everything under control when a tyre punctured with two laps left, robbing him of his first Grand Prix victory. Prost beat Michael Schumacher (Benetton) by 16.6 seconds. Fastest lap: Schumacher 149.7mph/240.9kph.

Speed decrease 1992–3: 0.4mph/0.6kph.

Ayrton Senna *chicane tightened.*

1994 Gerhard Berger (Ferrari) took pole. An explosive start, Mika Häkkinen's McLaren sideways into the first corner and cars spearing off everywhere. For a moment the images were horrendous but not as horrendous as Jos Verstappen's pit stop. The Benetton was engulfed by a huge sheet of molten yellow flame – remarkably, nobody badly hurt. Berger beat Olivier Panis (Ligier) by 54.7 seconds. Fastest lap: David Coulthard (Williams) 143.7mph/231.3kph.

1995 Damon Hill, pole, had everything under control – his Williams and Schumacher in the Benetton – when he spun off at the first corner on lap 2, not to return. A mechanical fault rather than driver error was diagnosed. Schumacher beat Coulthard (Williams) by 5.9 seconds. Fastest lap: Schumacher 140.2mph (-3.5)/225.7kph (-5.6).

Changing the circuit to suit modern times.

1996 Berger (Benetton) led to lap 43 of the 45 when the engine failed after sustained pressure from Hill, pole, who now led the Championship decisively (73 points against team-mate Jacques Villeneuve's 52). Hill beat Jean Alesi (Benetton) by 11.4 seconds. Fastest lap: Hill 143.3mph (+3.1)/230.6kph (+4.9).

1997 Berger led from pole throughout except his pit stops, giving Benetton their first win since Schumacher left. He beat Schumacher (Ferrari) by 17.5 seconds. Berger then confirmed he was leaving. Fastest lap: Berger 144.3mph (+1.0)/232.3kph (+1.7).

1998 McLaren's weekend as Häkkinen took pole from Coulthard, and ran 1-2 throughout. Häkkinen won by 0.4 of a second. The weekend belonged equally to the Mercedes engines in the McLarens. Schumacher, meanwhile, could get the Ferrari no higher than fifth. Fastest lap: Coulthard 143.8mph (-0.5)/231.5kph (-0.8).

1999 Häkkinen (McLaren) took pole. Schumacher had broken his leg at Silverstone and Ferrari summoned Mika Salo from BAR. He'd been driving in Grands Prix since 1994 but had a best finish of fourth, the year before. He ran second before ceding the lead to team-mate Eddie Irvine, who beat him by 1.0 second. Fastest lap: Coulthard 145.0mph (+1.2)/233.3kph (+1.8).

2000 David Coulthard (McLaren) took pole. Giancarlo Fisichella (Benetton) and Schumacher collided at the first corner while Rubens Barrichello worked his way up from the ninth row of the grid for his first win for Ferrari, beating Häkkinen (McLaren) by 7.4 seconds. Barrichello was so overcome he wept openly on the podium. Fastest lap: Barrichello 146.4mph (+1.4)/235.6kph (+2.3).

2001 Juan-Pablo Montoya (Williams) took pole. Schumacher's Ferrari had gear selection problems from the line and Luciano Burti (Prost) struck it hard enough to be pitched completely in the air, rotating above the rest of the grid before landing on Enrique Bernoldi's Arrows. Nobody was even hurt. Ralf Schumacher (Williams) beat Rubens Barrichello (Ferrari)

The memorial to Jim Clark had to be moved into the new circuit. When it was unveiled members of the family were in attendance.

ICH LIEBE WILLI WEBER

Schumis Erben fahren 2008
wieder auf dem Hockenheimring

Hockenheim lost Formula 1 although it was central to its character but, like so many businesses, it learnt to diversify.
(From the circuit's official magazine, courtesy Hockenheim-Ring GmbH)

by 46.1 seconds. Fastest lap: Montoya 150.0mph (+3.6)/241.3kph (+5.7).

Speed increase 1994–2001: 6.3mph/10.0kph.

The track was drastically revised, shedding the forest sections altogether and reducing the distance from 4.2 miles to 2.8. Designer Tilke says: 'The forest section was the old Hockenheim. For political reasons in the region, they wanted to have another circuit, a smaller one.'

Alexander Wurz (Benetton and McLaren) felt it had become like other tracks but offered certain challenges. He said: 'You reach Nordkurve at 270kph [168mph], brake briefly and need good turn-in to prevent understeer. The Parabolica is "strange" – slippery, uneven and again demanding brief braking. You need the power now because you're on the longest straight – 310kph [193mph]. The Spitzkehre hairpin is first gear 60kph [37mph] and the best overtaking place. Turn 7 is flat and the following left-hander taken at 280kph [174mph] with an elusive apex – the car slides.

'You lift a little for the next right and exit in fifth towards the Stadium. The Mobil 1 Kurve is the most challenging: fast entry, uneven and narrow coming out. Then: the banked Sachskurve, a gradient giving oversteer, a left-right flick, a compression into the final right-handers at Südkurve.'

2002 The Jim Clark Memorial, which had stood where he crashed, was moved and given a new backdrop (on which the year of his death, 1968, was given as 1967).

Astonishingly, Schumacher (pole) had secured his fifth World Championship at the race before, France, in *July*. Would he take it easy? The answer: pole then leading every lap except the pit stops to beat Montoya (Williams) by 10.5 seconds. Fastest lap: Schumacher 133.8mph/215.4kph.

2003 Montoya (Williams) took pole. The sprint to the first corner created yet another crash. Montoya's team-mate Ralf Schumacher, without ever intending to, squeezed Barrichello's Ferrari, Kimi Räikkönen's McLaren became involved, and the race opened to Montoya, who beat Coulthard (McLaren) by 1 minute 05.4 seconds. Fastest lap: Montoya 136.6mph (+2.8)/219.8kph (+4.4).

2004 Michael Schumacher (Ferrari) pole. Jenson Button (BAR) chased Schumacher hard in the closing laps

FACTS OF THE MATTER

4.218m/6.789km circuit

Year	Winner
1970	J. Rindt (Lotus)
1977	N. Lauda (Ferrari)
1978	M. Andretti (Lotus)
1979	A. Jones (Williams)
1980	J. Laffite (Ligier)
1981	N. Piquet (Brabham)
Fastest pole	A. Jones (Williams) 1980 (143.5mph/230.9kph)
Fastest lap	A. Jones 1980 (140.0mph/225.3kph)

Östkurve, 4.223m/6.797km circuit

1982	P. Tambay (Ferrari)
1983	R. Arnoux (Ferrari)
1984	A. Prost (McLaren)
1986	N. Piquet (Williams)
1987	N. Piquet (Williams)
1988	A. Senna (McLaren)
1989	A. Senna (McLaren)
Fastest pole	K. Rosberg (McLaren) 1986 (149.0mph/239.9kph)
Fastest lap	N. Mansell (Williams) 1987 (143.8mph/231.5kph)

Östkurve altered, 4.227m/6.802km circuit

1990	A. Senna (McLaren)
1991	N. Mansell (Williams)
Fastest pole	N. Mansell 1991 (156.7mph/252.2kph)
Fastest lap	R. Patrese (Williams) 1991 (146.9mph/236.4kph)

Tighter Östkurve, 4.235m/6.815km circuit

1992	N. Mansell (Williams)
1993	A. Prost (Williams)
Fastest pole	N. Mansell 1992 (155.6mph/250.4kph)
Fastest lap	R. Patrese (Williams) 1992 (150.1mph/241.5kph)

Ayrton Senna Kurve tightened, 4.240m/6.823km circuit 1994–9; 4.241m/6.825km 2000–1

1994	G. Berger (Ferrari)
1995	M. Schumacher (Benetton)
1996	D. Hill (Williams)
1997	G. Berger (Benetton)
1998	M. Häkkinen (McLaren)
1999	E. Irvine (Ferrari)
2000	R. Barrichello (Ferrari)
2001	R. Schumacher (Williams)
Fastest pole	J.-P. Montoya (Williams) 2001 (155.6mph/250.4kph)
Fastest lap	J.-P. Montoya 2001 (150.0mph/241.3kph)

Forest section removed, 2.842m/4.574km circuit

2002	M. Schumacher (Ferrari)
2003	J.-P. Montoya (Williams)
2004	M. Schumacher (Ferrari)
2005	F. Alonso (Renault)
2006	M. Schumacher (Ferrari)
2008	L. Hamilton (McLaren)
Fastest pole	M. Schumacher (Ferrari) 2004 (139.6mph/224.6kph)
Fastest lap	K. Räikkönen (McLaren) 2004 (138.7mph/223.2kph)

despite the fact that Button's helmet strap became loose and on the straights tried to strangle him. He finished only 8.3 seconds behind Schumacher. Fastest lap: Räikkönen (McLaren) 138.7mph (+2.1)/223.2kph (+3.4).

2005 Räikkönen (McLaren) took pole. In the sprint to the first corner Takuma Sato (BAR) went into the Williams of Mark Webber, who went into the Toyota of Jarno Trulli. Heartbreak for Räikkönen, however, when he commanded the race but had a hydraulic leak on lap 36. Fernando Alonso (Renault) beat Montoya (McLaren) by 22.5 seconds. Fastest lap: Räikkönen 136.7mph (-2.0)/219.9kph (-3.3).

2006 Räikkönen (McLaren) took pole. The Renault team's mass dampers were ruled illegal, hobbling Alonso (fifth) and team-mate Fisichella. Michael Schumacher (Ferrari), meanwhile, sailed

through the weekend majestically, beating team-mate Felipe Massa by 0.7 of a second. Fastest lap: Schumacher 134.0mph (-2.7)/215.6kph (-4.3).

2008 Lewis Hamilton (McLaren), pole, was in the process of confirming that his debut season in 2007 was a beginning rather than a fluke, and he confirmed it by leading every lap except his pit stops while Nelson Piquet Jnr (son of Nelson) came second after good fortune with the Safety Car: he'd pitted just before it came out and had a clear run to second place. Hamilton won by 5.5 seconds. Fastest lap: Nick Heidfeld (BMW) 134.7mph (+0.7)/216.7kph (+1.1).

Speed increase 2002–8: 0.9mph/1.3kph.

Footnotes
[1] *Autosport*. [2] *World Champion*, Andretti.

NÜRBURGRING

Location: 37 miles (60km) west of Koblenz.
Constructed: 1925.
World Championship Grands Prix: 37.

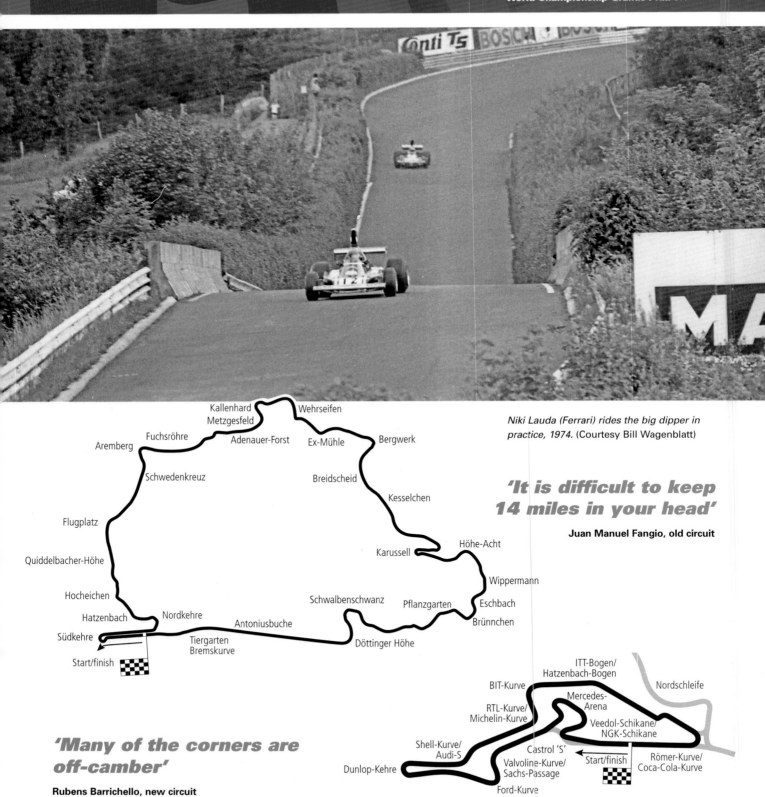

Niki Lauda (Ferrari) rides the big dipper in practice, 1974. (Courtesy Bill Wagenblatt)

'It is difficult to keep 14 miles in your head'

Juan Manuel Fangio, old circuit

Kallenhard   Wehrseifen
Metzgesfeld
Fuchsröhre   Adenauer-Forst   Ex-Mühle   Bergwerk
Aremberg
Schwedenkreuz   Breidscheid
Kesselchen
Flugplatz
Höhe-Acht
Quiddelbacher-Höhe   Karussell
Wippermann
Hocheichen   Eschbach
Schwalbenschwanz   Pflanzgarten
Hatzenbach   Nordkehre   Brünnchen
Antoniusbuche
Südkehre   Döttinger Höhe
Tiergarten
Bremskurve
Start/finish

'Many of the corners are off-camber'

Rubens Barrichello, new circuit

ITT-Bogen/
Hatzenbach-Bogen
BIT-Kurve   Nordschleife
Mercedes-
Arena
RTL-Kurve/
Michelin-Kurve   Veedol-Schikane/
NGK-Schikane
Shell-Kurve/
Audi-S   Castrol 'S'   Römer-Kurve/
Dunlop-Kehre   Valvoline-Kurve/   Start/finish   Coca-Cola-Kurve
Sachs-Passage
Ford-Kurve

There's a mystery about the Nürburgring, and a majesty, and a madness. You get all three together, as if your senses are being completely overwhelmed from different directions simultaneously.

I am speaking, of course, about the old Nürburgring, the one that guards its mysteries because for most of the 22.8km you cannot see it. It's somewhere beyond the high mesh fence, somewhere in those tall, endless trees, and only really reveals itself at certain vantage points – clearings – where the curious come to gaze through the fence. They are looking at short segments of the track, almost vistas, as it descends and ascends so tightly, contorting furiously as it goes.

Driving the old Nürburgring is lonely, private, secluded, and eternally dangerous.

Driving the new Nürburgring, the 4.5km that cling like an udder to the belly of its parent, is open and, as much as any racing circuit can be, eternally safe. It has no mystery, or majesty, or madness, because it was designed specifically to exclude them. You don't get any of the three at all, as if your senses are being completely underwhelmed from different directions simultaneously. Perhaps I am being too harsh and it is the inescapable comparison that is so destructive. If you put the new Nürburgring in some lost pastureland in the middle of Italy it'd probably be fine in the modern way. The problem remains the udder and the belly.

If you want to press the point, the 22.8km represent precisely the way the world was and the 4.5 what is has evolved into. The fact that ordinary motorists can pay a small sum and take their cars round the 22.8 while the Grand Prix drivers don't venture beyond the 4.5 merely reinforces the comparison.

There is a very real sense that the 22.8km represent an absolute – Pescara was longer at 25.5 but hosted only one Grand Prix, the last real road race, in 1957, and represented an end. Other circuits were faster. Lauda's pole in 1975, 122.0mph, would be slower that season than Silverstone (133.0), Austria (139.4) and, of course, Monza (140.1) *but* faster than all the others. The

The castle looms in the distance, and the cars take on the Ring with nothing but their skill to keep them safe. This is 1952. (Courtesy Thomas Horat)

absolute means you could not create a longer circuit that was faster and more crowded with different challenges – so many that drivers swore you could never learn the whole 22.8. The Nürburgring was *it*.

Because construction began in 1925 and the first Grand Prix was held there a year later, the circuit knew all the great interwar drivers, regularly attracted 300,000 spectators, and was exploited by Hitler, the Nazis, Mercedes, and Auto Union. You feel closer to all that at the old Nürburgring because the track has changed so little.

Here in 1935 Tazio Nuvolari beat both German teams in an Alfa Romeo, one of the greatest drives, and a sense of the absolute lingers over that, too.

The circuit was conceived to reduce unemployment in the Koblenz-Cologne area with the additional arguments that a circuit would promote the German car industry by giving it a permanent test track (for which it is still used) as well as opening the region to tourism. In its full form – the 14.17-mile *Nordschleife* (North Loop) and the 4.8-mile *Südschleife* (South Loop) – it confronted the driver with 172 corners, 88 left-handers, 84 right-handers. As Cyril Posthumus wrote in *The German Grand Prix:* 'Describing the Nürburgring always provides a vigorous exercise in superlatives, and sometimes expletives from those learning its intricacies the hard way.

'The Nürburgring had emerged in the French Zone of the West German

Republic, battered but basically intact [after the Second World War]. Tanks had left their marks on its surface; trees, hedges and grass had flourished; bombs, grenades and bullets had in passing spared little glass in the timekeeping and other circuit buildings, while a litter of shattered equipment and other debris betrayed the hurried passage of armies. Not until 1949 was the famous 14.1-mile *Nordschleife* circuit resurfaced and raced over again, at first for national events only.'

The German Grand Prix was run again in 1950, a gap of 11 years, but as a Formula 2 event. It attracted an entry of 35 and was won by Alberto Ascari (Ferrari). A year later the real Grand Prix was reinstated and continued (with the excursion to the Avus in 1959 and one to Hockenheim in 1970) until 1976, when Niki Lauda (Ferrari) almost died in a fiery crash. It demonstrated how outdated the circuit had become. Because of its length, rescue services could not reach every part of it in the way they could at the more modern circuit – Spa, similar in character, had not survived beyond 1970.

The old circuit was left as a sort of living museum as well as a valuable testing ground for production cars. The new circuit, modern in every aspect, lured the Grand Prix cars back in 1984.

Twist and shout, the Ring 1972.
(Courtesy Bill Wagenblatt)

COCKPIT VIEWS –
OLD CIRCUIT

Juan Manuel Fangio, who drove five Grands Prix there:

'In the Alfa Romeo coupé the firm had given me, a 6-cylinder 2½-litre machine, I set about doing a general reconnaissance. Then I tried to memorise the circuit from the start onwards. When the day of the race came, I knew it by memory as far as the eighth mile.

'It wasn't easy. We usually raced on much smaller tracks, where you simply had to go round a number of times, stop, and work out where you'd been making mistakes. You soon learn where you can go fast into a curve, so the next time round the better your time. But the Nürburgring is more than 14 miles long, and none of this applied. You got to know it by stages. You said to yourself: "Right, I know it up to the eighth mile. Now I must try to memorise it up to the 10th, the 12th mile."

'It's impossible to get to know it all in a short time. All you have are reference points: "Up to there, I can go at such and such a speed. From then on, there is a difficult succession of curves" – for example, after the "carousel" the first and second curves could be taken with confidence, accelerating; then came a downhill stretch where you saw a wooden hut; this was an alarm signal for difficult "S" bends...

'It is difficult to keep 14 miles in your head, so for that reason I tried to blot from my mind all the slow parts. What you had to keep in your mind were the fast bits, because dealing with slow curves is like driving in the mountains — you go by what you see, and take them as they come. That's why I always say that mountain driving is not so difficult; what is difficult is dealing with high-speed curves. There you can't afford the luxury of confusing one with another...'[1]

Piero Taruffi, who drove in three Grands Prix there:

'The 'Ring strains the transmission and suspension systems of a car to the utmost. This was brought home to me at the place called the *Fuchsröhre* [Fox's Earth]; the road plunges down a 1 in 6 gradient then shoots up an even steeper slope on the other side of the valley and disappears into the woods. The change from downhill to uphill takes place on a slight left-hand bend, and as one rounds it, owing to the slight delay while the springs are being compressed by "g" and before the better traction of the uphill stretch makes itself felt, the car feels as if it is being thrown off the road. At racing speeds the road seems to close in (although it is 40 feet wide); this, plus the increased impression of speed, and the sudden dive out of the open into a dark wood, all combines to make one feel like a fox being chased by hounds.'[2]

COCKPIT VIEW –
NEW CIRCUIT

Rubens Barrichello, Brawn, 2009:

'I have always enjoyed racing at the Nürburgring and it provides a good challenge for the drivers. The layout and flow is nice which allows you to get into a rhythm and there are some interesting undulations and bumps to look out for. I won the race here back in 2002 so the circuit always holds some good memories for me.

'The weather can be a little unpredictable due to its location right in the Eifel Mountains.

'The first corner is really important to set yourself up for a good lap and it's a bumpy run down from the start line. You have to get your approach absolutely right and position yourself well for a good exit. However it is also one of the best overtaking opportunities if the cars around you slide straight on so you need to be alert to take advantage of any opportunities.

'Many of the corners at the Nürburgring are off-camber so getting the correct line for your corner entry is important all round the lap.'[3]

EYEWITNESS

Gareth Rees, motor sport enthusiast:

'A few years ago I went back to the Nürburgring to see a touring car race on the new track but I made sure to drive a couple of obligatory laps on the *Nordschleife*. About 30 years before I'd done it once as a teenager in my parents' Hillman Minx but this time I just kept asking myself and my much less-obsessed passenger "Can you imagine that *F1 cars* used to *race* here?" It was truly a Grand Prix circuit like no other, a track where not only brave drivers but also those with good memories could make a difference.

'In the late 1960s and early 1970s Jacky Ickx was probably both and he was, for a few years, the star driver at the 'Ring. He was certainly a star without equal when I went there for the first time in 1972 on a Chequers Travel weekend trip from the UK, travelling overnight to arrive in time for Saturday practice and returning on the Sunday night ferry to Dover after the race.

'As it was quite impossible to see the whole track we just worked our way from the start/finish area down through the curves of *Hatzenbach* during practice, and then watched the race from the top of the hill at *Flugplatz*, where we had a panoramic view of the surrounding hills and could see the cars coming out of *Quiddelbacher-Höhe* in the distance, dropping down the hill and on up towards us.

'I think they'd already flattened out the jump at the brow of the hill because I don't recall any jumping cars like you can see on films of the 1967 race. What I do recall, though, is that from the outset it seemed like it was ages before the next cars came into view after Ickx had appeared and, then, long disappeared. It was a masterful display

of utter dominance as he certainly didn't have the best car that year.

'Two years later I went again and saw another Ferrari victory, this time for Clay Regazzoni, proving that he really was a driver who could be great on his day. This particular time, my mate and I discovered that we could see the race without paying for a ticket, simply by watching from the bridge of a public road crossing over the long straight back to the pits area.

'Today I regret that deeply because, only seeing the cars come past on the straight, I feel like I never even went to the race at the Nürburgring at all. What a wasted opportunity!'

MEMORIES AND MILESTONES

1951 There were no German cars and only one German driver, which cut the attendance to 180,000. Alberto Ascari (Ferrari), pole, beat Juan Manuel Fangio (Alfa Romeo) by 30.5 seconds. Fastest lap: Fangio 85.6mph/137.8kph.

1952 Ascari, pole, drove 'what he regarded as probably the finest car he'd ever driven (the Ferrari 500) on his favourite foreign track. By lap 4 he led Farina by 59.6 seconds, helped by the latter's stopping hurriedly for fresh goggles. By lap 5, it was 69 seconds. Lesser cars were retiring one after the other. By lap 9, his lead had gone down to 45 seconds, then he made a rear-wheel-change pit stop of 32 seconds. Soon after, Farina's mechanics beat this by a second, but then the Doctor [Farina] spoiled it by stalling twice. Alberto seemed assured of a win.'[4] He beat Farina by 14.1

seconds. Fastest lap: Ascari 84.3mph (-1.3)/135.7kph (-2.1).

1953 Ascari (Ferrari) took pole again but team-mate Mike Hawthorn led from laps 5 to 7, the first Briton to lead the German Grand Prix since Dick Seaman in 1938. Giuseppe Farina (Ferrari) beat Fangio by 1 minute 4.0 seconds, Hawthorn third. Fastest lap: Ascari 85.6mph (+1.3)/137.8kph (+2.1).

1954 Mercedes used the track to test drivers for their new Grand Prix team and now Fangio put one on pole and won but his protégé, Onofre Marimón, was killed during practice. Fangio beat Hawthorn (Ferrari) by 1 minute 36.5 seconds. Fastest lap: Karl Kling 85.7mph (+0.1)/138.0kph (+0.2).

There was no race in 1955 because of the Le Mans tragedy and great nervousness about any motor racing. Mercedes withdrew.

1956 Fangio had a Lancia Ferrari, which he put on pole and beat Stirling Moss (Maserati) by 47.0 seconds. Fastest lap: Fangio 87.7mph (+2.0)/141.2kph (+3.2).

1957 Fangio (Maserati) had pole again and created a masterpiece hauntingly similar to Nuvolari's: a long pit stop then a gathering, climactic pursuit of Hawthorn and Peter Collins in the Ferraris. Fangio broke the fabled 90mph barrier and progressively reduced the lap record until it reached 9 minutes 17.4 seconds, perhaps the greatest lap ever driven. He swept past the Ferraris on the second to last lap, beating Hawthorn by 3.6 seconds. Fastest lap: Fangio 91.5mph (+3.8)/147.3kph (+6.1).´

1958 The pace of progress took Hawthorn (Ferrari), pole, and Tony Brooks (Vanwall) to qualifying times faster than Fangio's 9:17.4. In the race Brooks caught Hawthorn and Collins but Collins went off, was thrown out and struck a tree. He died in hospital. Brooks beat Roy Salvadori (Cooper) by 3 minutes 29.7 seconds. Fastest lap: Stirling Moss (Vanwall) 92.9mph (+1.4)/149.5kph (+2.2).

The 1959 race went to the Avus and 1960 was for Formula 2 cars, run on the *Südschleife*.

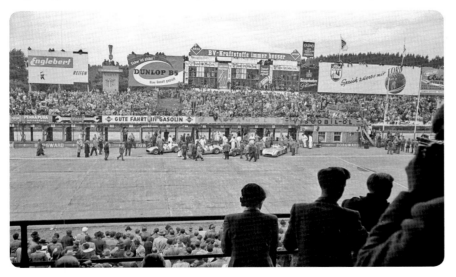

The Mercedes were not all-conquering in 1954, although Juan Manuel Fangio (18) would win the German Grand Prix. Hermann Lang (21) spun out and Hans Hermann (20) stopped with a fuel injection problem. (Courtesy Thomas Horat)

1961 The 100th Championship race. The pace of progress increased: Wolfgang von Trips (Ferrari) went round in under 9 minutes and Phil Hill in another Ferrari decreased that to 8 minutes 55.2 seconds for pole. Moss (Lotus) beat von Trips by 21.4 seconds. Fastest lap: Phil Hill 94.9mph (+2.0)/152.7kph (+3.2).

1962 Graham Hill (BRM) beat John Surtees (Lola) by 2.5 seconds and Dan Gurney (Porsche), pole, by 4.4 in a very wet race. 'All three drivers were completely exhausted by their ordeal, and could barely speak at first.'[5] Fastest lap: Graham Hill 83.3mph/134.1kph (no comparison).

1963 Jim Clark (Lotus), pole, dominated the season but had an engine problem and John Surtees (Ferrari) won, beating Clark by 1 minute 17.5 seconds – there were seven crashes. Surtees averaged 95.8mph/154.1kph, faster than the existing lap record. Fastest lap: Surtees 96.8mph (+1.9)/155.8kph (+3.1).

1964 Honda made their Grand Prix debut and Surtees (Ferrari) took pole at 98.4mph, within touching distance of the fabled 100mph. Carel de Beaufort, last amateur driver to race in Grands Prix regularly, died after his Porsche crashed in practice. Surtees beat Graham Hill (BRM) by 1 minute 15.6 seconds. Fastest lap: Surtees 98.3mph (+1.5)/158.2kph (+2.4).

1965 In Friday practice Clark did a lap of 8 minutes 22.7 seconds, which was 101.5mph/163.3kph, for pole, compared with Surtees' 8:38.4 the year before. Clark led every lap to become World

Hans Stuck takes the March (No 9) through shadowlands and Carlos Pace takes the Brabham (8) clean off the ground. (Courtesy Bill Wagenblatt)

Champion with three races to spare. He beat Graham Hill (BRM) by 15.9 seconds. Fastest lap: Clark 101.2mph (+2.9)/162.9kph (+4.7).

1966 Clark (Lotus) took pole. On the first lap a Briton, John Taylor, spun and crashed his Brabham, later dying of his injuries. Jack Brabham (Brabham) won a wet race, beating Surtees (Cooper) by 44.4 seconds. Brabham remembered: 'It was a shocking race, actually, and a very dangerous one; I guarantee we drove every lap under a different set of circumstances, because of rain showers on different parts of the circuit. One lap you would come round and the track was dry, and the next lap it would all be wet. And then you would come across rivers running across the road. There were quite a few times when the conditions were really dangerous – we were sliding all over the road in mud and water.'[6] Fastest lap: Surtees 96.5mph/155.2kph (no comparison).

Speed increase 1951–66: 15.6mph/25.1kph.

A curve (known as the Bremskurve*) was added to try and reduce speed as the cars approached the pits. It lengthened the track by 0.025km but the pace of progress, especially here, could not be halted.*

1967 Clark (Lotus) took pole. For the second year, Formula 2 cars competed concurrently and Jacky Ickx, in the Formula 2 Matra, lapped two and a half seconds faster than Clark had been doing in 1966. Denny Hulme (Brabham) beat Brabham (Brabham) by 38.5 seconds. Fastest lap: Dan Gurney (Eagle) 103.2mph/166.0kph.

1968 Ickx (Ferrari) took pole for a very wet, foggy race. For the only time in his life Ken Tyrrell ordered a driver –

Jackie Stewart – to go out and drive it to see where the water ran. Stewart did, then drove a consummate race to finish 4 minutes 03.2 seconds in front of Graham Hill (Lotus). As someone at Tyrrell remarked, waiting more than four minutes for the next car to come in is a *l-o-n-g* time. Fastest lap: Stewart 88.7mph/142.7kph (no comparison).

1969 The weather was warm and dry at last and Ickx (Brabham) took pole with 7 minutes 42.1 seconds (110.5mph/177.8kph). In practice, German Gerhard Mitter crashed his BMW fatally. Stewart (Matra) led the race to lap 6 before he and Ickx duelled, but Stewart had gear selection problems. Ickx beat him by 57.7 seconds. Fastest lap: Jacky Ickx (Brabham) 110.1mph (+6.9)/177.2kph (+11.2).

The 1970 race went to Hockenheim for safety reasons.

1971 The drivers returned to find improvements had been carried out. The track had had some of its most intimidating features – trees, hedges, rock faces – removed. Armco and catch-fencing had been extensively used. The tree-felling gave spectators and drivers a better view. Stewart (Tyrrell), pole, beat team-mate François Cevert by 30.1 seconds. Fastest lap: Cevert 116.1mph (+6.0)/186.8kph (+9.6).

1972 Ickx (Ferrari) took pole with 7 minutes 7.0 seconds (119.6mph/192.5kph) – Ascari in 1951 had been 9 minutes 55.8 seconds. Ickx beat team-mate Clay Regazzoni by 48.3 seconds. Fastest lap: Ickx 117.8mph (+1.7)/189.6kph (+2.8).

1973 The Tyrrells of Stewart, pole, and Cevert led immediately and finished in the same order an hour and 42 minutes later, Stewart winning by 1.6 seconds. Fastest

lap: Carlos Pace (Surtees) 118.4mph (+0.6)/190.6kph (+1.0).

1974 The objective now was to beat 7 minutes, although Niki Lauda (Ferrari) did 7 minutes 00.8 seconds on the Friday. That became pole but Regazzoni in the other Ferrari won, beating Jody Scheckter (Tyrrell) by 52.2 seconds. Fastest lap: Scheckter 118.5mph (+0.1)/190.7kph (+0.1).

1975 Lauda, pole, did go through the barrier with a pole of 6 minutes 58.6 seconds, cranking the speed up to 122.0mph/196.3kph. The drivers feared punctures and parts of the circuit were swept, but in the race Jochen Mass (McLaren) had a tyre disintegrate and the car hammered the Armco. Emerson Fittipaldi (in the other McLaren) had one and Vittorio Brambilla (March) had three. Of the 24 starters only ten finished. Carlos Reutemann (Brabham) beat Jacques Laffite (Williams) by 1 minute 37.7 seconds. Fastest lap: Regazzoni 119.8mph (+1.3)/192.8kph (+2.1).

1976 James Hunt (McLaren) took pole. Lauda (Ferrari) crashed approaching *Bergwerk* on lap 2 and almost died as the Ferrari became a fireball. At that instant the old Nürburgring died too: it was simply too long for rescue services to be able to get to crashes in an acceptable time. Hunt won the restart, beating Scheckter (Tyrrell) by 27.2 seconds and, from being given the Last Rites in hospital, Lauda began the greatest comeback in Formula 1 history. Fastest lap: Scheckter 118.6mph (-1.2)/190.8kph (-2.0).

Speed increase 1967–76: 15.4mph/24.8kph.

The new circuit, 2.8 miles and modern in concept. Nigel Roebuck in Autosport *was particularly scathing. 'They should have called it something else. To glorify this sanitised pre-packed autodrome with the name of "Nürburgring"' was, he insisted, like comparing a great claret with cooking wine. 'It is blandness personified, a series of short straights and constant-radius corners … you could roll pastry on the surface.' Roebuck pointed out the run-off areas were so enormous that when Gerhard Berger (ATS) hit the Armco there was general admiration that he had actually been able to reach it.*

1984 The first Grand Prix on it, dubbed the European. Lauda and Alain Prost in the McLarens were struggling for the World Championship with only

The old circuit stretched to infinity, the new compressed. Here David Coulthard (Williams) leads the pack through in the European Grand Prix, 1995.
(ICN U.K. Bureau)

Estoril to come. Piquet (Brabham) took pole. Lauda was asked how he'd feel returning to the scene of the fireball but he pointed out that (a) the 'new' was in no way comparable and (b) he didn't have any memory of the crash so how could it worry him? Prost beat Michele Alboreto (Ferrari) by 23.9 seconds, Lauda fourth. Fastest lap: Alboreto/Piquet 122.2mph/196.7kph.

1985 It became the German Grand Prix again and Teo Fabi (Toleman) took pole. Michele Alboreto (Ferrari) won but only after he had run into team-mate Stefan Johansson in the notorious first corner. Alboreto beat Prost (McLaren) by 11.6 seconds and went immediately to Johansson to apologise. Fastest lap: Lauda (McLaren) 122.7mph/197.5kph.

Speed increase 1984–5: 0.5mph/0.8kph.

Chicane altered.

1995 With Michael Schumacher (Benetton) the reigning World Champion, it made sense for Germany to have two races, the national Grand Prix (at Hockenheim) and the European here. David Coulthard (Williams) took pole. In damp, overcast conditions Schumacher caught Jean Alesi (Ferrari) and, with three laps to go, threaded through at the chicane – a move that needed courage, exquisite judgement, and a way of defying geometry. As someone said, at that moment he went from being a good driver to being a great one. Schumacher beat Alesi by 2.6 seconds. Fastest lap: Schumacher 125.5mph (+2.8)/202.0kph (+4.5).

1996 Damon Hill (Williams) took pole but team-mate Jacques Villeneuve led

every lap, although he was under intense pressure from Schumacher (now Ferrari) for half the race, trying to force an error. Villeneuve beat him by 0.7 of a second. Fastest lap: Hill 125.3mph (-0.2)/201.6kph (-0.4).

1997 It became the Luxembourg Grand Prix. Mika Häkkinen (McLaren) took pole and the race became instantly notorious because in the first corner Ralf Schumacher (Jordan) crashed into team-mate Giancarlo Fisichella and then brother Michael. Villeneuve (Williams) beat Alesi (Benetton) by 11.7 seconds. Fastest lap: Frentzen (Williams) 129.3mph (+4.0)/208.1kph (+6.5).

1998 Schumacher was level with Häkkinen (McLaren) – 80 points each – in the Championship and took pole. That brought huge crowds. They did not trouble Häkkinen, who drove a typically assured, understated race to beat Schumacher by 2.2 seconds and tilt the Championship. Fastest lap: Häkkinen 126.7mph (-2.6)/203.9kph (-4.2).

1999 The race became the European again although by now it could have been called anything. Heinz-Harald Frentzen (Jordan) took pole. The weather moved from dry to wet and, wonderfully, the little Stewart team (Johnny Herbert and Rubens Barrichello) finished first and third – Stewart's first win. Herbert guessed right at his first tyre stop and selected

1 A postcard of Jackie Stewart (BRM) at the 1965 race, but he only managed two laps before the suspension failed. *(Courtesy Martin Hadwen, National Motor Racing Archive)*

2 Then and now. You can peer through and watch as any day all manner of cars take it on – some from manufacturers measuring their creations against the Ring's total demands. Or you can stand and gaze at the empty track in all its silent, static majesty. *(Author)*

3 This postcard is from 1987 and therefore offering only memories. Grand Prix racing had been gone for a decade. *(Courtesy Martin Hadwen, National Motor Racing Archive)*

4 The people at the new circuit and the old are conscious of the history locked into everything around them. Fangio and the triumphant Mercedes, in place forever and standing guard over the past. *(Courtesy Filipp Gorelik)*

5 The circuit grows and grows. This is part of the construction work in summer 2009. *(Author)*

wets, which gave him a platform to beat Jarno Trulli (Prost) by 22.6 seconds. Fastest lap: Mika Häkkinen 125.4mph (-1.3)/201.8kph (-2.1).

2000 Coulthard (McLaren) took pole. In heavy rain, Michael Schumacher showed all his control and sensitivity, taking a decisive step towards the longed-for Championship at Ferrari. This was the sixth round and he'd already won three others. Only Häkkinen finished on the same lap, 13.8 seconds away. Fastest lap: Schumacher 123.9mph (-1.5)/199.4kph (-2.4).

2001 The weather was dry, hot, and sunny, and so was Schumacher, who led every lap from pole except one when he made his first pit stop. For more than half the race he had a lively duel with brother Ralf (Williams) who was given a ten-second stop'n'go penalty after a pit lane exit infringement. Schumacher beat Juan-Pablo Montoya (Williams) by 4.2 seconds. Fastest lap: Montoya 130.1mph (+6.2)/209.3kph (+9.9).

Speed increase 1995–2001: 4.6mph/7.3kph.

New section after first corner.

2002 Montoya (Williams) took pole. Barrichello beat Ferrari team-mate Schumacher by 0.2 of a second, the team definitely *not* applying team

orders after the fiasco in Austria (see A1-Ring). Fastest lap: Schumacher 124.8mph/200.9kph.

2003 Kimi Räikkönen (McLaren) led cleanly and crisply from pole and extended it deep into the race before his engine failed, opening the race to Ralf Schumacher (Williams), who beat team-mate Montoya by 16.8 seconds. Fastest lap: Räikkönen 124.3mph (-0.5)/200.1kph (-0.8).

2004 Michael Schumacher took pole and led every lap except his first pit stop to beat Ferrari team-mate Barrichello by 17.9 seconds. It meant that after this Round 7 he had made the Championship table a massacre. He had 80 points, Barrichello next on 46. Fastest lap: Schumacher 128.7mph (+4.4)/207.1kph (+7.0).

2005 Nick Heidfeld (Williams) took pole. Räikkönen commanded the race in the McLaren but he flat-spotted a tyre. He and the team felt it would get him to the end and victory but on the final lap it disintegrated and he went off at 170mph. Fernando Alonso (Renault) went by, worried only that he might pick up debris. He beat Heidfeld by 16.5 seconds. Fastest lap: Alonso 126.9mph (-1.8)/204.3kph (-2.8).

2006 Classic Michael Schumacher: behind Alonso (Renault), pole, he delayed his final pit stop for three laps and in them went so fast that he built a 7.7 second lead – his in-lap was fully three seconds faster than Alonso's had been. He won by 3.7 seconds. Fastest lap: Schumacher 125.0mph (-1.9)/ 201.2kph (-3.1).

2007 Räikkönen (Ferrari) took pole for a wild and wonderful race. A cloudburst decimated the field but Felipe Massa (Ferrari) emerged in the lead. Alonso (McLaren) tracked him and after more rain they banged wheels before Alonso overtook. He claimed Massa should learn to drive and Massa said *he* should learn to drive. At least they weren't on the real Nürburgring, which would have taught them both how to drive and very, very quickly. Alonso beat Massa by 8.1 seconds. Fastest lap: Massa 124.0mph (-1.0)/199.6kph (-1.6).

2009 Mark Webber (Red Bull), pole, drove a fiercely determined race and was able to beat team-mate Sebastian Vettel by 9.2 seconds despite a drive-through penalty for contact with Barrichello (Brawn). It was his first win in his 128th Grand Prix. Fastest lap: Alonso (Renault) 123.3mph (-0.7)/198.5kph (-1.1).

Speed decrease 2002–9: 1.5mph/2.4kph.

Footnotes
[1] *My Racing Life*, Fangio. [2] *Works Driver*, Taruffi. [3] Courtesy Brawn GP. [4] *The Man with Two Shadows*, Desmond. [5] *The German Grand Prix*, Posthumus. [6] *When the Flag Drops*, Brabham.

Sebastian Vettel (Red Bull) followed by Robert Kubica (BMW) and Rubens Barrichello (Brawn) – and if you look at the background you might almost be on the old Ring. (Courtesy Alain Vandaele)

FACTS OF THE MATTER

14.173m/22.810km circuit

Year	Winner
1951	A. Ascari (Ferrari)
1952	A. Ascari (Ferrari)
1953	G. Farina (Ferrari)
1954	J.M. Fangio (Mercedes)
1956	J.M. Fangio (Ferrari)
1957	J.M. Fangio (Maserati)
1958	T. Brooks (Vanwall)
1961	S. Moss (Lotus)
1962	G. Hill (BRM)
1963	J. Surtees (Ferrari)
1964	J. Surtees (Ferrari)
1965	J. Clark (Lotus)
1966	J. Brabham (Brabham)
Fastest pole	J. Clark (Lotus) 1966 (102.8mph/165.4kph)
Fastest lap	J. Clark (Lotus) 1965 (101.2mph/162.9kph)

Bremskurve added, 14.189m/22.835km circuit

1967	D. Hulme (Brabham)
1968	J. Stewart (Matra)
1969	J. Ickx (Brabham)
1971	J. Stewart (Tyrrell)
1972	J. Ickx (Ferrari)
1973	J. Stewart (Tyrrell)
1974	C. Regazzoni (Ferrari)
1975	C. Reutemann (Brabham)
1976	J. Hunt (McLaren)
Fastest pole	N. Lauda (Ferrari) 1975 (122.0mph/196.4kph)
Fastest lap	C. Regazzoni (Ferrari) 1975 (119.8mph/192.8kph)

New circuit, 2.822m/4.542km

1984*	A. Prost (McLaren)
1985	M. Alboreto (Ferrari)
Fastest pole	T. Fabi (Toleman) 1985 (131.2mph/211.2kph)
Fastest lap	N. Lauda (McLaren) 1985 (122.7mph/197.5kph)

Chicane altered, 2.831m/4.556km circuit

1995*	M. Schumacher (Benetton)
1996*	J. Villeneuve (Williams)
1997**	J. Villeneuve (Williams)
1998**	M. Häkkinen (McLaren)
1999*	J. Herbert (Stewart)
2000*	M. Schumacher (Ferrari)
2001*	M. Schumacher (Ferrari)
Fastest pole	M. Schumacher (Ferrari) 2001 (136.0mph/218.8kph)
Fastest lap	J.-P. Montoya (Williams) 2001 (130.1mph/209.3kph)

New section after first corner, 3.198m/5.146km circuit 2002; 3.199m/5.148km from 2003

2002*	R. Barrichello (Ferrari)
2003*	R. Schumacher (Williams)
2004*	M. Schumacher (Ferrari)
2005*	F. Alonso (Renault)
2006*	M. Schumacher (Ferrari)
2007*	F. Alonso (McLaren)
2009	M. Webber (Red Bull)
Fastest pole	M. Schumacher (Ferrari) 2004 (130.3mph/209.8kph)
Fastest lap	M. Schumacher 2004 (128.7mph/207.1kph)

* European Grand Prix.
** Luxembourg Grand Prix.

GREAT BRITAIN
AINTREE

Location: 6 miles (9km) from Liverpool city centre.
Constructed: 1954.
World Championship Grands Prix: 5.

The men with the power, 1955: Moss (12) and Fangio (10) will dominate. (LAT)

'It was three miles and the first mile and a bit was quite demanding but frankly the rest wasn't'

Stirling Moss

Waterway Corner

Canal Side

Anchor Crossing

Finishing Straight

Sefton Straight

Village Corner

Valentine's Way

Start/finish

Country Loop

Bechers Bend

Cottage Corner

Country Corner

Tatts Corner

Railway Straight

Melling Crossing

Aintree meant horse racing, which began in 1829, and came to mean the Grand National, which began in 1839. The racecourse was flat, with grandstands like a protective crook of an arm running along one side and some of its landmarks – the Melling Road, Becher's Brook, and The Chair – were deeply embedded in the national psyche. The Topham family, through Edward, a breeder and expert race handicapper, became involved in 1848 and 101 years later bought it outright. Edward's grandson Arthur married a former Gaiety Girl, Mirabel,[1] and although he didn't show much interest in Aintree, she did.

She became deeply embedded in the national psyche over the next 40 years when she ran the circuit as a fiefdom. After the Second World War she looked for ways to capitalise on the area and around 1952 began to consider motor racing. The Duke of Richmond owned the Goodwood circuit in Sussex, which hosted horse and motor racing, *and*

happened to be President of the British Automobile Racing Club. Mrs Topham approached him and offered to let the BARC run the racing.

Their 1952 magazine said: 'The great attraction of Aintree will be that the track will run almost side by side with the actual horse-race course, so that the fullest use can be made of the extensive permanent grandstand accommodation and other existing public facilities … in fact the "set up" is absolutely ideal … From the grandstands one will be able to see entirely round the circuit, and in one of the public enclosures there is a huge spectator bank which will offer wonderful and unrestricted views for many thousands of people.'

In 1954 an exploratory race was run for a mixed entry of Formula 1 and 2 cars, and run anticlockwise. The Grand Prix in 1955 was, however, clockwise.

Douglas Rutherford followed the 1955 motor racing season[2] and wrote: 'Although true road racing may not be

seen in Britain, the three-mile Aintree circuit is a very close equivalent. It was laid down and built exactly like the standard thirty-five foot [10.6m] highway. Its seven corners and one wiggly section make it an excellent test of driving skill. Sheer speed does not count for so much here. Even on the straight the fastest cars do not expect to reach more than 150 mph. The width and surface of the road is uniform the whole way round. There are no bumps, kerbstones or drain holes. The result is that each corner can be taken as its shape indicates without regard for local peculiarities.'

In 1964 the British Grand Prix went to Brands Hatch, which would alternate with Silverstone. Aintree went into the cold and stayed there because Mrs Topham wanted to sell to a property company. It was a complicated situation resulting in legal action for two years.

Racing continued on the Club Circuit until 1982.

COCKPIT VIEW

Sir Stirling Moss, winner, 1955:
'The circuit was very, very tough on brakes. It was three miles and the first mile and a bit was quite demanding but frankly the rest wasn't.

'The start/finish straight was very, very fast and you needed really hard braking into *Anchor*, the first real corner. You'd put them on lightly for *Waterways* to get a bit of warmth in. Then you'd get near the maximum speed, be hard on the brakes, be near the maximum, hard on the brakes again.

'That takes us to *Village Corner*. You'd come out of there flat out, then you'd come to *Becher's Bend*. You'd brake, get the car over to the left and once you came off the brakes it was absolutely flat out. It was a curve rather than a straight line but, because the road holding of the cars was so good, you could take it flat out. It's rather like the corner into the straight at Goodwood now which is taken flat out.

'The great long straight was boring: acceleration, brake, acceleration, brake.

'The *Melling Crossing* was where the road crossed the Grand National circuit and they laid something over it every year for the horses. It was no problem. In those days we were racing cars that

you could race on the road and if you went over a manhole cover or if you went over a tramline, no big deal. You've got to realise that a racing car then would accept anything that a road car would accept. Now it couldn't happen at all.

'Aintree was not one of my favourites. It wasn't challenging for a driver and the main thing, as I say, was how tough it was on the brakes. That was the thing you had to be careful about.'

EYEWITNESS

Tony Bagnall, spectator and author:
'As a child I was always interested in things mechanical, particularly cars and aeroplanes. Then, one day in July 1955, my father announced that he was going to a motor race at the nearby Aintree circuit and did my elder brother and myself wish to go? That race, of course, was the 1955 British Grand Prix, which the recently opened Liverpool circuit was hosting that year for the first time.

'Thus on 16 July 1955, one very excited 12-year-old, accompanied by his father and elder brother, attended his first motor race, along with the many thousands of enthusiasts who came to Aintree on that gloriously sunny Saturday.

'I was totally overcome by the sight

and sound of the cars and their drivers, and I became an immediate motor racing fan, which I remain to this day.

'I cannot recall why I did not go to the next meeting held in September that year, but from 1956 I attended every major motor race held there until 1964 when the final International 200 meeting was held. It was a terrible blow to me when major motor races were no longer held at Aintree, but I did have the consolation of Oulton Park not being too far away and I am still an attendee at meetings there if they appeal to me.'[3]

MEMORIES AND MILESTONES

1955 The Grand Prix season excited special interest because Stirling Moss joined Juan Manuel Fangio at Mercedes – with Karl Kling and, here, the Italian Piero Taruffi – and their cars seized Aintree. Taruffi would remember Fangio's genius. 'I had already begun taking the clockwise corner known as Becher's when the World Champion slashed past me at high speed on my right. I was practically into the corner, and seeing Fangio go past on the inside, with the handicap of having to take it on a much sharper radius, I quite expected him to go off the road; I

Mercedes bring their mighty horsepower to the horseracing circuit, 1955: Juan Manuel Fangio leads Stirling Moss with Karl Kling and Piero Taruffi behind them. (LAT)

dropped back, to keep out of harm's way. Instead of crashing, though, he resolutely threw the car into the most enormous drift angle – it looked to me about 30 degrees – which scrubbed off his excess speed on the way into the corner. In this phase, owing to imperceptible variations in road grip, I could see the car skidding, and with every tiny slide I could detect a change in the intensity of his exhaust note. At a given moment the engine revs began to mount gradually, and his car went on drawing away, yard by yard.'[4]

Moss, pole, led into the first corner but Fangio overtook him and led to lap 2, then Moss from 3 to 17, then Fangio from 18 to 25, then Moss to the final lap, 90. Fangio came fully up to Moss

Nose to tail in 1959 as Maurice Trintignant (Cooper) leads Moss (BRM) and Bruce McLaren (Cooper) past the famous old grandstands. (LAT)

on that lap and they crossed the line separated by less than a car's length – 0.200 of a second. Fastest lap: Moss 89.7mph/144.4kph.

1957 With Mercedes gone (they withdrew at the end of 1955) the British Vanwall cars excited the special interest now, not least because Moss was in one of them. He took pole and led but an engine problem forced him into the pits. Tony Brooks, in another Vanwall, had crashed at Le Mans and was still suffering from that. He was signalled in and Moss took the car

over, beating Luigi Musso (Ferrari) by 25.6 seconds. It was the first time a British car had won a Championship Grand Prix. Fastest lap: Moss 90.6mph (+0.9)/145.8kph (+1.4).

1959 The problem was tyre wear. Jack Brabham (Cooper), pole, remembered: 'We were all on Dunlops, but for some reason the Aintree circuit was very hard on tyres. The surface of the track had a lot to do with it, but also that year the cars were going so much faster than previously. The engines were developed to a point at which tyres were becoming

marginal. We needed bigger tyres and there were none available – little skinny things we had, and there was just not enough rubber on the road to cope with the power and speed.'[5] He led all 75 laps and beat Moss (BRM) by 22.2 seconds. Fastest lap: Moss and Bruce McLaren (Cooper) 92.3mph (+1.7)/148.6kph (+2.8).

1961 The race was wet and cars spun off but later the track dried, leaving Wolfgang von Trips to beat Ferrari team-mate Phil Hill, pole, by 46.0 seconds.

Fastest lap: Tony Brooks (BRM) 91.7mph (-0.6)/147.5kph (-1.1).

1962 Jim Clark (Lotus), pole, led all 75 laps and beat John Surtees (Lola) by 49.2 seconds. Fastest lap: Clark 93.9mph (+2.2)/151.1kph (+3.6).

Speed increase 1955–62: 4.2mph/6.7kph.

Footnotes

[1] Gaiety Girls were the chorus girls in Edwardian musical comedies. [2] *The Chequered Flag*, Rutherford. [3] *The Unfulfilled Dream*, Bagnall. [4] *Works Driver*, Taruffi. [5] *When The Flag Drops*, Brabham.

FACTS OF THE MATTER

3.000m/4.828km circuit

Year	Winner
1955	S. Moss (Mercedes)
1957	S. Moss/T. Brooks (Vanwall)
1959	J. Brabham (Cooper)
1961	W. von Trips (Ferrari)
1962	J. Clark (Lotus)
Fastest pole	J. Clark 1962 (95.1mph/153.0kph)
Fastest lap	J. Clark 1962 (93.9mph/151.1kph)

ABOVE: Aintree promoted itself in a very modern way, using every outlet. This is a large-size postcard.

RIGHT: A document of its time. The advance ticket sales brochure which wasn't coy about depicting Mike Hawthorn and Peter Collins, both killed the year before.

RIGHT: The build up to the 1961 race which Wolfgang (Taffy) von Trips – there he is in the ticket sales brochure – won.

LEFT: Aintree was still promoting itself in 1963 even though the Grand Prix had gone.

(All courtesy Martin Hadwen, National Motor Racing Archive)

BRANDS HATCH

Location: 7 miles (12km) south of Dartford, Kent.
Constructed: 1950.
World Championship Grands Prix: 14.

Even the magnificent occasion that was race day suggested the countryside was all around. (Courtesy Linda Carlson)

Paddock Hill Bend

Pilgrim's Rise/ Hailwood Hill

Hawthorn Bend

Portobello Straight/ Derek Minter Straight

Bottom Bend/ Graham Hill Bend

Druids Bend

Hawthorn Hill

Graham Hill

Bottom Straight

Pilgrim's Drop

Westfield Bend

Cooper Straight

Stirling's Bend

Dingle Dell

Start/finish

Dingle Dell Corner

South Bank Bend/ Surtees

Brabham Straight

Clearways

'There is hardly any respite, even down the main straight itself'

Graham Hill

Clark Curve

The contrasts were sharply drawn and always had been since some cyclists, moving down the road from London to Folkestone in 1926, noticed a natural bowl and thought it would be ideal for racing. The land was part of a farm called Brands Hatch, it had tracks made by the tractors, and the cyclists sought out the farmer. Permission was given. The bike riders followed two years later and a rough circuit measuring three-quarters of a mile followed that.

Brands Hatch was rural England, pastureland merging into grassland, copses of trees merging into heavy woodland with the natural bowl forming its heart. If the cyclists hadn't stopped, only sheep, cattle, wood merchants, and the farmer in Brands Hatch Farm would ever have known it. The slumber of centuries would always have held it.

The circuit never quite lost that feel, even when 100,000 gathered in the arc of grandstands facing the natural bowl to watch the Grands Prix and on those days the contrast was even more sharply drawn. On those days, the engines yearning, the circuit felt like the centre of the world and was *still* somehow the pastureland and the woodland.

It was quite a circuit, too…

The major step towards a real circuit happened in 1947 when Brands Hatch Stadium Limited was formed, initially for bike racing. John Surtees would remember:[1] 'when I was just 13 I had my first rides on a [Wolf] single-gear bike round Brands Hatch, on the cinder path which was used for public access on the outside of the grass circuit. This was at a time when [my father] was visiting Brands Hatch quite frequently, representing the riders in their dispute with the circuit owners and the ACU [Auto Cycle Union, the rule-making body] over the condition of the track.'

A proper surface was laid in 1950, creating a mile-long oval track. Surtees rode in 'the opening event on the newly resurfaced Brands Hatch track, running in an anticlockwise direction'.

That April cars raced on it but it was only really suitable for Formula 3, and Stirling Moss competed in that. 'I won five races in a day at Brands Hatch on 25 June.'[2]

The circuit was getting serious and in 1953 it was widened and the Druids loop included to give it a distance of 1.2 miles,

pits built, banks for spectators excavated. The races now went clockwise. There was also a racing school and, much later, the annual Formula Ford Festival would find a home at the circuit.

Graham Hill was an enthusiastic rower but in the autumn of 1953 someone 'threw a magazine across the desk to me and said, "Here, look at this, you ought to do this!" And there was an advertisement saying you could drive a Formula 3 car at Brands Hatch for five shillings per lap. Well, I didn't know what a Formula 3 car was, but as I had just learnt to drive a car I thought I would like to have a go. So the next afternoon I arrived at the racing drivers' school at Brands Hatch in my Morris – while most of my fellow pupils were arriving in their Healey sports cars and the like, complete with brand-new goggles, helmets, special shoes and so on. I was a bit green and I remember that I had to borrow a helmet as I had come without one. I had decided to have a quid's worth, which was four laps.'[3]

By 1956 the circuit was hosting Formula 2 races and John Webb, a press officer, became a leading figure.

In 1958 a driver from the Borders thought he'd like to buy a Formula 2 Lotus and contacted Colin Chapman, adding that he'd like a friend to try one too. Chapman agreed and was having a test session at Brands Hatch, which was how that October the friend – Jim Clark – first drove a racing car. 'The circuit was the old one which included *Druids* but not the new Grand Prix part.'[4]

The 2.6-mile (4.2km) Grand Prix circuit, now embracing the great loop into the woodland, was built in 1959. That allowed a major race meeting to be held in August 1960. A year later

Grovewood Securities bought the circuit and a company called Motor Racing Developments managed it. Webb had a seat on the board and pushed hard to get the British Grand Prix, which he did in 1964. It would alternate with Silverstone.

Several deaths, notably that of Jo Siffert in 1971, led to major safety improvements. Siffert's BRM crashed in the Race of Champions and he was burned to death.

The circuit became a major international centre of motor sport, regularly staging the Race of Champions, World Sports Cars, Formula 3000, and the Superbike World Championship.

The last Grand Prix was in 1986. That year a businessman and driver, John Foulston, bought the circuit but was killed testing an IndyCar at Silverstone. His daughter Nicola eventually ran it. The circuit was slowed with a chicane at *Dingle Dell* and other corners tightened.

There would be no more Grands Prix, although in a Formula 3000 race in 1988 Johnny Herbert crashed in *Pilgrim's Drop*, his Jordan thrashing from Armco to Armco in a scene from hell. He recovered to have a Grand Prix career but the invincibility he had felt was gone forever.

Nicola Foulston made an attempt to get the British Grand Prix but sold the circuit to a company who couldn't get planning permission for the work to bring it up to Grand Prix standard. A CART race, however, was held there in 2003. Former driver Jonathan Palmer bought the circuit in 2004.

The impressive panorama had always been essentially the same. This is 1964, with Mike Spence (Lotus) moving towards ninth place. (LAT)

Brands Hatch always retained a certain rural charm, reflecting its origins – even Paddock Hill Bend with its adverse camber. *(All courtesy David Corbishley).*

COCKPIT VIEW

Graham Hill, who drove in the Grand Prix five times:

'Brands Hatch is a pretty gruelling course and with six speeds in our gearbox we were kept very busy. There is hardly any respite, even down the main straight itself there is a kink about a third of the way along and then there is a sharp drop with a very bad dip at the bottom – and then you have to start braking for the next corner. The corners are all different from each other and the course is quite hilly.

'It is a most enjoyable track to drive on and the crowd is always very enthusiastic. They get particularly good viewing at Brands Hatch; the area of the pits and the main grandstand is a natural amphitheatre in a valley in the Kentish hills. The hills provide a perfect viewpoint for people to see any part of the track they wish and they can see a lot of it sitting in their own cars. It has always been a great favourite with the motor racing enthusiasts.'[5]

As late as the 1970s the pits and paddock were basic. (Both courtesy David Corbishley)

EYEWITNESS

Linda Carlson, Upstate New York:

'In 1978, my first full year as a Travel Agent, I was able to arrange for [husband] Gary and I to take a long-awaited trip to the UK. We were going over to visit friends and to hit many of the tourist sites that Anglophile Yanks long to see on a trip to Britain.

'Our main objective, however, was to attend the British Grand Prix. If our trip had fallen on an odd-numbered year Silverstone would have been our destination. Nothing against Silverstone, but we were happy that "our" race was to be at Brands Hatch. Having followed Formula 1 from the other side of the pond for so many years the great circuits of Europe were magic names to us: Spa, the Nürburgring, Zandvoort, Monza, Brands Hatch.

'My friends had a stand at Brands that weekend selling Clay Regazzoni's clothing line and accessories. As a bonus to that first experience I was able to help out at the stand through the race weekend.

'In order to help set up the stand and sort the merchandise we first set eyes

on Brands Hatch the Thursday before the Grand Prix when the track was relatively deserted.

'Up to that point our only live Grand Prix experiences had come from Mosport and Watkins Glen. Both were challenging tracks with a genuine beauty about them but Brands had such a sense of established permanence and real visual impact. On that July morning in 1978 I never could have imagined that its days as a Grand Prix circuit were numbered.

'There were the wonderful place names (names, not numbers!): *Hawthorn Bend, Dingle Dell, Stirling's, Clearways, Paddock Hill Bend, Hailwood Rise, Druids* – names we had heard so many times through the years and now here they were, in front of us.

'The natural bowl-like amphitheatre around the front straight area, hiking out to *Hawthorn* and *Westfield*, standing at *Hailwood* watching the cars climb the rise to enter *Druids* and around: what a fantastic spectator circuit!

'That rise from *Paddock* to *Druids* was a favourite place to stand. With the steep elevation change and the bright yellow

Well, where did you think the racing cars got their fuel from? (Courtesy Linda Carlson)

And this is the other way sponsors Shell made their presence felt. (Courtesy David Corbishley)

Dunlop sign on the bridge crossing the top of the rise, it was a natural picture-taking spot. Hard not to get a good shot there.

'Everywhere we looked, even the petrol station, was a pleasant sight with the white-haired gent in his white coat who seemed to be patiently awaiting the arrival of someone to serve. There didn't seem to be a bad view in the place. I fell instantly in love with it.'

MEMORIES AND MILESTONES

1964 Brands 'set a standard of pomp and ceremony for which they would become justifiably famous. The bands of the Royal Dragoons and the 1st Battalion Royal Scots marched and played. A demonstration of battle tactics involving armoured cars, helicopters, the troops of Eastern Command and the Royal Artillery gunners startled the unwary when a 25-pounder let rip just by the entrance to the tunnel. Then followed a cavalcade of historic army vehicles. Finally, a fanfare by the trumpeters of the Royal Artillery greeted the arrival of the Formula 1 cars. Another innovation was the use of a dummy grid, where the cars would be fired up before rolling forward on to the grid proper, pausing briefly to take the start itself.'[6] Clark had pole, led all the 80 laps and beat Graham Hill (BRM) by 2.8 seconds. Fastest lap: Clark 96.6mph/155.4kph.

1966 The new 3-litre Formula was known as 'the Return of Power'. In 1964 Clark (Lotus) had taken pole at 97.2mph/156.5kph. Jack Brabham (Brabham) took it now with 100.9mph/162.4kph. The race was devalued because Ferrari didn't go. Brabham beat team-mate Denny Hulme by 9.6 seconds. Fastest lap: Brabham 98.4mph (+1.8)/158.3kph (+2.9).

1968 Graham Hill (Lotus) took pole for what would be a British Grand Prix of sadness: the first without Clark. Jackie Oliver in the other Lotus led from the front row, Hill overtook him on lap 4 but had mechanical problems. Oliver led again (laps 27 to 43) then he had mechanical problems, opening the race to Jo Siffert (Lotus), who beat Chris Amon (Ferrari) by 4.4 seconds. Fastest lap: Siffert 106.4mph (+8.0)/171.2kph (+12.9).

1970 Brabham (Brabham) overtook Jochen Rindt (Lotus), pole, at *South Bank* bend – also known as *Surtees* – with 11 laps left, and powered away. Into the final lap he led by 14 seconds but, into *Clearways*, Rindt appeared in the lead with Brabham behind – he'd run out of fuel at *Stirling's Bend*. Rindt beat him by 32.9 seconds. Fastest lap: Brabham 111.1mph (+4.7)/178.7kph (+7.5).

1972 Jacky Ickx (Ferrari) took pole. John Player sponsored the race and insisted it was named after them. While Emerson Fittipaldi (Lotus) was winning Graham Hill (Brabham) was crashing, bringing one of his great comments: 'From a gentleman to a twit in a tenth of a second.' Fittipaldi beat Jackie Stewart (Tyrrell) by 4.1 seconds. Fastest lap: Stewart 113.6mph (+2.5)/182.8kph (+4.1).

1974 Lauda (Ferrari) took pole although Ronnie Peterson (Lotus) did the same time (1m 19.7s) – Lauda did his first. Lauda led to lap 69 of the 75 when a puncture slowed him and Jody Scheckter (Tyrrell) went by, beating Fittipaldi (McLaren) by 15.3 seconds. Fastest lap: Lauda 117.6mph (+4.0)/189.3kph (+6.5).

Speed increase 1964–74: 21.0mph/33.9kph.

South Bank *alterations*.

Jackie Stewart taking the Tyrrell to second place in 1972. (Courtesy David Corbishley)

The view that defined Brands Hatch and proved an intimate vantage point for spectators: the rise to Druids, the descent from it. This is Jean-Pierre Jabouille (Renault) in 1978. (Courtesy Linda Carlson)

1976 Niki Lauda (Ferrari) took pole. James Hunt's Championship year and the race became its most controversial. From the start a tremendous crash into and through *Paddock Hill Bend* left debris across the track. A restart was ordered

The perils of Paddock Hill Bend, demonstrated by Clay Regazzoni (Ferrari) in 1976 – creating mayhem and, later, nearly a riot. (LAT)

and Hunt, Clay Regazzoni (Ferrari), and Jacques Laffite (Ligier) had to take it in their spare cars. The officials tried to exclude Hunt and the crowd turned nasty. Hunt drove, beat Lauda by 52.0 seconds and, under Ferrari protest, 'lost' it in the autumn. Fastest lap: Lauda 117.8mph/189.5kph.
1978 Ronnie Peterson (Lotus) pole. A crowd of 84,000 watched team-mate Mario Andretti (Lotus) lead, then Jody Scheckter's Wolf, then Lauda's Brabham, before Carlos Reutemann (Ferrari) seized it on lap 60 of the 76 and held it to the end, beating Lauda by 2.2 seconds. Fastest lap: Lauda 119.7mph (+1.9)/192.7kph (+3.2).
1980 In testing three weeks before the race both Alan Jones (Williams) and

Didier Pironi (Ligier) destroyed Peterson's 1978 pole time, 1 minute 16.8 seconds. Jones did 1 minute 12.2 seconds, Pironi a tenth quicker. Pironi took pole. Ground effects had come, making *Paddock Hill Bend* a glorious and frightening sight. Pironi led from Laffite in the other Ligier but both had tyre failures and Jones beat Nelson Piquet (Brabham) by 11.0 seconds. Fastest lap: Pironi 130.0mph (+10.3)/209.3kph (+16.6).
1982 Keke Rosberg (Williams) took pole for the wonderfully notorious race when the little Toleman team fuelled their driver Derek Warwick light to make an impression on television, which they did when Warwick overtook Pironi's Ferrari into *Paddock Hill Bend*. He ran out of fuel after 41 laps. Lauda (McLaren) beat Pironi by 25.7 seconds. Fastest lap: Brian Henton (Tyrrell) 128.9mph (-1.1)/207.4kph (-1.9).
1983 Elio de Angelis (Lotus) took pole for the race, dubbed the Grand Prix of Europe because the New York Grand Prix was cancelled after planning problems. Nelson Piquet (Brabham) beat Prost (Renault) by 6.5 seconds. Fastest lap: Mansell (Lotus) 126.6mph (-2.3)/203.7kph (-3.7).
1984 Johnny Cecotto (Toleman) crashed in the first untimed session, injuring his legs so badly that his Grand Prix career ended. Piquet (Brabham) took pole. Lauda (McLaren) beat Warwick (Renault) by 42.1

FACTS OF THE MATTER

2.650m/4.265km circuit

Year	Winner
1964	J. Clark (Lotus)
1966	J. Brabham (Brabham)
1968	J. Siffert (Lotus)
1970	J. Rindt (Lotus)
1972	E. Fittipaldi (Lotus)
1974	J. Scheckter (Tyrrell)
Fastest pole	N. Lauda (Ferrari) 1974
	(119.7mph/192.6kph)
Fastest lap	N. Lauda 1974
	(117.6mph/189.3kph)

South Bank alterations, 2.614m/4.207km circuit

1976	N. Lauda (Ferrari)
1978	C. Reutemann (Ferrari)
1980	A. Jones (Williams)
1982	N. Lauda (McLaren)
1983*	N. Piquet (Brabham)
1984	N. Lauda (McLaren)
1985*	N. Mansell (Williams)
1986	N. Mansell (Williams)
Fastest pole	N. Piquet (Williams) 1986
	(140.5mph/226.2kph)
Fastest lap	N. Mansell (Williams) 1986
	(135.2mph/217.6kph)

* European Grand Prix.

seconds, and a certain Ayrton Senna in the other Toleman came third. Fastest lap: Lauda 128.6mph (+2.0)/206.9kph (+3.2). **1985** Senna (Lotus) took pole for the Grand Prix of Europe again. For the British, this was a deeply significant race because Nigel Mansell (Williams) won it, the first of his career and opening the way for him to become a leading driver. He beat Senna (Lotus) by 21.3 seconds. Fastest lap: Jacques Laffite (Ligier) 131.6mph (+3.0)/211.7kph (+4.8). **1986** Some 120,000 people watched a crash at the start. Mansell (Williams) wasn't involved but his driveshaft failed immediately and for the restart he had to take the spare, set up for team-mate and No1 driver Piquet. Mansell beat Piquet, pole, by 5.5 seconds amid extraordinary emotions. Fastest lap: Mansell 135.2mph (+3.6)/217.6kph (+5.9).

Speed increase 1976–86: 17.4mph/28.1kph.

Footnotes
[1] *World Champion*, Surtees. [2] *My Cars, My Career*, Moss. [3] *Life at the Limit*, Hill. [4] *At the Wheel*, Clark. [5] Hill, *ibid*. [6] *British Grand Prix*, Hamilton.

JOHN PLAYER GRAND PRIX
organised by the Royal Automobile Club
Brands Hatch,
Nr. Dartford, Kent
Saturday, 20th July, 1974.

In assembling officials for this event I am hoping that I will be able to look forward to your help as a OBSERVER

Unless otherwise notified, officials will be asked to be on duty from 9.00 a.m. to 6.00 p.m. on all three days of this meeting i.e. Thursday 18th July, Friday 19th July and Saturday 20th July, marshals who can assist on all three days will be given preference.

R. N. Eason Gibson,
Secretary of the Meeting

PLEASE RETURN IMMEDIATELY

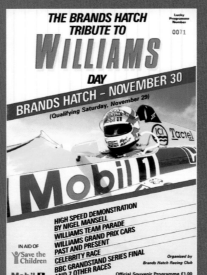

In 1986 the Williams were so successful (Mansell second in the Championship, Nelson Piquet third, the Constructors' won by 45 points from McLaren) that they were given their own tribute day. *(Courtesy Martin Hadwen, National Motor Racing Archive)*

And here are the people we met at Clermont-Ferrand, ready to film another episode. *(Courtesy Martin Hadwen, National Motor Racing Archive)*

GREAT BRITAIN

DONINGTON

Location: 8 miles (13km) south-east of Derby.
Constructed: 1933.
World Championship Grands Prix: 1.

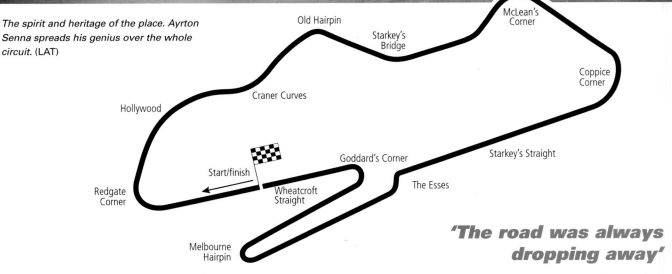

The spirit and heritage of the place. Ayrton Senna spreads his genius over the whole circuit. (LAT)

Old Hairpin

Starkey's Bridge

McLean's Corner

Coppice Corner

Craner Curves

Hollywood

Starkey's Straight

Redgate Corner

Goddard's Corner

The Esses

Start/finish

Wheatcroft Straight

Melbourne Hairpin

'The road was always dropping away'

Johnny Herbert

A single World Championship round hardly suggests that a sense of history hung heavy over Donington, but it did. There are special reasons. The track was built in 1933 through wooded countryside beside the stately pile of Donington Hall and, in 1937 and 1938, hosted two Grands Prix which, with the shadows of war approaching, pitted the good chaps of England in little sit-up-and-beg cars against Mercedes and Auto Unions of futuristic design and immense power.

The track featured a long descent to a U-turn – *Melbourne* corner – in what really was a field with the ascent running parallel. At the top of that the cars breasted a hump and the Germans were so powerful that they were airborne, all four wheels off the ground.

The 1937 race was won by Bernd Rosemeyer (Auto Union), one of the great drivers, and the 1938 race won by Tazio Nuvolari in another Auto Union. Many insist Nuvolari remains *the* greatest driver of all.

Donington was used for military storage during the Second World War and after it a local builder and racing enthusiast, the late Tom Wheatcroft, bought it, rebuilt the circuit, and campaigned for a Grand Prix. He finally got one, the European race, in 1993.

Anyone wandering to the rear of the paddock could see, suddenly spread before them, the parallel tracks and *Melbourne* corner, long disused but still there – something almost alive from another time.

If you go to Donington you'll see why history hangs heavy. The offices are in a stone house that you can see in film of the 1937 and 1938 races, cars passing just in front and straw bales protecting it, or protecting them. There's a museum where Wheatcroft assembled a magnificent collection of racing cars. Outside there's a statue of Senna and Juan Manuel Fangio standing together on a celestial podium, reaching out to clasp hands.

Nearby there's a memorial stone to Rosemeyer and a rosebush which, so the legend says, was originally part of a bouquet given to Nuvolari when he won. Someone planted one of the roses, it grew and was transplanted to Donington.

That single World Championship race rewarded Wheatcroft so richly and cost him so dear.

The circuit even obtained the rights to stage the British Grand Prix from 2010, but the company behind it ran into financial difficulties and the race went from them.

COCKPIT VIEW

Johnny Herbert, Lotus, 1993:

'For everything else, from Formula Ford to Formula Three – I never did Formula 3000 there – it was a good track and you could have some good races on it, but once you got Formula 1 you didn't have many opportunities, if any, to overtake. That was always its problem.

'The Donington everybody remembers is obviously the 1993 Grand Prix with Ayrton, and that was because it was wet. We know through the history of Formula 1 that when it is wet you always get more interesting races. A lot of people were staying out of Ayrton's way but that was the aura he had, what he was able to achieve.

'That weekend was interesting because, in the wet, it did bring opportunities to overtake. I think Alain [Prost] did about seven pit stops – drivers kept coming in thinking it was going to dry and when they came out it started to rain again, so they had to come back in and …

'I don't remember so many unscheduled pit stops happening *ever*, well, not in my time at least. In the dry, Donington was fairly easy, to be honest, but in that wet … the road was always dropping away from you through *Redgate*, then the right as you go down, then the left into the *Old Hairpin*. That was hellishly tricky and in the wet you had to get the car right. You needed the comfort factor – security and feedback – from the car to go through it on the edge although in a controlled way.

'It was one of those circuits where the racing line is the outside: you always went round the outside everywhere, you never actually went on to the [orthodox] racing line during the race. Brands Hatch used to be another one, old Silverstone used to be the same. You always went round the outside of the *Old Hairpin* and *Redgate*.

'It was a good track but I wouldn't class it as one of the most demanding.'

EYEWITNESS

Dave Fern, Press Officer:

'The news that after years of trying we finally had a Grand Prix, broke on the eve of the RAC Rally, where I was penning a preview for the *Daily Express*, but that was thrown out of the window with growing demands for the Donington story.

'For the next four months or so life was never the same for the small team of which I was proud to be a part – I reckon it was the least there has ever been to put together such a race – worked around the clock to make it happen.

'The dream was finally reality, albeit on the wettest Easter Sunday in memory – the rain lashed down in torrents but nothing was going to spoil the experience. There was Lady Di watching from a pit lane suite, gazing wistfully down towards what the gossip columnists reported as one of her beaux!

'Tom Wheatcroft took to his circuit in a pre-war Mercedes similar to those that raced in the great events of 1937 and 1938, only to spin off at the *Old Hairpin*, fortunately neither he nor the car suffering more than wounded pride. Adding to the drama he was taken ill but after an epic race watched by far too few people he was back to his old self to present the winner's trophy.

'The critics who reckoned the circuit was not wide enough to overtake on were silenced, possibly drowned, on the opening couple of laps as I stood, drenched to the skin, watching the amazing Ayrton Senna come through to take the lead, and then the victory, before escorting him to the media conference.

'For me then, it was case of ensuring the world's media had the facilities to file their stories and pictures, and, for those wanting a bit more, an interview with Wheatcroft who shook them by admitting he had lost more than £2 million on the day. "But lads, I've had my race and it was worth every penny," he explained to a stunned group of journalists from the national newspapers.

'It had been an epic day in every sense and sadly, it seems, not to be repeated.'

Rubens Barrichello (Jordan) rode the storm almost as well as Senna and got up to second before the fuel pressure stopped him. (LAT)

Sight just about unseen: Alain Prost leads from Williams team-mate Damon Hill with Karl Wendlinger (Sauber) between them – and the yellow of Senna's helmet just glimpsed behind Wendlinger. (LAT)

MEMORIES AND MILESTONES

1993 The grid contained four men who had been or would be World Champions – Ayrton Senna (McLaren), Damon Hill and Alain Prost (Williams), and Michael Schumacher (Benetton). Between them they'd win it 15 times.

Senna was about to create a masterpiece of such intensity on an afternoon of wild, ever-changing weather that many insist *he* remains the greatest driver of all. The sodden track meant that his Ford Cosworth engine was not at a disadvantage against the Williamses with their Renault engines.

Prost had pole from Hill, Senna on the second row. In the jostling start Senna

Something of the feeling of a park would always linger at Donington, although there were few reminders it had been a military depot during the war.
(Courtesy Andrew Clegg)

was forced to put two wheels off the track and ran fifth as the necklace of cars strung out towards the descending curves to the *Old Hairpin*. Nuvolari had passed this way. Senna caught Schumacher quickly and went inside him. Senna caught Karl Wendlinger (Sauber) quickly and went outside him, *a move that could not be done*. They travelled through the *Old Hairpin* and up to McLean's corner, a right. Senna went inside Hill. They travelled on, Senna gaining on Prost, who had a traditional dislike of driving in the wet. Senna caught him by the time they reached the left-right esses. Senna swept past, Prost choosing not to resist.

Senna crossed the line to complete the opening lap and Jo Ramirez, senior McLaren team member, watched, assuming the Williamses had got the tyres wrong and were on dries. They were on wets like everyone else. Senna had a lead, Ramirez concluded, *that could not be done*.

Senna drove away quite alone into his own mythology: at one point he led by a full lap, set fastest lap using the pit lane, and beat Hill by 1 minute 23.1 seconds, nobody else on the same lap.

The heritage of Donington: the mighty Mercedes and Audis came in 1937 and 1938 and crushed all opposition.

FACTS OF THE MATTER

2.500m/4.023km circuit

Year	Winner
1993	A. Senna (McLaren)
Pole	A. Prost (Williams)
	(127.7mph/205.6kph)
Fastest lap	A. Senna (115.3mph/185.6kph)

Location: 3 miles (2km) south of Towcester, Northants.
Constructed: 1948.
World Championship Grands Prix: 42.

Mansell Mania, centred on Silverstone, was an important chapter in the very English place – Mansell, from Birmingham, rousing base emotions from a huge English gathering. Here he wins the 1987 race. (ICN U.K. Bureau)

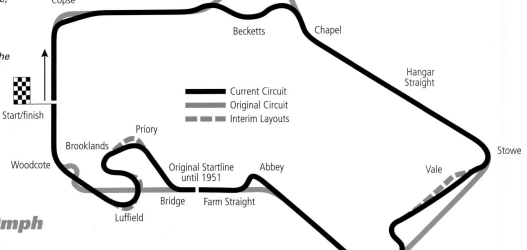

Copse
Maggotts
Becketts
Chapel
Hangar Straight
Start/finish
Priory
Brooklands
Woodcote
Original Startline until 1951
Abbey
Vale
Stowe
Bridge
Farm Straight
Luffield
Club

━━━ Current Circuit
━━━ Original Circuit
╍╍╍ Interim Layouts

'You're up to 200mph before Becketts'

Lewis Hamilton

Silverstone is a curious place because so much has happened since the World Championship began there in 1950, and yet it remains somehow a wartime airbase with a circuit superimposed on it. Perhaps that's because it's so flat and perhaps it's because memories linger of when the facilities for drivers, teams, and the paying public were so neglected. People get emotional *at* Silverstone but not emotional *about* Silverstone. Even when they're trying to save it, they're doing it because they want the British Grand Prix to survive, not because emotion dictates Silverstone.

The fact that its facilities have been dramatically transformed in the last ten years has not prevented it being a piece on a – here's that word again – curious boardgame, with Bernie Ecclestone, for reasons lost on everyone else, taking the British Grand Prix to Donington for ever and a day and, when Donington's unfinanced plans collapsed, playing the boardgame with Silverstone again.

It was never going to get government subsidy and without that was never going to rival the newer tracks being build in the Middle and Far East. Neither were Monza and Imola, the Nürburgring and Hockenheim, Budapest, Spa, or São Paulo, so why the constant goading of Silverstone and not them? That's a story for another book – about sports politics, sports money, and sporting personal enmity – but Silverstone itself, the teams based in the area around it, the companies who supplied them, and the British public, frankly deserved better.

The bomber base opened in 1943 and, lying deserted after the war, seemed ideal for motor racing. Evidently a local racer and friends staged an event in 1947 over a two-mile circuit, during which the local racer struck a sheep, doing it and his car no good.[1]

The RAC, who run the sport in Britain, came to investigate possibilities. They found 'the place had the forlorn look familiar to abandoned aerodromes of greater vintage: rotting wood, faded paintwork, weeds and grass sprouting freely in the concrete runways, the odd broken pane of glass to allow the chill wind access to deserted buildings and hangars.

Everywhere had a layer of dust and grit. It was clearly a place no-one had been sorry to leave.'

This may seem primitive now but the war had only been over for three years; Britain was an austere place, still ruled by rationing, and people took whatever pleasure they could where they could. More than that, British motor sport needed a focal point, a centre, and the obvious candidates were all unavailable for anything as serious as a Grand Prix. Donington had become a huge military vehicle storage depot, the banked Brooklands had been sold, Crystal Palace lay in

The royal stand but no standing on ceremony: The Queen waits for the cars to come by in the first World Championship round of all, 1950. (LAT)

disrepair, and Brands Hatch was in no sense ready.

If Silverstone didn't look ideal it was the best solution. The RAC contacted the Air Ministry, who owned it, and despite the fact that it was now a cereal farm and a piggery 'the RAC employed farmer James Wilson Brown to create the first Grand Prix circuit at the site and gave him just two months to build it.'[2]

The airbase had a perimeter road but if that became the track it would offer only medium-speed corners, so the runways were incorporated, linked by hairpins and marked out by straw bales.

The circuit created then has a resonance today, in shape and names. The pits and paddock were near the access to the circuit, midway between *Abbey* and *Woodcote*. *Abbey* was named for Luffield Abbey Farm, itself taking its name from the ruins of Luffield Priory close by. The start/finish was nearer *Abbey*.

Woodcote was named for the RAC's country club at Woodcote Park in Surrey. This was the perimeter road and it flowed on to *Copse* corner, named for the Seven Copses Wood that was nearby.

At *Copse* it turned hard right on to one of the old runways, named for the British pre-war driver Dick Seaman. Halfway down it turned hard left on to another of the runways, bringing the cars to the perimeter road and *Maggotts* corner, named for Maggotts Moor, also nearby. On the perimeter road it had a short straight to *Becketts* corner, named for the ruins of a chapel of St Thomas a' Becket.

It went along *Hangar Straight*, named for two hangars, to *Stowe* corner, named for a local school, and it turned hard right on to the other end of *Seaman Straight* then hard left to *Club* corner, named for the RAC Club, London. It ran through *Abbey* to the start/finish.[3]

The British Grand Prix was held on 2 October 1948 and Luigi Villoresi won it from Alberto Ascari, both driving Maseratis. The 1949 race was held in May and won by Emanuel de Graffenried in a Maserati.

It prepared the way for 1950 and the start of the Championship itself.

In 1949 the runways were abandoned and the perimeter road used with a chicane at *Club*. The circuit had, in fact, assumed its modern shape. In 1952 new pits were built after *Woodcote* and in 1975 a chicane added there. It became a challenge because, although it was designed to slow speeds, it was approached fast, and bravery (or folly) dictated what happened next.

Between the Grands Prix in 1990 and 1991 the new complex at *Luffield* was added. As part of a general tightening of safety after Ayrton Senna's death at Imola in 1994, the entry into *Stowe* corner from *Hangar Straight* – which had been spectacularly fast – was altered and the kink at *Abbey* made into a chicane.

Silverstone, however, remained fast and in 1985 Keke Rosberg (Williams) was able to lap it at an average of 160mph (259kph).

COCKPIT VIEW

Lewis Hamilton, McLaren, 2009:

'There are so many highlights around here: you're doing almost 190mph into *Copse*, you downshift one gear and briefly lift – no brakes – as the car bounces around under huge G-forces. You're up to 200mph before *Becketts* – there are four parts: the first two are flat-out, then it's down one gear for the left-hander before going down another gear for the right-hander that bends out on to the *Hangar Straight*. Because you're not braking, you're just pulling huge G at high speed and the car wants to step out all the time. It's probably the most exciting part of the track.

'*Stowe* is another quick corner and then the course starts to tighten up: *Club* is one of the slower corners but the exit opens up and, as you shift up through the gears, the rear is always stepping out. You have to constantly correct the car.

'*Abbey* is a tricky chicane: third gear, you slide through the first left-hander but need to miss the second apex because you're fully on the car. Hit it and you'll suffer an oversteer moment. Every time I went through there last year I could see the crowd jumping up and cheering me on, because other people were spinning.

'*Bridge* is flat but you need to get the car over to the right of the track for *Priory*, which is blind and tricky – it's a corner I always struggle with, for some reason. You're early on the brakes and turn-in for *Priory*, where it's easy to spin the car and end up in the gravel. The bumps on the entry to *Brooklands* unsettle the car but it's vital to get a good exit; you take all the kerb and some of the grass, to get up to maximum speed for the start/finish straight.'[4]

In 1988 Lotus were still a big name and so was former Champion Nelson Piquet, who said how much he liked the circuit. (Courtesy Camel)

EYEWITNESS

Roger Chapman, financial adviser, 1999:

'Silverstone is one of the most dull, boring and exciting places I have ever been.

'I arrived early one overcast July Sunday morning when everyone still appeared to be asleep and I felt as though I should be! Gradually the weather improved and the crowds increased, it began to feel like a day at any windswept boot market on an ancient airfield, with merchandisers and fast food vendors as far as the eye could see.

'The Formula 1 cars I had expected were nowhere to be seen, and, even when I eventually found the grandstand that I had arranged to view one of the greatest spectacles on earth from, there was still nothing apart from the odd saloon car touring round the circuit.

'Then it happened: the first Formula 1 cars howled on to *Hangar Straight* and my whole body started to tingle with adrenaline like a petrol-head junkie. This was a first for me and I could not believe the sound or the awesome braking ability of these cars. My only previous experience had been to watch the race on television. This was something very different.

'I had just experienced my first morning warm-up and my opinion of Silverstone had already been changed dramatically. The first lap of the race was even more body-tingling when all the cars appeared together. It was an incredible sight and the engine noise has to be heard to be believed.

'Then Michael Schumacher in the Ferrari went off and we had a clear view of that. He broke his leg.

'Silverstone is one of the few places in the world where you can get close to Formula 1 cars and that is why it is a truly exciting and magical place to be. It has to be experienced. There is no substitute, and if you are a motor sport enthusiast you must go there, if only once, to feel the earth tremble.

'I have been back since to drive high-performance cars, and although I really enjoyed the challenge and the thought that I was driving on the same tarmac as Ayrton Senna – which had great meaning to me – I will never forget my first visit to Silverstone. Like a spectacular firework display, the dull and boring bit is well worth enduring to get to the finale!'

MEMORIES AND MILESTONES

1950 Ferrari didn't come but Alfa Romeo did in force and filled the front row, which was then four cars wide. Giuseppe Farina took pole and, in front of the King and Queen, moved into an immediate lead. The Alfas swapped the lead, but deep into the race Juan Manuel Fangio made a rare mistake and hit a straw bale. It damaged the car enough to force him to retire. Farina beat Luigi Fagioli in another of the Alfas by 2.6 seconds. Fastest lap: Farina 94.0mph/151.3kph.

1951 The Ferraris did come and Froilan González put his on pole, averaging 100mph – which had not been done at the circuit before. Fangio (Alfa Romeo) seized the lead from González on lap 10 and held it to lap 38, when González regained it. He beat Fangio by 52 seconds. Fastest lap: Farina (Alfa Romeo) 100.0mph/160.9kph.

Speed increase 1950–1: 6.0mph/9.6kph.

The pits – of brick, and therefore permanent – and grandstand were built just after Woodcote. *Many corners were reprofiled, slightly increasing the length of the lap.*

Refuelling, 1951. This is Reg Parnell (BRM). Note the complete absence of protection for the pit lane and only straw bales in front of the grandstand opposite. (LAT)

Carlos Reutemann (Brabham) at close quarters in the days when you could get at close quarters. (Courtesy Gareth Rees)

1952 Farina took pole from Ferrari team-mate Alberto Ascari and 31 cars came to the grid, among them Stirling Moss (ERA). Ascari led all 85 laps and beat Piero Taruffi (Ferrari) by a lap. Fastest lap: Ascari 94.1mph/151.4kph.

1953 Ascari (Ferrari) took pole and duelled with González (Maserati) until he was black-flagged for dropping oil. After 'a stormy scene at the pits'[4] González continued, but Ascari was long gone. He led all 90 laps and beat Fangio (Maserati) by one minute exactly. Fastest lap: Ascari and González 95.8mph (+1.7)/154.2kph (+2.8).

1954 Fangio (Mercedes) took pole, González (Ferrari) next to him. Some 90,000 watched González take the

By 1963 the circuit had evolved to the point where its layout feels almost familiar to the modern eye – and by now it had slightly more protection with a pitlane wall – even glimpsed through the smokescreen laid by Innes Ireland's BRM. (LAT)

lead and Fangio began striking the oil drums that lined the circuit, because the wheels on the Mercedes were enclosed, making judgement of the corners difficult. González beat Hawthorn (Ferrari) by 1 minute 10 seconds. Fastest lap: Ascari (Maserati)/Jean Behra (Gordini)/Fangio (Mercedes)/González/Hawthorn/Onofre Marimón (Maserati)/Stirling Moss (Maserati) 95.8mph/154.2kph (no change).

1956 Moss (Maserati) took pole but Hawthorn (BRM) led to lap 15, when Moss overtook him at *Copse*. Moss was to suffer several mechanical problems, and Fangio (Ferrari) beat Alfonso de Portago/Peter Collins (who shared a Ferrari) by a lap. Fastest lap: Moss 102.1mph (+6.3)/164.3kph (+10.1).

1958 Moss in the very British Vanwall took pole but Collins, from the second row, had the lead by *Becketts* and never lost it across the 75 laps. He beat Ferrari team-mate Hawthorn by 24.2 seconds. Fastest lap: Hawthorn 104.5mph (+2.4)/168.2kph (+3.9).

1960 Jack Brabham (Cooper) took pole averaging 111mph/179kph, and a decade before Farina had done 94mph. A big difference. Farina did the lap in 1 minute 58.0 seconds, Brabham 1 minute 34.6. Brabham led, Graham Hill (BRM) caught and overtook him on lap 55 but with seven laps left spun at *Copse*. Brabham beat John Surtees (Lotus) by 49.6 seconds. Fastest lap: Graham Hill 111.6mph (+7.1)/179.6kph (+11.4).

1963 Jim Clark (Lotus) took pole but 100,000 saw him make a bad start so that across the opening lap Brabham (Brabham), Dan Gurney (Brabham), Bruce McLaren (Cooper), and Graham Hill (BRM) were ahead. Clark overtook Hill and McLaren on lap 2, Gurney on

lap 3, and Brabham on lap 4. He beat Surtees (Ferrari) by 25.8 seconds. Fastest lap: John Surtees (Ferrari) 109.8mph (-1.8)/176.6kph (-3.0).

1965 Clark (Lotus), pole, led all 80 laps to beat Graham Hill (BRM) by 3.2 seconds, although deep into the race his engine started cutting out. He managed to keep it going. Fastest lap: Graham Hill 114.3mph (+4.5)/183.9kph (+7.3).

1967 Clark took pole (of course) from Lotus team-mate Graham Hill. Clark led to lap 25 when Hill went by, but on lap 55 he had a suspension failure. Clark beat Denny Hulme (Brabham) by 12.8 seconds. Fastest lap: Hulme 121.1mph (+6.8)/194.9kph (+11.0).

1969 Jochen Rindt (Lotus) took pole from Jackie Stewart (Matra) and at the end of the first lap they'd pulled three seconds clear of the rest. Rindt led to lap 6 when Stewart outbraked him at *Stowe*. Rindt retook him on lap 16 and led to lap 61 but had to pit with an aerofoil problem. Stewart beat Jacky Ickx (Brabham) by one lap. Fastest lap: Stewart 129.6mph (+8.5)/208.6kph (+13.7).

1971 The Stewart era succeeded that of Clark. Clay Regazzoni (Ferrari) took pole, the average speed now 134mph/217kph, and led for three laps before Stewart (Tyrrell) outbraked him at *Stowe* and stole down the inside. He beat Ronnie Peterson (March) by 36.1 seconds. Fastest lap: Stewart 131.9mph (+2.3)/212.2kph (+3.6).

1973 Jody Scheckter (McLaren) was running fourth at the end of the opening lap and at *Woodcote* lost control, spun across the track, and bounced off the pit wall. That was in front of the oncoming traffic and – braking, thrashing, crashing – nine cars were involved. Ronnie Peterson (Lotus), pole, led from the restart before Peter Revson (McLaren) went past and won by 2.8 seconds. Fastest lap: James Hunt (March) 134.1mph (+2.2)/215.7kph (+3.5).

Speed increase 1952–73: 40.0mph/64.3kph.

The new chicane at Woodcote was in place, forced by the crash of '73 and events at the Spanish Grand Prix in April (see Montjuïc Park). It was not universally popular with the drivers.

1975 Graham Hill announced his retirement. Tom Pryce (Shadow) took pole but the race had seven leaders (including Pryce) as rain fell and a cloudburst stopped it after 56 laps with

Reine Wisell, the Swede who promised much but couldn't deliver. Here in 1971 he battles on through Silverstone's broad acres in the Lotus to finish running but not classified. (Courtesy Julian Nowell)

The most English place. Graham Hill, not so soft-spoken father of Damon, announced his retirement at the 1975 Grand Prix and did a lap of honour. (Courtesy Julian Nowell)

cars spinning everywhere. Only five were actually running at the finish, and although Emerson Fittipaldi (McLaren) had clearly won, Carlos Pace (Brabham) – one lap down – was only placed second after days of protest. Fastest lap: Clay Regazzoni (Ferrari) 130.5mph/210.0kph.

1977 Gilles Villeneuve made his debut and astonished everyone by spinning his McLaren because he was deliberately trying to find its limits. He qualified on the fifth row. James Hunt (McLaren) took pole but John Watson (Brabham) led the first 49 laps before his fuel system began to fail. Hunt swept by to beat Niki Lauda (Ferrari) by 18.3 seconds. Fastest lap: Hunt 132.6mph (+2.1)/213.4kph (+3.4).

1979 The Williams team, after years of poverty, were emerging as race winners, and Alan Jones, pole, who'd been a potent force in the emergence, ought to have been the winner, but after leading for 38 laps his engine failed and team-mate Regazzoni beat René Arnoux (Renault) by 24.2 seconds. Fastest lap: Regazzoni (Williams) 141.9mph (+9.3)/228.3kph (+14.9).

1981 Arnoux (Renault) took pole at 140mph (226kph). Team-mate Prost (Renault) led but his engine failed, Arnoux led but his engine failed, and, amid vast jubilation, Watson brought his McLaren safely home 40.6 seconds ahead of Carlos Reutemann (Williams). Fastest lap: Arnoux 140.6mph (-1.3)/239.2kph (-2.0).

1983 'Professor' Prost (Renault) calculated that the Ferraris of Arnoux, pole, and Patrick Tambay, ahead of him on the grid, would set off at tremendous speed and wear their tyres. By lap 20 he'd gone past them both into the lead to

beat Nelson Piquet (Brabham) by 19.1 seconds. Fastest lap: Prost 142.2mph (+1.6)/228.9kph (+2.6).

1985 Keke Rosberg (Williams) took the pole average to 160mph but Ayrton Senna (Lotus) led until an engine problem halted him, and that opened the race to Prost (McLaren), who beat Championship leader

The opening lap of the 1975 Grand Prix and James Hunt (Hesketh) challenges Niki Lauda (Ferrari) in Becketts, which was then V-shaped. Tom Pryce (Shadow) and Clay Regazzoni in the other Ferrari contest Becketts, too. (Courtesy Julian Nowell)

Michele Alboreto (Ferrari) by a lap. Fastest lap: Prost 151.0mph (+8.8)/243.1kph (+14.1).

Speed increase 1975–85: 20.5mph/33.1kph.

A dog-leg left-right under the bridge slowed the car enough for the Woodcote *chicane to be removed and the original corner restored.*

1987 Clearly Piquet, who led from pole, was going to win from Williams team-mate Mansell, who pitted with 29 laps left when a wheel balance flew off. The wheels changed, he emerged 28 seconds behind Piquet and created a gathering impetus, cutting and cutting the gap

until, with three laps left, he sold Piquet a dummy at the end of *Hangar Straight* and beat him by 1.9 seconds. Fastest lap: Mansell 153.1mph/246.3kph.

1988 A wet race and Berger (Ferrari) led gloriously from pole, but Senna (McLaren) was pacing himself behind, gauging that Berger wouldn't have enough fuel to sustain his pace. Senna took him at *Woodcote* on lap 14 and beat Mansell (Williams) by 23.3 seconds. Prost in the other McLaren retired after 25 laps because he judged the conditions too dangerous. Fastest lap: Mansell 128.3mph/206.5kph (no comparison).

1989 By now the central story of Grand Prix racing had become Senna versus Prost in the McLarens. Senna, pole, led Prost but spun off on lap 12 with a gearbox problem and although Mansell (Williams) tried mightily to catch Prost he couldn't. Prost won it by 19.3 seconds. Fastest lap: Mansell 148.5mph (-4.6)/238.9kph (-7.4).

1990 Mansell (Ferrari) took pole and announced his retirement. Senna (McLaren) led but Mansell powered by at *Bridge* then had a gearbox problem. Now Gerhard Berger (McLaren) led but he had a throttle problem. It was all Prost (Ferrari) needed and he beat Thierry Boutsen (Williams) by 39.0 seconds. 90 Fastest lap: Mansell 150.0mph (+1.5)/241.4kph (+2.5).

Speed decrease 1987–90: 3.1mph/4.9kph.

The complex was added, kinking right from the bridge (now called Bridge*) and looping left through* Priory *to a right-right called* Luffield, *feeding on to the start/ finish straight.*

1991 Mighty Mansell (Williams) led every lap from pole to beat Berger (McLaren) by 42.2 seconds and excite the crowd to the point where he was becoming a national talking point. Hadn't he retired from motor racing the year before? Hardly. Fastest lap: Mansell 135.3mph/217.8kph.

1992 From pole Mansell (Williams) over-excited the crowd, leading every lap from team-mate Riccardo Patrese and beating him by 39.0 seconds. The crowd invaded the track while the cars were still going round in an act of collective madness. Fastest lap: Mansell 141.6mph (+6.3)/227.9kph (+10.1).

1993 Damon Hill (Williams) might have succeeded Mansell (who'd gone to IndyCars) and he led for 41 laps before his engine failed, team-mate Prost, pole, profiting to beat Michael Schumacher (Benetton) by 7.6 seconds. Fastest lap: Hill 141.7mph (+0.1)/228.0kph (+0.1).

The pressure on safety increased, not just from Senna's accident at Imola but because, in May, Pedro Lamy (Lotus) was testing and at Bridge *somersaulted off into what was an area for spectators. Silverstone had plans to improve safety for 1995 but now, at a cost of £2.5 million, these improvements were carried out in time for testing before the French Grand Prix.* Copse, Stowe – *modified because its entry was considered so dangerous – and* Luffield *were reprofiled, and* Abbey Curve

1 **Damon Hill was never going to emulate Mansell Mania because he wasn't that kind of man but he captivated Silverstone in a different way. He won in 1994.**

2 **After that, he'd stir patriotic emotions whatever he did.**

3 **Jackie Stewart and son Paul (left) gave Silverstone a very Scottish flavour, too, as they discuss Hill's sixth place in 1997.**

4 **The most English place with the most English people. Soft-spoken Damon Hill wins the 1994 Grand Prix and Lady Di's presence crowns the occasion.** *(All ICN U.K. Bureau)*

The British Racing Drivers' Club HQ could look (nearly) as exotic as Sepang. Lewis Hamilton (McLaren), Giancarlo Fisichella (Force India) and Mark Webber (Red Bull), 2009. (Vodafone/LAT)

transformed into a chicane. Run-off areas were increased.

1994 Hill (Williams), pole, led to lap 15 when Schumacher (Benetton) got by at the pit stops *but* Schumacher had overtaken on the two parade laps and, after Ferrari had protested a stop'n'go penalty, he came in to serve it, passing the race to Hill who beat Jean Alesi (Ferrari) by 1 minute 08.1 seconds. Fastest lap: Hill 129.9mph/209.0kph.

1995 Hill (Williams), pole, tried to take Schumacher (Benetton) in the Complex with 15 laps left and they crashed. Paradoxically that created an enormously popular victory with Johnny Herbert in the other Benetton beating Alesi (Ferrari) by 16.4 seconds. Fastest lap: Hill 126.0mph/202.8kph.

Speed decrease 1994–5: 3.9mph/6.2kph.

Stowe Corner *was reprofiled, slightly increasing the length of the lap.*

1996 Hill (Williams) took pole but team-mate Jacques Villeneuve led, Hill running fifth then fourth. Villeneuve lost the lead to Alesi (Benetton) during his first pit stop, regained it when Alesi pitted and beat Berger (Benetton) by 19.0 seconds. Fastest lap: Villeneuve 127.1mph/204.5kph.

Luffield reprofiled.

1997 Villeneuve, pole, gave Williams their hundredth victory but only after Michael Schumacher (Ferrari) and Mika Häkkinen (McLaren) had had problems. He beat Alesi (Benetton) by 10.2 seconds. Fastest lap: Schumacher 136.1mph/219.0kph.

1998 Häkkinen (McLaren) took pole but Schumacher (Ferrari) beat him by 12.4 seconds although, as *Autocourse* reported, everything else in sodden Silverstone was 'surrounded by varying degrees of controversy and uncertainty' – including Schumacher completing the race by doing a stop'n'go penalty on the last lap. Fastest lap: Schumacher 120.1mph/193.3kph (no comparison).

1999 Häkkinen (McLaren) took pole. Schumacher (Ferrari) crashed at *Stowe* on the opening lap, breaking a leg. The restarted race had five leaders and six changes of lead before David Coulthard (McLaren) emerged to beat Eddie Irvine (Ferrari) by 1.8 seconds. Fastest lap: Häkkinen 130.2mph (-5.9)/209.5kph (-9.5).

2000 The race was moved to April and the English weather simply drowned it, or rather the car parks did. The public were even turned away from Saturday qualifying. Rubens Barrichello (Ferrari) took pole and Coulthard (McLaren) beat

team-mate Häkkinen by 1.4 seconds. Fastest lap: Häkkinen 133.4mph (+3.2)/214.7kph (+5.2).

2001 The race was returned to July and Schumacher (Ferrari) took pole from Häkkinen (McLaren). He led, but into the fifth lap Häkkinen (on two stops) cut past at *Becketts*. Schumacher (one stop) couldn't catch him and lost by 33.6 seconds. Fastest lap: Häkkinen 137.9mph (+4.5)/221.9kph (+7.2).

2002 Schumacher (Ferrari) won once he'd got past Juan-Pablo Montoya (Williams), pole, but the race belonged to Barrichello in the other Ferrari. He started last after having to change his steering wheel and by the end had cut a path to second, 14.5 seconds behind Schumacher. Fastest lap: Barrichello (Ferrari) 138.4mph (+0.5)/222.8kph (+0.9).

2003 Barrichello (Ferrari), pole, had been under criticism for his performances in the previous races and now answered his critics by beating Montoya (Williams) by 5.4 seconds. The race will be remembered,

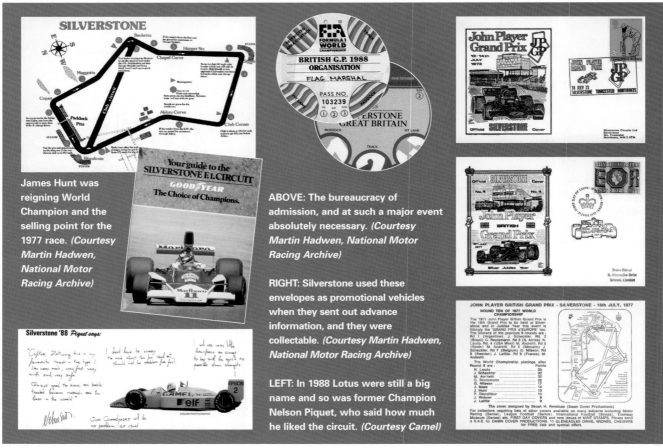

James Hunt was reigning World Champion and the selling point for the 1977 race. *(Courtesy Martin Hadwen, National Motor Racing Archive)*

ABOVE: The bureaucracy of admission, and at such a major event absolutely necessary. *(Courtesy Martin Hadwen, National Motor Racing Archive)*

RIGHT: Silverstone used these envelopes as promotional vehicles when they sent out advance information, and they were collectable. *(Courtesy Martin Hadwen, National Motor Racing Archive)*

LEFT: In 1988 Lotus were still a big name and so was former Champion Nelson Piquet, who said how much he liked the circuit. *(Courtesy Camel)*

An angry sky gathers over Silverstone's flatland in 2005 as Jarno Trulli (Toyota) goes through Copse in practice. (LAT)

however, for lap 12, when a Bible-crazed religious activist ran on to the track and towards the cars. Fastest lap: Barrichello 139.8mph (+1.4)/225.1kph (+2.3).

2004 Kimi Räikkönen (McLaren) took pole. Schumacher (Ferrari) had to withstand strong pressure from him – Räikkönen led to the first pit stops – and won by only 2.1 seconds. Fastest lap: Schumacher 146.1mph (+6.3)/235.0kph (+9.9).

2005 Räikkönen (McLaren) qualified second behind Fernando Alonso (Renault) but an engine change relegated him ten places. Montoya in the other McLaren beat Alonso by 2.7 seconds, Räikkönen third – and that meant he was now 26 points behind Alonso in the Championship. Fastest lap: Räikkönen 142.9mph (-3.2)/229.9kph (-5.1).

2006 Alonso came to Silverstone leading Schumacher (Ferrari) by 21 points and took pole from Räikkönen (McLaren). Alonso commanded the race – and clearly enjoyed Silverstone's mini-heatwave to hold off Räikkönen and in the later stages Schumacher to win by 13.9 seconds. He led every lap except one, for his second pit stop. and left with his lead increased to 23 points. Fastest lap: Alonso 140.9mph (-2.0)/226.8kph (-3.1).

2007 Lewis Hamilton (McLaren) took pole and led but emerged from the first pit stops third behind team-mate Alonso and Räikkönen (Ferrari). Alonso led to the second stops but Räikkönen stayed out longer, went faster, had the lead, and won by 2.4 seconds. Fastest lap: Räikkönen 142.6mph (+1.7)/229.5kph (+2.7).

2008 Hamilton qualified on the second row but by lap 5 of a wet-dry race had the lead from McLaren team-mate Heikki Kovalainen, pole, and never lost it, beating Nick Heidfeld (BMW) by 1 minute 08.5 seconds. This was the weekend when the FIA announced the Grand Prix was moving to Donington in 2010. Fastest lap: Räikkönen (Ferrari) 124.8mph/200.8kph (no comparison).

2009 Sebastian Vettel (Red Bull) took pole and dominated the race, team-mate Mark Webber initially trapped behind Barrichello (Brawn). Vettel beat Webber by 15.1 seconds and, of greater

significance, suggested the Championship was still alive. It wasn't, but we'd only know that by season's end. Whatever, Vettel – an anglophile – proved immensely popular at Silverstone. Fastest lap: Vettel 142.4mph (-0.2)/229.2kph (-03.).

FACTS OF THE MATTER

2.889m/4.649km circuit

Year	Winner
1950	G. Farina (Alfa Romeo)
1951	F. González (Ferrari)
Fastest pole	F. González 1951 (100.6mph/161.9kph)
Fastest lap	G. Farina (Alfa Romeo) 1951 (100.0mph/160.9kph)

New Woodcote, pits, 2.927m/4.711km circuit

1952	A. Ascari (Ferrari)
1953	A. Ascari (Ferrari)
1954	F. González (Ferrari)
1956	J.M. Fangio (Ferrari)
1958	P. Collins (Ferrari)
1960	J. Brabham (Cooper)
1963	J. Clark (Lotus)
1965	J. Clark (Lotus)
1967	J. Clark (Lotus)
1969	J. Stewart (Matra)
1971	J. Stewart (Tyrrell)
1973	P. Revson (McLaren)
Fastest pole	R. Peterson (Lotus) 1973 (138.1mph/222.3kph)
Fastest lap	J. Hunt (March) 1973 (134.1mph/215.7kph)

Woodcote chicane, 2.932m/4.719km circuit

1975	E. Fittipaldi (McLaren)
1977	J. Hunt (McLaren)
1979	C. Regazzoni (Williams)
1981	J. Watson (McLaren)
1983	A. Prost (Renault)
1985	A. Prost (McLaren)
Fastest pole	K. Rosberg (Williams) 1985 (160.9mph/259.0kph)
Fastest lap	A. Prost (McLaren) 1985 (151.0mph/243.1kph)

New Woodcote corner, 2.969m/4.778km circuit 1987–8; 2.970m/4.780km 1989–90

1987	N. Mansell (Williams)
1988	A. Senna (McLaren)
1989	A. Prost (McLaren)
1990	A. Prost (Ferrari)
Fastest pole	N. Piquet (Williams) 1987 (159.3mph/256.3kph)
Fastest lap	N. Mansell (Williams) 1987 (153.1mph/246.3kph)

New complex, 3.247m/5.226km circuit

1991	N. Mansell (Williams)
1992	N. Mansell (Williams)
1993	A. Prost (Williams)
Fastest pole	N. Mansell (Williams) 1992 (148.0mph/238.3kph)
Fastest lap	D. Hill (Williams) 1993 (141.7mph/228.0kph)

Safety revisions, 3.142m/5.057km circuit

1994	D. Hill (Williams)
1995	J. Herbert (Benetton)
Fastest pole	D. Hill (Williams) 1994 (133.1mph/214.3kph)
Fastest lap	D. Hill (Williams) 1994 (129.9mph/209.0kph)

Stowe reprofiled, 3.152m/5.072km circuit

1996	J. Villeneuve (Williams)
Pole	D. Hill (Williams) (130.6mph/210.2kph)
Fastest lap	J. Villeneuve (Williams) (127.1mph)/204.5kph)

Luffield reprofiled, 3.194m/5.140km circuit 1997–9; 4.141m/3.194km from 2000

1997	J. Villeneuve (Williams)
1998	M. Schumacher (Ferrari)
1999	D. Coulthard (McLaren)
2000	D. Coulthard (McLaren)
2001	M. Häkkinen (McLaren)
2002	M. Schumacher (Ferrari)
2003	R. Barrichello (Ferrari)
2004	M. Schumacher (Ferrari)
2005	J.-P. Montoya (McLaren)
2006	F. Alonso (Renault)
2007	K. Räikkönen (Ferrari)
2008	L. Hamilton (McLaren)
2009	S. Vettel (Red Bull)
Fastest pole	K. Räikkönen (McLaren) 2004 (147.0mph/236.6kph)
Fastest lap	M. Schumacher (Ferrari) 2004 (146.1mph/235.0kph)

Speed increase 1997–2009: 6.3mph/10.2kph.

Footnotes
[1] en.wikipedia.org/wiki/Silverstone_Circuit.
[2] www.silverstone.co.uk/about/history. [3] *British Grand Prix*, Hamilton. [4] Courtesy McLaren.

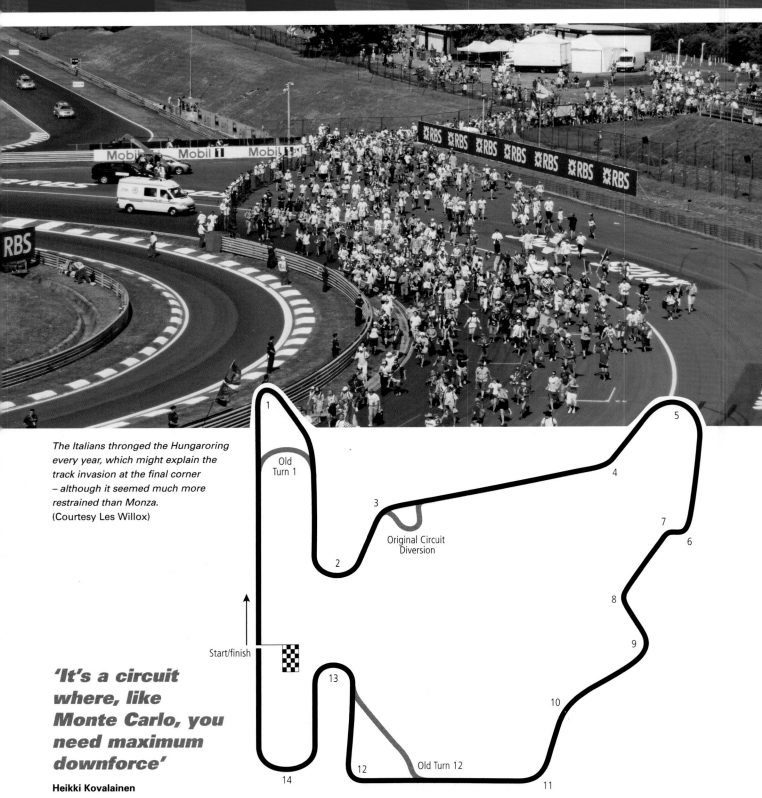

HUNGARY

HUNGARORING

Location: 12 miles (20km) north-east of Budapest.
Constructed: 1984.
World Championship Grands Prix: 25.

The Italians thronged the Hungaroring every year, which might explain the track invasion at the final corner – although it seemed much more restrained than Monza.
(Courtesy Les Willox)

Old Turn 1

1

5

4

3

Original Circuit Diversion

2

7

6

8

9

10

Start/finish

13

12

14

11

Old Turn 12

'It's a circuit where, like Monte Carlo, you need maximum downforce'

Heikki Kovalainen

To take Grand Prix racing – a defining symbol of capitalism, multinational corporations, extreme technology and, more broadly, the excesses of the Western world – to a Communist country behind the Iron Curtain seemed, in 1986, deeply amazing. That a Communist government would actively welcome Grand Prix racing seemed more remarkable still.

There were discreet clues, however. Since 1956, when the Hungarians rose against their own government and the Soviet Army crushed the revolt, the country had moved very cautiously towards creating space for itself. By the 1970s Hungarians could obtain passports (but not foreign currency, so they needed 'sponsors' in the West), small businesses and shops were privately owned and Budapest had the feel of an international city – with Italian restaurants, for example, and Shell petrol stations – rather than just another drab Eastern Bloc capital.

Bernie Ecclestone had been negotiating a possible street race in Moscow and when that didn't happen Tamas Rohonyi, an advertising man who'd been born in Budapest and was involved in the Brazilian Grand Prix, suggested he looked at Hungary.

Ecclestone went to Budapest in 1983 and found that the head of the *Magyar Autoklub* liked the idea. Evidently when a telegram reached the Ministry of Foreign Affairs they liked it too. The government considered street circuits but decided an entirely new track would be better and settled on a site in a valley. It would be good news for spectators.

In 1985 a consortium was established to supervise the construction and it opened in June 1986 after only seven months' work.

The first Grand Prix attracted 200,000, which answered the question of whether Hungarians, earning the equivalent of £75 a month, would pay £13 to watch. Many in that crowd, however, came from Czechoslovakia and East Germany, because they were allowed to travel to Hungary for their holidays and could now taste capitalist excess, so long denied them. West Germans and Austrians came too. That first race had a slightly intoxicating air about it but also a sense that, rather than amazement, this was a new normality.

The track, however, had one flaw: overtaking was almost impossible except at the end of the long start/finish straight.

Rubens Barrichello waltzes the Brawn round the circuit but 2009 wasn't to be his race. (Courtesy Les Willox)

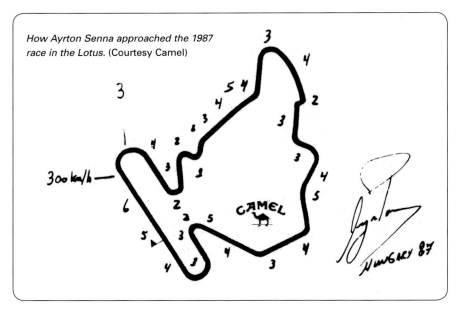

How Ayrton Senna approached the 1987 race in the Lotus. (Courtesy Camel)

COCKPIT VIEWS

Ayrton Senna, Lotus, 1987:

'I like the place. It's a hard-driving circuit with restricted level of grip. Most of it is low to medium speed corners. It's not too hard on tyres. You need lots of downforce for this type of circuit.'

Heikki Kovalainen, McLaren, 2009:

'The Hungaroring is a twisting, demanding track with few opportunities for overtaking: it's difficult to position your car alongside another car – the only real opportunity is into Turn 1, where you can use the slipstream to get past. But if you don't make it, you just have to follow the car for another lap.

'That means strategy is important. You've got to get the car as light as possible for qualifying, get a good grid position and run a short first stint. After that, it's common to run a longer second stint before switching to a shorter final stint. In Hungary, you sometimes struggle on the softer tyre, so you want to run it as briefly as possible.

'It's also a circuit where, like Monte Carlo, you need maximum downforce. There's only relatively long straight and lots of corners, where you don't want the car sliding around too much. Off the racing line it's very dirty and dusty – going offline means you pick up lots of rubber on the tyres and it can take a couple of laps to clean them up again.

'In fact, at the end of the race, it's usually better to slacken your pace by a few laps and be sure of running safely rather than risk pushing, going wide and picking up the dirty rubber. It's a tough race – but always an interesting one.'[1]

EYEWITNESS

Mónika Déri, Budapest, enthusiast:

'I'm a big Formula 1 fan since 1996. My first favourite was Jacques Villeneuve and then Jenson Button.

'I'd had the money to buy a ticket but couldn't find people with whom I could go and I didn't want to go alone. In 2005 my sister's boyfriend got four free tickets for the Friday practice and the pit lane visit. They were only three so I got the fourth ticket.

'I was very happy! I danced across my room, singing, with a smile on my face, but when we arrived my sister and the boys said that they didn't want to come inside [the pit lane] because there were many, many people there. I went inside alone.

'When I saw the starting grid I felt like I had arrived home and I was crying. It was a miracle!

'I went to the Honda pit. I was standing there about 15–20 minutes when a mechanic came and said "Hey, girl, would you like to go inside?" I was shocked. Me? There were many people, and *me?* I went into the garage and sat on Jenson's third car [the spare]. I got a baseball cap for free, and when I asked "Can I see Jenson?" they said "He's in the motorhome, come on." I went into the paddock and drivers and reporters were everywhere. I felt like a little girl who lost her way.

'At the Honda motorhome I thought *they are a big family, no one asked "who are you? Why are you here with your free standing ticket?"* I got a beer then sat down and waited for Jenson. Later he came, I stood up and said "Hi!" Jenson said "Hi!" and went away with Takuma Sato. This was our first conversation.

'Later at night, I met the guys at our hotel and got a free paddock pass, so the next day I was at the paddock too.

'People believe in miracles. I did it! I went to the paddock for free and I met very good friends, for example John Button.

'Next year I was inside too. I got a Honda umbrella and the guys took me home with the team's minibus. Jenson was standing next to me, I said "It is raining," and he said something very rude. That was our *second* conversation.

'When first I went on to a Hungarian internet forum and told my story everyone said "Ha-ha, you are lying." When they saw my pictures they said "Sorry. What a lucky girl you are" – and yes, I am a lucky girl. Every year when John Button comes to Hungary we meet and talk and I give him presents.

'This year [2009] I was invited to the Red Bull party. I had never heard of it before. I believed it would be big and expensive so I wore a very nice dress I bought in Paris and high heels. When we arrived I saw that everybody was in jeans and T-shirts. I had to go dancing in high heels!'

MEMORIES AND MILESTONES

1986 One of the drivers, Martin Brundle, seeing the circuit for the first time, memorably described it as 'Monaco without the houses.' The race produced a struggle between Nelson Piquet (Williams) and Ayrton Senna (Lotus), pole. Into lap 57 Piquet cut in front of Senna and shook his fist at him for good measure. Piquet beat him by 17.6 seconds. Fastest lap: Piquet 98.7mph/158.8kph.

1987 Nigel Mansell (Williams), pole, led imperiously but with four laps to go a wheel nut worked loose, marooning him on the circuit and giving the race to arch-rival Piquet, who beat Senna (Lotus) by 37.7 seconds. Fastest lap: Piquet 99.6mph (+0.9)/160.3kph (+1.5).

1988 Alain Prost made an inspired attempt to overtake McLaren team-mate Senna, pole, into lap 49 at the first corner. Senna gave him room, Prost took it and skated wide. Senna struck back and won the race by 0.5 of a second. Fastest lap: Prost 99.1mph (-0.5)/159.4kph (-0.9).

Speed increase 1986–8: 0.4mph/0.6kph.

Turn 3, a tight-right-left-right was eliminated, leaving the straight unencumbered.

1989 Riccardo Patrese (Williams) took pole but the race gave Mansell a rare and precious moment. On lap 56 a back-marker made Senna lift – fractionally, but enough for Mansell to ram his Ferrari past the McLaren using reaction, nerve, and balance. It was arguably the moment of the whole season: in 1989 people didn't overtake Senna or a McLaren. Mansell beat him by 25.9 seconds. Fastest lap: Mansell 107.4mph/172.9kph.

1990 Thierry Boutsen (Williams) took pole. Senna demonstrated how ruthless he could be by ramming Sandro Nannini's

Benetton – Nannini had had the temerity to be in front of him. Boutsen beat Senna by 0.2 of a second. Fastest lap: Riccardo Patrese (Williams) 108.2mph (+0.8)/174.1kph (+1.2).

You could stroll, sampling various different aspects of the circuit and yet even in 2009 it looked a modern facility, the buildings all clean lines but not overwhelming.
(Courtesy Les Willox)

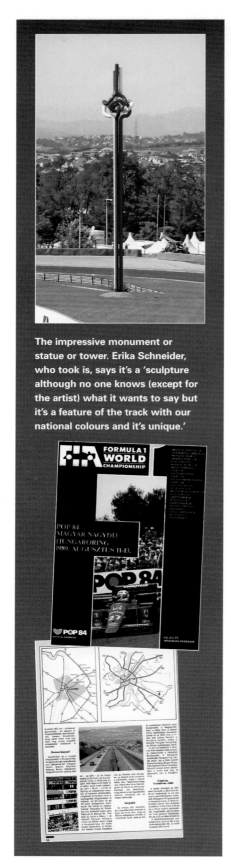

The impressive monument or statue or tower. Erika Schneider, who took is, says it's a 'sculpture although no one knows (except for the artist) what it wants to say but it's a feature of the track with our national colours and it's unique.'

Round the first corner and under the bridge in 1987, each driver knowing this is the moment to make up places: Nigel Mansell (Williams) leads from the Ferraris of Gerhard Berger and Michele Alboreto, Nelson Piquet (Williams), Alain Prost (McLaren) and Ayrton Senna in the Lotus. (LAT)

1991 Senna's Championship hopes were coming under increasing pressure from the Williamses. He responded by drawing a tremendous lap from his McLaren for pole and commanded every lap of the race from there, beating Mansell by 4.5 seconds. Fastest lap: Bertrand Gachot (Jordan) 108.8mph (+0.6)/175.2kph (+1.1).

1992 Patrese (Williams) took pole but team-mate Mansell took the Championship by finishing 40.1 seconds behind Senna (McLaren) and, in the emotion, seemed to have vindicated all the struggles of his life. Fastest lap: Mansell 113.3mph (+4.5)/182.4kph (+7.2).

1993 Prost (Williams) took pole but team-mate Damon Hill won the first Grand Prix of his career. Born in 1960, he'd done a couple of races in an uncompetitive Brabham the season before but now had a winning car. He beat Patrese (Benetton) by 1 minute 11.9 seconds. Fastest lap: Prost 111.5mph (-1.8)/179.4kph (-3.0).

1994 Hill (Williams) would find himself in heavy combat with Michael Schumacher's Benetton, this season and next. Schumacher, pole, swept round him to take the first corner – and the race – by 20.8 seconds. Fastest lap: Schumacher 109.7mph (-1.8)/176.6kph (-2.8).

1995 Hill needed to win – Schumacher led the Championship by 21 points – and did, from pole. Schumacher, running second with four laps to go, had a fuel pump failure. Hill beat David Coulthard (Williams) by 33.3 seconds. Fastest lap: Hill 110.6mph (+0.9)/178.0kph (+1.4).

1996 Schumacher (Ferrari) took pole. Hill needed to win because, although he led team-mate Jacques Villeneuve by 21 points in the Championship, Villeneuve (in his first season) was gaining in strength and experience. Villeneuve beat Hill by 0.7 of a second. Fastest lap: Hill 110.8mph (+0.2)/178.4kph (+0.4).

1997 Hill was now with Arrows and powered past Schumacher (Ferrari), pole, on lap 11. He got to within two miles of an astonishing victory – it was, as someone said, as if reality had been suspended – before a hydraulic problem slowed him. He finished 9.0 seconds behind Villeneuve (Williams). Fastest lap: Heinz-Harald Frentzen (Williams) 113.3mph (+2.5)/182.3kph (+3.9).

1998 Mika Häkkinen (McLaren) took pole. Schumacher ran behind both McLarens and Ross Brawn, the magical Ferrari strategist, switched him from a two-stop strategy to three in one of the most celebrated tactical ploys of all time. Schumacher drove one stint at qualifying speed and, on the circuit where you can't overtake, did some leapfrogging instead to beat Coulthard (McLaren) by 9.4 seconds. Fastest lap: Schumacher 112.1mph (-1.2)/180.3kph (-2.0).

1999 Häkkinen (McLaren) took pole. Schumacher had broken his leg in a crash at Silverstone and although Eddie Irvine put the Ferrari on the front row he couldn't hold the McLarens. Häkkinen beat Coulthard by 9.7 seconds. Fastest lap: Coulthard 110.1mph (-2.1)/177.2kph (-3.1).

FACTS OF THE MATTER

2.494m/4.014km circuit

Year	Winner
1986	N. Piquet (Williams)
1987	N. Piquet (Williams
1988	A. Senna (McLaren)
Fastest pole	A. Senna (McLaren) 1988
	(102.5mph/164.9kph)
Fastest lap	N. Piquet (Williams) 1987
	(99.6mph/160.3kph)

Turn 3 reconfigured, 2.466m/3.968km circuit 1989–97; 2.468m/3.972km 1998; 2.469m/3.973km 1999; 2.470m/3.975km 2000–2

1989	N. Mansell (Williams)
1990	T. Boutsen (Williams)
1991	A. Senna (McLaren)
1992	A. Senna (McLaren)
1993	D. Hill (Williams)
1994	M. Schumacher (Benetton)
1995	D. Hill (Williams)
1996	J. Villeneuve (Williams)
1997	J. Villeneuve (Williams)
1998	M. Schumacher (Ferrari)
1999	M. Häkkinen (McLaren)
2000	M. Häkkinen (McLaren)
2001	M. Schumacher (Ferrari)
2002	M. Schumacher (Ferrari)
Fastest pole	R. Barrichello (Ferrari) 2002
	(121.3mph/195.1kph)
Fastest lap	M. Schumacher (Ferrari) 2002
	(116.7mph/187.8kph)

Turns 1 and 12 alterations, 2.722m/4.381km circuit

2003	F. Alonso (Renault)
2004	M. Schumacher (Ferrari)
2005	K. Räikkönen (McLaren)
2006	J. Button (Honda)
2007	L. Hamilton (McLaren)
2008	H. Kovalainen (McLaren)
2009	L. Hamilton (McLaren)
Fastest pole	M. Schumacher (Ferrari) 2004
	(123.8mph/199.3kph)
Fastest lap	M. Schumacher (Ferrari) 2004
	(123.9mph/199.5kph)

2000 Häkkinen made a power play from the second row, engulfing McLaren team-mate Coulthard from the grid and Schumacher (Ferrari), pole, at the first corner, the race decided. He beat Schumacher by 7.9 seconds. Fastest lap: Häkkinen 111.1mph (+1.0)/178.8kph (+1.6).

2001 Schumacher won the World Championship when he beat Ferrari team-mate Rubens Barrichello into second place by 3.3 seconds and Coulthard (McLaren) into third. Fastest lap: Häkkinen (McLaren) 115.9mph (+4.8)/186.5kph (+7.7).

2002 Ferraris first and second: Barrichello led every lap (except one, when he refuelled) from pole, Schumacher behind him every lap (except two, when he refuelled). Barrichello won by 0.4 of a second. Fastest lap: Schumacher 116.7mph (+0.8)/187.8kph (+1.3).

Speed increase 1989–2002: 9.3mph/14.9kph.

Turn 1 was extended and tightened, Turn 12 eliminated.

2003 Fernando Alonso (Renault), pole, became the youngest winner of a Grand Prix at 22 years and 26 days when he beat Kimi Räikkönen (McLaren) by 16.7 seconds. Fastest lap: Juan-Pablo Montoya (Williams) 119.4mph/192.1kph.

2004 This was deep into the Ferrari era, Schumacher, pole, beating Barrichello by 4.6 seconds, Alonso (Renault) 44.5 seconds distant. Ferrari had their 14th Constructors' championship. Fastest lap: Schumacher 123.9mph (+4.5)/199.5kph (+7.4).

2005 Räikkönen's time. He qualified fourth but gained two places immediately, tracked Schumacher (Ferrari), pole, and

Kimi Räikkönen takes the Ferrari round the final corner on to the start-finish straight and moves towards second place in 2009. (Courtesy Les Willox)

just before the second pit stops was able to create a lap so intense that it brought him the lead after he stopped. He beat Schumacher by 35.5 seconds. Fastest lap: Räikkönen 120.7mph (-3.2)/194.2kph (-5.3).

2006 Jenson Button's time. He'd been a Grand Prix driver since 2000 but not won, and, in the Honda, didn't look like winning now. Räikkönen (McLaren), pole, led but had an accident. Alonso (Renault) led but a wheel nut worked loose and he spun. Button, who'd worked his way up from the seventh row of the grid, sailed by to beat Pedro de la Rosa (McLaren) by 30.8 seconds. Fastest lap: Felipe Massa (Ferrari) 117.3mph (-3.4)/188.8kph (-5.4).

2007 The new man, Lewis Hamilton, seized the race from pole, heaping pressure on McLaren team-mate Alonso, *the reigning World Champion.* Alonso was only fourth. Hamilton beat Räikkönen (Ferrari) by 0.7 of a second. Fastest lap: Räikkönen 122.4mph (+5.1)/197.0kph (+8.2).

2008 Hamilton (McLaren) took pole. Heikki Kovalainen, a new man with McLaren, beat Timo Glock (Toyota) by 11.0 seconds. It was Kovalainen's first win and he became the hundredth winner. Fastest lap: Räikkönen (Ferrari) 120.7mph (-1.7)/194.2kph (-2.8).

2009 Fernando Alonso (Renault) took pole. McLaren had been struggling but Hamilton demonstrated that he hadn't

lost any of his skills and that the team were coming back strongly. He held off Räikkönen (Ferrari) to win by 11.5 seconds. Fastest lap: Mark Webber (Red Bull) 119.6mph (-1.1)/192.5kph (-1.7).

Speed increase 2003–9: 0.2mph/0.4kph.

Footnote
[1] Courtesy McLaren.

IMOLA

Location: On the outskirts of the town of Imola.
Constructed: 1950.
World Championship Grands Prix: 27.

Senna (McLaren) leads from pole with Nelson Piquet (Lotus, No 1) and Sandro Nannini (Benetton, No 19) progressively squeezing Alain Prost in the other McLaren at the start in 1988. Senna led every lap.

'It's probably the most difficult circuit on fuel'

Ayrton Senna

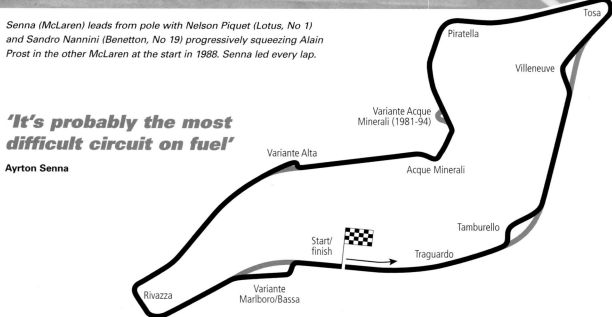

Central Italy is a very civilised place and the circuit of Imola, set in genteel parkland beside the Santerno river, seemed to reflect that year after year: good food, good wine, good circuit, good racing and (by a process difficult to explain) good spectators. The *tifosi* went to Monza as a lawless army prepared to pillage, they journeyed to Imola simply to savour the good things.

It is true that on the weekend culminating on 1 May 1994 a terrible brutality stalked the parkland and the circuit would never be a genteel place again. We'll come to that because it cannot be avoided.

Central Italy – this part of it, anyway – is Ferrari territory (Maranello not far away), as well as Lamborghini and Maserati. In the aftermath of the Second World War some local enthusiasts proposed linking public roads to make a circuit which could be used to test and develop cars. It made sense. In early 1950 construction began and it was first used a couple of years later when, fittingly, Enzo Ferrari sent one of his beautiful creations to what in effect was a baptism.

Bikes raced there from April 1953 and the cars a year later.

On 21 April 1963 a non-Championship Formula 1 race was run over 50 laps of the 3.2-mile circuit and Jim Clark (Lotus) won at an average speed of 99.3mph/159.8kph. He beat Jo Siffert in another Lotus by 40 seconds. Ferrari didn't enter.

The grandstand was built in 1965 and in 1969 the circuit hosted the bike World Championship (50cc, 125, 250, 350 and 500; Phil Read on a Yamaha won the 250 and 350 while the 500 yielded an average winning speed of 93.4mph/150.4kph).

Imola appeared to have limited ambitions, which was scarcely surprising because the Italian Grand Prix had always been at Monza and, even when Pescara was given a race in 1957, it did not become the Italian Grand Prix. That was run at Monza three weeks later.

However, the Imola Council cleverly decided to dedicate the circuit to Enzo Ferrari's son Dino, who died of leukaemia in 1956, by naming it after him. It guaranteed that Ferrari would support the circuit and in the early 1970s a state-of-the-art pits complex was built. More important, there were enough funds to build bypasses for ordinary traffic, enabling the track to become a proper circuit.

Significantly, another non-Championship Formula 1 race was held in September 1979. It attracted 16 entries (including Italian bike hero and sex symbol Giacomo Agostini in a Williams). Niki Lauda (Brabham) won it, beating Carlos Reutemann (Lotus) by seven seconds, averaging 117.5mph/189.2kph.

The significance became clear because controversy remained after Ronnie Peterson's death at Monza in 1978. In 1980 the Italian Grand Prix went to Imola and, although it returned to Monza the year after, Imola had been such a success that it justified a race. The solution proved simple. The tiny, hilly principality of San Marino was some 50 miles down the road and would lend its name.

The San Marino Grand Prix became one of the central pillars of the calendar. When Enzo Ferrari died in 1988 the circuit was renamed after him and Dino.

The facilities were beginning to become dated; evidently some teams complained and the circuit was dropped from the calendar from 2007.

View from the hill, always cloaked in the Ferrari faithful. The track flicks left-right on to the pit lane straight; the pit lane entrance is straight ahead. (ICN U.K. Bureau)

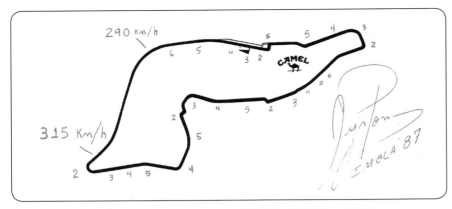

Ayrton Senna's lap, 1987. Note the speed through Tamburello – 290kmh. (Courtesy Camel)

COCKPIT VIEW

Ayrton Senna, 1987:

'It's probably the most difficult circuit on fuel and, as a consequence, very hard on the brakes. Normally we achieve quite high speed during the long straight.

'The Camel Lotus will need a lot of fuel to cover the race distance. We'll run as little wing as possible due to the fuel consumption. Cooling to the brakes is very important. Tyres are not normally a big problem.'

EYEWITNESS

Ann Bradshaw, PR expert:

'It was everything that Monza wasn't. I never liked Monza, never been a fan. You'd go to Monza and you felt threatened. You felt that somebody was going to pick your pocket, you felt that your car was going to be broken into.

'You got to Imola and the people were nice, everybody loved the circuit. It's just a nicer part of Italy, as Mugello is. You hardly saw a policeman because you didn't need them. The circuit always attracted a big crowd for testing too.

'OK, you had cramped garages and a cramped paddock but there was an amazing Italian restaurant in the main building where you could have wonderful pasta. From the Press Office you could look over the start/finish line.

'As a working environment it was easier than Monza because in those days you had to go out into the public area to get to the Media Centre at Monza.

'It was very heavy on fuel and we remember that well because they all ran out.'

MEMORIES AND MILESTONES

1980 René Arnoux (Renault) took pole. On lap 6 the right rear tyre on Gilles Villeneuve's Ferrari exploded at *Tosa* and the car was torn to pieces against the wall. Villeneuve emerged unhurt when he had regained consciousness. Clay Regazzoni, now in a wheelchair, attended a race for the first time since his horrific crash at Long Beach the year before. Nelson Piquet (Brabham) beat Alan Jones (Williams) by 28.9 seconds. Fastest lap: Jones 116.4mph/187.3kph.

The chicane at Acque Minerali *was added.*

1981 Villeneuve (Ferrari) took pole. Piquet (Brabham) won again, this time in the wet, beating Riccardo Patrese (Arrows) by 4.5 seconds. Fastest lap: Villeneuve 104.3mph/167.9kph.

1982 The FISA-FOCA power struggle was at its height – the FOCA team boycotted the race and only 14 cars came to the grid. The race would become notorious for another reason, however. Arnoux (Renault) took pole. With so few cars – at the end, five left running – Villeneuve imagined his Ferrari team-mate Didier Pironi was merely putting on a show by overtaking him. Traditional Ferrari orders were that if one of their drivers led a race the other would not challenge him. Villeneuve was wrong and never spoke to Pironi again. Pironi's winning margin was 0.3 of a second. Fastest lap: Pironi 118.6mph/190.9kph (no comparison).

1983 Arnoux (Ferrari) took pole. The most revealing race, because Riccardo Patrese, *Italian* of course, led in a Brabham from Patrick Tambay, *French* of course, but in a Ferrari. Patrese crashed and the crowd erupted with approval. They were nationalistic about Ferrari but not about the drivers. Tambay beat Alain Prost (Renault) by 48.7 seconds. Fastest lap: Patrese 119.4mph (+0.8)/192.1kph (+1.2).

1984 The little Toleman team and Pirelli were in dispute so Ayrton Senna didn't run in first qualifying and a misfire next day meant he didn't qualify for the race. Piquet (Brabham) took pole. Prost (McLaren) won despite a 360° spin (a master cylinder jammed), beating Arnoux (Ferrari) by 13.4 seconds. Fastest lap: Piquet 120.9mph (+1.5)/194.5kph (+2.4).

1985 Senna (Lotus) took pole. Imola was known as a thirsty track for fuel and when the fuel regulation changed to 220 litres drivers had to nurse their cars to the end. Prost crossed the line first but was disqualified when the McLaren was found to be below the minimum weight

A very Italian backdrop to a betrayal: Didier Pironi leads Ferrari 'team-mate' Gilles Villeneuve in 1982. (LAT)

limit. Elio de Angelis (Lotus) beat Thierry
Boutsen (Arrows) by a lap. Fastest lap:
Michele Alboreto (Ferrari) 123.9mph
(+3.0)/199.4kph (+4.9).

1986 Senna (Lotus) took pole. Prost
(McLaren) crossed the line to win, moving
the McLaren from side to side to force
the last of the petrol through. Prost beat
Piquet (Williams) by 7.6 seconds. Only 10
of the 26 starters finished. Fastest lap:
Piquet 127.2mph (+3.3)/204.6kph (+5.2).

1987 Senna (Lotus) took pole. In Friday
qualifying Piquet had a massive crash
in his Williams, striking the wall at the
Tamburello corner. He was concussed
and not allowed to race. Team-mate
Nigel Mansell beat Senna in the active-
suspension Lotus by 27.5 seconds.
Fastest lap: Teo Fabi (Benetton) 126.3mph
(-0.9)/203.3kph (-1.3).

1988 The beginning of the Senna-Prost-
McLaren-Honda domination. Senna,
pole, beat Prost by 2.3 seconds, nobody
else on the same lap. Fastest lap: Prost
125.7mph (-0.6)/202.3kph (-1.0).

1989 Senna (McLaren) took pole.
Gerhard Berger's Ferrari crashed at
Tamburello in a fireball and he survived.
At McLaren, Senna and Prost had an
agreement that whichever led from the

line would not be challenged until both
were safely through *Tosa*. Prost led,
Senna overtook into *Tosa* and nothing
was ever the same again. Senna beat
Prost by 40.2 seconds. Fastest lap: Prost
129.9mph (+4.2)/209.0kph (+6.7).

1990 Senna was on pole from Berger
in the other McLaren but Senna spun,
Berger's engine was down on power and
Patrese (Williams) won a victory that, in
historical context, atoned for 1983. He
beat Berger by 5.1 seconds. Fastest lap:
Alessandro Nannini (Benetton) 129.4mph
(-0.5)/208.2kph (-0.8).

1991 The McLaren domination continued,
Senna, pole, and Berger first and second
again, J.J. Lehto (Dallara) third a lap down,
everyone else much further back. Senna
won by 1.6 seconds. Fastest lap: Berger
130.3mph (+0.9)/209.7kph (+1.5).

1992 Mansell (Williams), pole, beat team-
mate Patrese by 9.4 seconds, becoming
the first man to win the first five races of
a season. Fastest lap: Patrese 130.9mph
(+0.6)/210.7kph (+1.0).

1993 Prost (Williams), pole, described
his victory: 'Going into *Tosa* I suddenly
found that the throttle stuck wide open
and I had a huge moment out there. Then
I took it carefully for two or three laps

*The pace car in 1994, Senna, Schumacher
and Berger following – and a disaster is only
moments away. (ICN U.K. Bureau)*

before I tried opening the throttle fully but
I had two more big moments after that
and, in the closing stages, I was being as
delicate with the throttle pedal as I dared.'
That's why he was called The Professor.
He beat Michael Schumacher (Benetton)
by 32.4 seconds. Fastest lap: Prost
130.9mph/210.7kph (no change).

1994 Friday, 29 April. Rubens Barrichello
(Jordan) unhurt after the car almost
cleared the fencing at *Variante Bassa*.

Saturday, 30 April. Roland
Ratzenberger (Simtek) killed in second
qualifying. Senna (Williams) pole.

Sunday, 1 April. Debris from a start-line
crash injured eight spectators.

Into lap 7, Senna crashed fatally at
Tamburello, cause still unknown.

Lap 41, Michele Alboreto (Minardi)
pitted, a wheel came off striking four
mechanics, who were taken to hospital.

Schumacher (Benetton) beat
Nicola Larini (Ferrari) by 54.9 seconds.
Fastest lap: Hill (Williams) 133.7mph
(+2.8)/215.1kph (+4.4).

Speed increase 1981–94: 29.4mph/47.2kph.

Imola changed fundamentally with chicanes at Tamburello *and* Villeneuve. Tamburello *demanded a car approaching at 170mph in sixth gear brake, change to fourth, and go in at 70mph. The days of taking it flat out were gone forever. The chicane at* Acque Minerale *was removed.* Mika Häkkinen *said: 'They've made changes to the corners which were extremely difficult and dangerous before. I never did enjoy those corners, because you were going so fast. These corners are gone, which is good.'*

1995 They came back sombre, came back with their memories. Schumacher (Benetton) took pole. Damon Hill (Williams) conquered whatever emotion he might have felt to beat Jean Alesi (Ferrari) by 18.6 seconds. Fastest lap: Berger (Ferrari) 122.3mph/196.7kph.

1996 Schumacher took pole, his first for Ferrari. David Coulthard (McLaren) led for 19 laps, Schumacher for one lap, and Damon Hill the rest to beat Schumacher by 16.4 seconds. Fastest lap: Hill 123.1mph/198.0kph.

Speed increase 1995–6: 0.8mph/1.3kph.

Further revision to the circuit.

1997 Jacques Villeneuve (Williams) took pole. Heinz-Harald Frentzen, in his fourth race for Williams, led 36 laps and won, his first victory in any form of motor racing since 1993. Suddenly he looked like a possible World Champion. He beat Schumacher (Ferrari) by 1.2 seconds. Fastest lap: Heinz-Harald Frentzen (Williams) 128.9mph/207.5kph.

1998 Coulthard (McLaren), pole, drove a tactical race – leading all 62 laps – to thwart the Ferraris and the 100,000 crowd. Suddenly he looked like a possible World Champion. He beat Schumacher by 4.5 seconds, Eddie Irvine in the other Ferrari third. Fastest lap: Schumacher 123.4mph (-5.5)/198.6kph (-8.9).

The race was going to be like any other but Formula 1 was never going to be the same again, and neither was Imola.
(All courtesy Martin Hadwen, National Motor Racing Archive)

It was the Schumacher era and the official programme reflected that.

Yes, the Schumacher era.

Michael y Ralf Schumacher

1999 Mika Häkkinen (McLaren) pole but in the race…

    Schumacher (Ferrari)   1h 33m 44.7s
    Coulthard (McLaren)   1h 33m 49.0s

    and Imola sounded just like Monza. Fastest lap: Schumacher 124.5mph (+1.1)/200.4kph (+1.8).

2000 The tumult returned like a vast echo when Schumacher held off Häkkinen (McLaren), pole, to win by 1.1 seconds. Fastest lap: Häkkinen 127.5mph (+3.0)/205.2kph (+4.8).

2001 Coulthard (McLaren) took pole. Just to break up the sequence, Ralf Schumacher won in a Williams, Barrichello (Ferrari) third – Schumacher out with a brake problem. Ralf beat Coulthard by 4.3 seconds. Fastest lap: Ralf Schumacher 129.0mph (+1.5)/207.6kph (+2.4).

2002 Ferrari were now becoming the dominant force in Grand Prix racing, and to an almost embarrassing extent. Only Ralf Schumacher (Williams) could get anywhere near them. Michael, pole, beat team-mate Rubens Barrichello by 17.9 seconds, Ralf almost two seconds further away. Fastest lap: Barrichello 131.1mph (+2.1)/211.0kph (+3.4).

2003 The Schumachers decided to race even though their mother had just died – they'd flown to Germany after qualifying to be with her but returned. Michael, (Ferrari) pole, beat Kimi Räikkönen (McLaren) by 1.8 seconds, Ralf (Williams) fourth. Fastest lap: Michael Schumacher 133.8mph (+2.7)/215.3kph (+4.3).

2004 Jenson Button (BAR) took pole. Michael Schumacher (Ferrari) and Juan-Pablo Montoya (Williams) had a lively skirmish on the opening lap, and a lively verbal skirmish afterwards, but Schumacher beat Button by 9.7 seconds. Fastest lap: Schumacher 137.2mph (+3.4)/220.8kph (+5.5).

2005 Räikkönen (McLaren) took pole. The race climaxed in 12 epic laps when young Fernando Alonso (Renault) kept his nerve as Michael Schumacher swarmed him in the Ferrari to win by 0.2 of a second. Fastest lap: Schumacher 134.8mph (-2.4)/216.9kph (-3.9).

2006 Role reversal – Schumacher, pole, held off Alonso, beating him by 2.0 seconds. 'With all my years of experience I knew what I wanted to do was to keep Alonso behind me – but at my pace, not pushing flat out, and that's

what I did.' Fastest lap: Alonso 131.2mph (-3.6)/211.1kph (-5.8).

    Speed increase 1997–2006: 2.3mph/3.6kph.

The start, 1995, and Michael Schumacher (Benetton) is on the power immediately – but many minds were on this moment a year before. (ICN U.K. Bureau)

FACTS OF THE MATTER

3.107m/5.000km circuit

Year	Winner
1980*	N. Piquet (Brabham)
Pole	R. Arnoux (Renault)
	(119.0mph/191.5kph)
Fastest pole	A. Jones (Williams)
	(116.4mph/187.3kph)

Acque Minerale chicane, 3.132m/5.040km circuit

Year	Winner
1981	N. Piquet (Brabham)
1982	D. Pironi (Ferrari)
1983	P. Tambay (Ferrari)
1984	A. Prost (McLaren)
1985	E. de Angelis (Lotus)
1986	A. Prost (McLaren)
1987	N. Mansell (Williams)
1988	A. Senna (McLaren)
1989	A. Senna (McLaren)
1990	R. Patrese (Williams)
1991	A. Senna (McLaren)
1992	N. Mansell (Williams)
1993	A. Prost (Williams)
1994	M. Schumacher (Benetton)
Fastest pole	A. Senna (Williams) 1994
	(138.3mph/222.5kph)
Fastest lap	D. Hill (Williams) 1994
	(133.7mph/215.1kph)

* Italian Grand Prix.

New chicane and other variations, 3.042m/4.895km circuit 1995; 3.040m/4.892km 1996

Year	Winner
1995	D. Hill (Williams)
1996	D. Hill (Williams)
Fastest pole	M. Schumacher (Ferrari) 1996
	(125.9mph/202.7kph)
Fastest lap	D. Hill (Williams) 1996
	(123.1mph/198.0kph)

Further revisions, 3.063m/4.930km circuit 1997–9; 3.065m/4.993km 2000–5

Year	Winner
1997	H.-H. Frentzen (Williams)
1998	D. Coulthard (McLaren)
1999	M. Schumacher (Ferrari)
2000	M. Schumacher (Ferrari)
2001	R. Schumacher (Williams)
2002	M. Schumacher (Ferrari)
2003	M. Schumacher (Ferrari)
2004	M. Schumacher (Ferrari)
2005	F. Alonso (Renault)
Fastest pole	J. Button (BAR) 2004
	(138.4mph/222.7kph)
Fastest lap	M Schumacher (Ferrari) 2004
	(137.2mph/220.8kph)

Further revisions, 3.081m/4.959km circuit

Year	Winner
2006	M. Schumacher (Ferrari)
Pole	M. Schumacher (Ferrari)
	(134.0mph/215.6kph)
Fastest lap	F. Alonso (Renault)
	(131.2mph/211.1kph)

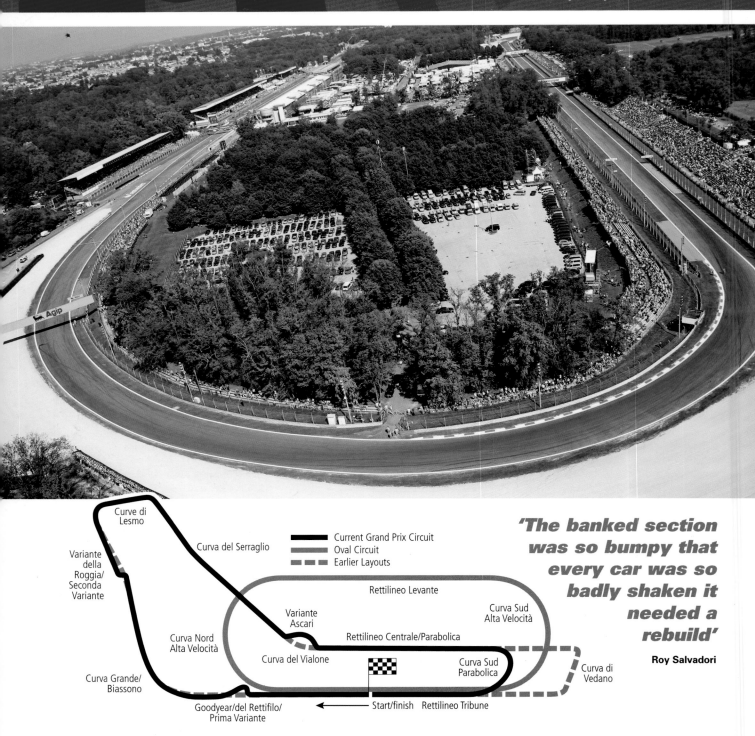

ITALY

MONZA

Location: 9 miles (15km) north-east of Milan.
Constructed: 1922.
World Championship Grands Prix: 59.

Curve di Lesmo

Variante della Roggia/ Seconda Variante

Curva del Serraglio

Curva Nord Alta Velocità

Curva Grande/ Biassono

Variante Ascari

Curva del Vialone

Goodyear/del Rettifilo/ Prima Variante

Rettilineo Levante

Rettilineo Centrale/Parabolica

Curva Sud Alta Velocità

Curva Sud Parabolica

Curva di Vedano

Start/finish Rettilineo Tribune

—— Current Grand Prix Circuit
—— Oval Circuit
- - - Earlier Layouts

'The banked section was so bumpy that every car was so badly shaken it needed a rebuild'

Roy Salvadori

Parabolica, 2007 and, at left, the old banking still flows in but like a river which has long been dammed.
(Courtesy Autodromo Nazionale Monza)

You are never alone at Monza even on those midweek days when nothing's happening and nobody's around. Ghosts stalk the emptiness, *all* the ghosts. Without exception, the great drivers have passed this way: the barely remembered Bordino and Nazzaro, the treasured Nuvolari and Varzi, the Mercedes and Auto Union cars which seemed in their might to herald war, Ascari and Farina, Fangio and Moss, Clark and Stewart, Senna and Schumacher.

To reach the circuit, known as the *Autodromo*, you'll probably come through the town of Monza itself. It's very Italian: a lot of church spires, a lot of old stone buildings, and a lot of narrow, mildly chaotic streets where pedestrians challenge motorists and vice versa. You'll come along a dual carriageway with chic apartments to one side and, after the royal palace on the other, parkland. You'll turn into the small, middle-class community of Vedano al Lambro and go through a stone arch. You're close now. The entry road runs through trees and under a tunnel to the paddock.

Those midweek days you can wander. The new pits complex is just over there, glistening and enormous. You can walk behind it and you'll find another tunnel, narrower, shorter,

Building the circuit, including horsepower.
(Courtesy Autodromo Nazionale Monza)

It would become this by 2003, a national outpouring through the medium of Ferrari.
(Courtesy Autodromo Nazionale Monza)

The start of the 1951 race, the grid four columns wide. (Courtesy Autodromo Nazionale Monza)

This is what it became in the modern era. (Courtesy Autodromo Nazionale Monza)

leading into the trees. Follow the path and you'll come upon a grandstand with a view across the end of the start/finish straight – itself a mighty thing – *and*, to the right, a wall of concrete curving into the distance. This is the old banking section and, even close up, it looks *vertical*. Is that the wind whispering through the trees or is it the ghosts?

You may experience many emotions at Monza during a Grand Prix meeting but loneliness certainly won't be one of them. You won't be hearing whispering either. Monza becomes, unashamedly, a tribal place, intimidating and suggesting a measure of lawlessness as the teeming thousands known as the *tifosi* tramp towards the *Autodromo* with their flags and banners. If you haven't witnessed it before you might think you're in the Middle Ages. They come uniquely and exclusively to pay their annual homage to Ferrari, though traditionally they don't always pay for admission. They come over the walls, under fences and, armed with bolt-cutters, slice through metal fences.

The British may throng Silverstone to anoint their latest hero, the Spanish may adore Fernando Alonso, Suzuka yearns for Japanese success, Interlagos enters into communion with any Brazilian doing well, and so it goes. The newer circuits – Turkey, Singapore, Bahrain, Abu Dhabi – attract the curious but don't deal in emotion at all.

Monza isn't like any of these.

Monza *is* emotion. Monza is fiercely, gloriously, blindly, impossibly partisan. The fact that the people generating this are Italian and (of course) fiercely and gloriously emotional in the first place creates a sort of three-day passion play.

They come *only* to see the Ferraris, and if the management at Maranello decided to dispense with drivers and put two Barbary Apes in the cockpits instead that would make absolutely no difference.

Monza is different in other ways. Once the winning car crossed the line huge numbers of spectators found ways to invade the track *while the other cars were still going round at racing speed.* Why? It seemed to make them happy.

(The *tifosi* have been photographed carrying inflatable women into the circuit. Why? Again, it seemed to make them happy. The tunnel to the paddock was reputed to be very unsafe for all women, inflatable or otherwise. Having walked through it many times, I don't believe a word of it, but myths don't need truth do they? They wouldn't be myths if they did.)

Italy needed a permanent circuit and the Automobile Club of Milan decided to build one. They considered a site near Malpensa airport and

another within Milan before choosing the parkland at Monza. The Opera Nazionale Combattenti, running the park, were happy to have the circuit. However, the idea of a 14km track came under criticism from the under-secretary for state education, who

The banking, immense, sudden and still very frightening. (Courtesy Julian Nowell)

Coming off the banking in 1957. That's today's Parabolica to your left. (Courtesy Autodromo Nazionale Monza)

ordered work to stop for reasons of 'monumental, artistic and landscape importance'. A 10km track was approved and built between 15 May and 15 August 1922.

That involved 3,500 workmen, 200 carts, 30 trucks, and a 5km railway with two engines and 80 wagons. They built a 5.5km road course and 4.5km oval, banked at both ends. In its essentials the track layout was as it is today, even though only the ghosts inhabit the banking now.

In fact, the first big event was a bike race, and it would continue to be a centre for that too.

Monza meant speed, and speed meant danger. In 1928 a car went into the crowd, killing 27; in 1933 three drivers were killed when they skidded on oil. During the 1930s the layout changed three times before a complete renovation in 1939 removed the banked oval altogether and extended the road track to 6.3km.

During the war the circuit was used to store official public motoring records and house wild animals evacuated from Milan's zoo.

More work was done after the war and in 1955 the banking rebuilt (and *Parabolica* built too). The banking was at 80° and 10.4 metres (34 feet) high.

Monza meant more and more speed, and in its rawest form the circuit was lined by trees, so close they almost overhung, so that drivers might suddenly find themselves engulfed by shadows.

The fastest lap in 1950 (117.3mph/188.9kph) had become 136.7mph/220.0kph in 1960, 150.9mhp/242.9kph in 1970 before the two chicanes constructed in 1972 cut that to 134.1mph/215.8kph. Two more chicanes in 1976 reduced the *increase* in speed again but by 1987 Senna touched 240kph/149mph. Schumacher in the Ferrari forced that to 254.8kph/158.3mph in 2003. The full fastest laps are given in 'Memories

and Milestones' below.

In 1989 reconstruction began on the pits complex while the medical centre expanded to embrace three surgeries and two intensive care units. In 1994–5 the track was modified to make it safer, at strategic points (like the second *Lesmo* bend) slower, and run-off areas were increased. Further work in 2000 – modifications, in fact – altered the first chicane from its esse shape to a sharp right-left. Since the drivers were approaching it at 210mph/337kph and needed to slow to 50mph in 4.3 seconds for the apex, the first chicane became what downhill ski racers call a *compression*.

The circuit has a presence that is very difficult to define. No doubt it's drawn from passion and promiscuity (don't leave anything unguarded, including the female of the species), from setting and scale to magnificent facilities that somehow blend into the parkland.

That's why you can see the ghosts.

COCKPIT VIEWS

Roy Salvadori, Maserati, 1956:

'The Italian Grand Prix was held on the combined road and banked track circuit at Monza and proved a complete fiasco for the Gilby [Engineering] team [for whom Salvadori drove]. The banked section of the circuit was so bumpy that every car in the race was so badly shaken that it needed a rebuild afterwards. I was trying to pick the best line on the banking to give the car the least hammering, the 250F was plagued by minor problems and after four pit stops I finished in 11th and last place, nine laps behind Stirling's winning 250F.'[1]

Derek Warwick, 1990:

'Monza is a very fast track which generally favours the multi-cylinder engines, and you want to set the car up for speed, with little downforce. However, you still need grip in the chicanes, so it's another of those places where you have to trade the two off against each other. The fact that you are running with little downforce makes *Lesmo* even more exciting.'

Jenson Button, Brawn, 2009:

'The circuit is very different to most that we race on because the car will be set up with the lowest levels of drag and

downforce possible to take advantage of the long straights.

'It always takes a few laps to get used to. *Ascari* is probably my favourite part of the track but also *Parabolica*, where the challenge is to brake as late as possible, particularly in qualifying when you're on a quick lap.'[2]

EYEWITNESS

Brian Hart, engine manufacturer:

'Monza is *Monza*. To me, in Europe, it was the most identifiable track. If you went to Monza it was better than Imola and it was better than Paul Ricard

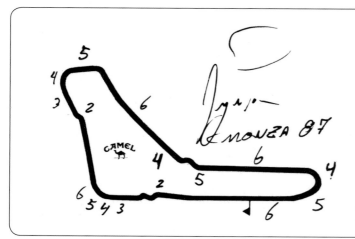

MONZA '87
Senna says:
"I hope to be up front at Monza and have a good finish position better than '85!!"

Ayrton Senna's own preview of the 1987 Grand Prix.
(Courtesy Camel)

because it had the heritage, the history. It had the banking – you look at it and think *oh my God.*

'The *tifosi* gave it a kind of electricity. They were not spectators, they were passionate Formula 1 enthusiasts. The enthusiasts knew what they were looking at.

'Can you imagine people at a racetrack on practice day at eight o'clock in the evening still cheering the mechanics? It didn't happen anywhere else we went to – so Monza was special.

'Every time you went under that tunnel to the paddock you felt something special, and then you read the history of it – of what had gone on there – and you went to the little museum…

'You look at some of the historic races, some of the classics of all time: all right, you've got Fangio at the Nürburgring in 1957, but at Monza they go on and on and on – Big John Surtees in the Honda, Peter Gethin [see 'Memories and Milestones', 1971], Clark gains a whole lap – who has ever gained a lap there?

'Then there was Brian Henton, and that was a part of it for me too. Brian qualified the Toleman and it was the first time in 18 months, more or less, from when we started. The sponsors had guests in the grandstand opposite and they were cheering as if we'd won the race.

'I went on the grid at races afterwards but not that first year because we'd only just qualified and we were tucked in at the back. When you were on the grid you could feel the passion. I used to leave the grid before the start and go up to the first chicane. I'd sit on the grass and watch the first lap. You knew there'd be a shunt – there was a famous shunt between Schlesser and Ayrton Senna, and McLaren didn't win all 16 races. *That* was Monza.'

MEMORIES AND MILESTONES

1950 Juan Manuel Fangio (Alfa Romeo) took pole. He went into the race with 26 points, Luigi Fagioli 24, and Giuseppe Farina 22 – they were in Alfas too. The historic circuit would provide a moment of history. Fangio decided he'd follow Farina – it would give him the Championship – but he had a tyre burst, a radiator problem, and switched to Piero Taruffi's car, which broke down. So Farina became the first World Champion when he beat the Ferrari of Dorino Serafini and

Alberto Ascari (they shared the drive) by 1 minute 18.6 seconds. Fastest lap: Fangio 117.4mph/189.0kph.

1951 Fangio (Alfa Romeo), pole, had an engine failure and Ascari won it from Froilan González by 44.6 seconds, opening up the Championship for the final round at Barcelona. Fastest lap: Farina (Alfa Romeo) 121.0mph (+3.6)/194.7kph (+5.7).

1952 Maserati brought new cars but Ferraris filled three of the first four places. Ascari, pole, had already won the Championship at the Nürburgring two races before and now beat González (in a Maserati) by more than a minute. Fastest lap: Ascari and González 111.8mph (-9.2)/179.9kph (-14.8).

1953 Ascari (Ferrari), pole, had already won the Championship two races before. Fangio (Maserati) captures Monza's mood: in practice 'my car was vibrating terribly, and so was … Onofre Marimón's, who asked me to try his as he didn't know what was wrong. … I was going at full speed along the main straight (there were no chicanes then). At the end of it, there was a chestnut tree, and that was the approximate marker for braking. Two seasons before, in the Alfetta, one had to brake 50 metres before the chestnut tree, because that car would be doing 186mph. The Formula 2 Maserati was slower, so I braked after passing the old tree ... I had no sooner pressed the pedal than my rear left tyre burst, the car went sideways, and instead of beginning to take the big curve, I found myself going off the track at 135mph, straight for the wooden post on which I had fixed my eyes...' He grazed the post – and went on to win the race, beating Farina (Ferrari) by 1.4 seconds.[3] Fastest lap: Fangio 113.2mph (+1.4)/182.2kph (+2.3).

1954 Fangio, pole, was at his peak, dominating the whole season with the mighty Mercedes-Benz. Monza developed into a slipstreaming contest. Fangio remembered getting into the lead 'several times, but with 20 laps to go I felt no great desire to be there. It was simply a matter of staying in the pack until the last corner. At the crucial moment, Farina came along the straight and out of my slipstream, and went well to the left to get behind Ascari. The two went very fast into the first curve of the "porfido" – this is not like the present-day "parabolica" (the "porfido" consisted of two bends that were sharply defined,

joined by a straight of about a hundred and fifty yards).' Ascari lost grip, Farina drifted wide, and Fangio had the race, beating Mike Hawthorn (Ferrari) by a lap.[4] Fastest lap: González (Ferrari) 116.7mph (+3.5)/187.7kph (+5.5).

1955 (banking): The banked circuit was bumpy – some spoke of ridges you couldn't see – and began to shred tyres. Suspensions needed adjusting and Stirling Moss described Mercedes' varied attempt as like 'musical chairs'. In testing on the road circuit Ascari went off and was killed. The corner where it happened, *Platano*, became the *Variante Ascari.* Fangio (Mercedes), pole, beat Taruffi in another Mercedes by 0.7 of a second. Fastest lap: Stirling Moss (Maserati) 134.0mph/215.7kph.

1956 (banking): Fangio (Ferrari) took pole. Moss, running out of fuel, cheekily signalled Luigi Piotti (both were in Maseratis) to push him to the pits. It worked. Moss won, beating Peter Collins/Fangio (Ferrari) by 5.7 seconds. Fangio had broken down and Collins, who – like Fangio and Moss – had a chance at the Championship, unselfishly handed his car to Fangio, literally giving it to him. Fastest lap: Moss 135.2mph/217.5kph.

Speed increase 1955–6: 1.2mph/1.8kph.

The tyre difficulties meant the race left the banking and returned to the road circuit, which had been shortened because the Curva di Vedano *became the* Parabolica.

1957 Stuart Lewis-Evans (Vanwall) took pole. Moss's victory in the other Vanwall was described as 'masterly' by Fangio, who had to 'make do' with second place. Moss beat him by 41.3 seconds. Fastest lap: Tony Brooks (Vanwall) 124.0mph/199.6kph.

1958 Moss (Vanwall), pole, led but his gearbox failed, opening the race to Tony Brooks (in another Vanwall) with Hawthorn (Ferrari) second, and that opened the championship to him in Morocco a month later. Brooks won by 24.2 seconds. Fastest lap: Phil Hill (Ferrari) 125.0mph (+1.0)/201.2kph (+1.6).

1959 Moss (Cooper), pole, drove a tactical race because Ferrari assumed – wrongly – he'd be making a late pit stop. He beat Phil Hill (Ferrari) by 46.7 seconds. Fastest lap: Phil Hill 128.1mph (+3.1)/206.2kph (+5.0).

Mike Hawthorn (14) has the Ferrari on the front row in 1958. Monza was still wide open then – look at the unprotected people under the trees. (Courtesy Thomas Horat)

1960 (banking): Phil Hill (Ferrari), pole, beat compatriot and team-mate Richie Ginther by 2 minutes 27.2 seconds to become the first American to win a Grand Prix and the last man to do it in a front-engined car. Fastest lap (comparison with 1956): Phil Hill 136.7mph (+1.5)/2 20.0kph (+2.5).

1961 (banking): Graham Hill remembered the banking was 'terribly steep – I tried once to run up it and failed. I could only just get to the top when I took my shoes off and my bare feet gave me a bit of extra grip.'[5] The ridges were so pronounced the BRM jumped 'most alarmingly' and the pounding so intense that 'you can hardly see'. Jim Clark

(Lotus) and Wolfgang von Trips (Ferrari), pole, crashed and 13 spectators were killed. Phil Hill (Ferrari) beat Dan Gurney (Porsche) to become World Champion. Fastest lap: Giancarlo Baghetti (Ferrari) 132.8mph (-3.9)/213.8kph (-6.2).

1962 Clark (Lotus) took pole. An entry of 30 was pruned to 22 for the race, and Masten Gregory (who qualified his Lotus on the third row) might not have been among them. A policeman arrested him over a paddock pass and he went to a cell for half an hour during final practice. Graham Hill (BRM) beat Ginther in another BRM by 29.8 seconds. Fastest lap (comparison with 1959): Graham Hill 125.7mph (-2.4)/202.3kph (-3.9).

1963 John Surtees (Ferrari) took pole. The organisers wanted to use the banking but during first practice it proved too dangerous. Clark (Lotus) emerged from the incessant slipstreaming to lead so commandingly that he allowed

Ginther (BRM) to unlap himself. He beat Ginther by 1 minute 35.0 seconds, Bruce McLaren a lap down, the next five two laps down. Then the Italian police said they wanted to see Clark about the 1961 crash, giving a 'rather miserable end to what should have been the most memorable day of my life' – his first Championship. Fastest lap: Clark 130.1mph (+4.4)/209.3kph (+7.0).

1964 John Surtees in a Ferrari was moving towards the World Championship – the USA and Mexico were to follow – and from pole he'd remember 'for the first 25 laps or so it was a real slipstreaming special.' He beat Bruce McLaren by more than a minute. Fastest lap: Surtees 130.2mph (+0.1)/209.5kph (+0.2).

1965 Clark's season. He didn't go to Monaco but won all the other six races in the Lotus. He took pole at Monza but the fuel pump failed. Jackie Stewart (BRM) beat Graham Hill in another BRM by 3.3 seconds. Stewart described it[6] as a 'tremendous thing. I had no illusions about it; if a new driver is going to do well in a Grand Prix he will do well at Monza because although it calls for a special kind of driving it does not make great demands on ability, at least not in the race. You need to be smooth and probably brave too' – staying on the power longer than the others. Fastest lap: Clark 133.4mph (+3.2)/214.7kph (+5.2).

1966 Monza surrendered to emotion. Ludovico Scarfiotti, Mike Parkes (pole) and Lorenzo Bandini in Ferraris led, and although Bandini's ignition failed Scarfiotti became the first Italian to win the race since Ascari in 1952, beating Parkes by 5.8 seconds. Fastest lap: Scarfiotti 139.2mph (+5.8)/224.0kph (+9.3).

1967 Clark (Lotus) took pole but wasn't involved in one of the great finishes, Surtees (Honda) taking Jack Brabham (Brabham) in the *Parabolica* and getting to the line 0.2 of a second ahead. That disguised the fact that Clark drove what engine manufacturer Brian Hart describes as one of the greatest races – the equal of Fangio at the Nürburgring in 1957 (see 'Eyewitness'). On lap 13 Clark had a puncture and emerged a lap down on a track where, in theory, you couldn't make up time because it was a full-out blast all the way for all of them. By lap 61 Clark had regained the lead but a fuel problem slowed him. Fastest lap: Clark 145.3mph (+6.1)/233.9kph (+9.9).

1968 Surtees (Honda) took pole. Denny Hulme (McLaren) was making a strong late-season push and won, beating Johnny Servoz-Gavin (Matra) by 1 minute 28.4 seconds. Chris Amon (Ferrari) crashed into the Armco backwards and the car flipped into the trees. He was unhurt. Fastest lap: Jackie Oliver (Lotus) 148.7mph (+3.4)/239.3kph (+5.4).

1969 Jackie Stewart (Matra) would say that 'Monza really shows how drivers behave under pressure.' He won, Jochen Rindt (Lotus), pole, at 0.08 of a second, Jean-Pierre Beltoise (Matra) at 0.17, and Bruce McLaren (McLaren) at 0.19. Fastest lap: Beltoise 151.0mph (+2.3)/243.0kph (+3.7).

1970 In final practice Rindt's Lotus suddenly swerved into the Armco at the *Parabolica*, tearing itself to pieces and killing Rindt. He would become the only posthumous World Champion. Jacky Ickx (Ferrari) took pole and team-mate Clay Regazzoni won from Stewart (March) by 5.7 seconds. Fastest lap: Clay Regazzoni (Ferrari) 151.0mph/243.0kph (no change).

1971 Chris Amon (Matra) took pole. In another frantic finish Peter Gethin (BRM) won with Ronnie Peterson (March) at 0.01 of a second, François Cevert (Tyrrell) at 0.09, Mike Hailwood (Surtees) at 0.18, and Howden Ganley (BRM) at 0.61. By now Colin Chapman of Lotus – suspicious of what the Italian police might do after the Clark and Rindt problems – took to leaving a spare car in the Formula 2 transporter just over the border in France. Fastest lap: Henri Pescarolo (March) 153.5mph (+2.5)/247.0kph (+4.0).

Speed increase 1957–71: 29.5mph/47.4kph.

To break up the slipstreaming two chicanes were added, one on the start/finish straight and the other at Vialone *before the run to* Parabolica. *It worked.*

1972 Ickx (Ferrari) took pole. Emerson Fittipaldi (Lotus) beat Hailwood (Surtees) by 14.5 seconds, although Hailwood, typically, said he didn't know anything about slipstreaming anyway. Fastest lap: Ickx 134.1mph/215.9kph.

1973 The Lotus transporter crashed on the *autostrada*, threatening Emerson Fittipaldi's Championship chances, but Chapman had that spare just over the border. Ronnie Peterson (in the other Lotus) took pole. Stewart (Tyrrell) had a puncture and dropped to 20th but worked his way to fourth by the end. Fittipaldi

was second, 0.80 of a second behind Peterson. It was enough. Fastest lap: Stewart 135.6mph/218.2kph.

Speed increase 1972–3: 1.5mph/2.3kph.

Vialone *was eased, slightly lengthening the lap.*

1974 Ferrari came to Monza leading the Constructors' Championship and Regazzoni leading the Drivers'. Neither Regazzoni nor team-mate Niki Lauda, pole, finished. Peterson (Lotus) beat Fittipaldi (McLaren) by 0.8 of a second. Fastest lap: Carlos Pace (Brabham) 137.3mph/220.9kph.

1975 Regazzoni did win, one of the most emotional moments of his life – and

The fantastical finish in 1971: Peter Gethin (BRM), Ronnie Peterson (March) at +0.01, François Cevert (Tyrrell) at +0.09, Mike Hailwood (Surtees) at +0.18. (Courtesy Autodromo Nazionale Monza)

Monza's life too. Lauda in the other Ferrari had taken pole. Regazzoni beat Fittipaldi (McLaren) by 16.6 seconds. Fastest lap: Regazzoni 138.9mph/223.5kph.

Speed increase 1974–5: 1.6mph/2.6kph.

This is what the first Lesmo looked like in 1972. (Courtesy Autodromo Nazionale Monza)

A chaotic start in 1976, drivers waiting for the '10 seconds' board when the green light went off. Here Rolf Stommelen (Brabham) will be under stack at any instant. (Courtesy Autodromo Nazionale Monza)

To decrease the speeds the cars were reaching – Regazzoni set fastest lap in 1975 at 138.8mph/223.5kph – as the speeds remorselessly increased towards what they had been before the 1971–2 chicanes, two further chicanes were added, at *Curva Grande* and Lesmo.

1976 Jacques Laffite (Ligier) took pole. Lauda (Ferrari) returned only six weeks after a crash so terrible that he was given the Last Rites. He finished fourth and, at his most phlegmatic, said 'some people thought that that was quite good'. Others thought it was a miracle. McLaren (with James Hunt as Lauda's Championship rival) were given the full Monza treatment: stories of illegal fuel, problems at the customs, the McLarens put to the back of the grid after a fuel inspection, *tifosi* signs condemning the 'English mafia', Hunt heckled and hissed at. Ronnie Peterson (March) beat Regazzoni (Ferrari) by 2.3 seconds. The chicanes cut the fastest lap – Peterson – to 128.1mph/206.1kph.

1977 Hunt (McLaren) took pole. Mario Andretti, of Italian origin, won in a Lotus but the crowd concentrated on the *Austrian* Lauda, second, because he was in a Ferrari. He finished 16.9 seconds

behind Andretti. Fastest lap: Andretti 130.9mph (+2.8)/210.7kph (+4.6).

1978 From the start, young Riccardo Patrese (Arrows) touched Hunt's McLaren, who touched Peterson's Lotus. It speared the Armco and bounced back on fire. At least seven other cars were involved. Peterson was taken to hospital and died there because bone marrow entered his bloodstream. Andretti, pole, was Peterson's team-mate and said 'unfortunately, motor racing is also this'. Lauda (Brabham) beat team-mate John Watson by 1.4 seconds. Fastest lap: Andretti 132.1mph (+1.2)/212.6kph (+1.9).

1979 Jean-Pierre Jabouille (Renault) took pole. Jody Scheckter won the Championship, Gilles Villeneuve in the other Ferrari following him home – 0.4 of a second behind – obeying team orders. Scheckter trusted Villeneuve but in the final laps put himself in a position where he didn't have to. The *tifosi* wouldn't see anything like this again for a generation. Fastest lap: Regazzoni (Williams) 135.7mph (+3.6)/218.4kph (+5.8).

1981 René Arnoux (Renault) took pole. The race returned – in 1980 it had gone to Imola as the furore over Peterson's death continued. Alain Prost drove a beautifully controlled race for Renault to beat Alan Jones (Williams) by 23.0 seconds while Villeneuve returned to his helicopter to find the radio equipment had been stolen. Fastest lap: Carlos Reutemann (Williams) 133.0mph (-2.7)/214.1kph (-4.3).

1982 Villeneuve had been killed at Zolder,

Didier Pironi crippled at Hockenheim, so, for Monza, Ferrari invited Andretti. He landed from the States at Milan wearing a Ferrari cap, a symbolic gesture that set Italian pulses racing and the pace for qualifying. He put the Ferrari on pole but René Arnoux (Renault) won, beating Patrick Tambay (in the other Ferrari) by 14.0 seconds, Andretti third. Since Arnoux was leaving Renault for Ferrari, a newspaper claimed the *whole* podium for Ferrari. Fastest lap: Arnoux 138.6mph (+5.6)/223.0kph (+8.9).

1983 Prost was going for the Championship. He'd fallen out with Arnoux at Renault and now, of course, Arnoux was with Ferrari and going for the Championship too. Prost arrived with the President of France's bodyguard – the *tifosi* disliked him so much that in earlier testing they'd thrown straw on to the track to try and make his Renault go off. Patrese (Brabham) took pole. Nelson Piquet (Brabham) beat Arnoux by 10.2 seconds. Fastest lap: Piquet 137.4mph (-1.2)/221.1kph (-1.9).

1984 Ayrton Senna was leaving Toleman for Lotus, and Toleman felt strongly that it had been improperly done. They took the car off him for Monza as the only way to punish him. Piquet (Brabham) took pole. Lauda (McLaren) beat Michele Alboreto (Ferrari) by 24.2 seconds. Fastest lap: Lauda 141.2mph (+3.8)/227.2kph (+6.1).

1985 Senna (Lotus) took pole. Prost (McLaren) made the Championship all but certain when he won, beating Piquet (Brabham) by 51.6 seconds, and challenger Alboreto (Ferrari) suffered an engine failure. Fastest lap: Mansell (Williams) 147.0mph (+5.8)/236.5kph (+9.3).

1986 Teo Fabi (Benetton) took pole. The Williams-Honda year – Piquet beating Nigel Mansell by 9.8 seconds, Prost disqualified for changing cars before the start. Evidently he used language about this that would have made the *tifosi* blush. Fastest lap: Fabi 147.3mph (+0.3)/237.0kph (+0.5).

1987 Senna (Lotus) led on lap 43 but went wide at *Parabolica* lapping a backmarker, and that let Piquet (Williams), pole, through. On worn tyres, Senna broke the lap record but couldn't get nearer than 1.8 seconds. Fastest lap: Senna 149.5mph (+2.2)/240.6kph (+3.6).

1988 The McLaren-Honda year. Senna, pole, and Prost should between them have won every race but Monza escaped them. Prost had an engine problem and forced the pace, obliging Senna to use too much fuel. Prost retired and Senna saw the Ferraris coming. He made a lunge at the first chicane to get past a backmarker, Jean-Louis Schlesser, and hit him. Gerhard Berger (Ferrari) beat team-mate Alboreto by 0.5 of a second. Fastest lap: Alboreto 145.7mph (-3.8) /234.4kph (-6.2).

1989 Senna (McLaren) took pole but team-mate Prost, leaving for Ferrari, beat Berger (Ferrari) by 7.3s and, from the podium balcony, dropped the trophy to the *tifosi* below – instead of making sure it went to the McLaren factory trophy room. Fastest lap: Prost 147.3mph (+1.6)/237.0kph (+2.6).

1990 After Senna, pole, had beaten Prost by 6.0 seconds a journalist asked how long their feud would go on. They made up, promising peace in our time. It lasted for six weeks, until Suzuka. Fastest lap: Senna 150.4mph (+3.1)/242.1kph (+5.1).

1991 Senna (McLaren) took pole but masterful Mansell beat him by 16.2 seconds. Fastest lap: Senna 150.8mph (+0.4)/242.6kph (+0.5).

1992 Masterful Mansell again, initially anyway: pole, leading to lap 19 when he let team-mate Patrese by – Patrese had naturally always wanted to win his own Grand Prix. They had problems, letting Senna in. He beat Martin Brundle (Benetton) by 17.0 seconds. Fastest lap: Mansell 150.7mph (-0.1)/242.5kph (-0.1).

1993 Prost (Williams), pole, was cruising to victory and his fourth World Championship when the Renault engine failed. Christian Fittipaldi ran into the back of another car and did a mid-air somersault in perhaps the most photogenic crash of all time. Damon Hill (Williams) beat Jean Alesi (Ferrari) by 40.0 seconds. Fastest lap: Hill 155.2mph (+4.5)/249.8kph (+7.3).

1994 Every circuit became the next to have a Grand Prix without Senna. Alesi (Ferrari) took pole. Benetton were banned for a refuelling irregularity the race before, so Schumacher had to watch Hill (Williams) win it, beating Berger (Ferrari) by 4.9 seconds. Fastest lap: Hill 151.0mph (-4.2) /243.0kph (-6.8).

Speed increase 1976–94: 22.9mph/36.9kph.

The first chicane had been drastically reshaped. Drivers had mixed feelings about it and how tight it was – especially when the cars arrived from the grid on the opening lap – but Schumacher said: 'I think it is a point of discipline between the drivers not to be crazy and just use the space available but no more than that.' Other work was 'carried out on the Grande curve and along the entire tract of Lesmo, from the entrance to the first curve to the exit of the second.' This had the 'objective of increasing the spaces of external escape, which went, in the most critical points, from 50 to 118 metres as far as regards the Grande curve and from 20 to 60 metres as far as regards the tract of the Lesmo curve. In addition, the first curve was tightened with a radius that passed from 98 to 75 metres and, a small amount, also that of the second from 36 to 35 metres. The Roggia curve was brought forward by 50 metres, maintaining, however, the same design to give more ample escape spaces. With these interventions, the length of the track was reduced from 5,800 to 5,770 metres.'[7]

1995 David Coulthard (Williams) took pole. Alesi (Ferrari) led to lap 45 of the 53 when a wheel bearing failed. In a towering rage he drove in his racing overalls from the circuit to Avignon at racing speed. 'I finished my Grand Prix on the way home.' He was about halfway back when Johnny Herbert (Benetton) beat Mika Häkkinen (McLaren) by 17.7 seconds. Fastest lap: Berger (Ferrari) 149.4mph/240.4kph.

1996 Hill (Williams) took pole in this, Schumacher's first season with Ferrari. Whether the *tifosi* could ever take him to their hearts as they had Alesi (now Benetton) was unclear, and made less clear when he beat Alesi by 18.2 seconds. Fastest lap: Schumacher 149.9mph (+0.5)/241.2kph (+0.8).

1997 Alesi (Benetton) took pole. Coulthard (McLaren) dedicated his victory to Diana, Princess of Wales. Her funeral had been the day before. 'It made me feel very emotional when the Union Flag was being raised behind me,' Coulthard said after he beat Alesi by 1.9 seconds. Fastest lap: Mika Häkkinen (McLaren) 152.2mph (+2.3)/244.9kph (+3.7).

1998 Häkkinen led, then Coulthard in the other McLaren. Both had problems, the *tifosi* in the various grandstands around the track cheering so loudly you could read the race by *sound* alone, not least because Schumacher, pole, and Eddie Irvine brought their Ferraris home first and second, 37.9 seconds apart. Fastest lap: Häkkinen 151.6mph (-0.6)/244.0kph (-0.9).

1999 Häkkinen (McLaren), pole, led to lap 30 when, at the first chicane, he changed down into first gear instead of second and the McLaren was gone from him. He was so upset by his own mistake that, when he was in the trees, he crouched and wept. Heinz-Harald Frentzen (Jordan) beat Ralf Schumacher (Williams) by 3.2 seconds. Fastest lap: Ralf Schumacher 150.8mph (-0.8)/242.7kph (-1.3).

Speed increase 1995–9: 1.4mph/2.3kph.
Modification to first two chicanes.

2000 Michael Schumacher (Ferrari), pole, dominated and, like Häkkinen, wept, but for different reasons. He was 'emotional' about being back on the pace and doing it here. Overlaid was the sombre news that a marshal had died when debris from a crash struck him. Schumacher beat Häkkinen (McLaren) by 3.8 seconds. Fastest lap: Häkkinen 151.4mph/243.6kph.

2001 More sombre news, this time the 9/11 attacks in the United States which had happened only five days before. Formula 1, like everyone else, wasn't quite sure how to react. Juan-Pablo Montoya (Williams), pole, beat Rubens Barrichello (Ferrari) by 5.1 seconds. Fastest lap: Ralf Schumacher (Williams) 152.3mph (+0.9)/245.1kph (+1.5).

2002 Montoya (Williams) set the fastest pole of all time with a lap of 1m 20.2s, which translated to an average speed of 161.4mph (259.7kph). Barrichello beat Ferrari team-mate Schumacher by 0.2 of a second. Fastest lap: Rubens Barrichello (Ferrari) 154.9mph (+2.6)/249.3kph (+4.2).

2003 Schumacher, pole, dominated, leading every lap except one during refuelling. He described it as 'one of the greatest days in my career' because Ferrari had been struggling. He beat Montoya (Williams) by 5.2 seconds. Fastest lap: Schumacher 158.4mph (+3.5)/254.8kph (+5.5).

2004 Ferrari dominated, Barrichello (pole) beating Schumacher by 1.3 seconds, Jenson Button (BAR) third but ten seconds away. Fastest lap: Barrichello 159.9mph (+1.5)/257.3kph (+2.5).

2005 McLaren faced a dilemma at the end: Montoya, pole, had worn tyres, and would they last, especially since in testing he'd been doing 231mph (372kph) on the straight? Montoya had no doubts,

The compression into the first chicane in 2007, Lewis Hamilton (McLaren) in the run-off area and running back on, Alonso in the other McLaren (left), the Ferraris of Felipe Massa and Kimi Räikkönen poised to pounce. (Courtesy Autodromo Nazionale Monza)

Sebastian Vettel rides the rain in 2008 to give Toro Rosso their first Grand Prix victory. (Courtesy Autodromo Nazionale Monza)

stayed out and beat Fernando Alonso (Renault) by 2.4 seconds. Fastest lap: Kimi Räikkönen (McLaren) 159.0mph (-0.9)/255.9kph (-1.4).

2006 Schumacher won his 90th Grand Prix, and immediately after he'd done it Ferrari confirmed he would retire at the end of the season. He beat Kimi Räikkönen (McLaren), pole, by 8.0 seconds. Fastest lap: Räikkönen 157.0mph (-2.0)/252.6kph (-3.3).

2007 Alonso (McLaren), pole, beat team-mate Lewis Hamilton by 6.0 seconds but Hamilton, in his first – astonishing – season led the Championship with 92 points to Alonso's 89. Fastest lap: Alonso 156.4mph (-0.6)/251.7kph (-0.9).

2008 A new star was born in 1h 26m 47.4s, the time it took young Sebastian Vettel, pole, to win his first Grand Prix, in drizzle, and give Toro Rosso their first win too. He led every lap except his first pit stop and beat Heikki Kovalainen (McLaren) by 12.5 seconds. Fastest lap: Räikkönen (Ferrari) 147.2mph/236.9kph (no comparison).

2009 Barrichello (with the new Brawn team) drove a controlled, mature race to hold off team-mate Button by 2.8 seconds and see off Hamilton (McLaren), pole, who crashed chasing him near the end. Fastest lap: Adrian Sutil (Force India) 152.9mph (-3.5)/246.1kph (-5.6).

Speed increase 2000–9: 1.5mph/2.5kph.

Footnotes
[1] *Racing Driver*, Salvadori. [2] Courtesy Brawn GP. [3] *My Racing Life*, Fangio. [4] *Ibid.* [5] *Life at the Limit*, Hill. [6] *World Champion*, Stewart. [7] *Monza: Una Grande Storia*, Montagna.

Monza was always Ferrari, of course, even on postcards, but Monza was also royal palace and historic churches. *(Courtesy Martin Hadwen, National Motor Racing Archive)*

Decorating the grid in the traditional way. *(Courtesy Brian Hart)*

FACTS OF THE MATTER

3.915m/6.300km circuit

Year	Winner
1950	G. Farina (Alfa Romeo)
1951	A. Ascari (Ferrari)
1952	A. Ascari (Ferrari)
1953	J.M. Fangio (Maserati)
1954	J.M. Fangio (Mercedes)
Fastest pole	J.M. Fangio (Alfa Romeo) 1951 (124.5mph/200.4kph)
Fastest lap	G. Farina (Alfa Romeo) 1951 (120.0mph/194.7kph)

Banked oval, 6.214m/10.000km circuit

1955	J.M. Fangio (Mercedes)
1956	S. Moss (Maserati)

Parabolica, 3.573m/5.750km circuit

1957	S. Moss (Vanwall)
1958	T. Brooks (Vanwall)
1959	S. Moss (Cooper)

Banked oval as 1956, 6.214m/10.000km circuit

1960	P. Hill (Ferrari)
1961	P. Hill (Ferrari)
Fastest pole	P. Hill 1960 (138.6mph/223.0kph)
Fastest lap	P. Hill 1960 (136.7mph/220.0kph)

Circuit as 1959, 3.573m/5.750km

1962	G. Hill (BRM)
1963	J. Clark (Lotus)
1964	J. Surtees (Ferrari)
1965	J. Stewart (BRM)
1966	L. Scarfiotti (Ferrari)
1967	J. Surtees (Honda)
1968	D. Hulme (McLaren)
1969	J. Stewart (Matra)
1970	C. Regazzoni (Ferrari)
1971	P. Gethin (BRM)
Fastest pole	C. Amon (Matra) 1971 (156.1mph/251.2kph)
Fastest lap	H. Pescarolo (March) 1971 (153.5mph/247.0kph)

Two chicanes, 3.588m/5.775km circuit

1972	E. Fittipaldi (Lotus)
1973	R. Peterson (Lotus)
Fastest pole	R. Peterson 1973 (136.3mph/219.3kph)
Fastest lap	J. Stewart (Tyrrell) 1973 (135.6mph/218.2kph)

Vialone eased, 3.592m/5.780km circuit

1974	R. Peterson (Lotus)
1975	C. Regazzoni (Ferrari)
Fastest pole	N. Lauda (Ferrari) 1975 (140.2mph/225.6kph)
Fastest lap	C. Regazzoni 1975 (138.9mph/223.5kph)

Two more chicanes added, 3.604m/5.800km circuit

1976	R. Peterson (March)
1977	M. Andretti (Lotus)
1978	N. Lauda (Brabham)
1979	J. Scheckter (Ferrari)
1981	A. Prost (Renault)
1982	R. Arnoux (Renault)
1983	N. Piquet (Brabham)
1984	N. Lauda (McLaren)
1985	A. Prost (McLaren)
1986	N. Piquet (Williams)
1987	N. Piquet (Williams)
1988	G. Berger (Ferrari)
1989	A. Prost (McLaren)
1990	A. Senna (McLaren)
1991	N. Mansell (Williams)
1992	A. Senna (McLaren)
1993	D. Hill (Williams)
1994	D. Hill (Williams)
Fastest pole	A. Senna (McLaren) 1991 (160.0mph/257.4kph)
Fastest lap	D. Hill 1993 (155.2mph/249.8kph)

Curva Grande, Lesmo altered, 3.585m/5.770km circuit

1995	J. Herbert (Benetton)
1996	M. Schumacher (Ferrari)
1997	D. Coulthard (McLaren)
1998	M. Schumacher (Ferrari)
1999	H. Frentzen (Jordan)
Fastest pole	M. Häkkinen (McLaren) 1999 (156.6mph/252.0kph)
Fastest lap	M. Häkkinen (McLaren) 1997 (152.2mph/244.9kph)

First two chicanes modified, 3.600m/5.793km circuit

2000	M. Schumacher (Ferrari)
2001	J.-P. Montoya (Williams)
2002	R. Barrichello (Ferrari)
2003	M. Schumacher (Ferrari)
2004	R. Barrichello (Ferrari)
2005	J.-P. Montoya (McLaren)
2006	M. Schumacher (Ferrari)
2007	F. Alonso (McLaren)
2008	S. Vettel (Toro Rosso)
2009	R. Barrichello (Brawn)
Fastest pole	R. Barrichello (Ferrari) 2004 (161.8mph/260.4kph)
Fastest lap	R. Barrichello 2004 (159.9mph/257.3kph)

ITALY
PESCARA

Location: North-west of the town of Pescara, Adriatic Coast.
Constructed: 1924.
World Championship Grands Prix: 1.

Masten Gregory (Maserati) goes up hill and down dale on his way to fourth. (LAT)

'It went up into the mountains and then wound down again'

Stirling Moss

Pescara was and remains the longest circuit in the Championship at 15.8 miles (25.5km). The Nürburgring was in second place, if you can put it like that, at 14.1 miles (22.8km) and Spa third at 8.7 miles (14.1km).

That is a deadpan way of describing a track that linked villages with Pescara, on the coast, and travelled up and down what looked like a mountain track. Pescara was very, very dangerous.

Jack Brabham would remember (in 1971!) that by its nature it represented the sort of circuit that had essentially disappeared in the modern era. He'd write of speeding past houses and chickens. He'd say a lap took ten minutes, so long that the Italians in the grandstands started fighting and the police were needed to sort it out.[1]

Stirling Moss would remember: 'I love road racing. Circuits like that, when the weather's good and so on, you suddenly find yourself on the most fantastic piece of road, very demanding, and to me that was what road racing was all about. You'd go to Spa, which was a proper road, and the Nürburgring – those, really and truly, were what motor racing was. You'd go to a town like Aix les Bains and you'd get there on the Thursday and they'd set up the circuit with straw bales to show you where it went. Usually it was just around one part of the town, and practice would start and the clerk of the course would go round to see that it was all right. You'd practise for a couple of hours and then they'd take the straw bales away and life would go back to normal. That's what it was.'[2]

The Pescara circuit formed a triangle. The start and finish was towards the end of the 6.4km straight that ran along the Adriatic coast from the railway station (at Montesilvano) to the outskirts of Pescara, an ancient fortress town. It turned hard right into an eight-mile (13km) hilly, twisty section 'past the *Villa Raspa*, through the village of *Spoltore* and on to *Cappelle sul Tavo*. Just outside this village the road curved right round through a hairpin bend which led on to the second straight. This led downhill to Montesilvano Station and was the fastest part of the course.'[3]

Ferrari would not be there. Enzo was under savage criticism because Eugenio Castellotti had been killed testing at Modena and a Ferrari had ploughed into the crowd during the Mille Miglia, killing nine spectators as well as the driver and co-driver. Enzo would not countenance Pescara, so his drivers Mike Hawthorn and Peter Collins were out. A third driver, Luigi Musso, pleaded and Enzo gave him a car that became what has been described as a semi-private entry (see 'Eyewitness').

Harry Schell (Maserati) goes round between the hedges on his way to third. (LAT)

COCKPIT VIEWS

Stirling Moss, who drove in the race:
'The circuit was like an Italian Nürburgring, 15.9 miles long and on the edge of the town. It went up into the mountains and then wound down again, narrow, bumpy and twisting through every sort of natural hazard. Altogether it was a true road circuit.

'It was a pretty good circuit, a bit hairy – but then all the races were a bit hairy in those days. You go to the old Spa and that was *bloody* hairy. Pescara? If there was a manhole cover and you didn't want to go over it you went round it – that's the way it was. And going through villages? Yes!'

Roy Salvadori, who drove in the race:
'The Pescara circuit was a very difficult 16-mile road course, very fast, loose at the edges and with the famous long straight along the sea front.'[4]

EYEWITNESS

Gregor Grant, *Autosport*:
'I went round the circuit a couple of times with Roy Salvadori and Tony Brooks in the former's Hillman Minx. That day every peasant in Pescara seemed to be out with donkeys, mules and oxen.

'Stirling Moss was going round in a Fiat "1100", Horace Gould in a Lancia, Scarlatti in a GT Lancia and Jean Behra in a very battered Porsche – the result of an argument with a couple of lorries near Modena. Fangio did several circuits in a borrowed Lancia.

'Luigi Musso, of the "unemployed" Ferrari team, tried hard to beg, borrow or steal an Fl machine in between telephoning Enzo Ferrari to please let him have a car.

'Late on Friday evening a Ferrari did arrive for Musso, but Enzo Ferrari insisted it was a private entry.'

MEMORIES AND A MILESTONE

1957 Because these were ordinary roads practice had to be restricted to morning and afternoon sessions on the day before the race. Juan Manuel Fangio (Maserati) took pole with 9 minutes 44.6 seconds from Moss (Vanwall, 9 minutes 54.7 seconds) and Luigi Musso (Ferrari, 10 minutes exactly).

Because this was August, and Italy can get extremely hot, the start was at 9:30 in the morning to avoid the worst of it: it would finish at 12:30. As the flag fell mechanics were still working on cars at the rear of the grid and one was struck, flipping into the air, by the Maserati of Horace Gould. He was unhurt. Gould, according to Brabham, 'went through a fence' on this opening lap and found himself in a chicken run. Brabham himself would run out of petrol and freewheel

FACTS OF THE MATTER

15.894m/25.579km circuit

Year	Winner
1957	S. Moss (Vanwall)
Pole	J.M. Fangio (Maserati)
	(97.9mph/157.5kph)
Fastest lap	S. Moss (97.9mph/157.5kph)

to a petrol station where the startled attendant filled his Cooper-Climax.

Musso led across the line to complete the first lap with Moss some three seconds behind and Fangio at 13.8 seconds. Moss took Musso on the straight towards the sea into the second lap and would lead to the end, beating Fangio by 3 minutes 13.9 seconds.

Footnotes
[1] *When the Flag Drops*, Brabham. [2] Moss quoted in *The Last Road Race*, Williams. [3] *Racing the Silver Arrows*, Nixon. [4] *Racing Driver*, Salvadori.

No pictures of donkeys, mules and oxen in *Autosport* – see 'Eyewitness'.

1 Pescara really was rural Italy. If offered moments like this.

2 This is the approach to the village of Spoltore,...

3 ... and this is what Spoltore looked like.

4 The approach to Cappelle...

5 ... entering Cappelle...

6 ... and deep in the heart of Cappelle.

7 The road out of Cappelle. *(All courtesy of Julian Nowell)*

AIDA

Location: 44 miles (70km) north-east of Okayama City.
Constructed: 1990.
World Championship Grands Prix: 2.

Noise abatement was truly not going to be a problem. (LAT)

Attwood
Curve

Moss
'S'

Revolver
Corner

The Hairpin

Williams Corner

Mike Knight
Corner

Hobbs
Corner

*'It wasn't, let's say, a
character-built track'*

Johnny Herbert

Piper
Corner

Redman
Corner

First
Corner

Last
Corner

← Start/finish

Hajime Tanaka built golf courses to his own design and in the 1980s an astonishing number of Japanese were obsessed by golf. Because there's so little land without a factory, office block or private dwellings already on it, golf driving ranges were built *vertically* so that, at night, tier after tier of people drove balls into the darkness. So what? So the courses made Tanaka rich enough for him to think he might do the same with a motor racing circuit. He found a place in an area of wooded mountains which wasn't going to trouble any noise abatement activists because it wasn't near anywhere except the village of Aida (population 3,700).

Tanaka financed it by creating a sports club with a life membership of $100,000 where people could garage their cars and take them on to the circuit – he had three Tyrrells himself and claimed the circuit lap record (until Senna came along in 1994).

The circuit opened in November 1990, with Stirling Moss in attendance – an esse had been named after him. Tanaka, of course, wanted a Grand Prix and the local state government were keen to publicise the region as a centre of technology as well as tourism. Money talks and money did talk, which is how the Pacific Grand Prix came there in 1994 and the Formula 1 travelling circus found itself travelling big distances to and from the track because the area had virtually no hotels. (Reportedly some Japanese spectators slept on tables.)

Schumacher described the whole facility as beautiful – clearly he wasn't sleeping on a table – and the track 'a little like Magny-Cours in that it is slippery and the corners are interesting. You have to drive a Formula 1 car a bit like a go-kart. It's small, tricky and pretty technical.'

The circuit hosted the Pacific Grand Prix twice but money talked less loudly: Tanaka had reportedly spent a lot of it and the race didn't go back.

However technical Aida was, however lost in deepest Japan, it was visually very striking. (ICN U.K. Bureau)

COCKPIT VIEW

Johnny Herbert, who drove in both Grands Prix:

'It was in the middle of nowhere and obviously specifically built to have a Grand Prix. The hotel on the circuit was more or less stacked up boxes, very, very typically Japanese basic. The track was very, very short.

'It was also not very demanding because everything was so slow. It was completely flat as well. It wasn't, let's say, a character-built track.

'I can't remember anybody really enjoying going there because (1) it was a pain to get to anyway, and (2) when you got there you did your bit, you left, and it was a pain to leave.

'The only feature was that long curve, the Attwood, and it wasn't high-speed anyway. There was one overtaking place out the back before you began to return towards the start/finish, the infield bit, and one opportunity in that last corner. And that was about it. It was all very, very tight as well, nothing special about it.'

EYEWITNESS

Steven Tee, LAT Photographic:

'I was working with Mild Seven and Schumacher won the World Championship there. I'd been doing a Mild Seven event beforehand with him and we flew in by helicopter from Osaka Airport.

'There were three helicopters: us in one, the Mild Seven people in the second, and the third had all our luggage in it. I'd been asked to take some pictures of Schumacher in the helicopter so I was sitting next to him. He was looking out of the window and I was on the seat inside, shooting his face looking out of the window.

'We suddenly came over this mountain and there was a racetrack. I remember his look: *well … I didn't expect that*. It was a racetrack literally in the middle of nowhere.

'I remember that helicopter because after that it was very much down to earth. We stayed 45 minutes away and had to be coached in every day.

'It was a funny little circuit and you wonder how that ever hosted a Grand Prix.'

MEMORIES AND MILESTONES

1994 Michael Schumacher (Benetton) won but Ayrton Senna (Williams), pole, was punted off at the first corner by

Coulthard leads at the start of the 1995 race, and the start/finish straight bears a strong resemblance to Suzuka. (ICN U.K. Bureau)

Michael Schumacher won the race and the Championship in 1995, beating the Williams team-mates David Coulthard (by 14.2 seconds) and Damon Hill (by 48.3 seconds). (ICN U.K. Bureau)

Bernie Ecclestone and Hajimi Tanaka, the power brokers. (ICN U.K. Bureau)

Mika Häkkinen (McLaren). Nobody knew that he would only ever drive five more Grands Prix laps. Schumacher beat Gerhard Berger (Ferrari) by 1 minute 15.3 seconds. Fastest lap: Schumacher 111.9mph/180.1kph.

1995 The race should have been run in the spring but an earthquake struck Japan, destroying the city of Kobe, and a Grand Prix was clearly inappropriate. The race was moved to October. David Coulthard (Williams) took pole. Schumacher had a barging match with Damon Hill (Williams) and dropped to fifth but Benetton (in an early example of what would happen at Ferrari in years to come) were able to exploit a three-stop pit strategy and, by beating Coulthard by 14.2 seconds, Schumacher became the youngest double World Champion. Fastest lap: Schumacher 108.5mph/174.5kph.

Speed decrease 1994–5: 3.4mph/5.6kph.

FACTS OF THE MATTER

2.301m/3.703km circuit

Year	Winner
1994	M. Schumacher (Benetton)
1995	M. Schumacher (Benetton)
Fastest pole	A. Senna (Williams) 1994
	(118.0mph/189.8kph)
Fastest lap	M. Schumacher 1994
	(111.9mph/180.1kph)

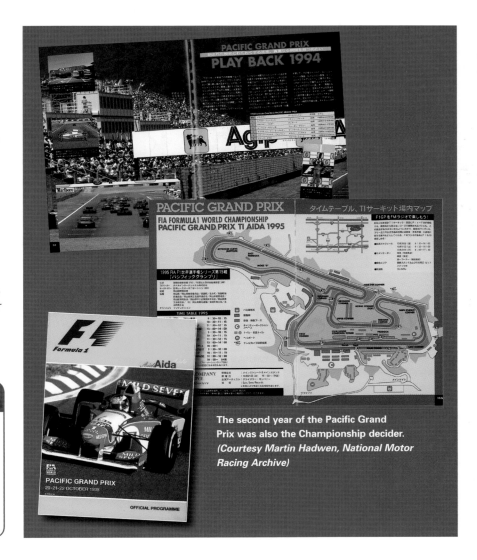

The second year of the Pacific Grand Prix was also the Championship decider. *(Courtesy Martin Hadwen, National Motor Racing Archive)*

FUJI

Location: 44 miles (70km) west of Yokohama.
Constructed: 1965.
World Championship Grands Prix: 4.

James Hunt, Mount Fuji, 24 October 1976.
(LAT)

OLD CIRCUIT

Coca Cola

Hairpin

Start/finish

Dunlop

300R

100R

Netz

Coca Cola

Hairpin

Panasonic

Start/finish

NEW CIRCUIT – 2007-on

'It was quite nice but it didn't get the juices flowing'

John Watson

Very rarely is a circuit defined by a single image. Fuji is, and perhaps always will be. James Hunt has risen from the cockpit of his McLaren and the team members, hemming the car, have hands raised and three fingers splayed to tell him that he emerged from a chaotic race third – making him World Champion.

Genuine drama seemed entirely appropriate to any race run in the shadow of a volcano – Mount Fuji itself – albeit a dormant one since December 1707. Mount Fuji habitually broods behind cloud. The area, however, is known for holidaymaking – part of it is called The Sea of Trees – and committing suicide.

The circuit was originally intended to run NASCAR-style races and built accordingly, as a 2.5-mile (4km) banked speedway, but the money ran out and only part of the banking was completed. The rest remained a road course, including a 0.9-mile (1.5km) straight, one of the longest ever used in Formula 1. The *Mistral* at Ricard was 0.7-mile (1.2km).

The banking was very dangerous and soon abandoned. The track was modified to circumvent the banking and now measured 2.7 miles (4.3km). It was to this that Hunt came at the climax of the 1976 season.

An horrific race in 1977 (see below) cost the circuit further Formula 1 races

Mount Fuji, the eternal presence.
(Courtesy Gareth Rees)

but the World Sportscar Championship was a regular visitor during the 1980s. It remained fast and two chicanes were added to cope with that.

Toyota bought it in 2000 and three years later it was closed for a major reworking to a design by Tilke. That made it ready for a Grand Prix again in 2007. Anthony Davidson, who

drove a Super Aguri, compared it to Indianapolis 'except that it's not flat'. He added: 'The undulations and camber change the character of the circuit. It's hard work on the balance of the car.'[1]

COCKPIT VIEW
John Watson:
'The first time I went there was in 1976, which was James Hunt's championship year.

'The biggest challenge was the final turn on to the main straight. The approach to it was quick, quite a long corner, then a long, long straight. The corner at the end was slow, second gear, then you accelerated out and dropped through a left then a long right to a hairpin bend. The descent continued to the lowest point of the circuit. The only real overtaking place was at the end of the main straight.

'It was quite nice but it didn't get the juices flowing.

'The big concern was rain, because if it does that it does it big time.

'Around the time these circuits were

built, Japanese racing was about their local championships. At Fuji they also had other layouts available to them and a banked corner somewhere (see 'Eyewitness'), so it may be that they had their championships on that one, not the Grand Prix circuit. Japanese racing was extremely dangerous at that time.'

EYEWITNESS
Gareth Rees, motor racing enthusiast:
'Having spent more than half of the last 20 years living in Tokyo I was a regular visitor to Fuji Speedway for the usual Japanese GT and Formula 3000 (later Formula Nippon) races. In the early 1990s I saw some of the last few Group C races where the works Nissans could hit 380kph [235mph] as they passed the grandstands!

'The place oozed history and until the

mid-1990s still had the old pits with the corrugated iron roofs that are so familiar in pictures of James Hunt's legendary Championship-winning race.

'Even better, at the end of the main straight, beyond what has for years now been Turn 1, you can still find most of the old downhill (!) banking used in the 1960s and early 1970s, which remain today as a monument to heroism or utter madness.

'I have a wonderful DVD of the Japan GP of 1969, where, among others, Jo Siffert drove one of the original Porsche 917s with David Piper and survived [in the 1960s it was a sports car race]. Many drivers in those days didn't survive, and the banking was already abandoned before the Formula 1 cars arrived for the first time in 1976.

'Come 2007 and 2008, when Formula 1 returned to Fuji, I was there both

Gareth Rees demonstrating how steep the banking was – and the circuit looks muscular, too. He says that 'the banking was never used for Formula 1. The fate of Fuji's banking was determined in June 1974, after Hiroshi Kazato and Seiichi Suzuki died in a multi-car accident at the start of a Grand Champion sports car race. By 1976 the first corner turned right well before the banking, which was the old first corner.'
(Courtesy Gareth Rees)

times. In the years previously Toyota had bought the circuit and reconstructed the lot to the latest Formula 1 standards but, thankfully, doing a good job of keeping the basic layout so that the traditional character of the circuit remained.

'I was a regular visitor for domestic races and what struck me most in 2007 was not the action on the track but the people running the show. In the paddock and hospitality areas there was no trace of

the usual, delightfully hesitant Japanese officials. All the people in "authority" seemed to be muscular ex-Army Brits in smart blazers who politely but sternly told you where you were allowed to be, and the message was very clear.

'Welcome to the warm world of Formula 1 in the 21st century. There was not a trace of local culture. If it hadn't been for the occasional glimpse of Mount Fuji we really could have been anywhere.'

MEMORIES AND MILESTONES

1976 Mario Andretti (Lotus) took pole. Torrential rain delayed the start and on lap 3 Lauda, face seared from his fiery crash at the Nürburgring in August, decided that the conditions were too dangerous, angled his Ferrari into the pits and retired. He had three more points than James Hunt (McLaren), who now needed at least third place for the Championship. Deep into the race a tyre shredded – Hunt thought the team should have called him in earlier, the team thought he should have made the decision – and after a pit stop he was sure the championship had gone. The splayed fingers at the end told him he was wrong. Andretti beat Patrick Depailler (Tyrrell) by a lap. Fastest lap: Jacques Laffite (Ligier) 121.9mph/196.2kph.

1977 Andretti (Lotus) took pole again. On lap 6 Gilles Villeneuve (Ferrari) missed his braking point at the end of the straight, rammed a Tyrrell and somersaulted off, killing a marshal and a photographer. Several other people were seriously injured. Hunt (McLaren) beat Carlos Reutemann (Ferrari) by 1 minute 02.4 seconds. Fastest lap: Scheckter (Wolf) 131.2mph/211.2kph (no comparison).

The circuit had been extended to 2.8

Fuji will always carry a specific sequence of images – of James Hunt riding the storm in 1976 to win the World Championship. Even The Times judged it big news.

Autosport magazine naturally carried their own sequence of images – and for them Champion James was very big news indeed.

FACTS OF THE MATTER

2.709m/4.359km circuit

Year	Winner
1976	M. Andretti (Lotus)
1977	J. Hunt (McLaren)
Fastest pole	M. Andretti (Lotus) 1977 (135.0mph/217.3kph)
Fastest lap	J. Scheckter (Wolf) 1977 (131.2mph/211.2kph)

2.835m/4.562km circuit

2007	L. Hamilton (McLaren)
2008	F. Alonso (Renault)
Fastest pole	L. Hamilton (McLaren) 2008 (130.1mph/209.5kph)
Fastest lap	F. Massa (Ferrari) 2008 (130.2mph/209.5kph)

CLOCKWISE FROM LEFT: The 2007 Grand Prix was wet but practice wasn't. Jenson Button (Honda) and Vitantonio Liuzzi (Toro Rosso) in parallel universes? Nico Rosberg gives a few words to the assembled media. The circuit wasn't packed and not everyone was excited. Felipe Massa (Ferrari). (Courtesy Gareth Rees)

miles with the addition of an 'infield' to the start/finish straight and the tightening of the Coca Cola corner.

2007 Almost hauntingly the race was run in a rainstorm, the Safety Car out for 18 laps. Anthony Davidson compared the conditions to being on a motorbike behind a truck at 70mph. 'Water was actually being driven in through the visor, through the vents in your helmet and into your face, dripping into your eyes.'[2] Lewis Hamilton (McLaren), pole, beat Heikki Kovalainen (Renault) by 8.3 seconds. Fastest lap: Hamilton 115.7mph/186.3kph.

2008 Hamilton (McLaren), pole, went to Fuji, round 16 of the 18, with 84 points, Felipe Massa 77 – but Hamilton got involved in a melee at the first corner. Robert Kubica (BMW) had started sixth but now led and commented cryptically: 'I think I was just about the only one to stay on the track, really.' However, Fernando Alonso (Renault) beat him by 5.2 seconds. Fastest lap: Massa 130.1mph/209.5kph (no comparison).

Footnotes
[1] *Autosport.* [2] *Ibid.*

JAPAN
SUZUKA

Location: 31 miles (50km) from the city of Nagoya.
Constructed: 1961.
World Championship Grands Prix: 21.

Because of the length of the straight the start at Suzuka was always charged with possibilities, especially when it rained. This is 1995, with Michael Schumacher (Benetton) leading Jean Alesi (Ferrari) and Mika Häkkinen (McLaren). (ICN U.K. Bureau)

'A real drivers' circuit just like Silverstone and Spa'

Jenson Button

Spoon Curve

Hairpin Curve

West Straight

130R

Crossover/ Underpass

Degner Curve

Casio Chicane/ Triangle

Last Corner

Dunlop Curve

S-Curves

Start/ finish

First Curve

Second Curve

The drivers adore Suzuka. The journalists who adore racing adore Suzuka. The Japanese who enjoy a fairground and a market of stalls and extensive leisure facilities as well as a motor race adore Suzuka.

There are problems, however, the first of them that Suzuka is not near anywhere. Tokyo is more than 160 miles away from Nagoya, which has been described as the Japanese equivalent of Wolverhampton. If you're French, substitute Lille. If you're German, substitute Duisberg. If you're Italian…

Before it was given a serious makeover for the 2009 season it shocked first-time visitors expecting a pristine, futuristic facility reflecting Japan's wealth and attitudes. They found instead somewhere cramped, rudimentary, with, for example, toilet facilities as primitive as any in France – a big statement.

The track, the only one shaped like a figure of eight with a crossover, compensated for everything.

The Williams team put it nicely enough: 'Suzuka is widely regarded as one of the most technically challenging tracks of the season where success lies in the balance of the car. Each of the 3.6-mile laps includes an unforgiving combination of 16 turns, ranging from the slow speed, twisty *Esses* and *Spoon* corner at the start of the lap to the high-speed *130R* and *Casio Triangle* towards the end.

'With such a variation of turns, aero efficiency and car stability are crucial to allow the driver to achieve fluidity through the corners and record a quick lap time. Suzuka ranks among the top five fastest tracks on the calendar, one which requires high revs and sees a high average speed over one lap. As such, engine power and torque are key variables.'

The circuit, designed by Dutchman John Hugenholz, was originally constructed for use by Honda for testing, and held its first race – for sports cars – in 1963. It continued to be used by sports cars and then Formula 2 but didn't get the first Japanese Formula 1 Grand Prix, which went to Mount Fuji in 1976 and again in 1977. Suzuka continued to host a wide variety of races.

Honda had now become a power

within Formula 1, supplying engines to Williams and Lotus, with McLaren to come. When Grand Prix racing did return to Japan in 1987, Suzuka was the chosen son, and because of its positioning on the calendar – the second to last race – the first five races there decided the Championships. That meant the circuit would be the stage for some of Formula 1's bitterest, most controversial and most dramatic moments.

In one important sense Suzuka distilled modernity because, if you had two evenly matched cars, the possibilities for overtaking were very

limited. It produced the bitterness, controversy and drama in 1989 when Ayrton Senna struggled to overtake his McLaren team-mate Alain Prost. It could only be done at the chicane before the start/finish straight and Senna knew if he didn't do it there he would lose the Championship. He tried, Prost refused to yield, and they collided – Prost out, Senna limping on towards disqualification.

The view which returned year after year: the big wheel from the fairground.
(ICN U.K. Bureau)

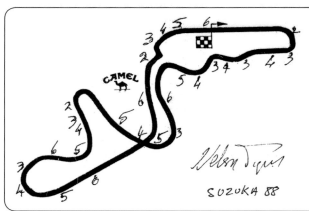

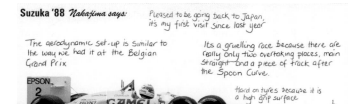

Suzuka '88 *Nakajima says:* Pleased to be going back to Japan, it's my first visit since last year

The aerodynamic set-up is similar to the way we had it at the Belgian Grand Prix

Its a gruelling race because there are really only two overtaking places, main straight and a piece of track after the Spoon Curve.

Hard on tyres because it is a high grip surface

Local knowledge. Satoru Nakajima (Lotus) sets out his view of the circuit and team-mate Nelson Piquet gives his gear changes. (Courtesy Camel)

COCKPIT VIEWS

Jenson Button, Brawn, 2009:

'Suzuka is such a fun circuit and I have lots of good memories from racing there over the years. It's a very fast-flowing lap and a real drivers' circuit just like Silverstone and Spa.

'*130R* is one of the fastest corners in Formula 1 and you really have to think about how you approach it. We might not be flat through there this year but it is still a real buzz to take the corner carrying speeds of 300kph [186mph]. I've had some moments there in the past.'[1]

Rubens Barrichello, Brawn, 2009:

'It's a tough circuit because of the corners and the track layout and you have to be precise, consistent and get the balance of the car absolutely right to have a good weekend.

'*Spoon* and *130R* are the undoubted highlights of the lap. Both turns are part of what makes Suzuka so demanding and such a great challenge for the drivers. Overtaking can be tough and generally happens into the slowest corner on the track, the *Casio Triangle*, into the fast fifth-gear *First Curve* or occasionally at the Turn 11 *Hairpin*.'[2]

EYEWITNESS

Steven Tee, LAT Photographic:

'It's a great circuit built at a time when they didn't over-plan them. Some of the new circuits have been over-planned.

'Where China is too big and too bland, Suzuka isn't. The drivers all love it – their three favourite tracks are Suzuka, Spa, and Silverstone, because they are *drivers'* circuits. They like Monaco, but for different reasons.

'In 1989 I went to the chicane because it is an obvious place to be. I was doing Formula 1 virtually on my own (for LAT), so you'd do a start shot from the first corner then you'd walk back up past the pits to the chicane where you could get some stuff during the race and you were easily located to get back for the podium shots. And if anyone was going to try and overtake at Suzuka, they were going to try it at that chicane.

'It is the slowest part of the circuit and you can try and out-brake people, which is exactly what Senna tried to do with Prost – but obviously Prost wasn't having any of it.

'The other thing was that you could get quite close. They've changed that chicane since but in those days you were on a bank probably 20 metres away.

'A year later I was at Turn 1 because you always did the start of a Grand Prix: somebody has to do a start picture. My mindset would have been the same as the year before: do the start then wander up and do the chicane.

'Funnily enough, the start tower – it was just taller than the debris fencing to protect the crowd – in those days wasn't in the best location. My pictures of that Senna-Prost shunt aren't as good as the chicane the year before because you were at the side of the track. Now they have the start tower at the end so you are looking back up the straight and the shunt would have come directly towards you. Literally Senna and Prost touched as they went past us.

'The most telling picture I got was the two of them walking back behind the Armco and you could see Senna's body language as opposed to Prost's. They didn't even look at each other, they were probably ten yards apart. I expect Senna was thinking *job done, there you go*, and Prost thinking *you little bastard*.'

MEMORIES AND MILESTONES

1987 The Championship was decided in qualifying when Nigel Mansell (Williams) slid off, struck a tyre barrier, was airborne and landed with great ferocity. He was taken to hospital and then flown home. Team-mate Nelson Piquet thus had the Championship by default. Gerhard Berger (Ferrari), pole, beat Ayrton Senna (Lotus) by 17.3 seconds. Fastest lap: Alain Prost (McLaren) 126.2mph/203.1kph.

1988 Senna, now partnering Alain Prost at McLaren, had pole – Prost alongside – but stalled at the green lights. His car freewheeled slowly forward and the engine fired. He was 14th but worked his way up to lead on lap 28 – Prost seemed to miss a gear – and won by 13.3 seconds, despite rain towards the end, to take the Championship. Afterwards Senna wept. Fastest lap: Senna 123.3mph (-2.9)/198.4kph (-4.7).

1989 At McLaren, Prost and Senna (pole) were locked into a feud as profound as any that Formula 1 had known, and it reached its first culmination on lap 47 when Senna dived down the inside into the chicane and Prost stayed on the racing line. They crashed, Prost out, Senna getting back to the pits for repairs and then 'winning'. Days later, however, Prost was declared Champion. (Sandro Nannini in a Benetton beat Riccardo Patrese's Williams by 11.9 seconds.) Fastest lap: Prost 126.6mph (+3.3)/203.8kph (+5.4).

1990 The notorious race when Senna (McLaren) took pole and wanted to move it to the cleaner side of the track. When he was refused he decided to go flat out into Turn 1 and if Prost (Ferrari, on the front row) was there, too bad. Prost was there and the crash reverberated

The aftermath of the infamous crash at the chicane, 1989. The McLarens are side by side, Senna looking at Prost – and Prost looking at Senna. (Courtesy Marlboro)

round the world, bringing great damage to the credibility of Formula 1. Piquet beat Benetton team-mate Roberto Moreno by 7.2 seconds. Fastest lap: Riccardo Patrese (Williams) 125.7mph (-0.9)/202.4kph (-1.4).

The chicane was tightened and moved so that it was further away from the white line indicating the entrance to the pit lane. This resolved one logistical problem: drivers stealing across the line when they were making overtaking moves.

1991 Mansell (Williams) was chasing Senna (McLaren) for the Championship and went off at Turn 1 with, as it seemed, a brake problem. The Championship was gone. Senna was ordered to let team-mate Berger, pole, through for his first win and Senna obeyed, reluctantly. Berger won by 0.3 of a second. 91 Fastest lap: Senna 129.2mph/207.9kph.

1992 The Williamses were *so* dominant that Mansell, pole, would give the race to Riccardo Patrese, who hadn't won during the season. Mansell fled into the lead, slowed for Patrese to catch him and then his engine blew. Patrese beat Berger (McLaren) by 13.7 seconds. Fastest lap: Mansell 130.3mph (+1.1)/209.7kph (+1.8).

1993 Senna conjured his fourth victory of the season from the McLaren and its Ford engine although, en route, he felt he was baulked by young Eddie Irvine (Jordan) and sought him out afterwards to explain the facts of life. Irvine was not impressed. Senna beat Prost (Williams), pole, by 11.4 seconds. Fastest lap: Prost 129.6mph (-0.7)/208.6kph (-1.1).

1994: Rain drowned the race, forcing it to be run in two parts with the aggregate to count. Damon Hill (Williams) resisted intense and growing pressure from Michael Schumacher (Benetton), pole, in the closing laps when the track was like ice, and won by 3.3 seconds. Fastest lap: Hill 112.5mph/181.1kph (no comparison).

1995 Schumacher's ninth win of the season gave Benetton the Constructors' Championship for the first time. From pole, Schumacher led every lap except his pit stops and beat Mika Häkkinen (McLaren) by 18.3 seconds. Fastest lap: Schumacher 127.4mph (-2.2)/205.0kph (-3.6).

1996 Jacques Villeneuve (Williams) took pole. Hill, who'd carried so much weight for so many years – starting with having Graham as a father, and endless comparisons between them – finally shed it. He put his Williams on the front row and led every lap, including his pit stops, to beat Schumacher (Ferrari) by 1.8 seconds and take the Championship.

Fastest lap: Villeneuve 126.1mph (-1.3)/202.9kph (-2.1).

1997 Villeneuve (Williams), pole and leading the Championship, was excluded for failing to slow during a waved yellow in practice. He appealed, raced, and finished fifth. Irvine led after lap 2 but ceded this to Ferrari team-mate Schumacher, who beat Heinz-Harald Frentzen (in the other Williams) by 1.3 seconds. That gave Schumacher 78 and Villeneuve 77 – and set up the final race, at Jerez, as the decider. Fastest lap: Frentzen 132.6mph (+6.5)/213.4kph (+10.5).

1998 Schumacher (Ferrari), pole, was four points behind Häkkinen (McLaren) but stalled on the line, aborting the start – two earlier starts had already been aborted. He started from the back of the grid, abandoned caution and reached third

The unique crossover, rarely photographed, could also be called the crossunder. (LAT)

Gianni Morbidelli (Footwork) learns all about the start and the perils of Turn 1. Karl Wendlinger (Sauber) has just tapped him in 1995. (ICN U.K. Bureau)

before a puncture on lap 32 ended it. Häkkinen had the Championship. He beat Irvine in the other Ferrari by 6.4 seconds. Fastest lap: Schumacher 130.9mph (-1.7)/210.7kph (-2.7).

1999 Irvine (Ferrari) 70 points, Häkkinen (McLaren) 66 coming to Suzuka –

The length of the straight is beautifully captured in this study of the 1997 race, Jacques Villeneuve (Williams) leading the crocodile. (ICN U.K. Bureau)

Schumacher, who'd broken his leg at Silverstone, ambivalent about whether he'd help Irvine or not. It never arose. Schumacher put his Ferrari on pole but Häkkinen led every lap except during his first pit stop and beat Schumacher by 5.0 seconds, Irvine third – and Häkkinen Champion. Fastest lap: Schumacher 129.5mph (-1.4)/208.4kph (-2.3).

2000 The year of consummation. After spending a fortune (nobody except Ferrari really knew how much) Schumacher finally created the succession to Jody Scheckter in 1979 by putting his Ferrari on pole from nearest rival Häkkinen and leapfrogging him at the second pit stops. The winning margin, 1.8 seconds, didn't mean much. The Championship meant everything. Fastest lap: Häkkinen 132.2mph (+2.7)/212.8kph (+4.4).

2001 Schumacher had won the Championship five races before – Hungary – so the end-of-season was a sort of triumphal procession. From pole at Suzuka he led every lap except pit stops and beat Juan-Pablo Montoya (Williams) by 3.1 seconds. Fastest lap: Ralf Schumacher (Williams) 135.2mph (+3.0)/217.6kph (+4.8).

Speed increase 1991–2001: 6.0mph/9.7kph.

The S-curves were modified, reducing the circuit length by 24 metres (78 feet).

2002 Another triumphal tour: Schumacher, pole, had won the Championship seven races before and now led every lap except during his first stop to beat Ferrari team-mate Rubens Barrichello by 0.5 of a second. Fastest lap: Schumacher 135.5mph /218.0kph.

130R and the chicane were reprofiled.

2003 Schumacher 92 points, Kimi

Räikkönen (McLaren) 83 going into this final round. Barrichello (Ferrari) took pole. Schumacher qualified 14th – thwarted by rain at the wrong time – and finished eighth. His Championship was saved by team-mate Barrichello who won, beating Räikkönen by 11.0 seconds: Schumacher 93, Räikkönen 91. Fastest lap: Ralf Schumacher (Williams) 139.1mph/223.8kph.

2004 Schumacher (Ferrari) took pole. Another triumphal tour: Schumacher had won the Championship four races before – Spa – and now led every lap from pole to beat brother Ralf (Williams) by 14.0 seconds. Fastest lap: Barrichello 140.1mph (+1.0)/225.4kph (+1.6).

2005 Ralf Schumacher (Toyota) took pole. Fernando Alonso (Renault) created one of the great overtakings by going past Schumacher (Ferrari) on the outside of 130R. That was lap 20, for fifth place – both had qualified far down the grid. Kimi Räikkönen (McLaren) beat Giancarlo Fisichella (Renault) by 1.6 seconds. Fastest lap: Räikkönen 141.9mph (+1.8)/228.4kph (+3.0).

2006 Felipe Massa (Ferrari) took pole. Team-mate Schumacher led from Alonso (Renault) for the middle section of the race then Schumacher had an engine failure – had he been pushing too hard to hold Alonso? At that moment, with only one race left, Schumacher's Championship was virtually gone. Alonso, 10 points ahead, beat Massa by 16.1 seconds. Fastest lap: Alonso 140.2mph (-1.7)/225.6kph (-2.8).

Speed increase 2003–6: 1.1mph/1.8kph.

The circuit needed modernising and this was carried out before the race returned. There were new pits, an improved paddock, and new grandstands. A section of the track had been resurfaced, and a new pit exit built. With other revisions the circuit was shortened.

2009 Sebastian Vettel (Red Bull), pole, had a slender chance of beating Jenson Button (Brawn) to the Championship but responded to this pressure with a tremendous win from pole, beating Jarno Trulli (Toyota) by 4.8 seconds. Two races to go and Button had 85 points, team-mate Barrichello 71, and Vettel 69. Fastest lap: Mark Webber (Red Bull) 140.3mph/225.8kph.

Footnotes
[1] Courtesy Brawn GP. [2] Ibid.

A view you rarely see: the full entertainment complex at Suzuka. *(Courtesy Martin Hadwen, National Motor Racing Archive)*

Formula 1 really is international and with international allegiances, as these supporters prove at Suzuka in 2009. *(Courtesy Michael Beran)*

FACTS OF THE MATTER

3.641m/5.859km circuit

Year	Winner
1987	G. Berger (Ferrari)
1988	A. Senna (McLaren)
1989	A. Nannini (Benetton)
1990	N. Piquet (Benetton)
Fastest pole	A. Senna (McLaren) 1990 (135.1mph/217.5kph)
Fastest lap	A. Prost (McLaren) 1989 (126.6mph/203.8kph)

Chicane moved, 3.644m/5.864km circuit

Year	Winner
1991	G. Berger (McLaren)
1992	R. Patrese (Williams)
1993	A. Senna (McLaren)
1994	D. Hill (Williams)
1995	M. Schumacher (Benetton)
1996	D. Hill (Williams)
1997	M. Schumacher (Ferrari)
1998	M. Häkkinen (McLaren)
1999	M. Häkkinen (McLaren)
2000	M. Schumacher (Ferrari)
Fastest pole	G. Berger (McLaren) 1991 (138.5mph/222.9kph)
Fastest lap	H.-H. Frentzen (Williams) 1997 (132.6mph/213.4kph)

Minor revision, 3.641m/5.859km circuit

2001	M. Schumacher (Ferrari)
Pole	M. Schumacher (141.7mph/228.1kph)
Fastest lap	R. Schumacher (Williams) (135.2mph/217.6kph)

S curve modification, 3.617m/5.821km circuit

2002	M. Schumacher (Ferrari)
Pole	M. Schumacher (142.6mph/229.5kph)
Fastest lap	M. Schumacher (135.5mph/218.0kph)

130R, chicane reprofiled, 3.608m/5.807km circuit

2003	R. Barrichello (Ferrari)
2004	M. Schumacher (Ferrari)
2005	K. Räikkönen (McLaren)
2006	F. Alonso (Renault)
Fastest pole	F. Massa (Ferrari) 2006 (145.0mph/233.3kph)
Fastest lap	K. Räikkönen (McLaren) 2005 (141.9mph/228.4kph)

Revisions, 3.387m/5.451km circuit

2009	S. Vettel (Red Bull)
Pole	S. Vettel (140.9mph/226.8kph)
Fastest lap	M. Webber (Red Bull) (140.3mph/225.8kph).

SEPANG

Location: 30 miles (48km) south of Kuala Lumpur.
Constructed: 1999.
World Championship Grands Prix: 11.

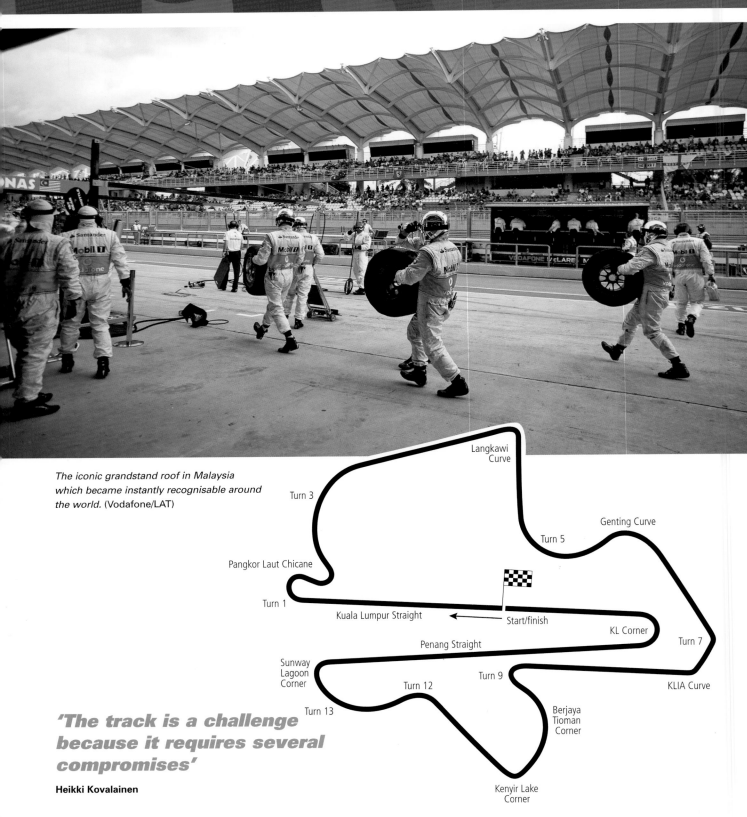

The iconic grandstand roof in Malaysia which became instantly recognisable around the world. (Vodafone/LAT)

Langkawi Curve

Turn 3

Genting Curve

Turn 5

Pangkor Laut Chicane

Turn 1

Kuala Lumpur Straight

Start/finish

KL Corner

Turn 7

Penang Straight

Sunway Lagoon Corner

Turn 9

KLIA Curve

Turn 12

Turn 13

Berjaya Tioman Corner

Kenyir Lake Corner

'The track is a challenge because it requires several compromises'

Heikki Kovalainen

Sepang is a town and district in southern Malaysia, and the Grand Prix circuit, designed by Tilke, has brought recognition to the area – that and Kuala Lumpur International Airport.

Malaysia does have a history of motor sport. They had a circuit called Shah Alam, which was 'originally known as Batu Tiga and sometimes referred to as Selangor in deference to the palace overlooking the circuit'. The Selangor 800 Sports Car race was, before 1999, the only World Championship race to have been held in Malaysia. 'It was run in the heat of the start of the monsoon season! Only 3,000 spectators paid to watch and so the exercise was not repeated. The circuit was closed in 1977 after an accident claimed the lives of six children. After improvements costing a reported £100,000 Shah Alam was reopened with better protection for spectators.'[1]

The circuit staged World Superbike rounds and the Malaysian bike Grand Prix but in 2003 was sold to a property developer.

Sepang, in the same province of

You can see why the roof was instantly recognisable: delicate like autumn leaves. (Vodafone/LAT)

Selangor, was to the south, and a fresh start. It was also a state-of-the-art facility when the Grand Prix first went, in 1999. Ecclestone described it as 'the best in the world' and its main grandstand was so spectacularly photogenic – especially its roof – that photographers took pictures of it year after year as if they'd just discovered it (or couldn't resist it).

Two long, broad straights, joined by a tight left-hand horseshoe, were a feature of the track. Its 15 corners came in all varieties: three to be taken in first or second gear, four in third gear, four in fourth gear, and two in fifth gear.

COCKPIT VIEWS

Heikki Kovalainen, McLaren, 2009:
'The track is a challenge because it requires several compromises to get the best set-up. There are plenty of long straights, where you ideally need lower downforce, but that gives the car a tendency to slide too much through the high-speed corners.

'The best corners are Turns 6 and 7 – the fast left-right esses behind the pits. In the car, you've not only got to find the optimum balance, but also make sure the brakes and cooling are efficient, otherwise you'll be in trouble before you get to the end of the race. The only difficulty for me is the heat; coming from Finland, we often see the same temperature readings – but with a minus in front…'[2]

Rubens Barrichello, Brawn, 2009:
'The Malaysian Grand Prix is always a really tough race but if you can cope well with the heat and humidity it is a track that the drivers enjoy.

'It's a real engineering challenge to find the right balance and you need to have a car with good aerodynamics to find time

around the lap. The intense heat puts pressure on the engine, brakes and the drivers as the temperature can rise above 50° in the cockpit so you have to be well-prepared and ensure you're fully-hydrated.'[3]

EYEWITNESS

Ann Bradshaw, PR expert:
'I have to be honest. Of all the countries I visit I do not enjoy Malaysia because I don't like hot, sweaty places – I hate high humidity.

'The circuit is close to the airport. In fact, it would take you about 10, 15 minutes to drive there and you can see it from the airport, but it's not very close to anything in terms of hotels. Apart from the Pan-Pacific at the airport you have to go 45 minutes or an hour to get to them.

'It's not really in a nice area. They obviously have problems with flash floods, so one minute you're roasting, the next minute the clouds darken and it tips down. That can happen in the middle of a race, and it did.

'It's one of those places which, when you go back to it for a race, you feel the

staff have arrived the day before, opened the offices, chased the spiders out then said *here we go again.* It does seem to be decaying.

'The people are nice enough and the track has produced some excellent racing.

'You didn't go there initially and think *oh, it's got everything* the way you do at Abu Dhabi. It was what I call the last of the nearly-theres. Ok, they have that lovely roof on the grandstand but I didn't get that *gosh, no money spared* feeling, and in terms of attendance nobody went.'

MEMORIES AND MILESTONES

1999 The race happened post-race. Eddie Irvine and Schumacher, pole, finished first and second in their Ferraris, Mika Häkkinen (McLaren) third – which meant Irvine went to the final race at Suzuka with a 4 point lead over Häkkinen. Then the Ferraris were found to have illegal bodywork and were disqualified. They were only reinstated on appeal after several days. Irvine beat Schumacher by 1.0 second. Fastest lap: Schumacher 123.6mph/199.0kph.

2000 Schumacher had already won the Championship at the race before and now, from pole, leapfrogged David Coulthard (McLaren) at the first pit stops for his 44th victory, equalling Nigel Mansell's nine in a season. He beat Coulthard by 0.7 of a second. Fastest lap: Häkkinen (McLaren) 125.8mph (+2.2)/202.5kph (+3.5).

2001 Schumacher (Ferrari), pole, led, but a tropical thunderstorm engulfed the circuit and he floated off with Ferrari team-mate Rubens Barrichello on lap 3. They recovered so strongly that they ran 1-2 by lap 16. Schumacher beat him by 23.6 seconds. Fastest lap: Häkkinen (McLaren) 122.8mph (-3.0)/197.6kph (-4.9).

2002 Schumacher took pole and chopped Juan-Pablo Montoya (Williams) from the lights. They crashed and that opened the race to brother Ralf, who seized the lead from Barrichello (Ferrari) at the first pit stops and beat team-mate Montoya by 39.7 seconds. Fastest lap: Montoya 126.5mph (+3.7)/203.5kph (+5.9).

2003 Young world: Fernando Alonso

There was an immensity as well as a delicacy to Sepang – and breadth to the start/finish straight, too. (LAT)

(Renault) became the youngest driver to take pole and Kimi Räikkönen (McLaren) the second youngest race winner when he beat Barrichello (Ferrari) by 39.2 seconds. Fastest lap: Schumacher (Ferrari) 128.6mph (+2.1)/207.0kph (+3.5).

2004 In steaming weather Schumacher (Ferrari) dominated from pole, and although Montoya (Williams) was able to exert some pressure it wasn't enough to prevent Schumacher beating him by 5.0 seconds. Fastest lap: Montoya 131.6mph (+3.0)/211.8kph (+4.8).

2005 The temperature reached 50° and Alonso (Renault) was even hotter. From pole he led every lap except his pit stops for his second career victory, although his overall control suggested he was older and much more experienced. He beat Jarno Trulli (Toyota) by 24.3 seconds. Fastest lap: Räikkönen (McLaren) 129.9mph (-1.7)/209.0kph (-2.8).

2006 Alonso was given more fuel than planned during final qualifying and had to haul that, offering Renault team-mate Giancarlo Fisichella, pole, his chance. They and Jenson Button (Honda) fought for the first two places throughout, Fisichella beating Alonso by 4.5 seconds and Button finishing a strong third. Fastest lap:

Alonso 130.8mph (+0.9)/210.5kph (+1.5).

2007 Felipe Massa (Ferrari) took pole. Alonso (McLaren) won and handsomely, but team-mate Lewis Hamilton was the story. This was only his second race and he ran second throughout except his pit stops, finishing 17.5 seconds behind Alonso. Fastest lap: Hamilton 128.2mph (-2.6)/206.4kph (-4.1).

2008 Felipe Massa took pole from Ferrari team-mate Räikkönen and led but Räikkönen produced a tremendous burst of pace at the first pit stops and leapfrogged him. Massa spun off and Räikkönen beat Robert Kubica (BMW) by 19.5 seconds. Fastest lap: Nick Heidfeld (BMW) 130.0mph (+1.8)/209.2kph (+2.8).

2009 A tropical storm of such intensity that drivers could barely control their cars *at any speed* did not prevent Button (Brawn), pole, from beating Nick Heidfeld (BMW) by 22.7 seconds – the race stopped, never to be restarted, so Button won it while he was static. Fastest lap: Button 128.3mph/206.5kph (no comparison).

Speed increase 1999–2009: 6.4mph/10.2kph.

Footnotes
[1] *The Guinness Guide to International Motor Racing,* Higham. [2] Courtesy McLaren. [3] Courtesy Brawn GP.

ABOVE: Formula 1 meets Malaysia. The locals demonstrating traditional wear and traditional methods, while one local demonstrates the on-track temperature. (LAT)

LEFT: Lewis Hamilton meets a local and she demonstrates just how warm they are. (Vodafone/LAT)

FACTS OF THE MATTER

3.444m/5.542km circuit 1999; 3.444m/5.543km from 2000

Year	Winner
1999	E. Irvine (Ferrari)
2000	M. Schumacher (Ferrari)
2001	M. Schumacher (Ferrari)
2002	R. Schumacher (Williams)
2003	K. Räikkönen (McLaren)
2004	M. Schumacher (Ferrari)
2005	F. Alonso (Renault)
2006	G. Fisichella (Renault)
2007	F. Alonso (McLaren)
2008	K. Räikkönen (Ferrari)
2009	J. Button (Brawn)
Fastest pole	F. Alonso (Renault) 2005 (132.1mph/212.7kph)*
Fastest lap	J.-P. Montoya (Williams) 2004 (131.6mph/211.8kph)

* The grid was decided by the aggregate of two sessions. Alonso did 3m 07.4s, with a first session time of 1m 32.5s.

MEXICO
MEXICO CITY

Location: Eastern suburbs of Mexico City.
Constructed: 1962.
World Championship Grands Prix: 15.

Horquilla

Esses

Curva Peraltada

Start/finish

The hairpin, 1965. Leader Richie Ginther (Honda) is far up the road as Dickie Attwood (21, Lotus) and Moises Solana (25, Lotus) come round. (LAT)

'It was damned bumpy but I think that just added a little bit more to it'

Johnny Herbert

You needed a strong stomach to take Mexico and that wasn't just the food, although the phrase Montezuma's Revenge was in no sense an historical joke (ask Nigel Mansell – he won't have forgotten).

Nobody knows how big Mexico City really is, although it sprawls like a smog-shrouded monster (and from the KLM flight at several thousand feet the hostess sniffed and asked 'Can't you smell it? Can't you smell Mexico City?')

The journey to the circuit in one of the millions of converted VW Beetles was itself a kind of event. They had wire from the horn to the gearlever so that every time the driver changed gear the horn sounded as a semi-permanent hostile warning to all the other Beetles around, who in turn were sending their hostile warnings in the same way. Even a few minutes of this was a long time and an hour became a torment.

You gained the strongest impression that the Mexican economy (if there was one) happened uniquely at traffic intersections where, during red lights, motorists could buy and sell an amazing range of goods as well as the car-washing by urchins (and not-so-urchins). A fire eater wandered up and down between the rows of cars while his assistant collected money. Someone said to the fire eater that he

must be inhaling some of the flames and it would eventually kill him. 'Yes,' he said, 'but what would you prefer: a short life with money or a long life without it?'

Not to mention that the buildings were so dilapidated that you couldn't really tell where a recent earthquake had torn through.

Against this backdrop the motor racing risked being eternally anti-climactic for those who survived the journey to the circuit. It wasn't, and for a variety of reasons.

The Autódromo Hermanos Rodríguez was named for the Mexican brothers Ricardo and Pedro Rodríguez who both drove in Grands Prix racing. It was originally called Magdalena Mixhuca and built in a municipal sports park on a dried-up lake bed. In 1962 it staged a non-championship Grand Prix won by Jim Clark and Trevor Taylor, sharing a Lotus drive. Ricardo Rodríguez was killed during practice.

The full Grand Prix came the following year. CSI (the governing body) delegates attended the 1962 race and were fully satisfied with the circuit.

Autocourse noted: 'The Mexico City Autodrome is one of the world's best, and while some drivers criticised the nature of the track itself, the appointments cannot be faulted. Each

pit is a permanent lock-up workshop, equipped with electricity and air lines so that the mechanics are not obliged to shift their equipment at all during the course of the whole meeting. The autodrome itself is only part of several hundred acres of sports arenas, swimming pools, etc. The pit straight is the only one of any real length (about 700 yards) and ends in a peculiar right-hander with an ever-tightening radius. Cars are underbraking almost right through the corner to take a very late apex, ready for exit through a left-hander and on to a short straight.

'This leads into a fastish left curve followed by a sharp right, so that once again most of the braking is done in the first corner. A couple of hundred yards later comes the banked hairpin and here cars are changed right down to first gear. Shortly after there is a sharp right and a faster left leading up to the Esses. These seem to be a never-ending series involving six changes of direction in several hundred yards.

'Careful choice of line here is vital and any inaccuracy on the part of the

The straight was long and immense and seemed to vanish into the smog. This is Stefano Modena (Tyrrell) in 1991. (Courtesy Braun)

driver, or any handling fault of the car, will result in a serious loss of time. Most drivers take a late apex on each of these curves so that they are on the correct line for the next curve.

'Speed through this section would be around 80 to 90mph. Then follows a period of acceleration to something like peak revs in fourth or fifth gear (depending on five- or six-speed gearbox) as the cars approach the long banked 180-degree turn which swings them back on to the pit straight. Most drivers lift off and take a dab at the brakes for the so-called banking and most have to feather the throttle

as understeer is inclined to set in about half way round. The surface was mainly very good, but a few curves – noticeably the banking – had surface ripples.'

The altitude of 7,500ft (2,285m) would cause breathing problems and unavoidably affect the cars. Graham Hill would describe it, explaining that the cars had to be specially set up and the engine specially tuned because the usual amount of air was not being sucked in. He estimated that this meant a 25% loss of power.

The race was run from 1963 to 1970 and by then there were financial

complications, and the crowd, creeping nearer and nearer the track, came on when the cars were still going round.

It returned in 1986 and survived to 1992, having been refurbished.

The circuit had one celebrated corner called *Peraltada*, a ferociously fast horseshoe from the back straight feeding on to the start/finish straight.

When Grand Prix racing departed a baseball stadium was built, and for the Champ Car series – which came in 2002 – *Peraltada* was bypassed in favour of three tight corners and two curves which snaked through part of the baseball stadium. NASCAR came in 2005.

COCKPIT VIEW
Johnny Herbert, who drove in three Grands Prix there:
'Mexico City was different. There was a nice area and a bad area. Unfortunately we stayed in the dodgy-ish area.

'I used to enjoy it. I went there in the early days of Lotus (after it had been relaunched) and visited the pyramids[1] a

couple of times, so at least there was something to do with a bit of history about it.

'The track was good. It was damned bumpy but I think that just added a little bit more to it because (1) you had to set the car up to ride those bumps and (2) physically it was very hard – because you had the bumps.

'You went down the main straight which was very long and very high speed, a good 200 miles an hour for sure. After that it was a very, very bumpy let's say infield all the way through until the last chicane on to the back straight. Then there was a massive bump on *Peraltada* – huge as you used to enter. That's what did Julian Bailey, and Ayrton as well.[2] I think over the years

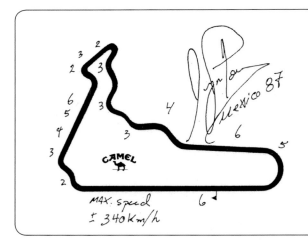

Two Brazilian views of Mexico – Senna invoking football! – but compare the gearchanges. (Courtesy Camel)

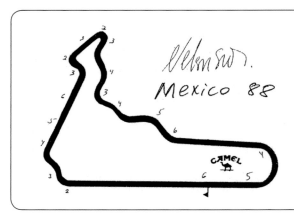

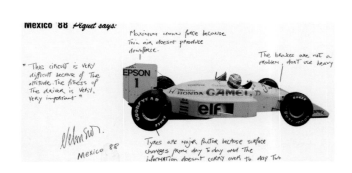

they tried to smooth it out but it never worked. In those days that's just what the track was. Everyone knew that. They tried once dragging stuff over it and that made it better but it was still quite a big bump.

'On a good car it was near flat. I can't remember if it was totally flat from the entry all the way in. Philippe Alliot had his big crash on the exit there so there was always a chance of incidents.

'In fact there was always something happening at Mexico. It was very hard physically and that knocks on to the mental side, a very tough circuit, and then it was very high. The altitude and thinner air was quite something. So you had all those normal physical things on the track itself, the car being very bouncy, and then the mental side.

'To me it was one of the great circuits that we went to.'

EYEWITNESSES

Ann Bradshaw, PR expert:
'I liked Mexico, I actually liked it. I liked the vibrancy of it, I liked going into the *Zona Rosa*,[3] I liked the people. The first time we went was not long after the earthquake and I remember being taken round that area. It was devastated but even so there was something vibrant about the place. You'd get to the street corner and a guy would leap out in front of your car and he'd be a fire eater.

'Of course, you had to be careful, and every shop you went into there was a guard on the door.

'At the circuit, you'd come out from the back of the garages and everybody had a little hut with a walkway between them so it was very sociable. The first morning the organisers always put on a breakfast and they'd have these great big pots of fried beans and so on.

'It was a great circuit. I remember that bump: they used to come round *Peraltada* and then hit it. Ayrton went off, Julian Bailey knocked himself out, Philippe Alliot had a big one coming out. If you caught that bump you were a passenger.

'It was an exciting circuit.'

Cynthia Tee, born in Mexico City, now married to LAT photographer Steven:
'I think it was 1987 I got invited to the Grand Prix by a guy I was going out with, who was half French and a big Alain Prost fan. So I went. I'd never been before and never watched a race. He was explaining

the whole thing to me. We were in the grandstand drinking beer and it was really good fun. You get there, nothing happens for a long time and the crowd were doing the Mexican wave!

'Then Ayrton Senna came off the track – this is on race day – just in front of us. The marshals tried to help him get out but I think there was a rule that if they pushed him he couldn't rejoin the race. So he was screaming "Go away, go away!" and the guys didn't know what to do. They pushed him and he had a complete fit, got out of the car and I thought it was fantastic. I wanted to find out about him and basically I became a fan.

'The next year I met the photographers – Steven and everybody – at a club. It was a Grand Prix party or something. In Mexico you go out at ten o'clock at night, very late, and I said "Let's get there early." I went with my cousin and we got there at 9:30 and the drivers had already gone to bed so it was a complete disaster.

'I wanted to go home but my cousin said "No, no, it's full of guys, let's go in." The photographers and the journalists

were still there and that's when I met them. They invited us to the Grand Prix and every single year after that. We could go into the pits and it was great to see everything so close.

'The Grand Prix was a big party all the time. Never a dull moment. There was always screaming and every time a photographer came past they screamed abuse – and everybody had a laugh.'

MEMORIES AND MILESTONES

1963 Jim Clark (Lotus), who'd won the Championship at Monza two races before, took pole from John Surtees (Ferrari) and led every lap to beat Jack Brabham (Brabham) by 1 minute 41.1 seconds. Fastest lap: Clark 94.7mph/152.4kph.
1964 A three-way Championship decider between Graham Hill (BRM) 39 points,

Jim Clark in the Lotus beats John Surtees (Ferrari) from the line in 1963 and will lead every lap. The crowd look fascinated – already. (LAT)

Surtees (Ferrari) 34, and Clark (Lotus) 30, although under the six-out-of-ten finishes to count Hill was dropping two points. He made a bad start (his goggle elastic snapped) and Surtees had a misfire. Hill eventually spun, Clark led to lap 63 of the 65 when he had an oil leak, and, although Dan Gurney (Brabham) beat Surtees by 1 minute 8.9 seconds, Surtees had the Championship. Fastest lap: Clark 94.5mph (-0.2)/152.1kph (-0.3).

1965 Clark (Lotus) had taken the Championship at the Nürburgring on 1 August, two months before. Honda were now into their second season of Grand Prix racing and Richie Ginther put their car on the second row (Clark, inevitably, pole). Honda had prepared at altitude and Ginther led every lap to give Honda their first victory. He beat Gurney (Brabham) by 2.8 seconds. Fastest lap: Gurney 96.6mph (+2.1)/155.4kph (+3.3).

1966 Brabham (Brabham) had won the

The Mexicans did love Formula 1 – in the background is a small part of a big crowd – and they had a chance to savour Riccardo Patrese (Williams) leading defending World Champion Alain Prost (Ferrari) in 1993.

Championship at Monza. In practice Innes Ireland (BRM) hit a stray dog, always a hazard here. Surtees (Cooper) took pole and the lead, beating Brabham by 7.8 seconds. Fastest lap: Ginther (Honda) 98.3mph (+1.7)/158.2kph (+2.8).

1967 Brabham (Brabham) could take the Championship but he needed to win and team-mate Denny Hulme to finish no higher than fifth. Hill (Lotus) led from his team-mate Clark, pole, who beat Brabham by 1 minute 25.5 seconds. Hulme was third a lap down – and Champion. Fastest lap: Clark (Lotus) 103.4mph (+5.1)/166.5kph (+8.3).

1968 Another three-way decider, now between Graham Hill (Lotus) 39, Jackie Stewart (Matra) 36, and Hulme (McLaren) 33. Jo Siffert (Lotus) took pole but Hulme crashed out on lap 10, Stewart's engine developed a misfire, and Hill, who led the race three times, beat Bruce McLaren (McLaren) by 1 minute 19.3 seconds to take the Championship. Fastest lap: Siffert 107.3mph (+3.9)/172.7kph (+6.2).

1969 The low kerbstones that allowed corner-cutting had been heightened and concrete ribs added. Stewart (Matra) already had the Championship. Brabham (Brabham) took pole but Hulme

(McLaren) moved into the lead on lap 10 and beat Jacky Ickx (Brabham) by 2.5 seconds. Fastest lap: Ickx 108.5mph (+1.2)/174.7kph (+2.0).

1970 Jochen Rindt had become posthumous champion at the race before. Clay Regazzoni (Ferrari) took pole but the 100,000 crowd were on the entire circuit before the start, rubbish and glass on it too. The drivers protested but the organisers said they were insured if anything serious happened. The drivers raced to prevent a riot. Ickx beat team-mate Regazzoni by 24.6 seconds but not before 'a bloody great dog' ran in front of Stewart's Tyrrell, which he hit 'fair and square'. Fastest lap: Ickx 108.5mph/174.7kph (no change).

Speed increase 1963–70: 13.8mph/22.2kph.

The circuit had been revised when Grands Prix returned after 16 years. The curve at the end of the start/finish straight became a right-left-right extended kink and the Horquilla hairpin became a right-left-right. This shortened the circuit by 0.4 of a mile.

1986 Ayrton Senna (Lotus) took pole. Nigel Mansell (Williams) went to this penultimate round leading team-mate

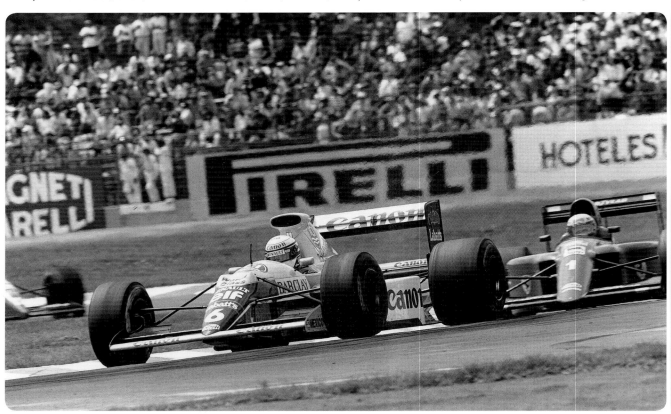

Nelson Piquet by four points but couldn't get first gear at the start. Gerhard Berger (Benetton) beat Alain Prost (McLaren) by 25.4 seconds, and the Championship went on to Australia. Fastest lap: Piquet 124.6mph/200.5kph.

1987 Derek Warwick (Arrows) had a major mechanical failure and crashed so heavily that the race had to be stopped. Mansell (Williams) beat team-mate Piquet by 26.1 seconds and the Championship went on to Japan. Fastest lap: Piquet 125.0mph (+0.4)/201.1kph (+0.6).

1988 The race was moved to May, and Philippe Alliott (Lola) crashed heavily in practice. Senna took pole from McLaren team-mate Prost, but Prost made the better start and led every lap, beating Senna by 7.1 seconds. Fastest lap: Prost 125.8mph (+0.8)/202.5kph (+1.4).

1989 Prost, deep into his rivalry with Senna at McLaren, made the wrong tyre choice and Senna beat Riccardo Patrese (Williams) by 15.5 seconds. Fastest lap: Mansell (Ferrari) 123.0mph (-2.8)/197.9kph (-4.6).

1990 Senna (McLaren) led to lap 60 of the 69 but had a slow puncture and Prost (Ferrari) went by to beat Mansell in the other Ferrari by 25.3 seconds. On the last lap Mansell overtook Gerhard Berger (McLaren) round the outside of *Peraltada*, a move of bravery, audacity and perfect car control. Fastest lap: Prost 126.9mph (+3.9)/204.2kph (+6.3).

1991 In practice Senna had a spectacular crash at *Peraltada*, the McLaren upside down as he emerged from it. Patrese took pole from Mansell in the Williamses. Patrese, running fourth, forced a way up and past Mansell, beating him by 1.3 seconds. Fastest lap: Mansell 128.8mph (+1.9)/207.3kph (+3.1).

1992 The new generation: Michael Schumacher put the Benetton on the second row. Mansell had pole from Williams team-mate Patrese and led every lap to beat him by 12.9 seconds, Schumacher third at 21.4 seconds. Fastest lap: Berger (McLaren) 127.3mph (-1.5)/204.8kph (-2.5).

Speed increase 1986–92: 2.7mph/4.3kph.

Footnotes
[1] Various civilisations built pyramids all over Mexico. [2] Bailey crashed so heavily in 1988 that next day he had to lift his own head off the pillow to go and try to qualify his Tyrrell. He didn't. Senna's crash in 1991 provided photographers with very spectacular images. [3] *Zona Rosa*, a lively area in central Mexico City featuring shops, hotels, restaurants and shops.

FACTS OF THE MATTER

3.107m/5.000km circuit

Year	Winner
1963	J. Clark (Lotus)
1964	D. Gurney (Brabham)
1965	R. Ginther (Honda)
1966	J. Surtees (Cooper)
1967	J. Clark (Lotus)
1968	G. Hill (Lotus)
1969	D. Hulme (McLaren)
1970	J. Ickx (Ferrari)
Fastest pole	C. Regazzoni (Ferrari) 1970 (109.8mph/176.7kph)
Fastest lap	J. Ickx (Brabham) 1969 (108.5mph/174.7kph)

Revisions, 2.747m/4.421km circuit

Year	Winner
1986	G. Berger (Benetton)
1987	N. Mansell (Williams)
1988	A. Prost (McLaren)
1989	A. Senna (McLaren)
1990	A. Prost (Ferrari)
1991	R. Patrese (Williams)
1992	N. Mansell (Williams)
Fastest pole	N. Mansell 1992 (129.5mph/208.5kph)
Fastest lap	N. Mansell (Williams) 1991 (128.8mph/207.3kph)

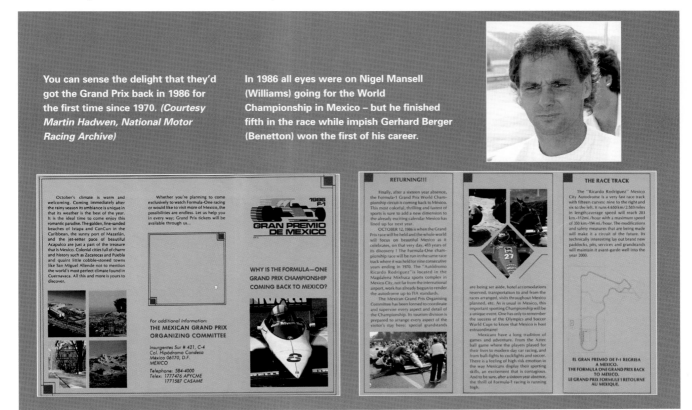

You can sense the delight that they'd got the Grand Prix back in 1986 for the first time since 1970. *(Courtesy Martin Hadwen, National Motor Racing Archive)*

In 1986 all eyes were on Nigel Mansell (Williams) going for the World Championship in Mexico – but he finished fifth in the race while impish Gerhard Berger (Benetton) won the first of his career.

MONTE CARLO

Location: Central Monte Carlo.
Constructed: 1929.
World Championship Grands Prix: 56.

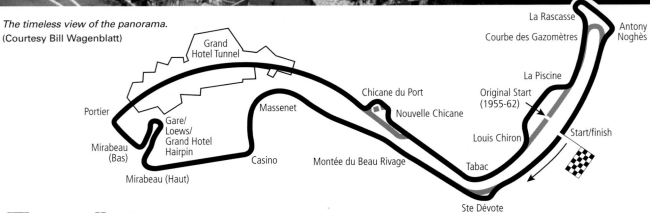

The timeless view of the panorama.
(Courtesy Bill Wagenblatt)

Grand Hotel Tunnel

La Rascasse

Courbe des Gazomètres

Antony Noghès

Massenet

Chicane du Port

La Piscine

Original Start (1955-62)

Portier

Nouvelle Chicane

Gare/ Loews/ Grand Hotel Hairpin

Casino

Louis Chiron

Start/finish

Mirabeau (Bas)

Montée du Beau Rivage

Tabac

Mirabeau (Haut)

Ste Dévote

'The smallest error will finish your race'

Jarno Trulli

You know Monaco. You may never have been near it but that doesn't matter. Just this once the television cameras give you an accurate representation of foreground and background. They are able to do this in a sort of totality because beyond the streets which form the racing circuit there isn't a great deal except the castle on the hill, more expensive apartments and a new commercial complex. If you add the ubiquitous football pitch and a tennis stadium, that's your lot.

You know it because, even through the television camera lenses, you have been transported there so many times: since 1929 when it all began, the race has been run every year except for the Second World War and four missing years between 1949 and 1954. The unbroken sequence begins in 1955 and reaches to this day. *Every* great driver from the 1930s has passed this way. To emphasise that, the circuit length has changed nine times since the world championship began but only from a shortest of 1.954 miles to a longest of 2.075. Monaco, teeming with buildings and every inch worth (literally) a fortune, imposes its own discipline on what the circuit can and cannot be.

In that sense it reaches back like an umbilical cord so that even old, flickering black and white film is amazingly familiar. You not only know Monaco, you know exactly what its history looks like.

The television cameras reach into the heart of the place in a way they don't elsewhere because, by definition, only street circuits offer that opportunity. If you watched the races in Detroit and Phoenix and Dallas and Long Beach you were seeing the hearts of those cities. You would in Singapore too, if they ran it in daylight. At the Nürburgring all you see is the Nürburgring. China's circuit could be anywhere and so could Malaysia's. Look at *any* photograph of Monaco and you can't be anywhere else. More than that, you probably know exactly where the picture has been taken.

The media, collectively and annually – and this certainly includes the television cameras – seek to portray Monaco as part tax refuge, part toytown, part harbour and yachts, part topless supermodels, part Hotel de Paris where

Monaco is magnificent from every vantage point. (Courtesy Greg Wesson)

a seaview room in high season will cost from 960 Euros *a night*, part Casino of global fame. The truth may disturb you but that can't be helped: Monaco is not only like that, *Monaco is that*. All clichés apply and, yes, they apply collectively and annually. You have heard them all and you'll be hearing them all again – and again.

For all these reasons, Monaco became a symbol of the World Championship and a selling point. Grand Prix racing offered itself as a genuinely glamorous human activity, Monaco offered itself as a genuinely glamorous setting and the sponsors *loved* the marriage. They were everywhere and if they did a bit of posing too they were not alone. The other part was barely reported at all: the officials who, far from being glamorous, seemed to have missed the milk of human kindness altogether, the impossibly cramped working conditions for the teams – the first time the little Toleman team went in 1981 they were given a distant garage and had to push the cars there – and the Media Centre which eventually moved from a theatre (complete with scenery) to a floor in a multi-storey car park.

There were genuine fears over crowd safety because, uniquely here, spectators could get so close to the cars, and if a car was airborne…

Once upon a time drivers were complaining about the manhole covers at Detroit and it made Ken Tyrrell angry

because, he said volubly, if you want to call yourself World Champion you have to be able to drive in the wet as well as the dry, Hockenheim as well as Monaco, Silverstone's broad acres and Adelaide's rectangles – and negotiate a few manhole covers as well.

Monaco principally enriches the calendar, however, because it holds out to every driver a unique challenge of his ability to manipulate a racing car. There are no hills in Singapore. There's no tunnel anywhere else (the Abu Dhabi pit tunnel isn't the same thing at all). Without Monaco, the World Championship would lose one of the most important elements that make it the World Championship. You'd get that from Ken Tyrrell, all right, if he was still here to tell you and, since he isn't, I am.

Ross Brawn, running his own team in 2009 and most perceptive of men in Grand Prix racing, summed it up. 'Monaco is a unique and unpredictable venue and you have to take a very controlled approach to the race weekend. The pit lane and paddock is an intense environment to work in due to the location at the heart of the city and it is therefore more stressful than any other race on the calendar. You can make just one mistake in Monaco and your race weekend will be compromised. However, we love that level of extra challenge and it is what makes Formula 1 and Monaco so special.'

The President of the Automobile Club of Monaco, Anthony Noghès, had the idea of a Grand Prix in 1928. It was a startling idea, too – remember that Grand Prix racing had begun in 1906, continued as a rough and ready affair over either specially built tracks (Monza, the Avus, Montlhéry) or vast tracts of ordinary country roads. *The Autocar* wrote:

'They have the most astounding audacity in some parts of Europe. For instance, there is going to be a Grand Prix at Monaco – a Grand Prix, mark you, in a Principality which does not possess a single open road of any length, but only has ledges on the face of a cliff and the ordinary main thoroughfares that everyone who has been to the Casino knows so well.'

The astounding audacity worked, of course, all the way to here.

A special atmosphere throughout a special place. (ICN U.K. Bureau)

COCKPIT VIEW

Jarno Trulli, Toyota, 2009:

'It's a great circuit and a great challenge. There is really nothing like it and the driver probably makes more difference around Monaco than on any other track, which always suits me.

'The atmosphere as well at Monaco is special because we are racing in the city so the fans are really close and you can feel the excitement. It is very enjoyable, although I must say I don't get many

Ayrton Senna liked Monaco and would live there. The circuit liked the active-suspension Lotus which Senna was driving, and now you know who won the 1987 Grand Prix. (Courtesy Camel)

chances to experience the glamour of Monaco because it is a race weekend after all so there is lots of work to do.

'The barriers are so close you have absolutely no room for even the smallest error. At other tracks you can maybe run a little wide and not suffer but in Monaco if you do that you are in the barriers so you need total concentration. Also, even though it is the slowest track we race on, it feels like one of the fastest because the barriers fly past you so quickly.

'You have to be completely focused to do a perfect lap and in the race it's quite challenging to stay so concentrated for the full distance, all the time knowing the smallest error will finish your race. I love this challenge and it really motivates me.'

EYEWITNESSES

Erika Schneider, Formula 1 follower:

'There's a Hungarian disco band from the '80s called Newton Family who wrote a wonderful song about Monaco. No wonder, because once you've been there it will inspire you. The same happened to me in 2008 as I entered the area of the Principality of Monaco just like in the kitschy American movies.

'We got off the bus we'd taken from Nice and were just standing there. *Bienvenue à Monaco.* We were amazed: the azure blue water, the shining sun and the feeling itself that we were at such a legendary racing track. It was Thursday, and one of the free practices was already over. We didn't have a ticket for that day so we explored the city (or

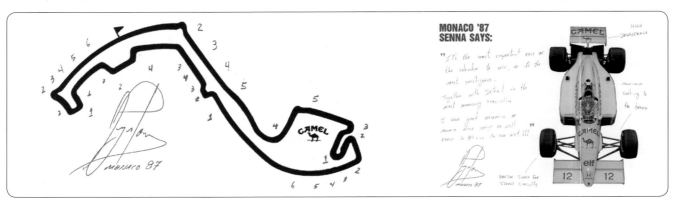

MONACO '87
SENNA SAYS:

country), looking for celebrities in every possible corner.

'We watched the second practice from up by the palace. Monaco's unique exposure, and the fact they only can build upwards, makes the noise of the cars much louder than a usual racing track, and you have the feeling the cars are everywhere, even behind you.

'On the Friday the drivers played hide and seek, or we were at wrong places at wrong times. On the way from Nice to Monaco we met an English gentleman. He was very interested in our stories, since he rarely meets girls who are hardcore Formula 1 fans, and are so fascinated by the sport they even travel to foreign Grands Prix. (Are we really something phenomenal? I mean, are there really just a few ladies who adore Formula 1?)

'We had our dinner at the famous Tip Top bar. If you have ever eaten a delicious three-cheese pizza anywhere else, forget about it. *This one* is the winner. After the dinner we headed downtown, and saw Mika Häkkinen and Martin Whitmarsh having their dinner as well. Naomi Campbell was answering her phone right next to me. Finally some celebrities! I don't know what happened to us, but as we checked the menu (16 Euros for a glass of champagne, well… we rather skipped this location), everyone disappeared.

'In the meantime we missed the last train and bus back to Nice. We could not decide for a while where to go and what to do. We had no better idea than to sit on one of the platforms and wait for the first train.

'Saturday and Sunday were a horror. It rained – heavily – but at least we learned the word umbrella in Portuguese from some lovely Brazilian Massa fans, saw a Lewis Hamilton cardboard figure acting as an escort for a couple of British guys, and had a great international time. And if you ask at the end *have you seen a single Formula 1 driver?*, fortunately I can say yes, we did – Kazuki Nakajima and Eddie Irvine, but we did.

'The summary of the trip: bad weather but, man, it was Monaco!'

Greg Wesson, enthusiast:

'Ever since I started watching racing as a child I have dreamt of going to the Monaco Grand Prix. It is more than just a car race.

'When I decided to go down to Monaco for the 2009 Grand Prix I wanted to make sure that I could see the marina while I was watching the race, to capture some of the glamour in my experience. I booked Grandstand L, which not only overlooked the marina but also had a view of the pit lane.

'Race day was beautiful – sunny and warm. Half the fans lathered up with sunscreen and put on hats. The other half stripped down to expose bare skin to the sun to work on their tans.

'Throughout the race, the echo of the cars bounced off the nearby rocky hills, doubling the noise of the cars and making Monaco louder than any race I'd previously seen. There was a large-screen TV in front of the grandstand but I spent most of my time watching the pit lane. On TV you only see the pit mechanics during the seven to ten seconds of the pit stop. Overlooking the pit I watched as they prepared, getting everything in place and waiting for the driver to speed down the pit lane and stop perfectly in their box.

'Similarly, I watched the track marshals clean up after Heikki Kovalainen hit the wall by our stands. It was an interesting opportunity to see behind the scenes, and I was amazed at the calm and professional demeanour of the pit crews and race marshals as cars race by at 100kph or more.

'The race ended with Jenson Button winning. I left and wandered through Monaco, past the Ferrari and yacht dealerships. The entire city shuts down and gives itself over to the Grand Prix. I grabbed a beer at one of the refreshment stands and headed back up towards the train station. I was about to cross a street when a police officer on a motorcycle pulled up and stopped the crowds from crossing. A few moments later, a convertible drove past. In the passenger seat was Charlotte Casiraghi, Prince Albert's niece and fourth in line to the throne of Monaco.

'I smiled. Monaco didn't disappoint. It delivered all the glamour I had expected.'

MEMORIES AND MILESTONES

1950 Juan Manuel Fangio (Alfa Romeo) took pole. The race was the second of the new World Championship, a week after the first at Silverstone. Nineteen cars set off but at *Tabac* on the first lap, where

the quayside was coated in spray that the wind had dragged from the harbour, one car spun and blocked the road. Eight others thrashed and crashed and a ninth got as far as the *Gasometer* before hitting a tree and catching fire. Fangio won and was the only driver, of the seven still running, to complete the 100 laps. He beat Alberto Ascari (Ferrari) by a lap.

It set a pattern. Monaco, which in theory didn't enable overtaking and thus ought to have been a predictable procession with the poleman winning every year, became an intense and tight yet panoramic expression of the unpredictable. Fastest lap: Fangio 64.1mph/103.1kph.

The race wasn't run in 1951 for financial reasons.

1952 Pierre Levegh (Talbot) took pole. The race was for sports cars, again for budgetary reasons. In practice Luigi Fagioli, a 54-year-old, touched a kerb in the tunnel and lost control of his Lancia. It crashed beyond the tunnel and went into the sea wall. He died later from his injuries. Vittorio Marzotto (Ferrari) beat Eugenio Castellotti in another Ferrari by 15.2 seconds.

The race wasn't run in 1953 or 1954.

1955 Mercedes returned, Fangio on pole in one, Stirling Moss on the front row in another (with Ascari's Lancia between them: the Monaco grid was alternate rows of three and two cars). Fangio led the race but the transmission failed. On lap 81 Ascari lost control at the harbour chicane. The car went between straw bales and sandbags and plunged into the sea, creating a cloud of steam. Moments later Ascari was seen swimming strongly for the shore. Maurice Trintignant (Ferrari) beat Eugenio Castellotti by 21.0 seconds. Fastest lap: Fangio 68.7mph/110.6kph.

1956 Fangio (Ferrari) took pole. The chicane had been tightened, forcing cars to go through more slowly and prevent a repetition of Ascari's dive. Moss (Maserati) led every lap to beat Peter Collins/Fangio (shared drive, Ferrari) by 6.1 seconds. 56 Fastest lap: 67.4mph (-1.3)/108.4kph (-2.2).

1957 Fangio (Maserati) took pole, Moss on the front row in a Vanwall. Emerging from the tunnel on lap 4 Moss 'hit the brake pedal as normal, and I swear there was a system failure … I am adamant the front brakes had gone when I hit that pedal. The now over-braked rears instantly locked, and my only course was to go straight on, smashing through a pole-and-sandbag barrier … Collins and Hawthorn crashed their Ferraris in the general confusion.' That opened the way for Fangio to win his final Monaco Grand Prix, beating Tony Brooks (Vanwall) by 25.2 seconds. Fastest lap: Fangio 66.6mph (-0.8)/107.2kph (-1.2).

1958 Brooks (Vanwall) took pole. This was Hawthorn's Championship year and although he set fastest lap he retired with a fuel pump problem. 'Walking past the hotel near the station I looked up into one of the rooms and a lovely blonde girl looked out. I stopped and asked if she had a glass of water – not the most original of remarks, but one that lovely blondes, whose answer to most questions is No, could hardly refuse. She asked me to come in … I had my glass of water, several of them, and then returned to the pits in a much better temper. I stood at the Gasworks urging on Luigi [Musso] and Pete [Collins, in the other Ferraris] who were now second and third respectively but too far behind to do much about Trintignant in the Cooper.'[1] Trintignant beat Musso by 20.2 seconds. Fastest lap: Hawthorn 69.9mph (+3.3)/112.5kph (+5.3).

1959 Moss (Cooper) took pole. Three cars crashed at *Ste Devote* on the second lap. Jean Behra (Ferrari) led but had engine problems, Moss led but had transmission problems, and now at lap 82 Brabham led. 'The only problem we had … was heat, the radiator being in the front and the pedals immediately behind it. The discomfort in that race from the physical point of view was very bad. I remember, when I eventually took the lead, wondering how I was going to keep going to the finish, because the actual brake pedal, clutch pedal and accelerator pedal were that hot I could barely keep a foot on them.'[2] He did. He beat Brooks (Ferrari) by 20.4 seconds. Fastest lap: Brabham 70.1mph (+0.2)/112.8kph (+0.3).

1960 A dry-wet race which Moss, pole, won in a Lotus-Climax 18, a car he described as 'just a biscuit box with a funny rear suspension'. He beat Bruce McLaren (Cooper) by 52.1 seconds. Fastest lap: McLaren 73.1mph (+3.0)/117.7kph (+4.9).

1961 Moss, pole, made history by becoming the first man to win the race three times, in Rob Walker's privateer

Lotus 18 – for contractual reasons Colin Chapman could not sell Walker the latest Lotus, the 21. Moss put the 18 on pole and 'we had a panic before the start as a chassis tube was found to be cracked, but Alf [Francis, mechanic] calmly welded it on the starting grid, despite thirty gallons of fuel still in the tanks within inches of his torch-flame because there was no time to empty them.'[3] He beat Richie Ginther (Ferrari) by 3.6 seconds. Fastest lap: Ginther and Moss 73.1mph/117.7kph (no change).

1962 Jim Clark (Lotus) took pole. The almost traditional early crashing at *Gasworks* (three cars out, two damaged) before Graham Hill – who in years to come would replace Moss as Mr Monaco – led to lap 92. The engine failed and Bruce McLaren brought the Cooper-Climax home, his first Championship win in Europe, 1.3 seconds in front of Phil Hill (Ferrari). Ginther's BRM crashed, killing a marshal. Fastest lap: Clark 73.7mph (+0.6)/118.6kph (+1.0).

1963 The grid returned from the harbour-side to its traditional position on the other side of *Gasworks*, where it is today. Clark (Lotus) took pole. Graham Hill (BRM) beat Ginther (also BRM) by 4.8 seconds. It was the first of five Hill wins here, and by then he'd be known as Mr Monaco. Fastest lap: John Surtees (Ferrari) 74.4mph (+0.7)/119.8kph (+1.2).

1964 Hill won for the second successive year. He'd remember starting well and trying to force his BRM between Brabham (Brabham) and Clark (Lotus), pole; they closed, trapping Hill's front wheels between their rears. Hill braked so violently he dug smoke from his tyres. He lifted, letting them go – but eventually beat Ginther in another BRM by a lap. Fastest lap: Hill 74.9mph (+0.5)/120.6kph (+0.8).

1965 Clark went to the Indianapolis 500 instead and while Hill, pole, was winning in a BRM, Paul Hawkins, an Australian in a Lotus, struck the barrier at the chicane and the car spun through the straw bales and into the harbour. Hill beat Lorenzo Bandini (Ferrari) by 1 minute 4.0 seconds, making history by winning for the third consecutive time. Fastest lap: Hill 76.7mph (+1.8)/123.5kph (+2.9).

1966 Clark (Lotus) inevitably took pole, from John Surtees (Ferrari), Jackie Stewart (BRM) on the second row. Surtees led to lap 14 but a rear axle was

failing, Clark had had a gear jam on the grid and Stewart won it by 40.2 seconds from Lorenzo Bandini (Ferrari). Fastest lap: Bandini 78.3mph (+1.6)/126.1kph (+2.6).

1967 Brabham (Brabham) took pole. On lap 82 Bandini crashed into the barrier at the chicane and his Ferrari was pitched, upside down, into straw bales, where it exploded into fire and lay in the middle of the track. He was burnt so badly that he died three days later. The race, of course, was not stopped. Graham Hill (Lotus) would remember driving through the smoke and foam unable to see if Bandini was still in the car. This was, he judged, 'one of the most sickening sights' he'd ever seen. Denny Hulme (Brabham) beat Hill (Lotus) by a lap. Fastest lap: Clark (Lotus) 78.6mph (+0.3)/126.5kph (+0.4).

1968 The chicane was reworked and tightened and the race distance reduced from the traditional 100 laps to 80. Hill (Lotus), pole, had his fourth win, beating Richard Attwood (BRM) by 2.2 seconds. Fastest lap: Attwood 79.9mph (+1.3)/128.5kph (+2.0).

1969 Jackie Stewart (Matra) took pole. Cars had been running with enormous rear wings but those on the Lotuses failed in Spain two weeks before. They were now banned *after* the Thursday practice session. Hill's fifth win, the Lotus finishing 17.3 seconds in front of Piers Courage (Brabham). Fastest lap: Stewart 82.7mph (+2.8)/133.0kph (+4.5).

1970 Stewart (March) took pole. Jochen Rindt (Lotus) mounted a tremendous late assault on the leader, Brabham (Brabham) who, at *Gasworks* on the final lap, braked too late and went into the straw bales. Rindt won it by 23.1 seconds – from Brabham. Fastest lap: Rindt 84.6mph (+1.9)/136.1kph (+3.1).

1971 Stewart (Tyrrell) took pole for the 200th Championship race. The number of cars allowed to start was increased from 16, deployed since 1955, to 18. The Thursday session was run in torrential rain that 'turned the sloping parts of the circuit into man-made rivers.'[4] In this, Chris Amon took his Matra round in 1 minute 48.8 seconds (which, as *Autocourse* pointed out, was faster than Fangio in 1950 in the dry) – next Reine Wisell (Lotus) in 1 minute 50.0 seconds. Stewart won the race, beating Ronnie Peterson (March) by 25.6 seconds. Fastest lap: Stewart 85.6mph (+1.0)/137.7kph (+1.6).

Apart from some well-placed clues you can drive Monaco on a week-day and it's … ordinary.
(Author)

Casino Square. 'Hey, they race cars round here?'

Emerging into daylight.

The approach to the grid.

Mirabeau, and this is not a bike race, they're just parked.

Looking back at the harbourside chicane.

Here's a clue – the white-painted grid places, but you have to look to see them.

From Mirabeau the view back to Casino.

The curve towards the Swimming Pool.

Ste Dévote, nice and easy does it.

The Loews hairpin.

Moving towards Rascasse.

The hill, steeper than you thought.

The entrance to the tunnel, construction work going on around it.

Juan Manuel Fangio stands guard over the approach to the start/finish straight and, right, the pits.

Well, they do call it a street race. (All courtesy www.fredlewisphotos.com)

Carlos Pace's March going into the underground car park for the night, 1972.

Monaco is dangerous, as Jackie Stewart might be about to discover.

1972 There was talk of a boycott when the organisers tried *not* to move the pit area 'which had been one of the most dangerous parts of any track in the world, openly inviting an accident which would have wiped out most of the Grand Prix entrants, team managers, mechanics, technicians, press and hangers-on'.[5] It was moved to after the tunnel – forcing the chicane to the harbour – with the paddock going to an underground car park. Emerson Fittipaldi (Lotus) took pole. A wet race and Jean-Pierre Beltoise (BRM) made a devastatingly fast start to lead every lap, beating Jacky Ickx (Ferrari) by 38.2 seconds. Fastest lap: Beltoise 70.4mph/113.2kph (no comparison).

Speed increase 1955–71: 16.9mph/27.1kph.

The circuit now assumed its modern face. The circuit 'incorporated a new, wider and straighter seafront road extending all the way from Portier Corner *to the* Gasworks Hairpin. *Gone was the familiar old tunnel and in its place a new and very modern tunnel had been*

built which was not only longer but also partially open to daylight. The chicane was moved back to its position prior to the 1972 race but the Tabac *corner was bypassed by a new corner on the same level as the rest of the road. From there the road projected further out into the harbour … and ran around the outside of the swimming pool by a sharp left-right turn followed by an even sharper right-left turn before swinging to the left again at the western side of the harbour. Then, after going through 180 degrees there was a short rise up to a point where the new road joined the existing one just past what was the* Gasworks Hairpin. *The area which previously formed part of the circuit from the* Tabac *to the* Gasworks Hairpin *was now used for the pits.*[6]

1973 Stewart (Tyrrell), pole, beat Fittipaldi (Lotus) by 1.3 seconds. Fastest lap: Fittipaldi 83.2mph/133.9kph.

1974 After a clean start there was chaos up the hill. Hulme's McLaren touched wheels with Beltoise (BRM). Three other cars were out and four more drove slowly

towards the pits. At the end of lap 5 the 25 who'd started had been reduced to 14. Peterson (Lotus) beat Jody Scheckter (Tyrrell) by 28.8 seconds. Fastest lap: Peterson 83.4mph (+0.2)/134.3kph (+0.4).

1975 The shadow of Montjuïc Park two weeks before (see under Spain) reached all the way to Monaco, where the Armco was reinforced with, at crucial places, another layer added. Chain-link fencing was intended to keep debris from flying into the spectators. Niki Lauda (Ferrari) took pole. The entry was reduced from 26 to 18 and the grid rows staggered to prevent a bunch reaching *Ste Devote* and crashing. Graham Hill (Hill) failed to qualify. Lauda beat Fittipaldi (McLaren) by 2.7 seconds. Fastest lap: Depailler 82.7mph (-0.7)/133.1kph (-1.2).

Speed decrease 1973–5: 0.5mph/0.8kph.

Ste Devote *and* Rascasse *were tightened.*

1976 Lauda (Ferrari), pole, led every lap to beat Scheckter (Tyrrell) by 11.1 seconds. Fastest lap: Clay Regazzoni (Ferrari) 82.1mph/132.1kph.

Stewart at the hairpin during practice in 1972, and these spectators had a truly amazing view. (Courtesy www.fredlewisphotos.com)

The start in 1972, wet and intimidating. Jean-Pierre Beltoise (BRM) will lead every lap. (Courtesy www.fredlewisphotos.com)

1977 John Watson (Brabham) took pole. Clay Regazzoni (Ensign) wished to compete in the Monaco Grand Prix *and* qualify for the Indianapolis 500 the same weekend: he'd get himself into the Grand Prix on the Thursday, miss Saturday qualifying to fly to Indianapolis, and fly back for the race on Sunday. It rained on Thursday, meaning all times on Saturday would be faster so he'd have to stay. Rain threatened again on Saturday and Regazzoni flew to Indianapolis, abandoning the Grand Prix. He didn't see Scheckter (Wolf) beat Lauda (Ferrari) by 0.89 of a second. Fastest lap: Scheckter 81.4mph (-0.7)/130.9kph (-2.2).
1978 Carlos Reutemann (Ferrari) took pole. Patrick Depailler (Tyrrell) won the first Championship race of his career, and led the Championship too. He beat Lauda (Brabham) by 22.3 seconds. Fastest lap: Lauda 83.6mph (+2.2)/134.5kph (+3.6).
1979 Scheckter (Ferrari) took pole. Regazzoni (Williams) created a long, gathering chase of leader Scheckter and by the final lap hounded him, pressing and feinting. Scheckter's tyres were worn but he kept his nerve to win by 0.44 of a second. Fastest lap: Depailler 83.4mph (-0.2)/134.2kph (-0.3).
1980 The race was, typically, oversubscribed: 27 entries for the 20 starting places but, of more immediate concern, with no pre-qualifying in practice all 27 cars might be on the circuit which was licensed for only 24. The drivers protested and the team owners told them: *get on with what you are paid to do.* They did, especially Didier Pironi (Ligier), who took pole, and Reutemann (Williams), who beat Jacques Laffite in the other Ligier by 1 minute 13.6 seconds. Fastest lap: Reutemann 84.8mph (+1.4)/136.4kph (+2.2).
1981 Because mythology envelops so much of what Gilles Villeneuve did, seeing it with a realistic eye is not always easy. The mythology is that he took a Ferrari turbo to an heroic victory – in fact Nelson Piquet (Brabham), pole, led to lap 53 when he had an engine problem, then Alan Jones (Williams) led but had fuel problems and let Villeneuve into the lead on lap 73 of the 76. Jones finished 39.9 seconds behind. Fastest lap: Jones 84.7mph (-0.1)/136.3kph (-0.1).
1982 René Arnoux (Renault) took pole for arguably the most dramatic and baffling race of all, because on the last lap Pironi

The Swimming Pool in 1973, a splendid aspect of the great panorama – Jackie Stewart (Tyrrell) leading – and Rascasse where the spectators almost overhung the car. (Courtesy Bill Wagenblatt)

(Ferrari) led but the electrics failed, Andrea de Cesaris (Alfa Romeo) was poised to win but ran out of fuel, and Riccardo Patrese (Brabham) was given a push-start after spinning. He crossed the line, had no idea he had won and disbelieved people when they told him. Officially he beat Pironi by a lap. Fastest lap: Patrese 85.8mph (+1.1)/138.1kph (+1.8).
1983 Alain Prost (Renault) took pole. The Williams team gambled on dry tyres on a wet afternoon and were right, giving the race to Keke Rosberg. He beat Piquet (Brabham) by 18.4 seconds. Fastest lap: Piquet 84.9mph (-0.6)/136.6kph (-1.5).
1984 Mythology envelops so much of what Ayrton Senna did, and seeing

it – specifically a storm-ridden afternoon at Monaco – with a steady eye remains difficult. In a Toleman he caught Alain Prost (McLaren), pole, and would have won if the race had not been stopped after 31 laps, although Stefan Bellof (Tyrrell) was catching *him* and was only 13.6 seconds away. The Tyrrell was subsequently disqualified for a fuel irregularity. Officially, Prost beat Senna by 7.4 seconds. Fastest lap: Senna 64.8mph/104.3kph (no comparison).
1985 A dispute between AC Monaco, the local governing body, and FISA over television rights threatened the race and was only resolved shortly beforehand. Senna (Lotus) took pole, Prost (McLaren)

beat Michele Alboreto (Ferrari) by 7.5 seconds. Fastest lap: Alboreto 89.7mph (+4.8)/144.3kph (+7.7).

Speed increase 1976–85: 7.6mph/12.2kph.

The organisers spent a reported £1 million to adapt the circuit to modern racing cars. A concrete 'extension' was built modifying the harbourside chicane from the tight left-right to something approaching a more orthodox corner. The topography of Monaco dictated this. Drivers complained in 1985 that the left-right, taken at up to 160mph, was a disconcerting experience and, because the width of the track was dictated by a sheer rock face to the right, the extension to the left was literally the only place to go. The new chicane might even be an overtaking place.

1986 Prost (McLaren), pole, gave a classic display of his precision, economy of movement, and concentration to lead every lap except his pit stop and beat team-mate Rosberg by 25.0 seconds. Fastest lap: Prost 86.0mph/138.3kph.

1987 Nigel Mansell (Williams) took pole. Lotus were running their fiendishly complicated 'active suspension' and

Senna leads through Ste Dévote in 1988 with Gerhard Berger (Ferrari), McLaren team-mate Alain Prost and Nigel Mansell (Williams) behind. (ICN U.K. Bureau)

when it worked it looked like the future become present. It worked at Monaco for Senna. Mansell led until a wastegate pipe problem halted him and Senna beat Piquet (Williams) by 33.2 seconds. Fastest lap: Senna 84.9mph (-1.1)/136.6kph (-1.7).

1988 Senna, now with McLaren, had pole in second qualifying but 'I was going faster and faster. One lap after the other, quicker, and quicker, and quicker. I was at one stage just on pole, then by half a second, and then one second and I kept going. Suddenly, I was nearly two seconds faster than anybody else, including my team-mate with the same car. And I suddenly realised that I was no longer driving the car consciously. I was kind of driving it by instinct, only I was in a different dimension. It was like I was in a tunnel, not only the tunnel under the hotel, but the whole circuit for me was a tunnel. I was just going, going more, and more, and more, and more. I was way over the limit, but still able to find even more. Then, suddenly, something just kicked me. I kind of woke up and I realised that I was in a different atmosphere than you normally are. Immediately my reaction was to back off, slow down. I drove back slowly to the pits and I didn't want to go out any more that day. It frightened me because I realised I was well beyond my conscious understanding.'[7] He led the race, lost concentration, crashed and was inconsolable. Prost in the other McLaren beat Gerhard Berger (Ferrari) by 20.4 seconds. Fastest lap: Senna 86.2mph (+1.3)/138.8kph (+2.2).

1989 Senna (McLaren), pole, led every lap, concealing a gearbox problem from team-mate Prost, second, and kept his concentration perfectly to win by 52.5 seconds. Fastest lap: Prost 87.1mph (+0.9)/140.1kph (+1.3).

1990 Senna (McLaren), pole, supreme but Jean Alesi (Tyrrell) announced himself after a feisty duel with Berger in the other McLaren. Senna beat Alesi by 18.3 seconds. Fastest lap: Senna 88.1mph (+1.0)/141.8kph (+1.7).

1991 Senna's hat-trick. He dominated both qualifying sessions and led every lap. Only Graham Hill and Prost had won three consecutively before this. He beat Mansell (Williams) by 18.3 seconds. Fastest lap: Prost (Ferrari) 88.2mph (+0.1)/142.0kph (+0.2).

1992 Mansell's year. In the Williams he took pole and led to lap 71 when he pitted

with a suspected puncture, emerged, and swarmed Senna – which impressed every televiewer in the world but did not impress A. Senna Esq, who drove the McLaren calmly to victory number four in a row, beating Mansell by 0.2 of a second. Fastest lap: Mansell 91.2mph (+3.0)/146.8kph (+4.8).

1993 Senna's lucky win: Prost (Williams), pole and leading, had a stop'n'go penalty for jumping the start and Michael Schumacher's Benetton had a suspension failure. Senna beat Damon Hill (Williams) by 52.1 seconds. Fastest lap: Prost 89.0mph (-2.2)/143.3kph (-3.5).

1994 Held two weeks after Senna's death at Imola, Monaco was sombre and nervous – and more nervous after Karl Wendlinger crashed his Sauber in free practice, receiving serious head injuries. Schumacher (Benetton), pole, beat Martin Brundle (McLaren) by 37.2 seconds. Fastest lap: Schumacher 91.8mph (+2.8)/147.8kph (+4.5).

1995 Hill (Williams) took pole but Schumacher (Benetton) won, which would become something ordinary in Formula 1. In Saturday morning free practice the Footwork of Taki Inoue was being towed back to the pits when a course car ran into it, which would remain something unique. Schumacher beat Hill (Williams) by 34.8 seconds. Fastest lap: Jean Alesi (Ferrari) 88.0mph (-3.8)/141.6kph (-6.2).

1996 A wet-dry race and Schumacher (now Ferrari) had pole but on the first lap slithered into the wall at *Portier*. Meanwhile Olivier Panis (Ligier) worked his way up from 12th. At the end only he and two other cars were still running. He beat David Coulthard (McLaren) by 4.8 seconds. Fastest lap: Alesi (Benetton) 87.4mph (-0.6)/140.6kph (-1.0).

Speed increase 1986–96: 1.4mph/2.3kph.

The approach to the Swimming Pool complex – the Esses – had been eased a little and opened a little.

1997 Heinz-Harald Frentzen (Williams) took pole. With the weather uncertain, Schumacher set the Ferrari up on an intermediate setting and by lap 5 led by 22 seconds. It was wet. He beat Rubens Barrichello (Stewart) by 53.3 seconds. Fastest lap: Schumacher 66.4mph/106.9kph.

1998 From pole, Mika Häkkinen (McLaren) led every lap to beat Giancarlo Fisichella (Benetton) by 11.4 seconds.

Fastest lap: Häkkinen 90.8mph/146.1kph (no comparison).

1999 Häkkinen (McLaren) took pole. By now Schumacher was building his own monument and his victory here increased that: it was his 16th for Ferrari, beating Lauda's 15, and with team-mate Eddie Irvine finishing second Ferrari had their first 1-2 since they first competed at Monaco in 1948 (with Prince Igor Troubetskoy – a Frenchman! – driving it; he crashed after 58 laps). Schumacher's margin was 30.4 seconds. Fastest lap: Häkkinen 91.6mph (+0.8)/147.4kph (+1.3).

2000 Schumacher (Ferrari) took pole but a cracked exhaust allowed Coulthard (McLaren) into the lead and he beat Barrichello in the other Ferrari by 15.8 seconds. Fastest lap: Häkkinen 92.4mph (+0.8)/148.7kph (+1.3).

2001 Coulthard (McLaren) took pole but the launch control misbehaved on the parade lap, giving him 'a long, lonely' afternoon and opening the race to Schumacher, who beat team-mate Barrichello by 0.4 of a second and described the victory as straightforward. It was his fifth at Monaco, which suggested Senna's record of six was now very vulnerable. Fastest lap: Coulthard 94.9mph (+2.5)/152.7kph (+4.0).

2002 Juan-Pablo Montoya (Williams) took pole. Coulthard (McLaren) atoned, leading every lap and resisting whatever pressure Schumacher laid on him for an hour and three-quarters to win by 1.0 second. Fastest lap: Barrichello (Ferrari) 96.6mph (+1.7)/155.5kph (+2.8).

Speed increase 1998–2002: 5.8mph/9.4kph.

Further revisions to the circuit.

2003 Jenson Button (Honda) crashed in the same place as Wendlinger had done in Saturday free practice but, because cockpits were now much safer, emerged with concussion and nothing more. Ralf Schumacher (Williams) took pole. Montoya (Williams) led towards the end but the team told him the engine was overheating and he had to cut the revs. He knew if he did that he'd lose the race so he kept on – and won, beating Kimi Räikkönen (McLaren) by 0.6 of a second. Fastest lap: Räikkönen 100.2mph/161.2kph.

2004 The notorious incident in the tunnel on lap 46 when, under the safety car, Michael Schumacher's Ferrari was struck by Montoya's Williams. Schumacher

The classic aerial view. This is 1997, and Giancarlo Fisichella (Jordan) is in front of Olivier Panis (Prost). (ICN U.K. Bureau)

The classic ground view. Johnny Herbert (Sauber) shows how any mistake carries a heavy penalty. This is lap 9 of the same race. (ICN U/K. Bureau)

Heikki Kovalainen crashed his McLaren at the Swimming Pool in 2009 and the crane took care of the rest. (Courtesy Greg Wesson)

A valuable commodity – but valueless on race day… (Courtesy Martin Hadwen, National Motor Racing Archive)

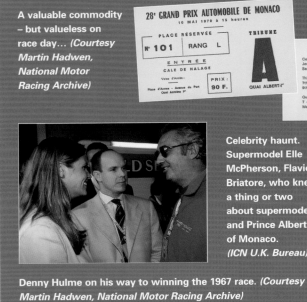

Celebrity haunt. Supermodel Elle McPherson, Flavio Briatore, who knew a thing or two about supermodels, and Prince Albert of Monaco. (ICN U.K. Bureau)

The 1967 programme, when Graham Hill ruled Monaco – for one day a year, at least – and look at the advertisements. Monaco was, and is, not for poor people. (Courtesy Martin Hadwen, National Motor Racing Archive)

Denny Hulme on his way to winning the 1967 race. (Courtesy Martin Hadwen, National Motor Racing Archive)

The second round of the new World Championship in 1950. (Courtesy Martin Hadwen, National Motor Racing Archive)

seemed to slow, leaving Montoya nowhere to go. Jarno Trulli (Renault), pole, beat Button (BAR) by 0.4 of a second. Fastest lap: Schumacher 100.4mph (+0.2)/161.5kph (+0.3).

2005 Räikkönen (McLaren) took pole and led but on lap 23 a multiple crash brought the Safety Car out. After it, while others pitted, he stayed out and drove a sequence of laps so fast that they decided the race. He beat Nick Heidfeld (Williams) by 13.8 seconds. Fastest lap: Schumacher 98.5mph (-1.9)/158.5kph (-3.0).

2006 Fernando Alonso (Renault) took pole. The notorious incident at *Rascasse* when Schumacher's Ferrari slewed and bumped the barrier at the end of qualifying, which effectively ended Alonso's hope of taking pole from him – but Schumacher was demoted to the back of the grid. Alonso beat Montoya (McLaren) by 14.5 seconds. Fastest lap: Schumacher 99.4mph (+0.9)/160.0kph (+1.5).

2007 The McLarens of Alonso, pole, and Lewis Hamilton dominated but the FIA investigated whether the team had issued orders forbidding Hamilton from challenging Alonso. McLaren were cleared. Alonso won by 4.0 seconds. Fastest lap: Alonso 99.2mph (-0.2)/159.7kph (-0.3).

2008 The race started in the wet and Felipe Massa (Ferrari), pole, led through *Ste Devote* while Hamilton surged past Räikkönen in the other Ferrari for second place. He had a puncture and pitted on lap 6, coming out fifth – but the track dried and everyone else pitted, giving him a lead he didn't lose. Hamilton beat Robert Kubica (Sauber) by 3.0 seconds. Fastest lap: Räikkönen 97.4mph (-1.8)/156.8kph (-2.9).

2009 The Brawn team, previously Honda, had given Button a winning car and from pole he won, his fifth from the first six races, with the other driver, Barrichello, second. Button's smooth style of driving enabled him to protect his tyres and in the end he was so fresh he *ran* from the car to the podium with a smile slightly bigger than the harbour. He won by 7.6 seconds. Fastest lap: Massa (Ferrari) 99.4mph (+2.0)/160.0kph (+3.2).

Speed decrease 2003–9: 0.8mph/1.2kph.

Footnotes
[1] *Champion Year*, Hawthorn. [2] *When the Flag Drops*, Brabham.
[3] *My Cars, My Career*, Moss. [4] *Autocourse*. [5] *Ibid.* [6] *Grand Prix!*, Lang. [7] *Grand Prix People*, Donaldson.

FACTS OF THE MATTER

1.976m/3.180km circuit

Year	Winner
1950	J.M. Fangio (Alfa Romeo)
Pole	J.M. Fangio (64.5mph/103.9kph)
Fastest lap	J.M. Fangio (64.1mph/103.1kph)

Chicane repositioned, 1.954m/3.145km circuit

1955	M. Trintignant (Ferrari)
1956	S. Moss (Maserati)
1957	J.M. Fangio (Maserati)
1958	M. Trintignant (Cooper)
1959	J. Brabham (Cooper)
1960	S. Moss (Lotus)
1961	S. Moss (Lotus)
1962	B. McLaren (Cooper)
1963	G. Hill (BRM)
1964	G. Hill (BRM)
1965	G. Hill (BRM)
1966	J. Stewart (BRM)
1967	D. Hulme (Brabham)
1968	G. Hill (Lotus)
1969	G. Hill (Lotus)
1970	J. Rindt (Lotus)
1971	J. Stewart (Tyrrell)
1972	J.-P. Beltoise (BRM)
Fastest pole	E. Fittipaldi (Lotus) 1972 (86.4mph/139.1kph)
Fastest lap	J. Stewart (Tyrrell) 1971 (85.6mph/137.7kph)

New layout, including Piscine and Rascasse, 2.037m/3.278km circuit

1973	J. Stewart (Tyrrell)
1974	R. Peterson (Lotus)
1975	N. Lauda (Ferrari)
Fastest pole	N. Lauda (Ferrari) 1974 (85.0mph/136.7kph)
Fastest lap	R. Peterson (Lotus) 1974 (83.4mph/134.3kph)

Ste Dévote, Rascasse tightened, 2.058m/3.312km circuit

1976	N. Lauda (Ferrari)
1977	J. Scheckter (Wolf)
1978	C. Reutemann (Ferrari)
1979	J. Scheckter (Ferrari)
1980	C. Reutemann (Williams)
1981	G. Villeneuve (Ferrari)
1982	R. Patrese (Brabham)
1983	K. Rosberg (Williams)
1984	A. Prost (McLaren)
1985	A. Prost (McLaren)
Fastest pole	A. Senna (Lotus) 1985 (92.1mph/148.2kph)
Fastest lap	M. Alboreto (Ferrari) 1985 (89.7mph/144.3kph)

New chicane, 2.068m/3.328km circuit

1986	A. Prost (McLaren)
1987	A. Senna (Lotus)
1988	A. Prost (McLaren)
1989	A. Senna (McLaren)
1990	A. Senna (McLaren)
1991	A. Senna (McLaren)
1992	A. Senna (McLaren)
1993	A. Senna (McLaren)
1994	M. Schumacher (Benetton)
1995	M. Schumacher (Benetton)
1996	O. Panis (Ligier)
Fastest pole	M. Schumacher (Benetton) 1994 (94.8mph/152.5kph)
Fastest lap	M. Schumacher (Benetton) 1994 (91.8mph/147.8kph)

Swimming Pool eased, 2.092m/3.366km circuit 1997; 2.092m/3.367km 1998–9; 2.094m/3.370km 2000–2

1997	M. Schumacher (Ferrari)
1998	M. Häkkinen (McLaren)
1999	M. Schumacher (Ferrari)
2000	D. Coulthard (McLaren)
2001	M. Schumacher (Ferrari)
2002	D. Coulthard (McLaren)
Fastest pole	J.-P. Montoya (Williams) 2002 (98.3mph/158.2kph)
Fastest lap	R. Barrichello (Ferrari) 2002 (96.6mph/155.5kph)

Further revision, 2.075m/3.340km circuit

2003	J.-P. Montoya (Williams)
2004	J. Trulli (Renault)
2005	K. Räikkönen (McLaren)
2006	F. Alonso (Renault)
2007	F. Alonso (McLaren)
2008	L. Hamilton (McLaren)
2009	J. Button (Brawn)
Fastest pole	K. Räikkönen (McLaren) 2005 (101.4mph/163.2kph)*
Fastest lap	M. Schumacher (Ferrari) 2006 (99.4mph/160.0kph)

* The grid was decided by the aggregate of two sessions. Räikkönen did 2m 30.3s, with a first session time of 1m 13.6s.

ÂIN-DIAB

Location: Western outskirts of Casablanca.
Constructed: 1957.
World Championship Grands Prix: 1.

Mike Hawthorn runs smoothly in second place and it will be enough. (LAT)

'Very nasty as the sun sinks'

Mike Hawthorn

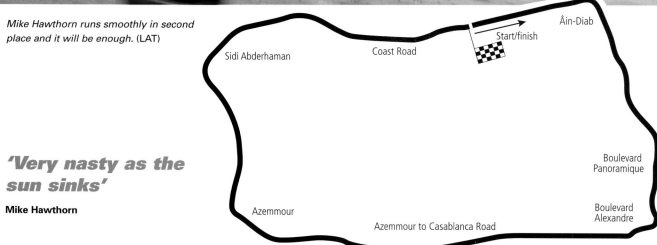

Âin-Diab

Start/finish

Sidi Abderhaman

Coast Road

Boulevard
Panoramique

Boulevard
Alexandre

Azemmour

Azemmour to Casablanca Road

The idea of having a Grand Prix in North Africa may seem bizarre now but it had its own context. There'd been one in Libya in the 1930s and, from 1925, a race in Morocco called the Casablanca Grand Prix. It resumed in 1954 after an interval of 19 years at Agadir, and in 1957 a non-Championship Grand Prix was held south-west of Âin-Diab, on the coast and a bus ride from Casablanca. This was a road circuit using the coast road itself and the main road from Casablanca to the city of Azemmour. It was completed in six weeks.

The race attracted a full entry, including Juan Manuel Fangio in a Maserati and Mike Hawthorn in a Ferrari, but Jean Behra (also Maserati) won from a Briton, Stuart Lewis-Evans (Vanwall).

The 1958 race was the Championship decider (and also featured Formula 2 cars on the grid, but running for their own championship). Hawthorn went into it clear favourite because his only rival, Stirling Moss (Vanwall), had to win and take the point for fastest lap while Hawthorn himself had to be no higher than third.

COCKPIT VIEW
Mika Hawthorn:

'The circuit measures 4.7 miles and is pretty fast. The start and pits, like Portugal, are opposite the Atlantic Ocean; from there one goes round a right-hand corner which winds inland and uphill to another right-hander on to the back straight, which like every straight past the pits, is very fast.

'This leads on to a vicious right-hander, quite fast and very nasty late in the day as the sun sinks and shines straight into your eyes; then there are a left- and right-hander, both of them fast, bringing you back along the straight parallel with the seashore.'[1]

EYEWITNESS
Gregor Grant, *Autosport*:

'All drivers were presented to the King of Morocco before the race, a most colourful spectacle, with a picturesque military band and the monarch's special bodyguard in close attendance. Tubby "Toto" Roche from Reims acted as starter, and, as usual, it was a bit of a nonsense. Without warning the flag fell, and bewildered drivers were left to sort things out as best they could – after the front row had left, with Moss and Lewis-Evans out-accelerating the rest,

and Phil Hill snapping ahead of team-mate Hawthorn.

'Long before the excited babble from the great crowd had died down the cars were round again, with Phil Hill in the lead – only just – from Moss, closely followed by Hawthorn and Bonnier; then came Brooks, Lewis-Evans, Behra, Schell and Gendebien in that order.'

MEMORIES AND A MILESTONE

1958 Stirling Moss found the track well surfaced but Graham Hill had other memories, including the luxury hotel he stayed in which had automatic doors, something he had never seen before. The social life was good, too, although 'in those parts they were able to provide some entertainments which one doesn't see elsewhere'.[2]

Moss went quickest from Hawthorn in first practice but weather for the Saturday session was cooler 'and a sea fog had rolled in which did not impair visibility and suited carburetion: times came down quite a bit'.[3]

Hawthorn had pole, Moss next to him. That night, the eve of the race, Hawthorn 'went straight to sleep with the sound of fog horns blowing' to alert shipping. He awoke to find the fog gone.

The story of the race was simple.

Moss set off in the lead and did set fastest lap but with 13 laps left Ferrari signalled their other driver, Phil Hill, to slow and let Hawthorn go. Hawthorn moved into second place.

Jack Brabham was in a Formula 2 car. 'While all this high-powered drama was going on at the front, we Formula 2 drivers were ploughing on, trying not to be worried by the fact that we were being lapped with monotonous regularity. It was really a bit dangerous to have some of the locals in such an important event in slow cars.'[4] Brabham would be lapped four times.

On lap 29 Tommy Bridger in a Formula 2 Cooper crashed and a lap later Olivier Gendebien (Ferrari) spun on oil and one of the Formula 2 drivers, François Picard (Cooper) rammed him.

On lap 42 Lewis-Evans was running fifth when the Vanwall's engine blew up. The car went off the circuit into sand and caught fire. Lewis-Evans got himself out but the fire had caught his overalls. He received burns that were to prove fatal.

Hawthorn finished second – 1 minute 24.7 seconds behind Moss – which was enough. At the end of a sad and savage season – his friend and team-mate Peter Collins killed, his team-mate Luigi Musso killed, and now a sense of foreboding about Lewis-Evans – Hawthorn felt emptied. He decided never to race again.

Footnotes
[1] *Champion Year*, Hawthorn. [2] *Life at the Limit*, Hill.
[3] *A Turn at the Wheel*, Moss. [4] *When the Flag Drops*, Brabham.

Big news in Italy, too – it was a win for Ferrari, of course.

FACTS OF THE MATTER

4.734m/7.618km circuit

Year	Winner
1958	S. Moss (Vanwall)
Pole	M. Hawthorn (Ferrari)
	(119.1mph/191.6kph)
Fastest lap	S. Moss (119.6mph/192.5kph)

ZANDVOORT

Location: 6 miles (9km) west of Haarlem.
Constructed: 1948.
World Championship Grands Prix: 30.

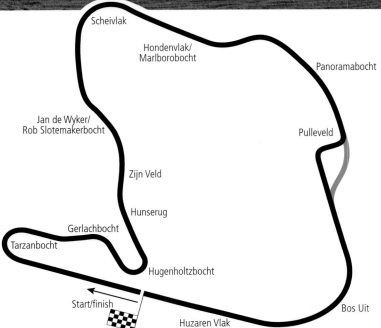

Tarzan today – the same shape and of necessity sanitised for a modern era. (Courtesy Filipp Gorelik)

Scheivlak

Hondenvlak/
Marlborobocht

Panoramabocht

Jan de Wyker/
Rob Slotemakerbocht

Pulleveld

Zijn Veld

Hunserug

Gerlachbocht

Tarzanbocht

Hugenholtzbocht

Start/finish

Bos Uit

Huzaren Vlak

'If you went off the track you were in the sand dunes'

John Watson

Everybody liked Zandvoort except the residents, or at least some of them. They didn't mind the wind brushing in off the North Sea but they didn't appreciate the shriek of engines being borne on it. It took the slumber out of slumbering summer afternoons.

Those who did like Zandvoort, the circuit on the rim of the seaside town of that name, proclaimed its virtues as a thoroughbred racetrack of great speed and differing demands. They also liked the fact that you might spend countless hours in traffic jams getting into and out of other circuits but here you either strolled from the town (if you were lucky enough to find a hotel there) or came in by train and strolled from the station. All very civilised. Amsterdam and its delights – many of them very, very dubious – were within comfortable commuting distance.

The circuit itself threaded a path through sand dunes and the wind sometimes dragged the sand on to the main straight.

During the Second World War the North Sea coastline, from Normandy to Holland, was fashioned into the Atlantic Wall by the Germans to repulse any invasion from Britain. They built thick-set concrete command posts, look-out posts, bunkers and gun emplacements, and many remain as historical artefacts both as a reminder of war and occupation and a problem of what to do with the damned things.

Zandvoort's circuit was built incorporating a link road between gun emplacements. Folklore suggests the local mayor persuaded the Germans not

A circuit threaded between the dunes and now you know why blown sand was a hazard. This is 1955, Juan Manuel Fangio leading Stirling Moss in the Mercedes. (LAT)

to send the menfolk to Germany to work but, instead, construct a long, straight road through the dunes for victory parades. Feeder roads were added by a group of officials from the Royal Dutch Motorcycle Association, with advice from Bentley Boy Sammy Davis (who had won the Le Mans 24 Hours in 1927). The architect John Hugenholtz exploited the topography as well as these roads to fashion his circuit.

The circuit staged its first race in 1948 and joined the World Championship in 1952. It stayed until 1985 when the environmentalists won.

'In the 1970s and 1980s, noise was a major issue in the racing world. Drivers used silencers from 1979 onwards but opponents believed it was not enough. Although the circuit generated tens of millions of guilders for the economy, the opposition persisted. In 1983, the mayor and aldermen of Zandvoort once again took a positive approach to the circuit. A key change occurred

in 1985 – The Council of State decided that the track's presence did not obstruct house-building in Zandvoort.

'Nonetheless, at the end of 1985 came a new problem: a bungalow development was proposed right next to the track. However, the circuit management devised a ready-made solution, and on 27 March 1986 presented the Columbus Egg, which involved repositioning the circuit by moving the section of track closest to residential buildings some 400 metres further away.'

In 1994 an action plan was approved, building new pits and extending the track to 4,300 metres. In 2001 the new main grandstand was completed.[1]

COCKPIT VIEW

John Watson, who drove in ten Grands Prix there:

'It was a sea-level circuit, on the beach – and a very clever circuit designed by a very clever man, John Hugenholtz. I drove it two or three years ago in an A1GP car, not on the original layout because half of it has gone, but again I thought a wonderful racetrack.

'It was dominated by a long main straight and then a series of sinuous corners after *Tarzan*, a hairpin bend and a key corner, but out the back of the circuit you had a sequence of quick corners – and these were quick fourth-

and fifth-gear corners, which in our cars were taken at 160 miles an hour. There was little in terms of safety for the driver because if you went off the track you were in the sand-dunes and Roger Williamson and Piers Courage paid with their lives consequently.

'It was a racetrack in the Watkins Glen mould. You could let the car *float* through these corners, and it was a balance of steering and throttle as opposed to the stop-start matrix of Long Beach and Detroit. So, to me, it was thoroughly enjoyable.

'The weather wasn't always favourable and the other big thing, of

course, was that you had sand blowing across the track.

'I was at a function recently amongst the old McLaren boys and some of them were talking about the last Grand Prix I did there in 1983. Just watching my car with its Cosworth engine as opposed to the car Niki Lauda had, which was the TAG turbo, they could see the Cosworth flying through the corners round the back. You were on that lovely *is-he, isn't-he?* edge. A little bit more and you were out of control, you were history. You had that sense of what your body feels when you know you're extracting the maximum out of the car and yourself.'

The feel of the dunes, which gave old and new circuits their distinctive character. (Both courtesy Filipp Gorelik)

EYEWITNESS

Gareth Rees, motor sport enthusiast:
'My earliest memories of Zandvoort are from seeing the Dutch Grand Prix on television as a kid, first in 1966 with Jim Clark's heroic battle for the lead in a 2-litre Lotus 33 against the 3-litre Brabhams, and then again in 1967 when Clark won on the debut of the Lotus 49 and its new DFV engine.

'I first went to the Dutch GP at Zandvoort on a Page & Moy overnight trip in 1971, taking my school homework to do on the coach. It was a miserably wet day when Jacky Ickx and Pedro Rodríguez had that historic race-long battle to the finish, lapping the rest of the field.

'Sadly, I missed much of this. We went to watch at the *Scheivlak* corner at the back of the circuit and simply lost count of the number of laps. Soaked through, we could neither hear nor understand any commentary and believed (hoped!) that the race must be almost over. We were worried that the bus might leave without us so we started walking back only to discover later that the race had barely reached half-distance!

'Much later in life I found myself living in the Netherlands and Zandvoort became my "home" track. In 1982 I watched from a temporary grandstand erected on the outside of *Bos Uit*, the fast undulating and crucial curve which led on to the long front straight. The sight of these last-generation ground-effect cars in the swooping *Bos Uit* was all the more spectacular because, despite having no suspension to speak of, the Cosworth cars of Rosberg and Lauda had to give it their all, just to stand a chance of keeping in the slipstream of a turbo on the long straight.

'From my seat I could see them burst over the brow from the *Panoramabocht*, drop flat out into the long sweeper and then watch the cars all the way down the straight until they turned into *Tarzan* hairpin. It was the first time I had ever experienced the weird phenomenon of my eyes seeing the cars turning into the corner, well before the sound of them lifting off the gas reached my ears. Sadly, in the name of progress, the Zandvoort of today has a shorter straight and the original *Bos Uit* is now underneath a bungalow park.

'In 1985, at the last Dutch Grand Prix, I watched from the outside of *Scheivlak*. The defining moment came late in the race when the soon-to-be-champion Prost caught and passed his wilting team-mate Lauda into the *Marlboro* chicane. It was a bit like witnessing the changing of the guard and the end of an era.'

MEMORIES AND MILESTONES

1952 A small entry, 18, included the Ferraris of Alberto Ascari (pole) and Giuseppe Farina, while Mike Hawthorn put his Cooper on the front row. Ascari was fast away and so was Hawthorn but on lap 2 Farina swept by him. However, Ascari led all 90 laps and beat Farina by 40.1 seconds. Fastest lap: Ascari 85.4mph/137.5kph.
1953 The circuit had been resurfaced the previous week and that meant loose grit. Ascari (Ferrari) took pole again, this time from Juan Manuel Fangio (Maserati), and led all 90 laps to beat Farina in another Ferrari by 10.5 seconds. Fastest lap: Luigi Villoresi (Ferrari) 83.2mph (-2.2)/133.8kph (-3.7).
1955 A race of enormous significance because it was run the week after the Le Mans disaster when at least 80

The old Zandvoort, the sand at the rim of the track. Jo Bonnier (Porsche) moves to seventh place

spectators were killed and the future of motor sport called into question. Mercedes filled the front row (three abreast) with Fangio taking pole from Stirling Moss. Fangio led all 100 laps and beat Moss by two tenths. Fastest lap: Robert Mières (Maserati) 93.0mph (+9.8)/149.6kph (+15.8).

1958 Stuart Lewis-Evans took pole, one of three Vanwalls on the front row (Moss alongside him) although the whole grid was tight: 2.7 seconds embraced the first 13 cars. Moss dominated the race, leading into *Tarzan*, and then all 75 laps to beat Harry Schell (BRM) by 47.9 seconds. It produced a curiosity. The first four Dutch Grands Prix comprised 355 laps but had had only four leaders. Fastest lap: Moss 96.1mph (+3.1)/154.7kph (+5.1).

1959 A sign of the times: BRM tested extensively at the circuit in the week before the race, using Moss, who in the race would be in his usual Cooper. Jo Bonnier (BRM), benefiting from Moss's testing, took pole and although the lead changed seven times among four drivers beat Jack Brabham (Cooper) by 14.2 seconds. Fastest lap: Moss 97.0mph (+0.9)/156.1kph (+1.4).

1960 Moss (Lotus) took pole from Brabham (Cooper) and they pulled cleanly away from the rest, Brabham leading and 17 seconds clear at lap 10. On lap 12 Dan Gurney's BRM had a brake failure approaching *Tarzan* and it went off, killing a spectator and injuring others. Later Brabham touched a kerbstone on the rim of the track in *Bos Uit* so hard he dislodged it, casting it back and destroying one of Moss's tyres. Brabham beat Innes Ireland (Lotus) by 24.0 seconds. Fastest lap: Moss 100.0mph (+3.0)/160.9kph (+4.8).

1961 Wolfgang von Trips (Ferrari) was a very popular German and, from the middle of the front row (Phil Hill in the other Ferrari had pole) led all 75 laps to win the first race of his career. He beat Hill by 0.9 of a second. Fastest lap: Jim Clark (Lotus) 98.2mph (-1.8)/158.1kph (-2.8).

1962 The first race of the season and John Surtees (Lola) took pole but Clark (Lotus) led into *Tarzan* and kept the lead to lap 12, when he pitted with a clutch problem. Graham Hill (BRM) beat Trevor Taylor (Lotus) by 27.2 seconds. Fastest lap: Bruce McLaren (Cooper) 99.4mph (+1.2)/159.9kph (+1.8).

1963 Clark (Lotus) took pole, the only man into 1m 31s. He led all 80 laps and beat Gurney (Brabham) by a *lap*. Fastest lap: Clark 100.1mph (+0.7)/161.1kph (+1.2).

1964 Clark (Lotus) *not* pole – Gurney (Brabham) 1m 31.2s, Clark 1m 31.3s – but emerged from *Tarzan* in the lead. He led all 80 laps and beat Surtees (Ferrari) by 53.6 seconds. Fastest lap: Clark 101.1mph (+1.0)/162.7kph (+1.6).

1965 Clark (Lotus) *not* pole – Graham Hill (BRM) 1m 30.7s, Clark 1m 31.0s – and Clark *not* into the lead at *Tarzan* but following Richie Ginther (Honda) and Hill. Hill outbraked Ginther, Clark outbraked Ginther and then Hill and led from lap 6 to lap 80, beating Jackie Stewart (BRM) by 8.0 seconds. The race is remembered for other reasons – Colin Chapman, who owned and ran Lotus, spent a night in jail after punching a policeman who didn't see his pit pass and tried to force him to leave. Fastest lap: Clark 103.5mph (+2.4)/166.6kph (+3.9).

1966 Brabham (Brabham) took pole. He'd already won France and Britain and now added the Dutch, after a lively duel with Clark (Lotus): Brabham led laps 1–26 and 76–90, Clark 27–75. Clark had a water pump problem and Brabham beat Graham Hill (BRM) by a lap. Fastest lap: Denny Hulme (Brabham) 103.5mph/166.6kph (no change).

1967 The race that changed motor racing history. Lotus had the new Cosworth engines. Graham Hill took pole but Clark had mechanical problems and qualified on the third row, eighth. Clark took the lead from Brabham (Brabham) on lap 16 and

beat him by 23.6 seconds. Fastest lap: Clark 106.5mph (+3.0)/171.4kph (+4.8).

1968 Chris Amon (Ferrari) took pole but, in drizzle, Jochen Rindt (Brabham) led into *Tarzan*. Graham Hill (Lotus) and Jackie Stewart (Matra) overtook him and, on lap 4, Stewart stole through at *Tarzan*, beating Jean-Pierre Beltoise in the other Matra by 1 minute 33.9 seconds. (Note: in a Formula 2 race a month later Clay Regazzoni and Englishman Chris Lambert crashed, and Lambert died.) Fastest lap: J.-P. Beltoise 88.5mph/142.5kph (no comparison).

1969 A five-week break between races because the exaggerated rear wings had broken in Spain and safety concerns could not be settled in time for Spa. Rindt (Lotus) took pole, team-mate Graham Hill led to lap 3 when Rindt forced his way through and pulled away until a driveshaft failed. Stewart (Matra) beat Jo Siffert (Lotus) by 24.5 seconds. Fastest lap: Stewart 113.1mph (+6.6)/182.0kph (+10.6).

1970 The seared race. Piers Courage (de Tomaso) crashed fatally on lap 23, the car overturned and burst into a hellish sheet of flames and smoke. Rindt (Lotus) beat Stewart (March) by 30.0 seconds. Fastest lap: Jacky Ickx (Ferrari) 118.4mph (+5.3)/190.5kph (+8.5).

1971 Clay Regazzoni and Mario Andretti (both Ferrari) crashed heavily in practice with tyre failures. Ickx in another Ferrari took pole and, in a wet race, duelled

The whole crocodile out among the dunes in 1973. (Courtesy Bill Wagenblatt)

James Hunt in the Hesketh, out among the dunes in 1974.
(Courtesy Bill Wagenblatt)

The Lotuses of Elio de Angelis and Roberto Moreno on the loop
behind the pits, 1982. (Courtesy Gareth Rees)

with Pedro Rodríguez (BRM) – the lead changed four times – before Ickx beat him by 7.9 seconds. Fastest lap: Ickx 98.8mph/159.0kph (no comparison).

Speed increase 1952–70: 33.0mph/53.0kph.

The 1972 race was lost because safety improvements weren't made, but, at considerable expense, they were just about complete for the 1973 race, although work was still being done on the Friday. The improvements included complete resurfacing, guardrails throughout, widening at strategic points, and the sand dunes at the side of the track removed. At Panoramabocht a new corner had been created to slow the cars. It turned right and had a wide left-hand exit.

1973 Ronnie Peterson (Lotus) took pole and led. On lap 8 Roger Williamson (March) crashed so heavily the guardrail launched it and it landed upside down on fire. David Purley (March) stopped and tried to get him out while the fire marshals watched. Williamson died. The race was not stopped. Peterson's gearbox failed and Stewart (Tyrrell) beat team-mate François Cevert by 15.8 seconds. Fastest lap: Ronnie Peterson (Lotus) 117.7mph/189.4kph.

1974 Niki Lauda (Ferrari) took pole and led all 75 laps, beating team-mate Regazzoni by 8.2 seconds. Fastest lap: Peterson (Lotus) 116.1mph (-1.6)/186.8kph (-2.8).

1975 The tiny Hesketh team, portrayed in the British media as errant public schoolboys, were very serious. Their only driver, James Hunt, put the car on the

second row (Lauda pole in the Ferrari), took the lead on lap 15 and beat Lauda by 1.0 seconds. Fastest lap: Lauda 115.9mph (-0.2)/186.5kph (-0.3).

1976 Lauda crashed at the Nürburgring on 1 August, his Ferrari consumed by fire and his survival uncertain. Now, as the team gathered at Zandvoort, the word was he'd come out of hospital. Peterson (March) took pole from Lauda's championship rival Hunt (McLaren) and led to lap 11 when Hunt went past and led to the end, beating Regazzoni (Ferrari) by 0.9 of a second. Fastest lap: Regazzoni 114.5mph (-1.4)/184.2kph (-2.3).

1977 An immense entry (34) had to be pruned on a special day of practice. Andretti (Lotus) took pole but Hunt (McLaren) made the better start, Andretti matching him wheel to wheel round *Tarzan* before being put on to the grass. Hunt led to lap 5 when they collided, and Jacques Laffite (Ligier) led until Lauda took him inside into *Tarzan*. He beat Laffite by 1.8 seconds. Fastest lap: Lauda (Ferrari) 118.2mph (+3.7)/190.2kph (+6.0).

1978 Andretti's Championship year with Lotus. He took pole from team-mate Peterson, led all 75 laps and beat Peterson by 0.3 of a second. Fastest lap: Lauda (Brabham) 118.8mph (+0.6)/191.2kph (+1.0).

Speed increase 1973–8: 1.1mph/1.8kph.

A chicane along the back straight at Marlborobocht had been built to slow the cars but it turned out to be an esse and bumpy. The drivers didn't like it.

1979 René Arnoux (Renault) took pole but Alan Jones (Williams), alongside

him, led to lap 10 when Gilles Villeneuve (Ferrari) took him on the *outside* round *Tarzan.* Jones took him at the new chicane and then Villeneuve's rear tyre exploded. He took it round to the pits on three wheels, wrecking the underside. Jones beat Villeneuve's team-mate Jody Scheckter by 21.7 seconds. Fastest lap: Villeneuve 119.0mph/191.5kph.

The chicane at Marlborobocht was made permanent.

1980 Arnoux (Renault) took pole but Jones (Williams) led, then Arnoux, then Jacques Laffite (Ligier), before Nelson Piquet (Brabham) out-nerved Laffite at *Tarzan*. Piquet beat Arnoux by 12.9 seconds. Fastest lap: Arnoux 119.9mph/192.9kph.

1981 Alain Prost took pole from Arnoux, two Renaults on the front row, but the race developed into a wrestling match between Prost and Jones (Williams), which Prost won because Jones's tyres went off, letting Piquet (Brabham) into second place. Prost beat him by 8.2 seconds – and only one other car, Jones, on the same lap. Fastest lap: Jones 116.2mph (-3.7)/187.1kph (-5.8).

1982 Arnoux (Renault) took pole but team-mate Prost led to lap 4, when Didier Pironi used all his Ferrari's power on the straight. Pironi beat Piquet (Brabham) by 21.6 seconds. Fastest lap: Derek Warwick (Toleman) 119.2mph (+3.0)/191.9kph (+4.8).

1983 Piquet (Brabham) took pole but Tambay (Ferrari), alongside him, got the start wrong and ran 21st. Piquet led to lap 42 when Prost (Renault) challenged him at *Tarzan* and they crashed out.

By 1985 the circuit had been manicured with grass - and cloaked in Armco, of course – but it still felt like the seaside. Here Ayrton Senna (Lotus) harrasses the McLaren of Niki Lauda. (LAT)

Arnoux in the other Ferrari beat Tambay, who fought his way back, by 20.8 seconds. Fastest lap: Arnoux 119.1mph (-0.1)/191.7kph (-0.2).

1984 Prost and Lauda at McLaren: Prost pole, Lauda the third row and ninth after the opening lap, Piquet (Brabham) leading Prost. Piquet had an oil pressure problem, Lauda had made the wrong tyre choice and couldn't catch Prost, who beat him by 10.2 seconds. It was McLaren's ninth win of the season, beating the eight of Lotus in 1978. Fastest lap: Arnoux (Ferrari) 119.7mph (+0.6)/192.6kph (+0.9).

1985 Piquet (Brabham) took pole but Keke Rosberg (Williams) led, then Prost, then Lauda, who leapfrogged him at the tyre stops in the McLarens. Prost came up behind and they circled in a glorious concentration of controlled power at close quarters to the end, 0.2 of a second between them. Afterwards, Lauda said he would indeed help Prost to the Championship but not yet. Fastest lap: Prost 124.3mph (+4.6)/200.0kph (+7.4).

Speed increase 1980–5: 4.4mph/7.1kph.

Footnote
1 www.circuit-zandvoort.nl/info/historie.

Teo Fabi in the Toleman which was really a Benetton, 1985, and Zandvoort wasn't all sand. (Courtesy Gareth Rees)

FACTS OF THE MATTER

2.605m/4.193km circuit

Year	Winner
1952	A. Ascari (Ferrari)
1953	A. Ascari (Ferrari)
1955	J.M. Fangio (Mercedes)
1958	S. Moss (Vanwall)
1959	J. Bonnier (BRM)
1960	J. Brabham (Cooper)
1961	W. von Trips (Ferrari)
1962	G. Hill (BRM)
1963	J. Clark (Lotus)
1964	J. Clark (Lotus)
1965	J. Clark (Lotus)
1966	J. Brabham (Brabham)
1967	J. Clark (Lotus)
1968	J. Stewart (Matra)
1969	J. Stewart (Matra)
1970	J. Rindt (Lotus)
1971	J. Ickx (Ferrari)
Fastest pole	J. Ickx (Ferrari) 1971 (121.2mph/195.0kph)
Fastest lap	J. Ickx (Ferrari) 1970 (118.4mph/190.5kph)

New corner at Panoramabocht, 2.626m/4.226km circuit

1973	J. Stewart (Tyrrell)
1974	N. Lauda (Ferrari)
1975	J. Hunt (Hesketh)
1976	J. Hunt (McLaren)
1977	N. Lauda (Ferrari)
1978	M. Andretti (Lotus)
1979	A. Jones (Williams)
Fastest pole	R. Arnoux (Renault) 1979 (125.3mph/201.6kph)
Fastest lap	G. Villeneuve (Ferrari) 1979 (119.0mph/191.5kph)

Marlborobocht, 2.642m/4.252km circuit

1980	N. Piquet (Brabham)
1981	A. Prost (Renault)
1982	D. Pironi (Ferrari)
1983	R. Arnoux (Ferrari)
1984	A. Prost (McLaren)
1985	N. Lauda (McLaren)
Fastest pole	N. Piquet (Brabham) 1985 (133.8mph/215.4kph)
Fastest lap	A. Prost (McLaren) 1985 (124.3mph/200.0kph)

ESTORIL

Location: 4 miles (6.5km) north of Estoril.
Constructed: 1972.
World Championship Grands Prix: 13.

The first start in 1995 was halted
by a multiple crash. In the second
David Coulthard (Williams) exploits
the long straight to lead, Michael
Schumacher (Benetton) is directly
behind and Hill in the other
Williams is squeezed out.
(ICN U.K. Bureau)

Curva do Tanque

Orelha *Saca-Rolhas* *Esses*

VIP *Parabolica Interior* *Parabolica Ayrton Senna*

Curva 1

Start/finish *Recta da Meta*

'Turn 5 is a bit strange because it's tight on the entry and wide at the exit'

Rubens Barrichello

The backdrop is rocky, barren, almost prehistoric. The foreground is much more interesting: a circuit with a long straight, switch back corners, and changes in elevation. High winds can sweep the circuit and sometimes it rains.

The circuit was a brief journey from the coast and Cascais, a town of easy charm – not forgetting Estoril itself and its casino – which made the Grand Prix weekend a pleasure. Portugal was popular, Cascais was popular, and the circuit was popular.

There'd been Oporto in 1958 and 1960, Monsanto in 1959 and then nothing. Estoril was beset by problems after its construction, including the fuel crisis and political upheaval.

A Formula 2 race was held in March 1975 and it attracted an entry of 16, including Jacques Laffite, Jean-Pierre Beltoise, and Patrick Tambay. It rained and Laffite (Martini) won easily. Further Formula 2 races followed in 1976 (René Arnoux in a Martini beat Beltoise) and 1977 (Didier Pironi beat Arnoux, both in

Martinis). Then the circuit deteriorated.

It was refurbished extensively with the incentive of a Grand Prix and as a venue for winter testing. It hosted 13 Grands Prix to 1996 but then lost it on safety grounds. It did continue to host a variety of races and in 2000 was redesigned to secure

Ayrton Senna and Nigel Mansell locked in combat, 1989.

FIM homologation. That year the Portuguese bike Grand Prix came and subsequently a round of the A1GP championship.

COCKPIT VIEW

Rubens Barrichello, who drove in the Grand Prix four times:

'When you get to the end of the start/finish straight you are very exposed to wind and your speed depends on this wind. In testing we were reaching 320kph but other times you reach just 310.

'You then change down from sixth to fifth and head along a short straight to Turn 2, which is a *really* fast corner we take at about 270kph. You don't have much run-off area.

'Exiting Turn 2 you go downhill and reach almost 300kph again before changing down to second for Turn 3. This

is a very tight corner and you have to take care because it is very easy to spin on the exit. Then you go up to third and then back to second for another very tight corner where you think you cannot gain much time, but you then have a long straight so it is an important corner to get the exit right. You need to be very smooth there because there is a very high kerb on the inside. On the outside also the kerb is high but actually you can go over it.

'Then you accelerate through the gears to sixth and you reach something like 290kph. I like this bit, but it is a bit bumpy: it could be a little bit better. Turn 5 is a third-gear corner and it is a bit strange

because it's tight on the entry and wide at the exit. Here you use the tyres most. If you have to stop in the race [for new tyres] one of the reasons is this corner.

'Then you go up to fourth, then fifth before changing down to second and braking for Turn 6. This corner is tight with high kerbs which you mustn't touch. You just follow it through and change up to fourth gear for Turn 7, which is 200kph absolutely blind with no run-off either! It's a bit like Turn 2.

'Then another blind corner, where we go almost flat out to the right and then you turn to the left. You see many people spinning there because you are braking and

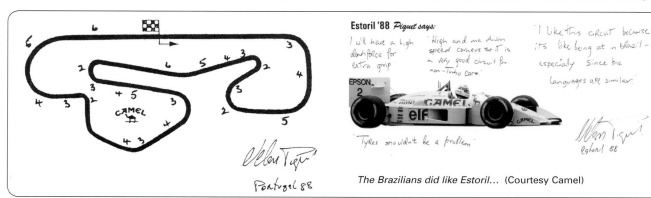

Estoril '88 *Piquet says:*

I will have a high downforce for extra grip

High and me down speed corners so it is a very good circuit for non-Turbo Cars.

I like this circuit because it's like being at in Brazil – especially since the languages are similar

Tyres shouldn't be a problem

Portugal 88

Estoril 88

The Brazilians did like Estoril... (Courtesy Camel)

turning at the same time but it is a nice part of the track because it is quite quick.

'Then you go through the gears. Which one you choose for the first corner depends on your gear ratios. It is a nice corner but you need to keep the car on the inside, so how you take that corner depends on the car. You should be exiting at about 260kph on to the start/finish straight.'

EYEWITNESS

Ann Bradshaw, PR expert:

'I love Estoril because I love Portugal. I've been to Estoril a lot because I go there for WTCC races and A1GP.

'The first time I went was for the Portuguese Rally. They used to do a stage there and finish it in the hills at Sintra. You'd get the service people doing slaloms down the pit straight.

'There were lots of poor dogs running around and I used to feed them and they used to come and pee on the awnings of the motorhome so I'd get told off. In 1985 I worked at a race for Williams for the first time. That was the year Ayrton Senna won, Keke Rosberg broke his thumb, it peed with rain, it dried and it peed with

rain again! The circuit saw some racing: Villeneuve doing an overtaking manoeuvre round the back, and there were some amazing things – *amazing* things – on the straight.

'Socially I remember we'd go to this little shack overlooking the sea and have amazing seafood. We paid a fiver a head and now it's probably about £500 or something…'

MEMORIES AND MILESTONES

1984 The Championship decider between Alain Prost and Niki Lauda in the McLarens. Nelson Piquet (Brabham) took pole, Prost alongside, Lauda 11th. Prost led from lap 9, Lauda working a patient path through the field to finish 13.4 seconds behind him, enough to take the Championship by half a point. Fastest lap: Lauda 117.2mph/188.7kph.
1985 Ayrton Senna's second race for Lotus and from pole, in atrocious conditions, he led every lap to beat Michele Alboreto (Ferrari) by 1 minute 2.9 seconds. Fastest lap: Senna 93.5mph/150.4kph (no comparison).
1986 Nigel Mansell (Williams) rampant.

Senna (Lotus) took pole but Mansell led all 70 laps and beat Prost (McLaren) by 18.7 seconds. Fastest lap: Mansell 120.2mph (+3.0)/193.5kph (+4.8).
1987 Masterclass from the Professor, as Prost was known. Gerhard Berger (Ferrari) took pole, Prost from the second row tracking him and pressuring him so relentlessly that he spun with three laps left. Prost beat him by 20.4 seconds. Fastest lap: Berger 122.7mph (+2.5)/197.5kph (+4.0).
1988 Prost pole from Senna, and their relationship at McLaren under strain. They raced wheel to wheel and along the pit lane straight Senna moved over on Prost – a deeply terrifying moment. Senna had mechanical problems and Prost beat Ivan Capelli (March) by 9.5 seconds. Fastest lap: Berger (Ferrari) 118.7mph (-4.0)/191.1kph (-6.4).
1989 Senna (McLaren) took pole but Mansell (Ferrari) moved into the lead, had a tyre stop which went wrong so that he had to reverse in the pit lane, was shown a black flag he claimed he couldn't see and was disqualified. Berger (Ferrari) beat Prost (McLaren) by 32.6 seconds. Fastest lap: Berger 123.2mph (+4.5)/198.3kph (+7.2).
1990 Mansell took pole from Prost, the two Ferraris forming the front row, but Mansell made the better start and the McLarens of Senna and Berger went through. Mansell took the lead from Senna on lap 50 and beat him by 2.8 seconds, Prost third. With three rounds to go the Championship was moving towards Senna. He had 78 points, Prost 60. Fastest lap: Riccardo Patrese (Williams) 124.3mph (+1.1)/200.0kph (+1.7).
1991 Nightmare for Mansell. Williams team-mate Patrese took pole and they shared the lead – Patrese first, then Mansell but at his pit stop a wheel wasn't properly tightened and it had to be re-attached down the pit lane. He was black-flagged and Patrese beat Senna (McLaren) by 20.9 seconds. Fastest lap: Mansell 124.5mph (+0.2)/200.3kph (+0.3).
1992 Mansell was at the height of his powers and the Williams a superb car. He took pole from team-mate Patrese, led all 71 laps, and beat Berger (McLaren) by 37.5 seconds. It was Mansell's ninth victory of the season, a record. Fastest lap: Senna (McLaren) 127.6mph (+3.1)/205.3kph (+5.0).
1993 Damon Hill (Williams) took pole but Michael Schumacher (Benetton)

The launch that everybody remembers. Senna joins Damon Hill at Williams in 1994 and it was all unveiled at Estoril where he, like Piquet, felt very much at home. (ICN U.K. Bureau)

FACTS OF THE MATTER

2.703m/4.350km circuit

Year	Winner
1984	A. Prost (McLaren)
1985	A. Senna (Lotus)
1986	N. Mansell (Williams)
1987	A. Prost (McLaren)
1988	A. Prost (McLaren)
1989	G. Berger (Ferrari)
1990	N. Mansell (Ferrari)
1991	R. Patrese (Williams)
1992	N. Mansell (Williams)
1993	M. Schumacher (Benetton)
Fastest pole	D. Hill (Williams) 1993 (136.1mph/219.0kph)
Fastest lap	D. Hill 1993 (130.0mph/209.2kph)

New corner at Saca-Rolhas, 2.709m/4.360km circuit

1994	D. Hill (Williams)
1995	D. Coulthard (Williams)
1996	J. Villeneuve (Williams)
Fastest pole	D. Hill (Williams) 1996 (121.4mph/195.4kph)
Fastest lap	D. Coulthard (Williams) 1994 (118.3mph/190.4kph)

held off Hill's team-mate Prost by a combination of weaving and blocking to win by 0.9 of a second. Second gave Prost the Championship and he promptly announced his retirement. Fastest lap: Hill 130.0mph (+2.4)/209.2kph (+3.9).

Speed increase 1984–93: 12.8mph/20.5kph.

In the wake of Senna's death at Imola, safety concerns were everywhere – Estoril truncated Turn 8 by adding a chicane, called Saca-Rolhas.

1994 Berger (Ferrari) took pole from Hill (Williams), but the race had five leaders before Hill beat team-mate David Coulthard by 0.6 of a second. British drivers hadn't finished first and second since Damon's father Graham and Piers Courage at Monaco in 1969. Fastest lap: Coulthard 118.3mph/190.4kph.

1995 Coulthard took pole from Williams team-mate Hill but a crash at the start, when Ukyo Katayama's Tyrrell finished upside down, halted it. Coulthard led the restart but Schumacher (Benetton) ran second, Hill third. It finished in that order, Coulthard winning by 7.2 seconds, and with four rounds left the Championship was moving from Hill (Schumacher 72 points, Hill 55). Fastest lap: Coulthard 117.2mph (-1.1)/188.6kph (-1.8).

1996 Hill took pole from Williams team-mate Jacques Villeneuve and led, but Villeneuve leapfrogged him at the second pit stops and beat him by 19.9 seconds. With one round left, the Championship still favoured Hill, who now had 87 points against Villeneuve's 78. Fastest lap: Villeneuve 117.7mph (+0.5)/189.4kph (+0.8).

The end of the long, long straight proved an ideal overtaking place if you could find the speed. Stefano Modena (Tyrrell) waits to see if Gianni Morbidelli (Minardi) can do it. (Courtesy Braun)

Speed decrease 1994–6: 0.6mph/1.0kph.

The programme that sombre 1994, Senna gone – safely into memory. *(Courtesy Martin Hadwen, National Motor Racing Archive)*

The way it was before the major circuit development. *(Courtesy Martin Hadwen, National Motor Racing Archive)*

MONSANTO PARK

Location: 3 miles (5km) west of city centre.
Constructed: 1953.
World Championship Grands Prix: 1.

Dan Gurney (Ferrari) doesn't get too near the straw bales as he finishes third in front of Maurice Trintignant (Cooper). (LAT)

'The circuit was quite a dangerous one really'

Jack Brabham

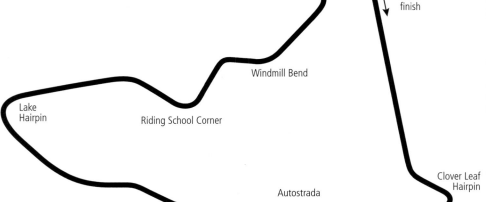

Pits Hairpin

Start/ finish

Windmill Bend

Lake Hairpin

Riding School Corner

Autostrada

Clover Leaf Hairpin

The circuit, first used in 1954, was in a park with its main straight one carriageway of the Estoril-Lisbon road. It ran across tramlines and Graham Hill described it as 'a very nice circuit outside the town – a true road circuit'. Jack Brabham held a different view, and we'll come to that in a moment.

'The Monsanto Forest Park is misleading; it contains numerous attractions and is much more than a park in the traditional sense. One of Monsanto's attractions is the Ecological Park. This special park is centrally located in the largest green patch in Lisbon, with more than 1,000 hectares. In addition, the park contains the Monsanto Park Circuit, a 5.440 kilometre racetrack. This circuit hosted the famous 1959 Formula 1 Portuguese Grand Prix, which helped to put the park on the map in the world of auto racing.

'The Monsanto Forest Park is one of the many protected forests in Portugal. This forest is remarkable for its biodiversity and for the number of species that have been gradually reintroduced into the park over time. This park is one of the most unique and interesting aspects of Lisbon.'[1]

After 1959 Formula 1 didn't go back, but national racing continued until 1971.

COCKPIT VIEW

Jack Brabham, who put his Cooper on the front row:

'The circuit was quite a dangerous one really, lots of trees and straw bales and dogs running across the road. In fact I had a pretty nasty experience there just before my accident [in the race].

'A little boy of probably seven or eight ran across the track in front of me, and I had to stand on the brakes and do a little swerving on a very fast part of the circuit. It gives you an awful jolt, because the last thing you want to run over is a kiddie; if it is a dog or something you might press on, but to see a little kid run across the track just as a straying dog would is quite upsetting.'[2]

EYEWITNESS

Diario de Lisboa, 14 August 1959

'It's been a dozen years since the management of the Automobile Club of Portugal gave the racing circuit at Monsanto a regular place. The people of Lisbon began by according it an intensity and a broader appeal than sometimes happens abroad.

'When therefore across that span of time the effect of motor racing is proved, it stirred the interest of thousands of enthusiasts who went to Monsanto to be present at one of the most emotional sporting occasions.'

MEMORIES AND A MILESTONE

1959 On lap 23, Brabham was chasing Stirling Moss in another Cooper, pole, for the lead when, lapping a backmarker who doesn't seem to have seen him, he was pitched into the straw bales. He would remember vividly rearing over the bales, seeing trees and thinking he couldn't avoid them. In fact the Cooper struck a telegraph pole with enough force to fling the car back on to the track, rolling and rolling. He waited for the impact of whatever it would hit next – which never came – and rolled out of the car instead. He found the Cooper of Masten Gregory bearing down on him. Gregory missed him, just as he'd missed the child. Moss beat Gregory by a lap. Fastest lap: Moss 97.3mph/156.6kph.

FACTS OF THE MATTER

3.380m/5.440km circuit

Year	Winner
1959	S. Moss (Cooper)
Pole	S. Moss (99.0mph/159.4kph)
Fastest lap	S. Moss (97.3mph/156.6kph)

Footnotes
[1] www.lisboa.in/sights/monsanto-forest-park. [2] *When the Flag Drops*, Brabham.

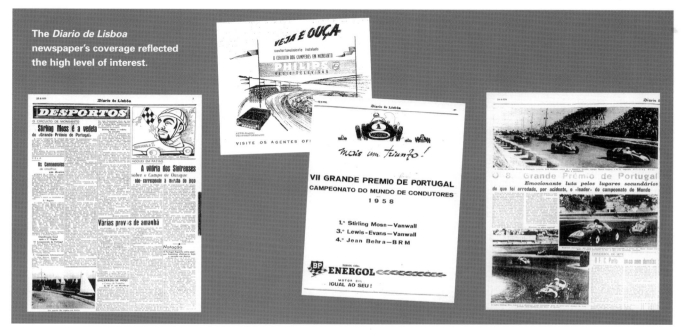

The *Diario de Lisboa* newspaper's coverage reflected the high level of interest.

PORTO

Location: Western outskirts of the city.
Constructed: 1950.
World Championship Grands Prix: 2.

Stirling Moss, the maestro, has everything under control as he wins – ignoring the 'useless' straw bales. (LAT)

Start/finish

Estrada da Circunvalaçao

Rua par da Fonleda

Rua do Lidador

Esplanada do Rio de Janeiro

Avenida Dr Antunes Guimaraes

Avenida da Boavista

'Porto was a street circuit, proper, normal streets. There was no protection'

Stirling Moss

Porto, sometimes known as Oporto – both are fine – is the second biggest city in Portugal and, by definition, intimately associated with the Port industry. 'Porto has for its long history been known as a cosmopolitan trading centre. It still has a blue collar working class feel, but it's a sort of Vasco de Gama working class with a timeless style.'[1] The Portuguese Grand Prix had been run six times as a sports car event since 1951, twice at Monsanto and the rest at Porto. The Porto circuit started beside the harbour on the Atlantic and stretched for 4.6 miles.

Mike Hawthorn, facing it in a Ferrari in 1958, described it as a true road circuit. Leaving the pits you went into a wide square, crossing tramlines, to a left-hander that fed you into a narrow straight. That was the uphill *Avenida da Boavista* and it led to another left-hander, still uphill.

The track turned left again and you were on to tramlines again. A left-right curve flowed between rows of trees and was lined with straw bales at intervals. He'd have preferred the bales to be a solid wall because if you lost the back end of the car it would bounce off the wall but might get between bales and flip the car.

That brought you back to the pits.

'In addition to the tramlines,' Hawthorn concluded, 'there were all the normal hazards of a road circuit, kerbstones, lamp standards, trees, the lot.'[2]

COCKPIT VIEW

Sir Stirling Moss, who drove in both Grands Prix there:

'I was down there quite recently but racing on a fantastic new circuit, not the old one. I've got a 1500 OSCA, a 1956 car,[3] and the circuit is certainly good enough for Formula 1 now.

'Porto was a street circuit, proper, normal streets. There was no protection but in those days they were all like that. You'd have a few people standing around on the pavement and the only protection was straw bales lining parts of it. I never felt anything going past people at racing speed, because it's what one did. Now you can't understand it because we've gone all cissy and you can't get near.

'What good were the straw bales? Nothing! They just stopped you going there but the point is you're not going to go into the straw bales, are you, if you're in control?

'It was a left-hand circuit, which was quite interesting, and had a long dual carriageway. We also went across tramlines, but again that's the way it was.

'The circuit was actually quite quick and there were places where you could get up speed. It wasn't like Monte Carlo, demanding absolute precision: the roads were much, much wider and you could overtake. The context is that so many circuits were like that: Naples, Reims, Spa. That was what was so good about racing then. We didn't have manufactured circuits and the cars were much easier because we had suspensions, so they soaked up cobblestones and tramlines.'

EYEWITNESSES

Gregor Grant, *Autosport*:

'Webbair organised quite a considerable air-lift to transport the British party to Oporto, using two aircraft. Drivers Fairman, McLaren, Gurney, Graham [were in one, while the other] comprised Moss, Ireland, Clark, Surtees, Hill, Brooks, Henry Taylor, Bonnier and Gregory.

'Also present were entrants John Cooper, Colin Chapman, Rob Walker and William Samengo-Turner, and a large party of press, trade and others connected closely with the motor racing game. 'Jack Brabham flew down in his Cessna, accompanied by Betty Brabham and RAC representative Dean Delamont.

'Training for the Formula 1 drivers began at 6 pm on Friday, 12th August, and all 16 reported with the exception of Jø Bonnier who had Asian 'flu.'

Diaro de Lisboa, 24 August 1959:

'The Grand Prix was a big fight in the campaign for somebody to take over from Fangio [who'd retired in France in July]. That was the atmosphere at the Grand Prix.

'The seventh Grand Prix of Portugal did not give the answer to a lot of the correspondents.

'Stirling Moss was the big driver in the Grand Prix. The Englishman's regularity spoke for itself and because of him, at the end of the day the race was very emotional and a thing of great motivation.

'He accepted the responsibility of leading straight away in the opening lap although there were another 49 laps to go. Although Hawthorn overtook him, Moss was more efficient and retook the lead on lap 8.

'This type of Grand Prix was good for Moss because he was driving at 150 kilometres an hour in cold weather and always making progress in terms of speed lap after lap after lap. He achieved 170 kilometres an hour. He gave the other drivers no chance to pass him.'

MEMORIES AND MILESTONES

1958 The race from another age (and anticlockwise too). Stirling Moss (Vanwall), pole, and Hawthorn were locked into a struggle for the World Championship. Moss won the race by 5 minutes 12.8 seconds – Hawthorn had a brake failure on the final lap. He pushed the Ferrari, trying to restart it, and angrily brushed away a spectator trying to help because that would have meant disqualification. He was also going in the opposite direction to the circuit, which also meant disqualification. Moss, on his slowing-down lap, saw that Hawthorn was in the escape road, technically not part of the circuit. He told officials this, Hawthorn became second and Moss went on to lose the Championship by a single point. Fastest lap: Hawthorn 108.7mph/175.0kph.

1960 The incident from another age. On the first lap Jack Brabham in a Cooper was behind Moss (Lotus). He tried to overtake, found himself *in* the tramlines and had a momentary vision of having to follow them to the depot. He didn't. He beat Bruce McLaren (Cooper) by 57.9 seconds and went on to retain the World Championship. Fastest lap: John Surtees (Lotus) 112.3mph/180.7kph.

Speed increase 1958–60: 3.6mph/5.7kph.

Footnotes
[1] goeurope.about.com/cs/oportoportugal/a/porto_guide.htm.
[2] *Champion Year*, Hawthorn. [3] OSCA racing cars (*Officine Specializzate Costruzioni Automobili*) were constructed in Bologna for 20 years from 1947.

FACTS OF THE MATTER

4.602m/7.407km circuit

Year	Winner
1958	S. Moss (Vanwall)
1960	J. Brabham (Cooper)
Fastest pole	J. Surtees (Lotus) 1960 (113.8mph/183.2kph)
Fastest lap	J. Surtees 1960 (112.3mph/180.7kph)

SINGAPORE

Location: Central Singapore.
Constructed: 2008.
World Championship Grands Prix: 2.

The night people, Singapore, September 2009.
(Vodafone/LAT)

Start/finish

23 22
21
20   18
19
17
5   16   15
1   13
2   4   6   14   11   12
3   8   10
7   9

**'You can feel quite
enclosed particularly
with the bright
floodlights shining down'**

Rubens Barrichello

A night race, or even the idea of a night race, was as outrageous as cricketers wearing coloured pyjamas and playing 20-over matches, tennis players looking as if they wore coats-of-many-colours and couldn't find a hairdresser, the Olympic Games going commercial, a venerated soccer ground (St James's Park) being renamed after a website, or Rugby League agreeing to move their whole season to the summer for reasons of television revenue.

The outrage (if there really was any) didn't survive the reality.

For obvious reasons a night race needed to be on a street circuit and Singapore offered that, allied to prosperity, the work ethic, and a way of making things happen. Formula 1 loved Singapore and Singaporeans loved Formula 1. An Italian specialist was hired to do the lighting, which had by definition to be bright enough for the drivers to see where they were going, even at 185mph, yet not produce glare for the television audience. He had, too, the job of making sure there were no shadows, and to do it he wasn't allowed to tear the roads up.

The race actually had history, beginning in 1961 as the Orient Year Grand Prix and becoming the Malaysian Grand Prix a year later. It was run on what was called the Thomson Road circuit and eventually became the Singapore Grand Prix after independence in 1965. It was a Formule Libre event and lasted until 1973. There'd been fatalities and evidently the locals objected to the roads being closed for the race.

Singapore wanted a modern Grand Prix and signed a five-year deal with Bernie Ecclestone – the Government provided most of the funds (90 million Singapore Dollars out of 150 million).

All 110,000 tickets were sold and corporate hospitality flourished.

Felipe Massa (Ferrari) caught the drivers' mood in 2008 when they'd had a good look at it for the first time. 'It will be a very tough race. We'll need to concentrate about ten times harder than we do in Monaco. It has nothing to do with the visibility, which is fine, but there are a lot more corners.'

Because the race was at night (starting at 8:00pm local time) the drivers decided to remain on body time, going to bed at breakfast and rising during the afternoon. In 2009 Jenson Button said: 'As last year, we will stay on European timing for the race weekend, which means staying awake throughout the night and sleeping most of the day to ensure that we are alert and the body is ready to react in the right way for the evening timetable.'

COCKPIT VIEW

Rubens Barrichello, Brawn, 2009:
'It's always good to have new challenges, and racing under the lights for the first time certainly provided that. I really enjoyed the circuit as it felt like a proper street circuit should with public roads, bumps, barriers and passing some of the famous city landmarks.

'It's very narrow in places and you can feel quite enclosed, particularly with the bright floodlights shining down. It's a very slow track so you need a high downforce aerodynamic configuration on the car, and with so many corners you have to maintain your concentration at all times.'[1]

EYEWITNESS

Steven Tee, LAT Photographic:
'I think Singapore at night is a brilliant addition to Formula 1. Photographically it opens up loads of interesting possibilities – and complications, obviously. It's a good circuit actually right in the middle of a city – which is exactly where it should be if you are going to have a city race – so you have the city as a backdrop.

'I had taken pictures at night before, at Le Mans in the old days, and I am glad that the digital age has come because the night race would have been a nightmare shooting film and trying to get the images that we can now get on digital. The cameras are so much more sophisticated.

'It's a great location and I wish we had a few more of those.'

MEMORIES AND MILESTONES

2008 The 800th championship race. Massa took pole. 'At every corner and every braking point I tried to get the most out of the car and I think I managed it. I'm pleased to be the first driver to be on pole for this Grand Prix, taking place in such a special and unusual atmosphere.' In the race Nelson Piquet Jnr crashed after 13 laps, benefiting his Renault team-mate Fernando Alonso who'd qualified 15th, just pitted, and now under the Safety Car rose to fifth as others pitted. When Massa had a refuelling problem the race

The spectacular setting from above.
(Courtesy David Corbishley)

ABOVE: The setting from just above ground level.
(Courtesy David Yeang)

RIGHT: Never try to hustle the East, as the saying goes. One unhustled Singaporean going about his business.
(Courtesy David Yeang)

BELOW: The setting from exactly eye level.
(Courtesy Sebastien Carter)

opened to Alonso. Some people were suspicious about aspects of this victory and made dark hints, but who knew? Alonso beat Nico Rosberg (Williams) by 2.9 seconds. Fastest lap: Kimi Räikkönen (Ferrari) 107.3mph/172.7kph.

2009 Long before the race everybody knew what had happened in 2008: Piquet had deliberately crashed to bring the Safety Car out and this implicated Flavio Briatore, running the team, who was given a life ban, and Pat Symonds, the tactician, who was banned for five years. Lewis Hamilton (McLaren) went some way to mitigating this awful episode by taking pole and leading every lap but four (pit stop) to beat Timo Glock (Toyota) by 9.6 seconds. Fastest lap: Alonso (Renault) 104.8mph/168.7kph.

Speed decrease 2008–9: 2.5mph/4.0kph.

Footnote
1 Courtesy Brawn GP.

FACTS OF THE MATTER

3.148m/5.067km circuit 2008; 3.152m/5.073km 2009

Year	Winner
2008	F. Alonso (Renault)
2009	L. Hamilton (McLaren)
Fastest pole	F. Massa (Ferrari) 2008 (108.2mph/174.1kph)
Fastest lap	K. Räikkönen (Ferrari) 2008 (107.3mph/172.7kph)

ABOVE: The pits complex looked surprisingly like – well, the pits complex at any circuit. (Courtesy Dan Diaz)

ABOVE RIGHT: The aftermath of Nelson Piquet's crash, one of the most extraordinary and damaging events in Formula 1 history. The man who took the photograph, David Yeang, says: 'I can still remember the commotion and the millions of flashbulbs that night.' (Courtesy David Yeang)

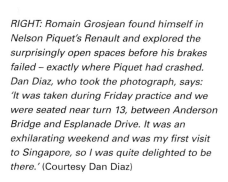

RIGHT: Romain Grosjean found himself in Nelson Piquet's Renault and explored the surprisingly open spaces before his brakes failed – exactly where Piquet had crashed. Dan Diaz, who took the photograph, says: 'It was taken during Friday practice and we were seated near turn 13, between Anderson Bridge and Esplanade Drive. It was an exhilarating weekend and was my first visit to Singapore, so I was quite delighted to be there.' (Courtesy Dan Diaz)

EAST LONDON

Location: Cape Province, on the outskirts of East London.
Constructed: 1959.
World Championship Grands Prix: 3.

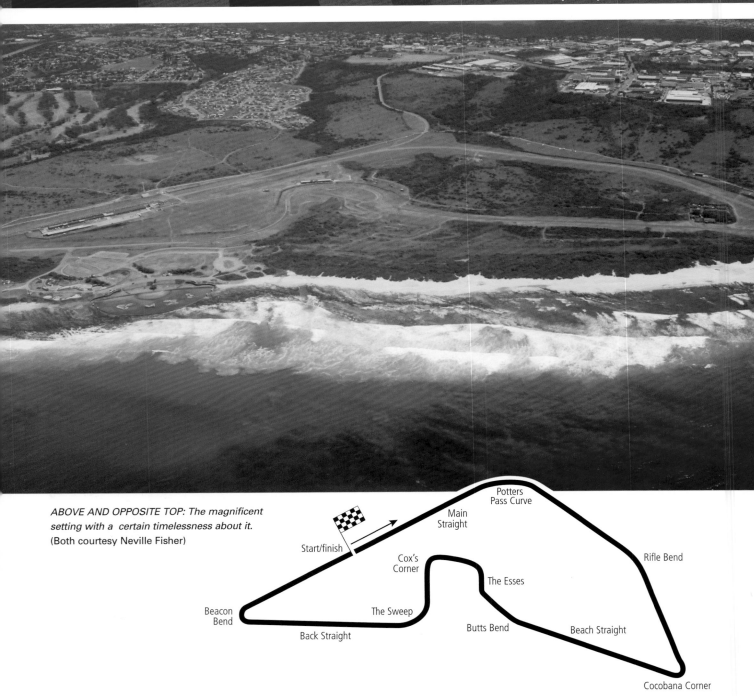

ABOVE AND OPPOSITE TOP: The magnificent setting with a certain timelessness about it. (Both courtesy Neville Fisher)

Potters Pass Curve

Main Straight

Rifle Bend

Cox's Corner

The Esses

Start/finish

Beacon Bend

The Sweep

Butts Bend

Beach Straight

Back Straight

Cocobana Corner

'The circuit was quite quick, a performance circuit'

John Surtees

As someone pointed out, motor racing flourished in South Africa because it was the one country on the continent that could afford it. The South African 'Grand Prix' began on the outskirts of the town of East London in 1934 at a circuit known as the Prince George. In 1934 it measured 15 miles but was shortened to 11 for 1936.

I'm indebted to journalist Roger McCleery for this circuit background: 'Grand Prix Racing first put East London on the world map thanks to the vision of Brad Bishop, the motoring editor of the *East London Daily Despatch* in 1932, who said East London should run a Grand Prix as East Londoners love their city and are ready to make strenuous efforts to increase its greatness without personal reward.

'They got the East London City Council to spend £30,000 to make a suitable set of roads available for Grand Prix racing. Bishop marked out a 15-mile circuit that was eventually shortened to 11 miles using the same main straight and *Potters Pass* corner of the current track, except this is now run in the opposite direction.

'Average speed in 1935 by a V16 Supercharged Auto Union was well over 160kph [100mph]. The field also included Maseratis and ERAs with the cars reaching speeds up to 310kph [192mph].

'The first South African Grand Prix was a 1934 Border 100 [100-mile] Handicap won by the American Whitney Straight. Race two was held in 1936 and won by "Dr Mario" Mazzacuratti in a Bugatti. Pat Fairland took race three in 1937 in an ERA, with the fourth event won by a local garage owner, Buller Meyer, in a Riley. With the Second World War imminent, Luigi Villoresi (Maserati) took the fifth Grand Prix from Cortese and "Dr Mario". All three drove Maseratis.'

The race fell victim to the Second World War, as did other South African circuits – in Johannesburg, Pietermaritzburg, and Cape Town.

East London was subsequently the leader in creating a new generation of circuits, this one in a park in a natural hollow by the sea (and a rifle range part of it). It retained sections of the old circuit. The 'Grand Prix' returned, but to Formule Libre regulations. Two years later they got the real thing, a race that was, as it happened, the Championship decider between Graham Hill (BRM) and Jim Clark (Lotus).

Hill would remember how strong the wind was in the quicker corners, so strong the cars would twitch. The wind could move the cars sideways and that made the two quick corners following the pits particularly tricky. It also played havoc with the gear ratios, because if it was behind you on the straight you'd tend to over-rev the engine, and if it was coming at you it would leave you short of revs. He used a single word – 'confusing'[1] – but thought the circuit 'nice', even if narrower than he'd have liked.

Hill said 'after I have gone through *Potters Pass* and *Rifle Bend* corners flat out and then got heavily on to the brakes for the steep downhill approach to the *Cocobana Corner* with the Indian Ocean just 100m in front of you, you know you are in a very special place.'

Potters Pass, the curve nestling at the far end of the straight after the start/finish line, and then *Rifle Bend* were taken at speed, and the *Cocobana Corner* made a vivid impression on spectators.

Even before the 1962 race a shadow began to creep across the circuit's

future: the South African Motor Racing Club bought land near Pretoria – Kyalami. A new, ambitious track was planned there.

'Unique in South Africa are cars and motorcycles racing on the same

Jim Clark (Lotus) leads the start of the 1963 race. (LAT)

programme,' McCleery says. 'It happens to this day. At Grands Prix there were riders like Jim Redman on a Works Honda 4, Gary Hocking on a Works MV, Paddy Driver, Phil Read plus Aussies and New Zealanders and the like on a mixture of AJSs, Nortons and Matchlesses, who put on an unforgettable show.

'The circuit still hosts National and Regional, plus International Historic events. The main purpose of the passionate people who still run the East London Grand Prix circuit in 2010 is to get a long-term lease of the property.

Once this is done they can close off the few public roads that are used and build a classic racing circuit with all its facilities. Unfortunately, dealing with the local council, which has had three different mayors in three months and 21 members suspended for various reasons, it will be an uphill task.

'East London has had a history of top motor racing for 80 years and this will continue.'

This was to be proved in February 2010 when the circuit would hold the final round of the SAFMARINE Historic SA Motorcycle TT Day of Champions,

featuring legendary riders like Mick Grant and Phil Read as well as 'The Stars of Africa' former local national champions riding some of their original machines.

Legendary bikes were being shipped from the UK by SAFMARINE too, including Carl Fogarty's Ducatis, an MV Augusta, Hondas, and a Suzuki RG500.

There'd be a round of the highly competitive National Formula Vee championship series and an array of historic racing cars.

East London, of such distant memory to Grand Prix racing, didn't die.

COCKPIT VIEW

John Surtees, who drove in all three races there:

'We used to stay at an hotel which was right on the front and I think it was owned by the Vice Brothers. Yes, a promising name! That clicks in my mind.

'The circuit was quite quick, a performance circuit. Obviously, with the two longish straights coupled with two corners, you have to think that both of those corners are followed by a quick section, so if you didn't have good grunt from the engine – good torque – you had a problem. This is one of the areas where the Ferrari was a little bit at a loss. It didn't have the middle range.

'It had a main straight then a quick corner – *Potters Pass*. You had two pretty tight corners which was a bit of a bugbear because the punch – the torque – wasn't very good. We are talking about the one

You can trace the evolution of the circuit but in all its guises it has been dramatic. (Courtesy Neville Fisher)

and a half litre engines. *Rifle Bend* didn't count: it was just a curve.

'One of the things was that at least we had whatever power was available from the car. If you did Kyalami you immediately lost horsepower because of the altitude. At East London, sea level, the engines performed as well as they could perform and as always with circuits which are close to the sea there was the question of the direction of the wind and the effect that had on the speed. We weren't too involved with aerodynamics in those days.

'I think the main thing about East London was that the setting was rather nice, a good hotel up the road, and the circuit was not protected in any way so the wind did play a part.

'In the Ferrari you'd have been taking *Cocobana* and *Beacon Bend* in second gear. Rarely did you use first gear. Then you've got the main straight and depending on the kind of power characteristics I'd have thought the Climax engines might even have stayed in top gear. Certainly with the narrower

power band of the V6 Ferrari it would probably have meant having to drop it down a gear.

'*Potters Pass* flat? In its own way it was rather like the old *Curva Grande* at Monza where you always intended to take it flat the next lap [see 'Eyewitness']. Some drivers tried to fool people because they'd be going along flat on the accelerator but with the other foot on the brake. At any one time there was only ever a maximum of half a dozen drivers in Formula 1 who would get the utmost out of a car...

'Remember, cars as such ran a lot lighter on the road because they didn't have aerodynamics. That sort of corner just wouldn't count today but when you didn't have aerodynamics it was a different thing.

'The circuits were not tailored to cars and you had the old circuits which were straightforward roads. In Portugal you had tramlines, in Belgium you had farmhouses. Circuits were much more natural and I think the word natural is an important one. They were not purpose-made or adapted.'

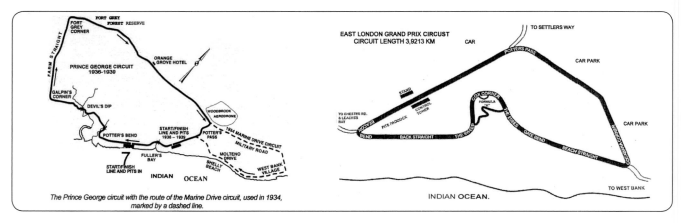

The Prince George circuit with the route of the Marine Drive circuit, used in 1934, marked by a dashed line.

EYEWITNESS

Roger McCleery, journalist:

'Grand Prix days in the 1960s were magic: good weather and races run in front of huge crowds from all over South Africa. Some of the top drivers in the world arrived to enjoy the sunshine and their holidays – Stirling Moss, Jo Bonnier, Jim Clark, Trevor Taylor, Jack Brabham, Graham Hill, John Surtees to name just a few. It was a Who's Who of the racing world, just as you'd had before the war with the Rosemeyers and so on.[2]

'They loved the GP circuit, which has everything – fast straights and corners, hairpins and tricky sweeps. It's also a track that goes up and down hill. It's still rated as one of the best circuits in the world.

'Cars used to be housed in garages all over the city so you could get a close look at them. They were driven out to the track on Grand Prix morning in a convoy.

'It's a wonderful place on the sea. You can actually see whales and dolphins at times and you couldn't get a better place. It's like an arena coming down from a hill and the original *Potters Pass* curve – named after an engineering guy from before the war – it still there. It's a most awesome corner, a corner that you say "OK, I'll go through it flat out *next time*," you go round and say "OK, I'll go through it flat out *next time*," again, you go round…

'If you do go through it flat out just once, however, you can do it again.

'My son used to race touring cars and he'd say that by the time he got to *Cocobana Corner*, which is about a kilometre away, "My chest was sore." I asked why and he said "From holding my breath!"'

'That was wonderful and at just a wonderful place.

'The circuit is an open road and the only thing you have is the control and the pits, which get broken into and things get stolen. They need to fence it off and make it into a true motor racing circuit. If they got the World Superbikes it would be like Phillip Island in Australia.

'Incidentally, I first went to the city of East London in, I suppose, 1959, and it's the same today. It hasn't changed. The world had passed it by. Both South African circuits – East London and Kyalami – were fantastic. Except for some advertising boards East London is the same circuit as it was then. The formula juniors came last year [2008] – from San Francisco, Australia, from all over the world – and they said "Don't change a blade of grass, it's just perfect." It was our era of circuits, our era of motor cars, and they just loved it.

'I reckon (under the pace of progress) those juniors – of course, there are new tyres and so on – would have won the Grand Prix in 1961!

'The circuit celebrated 50 years in 2009. It is one of the only few racing circuits in the world that has remained unchanged since it was originally opened in 1959 next to the sea.'

MEMORIES AND MILESTONES

1962 Amazingly, the US Grand Prix was on 7 October but East London not until 29 December, a wait that Jim Clark (Lotus) found unnerving. Graham Hill (BRM), without comment or irony, wrote that 'one particular section was wired off for coloured people'. Clark took pole but an oil leak stopped him on lap 62 of the 82 and Hill had the Championship. He beat

Bruce McLaren (Cooper) by 49.8 seconds. Fastest lap: Clark 96.4mph/155.1kph.

1963 The Championship had gone to Clark at Monza, four races before, but East London attracted a big entry – 20. Clark (of course) had pole, Clark led every lap (of course), and Clark won (of course), beating Dan Gurney in a Brabham by 1 minute 6.8 seconds, which was a lot then and is a lot now. Fastest lap: Gurney 98.4mph (+2.0)/158.4kph (+3.3).

1965 In complete contrast to 1962 this race began the season on 1 January, although there's a delicious tale explaining that. The organisers moved the race forward by one week, so that at that instant it ceased to be the final race of 1964 and became the first of 1965. Clark was at the height of his powers, took pole (of course), led every lap (of course), and beat John Surtees (Ferrari) by 29.0 seconds. Fastest lap: Clark 100.1mph (+1.7)/161.1kph (+2.7).

And then the race went to Kyalami, never to return.

Speed increase 1962–5: 3.7mph/6.0kph.

Footnotes

[1] *Life at the Limit*, Hill. [2] Bernd Rosemeyer, regarded as one of the great drivers of all time, is synonymous with Auto Union. He raced at the Prince George circuit at East London in 1937 and (according to Chris Nixon in *Racing the Silver Arrows*) also raced that year at Grosvenor, Cape Town. This was a handicap scratch, as East London had been, and Rosemeyer (scratch) had to give an MG Midget nine laps' start of the 4.6-mile circuit.

The South African Grand Prix had a rich history before it hosted a round of the World Championship. *(Courtesy Neville Fisher)*

Jim Clark (Lotus) passes local hero Bill Jennings (Porsche) as he wins the 1961 Grand Prix – the last before it became a round of the Championship. *(Courtesy Norman Hickel)*

SOUTH AFRICA

KYALAMI

Location: 15 miles (24km) north of Johannesburg.
Constructed: 1961.
World Championship Grands Prix: 20.

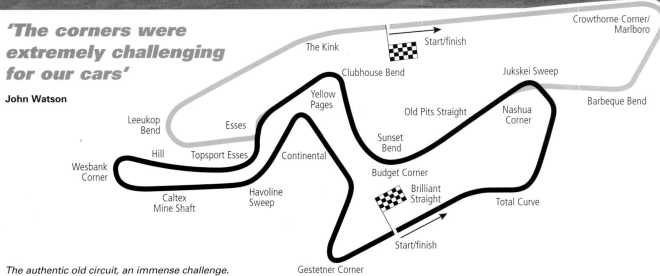

'The corners were extremely challenging for our cars'

John Watson

The authentic old circuit, an immense challenge.
This is 1982, with the Renaults of René Arnoux and
Alain Prost leading from the grid. (LAT)

Crowthorne Corner/
Marlboro

The Kink
Start/finish

Clubhouse Bend
Jukskei Sweep

Yellow
Pages
Old Pits Straight
Nashua
Corner
Barbeque Bend

Leeukop
Bend
Esses
Sunset
Bend

Hill
Topsport Esses
Continental
Budget Corner

Wesbank
Corner
Brilliant
Straight
Total Curve

Caltex
Mine Shaft
Havoline
Sweep
Start/finish

Gestetner Corner

South Africa was never an easy country to get into focus. There were too many contradictions, too many complications, too many – forgive me – shades. The countryside around Johannesburg looked like Africa and Johannesburg looked like America. Apartheid was more insidious than the Berlin Wall because it dispossessed on racial lines – the Wall simply dispossessed everybody it imprisoned and didn't discriminate.

Among the contradictions was this: apartheid stirred revulsion throughout the civilised world and a South African Rugby tour to Britain became a battleground, with passionate protesters storming stadiums. An international global boycott was instituted in 1971.

There were seven rebel cricket tours to South Africa between 1982 and 1990, each proving controversial and divisive. South Africa was excluded from the Olympics in 1968 and also from the international soccer governing body FIFA.

During this time – 1967 to 1985 – Grand Prix racing went to Kyalami every year except 1981, without condemnation, rioting, or anything approaching international vilification. It was an extraordinary contradiction and very difficult to explain. There were misgivings towards the end, however, as we shall see.

Perhaps the explanation was that the world at large did not regard Grand Prix racing as sport but a curious fusion of commerce, technology, and the global automotive industry with *everything* sponsored, so it was left alone and went, quite normally, to Kyalami out on the Veldt in the middle of nowhere.

Certainly having a Grand Prix in Africa added to the plausibility of calling it a *World* Championship. The first year they hosted one (1967) there would also be races in Canada, the United States, and Mexico, as well as the European standards.

The story of Kyalami is interesting in itself and I'm indebted to journalist Roger McCleery for telling it.

'In 1960 the Mayor of Johannesburg, Dave Marais, and the Chairman of the Sports Car Club, Francis Tucker, seeing the success of the East London

Grand Prix circuit, felt it was time that Johannesburg had an international motor racing track. It should be built in a valley to increase spectator viewing and friendliness.

'A 330-acre piece of land was found between Pretoria and Jo'burg on the Kyalami Country Estate. It was also situated halfway between the crowded East and West Rand close to the Pretoria to Johannesburg motorway. £6,500 (at today's exchange rate with the Rand) was paid for this property. Samrac, the South African Motor Racing Club, was formed to organise races and to encourage corporates like Caltex, the *Rand Daily Mail* newspaper, United Tobacco, and the Road Engineering Company, Basil Read, to come on board.

'The first race meeting was held on 4 November 1961, with the first Grand Prix (the Rand Grand Prix) won by Jim Clark in his Lotus Climax. The first World Championship Grand Prix was held in 1976 and continued uninterrupted until 1980, when due to financial troubles the circuit was bought by Max Mosley, on behalf of Bernie Ecclestone.

'The next Formula 1 World Championship event was held in 1982, until political pressure – with the French refusing to send their cars to the event – encouraged FISA to take South Africa off the Grand Prix calendar.

'In 1987 a new company, MRE (Motor Racing Enterprises), took over running the track, which they

remodelled into a 3.89km facility running in the opposite direction. They also sold half the property to Anglo-American Properties, who'd had their eye on the ground for years.

'In 1988 the gates opened again on July 1 and International Motor Racing returned with C1 and C2 sports car racing. The Porsche Turbo Cup series took place there in 1989 with DTM Saloon Cars following in 1991. Brabham, Benetton, Williams, and Tyrrell came to test in these years, which drew Grand Prix-sized crowds, as South Africans are motor sport mad.

'Before the return of World Championship Grand Prix racing again in 1992 (Nelson Mandela had now been released) a 20 million Rand development programme was put in place. Here a further 400 metres was added to its length (now 4.2km), more opportunities for passing were introduced, and a new pit complex was built. Grand Prix racing lasted two years before, in 1993, the event was pulled due to fraud charges against the track owners at the time.

'The circuit was bought by the AA of South Africa and eventually sold to Greek property developers who, surprisingly to many, kept the racing

Rural and rudimentary – notice the fire extinguisher all by itself – as Graham Hill moves to second place in the Lotus behind (of course) Jim Clark. (LAT)

going for international events. These include the Moto-GP, World Superbikes, A1 Grand Prix, and Superbike test matches between the Australians and the UK. Successful national and regional racing series are held throughout the year.

'Competitors from all over the world love the testing twists and turns of the new Kyalami and the massive hill up to the *WesBank* shelf, before vehicles dive down the *Mine Shaft*, where Grand Prix cars hit 310kph. The circuit flows, now that an irritating kink behind the pits – built to slow competitors down after Ivan Capelli crashed his Formula 1 car – has been changed to a full-bore right-hander.

'Kyalami is still the home of motor sport in South Africa and is one the country's eight operational circuits.'

COCKPIT VIEW
John Watson, who drove in eight Grands Prix there:
'A great racetrack for that generation of cars from the 1970s to the early 1980s. It was dominated by two things, altitude – five and a half thousand feet above sea level – and that very long straight from *Leeukop Bend* to *Crowthorne* corner. That was about a mile and downhill.

'The layout was super, one of those places you really enjoyed driving. The corners were extremely challenging for our cars because of the (low!) level of downforce, so you were going out of *Crowthorne* down the hill through *Jukskei Sweep* – downhill right then a left – in real tippy-toes corners.

'If you look at photographs or films of those cars, look at the slip angle they were achieving. If you overlap that with a modern Formula 1 car the difference is night and day. It meant our cars were slipping and sliding through those corners and the big thing on that circuit was not to wear your tyres out, particularly the front left because that was the one that suffered the most.

'There was a great atmosphere. Because of the politics of South Africa, the era when apartheid was gradually coming to an end, South Africa was welcoming as much entertainment as they could get. Whilst I wasn't taking it on board particularly, and I never saw any ill treatment of the black population at the racetrack, clearly there was a dichotomy going on within the country and the international community at large.

'It was only when a group called Samrac started getting very agitated about anybody in show business visiting South Africa that it became a bit of an issue. I remember doing an interview on radio on the BBC's *Today* programme trying to justify why I was racing there.

'It was attractive to go because it was coming towards the end of their summer and normally the weather was lovely. The white population, which had the affluence, were extremely friendly and welcoming in every sense.'

EYEWITNESS
Roger McCleery, journalist:
'Kyalami in Zulu means "My home". It certainly has been the home of South African international and local motor sport for 48 years.

'Like Spa, Monza, the Nürburgring, and Silverstone, it was recognised as one of the greatest and fastest Grand Prix circuits in the world. It was probably better known than Johannesburg, or indeed South Africa, at the time, along with [golfer] Gary Player and [heart transplant surgeon] Chris Barnard.

'Its 4.1km length had the longest straight in GP racing and its corners all provided challenges to the host of international drivers who took part in the South African Grand Prix, the 9-Hour, DTM Porsche Turbo Cup Races, and GP motorcycle races.

'The track was close to spectators. Nowhere else in the world could you enjoy a full field of 30 Formula 1 Grand Prix cars or World Championship sports cars coming at you at full speed and going left as you sat on the outside of *Jukskei* in safety, with less than ten metres [30 feet] between you and the action, or see cars and Grand Prix motorcycles fly up the hill to *Leeukop* at the top of the circuit, where they exited at 160kph [100mph] within touching distance. You could look down into cockpits and see the rev counters! Plus you could virtually see the vehicles in action all the way around the track.

'Fastest speed recorded was 327kph [203mph] by Nelson Piquet in the Williams Honda, when he and Nigel Mansell came to test. Ignazio Giunti did 287kph [178mph] at night in a V12 Ferrari in the 9-Hour Sports Car Race. As a commentator close to the track, nothing could match the spectacle and pent-up energy, speed, power, and excitement of every known Porsche 956 racing at Kyalami, the factory Ferraris, GT40 Fords, Gulf Mirages, T70 Lolas, Alfas, and Chevrons at war with each other. It virtually left you speechless. Or the world's greatest motorcyclist – Mike Hailwood – giving a solo demonstration on his Honda 6 to a wildly cheering crowd, or seeing him pass Jackie Stewart on the outside at *Barbeque* in a Formula 1 Grand Prix Surtees to the cheers of the many motorcyclists who had come to see him.

'Another highlight, or lowlight, was John Love suffering fuel pump problems in sight of the chequered flag on his way to winning the first South African Grand Prix in 1967 at Kyalami, before handing the win to Pedro Rodríguez. Ironically Love had lent the Mexican a fuel pump for his Cooper Maserati just before the race. Love finished second, ahead of Surtees in his Honda.

'Jody Scheckter winning the South African Grand Prix in 1975 was one of the most extraordinary days, as it was also the last time that victory laps were held, as the crowd mobbed on to the circuit to cheer him and he couldn't complete the lap.'

MEMORIES AND MILESTONES
1967 A Brabham front row, Brabham himself on pole from Denny Hulme – who led for the first 60 laps but pitted for brake fluid. Rhodesian John Love (Cooper) inherited the lead and kept it for 13 laps before pitting for fuel. Pedro Rodríguez (Cooper) went by and beat Love by 26.4 seconds. Fastest lap: Hulme 101.9mph/163.9kph.

The track had been widened and resurfaced and conditions for the spectators were improved.

1968 Jim Clark (Lotus) took pole from team-mate Graham Hill, and although Jackie Stewart (Matra) led the opening lap Clark went by, led all the other 79, and beat Hill by 25.3 seconds. Fastest lap: Clark 109.7mph/176.5kph.

1969 Brabham (Brabham) took pole but Stewart (Matra) had the lead by *Barbeque*

Bend and never lost it, beating Hill (Lotus) by 18.8 seconds. Fastest lap: Stewart 112.5mph (+2.8)/181.1kph (+4.6).

1970 Stewart (March) pole but a second covered the first ten cars. Stewart and Brabham (Brabham) disputed the lead into Crowthorne but Stewart had it and held it until lap 19 when Brabham went by, to be followed by Hulme in the McLaren. Brabham beat him by 8.1 seconds. Fastest lap: John Surtees (McLaren) and Brabham 113.6mph (+1.1)/182.8kph (+1.7).

1971 Stewart (Tyrrell) took pole but Clay Regazzoni (Ferrari) went into the lead while a shoal of cars jostled behind, taking and retaking each other. On lap 17 Hulme (McLaren) went by and pulled away. Mario Andretti (Ferrari) caught him by hurling the Ferrari at the circuit and when Hulme had a mechanical problem Andretti beat Stewart by 20.9 seconds. Fastest lap: Andretti 114.3mph (+0.7)/184.0kph (+1.2).

1972 Stewart (Tyrrell) took pole but Hulme (McLaren) led into *Crowthorne* from the second row. Stewart took him on the second lap. He went to lap 45 when the gearbox failed, and Emerson Fittipaldi (Lotus) led to lap 56, then Hulme went past him to win by 14.1 seconds. Fastest lap: Mike Hailwood (Surtees) 116.4mph (+2.1) /187.3kph (+3.3).

1973 Hulme (McLaren) took pole but Stewart (Tyrrell) dominated the race, beating Peter Revson in the other McLaren by 24.5 seconds. The race is remembered for Regazzoni's crash in the BRM, which exploded in fire, and Hailwood (Surtees) running into the flames to try and pull him out. Fastest lap: Fittipaldi (Lotus) 119.1mph (+2.7)/191.6kph (+4.3).

1974 In testing the week before, Revson crashed fatally at *Barbeque Bend* when his Shadow went through the guardrail. Niki Lauda (Ferrari) took pole and led to lap 8, when Carlos Reutemann (Brabham) passed him on the inside at *Crowthorne* and beat Jean-Pierre Beltoise (BRM) by 33.9 seconds. Fastest lap: Reutemann 117.5mph (-1.6)/189.0kph (-2.6).

1975 Carlos Pace (Brabham) took pole and the lead until Jody Scheckter (Tyrrell) outbraked him at *Crowthorne* and led the remaining 76 laps to beat Reutemann (Brabham) by 3.7 seconds. Fastest lap: Pace 118.9mph (+1.4)/191.4kph (+2.4).

1976 James Hunt (McLaren) took pole with 1m 16.10s, Lauda (Ferrari) alongside on 1m 16.20s. This set the tone and

A lap of the new circuit, 1990.
(Courtesy Andrew Clegg)

direction of the season. Hunt was given the option of which side to start from and chose the right but Lauda led and kept it, beating Hunt by 1.3 seconds. Fastest lap: Lauda 117.7mph(-1.2)/189.5kph (-1.9).

1977 Hunt (McLaren) took pole from Lauda (Ferrari) and led to lap 7 when Lauda went by into *Crowthorne*. On lap 23 a fire

marshal, running across the track to reach a stricken car, was struck by Tom Pryce's Shadow. Both men died, Pryce when the

Shorts, parasols and spooky looking cars – that was Kyalami, 1969. Jackie Stewart (Matra) will win it comfortably. (LAT)

Gilles Villeneuve makes the Veldt vanish when his Ferrari engine blows in 1982. He would never pass this way again. (LAT)

fire extinguisher struck him. Lauda beat Scheckter (Wolf) by 5.2 seconds. Fastest lap: John Watson (Brabham) 118.3mph (+0.6)/190.3kph (+0.8).

1978 The 300th Championship race.

They couldn't change the backdrop but the new circuit was a very distant cousin of the old. Giovanna Amati tries – and fails – to qualify the Brabham in 1992. (LAT)

Lauda (Brabham) took pole but the race would have five leaders, including Riccardo Patrese (Arrows) from laps 27 to 63 when the engine failed. Ronnie Peterson (Lotus) beat Patrick Depailler (Tyrrell) by 0.4 of a second. Fastest lap: Andretti (Lotus) 119.1mph (+0.8)/191.7kph (+1.4).

1979 Jean-Pierre Jabouille (Renault) took pole but a storm ravaged the circuit after two laps and the race had to be restarted. Gilles Villeneuve beat Ferrari team-mate Scheckter by 3.4 seconds. Fastest lap: Villeneuve 123.4mph (+4.3)/198.5kph (+6.8).

1980 The French-accented race,

Jabouille pole from Renault team-mate René Arnoux and leading to lap 62, when a tyre failed. Arnoux beat Jacques Laffite (Ligier) by 34.0 seconds, Didier Pironi (in the other Ligier) third. Fastest lap: Arnoux 125.5mph (+2.1)/202.0kph (+3.5).

1982 The drivers went on strike over the terms of their superlicences, creating bitterness and chaos. Eventually Arnoux (Renault) took pole and he and team-mate Prost exchanged the lead twice before Prost won, beating Carlos Reutemann (Williams) by 14.9 seconds. Fastest lap: Prost 134.5mph (+9.0)/216.4kph (+14.4).

1983 The final race of the season and a three-way Championship between Nelson Piquet (Brabham), Prost (Renault), and Arnoux (Ferrari). Piquet was fuelled light to gain a decisive advantage, pit, and still lead. Arnoux's engine failed, Prost's turbo failed, and Piquet moved aside to let team-mate Patrese beat Andrea de Cesaris (Alfa Romeo) by 9.3 seconds, Piquet third – and Champion. Fastest lap: Piquet 131.2mph (-3.3)/211.2kph (-5.2).

1984 Piquet (Brabham) took pole but Lauda (McLaren) took the lead on lap 21 and flowed masterfully into the distance, beating team-mate Prost by 1 minute 5.9 seconds. Fastest lap: Patrick Tambay (Renault) 133.3mph (+2.1)/214.5kph (+3.3).

1985 Nigel Mansell's career, now in its fifth season, suddenly blossomed. He won his first race (Europe, Brands) on 6 October and now two weeks later took pole. From there he led every lap except

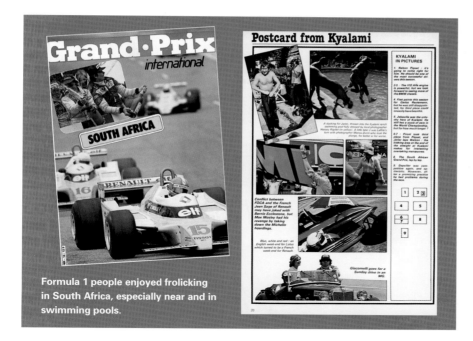

Formula 1 people enjoyed frolicking
in South Africa, especially near and in
swimming pools.

one (lap 8) when he waved Williams
team-mate Keke Rosberg through
confident he could retake him. Rosberg
spun on oil and Mansell beat him by 7.5
seconds. Fastest lap: Rosberg 134.7mph
(+1.4)/216.8kph (+2.3).

Speed increase 1968–85:
25.0mph/40.3kph.

*A new circuit although overlapping
the old. The fabled corners* Sunset *and*
Clubhouse *survived, as did the esses,
but they now bore sponsors' names:*
Budget, Yellow Pages, *and* Topsport. *The
circuit – sanitised, as someone noted –
was slightly longer than the original, had
nothing to compare with the*

great, imperious straight from
Leeukop *to* Crowthorne, *and unusually
went anticlockwise.*

1992 Mansell (Williams) might never
have been away. He took pole from
Ayrton Senna (McLaren) and led all 72
laps from team-mate Patrese to win
by 24.3 seconds. Fastest lap: Mansell
122.9mph/197.7kph.

1993 Prost was back racing after a
year's sabbatical, put the Williams on pole
(inevitably from Senna, McLaren), moved
into the lead from team-mate Damon
Hill at the pit stops and beat Senna by 1
minute 19.8 seconds. Fastest lap: Prost
119.9mph (-3.0)/193.0kph (-4.7).

FACTS OF THE MATTER

2.544m/4.094km circuit

Year	Winner
1967	P. Rodríguez (Cooper)
Pole	J. Brabham (Brabham)
	(103.7mph/166.9kph)
Fastest lap	D. Hulme (Brabham)
	(101.8mph/163.9kph)

Widened, 2.550m/4.104km circuit

1968	J. Clark (Lotus)
1969	J. Stewart (Matra)
1970	J. Brabham (Brabham)
1971	M. Andretti (Ferrari)
1972	D. Hulme (McLaren)
1973	J. Stewart (Tyrrell)
1974	C. Reutemann (Brabham)
1975	J. Scheckter (Tyrrell)
1976	N. Lauda (Ferrari)
1977	N. Lauda (Ferrari)
1978	R. Peterson (Lotus)
1979	G. Villeneuve (Ferrari)
1980	R. Arnoux (Renault)
1982	A. Prost (Renault)
1983	R. Patrese (Brabham)
1984	N. Lauda (McLaren)
1985	N. Mansell (Williams)
Fastest pole	N. Mansell (Williams) 1985
	(147.2mhp/236.9kph)
Fastest lap	K. Rosberg (Williams) 1985
	(134.7mph/216.8kph)

New circuit, 2.648m/4.261km

1992	N. Mansell (Williams)
1993	A. Prost (Williams)
Fastest pole	N. Mansell (Williams) 1992
	(126.3mph/203.2kph)
Fastest lap	N. Mansell (Williams) 1992
	(122.9mph/197.7kph)

*Grand Prix racing came back and so did the
crowd – to see Nigel Mansell beat Williams
team-mate Riccardo Patrese. (Courtesy Camel)*

*The new has replaced the old.
(Courtesy Andrew Clegg)*

SPAIN

JARAMA

Location: 17 miles (28km) from Madrid.
Constructed: 1967.
World Championship Grands Prix: 9.

'It is perhaps a little short and tight for Grand Prix cars'

Jackie Stewart

Emerson Fittipaldi (Lotus) wins the 1972 race and the man with the chequered flag could almost be a bullfighter. (LAT)

Ascari
Portago
Rampa Pegaso
Monza
Bugatti Esses
Farina
Varzi
Fangio
Le Mans
Pegio/ Bugatti
Tunel
Nuvolari
Start/finish

The circuit, in arid, rolling scrubland north of Madrid, was designed by John Hugenholtz, who'd designed Zandvoort and Suzuka. (Jarama is a river in central Spain, flowing north to south. It passes east of Madrid.)

The area of the circuit was cramped, which dictated its essential character: 'tight, near-hairpin corners with just one half-mile straight. Most of the drivers regard it as a glorified kart-track, but there are several good viewing areas for spectators and the pits-cum-lock-up garages are the best in Europe.'[1]

The start/finish was halfway along the straight. From it the cars went into a tricky double right-hander, then a right-hand kink, feeding into a left-hand hairpin. This fed into a right-hand hairpin then a fast, climbing left-hander leading to a shorter straight. At the top the cars had to negotiate another tight right-hander feeding into another double right-hander. The right-hander on to the straight was fast.

Jarama hosted a non-Championship Grand Prix in 1967, which Jim Clark (Lotus) won. It

The front of the grid, 1974, and Ronnie Peterson in the Lotus is getting away ahead of Niki Lauda (Ferrari) on pole. (LAT)

opened the way to a full Grand Prix, alternating with Montjuïc Park and thus placating the sensibilities of Madrid and Barcelona.

Jarama hosted its last Grand Prix in 1981. After that it was considered too narrow for modern racing, although occasional sports car and bike races continued.

COCKPIT VIEW
Jackie Stewart, who drove in two Grands Prix there:
'It is perhaps a little short and tight for Grand Prix cars. It is a fatiguing track to drive on, demanding a lot of arm work and a lot of back-and-forward movement of the head, with braking and accelerating between the corners. I don't rate Jarama among my favourite tracks, but the great thing about Grand Prix motor racing is that no two tracks are the same and you

have to adapt yourself to the different characters of the tracks.'

EYEWITNESS
Ann Bradshaw, PR expert:
'We used to go testing with sports cars when I was working with Tom Walkinshaw. It's not a bad circuit, it's quite fun – had a nice feel about it – and you're near Madrid.

'There's a convention centre where you stay, a bit like the NEC at Birmingham, then you can get on a tube

and go into the centre of Madrid, so it's very well positioned.'

MEMORIES AND MILESTONES
1968 Jim Clark had been killed in a Formula 2 race at Hockenheim on 7 April and Jarama was on 12 May. Colin Chapman could not bring himself to go and only Graham Hill's strength of personality and willpower hauled the team through the ordeal. Nor was it helped by

Jackie Stewart wins the 1970 race from Bruce McLaren (left) and Mario Andretti. (LAT)

the drivers threatening a boycott because they considered the Armco too high, and rubber marker cones and loose gravel beside the track too dangerous. Chris Amon (Ferrari) took pole but Hill won the race, itself an extraordinary feat, beating Denny Hulme (McLaren) by 16.0 seconds. Fastest lap: Jean-Pierre Beltoise (Matra) 86.2mph/138.8kph.

1970 A big entry had to be pruned to 16, which meant five didn't qualify. An extra practice session was arranged for the Friday but did the times count for the grid? Nobody was sure, leading to protests. Jack Brabham (Brabham) took pole. More chaos followed on race day when the non-qualifiers were allowed on to the grid and then banished from it. Jackie Stewart (March) won by a lap from Bruce McLaren (McLaren). Fastest lap: Brabham 90.3mph (+4.1)/145.4kph (+6.6).

1972 Jacky Ickx (Ferrari) took pole. The rain fell on Spain and 14 of the 25 starters broke down or crashed. The race had three leaders, Hulme (McLaren), Stewart (Tyrrell), and Emerson Fittipaldi (Lotus), who beat Ickx by 18.9 seconds. Fastest lap: Ickx 94.0mph (+3.7)/151.3kph (+5.9).

Denny Hulme's McLaren would only cover ten laps before a rotor arm shaft failure. Henri Pescarolo (Matra) passes the burning wreck of Jackie Oliver's BRM – Oliver was unhurt. (Courtesy Martin Hadwen, National Motor Racing Archive)

Gilles Villeneuve (Ferrari) spins in 1979 and lets Carlos Reutemann (Lotus) through. (LAT)

1974 In practice Hulme (McLaren) veered off, striking a marshal a fatal blow. The marshal had been trying to warn other cars about oil on the track. Niki Lauda (Ferrari) took pole. Again the race had heavy attrition (12 of the 25 cars out) and three leaders, Ronnie Peterson (Lotus), Lauda, and Ickx (Lotus), Lauda from laps 21 to 22 and 25 to 84. He beat team-mate Clay Regazzoni by 35.6 seconds. Fastest lap: Lauda 94.2mph (+0.2)/151.6kph (+0.3).

1976 The fourth race of a season sunk in politics, protests, and accidents. James Hunt (McLaren), pole, won from Lauda (Ferrari) by 30.7 seconds, was disqualified because his car was too wide and reinstated on appeal. This was the first time a six-wheeler had run (Patrick Depailler in the Tyrrell). Fastest lap: Jochen Mass (McLaren) 94.1mph (-0.1)/151.4kph (-0.2).

1977 31 drivers vied for the 24 places. From pole, Mario Andretti (Lotus) led every lap and beat Carlos Reutemann (Ferrari) by 15.8 seconds. Fastest lap: Jacques Laffite (Ligier) 94.2mph (+0.1)/151.6kph (+0.2).

1978 Andretti (1m 16.39s) took pole again from Lotus team-mate Peterson (1m 16.68s) and they finished the race in that order, although Peterson was 19.5 seconds behind. Fastest lap: Andretti 95.1mph (+0.9)/153.1kph (+1.5).

1979 Jacques Laffite (Ligier) took pole. Patrick Depailler (Ligier) won only the second race of his career (which had begun in 1972), beating Carlos Reutemann (Lotus) by 20.9 seconds. Fastest lap: Gilles Villeneuve (Ferrari) 99.6mph (+4.5)/160.3kph (+7.2).

1980 Laffite (Ligier) took pole. Alan Jones (Williams) beat Mass (Arrows) by 51.0 seconds, but the race was declared illegal, a victim of the power struggle between the constructors (FOCA) and the governing body (FISA).

1981 Laffite (Ligier) took pole. Jones (Williams) led easily but on lap 14 locked his brakes at the *Virage Ascari* and went off. Villeneuve in a deeply uncompetitive Ferrari inherited the lead and you'd have imagined he'd have been able to keep it for only a lap or two. By audacity, nerve, concentration, and bloody-mindedness he wrestled the Ferrari through the next 67 laps, the cars behind so bunched that at the end 1.2 seconds covered the first five. Villeneuve beat Laffite by 0.21 of a second. Fastest lap: Jones 95.2mph (-4.4)/153.2kph (-7.1).

Speed increase 1968–81: 9.0mph/14.4kph.

Footnote
[1] *Autocourse.*

FACTS OF THE MATTER

2.115m/3.404km circuit

Year	Winner
1968	G. Hill (Lotus)
1970	J. Stewart (March)
1972	E. Fittipaldi (Lotus)
1974	N. Lauda (Ferrari)
1976	J. Hunt (McLaren)
1977	M. Andretti (Lotus)
1978	M. Andretti (Lotus)
1979	P. Depailler (Ligier)
Fastest pole	J. Laffite (Ligier) 1979 (102.2mph/164.5kph)
Fastest lap	G. Villeneuve (Ferrari) 1979 (99.6mph/160.3kph)

2.058m/3.312km circuit

1981	G. Villeneuve (Ferrari)
Pole	J. Laffite (Ligier) (100.5mph/161.7kph)
Fastest lap	A. Jones (Williams) (95.2mph/153.2kph)

Location: 22 miles (35km) north-east of Cadiz.
Constructed: 1986.
World Championship Grands Prix: 7.

ABOVE AND OPPOSITE: Senna leads into the first corner in the 1989 race and would stay there to the end, however much McLaren team-mate Prost tried to hustle him. (Both ICN U.K. Bureau)

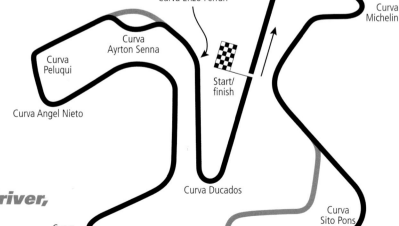

Curva Expo '92
Curva Enzo Ferrari
Curva Michelin
Curva Ayrton Senna
Curva Peluqui
Start/finish
Curva Angel Nieto
Curva Ducados
Curva Sito Pons
Curva Dry Sack

'It's very hard on the driver, quite hot, bumpy'

Ayrton Senna

A glance at the map shows you the problem. Jerez is a long way from anywhere, and that was reflected in the attendances, although the teams liked it for testing.

The Spanish Grand Prix had languished, the last one at Jarama in 1981, when Gilles Villeneuve won.

The Mayor of Jerez de la Frontera, Pedro Pacheco, hit upon the idea of a Grand Prix as a promotional vehicle for the town, already world famous for its sherries, of course.

'The sherry country, between the romantic-sounding cities of Cádiz and Seville, is almost a caricature of grandee Spain. Here are the bull ranches, the castles on the skyline, the patios, the guitars, the flamenco dancers, the night-turned-into-day.

Jerez de la Frontera, the town that gives its name to sherry, lives and breathes sherry as Beaune does burgundy and Epernay champagne.'[1]

The circuit was in 'a natural amphitheatre in the dry and underpopulated region where life is slow, relaxed and *mañana* is never too late'.[2] It was finished shortly before the first Grand Prix in April 1986.

COCKPIT VIEWS

Ayrton Senna, Lotus, 1987:
'Lots of downforce needed. It's very hard on the driver, quite hot, bumpy – and quite hard on the tyres.'

Nelson Piquet, Lotus, 1988:
'Very bad for turbos – 40 kilos heavier – and in the car the circuit seems as if it is nothing but corners. It's very bumpy, very tight.'

EYEWITNESS

Ann Bradshaw, PR expert:
'I remember when Jerez was going to go on to the calendar and we all thought *we're going back to Spain.* We'd been away a long time. Nobody was quite sure why because of the simple fact that we hadn't got any Spanish drivers and the circuit was in the middle of nowhere. The initial reaction was the same as it had been for Adelaide: *well, where* is *Jerez?* It wasn't Barcelona, it wasn't Madrid, it was where the sherry came from and we weren't quite sure where that might be.

'Everybody said the circuit wouldn't be ready in time. A Spanish journalist, Javier Del Arco [*Solo Auto Actual*], came to all the races and he was so certain that it wouldn't happen he booked his holidays that week!

'You have to say the stories were legion that it *wouldn't* get finished and it *did* get finished.

'We flew into Seville because this was before Ryanair and EasyJet and you couldn't just go to Jerez Airport. Nobody had been to the circuit before and when we got there the place was empty. On race day they actually opened the entrances to the grandstands and shooed everybody in.

'It became the preferred test track and it could be very cold – I remember once it was bloody cold. Obviously in the summer it was lovely and it's right

A Williams front row in 1987, Nelson Piquet (left) and Nigel Mansell, who'd win – Piquet fourth. (ICN U.K. Bureau)

next door to a PGA golf course. There'd be testing and there'd be the Seve Ballesteroses of this world coming to watch the cars.'

Senna's preview of his laps at Jerez in 1987, when he'd finish fifth. (Courtesy Camel)

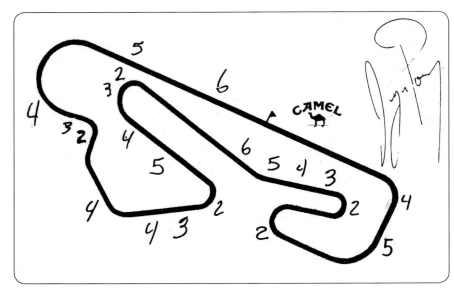

MEMORIES AND MILESTONES

1986 An extraordinary finish, Ayrton Senna (Lotus), pole, holding off Nigel Mansell (Williams) by 0.014 of a second, and only Italy in 1971 had been closer (0.010). Fastest lap: Mansell 108.2mph/174.2kph.

1987 Nelson Piquet (Williams) took pole but team-mate Mansell led easily enough from the front row while Senna (Lotus), running literally non-stop, had a frustrated column of cars behind him. He resisted

their pressure until his tyres went off on lap 63 of the 72. Mansell beat Alain Prost (McLaren) by 22.2 seconds. Fastest lap: Gerhard Berger (Ferrari) 108.5mph (+0.3)/174.6kph (+0.4).

1988 In qualifying, Riccardo Patrese (Williams) gave Julian Bailey (Tyrrell) such a blatant 'brake test' that he was fined $10,000. Prost's race, because McLaren team-mate Senna, pole, was worried about fuel consumption so that Mansell (Williams) ran second and even pressured Prost early on, but Prost won by 26.2 seconds. Fastest lap: Prost 107.4mph (-1.1)/172.9kph (-1.7).

1989 Mansell (Ferrari) was excluded after a black flag at Estoril two weeks before, removing a whole layer of pressure from Senna (McLaren), who led every lap from pole and beat Berger (Ferrari) by 27.0 seconds. Fastest lap: Senna 110.0mph (+2.6)/177.0kph (+4.1).

1990 The defining image of the weekend was not Senna (McLaren), pole, beating Mansell (Ferrari) by 22.0 seconds, but Martin Donnelly on the track after his Lotus hit the Armco at 140mph in practice and he was thrown from it. He survived but with horrific injuries. Fastest lap: Riccardo Patrese (Williams) 111.6mph (+1.6)/179.7kph (+2.7).

Speed increase 1986–90: 3.4mph/5.5kph.

FACTS OF THE MATTER

2.621m/4.218km circuit

Year	Winner
1986	A. Senna (Lotus)
1987	N. Mansell (Williams)
1988	A. Prost (McLaren)
1989	A. Senna (McLaren)
1990	A. Prost (Ferrari)
Fastest pole	A. Senna (McLaren) 1990 (120.4mph/193.7kph)
Fastest lap	R. Patrese (Williams) 1990 (111.6mph/179.7kph)

New corner at Sito Pons and chicane, 2.751m/4.428km circuit

1994*	M. Schumacher (Benetton)
1997*	M. Häkkinen (McLaren)
Fastest pole	J. Villeneuve (Williams) 1997 (122.2mph/196.6kph)
Fastest lap	H.-H. Frentzen (Williams) 1997 (119.1mph/191.7kph)

* European Grand Prix.

The authentic flavour of Jerez, Alain Prost (McLaren) passing by. (ICN U.K. Bureau)

The track returned to Grand Prix racing, at the last minute, as the European Grand Prix. A new curve, named after Ayrton Senna, was added and the Sito Pons right-left made into a horseshoe.

1994 Michael Schumacher (Benetton), pole, and Damon Hill (Williams) were fighting for the Championship, verbally as well as on the track, and significantly Schumacher beat Hill by 24.6 seconds. Fastest lap: Schumacher 116.5mph/187.4kph.

1997 Jacques Villeneuve (Williams) took pole. The defining image of this weekend was Schumacher turning his Ferrari into Villeneuve in a desperate bid to stop him overtaking and winning the Championship. Schumacher damaged the Ferrari, Villeneuve continued and finished a comfortable, unstressed third. It was all he needed. Mika Häkkinen beat McLaren team-mate David Coulthard by 1.6 seconds. Fastest lap: Heinz-Harald Frentzen (Williams) 119.1mph/191.7kph.

Speed increase 1994–7: 2.6mph/4.3kph.

Jerez proved a popular testing ground. Gerhard Berger in the Ferrari, 1989, and David Coulthard in the Williams, 1994. (ICN U.K. Bureau)

Footnotes
[1] *World Atlas of Wine*, Hugh Johnson. [2] *The World Atlas of Motor Racing*, Saward.

SPAIN
MONTJUÏC PARK

Location: West of Barcelona city centre.
Constructed: 1933.
World Championship Grands Prix: 4.

*Jackie Stewart (Tyrrell) led all 75 laps of the
1971 race and the crowd were close enough
to savour his mastery. (LAT)*

Viraje

La Pergola

Pueblo
Español

Riug y Taulet

Palico
Agricultura

Tecnica

Teatro
Griego

San Jordi

'**Without
hesitation, the
best street
track I have
ever raced on**'

John Watson

Start/
finish

Estadio

A picturesque place, undulating through a public park and bearing the name Jewish Mountain because it was the site of an ancient cemetery.

'It took all of a decade of pleading, coaxing, bribing, but in the end it was nothing but the enduring goodwill of the Catalan people that was the ultimate catalyst which managed to overpower the insurmountable obstacle of global economic insecurity and financial depression, to secure the first Historic Gran Premio Penya Rhin event in June, 1933. The acceptance by "The Little Great Man" – Tazio Nuvolari – to race in the event, triggered off the required enthusiasm of the financiers to proceed with the race and fund it.'[1]

A turbulent beginning, and it would lead to a turbulent end.

The Spanish Civil War and subsequent isolation of Spain under General Franco had a direct impact on motor sport but that started to change in the 1950s, although racing at Montjuïc was on a modest scale involving touring cars. It was properly revived in 1954 with a sports car race.

By 1966 Formula 2 cars were going. That year Jack Brabham, Jackie Stewart, Denny Hulme, Graham Hill, and Jim Clark competed and it proved a preliminary to a Grand Prix in 1969.

The track, or rather the road, 'curves uphill to a tight left-hand hairpin and then plunges down to a very tight right-hander. Four more sharp corners follow and then comes a short, wide straight which leads into a climbing left-hander and a series of fast swerves which climb back to the pit area.'[2]

Before they'd consent to a Grand Prix the drivers and the CSI, the governing body, insisted on certain safety precautions, including lining the whole circuit with Armco. Rindt checked it out, was satisfied, and Montjuïc had the race.

It would alternate with Jarama.

Sir Frank Williams[3] remembers that the 1969 race was the first Grand Prix 'in which I participated as a car owner and entrant'. He described it as 'a great circuit for drivers requiring much courage, but also a dangerous track for spectators, as witnessed in a spectacular accident at the end of the pit straight. The circuit was definitely for men and not for boys. A series of high-speed sweeping corners up hill to the pit straight were as challenging as those at Spa.'

Glimpses of 1975. (All courtesy Julian Nowell Archive)

Clay Regazzoni in the Ferrari, but he wouldn't finish.

Tom Pryce in the Shadow, but he'd crash.

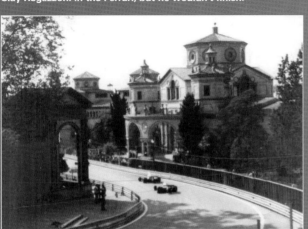

The Teatro del Griego corner.

Mario Andretti in the Parnelli, exiting the hairpin, but he'd crash.

The circuit today. Ted Tofield, who took these pictures, says 'my favourite is the corner picture showing just how steep the track was. The corner itself is very tight as well although the road is wide here.' *(Courtesy Ted Tofield)*

COCKPIT VIEW

John Watson, who drove in the 1975 Grand Prix:

'Both thumbs up! Without hesitation, the best street track I have ever raced on. Magic. It had a combination of scale and was what Monaco isn't.

'The harbour at Monaco is nicer but Montjuïc Park was built on like a terrace. It was quick and for a street track it had proper corners. It wasn't matrix stop-go, stop-go.

'When you got to the bottom of the circuit you started this process of climbing, a bit like going up one of these estates you see where they grow things in tiers. You get up to one and there's another one and another one, *and* of course you were running close to barriers.

'Whereas at Monaco there wasn't a single quick corner other than the tunnel's exit, there were a lot of quick corners in Montjuïc Park. I went there in 1970 in a Formula 2 car and loved it to bits because I found it my kind of racetrack.

'I had a good run going in 1975 but unfortunately I locked up a brake and flat-spotted a tyre. The race was stopped anyway because of Stommelen's accident [see 'Memories and Milestones'].

'The cars got airborne. You came past the start/finish straight, climbed up to the left and then the road dipped away very quickly and literally the cars were flying, they were maybe the best part of a foot off the ground. Then on to the brakes, down the gears, turn left downhill through a right then down again.

'It was a circuit that was lost and we ended up going to places like Jarama, Jerez, and Barcelona. It would be impossible, *impossible*, to run a modern Grand Prix at the old circuits we talk about, like Montjuïc Park. The speeds would be beyond the capacity of the circuit and the drivers wouldn't accept it. If you take that sequence of corners coming up to the start/finish – lefts, lefts, lefts – probably a lot of Formula 1 cars today would not be far short of flat out through there – and then consider the pit straight, then up over the top. I mean, they'd be doing 190 miles an hour…

'It's one of the great racetracks of the world, forgotten.'

EYEWITNESS

Ted Tofield, enthusiast:

'I have long planned to visit some of the world's greatest racetracks. This passion started for me when I went to my first Grand Prix in Suzuka: a long way from home, but I was overwhelmed by the track itself, so different from my local track of Brands Hatch and those others like Castle Combe and Thruxton. Whenever I've travelled I've made sure that I do my research first.

'It's meant a diversion here and long way round there, and occasionally the chance to drive my car on a long-forgotten piece of tarmac that was once a Grand Prix circuit.

'In October 2009 I took my darling wife on a weekend break in Barcelona. We had several aims: to gorge on Tapas, to gorge on Gaudí,[4] and to find the Montjuïc circuit. After much art and food we found ourselves on the Red Route of the *Bus Touristique*. As the bus heads back from the football stadium it takes a right turn and joins the old racing track in Montjuïc Park. When it swung on to the pit straight I was dumbstruck. Cars used to race *here*? Wow.

'I began to realise how daunting this circuit would be at full pelt in a Formula 1 car. There didn't seem to be a straight piece of road anywhere. To commit a Grand Prix car at full speed around these bends, in a four-wheel drift, would take more courage than I could imagine. The cars that used to race here were dangerous beasts with low-grip, fat, cross-ply tyres, 400-odd horse power, and next to no aerodynamics. They also tended to explode into flames at the slightest touch and would break your legs if you hit anything head on … God help you if you rolled it.

'The circuit itself is little changed, of course, except now swarming with visitors to Barcelona unaware they are walking along one of the greatest circuits ever raced on.

'What struck me first was that almost the whole track is on a curve, and from the straight round to the hairpin is awe-inspiring. The circuit rises and falls horrifically and, in a car with little care for safety measures at Grand Prix speeds, this must have been a track where bravery was a necessity.

'To plunge downhill at high speed towards the hairpin would requires nerves of steel or perhaps a certain foolhardiness to even touch the brakes where required. The corner itself is very tight as well, although the road is wide here. I think over the weekend we did three laps of the circuit by bus and by foot and enjoyed every minute of it. Sipping a beer in the sunshine on the steps of the museum at the top looking down at the start/finish straight is highly recommended…

'It was only when I came back (and watched a few old videos) that the fact that the big one had happened at my favourite corner struck home. This, of course, was where Stommelen crashed so terribly and went over the barrier into the crowd. This was where the drivers and mechanics had gone round the morning of the race and tightened up the bolts holding the Armco together themselves ... this was where the drivers tried to say it was too dangerous ... this was where members of the public were killed.

'Grand Prix racing never returned to Montjuïc Park.

'It's right, too. It was far too dangerous.'

MEMORIES AND MILESTONES

1969 There was an immediate omen. Practice began on the Thursday and after a few minutes Rindt brought his Lotus back with suspension damage after he'd hit a dog. Rindt took pole from Chris Amon (Ferrari) and Graham Hill (Lotus). It was the era of enormous rear wings – aerofoils. The ones on the Lotuses both failed, pitching Hill then Rindt horrifically into the Armco. Jackie Stewart (Matra) beat Bruce McLaren (McLaren) by two *laps,* making it the biggest winning margin at the time (to be equalled by Damon Hill in Australia in 1995). Fastest lap: Rindt 96.0mph/154.6kph.

1971 Jacky Ickx (Ferrari) took pole from team-mate Clay Regazzoni, but Stewart took Ickx for the lead on lap 6 when Ickx went wide in one of the fast corners. He never lost it. He rarely did. He beat Ickx by 3.8 seconds. Fastest lap: Ickx 99.6mph (+3.6)/160.4kph (+5.8).

1973 A tight finish: Ronnie Peterson (Lotus), pole, led to lap 56 of the 75 but his gearbox stuck in first. That passed the lead to Emerson Fittipaldi in the other Lotus but he had a slow puncture. Carlos Reutemann (Brabham) was closing but a driveshaft broke. Fittipaldi crossed the line to win with the tyre flat, beating François Cevert (Tyrrell) by 42.7 seconds. Fastest lap: Peterson 101.2mph (+1.6)/162.9kph (+2.5).

1975 The drivers were unhappy with how the Armco had been installed – loose and missing bolts – and on the Friday all but two refused to go out. Workmen toiled through the night but the drivers were still unhappy. The organisers pointed out the team's contractual obligations

(and threatened to impound the cars). There was a practice, Niki Lauda taking pole from Ferrari team-mate Regazzoni. Fittipaldi decided the circuit was unsafe and headed for home. By lap 25 nine cars had had accidents, and worse – much worse – was coming. The aerofoil on Rolf Stommelen's Hill-Ford broke, pitching the car out of control at more than 120mph. It made another car swerve, it ran along the Armco, rode over it killing three officials and a photographer. The race was not stopped for another four laps. Jochen Mass (McLaren) was declared the winner, beating Ickx (Lotus) by 1.1 seconds. Fastest lap: Mario Andretti (Parnelli) 99.6mph (-1.6)/160.4kph (-2.5).

Grand Prix racing at Montjuïc was dead.

Speed increase 1969–75: 3.6mph/5.8kph.

Footnotes
[1] montjuich.speedgeezers.net/history.html. [2] *Autocourse.* [3] *Montjuïc: 40 Years of Motor Racing,* de Izco. [4] Antonio Gaudí (1852–1926) was an architect of the modern school from Catalunya, where Barcelona is. Among his designs in the city, the most famous is the Sagrada Família, an eccentric-looking cathedral. Work began in 1883 and is due to be completed around 2030.

FACTS OF THE MATTER

2.356m/3.791km circuit

Year	Winner
1969	J. Stewart (Matra)
1971	J. Stewart (Tyrrell)
1973	E. Fittipaldi (Lotus)
1975	J. Mass (McLaren)
Fastest pole	R. Peterson (Lotus) 1973 (103.7mhp/166.8kph).
Fastest lap	R. Peterson (Lotus) 1973 (101.2mph/162.9kph)

The 1973 programme and a pictorial celebration of 60 years of the Spanish Grand Prix. *(Courtesy Martin Hadwen, National Motor Racing Archive)*

MONTMELÓ (Barcelona)

Location: 12 miles (20km) north of Barcelona.
Constructed: 1991.
World Championship Grands Prix: 15.

The extraordinary temporary chicane which the drivers insisted on in 1994 – the race took place only four weeks after the tragedies at Imola. (ICN U.K. Bureau)

Campsa
* Tyre chicane in 1994
Repsol
Nissan
Europcar
Renault
Banc de Sabadell
Seat
Würth
La Caixa
Elf
Start/finish
New Holland

'Traditionally, always one of the most difficult circuits for overtaking'

Pedro de la Rosa

Once upon a time, winter seemed to be the longest season for any Formula 1 driver because he'd spend large tracts of it pounding round the track (sometimes known simply as Barcelona, occasionally as Catalunya) testing. It was in the right place (not too far away, since all the Formula 1 teams were based in Europe), it was an interesting track in itself, and if you were from anywhere up north the weather was (a lot) better. Of course,

you can have too much of a good thing, which prompted Damon Hill when he retired to say that he was looking forward to a great deal, including *not* going round Barcelona any more... (see Button, 'Cockpit View').

The Spanish Grand Prix, as we have seen, was as itinerant as the French (Jarama, Jerez, Montjuïc, here, and Pedralbes). It needed a *permanent* home, and in October 1986 Catalan's parliament voted to

form an organisation which could do precisely that.

Just over a year later the Royal Automobil Club de Catalunya bought land which had good access in the municipality of Montmeló and secured finance from local government and Montmeló town council. Work began in early 1989 and was completed shortly before the first Grand Prix there in 1991.

Its facilities were extremely modern and it had a capacity of 67,730.

COCKPIT VIEW

Jenson Button, Brawn, 2009:
'I know the track inside out. You need to have a car with good downforce for a really quick lap there and we are fortunate that our car behaves so predictably, which enables you to feel completely confident when committing to high-speed corners.

'This can be a very difficult circuit for overtaking so you have to make the most of the run down to the first corner to capitalise on any opportunities at the start of the race.'

Pedro de la Rosa, McLaren test driver and Barcelona native, 2009:
'The circuit is extremely hard on tyres, one of the toughest on the calendar. As a result it's vital to have a good balance to keep your tyres alive for as long as possible. You can't be too aggressive on the tyres too early in the race or else you'll lose a lot of time during the stint.

'Tyres are so important because of the nature of the long, fast corners such as Turns 3 and 9. Turn 3 is a very long high-speed corner where you're loading the outside of the car for a long time. Load that front tyre for too long and it will grain. The track is also hard on the rears because there are a couple of low-speed corners where traction is important. This means Bridgestone brings its hardest compounds to the Spanish Grand Prix.

'Traditionally, Barcelona is always one of the most difficult circuits for overtaking. The new regulations will help, as will the new chicane before the final corner, but only to a small extent.'

EYEWITNESS

Erika Schneider, Hungarian enthusiast:
'Barcelona. My very first foreign Formula 1 race, and at such a famous and beloved racing track. It was the first European

race in the season of 2007 and Alonso [McLaren], as a local hero, attracted a huge mass of fans.

'The track was easy to approach by train and the infrastructure itself excellent as well.

'The temper of the Mediterranean people and their love that they show and spread was absolutely enchanting. Even a taxi driver who did not speak a word of English and who saw us standing alone, lost, showed us where to go and was yelling *Aloooooooonso, Aloooooooonso*. We, as non-Alonso fans, were kind of outsiders but it wasn't bothering at all, in fact the opposite. It was funny to see: whoever wasn't wearing McLaren team clothing surely wasn't Spanish.

'The organisers did everything to please the fans: two pit lane walks on Thursday – one in the morning, and one in the afternoon – driver appearances on Saturday and Sunday, at Scuderia Toro Rosso [Tonio Liuzzi and Scott Speed], and at Toyota [Ralf Schumacher and Franck Montagny]. I guess they collaborated with the good-weather gods up above too, since we had such nice temperatures during the whole week we spent in Spain.

'Finally there was a GP2 race after the long winter pause, so we had the opportunity to meet almost all of the youngsters, like Bruno Senna, Timo Glock, Javier Villa, and Luca Filippi.

'On Sunday the first 10,000 entrants received free breakfast and a T-shirt with the track logo and a racing car on it.

'It was an up-and-down of feelings during the race. Alonso slipped out right after the start, colliding with Massa. We received some very bad Spanish words and evil looks as we celebrated, but what comes around goes around. Kimi's retirement from the race [Räikkönen, Ferrari, had an electrical fault after nine

laps] caused the same: very bad words in Hungarian and a lot of gloating Spanish smiles. But that's the salt and the pepper of the race, the rise and the fall.

'And I can proudly tell you, we – four little girls from all around Hungary – were a part of a record, the race day attendance of 140,300. Amazing, isn't it?

'But the Catalan capital isn't just about Formula 1. It's a must to visit at least one of Antonio Gaudí's incredible houses, the *Sagrada Familia* church, the *Nou Camp* stadium, no matter if you're a fan of FC Barcelona or not. The fish market, the *Diagonal*, the *La Rambla*

The start in 1995, and Michael Schumacher (Benetton) is leading Jean Alesi (Ferrari). (ICN U.K. Bureau)

The circuit as it is today. *(Courtesy Erika Schneider)*

with its restaurants and food. The narrow medieval streets and the churches are in perfect harmony with the Louis Vuitton, Gucci and other luxury designers' stores.

'Did you know that Franck Montagny has a hairdressing saloon in Barcelona?

Street race, 1995? No, just a nice way to let bystanders savour a Formula 1 car – David Coulthard in the Williams. (ICN U.K. Bureau)

'We've been there. We've been everywhere.

'Culture, sunshine, Latino temperament and Formula 1. You don't need a better combination.'

MEMORIES AND MILESTONES

1991 Gerhard Berger (McLaren) took pole. Nigel Mansell (Williams) went head-to-head with Ayrton Senna (McLaren)

down the straight at 180mph, only inches between their wheels. Mansell had the inside line and took the corner at the end. Frank Williams, asked (by the author) if he wasn't worried, replied: 'I wish it was like that every race!' Mansell beat Alain Prost (Ferrari) by 11.3 seconds. Fastest lap: Riccardo Patrese (Williams) 128.2mph/206.3kph.

1992 The rain in Spain brought a thoroughly wet race and while Mansell (Williams), pole, was beating Schumacher (Benetton) by 23.9 seconds 12 cars spun off. Fastest lap: Mansell 103.6mph/166.7kph (no comparison).

1993 Prost was now with the dominant Williams team and took pole, though team-mate Damon Hill pressured him very hard before an engine failure decided the race. Prost beat Senna (McLaren) by 16.8 seconds. Fastest lap: Schumacher (Benetton) 131.1mph (+2.9)/211.0kph (+4.7).

Speed increase 1991–3: 2.9mph/4.7kph.

In the wake of Senna's death at Imola on 1 May in a Williams, everyone was still nervy at the end of the month and the drivers insisted on a chicane being made (of tyres, actually) at the Nissan *curve.*

1994 Hill, in an echo of what his father had done at Jarama after Clark's death, won in his Williams, beating Schumacher (Benetton), pole, by 24.1 seconds. Fastest lap: Schumacher 124.7mph/200.7kph.

The Nissan *corner was bypassed, making a straight between* Campsa *and* La Caixa. *That had twin effects: it made the entry to* La Caixa *more challenging but created a possible overtaking place.*

1995 Schumacher (Benetton) led every lap from pole to beat team-mate Johnny Herbert by 51.9 seconds and move one point ahead of Hill (Williams) in the Championship. Fastest lap: Hill 125.1mph/201.3kph.

1996 Hill (Williams) took pole. The rain in Spain fell a lot harder, so hard that it gave Schumacher a chance to prove he could walk on it while 14 others didn't finish. It was his first win for Ferrari – a measure of his extraordinarily sensitive skills is that he beat Jean Alesi (Benetton) by 45.3 seconds. Fastest lap: Schumacher 100.2mph/161.3kph (no comparison).

1997 Schumacher (Ferrari) made a dynamic (almost dynamited) start from seventh on the grid to be second, but

Jacques Villeneuve (Williams), pole, led every lap (except pit stops) to move past Schumacher in the Championship. Schumacher finished the race fourth, Villeneuve beating Olivier Panis (Prost) by 5.8 seconds. Fastest lap: Giancarlo Fisichella (Jordan) 128.6mph (+3.5)/207.0kph (+5.7).

1998 The power lay with the McLarens now. Mika Häkkinen, pole, beat team-mate David Coulthard by 9.3 seconds and only two other cars (one of them inevitably Schumacher's Ferrari) finished on the same lap. Fastest lap: Häkkinen 125.5mph (-3.1)/202.0kph (-5.0).

1999 An encore. Häkkinen, pole, beat Coulthard by 6.2 seconds and only two other cars (one of them inevitably Schumacher's Ferrari) finished on the same lap. Fastest lap: Schumacher 124.5mph (-1.0)/200.3kph (-1.7).

2000 And the hat-trick. Häkkinen beat Coulthard by 16.0 seconds and only four other cars finished on the same lap, although Schumacher (Ferrari) had had pole. Fastest lap: Häkkinen 125.3mph (-0.8)/201.6kph (-1.3).

2001 Schumacher (Ferrari), pole, and Häkkinen (McLaren) exchanged the lead four times but Häkkinen led into the last lap. Then the clutch failed and the Ferrari moved past to win it by 40.7 seconds from Juan-Pablo Montoya (Williams). Fastest lap: Schumacher 130.4mph (+5.1)/209.8kph (+8.2).

2002 Schumacher put the Ferrari on pole, led every lap and set fastest lap to win from Montoya (Williams) by 35.6 seconds – his fourth of the five races so far. Fastest lap: Schumacher 131.7mph (+1.3)/211.9kph (+2.1).

2003 Schumacher's encore: pole and leading every lap except five (pit stops), although fastest lap went to Ferrari team-mate Rubens Barrichello, and Fernando Alonso (Renault) stirred Spanish passions by finishing second, by 5.7 seconds. Fastest lap: Barrichello 132.0mph (+0.3)/212.5kph (+0.6).

Speed increase 1994–2003: 7.3mph/11.8kph.

The La Caixa *corner was revised so that what had been a left-handed V became in Jenson Button's words 'the tightest corner on the circuit'. It was taken in second gear and a driver risked front-locking his tyres.*

2004 Schumacher's hat-trick, although Jarno Trulli (Renault) made a huge

The start in 1996, Jacques Villeneuve (Williams) into the lead. (ICN U.K. Bureau)

start from fourth to lead. Schumacher, pole, exploited his speed at the pit stops to lead a total of 51 laps and beat team-mate Barrichello by 13.2 seconds. Fastest lap: Schumacher 133.6mph/215.1kph.

2005 Kimi Räikkönen (McLaren), pole, led every lap and beat Alonso (Renault) by 27.6 seconds. Fastest lap: Giancarlo Fisichella (Renault) 136.8mph (+3.2)/220.2kph (+5.1).

2006 Alonso (Renault) stirred Spanish passions, 130,000 of them, a great deal more than he had done the year before. He took pole and stormed the race, leading every lap except 12 (pit stops) to beat Schumacher (Ferrari) by 18.5 seconds. Afterwards he spoke quite naturally of 'my people, my supporters'. Fastest lap: Felipe Massa (Ferrari) 135.0mph (-1.8)/217.3kph (-2.9).

Speed increase 1995–2006: 9.9mph/16.0kph.

Revisions, extending the circuit from 2.875 miles to 2.892.

2007 Lewis Hamilton (McLaren) finished a strong second to Massa (Ferrari), pole – 6.7 seconds behind – and now led the Championship by two points from Alonso (McLaren). He was the youngest driver ever to do that. Fastest lap: Massa 125.9mph/202.7kph.

2008 Alonso (Renault) ran third but an engine problem halted him. Räikkönen (Ferrari), pole, was never really under pressure from Ferrari team-mate Massa, although a margin of 3.2 seconds might suggest he was. Fastest lap: Räikkönen 127.5mph (+1.6)/205.2kph (+2.5).

2009 The Brawn season, but controversial here because the team switched Button (leading the championship), pole, to a two-stop

strategy while Barrichello remained on three. Barrichello led three times but Button won. Barrichello was not pleased. Button beat him by 13.0 seconds. Fastest lap: Barrichello 125.8mph (-1.7)/202.5kph (-2.7).

Speed decrease 2007–9: 0.1mph/0.2kph.

FACTS OF THE MATTER

2.950m/4.747km circuit

Year	Winner
1991	N. Mansell (Williams)
1992	N. Mansell (Williams)
1993	A. Prost (Williams)
1994*	D. Hill (Williams)
Fastest pole	A. Prost (Williams) 1993 (136.5mph/219.6kph)
Fastest lap	M. Schumacher (Benetton) 1993 (131.1mph/211.0kph)

Nissan straightened, 2.937m/4.727km circuit 1995–6; 2.938m/4.728km 1997–9; 2.939m/4.730km 2000–3

1995	M. Schumacher (Benetton)
1996	M. Schumacher (Ferrari)
1997*	J. Villeneuve (Williams)
1998	M. Häkkinen (McLaren)
1999	M. Häkkinen (McLaren)
2000	M. Häkkinen (McLaren)
2001	M. Schumacher (Ferrari)
2002	M. Schumacher (Ferrari)
2003	M. Schumacher (Ferrari)
Fastest pole	M. Schumacher (Ferrari) 2002 (138.6mph/223.0kph)
Fastest lap	R. Barrichello (Ferrari) 2003 (132.0mph/212.5kph)

La Caixa revised, 2.875m/4.627km circuit

2004	M. Schumacher (Ferrari)
2005	K. Räikkönen (McLaren)
2006	F. Alonso (Renault)
Fastest pole	F. Alonso (Renault) 2006 (138.7mph/223.1kph)
Fastest lap	G. Fisichella (Renault) 2005 (136.8mph/220.2kph)

Further revisions, 2.892m/4.655km circuit

2007	F. Massa (Ferrari)
2008	K. Räikkönen (Ferrari)
2009	J. Button (Brawn)
Fastest pole	J. Button (Brawn) 2009 (129.3mph/208.1kph)
Fastest lap	K. Räikkönen (Ferrari) 2008 (127.5mph/205.2kph)

* European Grand Prix.

SPAIN
PEDRALBES

Location: 4 miles (7km) north-west of Barcelona city centre.
Constructed: 1946.
World Championship Grands Prix: 2.

'Broad avenues and wide streets and some very fast stretches'

Mike Hawthorn

The start of the 1951 race and Alberto Ascari (Ferrari) has the lead – which he'd hold to lap 3, when Juan Manuel Fangio (Alfa Romeo) went by and won. (LAT)

Avenida de la Victoria

Carretera de
Cornella a Fogas
de Tordera

Paseo de Manuel Girona

Calle de
Numancia

Avenida del Generalissimo Franco

Start/finish

There was racing at Montjuïc Park, Barcelona, in the 1930s but it became an immediate casualty of the Spanish Civil War, which began in 1936. Pedralbes continued the tradition of racing, but not until 1946. It held the non-championship Penya Rhin Grand Prix, attracting a strong entry.

It was a street circuit run down wide streets and what have been described as 'expansive, sweeping corners' near the Pedralbes monastery.

The start/finish line was on the *Avenida del Generalissimo Franco* 'leading into a right-hand hairpin. A flick left led into a looping right-hander down the *Avenida de la Victoria*, followed by a left-hander after which the cars ran parallel to the main straight. Two right-handers brought the cars back to the start/finish area.'[1]

The Mercedes returned in 1954 at the French Grand Prix and were quickly dominant. 'Having won at Monza only by the skin of their teeth, Daimler-Benz were distinctly worried about Barcelona. They had no experience of the circuit to fall back on and as it comprised long straights and tight corners they took six cars to Spain, three streamliners and three open-wheelers. All three drivers opted for the latter models in the race.'[2]

After the tragedy of Le Mans in 1955 safety standards and provision were suddenly brought to the forefront and Pedralbes became a casualty.

COCKPIT VIEW

Mike Hawthorn, who drove a Ferrari:
'The circuit is composed of broad avenues and wide streets and there are some very fast stretches, but it is also bumpy in parts. I went out to do some fast laps in the [Ferrari] Squalo, lost it on a corner at the top of a hill and spun backwards into the straw bales, smashing up the tail end.'[3]

EYEWITNESS

Motor Sport, **November 1951:**
'There was no practice on the Saturday but hospitality of the most charming and generous sort was forthcoming from Señor A.F. Nava, a well-known local enthusiast, and we went to look over the splendid Pegaso factory – but that is another story!

'Sunday dawned fine and very warm and in one of two most imposing Pegaso coaches we were driven the short distance to the Press box – this Penya Rhin GP is rather as if we closed the arterial part of our Great West Road for

Mike Hawthorn (Ferrari) skirts the straw bales in 1954 on his way to a convincing win. (LAT)

a race, letting disinterested parties leave London via Hounslow and Isleworth!

'The scene was as any other great motor race in Europe – very picturesque. Perhaps more so, by reason of the dusky troops who guarded the pit area, the mounted police, the trailer-trains crammed and festooned with humanity, and an occasional Hispano-Suiza! The stands, like those at Silverstone, are of steel scaffolding, but far better disguised!'

MEMORIES AND MILESTONES

1951 Juan-Manuel Fangio arrived for this, the final race of the season, with the Championship in play. His Alfa Romeo had had an engine failure in the race before, Monza, and he would remember his state of mind: worried. The Ferraris of Alberto Ascari, pole, and Froilan González were strong.

'Alberto took the lead right from the start, with Farina and I right behind … The *Avenida General Franco*, known more familiarly by the people of Barcelona as the diagonal, was an extraordinary straight on which our cars could touch nearly 160mph. Ascari, just ahead of me, was going like an arrow. I decided not to duel immediately but to hold on, up in front, without pushing my car too hard. My main worry was refuelling. The Ferrari had huge extra tanks, which meant a minimum number of stops, while our Alfas would have to refill more often.'[4] He beat González by 54.3 seconds. Fastest lap: Fangio 103.2mph/166.1kph.

1954 In practice, Peter Collins crashed his Vanwall, Stirling Moss crashed his Maserati (it 'had a centre throttle and I muddled up the pedals'), and Hawthorn (Ferrari) lost control and went into the straw bales backwards. A British journalist had been boasting about how good the British drivers were and now three crashed within 300 yards. Ascari (Lancia) took pole. This, again, was the last race of the season but the Championship had been decided two races before. Hawthorn beat Luigi Musso (Maserati) by 1 minute 13.0 seconds. The Mercedes were *not* dominant: Fangio third, Karl Kling fifth, Hans Hermann out when the fuel injector pump failed. Fastest lap: Ascari (Lancia) 100.6mph/161.9kph.

Speed decrease 1951–4: 2.6mph/4.2kph.

Footnotes
[1] www.f1fanatic.co.uk. [2] *Mon Ami Mate*, Nixon. [3] *Challenge Me the Race*, Hawthorn. [4] *My Twenty Years of Racing*, Fangio.

FACTS OF THE MATTER

3.925m/6.316km circuit

Year	Winner
1951	J.M. Fangio (Alfa Romeo)
1954	M. Hawthorn (Ferrari)
Fastest pole	A. Ascari (Ferrari) 1951 (108.2mph/174.1kph)
Fastest lap	J.M. Fangio (Alfa Romeo) 1951 (103.2mph/166.1kph)

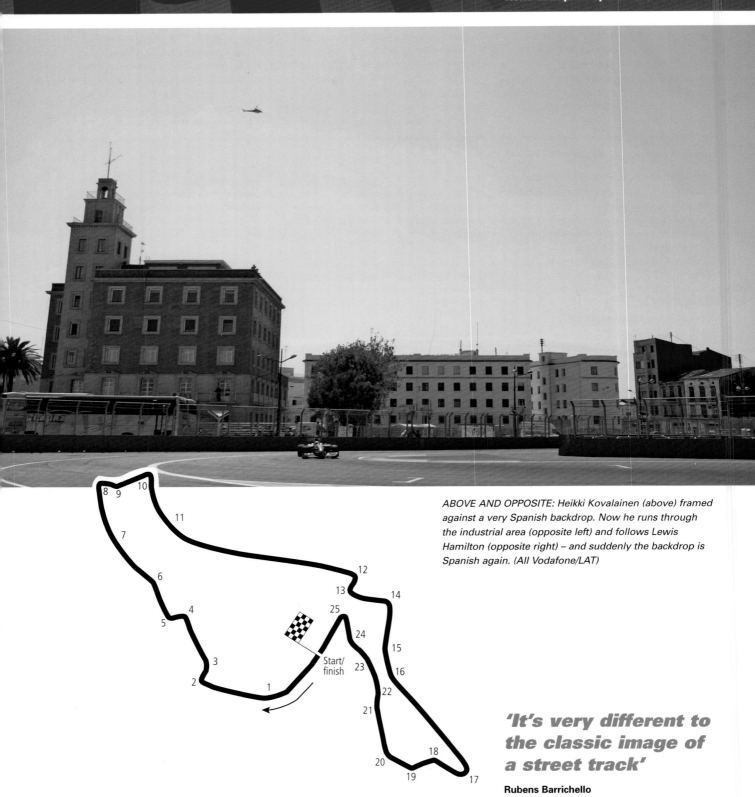

VALENCIA

Location: Central Valencia.
Constructed: 2008.
World Championship Grands Prix: 2.

ABOVE AND OPPOSITE: Heikki Kovalainen (above) framed against a very Spanish backdrop. Now he runs through the industrial area (opposite left) and follows Lewis Hamilton (opposite right) – and suddenly the backdrop is Spanish again. (All Vodafone/LAT)

Start/finish

'It's very different to the classic image of a street track'

Rubens Barrichello

The circuit runs round the port and includes the swing bridge (at 86 yards/140 metres), provoking a criticism that it *looks* too much like a port rather than somewhere more exotic. Some of the roads were designed by the ubiquitous Tilke. It's 3.3 miles (5.4km) and embraces 25 corners (14 left-handers, 11 right-handers).

The race was the product of a deal between Bernie Ecclestone and the Valmor Sport Group in 2007 and the first races, Spanish Formula 3 and International GT Open, were run in July a month before the first Grand Prix.

'Valencia presents an unusual engineering challenge because the circuit is quite different from anywhere else on the calendar,' Ross Brawn says. 'It's not the type of street circuit that we have been used to racing around in Monaco, it's much more open and quite fast-flowing with higher top speeds.

'The tall barriers give the lap the feel of a street circuit but the run-off areas are quite generous compared to Monaco, helping to improve safety and giving the drivers some margin for error at certain places of the lap.

'Traction is important here and the sectors of the lap which have a stop-start nature make Valencia tough on the brakes. Cooling is also a consideration in the high ambient temperatures.'

The races were billed as the European Grand Prix because Spain already had its own race at Barcelona.

COCKPIT VIEW
Rubens Barrichello, Brawn, 2009:
'The first part of the lap is quick with the long pit straight followed by a curved right-hander before the slower section leading up to the bridge over the marina, and then you're down on to another curved straight.

'The second half of the lap feels more like a street circuit as you head away from the water and the third long straight ends with a tight hairpin at Turn 17 which is the best overtaking opportunity.

'The final part of the lap is quite fast with some sweeping corners before the tight left-hander which takes you back out on to the pit straight. It's a very different type of circuit to the classic image of a street track such as Monaco.'[1]

EYEWITNESS
Steven Tee, LAT Photographic:
'The jury is still out on Valencia. I don't completely dislike it but it is a bit soulless. I think the plan is that the parts which are a bit like a building site will have buildings, so it will look more like a street race.

'It is basically a race around a massive commercial port. There are no boats. You get container ships in the background. The Americas Cup yard is there but they are not allowed to have their boats in the harbour.

'It's a bit of a weird race, really.

'They had a big crowd the first year and virtually no one last year. The problem they have is scheduling. It's in the middle of the Spanish holidays so everyone is on the beach. They're not necessarily going to come to a Grand Prix at that time of year.'

MEMORIES AND MILESTONES
2008 Felipe Massa liked Valencia and his Ferrari did too. He took a powerful pole ('I think my performance in Sector 1 was the key') and led every lap except for the pit stops, beating Lewis Hamilton (McLaren) by 5.6 seconds. The crowd, who hadn't forgotten that their very own Fernando Alonso did not survive at McLaren in 2007 against Hamilton, let Hamilton know all about it. Alonso (Renault) qualified 12th and, struck from behind, didn't complete a lap. Fastest lap: Massa 122.8mph/197.6kph.
2009 Rubens Barrichello had staged an extraordinary recovery after Brawn team-mate Jenson Button utterly dominated the first part of the season. McLaren got their second pit stop for Hamilton, pole, wrong (a mix-up over team-mate Heikki Kovalainen coming in) but by then Barrichello was flinging the Brawn round the 25 corners with the verve and audacity of a young man grafted on to the precision and control of the 37-year-old that he was. In beating Hamilton by 2.3 seconds he opened the Championship – Button seventh and far from the pace. Fastest lap: Timo Glock (Toyota) 122.8mph/197.6kph.

Speed increase 2008–9: no change.

Footnote
[1] Courtesy Brawn GP.

FACTS OF THE MATTER

3.367m/5.419km circuit

Year	Winner
2008*	F. Massa (Ferrari)
2009*	R. Barrichello (Brawn)
Fastest pole	F. Massa (Ferrari) 2008 (122.5mph/197.1kph)
Fastest lap	T. Glock (Toyota) 2009 (122.8mph/197.7kph)

* European Grand Prix.

ANDERSTORP

Location: 50 miles (80km) south of Jönköping.
Constructed: 1968.
World Championship Grands Prix: 6.

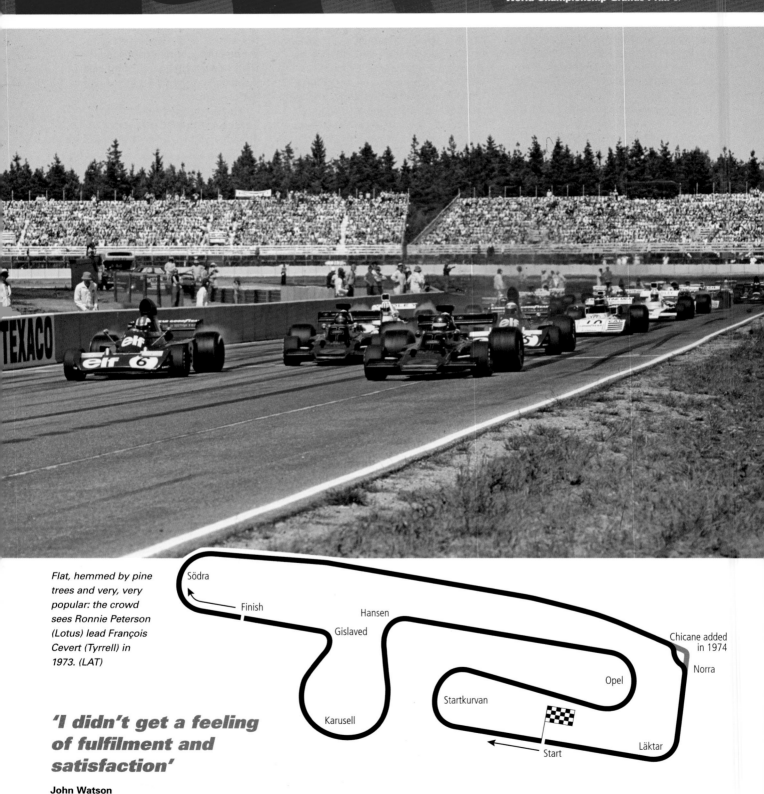

Flat, hemmed by pine trees and very, very popular: the crowd sees Ronnie Peterson (Lotus) lead François Cevert (Tyrrell) in 1973. (LAT)

Södra

Finish

Hansen

Gislaved

Chicane added in 1974

Norra

Opel

Startkurvan

Karusell

Läktar

Start

'I didn't get a feeling of fulfilment and satisfaction'

John Watson

Everything ought to have been predictable and maybe plain uninteresting: marshland with, as its back straight, an airstrip enabling people to get there. It was, after all, 250 miles from Stockholm, itself not exactly the centre of the universe, and 100 miles south-east of Gothenburg. It was also known as the Scandinavian Raceway.

In fact, the circuit proved to be home to highly unpredictable racing. It had a twisting infield section, slightly banked curves, and finding a set-up for the cars proved elusive. Tyre combinations were elusive too.

Three local enthusiasts – Sven Åsberg, Bertil Sanell and Åke Bengtsson – were behind it and Åsberg prophesied, to much scepticism, that a Grand Prix would be run there within five years.

I'm indebted to Mattias Persson of *Motorsport Publication* and Thyrone 'Ticko' Persson of the Scandinavian Raceway for the background that follows. It is in their words.

Sven 'Smokey' Åsberg, originally from central Sweden, was the driving force behind Scandinavian Raceway. 'Smokey', nicknamed after the cigars he always seemed to enjoy, ran a chrome business and saw huge potential in what was called the Gnosjö Region, a fast-growing part of the country. He decided to move there, to Anderstorp.

He met Bertil Sanell, who had set up his own varnishing venture, and together the two businessmen, who shared an interest in motor sport, created Team Mosarp (leaving one 's' out due to a spelling mistake). They set off in their hats and white shirts to go rallying!

Soon Team Mosarp was joined by former amateur rally driver Åke Bengtsson, but the police began to object to the trio making practice runs on local roads. Something needed to be done and it sowed the seeds of a circuit in Anderstorp: the Scandinavian Raceway.

Sitting at Bladh's Café (in central Anderstorp, now gone), plans were made to finance the project. After establishing that a piece of land was suitable for construction, 'Smokey' and co came up with the idea of trying to sell shares to local companies. They knew that motor sport wasn't very attractive and officially argued that the main project would revolve around the 1,000-metre straight – acting as an airport! This major project made Anderstorp the centre of attention and in 1967 construction began.

The circuit layout was drawn by Holger Eriksson, 'Smokey's' own designer. Eriksson's first proposal wasn't approved by the Swedish governing body, which upset him so much that he took the ruler and just drew straight lines with a few corners in frustration. The new version was accepted!

The first race took place on 16 June 1968, attracting 30,000 spectators. In 1969, the Raceway became the first in Sweden to host drag racing, but fights and alcohol largely ruined the events. Portable toilets were set on fire and police cars turned over. Interestingly, all liquor stores in the region closed one week ahead of the inaugural Grand Prix in 1973. A lesson learnt from drag racing, perhaps?

About 30km from Anderstorp, a Wild West-themed funfair called High Chaparral was completed in 1966. When the Grand Prix circus came in 1973 the local hotels couldn't cope but 'Smokey' teamed up with the Chaparral founder to build a hotel inside its gates. Every Formula 1 driver stayed there during the event and history has it that there was never so much fun before or after they finally left.

Picko Troberg was a famous Swedish international driver of the 1960s and '70s. When funding was needed for a new grandstand at the *Atlas* corner he offered to pay for the construction if he could take 50% of the circuit's income for the next five years. This was when Formula 1 came to Sweden, and when the (bike) Road Racing World Championship decided to have a round at Anderstorp as well the grandstand became Picko's best-ever deal.

The circuit hosted many other events, most during the golden years of 1967–85. They included an AC/DC concert at the camp site beside the circuit, a display of 172 aeroplanes on the landing strip at one of the Grands Prix – still the highest known number of planes gathered at the same place in Sweden at the same time – wheelchair races, and the world's biggest orienteering competition, with 23,000 participants.

Bernie Ecclestone briefly negotiated to buy the Raceway in 1981. Plans were made to take Formula 1 back to Anderstorp but ultimately it all came to nothing.

All you needed in 1978 was a parasol, a couple of deckchairs and a (protected) platform, and you could watch Niki Lauda (Brabham) win very comfortably. (LAT)

COCKPIT VIEW

John Watson, who drove five Grands Prix there:

'It was in the middle of nowhere, it was basically a military airport base and usually very dusty. It had these long, slightly-banked, parabolic-type corners and didn't do an awful lot for most drivers.

'Ironically, to call it tricky wouldn't be entirely fair but certain cars, for a variety of reasons, seemed to work on it, whereas others which worked well everywhere else didn't work at Anderstorp.

'It wasn't a circuit that I would call a favourite. It was, rather, another racetrack that we had to go and compete on.

'Somewhere like Watkins Glen, for instance, oozed atmosphere, oozed all the things that really made you feel great about being a racing driver, but Anderstorp didn't do any of that. On a personal level, I didn't get a feeling of fulfilment and satisfaction.

'The whole thing about going to Sweden in the late 1970s was experiencing the freedom that that country had within its society, which we in Britain didn't have – at that point Sweden was a more advanced society

A bit rural but effective.

The cigar tells you who this is.

ABOVE: Something about Sweden encouraged physical abandon – in several forms, even in the late 1980s. World 250cc Motorcycle Champion Sito Pons is being thrown into the pool by Carlos Lavado of Venezuela.

RIGHT: The museum at the circuit, keeping memories alive.

LEFT: John Watson's Penske goes off on the first lap in 1976 when the throttle jammed.

RIGHT: This is 1976 and the podium parade: Niki Lauda (Ferrari), Carlos Reutemann (Brabham) and Clay Regazzoni (Ferrari) with Swedish artist Barbro 'Lill-Babs' Svensson handing out the garland.

than we were, more liberal, and you had the Scandinavian blondes, gorgeous, and the Swedes were nice people. It was quite different to what an Anglo-Saxon society might be – but as a racetrack it didn't tick very many boxes.'

EYEWITNESS

Anette Claesson, who lived on a farm close to the circuit:

'As most of the major races at Scandinavian Raceway were run in the middle of the Swedish summer, the heat was always a factor for competitors and visitors alike. In fact, the paddock itself featured a very popular swimming pool that became like a second home for team members throughout the weekends, although it has now been dismantled.

'The Formula 1 and Road Racing World Championship events really were very big happenings in the region and a point of interest for visitors from all the neighbouring Scandinavian countries. Such was the attention that all roads and streets surrounding the circuit were filled to, and over, their maximum capacity, and ever-growing queues became an almost inevitable reality.

'I remember standing in the garden of my family's farm in Bredaryd, some *15km* from Anderstorp, and watching the slow-running line of cars on their way to the circuit. Of course, in that day and age cars lacked the cooling capabilities of today and weren't made to stand still for what seemed like an eternity with their engines constantly running. Many cars literally began to boil!

'As everyone was excited and happy about the big guns rolling into town, there was a common feeling of responsibility to try and help in whatever way you could. I can still recall my family and I running to our well to grab some water for cooling, and the drivers, needless to say, were very thankful.

'Scandinavian Raceway turned into something that united us, and the people of Småland [the region in Sweden where the circuit is located] really woke up and contributed during those hectic summer months!'

MEMORIES AND MILESTONES

1973 Åsberg was right and the timing was good. Ronnie Peterson put his Lotus on pole and led to lap 78 of the 80 when

he had a puncture and couldn't stop Denny Hulme (McLaren) going by. He beat Peterson by 4.0 seconds. Fastest lap: Hulme 104.3mph/167.9kph.

1974 The circuit had been slightly modified for safety reasons. The corner at the end of the straight became an esse (right then left then right). James Hunt (Hesketh) pressured the Tyrrells of Jody Scheckter and Patrick Depailler, pole, towards the end but he couldn't catch them. Scheckter beat Depailler by 0.3 of a second. Fastest lap: Depailler 103.0mph (-1.3)/165.8kph (-2.1).

1975 The pits and access to them from the track had been improved. Vittorio Brambilla (March) took pole and led to lap 15 but had understeer and Carlos Reutemann (Brabham) went by. Niki Lauda (Ferrari) drove a beautifully tactical race from the third row and outpowered Reutemann on the straight on lap 70 of the 80 to win by 6.2 seconds. Fastest lap: Lauda 101.8mph (-1.2)/163.9kph (-1.9).

1976 Tyrrell had taken an astonishing step in building six-wheeled cars (four small at the front, two large at the back), although Mario Andretti (Lotus) led to lap 45 when he had an engine problem. The six-wheelers of Jody Scheckter, pole, and Patrick Depailler finished first and second 19.7 seconds apart. This was deceptive because the circuit suited them. Other circuits didn't. Fastest lap: Andretti 102.1mph (+0.3)/164.4kph (+0.5).

1977 Gunnar Nilsson (Lotus) won the Belgian Grand Prix two weeks before, which guaranteed the sort of attendance the race hadn't had in the previous couple of years. His team-mate Mario Andretti took pole. Maintaining the race's sense of difficulty and surprise, Jacques Laffite steered the Ligier to victory from the fourth row of the grid, beating Jochen Mass (McLaren) by 8.4 seconds. Fastest lap: Andretti 102.6mph (+0.5)/165.1kph (+0.7).

(On the original 1977 event poster for the race, Lauda's Ferrari carried Goodyear logos. Gislaved, a Swedish tyre manufacturer, were the main sponsors and so a second set of posters had to be printed. Although the biggest Goodyear logos were removed from the rear wing, smaller ones can still be found on the front of the car…)

Speed decrease 1973–7: 1.7mph/2.8kph.
Revisions to the circuit, increasing its length.

Patrick Depailler in the six-wheeled Tyrrell in 1976.

1978 Andretti (Lotus) took pole. Gordon Murray eclipsed the Tyrrell six-wheeler by introducing rear fans on the Brabhams, Lauda and John Watson driving them. At first they were regarded with light amusement but once they went out on to the track drivers following them found the fans sucked up debris and blew it back. The cars proved fast and while a crowd of 50,000 came the fans were being protested from half a dozen directions. The cars raced. Andretti (Lotus) led to lap 38 then Lauda led to the end (Watson spun off on lap 20), beating Riccardo Patrese (Arrows) by 34.0 seconds. The fans were banned. Fastest lap: Lauda 106.3mph/171.1kph.

Peterson died after the Italian Grand Prix at Monza in 1978, Nilsson from cancer a month later and, without them, the race was no longer viable.

FACTS OF THE MATTER

2.497m/4.018km circuit

Year	Winner
1973	D. Hulme (McLaren)
1974	J. Scheckter (Tyrrell)
1975	N. Lauda (Ferrari)
1976	J. Scheckter (Tyrrell)
1977	J. Laffite (Ligier)
Fastest pole	R. Peterson (Lotus) 1973 (107.2mph/172.6kph)
Fastest lap	D. Hulme (McLaren) 1973 (104.3mph/167.9kph)

2.505m/4.031km circuit

1978	N. Lauda (Brabham)
Pole	M. Andretti (Lotus) (109.9mph/176.8kph)
Fastest lap	N. Lauda (106.3mph/171.1kph)

BREMGARTEN

Location: Near Berne.
Constructed: 1931.
World Championship Grands Prix: 5.

The start, 1953: 24 is Giuseppe Farina (Ferrari), 46 Alberto Ascari in another Ferrari, 32 Juan Manuel Fangio (Maserati). (Courtesy Thomas Horat)

'It put a premium on driving skill, with uphill and downhill stretches, and very fast bends'

Piero Taruffi

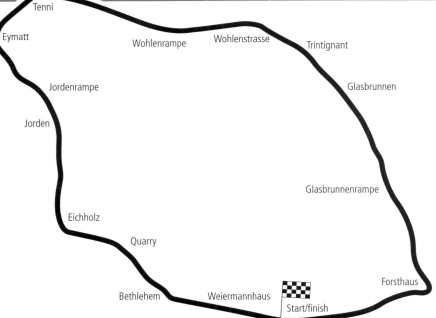

Tenni
Eymatt
Wohlenrampe
Wohlenstrasse
Trintignant
Jordenrampe
Glasbrunnen
Jorden
Glasbrunnenrampe
Eichholz
Quarry
Forsthaus
Bethlehem
Weiermannhaus
Start/finish

The way it was in the early 1950s, the long straight and Grandstand Bend.
(Courtesy Thomas Horat)

Fragments remain but not enough to recreate a circuit measuring 4.5 miles (7.2km). More confusing still, the fragments are ordinary roads, so that the route the circuit took is itself difficult to determine. Was it this road or that? Where could the pits and grandstands have been?

The last Grand Prix run at Bremgarten, which nestles into the outskirts of Berne in central Switzerland, was in 1954. If you watched as a ten-year-old you're a pensioner now. It was a long time ago, long enough for the soul of the circuit to have gone and been replaced by all manner of development. The pits and grandstands are now a motorway junction with slip roads and traffic lights.

It was originally built for racing motorbikes, and cars didn't come until 1934. Into the 1950s bikes and cars shared the Grand Prix meeting, creating a festival of speed.

There is a vivid description of the circuit.[1] It was 'equipped with a magnificent grandstand and well-built pits. The circuit was almost oblong in shape, but consisting of many slight bends which could be taken at great speed. The pits being situated on a loop road further behind the actual course, signalling from the pits themselves was impossible. Thus signalling stations were arranged on a bend before the grandstands and these were connected with the pits by special telephones. As the signalling stations were protected by sandbags they had the martial appearance to which we had not yet become accustomed in 1934.'

The track had no straight, its surface changed as it looped out into the woodlands – sometimes it was cobbled – and the screen of overhanging trees could create a dangerous shadowland in sunshine.

The descent through a place called *Eymatt* still exists (as a road with suburban houses down it). It's narrow and contorting. In the days of the circuit it was in the shape of a gentle slope with trees running towards the edge of the road, where there was a deep grassy verge and a wire fence strung between posts.

Today, after it has crossed a new main road it snakes into the wood, still narrow and hemmed by trees. The notion of Grand Prix cars in there is deeply alarming.

In the wet it could be lethal.

During the 1934 Grand Prix, in 'pelting rain', Briton Hugh Hamilton 'went into a wild skid in the wooded section'. His car, out of control, struck a tree, killing him instantly. In 1948 the great Italian Achille Varzi, practising for the Grand Prix, skidded on a damp surface. His Alfa Romeo almost halted after several spins but then rolled, crushing him. From this time on drivers were forced to wear crash helmets in Grands Prix.

The Swiss Grand Prix was a casualty of the Le Mans disaster when at least 80 people were killed after a Mercedes vaulted into the crowd and broke up. Motor racing in all but the most limited way ended and the 1982 'Swiss' Grand Prix was held at Dijon, a thinly disguised way of giving France another race. There have been none since, in Switzerland, France, or anywhere else.

COCKPIT VIEW

Piero Taruffi, who drove in two Grands Prix there:
'I like the Bremgarten course, because, like the Nürburgring and Spa, it put a premium on driving skill, with uphill and downhill stretches, and very fast bends; at the same time it was rather dangerous. Several of the fastest bends ran alongside sheer drops, and on top of all this the road was bordered by hefty fully grown trees ready to welcome anyone who went off the road. Many drivers fell victim to these, which, as so often happens, were retained for scenic reasons, without considering the toll of human life.'[2]

Mike Hawthorn, who drove in two Grands Prix there:
'It is a fast winding main-road circuit through a forest which has seen many spectacular crashes. There are various changes of surface, it is often wet and the trees keep some parts of the course damp long after others have dried out; if you leave the road you are almost certain to hit a tree or some other solid object and on fine days the rapid changes from light to shade make it difficult to see clearly.

'Personally I like the circuit, but the full two-day programme with motorcycle and sports car events before the Grand Prix meant that apart from the rubber and drops of oil which made the corners slippery, our race finished late, and we

The track remnants today, but the images remain almost terrifying – racing cars in exactly this. *(Author)*

had the setting sun right in our eyes on the most dangerous part of the course. It was blinding on the straight past the pits and came filtering through the trees past *Bethlehem Corner* and the chalk pits which followed and on up the hill to the *Eichholz Bridge.'*[3]

EYEWITNESS
Charles Riesen, resident of Berne:
'I was born in 1943 and lived in Berne.

My father managed a garage in the town, a BMW agency. From 1937 he raced, at the Avus [Germany], and at Hamburg, and plenty of mountain races. He was very successful. After the war he did mountain races again. So petrol came into my blood and Castrol R into my bones.

'I was there at the 1953 as a ten-year-old and again at the 1954 Grand Prix. In our house there were only two talking points, football and car races. I was interested in the races in Bremgartenwald [Bremgarten woods].

'In August 1953 I saw Farina and Ascari in their Ferraris fill the front row with Fangio's Maserati. I had an armband [pass] and could get near the pits. Before that there was the sports car race and my father started on the third row but as the first BMW driver. He finished fourth.

'The Grand Prix started at 14:50 and more than 75,000 spectators were round the circuit. They went mad – Ferrari finished first, second, and third. That third was Hawthorn in a perfect bow tie.

'I remember so well how I was sitting at the pits and watched from start to finish. I was so close that whenever a car was coming in I was told to move my legs!

'In August 1954 my father's BMW did not run properly. A good customer, a baker, was looking for people to go round with vendors' trays selling his wares and I was not able to get out of doing it. On the Saturday I had one full of cheese biscuits. I only saw parts of the sports car and motorbike races.

'About 4:00 I sold the last little biscuit – perhaps I even ate it, I can't remember – and I went across the track to the pits. I was wearing my father's armband so nobody stopped me. I was able to get very close to the legendary Mercedes team manager Alfred Neubauer and I had a good view of the drivers – and the wonderful Mercedes and Ferraris.

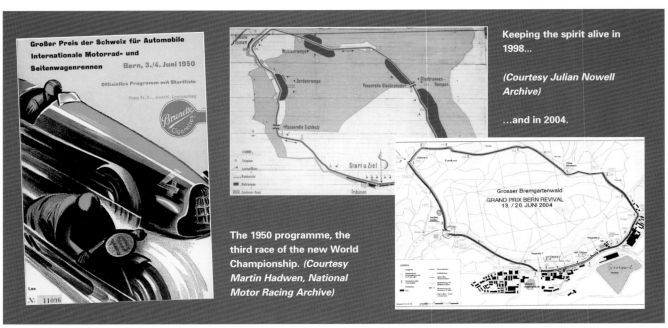

The 1950 programme, the third race of the new World Championship. *(Courtesy Martin Hadwen, National Motor Racing Archive)*

Keeping the spirit alive in 1998...

(Courtesy Julian Nowell Archive)

...and in 2004.

'On the Sunday I made a big detour to avoid the baker and I took up a place first at *Glasbrunnen*. You didn't have to pay to go in because most of the circuit is inside a big forest. So we had a lot of opportunities to go there via the forest. You could stand in the trees and watch the cars. It was extraordinary to be so close and it was not a problem. No fences, no barriers, no policemen, nothing!

'Then I went to the *Forsthaus* bend. I shall never forget the speeds: Juan Manuel Fangio followed closely by Karl Kling and Froilan González, and the young Hans Hermann behind the 3.4 Ferraris and Maseratis. Fantastic. I *lived* with Kling when he spun at *Forsthaus* and hit straw bales. He got out, restarted the dead Mercedes engine, jumped in, and set off again last. He drove sensationally to catch up with the others again.

'I saw Neubauer holding out a sign *RG* [*regolare* – steady!] to Kling, but unfortunately a technical problem [fuel injection pump] stopped the old master.

'I went to compete from 1962 to 1970, I was an aerobatic pilot and flying instructor. The petrol in my blood has not evaporated even today. I am a regular visitor to the Goodwood Festival of Speed and I have had great pleasure in being a member of the committee for the Swiss Grand Prix revival meetings [starting in 1998]. On the race weekends we get between 70,000 and 100,000 paying spectators.

'We can't use the original circuit any more because they have built modern roads. It's a little bit sad, but the new circuit that we have is very good. It's on the western side of the city of Berne near the original.'

MILESTONES AND MEMORIES

1950 This was only the third race of the new World Championship (excluding the Indianapolis 500). Juan Manuel Fangio put his Alfa Romeo on pole and led but a valve failed on lap 33. The Alfas, however, were supreme: Giuseppe Farina in one beat Luigi Fagioli in another by 0.4 of a second. Fastest lap: Farina 100.8mph/162.2kph.

1951 Stirling Moss's first visit and he judged the circuit as one which 'really sorted the men from the boys. I regarded it as a terrific challenge'.[4] In the wet, Fangio (Alfa Romeo), pole, beat Piero Taruffi (Ferrari) by 1 minute 15.3 seconds. He remembered it mainly 'because I had resisted the temptation to let myself be dragged down by superstition'. On the eve of the race, late, 'I invited two friends to take one or two laps of the track with me in my own car, as I wanted to memorise it down to the last detail, as it was rather tricky. Suddenly, what should happen but a cat darts out from some shrubs, and I ran it over! "You've killed a black cat!" they shouted in unison. They began to make jokes about how unlucky it was to kill a black cat, especially just before a race.'[5] Moss finished eighth. Fastest lap: 95.2mph (-5.6)/153.2kph (-9.0)

1952 The race was for Formula 2 cars. Farina (Ferrari), pole, led to lap 17 of the 62 when the magneto failed and Taruffi (Ferrari) beat Rudi Fischer (also Ferrari), a restaurant owner and useful amateur driver, by 2 minutes 37.2 seconds. Fastest lap: Taruffi 96.3mph (+1.1)/155.0kph (+1.8).

1953 Fangio (Maserati) took pole and Hawthorn (Ferrari) finished third – Alberto Ascari beat Farina by 13.2 seconds, both in Ferraris [see 'Eyewitness']. Fastest lap:

Ascari 101.0mph (+4.7)/162.5kph (+7.5).

1954 Froilan González (Ferrari) took pole. Hawthorn's Ferrari had a fuel pump failure. 'I took a look at the engine to make sure there was no escaping oil and no holes in the crankcase and then set off to walk back to the pits through the woods in the centre of the course. These woods are barred to the public during the race and the Swiss police use fierce Alsatian dogs to enforce the ban. One of them went for me, snarling and snapping, and it took the policeman in charge of it some time to calm it down.'[6] Fangio (Mercedes) beat González by 58.0 seconds. Fastest lap: Fangio 102.0mph (+1.0)/164.1kph (+1.6).

Speed increase 1950–4: 1.2mph/1.9kph.

Footnotes
[1] *Dick Seaman*, Chula. [2] *Works Driver*, Taruffi. [3] *Challenge Me the Race*, Hawthorn. [4] *My Cars, My Career*, Moss. [5] *My Racing Life*, Fangio. [6] *Challenge Me the Race*, Hawthorn.

The track is swept just before the start of the 1954 race and now Fangio (Mercedes) leads it, as he will every lap. (Courtesy Thomas Horat)

FACTS OF THE MATTER

4.524m/7.280km circuit

Year	Winner
1950	G. Farina (Alfa Romeo)
1951	J.M. Fangio (Alfa Romeo)
1952	P. Taruffi (Ferrari)
1953	A. Ascari (Ferrari)
1954	J.M. Fangio (Mercedes)
Fastest pole	J.M. Fangio 1951 (104.5mph/168.1kph)
Fastest lap	J.M. Fangio 1954 (102.0mph/164.1kph)

ISTANBUL

Location: 30 miles (48km) from Istanbul.
Constructed: 2005.
World Championship Grands Prix: 5.

Istanbul had everything except spectators. (Courtesy David Corbishley)

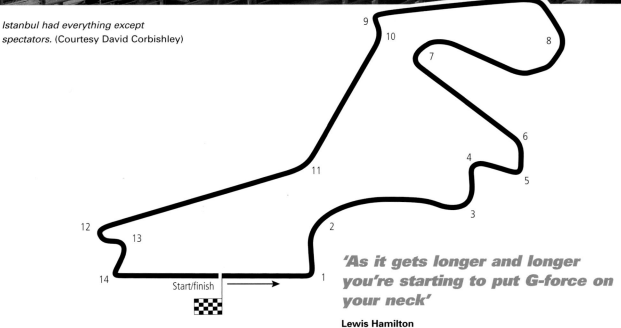

'As it gets longer and longer you're starting to put G-force on your neck'

Lewis Hamilton

In a sense a Turkish Grand Prix symbolised Grand Prix racing's direction, because Turkey straddled Europe and Asia. Grand Prix racing was doing the same.

The circuit, running anticlockwise and undulating, was designed by the ubiquitous Hermann Tilke. It runs across four level sections with rising and descending gradations. It has 13 corners (six right-handers, seven left-handers), some of them reflecting famous corners on long-established tracks.

The main stand seats 30,000, and other stands, plus what have been described as 'natural ground stands', bring the capacity to 155,000.

A backdrop we have come to know on our journey through the circuits: sloping countryside dense with trees. In the foreground Jarno Trulli leads Toyota team-mate Timo Glock in 2009. Trulli would be fourth, Glock eighth. (LAT)

COCKPIT VIEW

Lewis Hamilton, McLaren, 2009:
'If you don't get the first apex right here you will miss the other two and either lose a lot of time or possibly run wide and go off. The speed is very scary. Imagine going straight on there. What's the fastest you have driven on the motorway? Imagine doing 170mph around this bend with that run-off and not lifting off the pedal. Most people would get hesitant and start lifting. For sure if any of you drove this track you would be doing it at 60mph.

'Turn 8 gets tighter and tighter and heavier and heavier on the steering wheel. The first part is not that physical but as it gets longer and longer you're starting to put G-force on your neck. The corner lasts for seven or eight seconds. The compression on your body and your guts – they are shot to the right side of your body.

'You can certainly feel the compression, especially when the car starts to bottom out at about 150mph. If you can't take it flat out you have to compromise. But I reckon the Red Bulls, the Ferraris, and the Brawns will be able to take it flat here – certainly the Red Bulls. I reckon I will lose two- or three-tenths on this corner compared to the guys taking it flat this weekend.'[1]

EYEWITNESSES

Steven Tee, LAT Photographic:
'I know the drivers all love it because it's got that Turn 8 and they built it with quite challenging corners. We've had some good races there – it's where Hamilton

had his mega race in GP2 so it does allow overtaking to a degree.

'Again in a similar vein to China, and built after China, I think it was the ultimate extension of race circuits being ridiculously too big, too wide, and with too big run-off areas. They're like Sainsbury's car parks. If you're a photographer, imagine you're trying to shoot a tiny little car on the far side of the car park.

'I think they have all the perspectives wrong. It doesn't come across on

television or in pictures as the exciting lap that all the drivers talk about experiencing, and it's so difficult to take pictures which allow the readers of our magazine [*Autosport*] any indication that you're in Turkey. There's nothing to hang it on.'

David Corbishley, New Jersey:
'We were watching the hamburger stand at the Turkish race as the fire fighters tried to put out the fire, and a number of us started a conversation on Formula 1 food. The

The fire which provoked the discussion about circuit food. (Courtesy David Corbishley)

ABOVE: East meets West in Turkey and Grand Prix racing has another crossroads. (Courtesy David Corbishley)

RIGHT: Scaling the heights, Istanbul, 2009. They'd see Jenson Button in the Brawn command the race. (LAT)

BELOW: The turn into the start/finish straight. (Courtesy David Corbishley)

consensus among the more widely travelled was: Spa the worst, Monza the best.

'At Spa the only food was sausage and chips, and you had to go through two lines to get them both. Monte Carlo was highly rated because they control prices to everyday level.

'At Indy the prices are very reasonable, the labour provided by local charities as a fund-raising activity. After the problems the first year [see Indianapolis entry] they sent us a letter offering a cooler with a selection of beer, soft drinks, and food that could be picked up at the track on race day.'

MILESTONES AND MEMORIES

2005 Kimi Räikkönen (McLaren) totally dominated this first Grand Prix, taking pole from Giancarlo Fisichella (Renault), leading every lap of the race – even his two pit stops – to beat Championship leader Fernando Alonso (Renault) by 18.6 seconds. Fastest lap: Juan-Pablo Montoya (McLaren) 140.9mph/226.7kph.
2006 Young Felipe Massa did something extraordinary. He out-qualified his Ferrari team-mate Michael Schumacher for

pole, led every lap except four during his second pit stop, and beat Alonso (Renault) by 5.5 seconds, Schumacher third. Fastest lap: Schumacher 135.7mph (-5.2)/218.4kph (-8.3).
2007 Massa took pole again, this time from Lewis Hamilton (McLaren), and led every lap except four (pit stops) – although on lap 43 during his second stop Hamilton led briefly before his right-front tyre exploded. He nursed the car back to the pits with fingertip control and finished fifth. Massa beat Ferrari team-mate Kimi Räikkönen by 2.2 seconds. Fastest lap: Räikkönen 136.8mph (+1.1)/220.1kph (+1.7).
2008 The Suzuki team travelled to the circuit but had gone bust and didn't get in. Massa (Ferrari) confirmed his emotional attachment to the circuit by taking another pole and leading all but 16 laps to beat Hamilton (McLaren) by 3.7 seconds. Fastest lap: Räikkönen (Ferrari) 138.0mph (+1.2)/222.1kph (+2.0).
2009 Sebastian Vettel (Red Bull) took pole. The Brawn year, and that meant the Jenson Button year. He equalled the record of six wins from the first seven races held by Jim Clark and Michael

FACTS OF THE MATTER

3.317m/5.338km circuit

Year	Winner
2005	K. Räikkönen (McLaren)
2006	F. Massa (Ferrari)
2007	F. Massa (Ferrari)
2008	F. Massa (Ferrari)
2009	J. Button (Brawn)
Fastest pole	K. Räikkönen (McLaren) 2005 (137.6mph/221.4kph)
Fastest lap	J.-P. Montoya (McLaren) 2005 (140.9mph/226.7kph)

Schumacher after leading all but one lap (pit stop). He beat Mark Webber (Red Bull) by 6.7 seconds. Fastest lap: Button 136.3mph (-1.7)/219.4kph (-2.7).

Speed decrease 2005–9: 4.6mph/7.3kph.

Footnote
[1] Courtesy McLaren.

All the Armco in the world can't prevent this: Giancarlo Fisichella (Force India) meets Kazuki Nakajima (Williams) on the first lap in 2008. (LAT)

ABU DHABI

Location: Yas Island on the east coast of Abu Dhabi.
Constructed: 2009.
World Championship Grands Prix: 1.

ABOVE AND OPPOSITE TOP: Grand Prix racing's new world, futuristic, stunning and impossibly remote from the beginning of the World Championship at Silverstone 1950. (Vodafone/LAT)

'There is enough overhead lighting to make it blend seamlessly from day into night'

David Coulthard

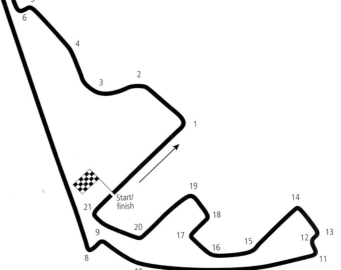

The Yas Marina Circuit set a completely new standard for Grand Prix racing. That is almost an understatement. It was billed as the $1 billion circuit and Bernie Ecclestone was moved to say nothing could top it although he hoped somebody would try.

It was announced at a Formula 1 Festival at Abu Dhabi in 2007, with a contract running from 2009 to 2016. It would become the sport's first day-night race (start 17:00 local time).

Hermann Tilke designed the 3.4-mile (5.5km) track, incorporating nine right-hander corners and 11 left. They are driven anticlockwise. The width ranged between 12 and 15 metres and the start/finish straight (546 yards/500 metres long) was the widest.

Up to 50,000 spectators could watch from permanent, covered grandstands or VIP suites.

A marina was built to accommodate more than 150 yachts, with space for 20 at 100 feet or more and six of what were described as mega yachts.

COCKPIT VIEW

David Coulthard, previewing the Grand Prix:

'Having had the opportunity to drive the circuit, what struck me is that it's a two-stage track. The first half of the lap, until corner Nine, is typical of the new type of track. There's the fast section at the beginning from Turn One to the Turn Four tight hairpin with the grandstand literally overhead, giving great viewing for the spectators.

'The 1.2 kilometre back straight should give an opportunity for some slipstreaming and overtaking and then the back section of the circuit has a real street circuit feel to it where you come along the section that takes you to the hotel and then passes underneath it, via a series of 90-degree right-handers and left-handers before opening out to the end of the lap and a medium speed corner on to the start/finish straight.

'The pit lane entry is very challenging, as is the exit, which is actually in a tunnel under the circuit and is going to make it particularly challenging for the drivers coming out of pit stops. There are great facilities and air-conditioned garages which will make working conditions in the heat a little bit easier, and also having an evening race will obviously take some of the heat out of what can be a very hot venue.

'I think the twilight aspect of the race will be more of a visual treat for the spectators and the TV audience but for the drivers it will be absolutely fine because there is enough overhead lighting to make it blend seamlessly from day into night, no problem.'

EYEWITNESS

Steven Tee, LAT Photographic:

'I had no idea what to expect going there for the first time. I'd been to Dubai and I didn't really like it and I think I expected it to be an extension of that.

'They couldn't have looked after us better. We were staying literally two minutes away from the paddock in a very nice hotel and you could walk to the track from it every day. I didn't come off Yas Island the whole time I was there because I didn't need to.

'The working conditions – the Media Centre and the photographers' area – were 21st century. They'd listened to everybody and done it absolutely right.

'The actual circuit is fantastic for photographs. Obviously you have this modern moonscape and then you add a day-night race so you've got the sunset. Just brilliant.

'I always walk a new circuit on the Thursday to have a look around. I did it at dusk, which was when the cars were going to be running, and you really did feel as if you had been transported into one of those video games.

'The whole place is just perfect. They couldn't have been nicer people and it is another great addition to Formula 1.'

MILESTONES AND MEMORIES

2009 Lewis Hamilton (McLaren) took pole and looked likely to win but a brake problem halted him. Sebastian Vettel (Red Bull) won what, in truth, was an uninspiring race against an inspiring backdrop, enlivened at the end by Jenson Button (Brawn) launching determined – and fruitless – assaults on Mark Webber, Vettel's team-mate. Button, in feisty mood, had overtaken team-mate Rubens Barrichello on the opening lap after Barrichello and Webber touched. Vettel beat Webber by 17.8 seconds, Button an eye-blink further back. Fastest lap: Vettel 123.9mph/199.4kph.

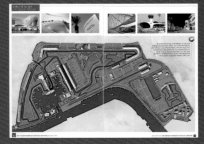

The British Automobile Racing Club were prominent as marshals at the inaugural Abu Dhabi Grand Prix.

FACTS OF THE MATTER

3.451m/5.554km circuit

Year	Winner
2009	S. Vettel (Red Bull)
Pole	L. Hamilton (McLaren)
	(123.1mph/198.1kph)
Fastest lap	S. Vettel (123.9mph/199.4kph)

USA

DALLAS

Location: Dallas city centre.
Constructed: 1984.
World Championship Grands Prix: 1.

The big dipper in the background – and foreground. René Arnoux (Ferrari) stays ahead of Niki Lauda (McLaren), and both keep away from the walls. (All pictures courtesy of David Corbishley)

'It was a good circuit, a tough circuit'

Derek Warwick

Start/
finish

UNITED STATES OF AMERICA

There is a deeply astonishing statistic: nine. Since 1950 that is the number of different circuits the World Championship has visited in the United States – more than any other country, even France (seven), Spain (six), or Britain (a mere four). The statistic reflects the nomadic nature of the attempt to interest Americans in it, and their ambivalence to it. The nine circuits hosted a total of 44 races – fewer than Monza or Monaco. On the nine, only Watkins Glen in upstate New York became anything like a regular, with an unbroken run between 1961 and 1980. Others might have done – Long Beach (eight) and Detroit (seven) – but they are memories now.

Between 1950 and 1960 the Indianapolis 500 was regarded as a round of the Championship (making it more authentically a World Championship), even though it was entirely self-sufficient and nothing to do with Formula 1. This has cluttered and complicated the record books ever since. Paradoxically, when the Brits went there and did well – Jim Clark, Graham Hill, Jackie Stewart – it was no longer a round of the Championship.

The race at Dallas captured the overall ambivalence between Grand Prix racing and the United States. It was a road circuit round the Cotton Bowl stadium,[1] and the speeds reflected that. In first qualifying Mansell (Lotus) was fastest with a lap averaging 89.9mph (144.7kph) while team-mate de Angelis had the fastest speed crossing the line, 133.7mph (215.2kph). That was 6 July. Five weeks before, 117 cars entered the Indy 500 and Chris Kneifel became the last driver – ever – to qualify at *under* 200mph.

What did Americans, who knew all about the Indy 500 and nothing about Formula 1, make of the 89.9mph lap? Nor would the words of Niki Lauda have mollified them much. 'This layout, particularly for a city circuit, is a very quick one but there are no run-off areas, which can make it more dangerous at the speeds we are running out there, and the surface is very bumpy. If you are going quick then you will hit the wall quick.'

The organisers of the race wanted to promote the city, and money talks. 'The awareness that will be raised, not just by television coverage but by people coming from all over the world, will help a lot of people to learn that Dallas is more than the television program,' said Donald R. Walker, a real estate investor and moving force driving the race, while the Mayor, A. Starke Taylor Jr, added that 'the Grand Prix will show that Dallas is an international city and an action city'.

The promoters spent an estimated $2.5 million resurfacing the roads, putting in the concrete barriers, and constructing temporary stands. There was a social dimension, too, with events like a chilli cook-off[2] and a charity ball.

Not everyone was happy, as Peter Applebome of *The New York Times* reported. 'International glamour notwithstanding, the event is getting a cooler reception from the people in the predominantly black, low-income neighborhoods surrounding the park. Many have complained that the race is a noisy intrusion about which they were never consulted.

'"It shows a total disrespect for the neighborhood,"' said a black Dallas City Councilwoman, Diane Ragsdale. "It's an age-old problem here."

'The Dallas Black Chamber of Commerce, which has worked with the Grand Prix to get some contracts for minority businessmen, says it supports the event and thinks it will be good for black businesses. But Tom Houston, the chamber's executive director, stopped short of enthusiasm. "We're in the ghetto here," he said. "Having the Prince of Monaco come to Fair Park and hobnob with folks at the Cotton Bowl isn't that important to black businessmen or black people in the area."'

The drivers were confronted by 100° heat and a concrete-lined circuit. The concrete, they complained, concealed potential hazards, the surface was too bumpy, and there weren't enough run-off areas. That Friday during first qualifying the track temperature rose to 150° and the track surface began to break up. This became so bad that an hour before the race new concrete was being laid. The drivers asked for ten reconnaissance laps but this was refused, no doubt because of television schedules. (Jacques Laffite arrived at the circuit at seven in the morning for the warm-up in his pyjamas, as a protest against this scheduling, the race due to begin at 11:00am.)

The fight for second place in 1984, Elio de Angelis (Lotus) holding off René Arnoux (Ferrari) – for the moment.

COCKPIT VIEW

Derek Warwick, Renault, 1984:

'Everybody remembers two things about Dallas. One, how hot it was because of the humidity – as soon as you walked outside you were absolutely dripping wet, but, two, it was good to go to Dallas because at the time you had the soap on British TV.[3] Everybody had it in their minds.

'The circuit was at a place called Fair Park, a typical street circuit. It had something like 14 corners and, being a street circuit, it was obviously tight. You had two straights but with chicanes in the middle so they weren't really straights.

'In fact, it was a good circuit, a tough circuit, and generally in our day winning meant somebody who was easy on their cars because the cars were unreliable and you had to look after them on the way.

'Overtaking is an art form on street circuits and you can be two or three seconds faster *or* slower than the car in front and still not get by, so Dallas was a very difficult circuit and passing almost impossible – I got a good run on Nigel Mansell to take the lead in the race but I got caught out on the loose and just clipped the barrier with my rear wheel – it could have been my first win but for that bit of stupidity. The circuit was breaking up and it did catch me out.

'I loved street circuits, because they were more difficult in some ways than any other kind. A lot of people talk about the fantastic Spa, the amazing Nürburgring and places like that but I think that when you go to a street circuit you have to be on your game, you have to be completely focused and if you lose concentration for one split second you hit the wall. That, to me, made a big difference.

'You had Graham Hill winning Monaco five times and that's extraordinary.'

For once the mechanics had their own audience but the actual pits were … standard.

EYEWITNESSES

Didier Braillon: *Grand Prix International* magazine, July 1984:

'The man has collapsed on a canvas folding chair under the dubious shade of a makeshift plastic tent. Sprawled there like a limp rag doll, his overalls around his waist, Ayrton Senna sweats. The ice pack on his head has a hole in it and rivulets of ice water are trickling down his face. "I've had it," he says. The Toleman-Hart has just done about ten laps around the circuit.

'Over at Brabham, Corrado Fabi has a wet towel wound round his neck. In a few minutes he'll be putting on his helmet, which has been covered with an asbestos foil, and wedging himself into the car's cockpit. Looking at it, one sees several places where the carbon fibre has white spots here and there surrounded by little puffs of smoke. The thin tube has been packed with pounds of dry ice.

'A few metres away, at Renault, work is going on underneath the steel overpass crossing the track. "They've even bought up the shade," complains someone, not in the best of faith.'

Mike Harris, *The Associated Press*, 8 July 1984.

'The start of the opening practice was delayed more than 3½ hours because a violent thunderstorm early Thursday morning knocked out communications around the circuit. And the delay was extended when track maintenance crews had to weld some manhole covers in place so the suction from the speeding race cars wouldn't pull them up.

'[9 July] Track crews had to work throughout the night and into the morning hours Sunday to repair portions of the temporary 2.424-mile, 16-turn circuit which had crumbled from the pounding of the 900-horsepower cars. In fact, the usual 30-minute warm-up session was canceled and the drivers were given just three laps of warm-up prior to the start of the race.'

Unsigned, *New York Times*:

'The heat turned the race into a survival course and a test of endurance for the drivers and tires. Two days of time trials and air temperatures as high as 104 degrees caused the track's asphalt to crumble in the corners, causing spinouts. Several drivers pounded into the concrete walls. No serious injuries were reported.

'At 3 a.m., crews attempted to repair the damaged track by digging out the corners and pouring in a special epoxy cement, which was expected to dry in 45 minutes. One of the batches of cement was faulty, however, and the cement had to be reapplied before the race's scheduled start at 11 a.m.'

MILESTONES AND MEMORIES

1984 Nigel Mansell (Lotus) took pole. Larry Hagman, the undisputed star (and villain) of the TV series, started the race while nearby people watched from private, white-tented boxes at $25,000 each. Fourteen cars spun off and/or hit the walls and only seven were running at the end. They deserve naming: Keke Rosberg (Williams), René Arnoux (Ferrari), Elio de Angelis (Lotus), Jacques Laffite (out of his pyjamas by now, Williams), Piercarlo Ghinzani (Osella), Corrado Fabi (Brabham), and Manfred Winkelhock (ATS).

Ayrton Senna (Toleman) had a driveshaft failure after clipping a wall. In the debrief he was adamant that the wall must have moved and, to placate him, team-member Pat Symonds walked with him to where it had happened. He and Senna saw that another car must have hit the block earlier, fractionally disturbing it so that one edge now protruded a tiny amount. That tiny amount was what Senna hit. The wall *had moved.*

Eddie Cheever (Alfa Romeo), who crashed after eight laps, said crisply: 'It's a feat just to stay on the track the whole race.'

FACTS OF THE MATTER

(2.424m/3.901km circuit)

Year	Winner
1984	K. Rosberg (Williams)
Pole	N. Mansell (Lotus)
	(89.9mph/144.7kph)
Fastest lap	N. Lauda (McLaren)
	(82.8mph/133.3kph)

Rosberg beat Arnoux by 22.4 seconds. Neither they, nor Senna, nor Symonds, nor anyone else in Grand Prix racing would pass this way again. Fastest lap: Niki Lauda (McLaren) 82.8mph/133.3kph.

Footnotes
[1] The Cotton Bowl Classic, a college football game played every year from 1937 at the stadium called after it. [2] I had no idea what a chilli cook-off might be. I am grateful to an American journalistic colleague, E.L. Gordon, for enlightenment. 'Chili cook-off is exactly what you think. People make what they think is their best chili (there's a raging debate on whether chili can include beans or not), following the contest rules, and then a panel of judges tastes the entries and declares a winner. For example, a food company that makes a hot sauce or Tabasco can stipulate that the entrants must use their product in the chili. Or a company that makes beans, etc. Texans make a big deal of chili cook-offs, but they are not the only ones. Some of these contests offer prize money.' [3] The *Dallas* soap opera – revolving round oil, money, and beautiful women – became compulsive television viewing in Britain.

The traditional way to move a Formula 1 car on any circuit.

DETROIT

Location: Detroit city centre.
Constructed: 1982.
World Championship Grands Prix: 7.

The towering presence of Ayrton Senna prepares to go round the towering presence of downtown Detroit, 1986 – and win, of course. (LAT)

Turn 8
Beaubien Street
Turn 9
Congress Street
Turn 7
Turn 6
Turn 5
Turn 10
Woodward Avenue
Larned Street
Turn 4
Jefferson Avenue
Turn 12
Woodbridge Street
Washington Boulevard
Turn 14
Turn 11
St Antoine Street
Turn 13
Kodak Camera Corner
Goodyear Tunnel
Atwater Street
Turn 2
Turn 16
Turn 3
Turn 15
Ford Corner
Turn 19
Turn 17
Turn 18
Turn 20
Start/finish
Turn 1

'You turned 90 degrees, sprinted, turned 90 degrees, sprinted'

Patrick Tambay

The idea of a Grand Prix round downtown Detroit made little sense at one level and very good sense at another. The race could never escape that paradox.

Little sense: the nature of the track prevented overtaking and real speed, which – like Dallas to come, and Phoenix – caused bemusement to an American public weaned on the Indy 500. It also offered manhole covers, which modern Formula 1 cars had not encountered before and which they did not like. Truth to tell Alain Prost, a purist, didn't like the place at all and he was not alone.

Very good sense: any Grand Prix in the United States was better than none (and two, Long Beach and Detroit, better than one). Detroit – the Mo-town of song – was looking elderly and exhausted and haunted by inner city problems, its automotive giants harried by the Japanese and Germans. What better way to symbolise rejuvenation than by having a Grand Prix, with all that that brought with it?

The track would zigzag through the grid pattern of streets round the giant Renaissance Center skyscraper, itself symbolising rejuvenation. There were, however, immediate problems, which prompted the locals to ask *what are they doing here?* And

Mauricio Gugelmin in the March.
(Courtesy Kris Heber)

the Formula 1 fraternity to ask *what are we doing here?*

The track had six 90° turns, a hairpin after the pits, bridges, a tunnel, and the concrete-clad walls which punished error.

COCKPIT VIEW
Ayrton Senna, Lotus, 1987:
'It's probably the hardest circuit physically because of difficult breathing and high humidity. Hopefully this year with the new surface we will have a lot less bumps?

'You need high downforce because of the low grip surface and low average speed. It's quite hard on brakes and you need maximum cooling because of the hot weather.'

Ayrton Senna would win the 1987 race.
(Courtesy Camel)

Patrick Tambay, who drove three Grands Prix there:
'It was narrow and used the roads which ordinary Americans used. It wasn't resurfaced. You turned 90°, sprinted, turned 90°, sprinted between concrete walls with fencing and chicken wire on top. The crowd was used to IndyCar racing but it was important that Formula 1 had a presence in the United States.'

EYEWITNESSES
Kris Heber, from Detroit, now living in Windsor, Ontario.
'I am 36 years old and I became hooked on Formula 1 after going to Watkins Glen in 1979. Detroit was an entirely different experience but the allure was still there. I always loved the fact that the teams all had different-looking cars, and back in those days, they all sounded different too.

'The Detroit Grand Prix is not going down in history as an all-time classic event but it did serve the purpose of bringing the series to many fans in the area. Yes, the drivers complained about the track being dull and bumpy, and they were probably right to do so, but they got on with it for seven years and I was there for every session.

'On Friday, 4 June 1982, we filed into the stands at the end of the pit straight and waited for the first ever practice session to begin … and waited … and waited. The track wasn't even close to being ready. Finally, at 4pm, the ATS-Ford of Eliseo Salazar emerged and accelerated towards the first left-hander. The next time around, seeing an F1 car scream down Atwater Street along the Detroit River for the first time was an awesome sight. It was Formula 1 in our own backyard.

'The drivers probably enjoyed the relative anonymity here. Some made the leisurely walk to the track right down the sidewalk in front of the

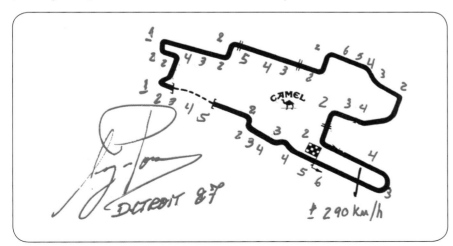

RenCen [Renaissance Center] without disruption other than an occasional autograph seeker.

'Another unique aspect of Detroit was that, because there were no pit garages of any kind, the teams had to pack everything up and move to Cobo Hall (a building like an aircraft hangar) every night. The public was allowed to walk around the aisles and watch the teams disassemble their cars up close.

'My favorite driver was René Arnoux and one year I watched as he and his Ligier mechanics pored over telemetry data (maybe trying to figure out why his left-front wishbone returned to the pits with a 90° bend!) before turning around to pose for some quick shots.

'Some teams were always swarming with activity (Ferrari), and others … not so much. Once, it looked like the AGS crew just parked the car and took off for dinner. The Tyrrell team actually demonstrated some of the capabilities of their new Data General computers for us one year. Even as a young kid, I thought it a very nice gesture.

'The race itself generated some heroic drives over the years. John Watson passed everyone in sight as he climbed from 17th to win the 1982 race of course. Two years later, Martin Brundle had the crowd on edge as he nearly reeled in Nelson Piquet in the closing stages. Most memorable for me though was Arnoux and team-mate Jacques Laffite running 1-2 for a few laps in 1986 after Ayrton Senna had to pit with a puncture.

'We were certainly the only ones in the stands actually cheering loudly for Ligier. Arnoux eventually stopped coming past and we knew he was done for the day (no big screen TVs back then). It turned out he hit the back of a broken down Williams while pushing too hard. It was one of René's last great drives and sadly had no result to show for it. I bet he was one that never claimed the circuit was dull.'

Roger Hart, AP Photographer:
'The start of a Formula 1 race is arguably the most exciting and dangerous time of the race. I knew the pressure was on me to make sure I had the photo if something were to happen. But because that position would be staffed only on race day, I talked my way into getting to shoot from the pits for the two qualifying days

before the race. I convinced the photo editor, who would later become a good friend, that I understood racing and should get the assignment.

'No question about it, both of these assignments, working the pits during qualifying and shooting from the tower on race day, were plum. Most of the AP photographers were covering corners, waiting for "incidents" of cars contacting the wall. For all seven Formula I races in Detroit, this was my routine: Friday and Saturday I worked the pits during practice and qualifying, occasionally getting a chance to walk around some of the circuit, then the stint in the Turn one tower for the race. During practice and qualifying, unless there was a crash in a corner, the majority of the photos sent out on the AP wire came from the pits. Candid shots of drivers and their cars were what photo editors wanted. But in seven years of covering this race, shooting more than 100 rolls of film, only about 30 or so of my photos were ever published.

'So, you will not see any photos of race winners spraying champagne or hoisting a trophy or being kissed by a beauty queen. I never had a chance to shoot victory circle. The closest thing I have to a celebration shot is a

driver raising a hand acknowledging the checkered flag. And it was not until Formula 1 abandoned Detroit and the race was run with cars and drivers from CART that I had a chance to shoot what became a signature shot from the race: a car making a turn in front of the *Spirit of Detroit* sculpture.'[1]

MILESTONES AND MEMORIES

1982 A special untimed practice on the Thursday had to be cancelled because the track wasn't ready. During Friday, concrete blocks and tyre walls were added and the cars didn't go out until late afternoon. Two qualifying sessions were scheduled for the following day but rain prevented the second of them.

Reigning champion Nelson Piquet had turbo problems and didn't make the grid at all. Alain Prost (Renault) took pole from Andrea de Cesaris (Alfa Romeo). Crashes halted the race and from the restart John Watson (McLaren) – using all his race craft in overtaking – worked his way into the lead and kept it. Watson beat Eddie Cheever (Ligier) by 15.7 seconds. Fastest lap: Prost 81.3mph/130.8kph.

1983 Piquet (Brabham) ought to have won it from the front row (René Arnoux, Ferrari, pole) but a puncture on lap 51

The iconic emblem of Detroit, the Renaissance Center with Nelson Piquet (Williams) in the foreground, 1986, and Satoru Nakajima, who had the most unenviable job in Formula 1 – partnering Senna. (Courtesy Camel)

FACTS OF THE MATTER

2.493m/4.012km circuit

Year	Winner
1982	J. Watson (McLaren)
Pole	A. Prost (Renault)
	(82.7mph/133.1kph)
Fastest lap	A. Prost (81.3mph/130.8kph)

Corners eased, 2.500m/4.023km circuit

1983	M. Alboreto (Tyrrell)
1984	N. Piquet (Brabham)
1985	K. Rosberg (Williams)
1986	A. Senna (Lotus)
1987	A. Senna (Lotus)
1988	A. Senna (McLaren)
Fastest pole	A. Senna (Lotus) 1986
	(91.6mph/147.3kph)
Fastest lap	A. Senna (Lotus) 1987
	(89.6mph/144.2kph)

of the 60 took that from him and young Michele Alboreto (Tyrrell) inherited it. Alboreto beat Keke Rosberg (Williams) by 7.7 seconds. Fastest lap: Watson (McLaren) 83.6mph (+2.3)/134.5kph (+3.7).

1984 Nigel Mansell (Lotus, second row) made a dynamic start, trying to get between Prost's McLaren and Piquet's Brabham, pole. Mansell and Piquet touched. Other cars became involved and the race had to be stopped. Piquet won the restart from Martin Brundle (Tyrrell) – later stripped of the result because of a Tyrrell fuel irregularity. So Piquet beat Elio de Angelis (Lotus) by 32.6 seconds. Fastest lap: Derek Warwick (Renault) 84.7mph (+1.1)/136.4kph (+1.9).

1985 Senna (Lotus), pole, led but chose the wrong tyres. Rosberg (Williams) chose the right tyres and led but with 13 laps left pitted. The engine temperature was rising alarmingly – a plastic bag was blocking an air intake. The pit crew changed tyres – which Rosberg did not want – but he came out ahead and stayed ahead. He beat Stefan Johansson (Ferrari) by 57.5 seconds. Fastest lap: Senna 85.2mph (+0.5)/137.1kph (+0.7).

1986 Senna took pole in the Lotus because precision was everything and he was very, very precise. In the race he had an early puncture but, again using precision, moved from eighth to the lead. He beat Jacques Laffite (Ligier) by 31.0 seconds. Fastest lap: Piquet (Williams) 88.9mph (+3.7)/143.1kph (+6.0).

1987 Senna had the Lotus 'active' suspension and it liked Detroit a lot: from the front row he ran second to half-distance when Mansell (Williams, pole,

The 1988 race. Sandro Nannini in the Benetton (Courtesy Kris Heber)

leading) made a pit stop for tyres. Senna didn't stop. He beat Piquet (Williams) by 32.8 seconds. Fastest lap: Senna 89.6mph (+0.7)/144.2kph (+1.1).

1988 Turbo engines ought to have been at a disadvantage round Detroit but Senna, pole, won it from Prost by 38.1 seconds and, of course, both their McLarens had

turbos. No other car finished on the same lap. Fastest lap: Prost (McLaren) 85.8mph (-3.8)/138.2kph (-6.0).

Speed increase 1982–8: 4.5mph/7.4kph.

Footnotes
[1] In *Postcards from Detroit*, reproduced by kind permission.

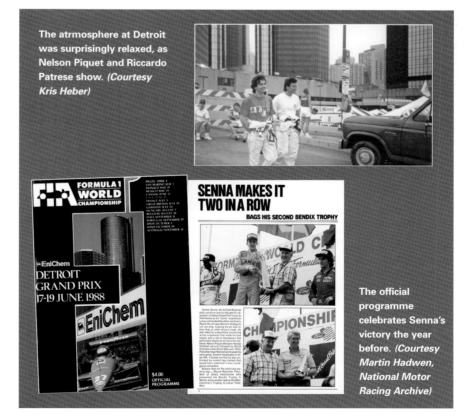

The atrmosphere at Detroit was surprisingly relaxed, as Nelson Piquet and Riccardo Patrese show. *(Courtesy Kris Heber)*

The official programme celebrates Senna's victory the year before. *(Courtesy Martin Hadwen, National Motor Racing Archive)*

USA

INDIANAPOLIS

Location: 6 miles (10km) west of city centre.
Constructed: 1909.
World Championship Grands Prix: 6.

ABOVE AND OPPOSITE: The first banking for Formula 1 cars since Monza in the 1950s. (Courtesy David Corbishley)

'We Europeans are probably a bit more chicken than Americans!'

Michael Schumacher

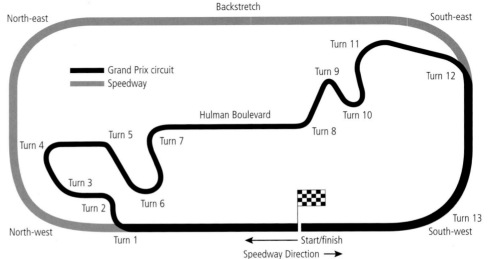

North-east Backstretch South-east

Grand Prix circuit
Speedway

Turn 11
Turn 9
Turn 12
Hulman Boulevard
Turn 10
Turn 8
Turn 5
Turn 7
Turn 4
Turn 3
Turn 2
Turn 6
Turn 1
North-west
Turn 13
South-west
Start/finish
← Speedway Direction →

The Brickyard, originally constructed of three million bricks in 1909, had arguably the richest history of any circuit in the world. It was the oldest and its annual 500-mile race attracted the largest one-day crowd (400,000) for any sporting event on earth.

Until the year 2000, that history involved being entirely self-sufficient and linked to Grand Prix racing tenuously. As we saw in the introduction, the 500 counted as a round of the World Championship from 1950 to 1960 although the winners sound unfamiliar to Grand Prix followers. One man, Troy Ruttman, spanned both, however briefly. He won the 500 in 1952 and competed in the 1958 French Grand Prix at Reims in a Maserati (and did not start in Germany after an engine problem).

It is true that in the 1960s British drivers went to the Indy 500, reaching a climax in 1966 when Graham Hill beat Jim Clark, Jackie Stewart sixth, and Hill said sardonically 'We'd better have a special prize for the leading American finisher.' This, of course, was not to be confused with or even made an extension of Grand Prix racing.

Tony George, who owned the speedway, decided to bid for a proper Grand Prix in 2000 and built a track using about a mile of the oval, including the banked south-west corner, with the rest snaking through the infield. It cost an estimated £30 million, measured 2.6 miles (4.1km) and went clockwise, in contrast to racing in the United States.

George had made an astute move. Some five years before, he'd set up his own championship, the IRL (Indy Racing League), to promote oval racing, breaking it away from the traditional IndyCar championship (CART, Championship Auto Racing Teams).

George came under pressure to make conciliatory moves but instead reached for the Grand Prix.

COCKPIT VIEW

Michael Schumacher, Ferrari, 2000:
'I did not find it difficult to adapt to the track. Going round the turns on the oval is not as exciting as it might look outside the cockpit because the entry speed is not so high. This means the element of danger is also reduced compared to what we might have expected.

'You can imagine that if you went faster how much the banking would help and satisfy you but on the other hand you have the wall right next to you. You know, we Europeans are probably a bit more chicken than Americans!

'The fact that the track is so flat means that it takes a few laps to find the right turn-in point for the corners.'

EYEWITNESSES

Steven Tee, LAT Photographic:
'I'd never been to Indy before we went for the first Grand Prix. I'd love to go to the Indy 500 but it always clashes with Monaco.

'My abiding memory of going, especially in the first couple of years, was that real feeling of Americana about the whole place. You stood on the grid and the girls holding the pit boards were dressed in stars and stripes outfits with great long red boots with stars on them.

'Then somebody sang – the way they do at American sports events – the national anthem, and the whole place went completely silent. Everybody stood up and they were hands on chests – everybody in the crowd. At the end they all went mental! You did feel that you were at a big event and that it mattered. That was with 250,000 people. Imagine what the Indy 500 would be like with 400,000.

'The old grandstands had a genuinely iconic sense about them and you'd got the cars going over the bricks, that classic vertical scoreboard, although the infield was Mickey Mouse. Basically they were passing time until they came back on to the straight again.

'There was always something going on in those Indy years, like the debacle over the tyres.

'It was a good addition to the calendar.

We'd go from Montréal (and the Canadian Grand Prix) to New York or Chicago and you'd get your little fix of America. The last couple of years we drove down from Chicago through the West to Indy and you had a real feeling of America. You were doing it the American way.

'Indianapolis is a small city, good restaurants, reasonable hotels, and lots of people who flew in for the race, Colombians when Montoya was racing, Brazilians, Canadians, and people from all over the place. Friday and Saturday night the city had a vibe about it: the Grand Prix was the only thing in town.

'You go to Shanghai, for instance, you wouldn't really know there was a Grand Prix going on. You did at Indianapolis.'

David Corbishley, New Jersey:
'They ran out of *beer*, and food, too, for that matter. I mention this because it points out how traditional Indianapolis is, especially the first year the US Grand Prix was there. As we constantly heard over the public address system, "Well, at the 500 we…"

Indianapolis felt like a big deal – and was.
(Courtesy David Corbishley)

'Indianapolis is famous for the 500-mile race every year around the US Memorial Day holiday and takes the full month of May between practice sessions, Fast Friday, Pole Day, Bump Day, carburetion day (even though the cars don't use carburetors) and finally the actual race. And why is *Gasoline Alley* called that when the cars in the 500 haven't used gasoline in decades? Tradition, of course.

'Because of the 500, Indianapolis is a great place to go for a race. Numerous hotels, more seats than any race track in Formula 1 (at the time anyway, with 257,325 permanent seats, over 400,000 with temporary in-field seating), friendly people and a location experienced in running a race and having large crowds. Compared to any of the other racetracks I have been to in recent times the prices for hotel rooms, race tickets, and food are a bargain. After a small general admission fee, seats were free for practice and qualifying and a great seat on race day was only $85.

'You arrive at the racetrack, and around the exterior, hanging from the grandstands, are giant banners honoring Indy 500 winners such as Jimmy Clark, and Graham Hill. From street level you enter and go down a tunnel that passes underneath the racetrack and resurfaces

to present the Speedway Museum (a great place to visit for only a few dollars).

'To your left is the new pit structure, paddock, and race control. On your right you will find the Formula 1 Experience vendor area and rolling landscape where you can sit and watch the proceedings for no extra charge.

'The run through the oval curve and down the start/finish straight before heading into the road section allowed for great drafting and exciting braking into that tight right-hand turn into the road course. With most people sitting along both sides of the start/finish line straight, everyone was standing for the start and the first lap coming off the banked, sweeping curve with engines at full scream. One of the most exciting experiences I've had in attending Formula 1 racing.

'So why did they run out of beer and food? The tradition at the 500 – a tradition I had never heard of, like most of the Europeans attending, I'm sure – is for people to bring their own. You are allowed a cooler measuring no more than 14 inches by 14 inches by 6 inches containing up to 24 cans of beer, your fried chicken and potato salad, or whatever you choose.

'At Watkins Glen we were always able to bring our own food, but if I go to a football game beverages will be taken away. The teams want to sell as much over-priced food and drink as they can. In America we are so used to *not* being allowed, and others from around the world

didn't know, that we didn't bring anything to Indy. The Speedway, however, expected the Formula 1 crowd to be like the 500 crowd … and didn't have enough beer and food vendors open to meet the demand.'

MILESTONES AND MEMORIES

2000 The first United States GP for a decade (Phoenix, 1991, the last) attracted a crowd of some 225,000. They saw Michael Schumacher (Ferrari) on pole but David Coulthard (McLaren) took the lead and held it to lap seven, when he was penalised for jumping the start. Schumacher beat team-mate Rubens Barrichello by 12.1 seconds to lead the Championship. Fastest lap: Coulthard 125.5mph/202.0kph.

2001 The race was run three weeks after 9/11 and there was a question over whether it would be run at all. A crowd estimated at 170,000 came to show their appreciation that it was. Schumacher had pole again but this time brother Ralf (Williams) alongside him. Michael led, team-mate Rubens Barrichello led, Michael again, Juan-Pablo Montoya (Williams), Michael, Mika Häkkinen, Barrichello, then Häkkinen to the end – a triumph for his one-stop strategy (he only pitted on lap 46). Fastest lap: Montoya 126.0mph (+0.5)/202.7kph (+0.7).

2002 The race of stupidity. Ferrari had been vilified for ordering Barrichello to pull over and give the Austrian Grand Prix to Schumacher. Now Schumacher, pole, and Barrichello were so dominant that they decided to try and stage a dead heat: how to lose friends and uninfluence people, especially Americans who'd paid hard cash to witness what they assumed would be a race. Fastest lap: Barrichello 128.9mph (+2.9)/207.5kph (+4.8).

2003 Kimi Räikkönen (McLaren) took pole. There were six leaders during the 73 laps but Schumacher (Ferrari) emerged as the winner and Montoya (Williams) finished sixth, removing him from the Championship. Fastest lap: Schumacher 131.2mph (+2.4)/211.1kph (+3.6).

2004 Barrichello (Ferrari) took pole. The race moved to June for the first time. Team-mate Schumacher, a man for all seasons, of course, won but only after brother Ralf (Williams) crashed after nine laps, striking the wall with terrible ferocity. Fastest lap: Barrichello 133.2mph (+1.0)/214.4kph (+3.3).

2005 Jarno Trulli (Toyota) took pole. The race of shame, which wasn't a race at all. Michelin's tyres couldn't cope with the banking (Turn 13) and the company was forced to advise its customers (all but Ferrari, Jordan, and Minardi) that it was dangerous unless speeds could be slowed at the Turn. They all withdrew after the parade lap, leaving the six Bridgestone runners on a ghostly grid. The great American public, 130,000 of them, made their feelings very, very clear. Fastest lap: Schumacher 131.2mph (-2.0)/211.1kph (-3.3).

2006 After 2005, would there be a 2006? Yes, and the race was entirely normal: seven cars crashed on the opening lap and Schumacher, pole, won from new Ferrari team-mate Felipe Massa. Fastest lap: Schumacher 129.0mph (-2.2)/207.5kph (-3.6).

2007 Lewis Hamilton, pole, won after a wheel-to-wheel moment with McLaren team-mate Fernando Alonso as they veered together at almost 200mph on the straight. The race, however, was overshadowed by Tony George and Bernie Ecclestone failing to reach an agreement over the race's future. It had no future, immediately anyway. Fastest lap: Räikkönen (Ferrari) 128.2mph (-0.8)/206.4kph (-1.1).

Speed increase 2000–7: 2.7mph/4.4kph.

FACTS OF THE MATTER

2.605m/4.192km circuit

Year	Winner
2000	M. Schumacher (Ferrari)
2001	M. Häkkinen (McLaren)
2002	R. Barrichello (Ferrari)
2003	M. Schumacher (Ferrari)
2004	M. Schumacher (Ferrari)
2005	M. Schumacher (Ferrari)
2006	M. Schumacher (Ferrari)
2007	L. Hamilton (McLaren)
Fastest pole	R. Barrichello (Ferrari) 2004 (133.5mph/214.9kph)
Fastest lap	R. Barrichello (Ferrari) 2004 (133.2mph/214.4kph)

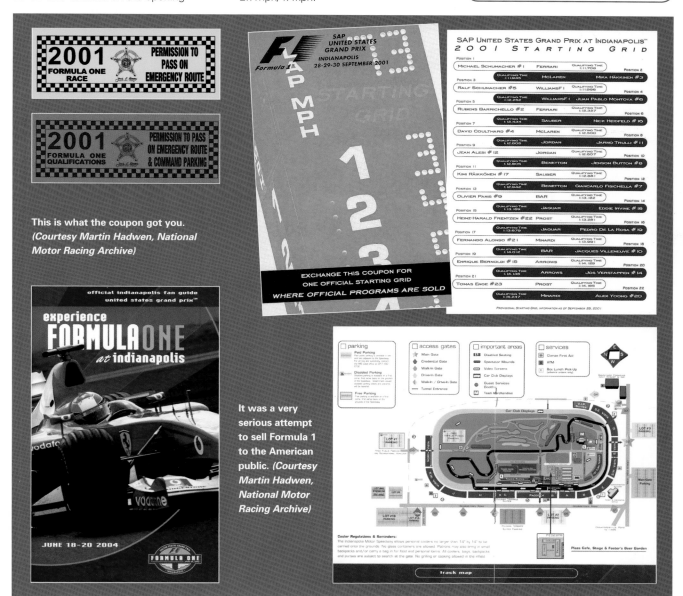

This is what the coupon got you. *(Courtesy Martin Hadwen, National Motor Racing Archive)*

It was a very serious attempt to sell Formula 1 to the American public. *(Courtesy Martin Hadwen, National Motor Racing Archive)*

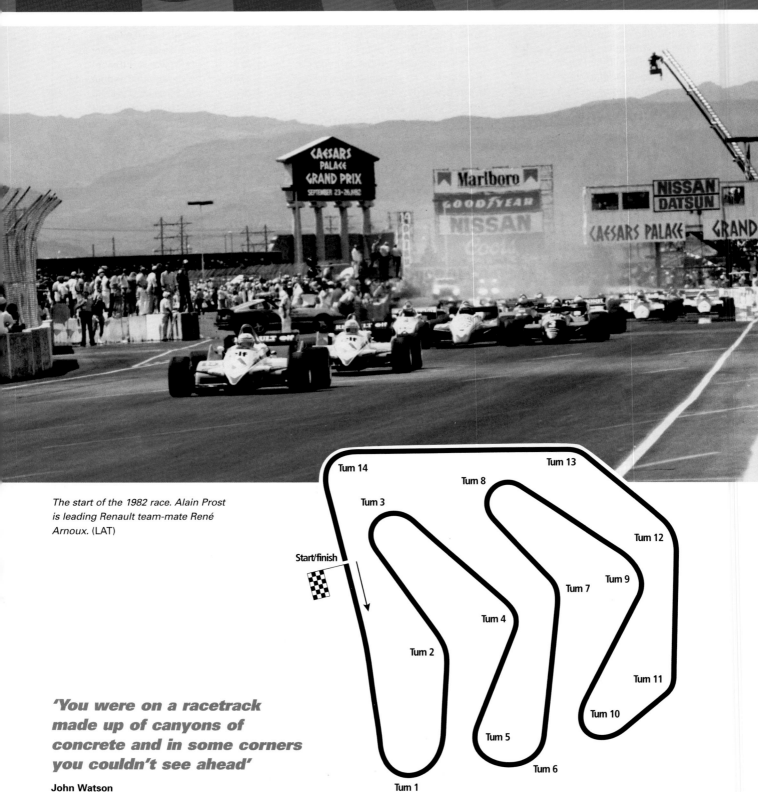

USA
LAS VEGAS

Location: West side of the Las Vegas 'Strip'.
Constructed: 1981.
World Championship Grands Prix: 2.

The start of the 1982 race. Alain Prost is leading Renault team-mate René Arnoux. (LAT)

Turn 14

Turn 13

Turn 8

Turn 3

Turn 12

Start/finish

Turn 4

Turn 7

Turn 9

Turn 2

Turn 5

Turn 11

Turn 6

Turn 10

Turn 1

'You were on a racetrack made up of canyons of concrete and in some corners you couldn't see ahead'

John Watson

If you look at the circuit map you wonder what the Grand Prix fraternity, never mind the Grand Prix cars, would make of something resembling an octopus in agony. In fact, as *Autocourse* pointed out: 'The organisers, with guidance from Chris Pook and his Long Beach team, had done a surprisingly good job. The track was wide, the surface smooth and local taxi drivers had been called in to season the tarmac. The corners were not too tight: first gear would not be necessary after all; the back section could be taken flat although the organisers did not plan it that way.'

Of it, Keke Rosberg would say: 'The track itself was sandy but tracks that were specially built and only used for that were always sandy. I think it was the first time computer analyses were used for a brand new track where we had never been before and it worked unbelievably well in terms of the aero package and things like that. It was a hard circuit on the driver, physically tough. You were constantly turning left.'

It was within the car park of Caesars Palace Hotel and was lined with interconnecting concrete barriers. The cars went anticlockwise.

Both races there, as it happened, were not only the final races of the season but the Championship deciders.

COCKPIT VIEW

John Watson, who drove in both Grands prix there:

'Racing round a car park is not exactly motor racing. You'd got these totally artificial corners. Once the tarmac and concrete we were racing on got rubber down the grip improved and some of the corners were actually challenging corners.

'The biggest difficulty was that you were on a racetrack made up of canyons of concrete and in some corners you couldn't see ahead – see if somebody had spun on the exit, because the barriers were higher than the level of the cars. That was a downside.

'The challenging corners were 4, 8, 9 and then coming through 11, 12 and 13. The quicker corners were the problem in that if you got it wrong you were going to go off very quickly and hit something very hard. The maximum speed was 150mph coming down through 14.'[1]

EYEWITNESS

Eric Bhat, *Grand Prix International*, 28 October 1981:

'It's becoming increasingly clear that Grands Prix of the future will take place where there is money, where racing can capture the public's imagination. Formula 1 has often been referred to as a circus, but that circus is becoming increasingly flexible. If you can run a Grand Prix in a car park, then the circus can come to any town. Today Las Vegas, where tomorrow? Probably New York. And, after that, who knows: London? Paris? Tokyo? Los Angeles?

'It seems that any promoter who can guarantee the money demanded by the constructors can host a Grand Prix. After that, it's simply a matter of finding a wide road, some concrete blocks to mark out the track, a big garage to house the cars, and you've got a race. But we'd like to think that real street racing takes place in streets used by the public every day, not in car parks.

'The Caesars Palace Grand Prix proved that the circus can come to town. It was a real race, tough on the drivers and hard on the cars. In a word, it was demanding, just what a Grand Prix should be. But it's a policy that some will find hard to stomach. Formula 1 is resolutely turning its back on traditional circuits like Spa, Nürburgring and Clermont-Ferrand. Its future appears to be in the circus that comes to town.'

MILESTONES AND MEMORIES

1981 Reportedly the residents of Las Vegas (who you'd have thought would have been shockproof) were shocked when Derek Daly took his March out to baptise the circuit, the suggestion being that they didn't know Formula 1 was in their midst and didn't know how loud Formula 1 engines were. Carlos Reutemann (Williams) took pole. Alan Jones (Williams) won, beating Alain Prost (Renault) by 20.0 seconds. Nelson Piquet (Brabham) finished fifth, enough for the Championship. Fastest lap: Didier Pironi (Ferrari) 101.9mph/163.9kph.

1982 Rosberg 42 points going in, John Watson (McLaren) 33, Prost (Renault) 31, and Niki Lauda (in the other McLaren) with 30 but appeals were pending over his exclusion from the Belgian Grand Prix so he was not necessarily out of it. Prost took pole. Watson finished a gallant second 27.2 seconds behind Michele Alboreto (Tyrrell). Prost was fourth, but fifth was enough for Rosberg. Fastest lap: Alboreto 102.5mph/165.0kph.

Speed increase 1981–2: 0.6mph/1.1kph.

Footnote
[1] *1982*, Hilton.

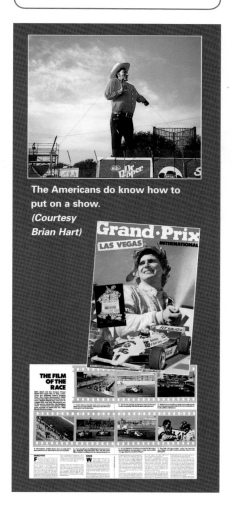

The Americans do know how to put on a show. *(Courtesy Brian Hart)*

USA
LONG BEACH

Location: Waterfront, southern Los Angeles.
Constructed: 1975.
World Championship Grands Prix: 8.

'You could imagine the film Bullitt and Steve McQueen driving that Mustang'

John Watson

Californians did seem interested in Formula 1 – look at them looking at Carlos Reutemann (Williams) and René Arnoux (Renault) in practice in 1980. (Courtesy Bill Wagenblatt)

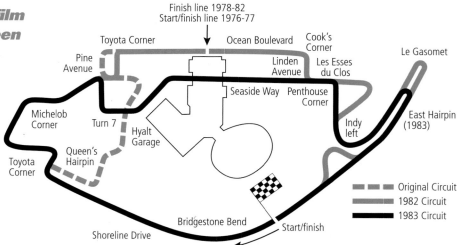

Finish line 1978-82
Start/finish line 1976-77

Toyota Corner

Ocean Boulevard

Cook's Corner

Pine Avenue

Linden Avenue

Les Esses du Clos

Le Gasomet

Seaside Way

Penthouse Corner

Michelob Corner

Turn 7

Hyatt Garage

East Hairpin (1983)

Indy left

Queen's Hairpin

Toyota Corner

Bridgestone Bend

Start/finish

Shoreline Drive

- - - Original Circuit
—— 1982 Circuit
—— 1983 Circuit

The talk, inevitably perhaps, was of recreating Monaco to rejuvenate the rather run-down Long Beach area. British entrepreneur Chris Pook was the moving force behind the idea and the City Fathers liked it.

The circuit measured 2.02 miles and *felt* Californian – the *Queen Mary* was forever moored nearby with a red British phone box on the quay beside it (so this had to be California), and where else could you find *Penthouse Corner?*

The track itself would evolve into something highly unusual with the start and finish at different points. In its original configuration – a Formula 5000 race in 1975 (won by Brian Redman) opening the way for a Grand Prix in 1976 – it had five 90° corners, two hairpins, and a long, curving spine called Shoreline Drive. Since the 5000 race, however, the track had been slowed by tightening the corners.

Autocourse recorded its satisfaction about how the track was physically put together, finding 'the short lengths of stout concrete blocks that formed the basic barrier system' was just one example. 'Lifted into place by truck-mounted cranes, joined by lengths of debris fencing, they were something that seemed safer and at the same time more practical than the standard

Armco-in-a-socket in use at European street circuits.

'Armco there was, at certain points, but mounted not on posts but on 50-gallon oil drums weighted with sand and connected with brackets hooked over the rims. Instead of catch-fencing, walls exposed to head-on attack by cars were protected by nests of interlaced discarded tyres. The very layout of city streets meant that almost every sharp corner was easily provided with an escape road. Altogether, it was

The start in 1980. Nelson Piquet (Brabham) leads Patrick Depailler (Alfa Romeo, 22) and René Arnoux (Renault, 16). (Courtesy Bill Wagenblatt)

a barrier system that could easily be put into use in any town in the world.'

The Grand Prix lasted until 1983 when it moved to CART. The 1984 race attracted an entry of 39 and was won by Mario Andretti, which gave it a familiar feeling.

COCKPIT VIEW
John Watson, who gave an astonishing performance in 1983:
'It was very much a matrix street track, almost the antithesis of Watkins Glen in terms of its layout. Principally it was stop-go, stop-go.

'The circuit went through a few metamorphoses in the years when the Grand Prix was held there but essentially it was like any street track – in America, particularly: zero grip when you start but picking up grip as you go through the Grand Prix weekend.

'In its original guise we went up on to what was a main street. You climbed up to it and you could imagine the film *Bullet* and Steve McQueen driving that Mustang round the streets of San Francisco. You had that little bit of elevation, and the sharp turns right and then right again at the end of the straight. Then you had

to go down again and that was exciting because the car would get elevated, light on its toes and so on, but effectively there was not a single what I'd call quick corner on it. There were challenging corners but they were low-speed.

'You had the concrete straightaway then you'd go on to a variety of different surfaces – almost like an infield. It was a bit of a *scratcher's* circuit – but it was a racetrack, same for everybody, got to make the best of it and on some occasions I achieved that, on other occasions I didn't.

'However, the whole thing wasn't just about racing. It was not far from Hollywood, it was just outside Los Angeles in California with the sunshine, the *Queen Mary* in the harbour and so on. It was very exciting. If you want to call it the Monaco of the west coast of America, you can.'

EYEWITNESS
Martyn Pass, now PR Manager, Audi UK Sport Press
'I'd been attending motor races throughout Europe for almost 20 years but nothing could have prepared me for my first race in North America in 1980 – for a combination of reasons.

'Long Beach is a coastal suburb of Los Angeles and so, unusually, I used public transport – a bus – to get to the track each day. Another unusual aspect was wearing a T-shirt and shorts, especially in March.

'I'd been to a number of Grands Prix, including Monaco, but this was totally different. The *Queen Mary* liner was moored close by to the track while Howard Hughes' Flying Boat, the *Spruce Goose*, was housed in a massive hangar, but the overriding memory was that of superb organisation, excellent food outlets, the F1 "paddock" housed inside one massive building ... and the American "fans".

'Hundreds, probably thousands, of massive motorhomes lined much of the perimeter of the circuit. Spectators sat in deckchairs on top of these huge, beautifully liveried machines or cooked all manner of food on barbecues.

'The interesting thing was that it was as if the motor racing, or specifically the Grand Prix, was of secondary importance – the vast majority of "home" US fans hadn't a clue about the cars or drivers contesting the "main" event.

'I'm sure the Toyota Celebrity race was more interesting to the majority of casual US spectators. And then there were the signs being held up by males who had been drinking alcohol for much of the day, suggesting the local Californian female fans showed off their assets! Simply ... unbelievable.'

MILESTONES AND MEMORIES

1976 A tumult of an introduction because only 20 cars could start (like Monaco the circuit couldn't accommodate a full grid) and seven failed to qualify. Of those who raced five had accidents, including James Hunt (McLaren), who claimed very loudly that Patrick Depailler (Tyrrell) shoved him off. Clay Regazzoni, pole, beat Niki Lauda in the other Ferrari by 42.4 seconds. Fastest lap: Regazzoni 87.5mph/140.8kph.

1977 The tumult continued. Carlos Reutemann (Ferrari) left his braking late for the first corner, creating a concertina of chaos behind and allowing the three cars in front – Jody Scheckter (Wolf), Mario Andretti (Lotus), and Lauda (Ferrari), pole – to escape. Scheckter led to lap 76 of the 80 but a deflating tyre let Andretti through. He beat Lauda by 0.7 of a second. Fastest lap: Lauda 87.9mph (+0.4)/141.4kph (+0.6).

The chaos brought a new starting point on Ocean Boulevard which was on the opposite side of the circuit to Shoreline Drive, where it had been.

1978 Reutemann (Ferrari) took pole. Of the 22 starters only 11 were running at the finish. Reutemann (Ferrari) beat Andretti (Lotus) by 11.3 seconds. Fastest lap: Alan Jones (Williams) 88.5mph (+0.6)/142.4kph (+1.0).

1979 The tumult endured. Reutemann's

Long Beach was an authentic street circuit, even if it really wasn't Monaco. (Courtesy Linda Carlson)

The grid at Long Beach was very Californian: relaxed. Keke Rosberg doing what he invariably did – talking. (Courtesy Brian Hart)

FACTS OF THE MATTER

2.020m/3.251km circuit

Year	Winner
1976	C. Regazzoni (Ferrari)
1977	M. Andretti (Lotus)
1978	C. Reutemann (Ferrari)
1979	G. Villeneuve (Ferrari)
1980	N. Piquet (Brabham)
1981	A. Jones (Williams)
Fastest pole	N. Piquet (Brabham) 1980 (93.6mph/150.6kph)
Fastest lap	N. Piquet 1980 (91.1mph/146.6kph)

Major reconstruction, 2.130m/3.428km circuit

1982	N. Lauda (McLaren)
Pole	A. de Cesaris (Alfa Romeo) (87.8mph/141.3kph)
Fastest lap	N. Lauda (84.4mph/135.9kph)

Shortening, 2.035m/3.275km circuit

1983	J. Watson (McLaren)
Pole	P. Tambay (Ferrari) (85.1mph/136.9kph)
Fastest lap	N. Lauda (McLaren) (82.9mph/133.5kph)

Lotus failed on the warm-up lap and after he pitted he wanted to take his place on the dummy grid. He was told he'd start from the pit lane after the racing cars had gone by – since the pits were still on Shoreline Drive they'd have covered half a lap by then. The racers did the parade lap but Gilles Villeneuve (Ferrari), pole, found nobody waving him to his position on the grid and took them round on a second parade lap. The gearbox on Jacques Laffite's Ligier locked, the car marooned across the track. The start had to be restarted. Twenty-four cars did that and only nine finished, Villeneuve beating team-mate Jody Scheckter by 29.3 seconds. Fastest lap: Villeneuve 89.6mph (+1.1)/144.1kph (+1.7).

1980 A repeat: 24 started, but ten finished. Regazzoni (Ensign) was not among them. His brakes failed along Shoreline Drive and he went into the short escape road at high speed, scattering a tyre wall and striking concrete blocks so hard he moved them. He never walked again. Nelson Piquet (Brabham), pole, beat Riccardo Patrese (Arrows) by 49.2 seconds. Fastest lap: Piquet 91.1mph (+1.5)/146.6kph (+2.5).

1981 Patrese (Arrows) took pole. Twenty-four started, eight finished, led by Jones, the defending Champion, whose Williams beat team-mate Reutemann by 9.1 seconds, Piquet (Brabham) third at 34.9 seconds. Fastest lap: Jones 89.9mph (-1.2)/144.7kph (-1.9).

Speed increase 1976–81: 2.4mph/3.9kph.

The circuit changed because a major construction project was being undertaken in Long Beach. The hairpin at the end of Shoreline went and among the changes a new section – a right, a left, two rights – added. The finishing line followed the starting line from Ocean Boulevard to Shoreline Drive.

1982 Andrea de Cesaris (Alfa Romeo) took pole to general astonishment but Lauda (McLaren) won the race, beating Keke Rosberg (Williams) by 14.6 seconds. Fastest lap: Lauda 84.4mph/135.9kph.

The hairpin feeding on to Shoreline Drive was shortened.

1983 Subsidence created a bump on steep Linden Avenue, which pitched Formula 1 cars into the air and made the drivers very, very unhappy. Quick-setting cement applied overnight solved the problem. Patrick Tambay (Ferrari) took pole. The McLarens had qualifying problems (John Watson on the 11th row, Lauda the 12th). They finished in that order – but first and second, disproving absolutely the notion that you can't overtake on street circuits. The margin was 27.9 seconds. Fastest lap: Lauda 82.9mph/133.5kph.

The beautiful people came, just like Monaco. This is Linda Vaughn, described as auto racing's Golden Girl. (Courtesy Linda Carlson)

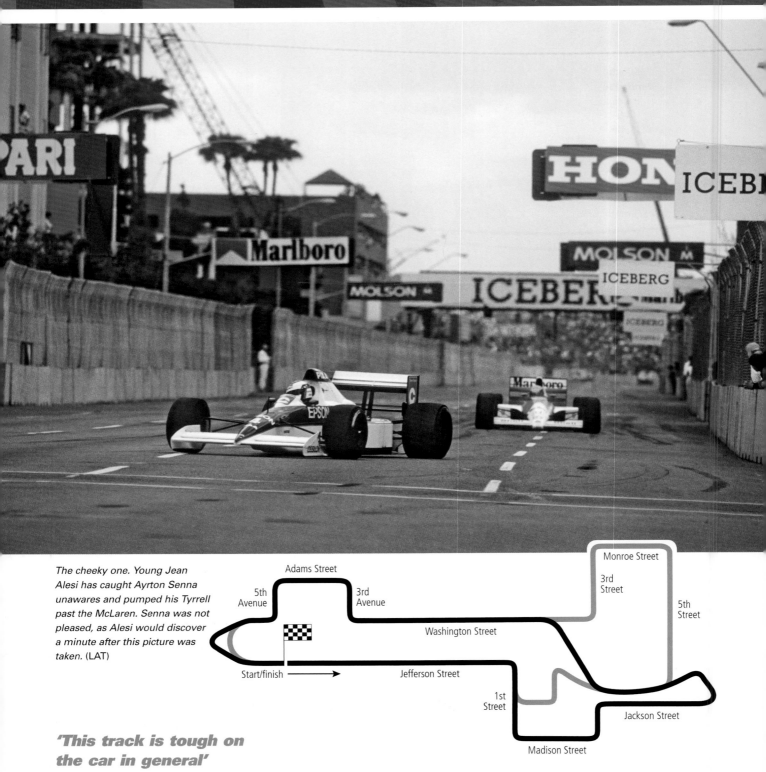

USA

PHOENIX

Location: West of city centre.
Constructed: 1989.
World Championship Grands Prix: 3.

The cheeky one. Young Jean Alesi has caught Ayrton Senna unawares and pumped his Tyrrell past the McLaren. Senna was not pleased, as Alesi would discover a minute after this picture was taken. (LAT)

Monroe Street

3rd Street

Adams Street

5th Avenue

3rd Avenue

5th Street

Washington Street

Start/finish →

Jefferson Street

1st Street

Jackson Street

Madison Street

'This track is tough on the car in general'

Derek Warwick

Another street circuit, and another which didn't interest Americans much – a (hopefully scurrilous) source suggests that one year an ostrich race attracted a bigger crowd.

Autocourse dismissed the track as 'simply another stultifying street circuit charting an anonymous path between featureless concrete barriers with mesh catch-fencing.'

Derek Warwick all alone and avoiding all that other traffic – but the Lotus would have a rear suspension failure. (LAT)

COCKPIT VIEW

Derek Warwick, who drove in the 1989 and 1990 Grands Prix:

'Phoenix is a nice circuit, fairly difficult, but interesting. This track is tough on the car in general; on the gearbox because there are so many changes, and on the tyres because you take a lot out of them with wheel spin in each of the corners. The brakes play a great part as well. For the driver, it's definitely tough to start the season with a street circuit.'

EYEWITNESS

Steven Tee, LAT Photographic:

'It was like Detroit: they built it right in the downtown business district, not where anybody lived. They lived in Scottsdale (a suburb) and the hotels were there.

'It was a 90° point-and-squirt circuit: straight, 90° turn, straight, but above the debris fencing – always mandatory in America because of all the insurance problems – you did have an American city, skyscrapers, great big, shiny glass buildings.

'I quite liked it, actually, even though the locals didn't care. We got there a few days early and we went off and did the favourite pastime in Phoenix, a thing called tubing: you take a lorry tyre up to the top of a fast-flowing river, you jump in, sit, and cruise down the river all day, watching the desert either side of you.

'The resort hotels out in Scottsdale

were brilliant and it was a good race from a social point of view. It was a real shame the Phoenixers, or whatever they call themselves, didn't give a damn about it. And Phoenix is a long way from anywhere, so people weren't necessarily going to travel to watch it.

'Phoenix has grown massively since we were there and maybe now it has a big enough catchment area that they would care about it.'

MILESTONES AND MEMORIES

1989 McLaren were mighty and this is what they made of the circuit after first qualifying. Ayrton Senna: 'It was obviously extremely hard work on what was a very low grip surface.' Ron Dennis: 'As you would expect on a street circuit like this, getting a quick lap is a most difficult challenge. The qualifying rubber seems to throw the cars a little bit out of balance, but that might have been partly due to the increase in ambient temperature this afternoon.' Senna took pole. Alain Prost (McLaren) beat Riccardo Patrese (Williams) by 39.6 seconds. Fastest lap: Senna 90.4mph/145.5kph.

1990 Gerhard Berger (McLaren) pole. The race became Round 1, the move bringing temperatures of 80° rather than the 105° of the year before. The race also became famous (briefly) because Senna

(McLaren) overtook Jean Alesi (Tyrrell) into Turn 1, ran fractionally wide and, with the speed and venom of a rattlesnake, Alesi almost instantaneously took him back. Senna beat Alesi by 8.6 seconds. Fastest lap: Berger 93.3mph/150.2kph.

Speed increase 1989–90: 2.9mph/4.7kph.

The track was revised, a curve bypassing three 90° corners at Monroe street and making the near hairpin final corner into a loop. The idea was to have fewer right-angle corners.

1991 The drivers preferred the new layout, although the American public weren't aware of it or anything else that happened during the meeting again. Senna (McLaren), pole, beat Prost (Ferrari) by 16.3 seconds. Mika Häkkinen, looking almost a teenager, made an assured debut, putting his Lotus on the seventh row. Fastest lap: Alesi (Ferrari) 95.9mph/154.4kph.

The 1991 programme. (*Courtesy Martin Hadwen, National Motor Racing Archive*)

FACTS OF THE MATTER

2.360m/3.798km circuit

Year	Winner
1989	A. Prost (McLaren)
1990	A. Senna (McLaren)
Fastest pole	G. Berger (McLaren) 1990 (95.8mph/154.2kph)
Fastest lap	G. Berger 1990 (93.3mph/150.2kph)

Monroe Street bypass, 2.312m/3.721km circuit

1991	A. Senna (McLaren)
Pole	A. Senna (102.2mph/164.5kph)
Fastest lap	J. Alesi (Ferrari) (95.9mph/154.4kph)

USA

RIVERSIDE

Location: 60 miles (100km) east of Los Angeles.
Constructed: 1957.
World Championship Grands Prix: 1.

It could only have been America, couldn't it? – and it truly was. (Courtesy Thomas Horat)

Turn 8
Turn 9
Turn 7
Start/finish
Turn 1
Turn 6
Turn 4
Turn 2
The Esses
Turn 5
Turn 3

'The dust and the sand were all over the place'

John Watson

In October 1958 a crowd of 70,000 watched what was billed as the First United States Grand Prix for sports cars, but the real Grand Prix cars in 1960 didn't attract so much interest. One source gives the crowd as 20,000.

The track, in barren desert country, was originally designed for versatility, with long and short courses and a NASCAR course. The Grand Prix cars used the long one. The track had a long, downhill straight to the horseshoe Turn 9, a lethal place where brakes were tested to the full.

In 1960 the championship had already been decided, which can't have helped ticket sales.

Turn 9 remained dangerous and in subsequent years A.J. Foyt crashed so heavily there he was assumed to be dead. The Turn was redesigned in 1969. However, Rolf Stommelen crashed fatally approaching it at an IMSA race.[1]

The circuit hosted its final race in 1989, although it has been used frequently by Hollywood for feature films and television dramas. A retail park consumed one end and, later, housing consumed the other so that nothing remains.

COCKPIT VIEW

Sir Stirling Moss, who drove a Lotus:
'To cross the Atlantic in those days you were talking 15, 16 hours and then another seven or eight hours to get to California. I suffered from a certain amount of jetlag, not terribly, but I'd normally get to the place on the Wednesday depending, obviously, on where one had been racing the week before.

'I could learn circuits pretty quickly. I would get to within half a second of my ultimate speed in probably 15 laps or so, 15 or 20. I never walked or cycled circuits to learn them. I'd go round in the hire car and stop at certain corners, get out and have a look. Obviously in a hire car you are higher up but you could still see it was as it would be in the racing car.

'There was an enormous difference between a professional and an amateur, which people nowadays forget. If Lewis Hamilton came to Goodwood for the Revival meeting, if he was driving cars he knew, he would be so much quicker than anybody else – because he is a professional. Good amateurs do a jolly good job amongst themselves but if you took the best of them and put them against a proper professional they'd be wiped out.'

John Watson:
'I raced it in an Iroc car, which was a one-make-for-TV type meeting. I liked Riverside very much, again for a lot of reasons outside the racetrack – California! Ironically in many respects it was not dissimilar to Zandvoort, because the dust and the sand were all over the place. And of course you had Linda Vaughn as well and her twin peaks were probably the highest things on the racetrack.

'It was a pit straight, a quick left flat out, down to a sequence of four or five lefts and rights. It was about finding the rhythm because rhythm is everything in motor racing. Then you ended up in a hairpin bend. It was one of those racetracks that gave you a level of satisfaction and fulfilment even in an Iroc car that many other circuits didn't provide.'

EYEWITNESS

Dick Hyland, *Los Angeles Times*:
'Riverside – A 25-lap Formula Jr race is scheduled to start at 11:30 am today on the 3.275-mile Riverside Raceway circuit.

'This event, exciting enough itself, should but whet the appetites of road racing fans for the Formula One class 75-lap Grand Prix of the United States scheduled to start at 2 pm Sunday.

'Both races are loaded with star drivers. Headlining today's small bore race is Billy Krause, winner of the recent Times-Mirror Grand Prix for Sports Cars. He will find worthy competition for his Lotus from Walt Hansgen, eastern SCCA champion, in a Cooper; Ken Miles, driving a Dolphin; Texan Jim Hall in another Lotus; Arizonan Bob Devlin in a Stanguellini and Briggs Cunningham in a Cooper.

'Following today's race the Formula One cars and drivers will do their final qualifying for Sunday's big Grand Prix and the 25 starting positions.

'The favorites in the 230-lap US Grand Prix include England's Stirling Moss (Lotus), Australia's Jack Brabham and New Zealand's Bruce McLaren (Coopers), and Dan Gurney (BRM).

'Moss again smashed the track record Friday, bombing his Lotus around the tricky course in 1:34.6. On Thursday Moss cracked Gurney's mark of 2:00.9 with a time of 1:54.9, hitting top speeds of approximately 180 mph.'

MILESTONES AND MEMORIES

1960 Stirling Moss (Lotus) took pole. Brabham put his Cooper on the front row and wouldn't forget what happened next, principally because (see Sebring) the year before he'd run out of fuel. Now his car was over-filled to make sure it didn't happen again. Brabham took the lead and held it to lap 4 but in the hot weather fuel was coming out across the engine and his Cooper burst into flames. He got it to the pits – by then the fire had gone out – and naturally he went out again. He finished fourth. Moss took what he'd describe as a comfortable win, beating Innes Ireland (Lotus) by 38.0 seconds.

Footnote
[1] IMSA, the International Motor Sports Association.

The *Los Angeles Times* wasn't quite sure what to make of the Grand Prix.

Pete Lovely leads Bruce McLaren, both Coopers. (*Courtesy Thomas Horat*)

FACTS OF THE MATTER

3.275m/5.271km circuit

Year	Winner
1960	S. Moss (Lotus)
Pole	S. Moss (103.1mph/165.9kph)
Fastest lap	J. Brabham (Cooper) (101.4mph/163.1kph)

![USA flag] **USA**

SEBRING

Location: 4 miles (6km) south-east of Sebring.
Constructed: 1950.
World Championship Grands Prix: 1.

Jack Brabham (Cooper) leads Bruce McLaren (also Cooper) past the semi-submerged tyres which weren't easy to see. (LAT)

'It was completely without boundaries'

Stirling Moss

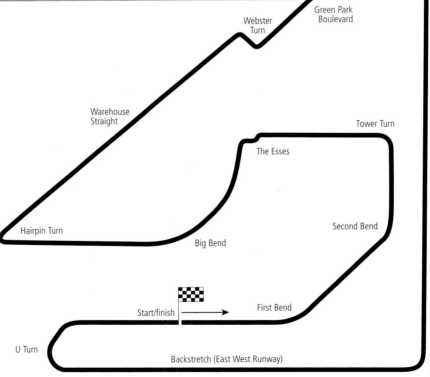

Sebring was, from 1941 to 1946, a United States Army Air Force training centre. Then a man called Alec Ulmann started to find civilian uses for such sites. Ulmann was 'Russian-born, son of St Petersburg's public utility plant director. In 1908 he was taken by the family to Moscow to see Victor Hemery win the St Petersburg Moscow road race in the mighty Benz later taken to Savannah for the first Grand Prize. Ulmann's family fetched up in America following the Revolution, and between the wars he took a post

with the Goodyear Tire & Rubber Co, was assigned to Europe and became steeped in motor racing. He was a member of the Automobile Racing Club of America which kept an amateur road-racing spark alive in the thirties, and in 1950 he founded what became the Sebring 12-Hours endurance classic run on the runways and perimeter track of Hendrick Field airbase in Florida.'

The 12-Hours, first run in 1952, grew into a major event.

'Ulmann's work at Sebring, which depended for its success upon

attracting the professional teams of Ferrari, Maserati, Aston Martin, Jaguar and Porsche from Europe, clashed with the parochial outlook of Sports Car Club of America road-racing amateurism, but in 1959 it was Ulmann who brought the first-ever Championship Grand Prix race to the United States, and revived a spirit dead since the last truly international Grand Prize of 1911.'[1]

For the Grand Prix, the crowd was small, the costs of staging the race high, and the Grand Prix didn't ever go back.

COCKPIT VIEW

Sir Stirling Moss, who drove a Cooper:
'Sebring was actually a difficult circuit in as much as that it was completely without boundaries. You could go down *Warehouse Straight* and it was a runway. An aeroplane might come down to land, not literally beside you but a little way over. The runways were enormously wide, overgrown with grass and you couldn't really see much. And don't forget the sports cars raced at night as well – a 12-hour race.

'The trouble with the sports cars was because it was a wide open area it hadn't got much character. You had to learn where to brake because it wasn't just a nice little track. You could go way out if you wanted to because the runways were probably a hundred yards wide.

'You see the esses. That made me laugh. We arrived there the first year and they said 'look, it's a no-overtaking zone. It's dangerous there.' We said 'what are you talking about?' Of course they couldn't do that because it was an FIA race.

'I'll tell you an interesting thing. It got quite hot and I was driving the OSCA, which I did quite a lot of 12-hours in. I was hot and I saw, I think, the photographer Bernard Cahier who was taking pictures at The Hairpin. I made a sign for *hot* and next time he held up a Coke bottle. I said yes and the next time I grabbed the Coke bottle, drank it and the lap after that gave it back to him.

'I remember in the Grand Prix a very, very nice American driver, Roger Ward, who was entered in a Midget – a Midget against Formula 1 cars was ridiculous! In a Formula 1 car you had quite a lot of speed going round Riverside and it wasn't very interesting – in fact a very boring

circuit. There was no character to it and the surface was bad.

'The Americans aren't really Formula 1 people. It was nice to be there because they are nice people and nice weather but the circuit – that was in the middle of nowhere.

'I won a 12-hours and one of the prizes was a homestead lot about 15, 20 miles up the road. I had this since 1953. In the 1970s – or it even might have been the 1980s! – I thought I'd better go and see it. Every year I'd paid about $100 tax on this piece of land, which I had never seen. We went and there was this place in the middle of nothing. They said if I was prepared to build they would give me a lot of the golf course. I said to my wife Susie what do we do? In the end I managed to find someone who bought it for 900 bucks but I'd spent a fortune at $100 a year. If they'd struck oil on it…'

EYEWITNESS

Gregor Grant, *Autosport*:
'There was plenty of excitement when [Harry] Schell found himself relegated to row four. He protested vociferously that he had done a 3 mins 0.5.2 secs, and he was going to get in his rightful place on the front row.

'After much bickering, the timekeepers admitted their error. Harry pushed his car jubilantly alongside Brabham's and Brooks's [Ferrari] was moved back.

'The fun then started again, and as the girls of the Sebring band and the majorettes tried to get into line, they were swept aside by an angry bunch of gesticulating Italians, with Tavoni[2] almost doing his nut. Arguments raged to and fro, with Alec Ulmann, Bill Smith and Reggie Smith doing their best to restore order.

'It looked exactly like a free-fight in a Glasgow dockside pub – and even noisier. Then the majorettes started up the band and the girls stamped their shapely legs. As if by magic the jostling and shoving ceased, although Tavoni and Co. shuffled off with black looks for Harry Schell, and both Moss and Brabham were trying unsuccessfully to keep their faces straight.'

MILESTONES AND MEMORIES

1959 Stirling Moss (Cooper) took pole for one of the most dramatic Championship-deciding races ever run. The track's edges were marked out by rubber pylons, whatever they were, and semi-submerged tyres which weren't necessarily easy to see. Jack Brabham found it a dull expanse of the flat and featureless. On this, he led from lap 6 to 41, when he felt the car go on to two cylinders. He kept on until it ran out of fuel, got out and pushed. Once he'd got it over the line – fourth, but enough for the Championship, he collapsed and had to be revived with Coca-Cola. Bruce McLaren (Cooper) beat Maurice Trintignant (also Cooper) by 0.9 of a second.

Footnotes
[1] *The United States Grand Prix*, Nye. [2] Romolo Tavoni, Ferrari team manager.

FACTS OF THE MATTER

5.200m/8.369km circuit

Year	Winner
1959	B. McLaren (Cooper)
Pole	S. Moss (Cooper)
	(104.0mph/167.4kph)
Fastest lap	M. Trintignant (Cooper)
	(101.2mph/162.8kph)

USA
WATKINS GLEN

Location: 18 miles (30km) from Elmira, New York State.
Constructed: 1956.
World Championship Grands Prix: 20.

'It gave you a real feeling of what driving a Grand Prix car was about'

John Watson

Brian Henton (Lotus) and Clay Regazzoni (Ferrari) duelling. (Courtesy Bill Wagenblatt)

Turn 4

Wedgewood/Front Straight

The Loop

The Esses

The Fast/Back Straight

The Dip/Chute

Turn 2

Turn 3

Turn 9

Turn 6

Turn 10

Original Startline until 1971

Turn 7

Turn 11

Turn 8

The Anvil

Big/Fast Bend

The Speed Trap

The Hard Right/The 90°

Start/finish

The Grand Prix circuit, which was to become the nearest thing to a permanent home that Formula 1 would find in the United States, was in fact the third circuit. The original, much longer, was on roads near the shores of Lake Seneca to the north and a hilltop course on the site, which became the circuit followed in the mid-1950s.

The third circuit was designed by Bill Milliken, a legendary figure involved in automotive engineering and fighter planes, with the help of technicians at Cornell University. 'The result was a magnificent 2.3-mile track which wound its way around a wooded hilltop.'[1]

Sebring and Riverside had not been financial successes, bringing the race to Watkins Glen.

During the 1969 race Graham Hill (Lotus) crashed. It would have profound and long-lasting consequences for the whole of Formula 1. He was on experimental tyres and the right-hand rear gave way. He went off into a bank and rolled several times before coming to rest upside down.

Professor Sid Watkins, to become Formula 1's own doctor, was working in the United States and officiated at the Glen with a team of specialist medical volunteers he'd put together. He'd remember that 'ambulances were sometimes a problem, particularly at Watkins Glen. One year they did not want to come as they had not been paid for the previous year! When the roads are crowded with race traffic it is difficult for them to make progress and certainly they are not a fast form of transport. I remember Carlos Reutemann complaining after his accident in Spain in 1978 that the

The pits in 1969, rustic and rudimentary.
(Courtesy Fred Lewis)

ambulance taking him to the hospital was very slow and, in addition, stopped at all the traffic lights! At Watkins Glen in 1969, the ambulance taking Graham Hill took to the field to get round the traffic, got lost, and finally went to a hospital that did not expect any business. Eventually he had to be taken on to Corning, a further 20 miles away.'[2]

In time, Watkins would set up a highly professional and sophisticated medical system for each race, and it was incidents like Hill's that showed him the necessity.

After the crash, too, the track was extensively reconfigured.

'For many drivers the revised version was much better than the original. The circuit had been resurfaced and widened and the pits moved. But there was also an extra 1.1-mile section of track – which took

the length out to 3.3 miles – which added an extra four corners. This new section dived down through the trees into a curling downhill left-hand turn which took the cars along the edge of the hillside until they reached a right-hander which led the circuit back up the old track – over an exciting blind brow.'[3]

Watkins Glen would know the death of two drivers, and the circuit declined in the 1970s. The area known as The Bog, where vehicles were burnt, was not the kind of symbol Formula 1 wanted, the facilities – including lack of hotels – didn't help, and Grand Prix racing moved away after 1980, to be replaced by stock cars, CART, NASCAR and, in 2005, the IRL (Indy Racing League).

COCKPIT VIEW

John Watson, who drove nine Grands Prix there:

'The first time I went there, July 1973, I thought it was one of the best racetracks I have ever raced on. I still believe it to this day. Of all the ones I have been on, in Formula 1 and in other forms of motor racing, I put it in my top six without hesitation.

'I was first in a Gulf Mirage in a six-hour sports car race but what was more relevant was going back there in the late

autumn of 1973 as part of the Brabham team. I was the driver in the third car.[4]

It was the circuit layout, the location, the atmosphere, the whole deal of upper New York State, including places with names like Ithaca, Elmira, and Syracuse.[5]

'For the Formula 1 cars being raced there it was the perfect track. I say that because of the nature and speed of the corners. There was a good straight and very quick uphill esses, which, of course, were very difficult and potentially very dangerous – as, tragically, we found out

with François Cevert [see 'Milestones and Memories', 1973].

The layout fulfilled the balance of what a circuit should provide in terms of buzz and in terms of the performance of the cars we had, the horsepower we had, and the levels of grip that we had.

'The last time I raced there in a Formula 1 car was 1980, at the point where ground effects were just about at their peak. That changed the whole dynamic of the circuit. For example, the final two Turns – 10 and 11 – were

(Courtesy Linda Carlson)

The infamous Bog, and a glance will tell you why it was called that.

(Courtesy David Corbishley)

corners where in 1973 [Brabham designer] Gordon Murray went to watch how Reutemann, Pace and myself were getting on. You needed the ability to "float" the car through and that gave you a real feeling of what driving a Grand Prix car, or what being a Grand Prix driver, was about.

'They were quick corners in those cars but the cars of today would be far too quick for the circuit and safety as it currently stands. I went back there recently and, other than the chicane at the end of the main straight, the place is fundamentally unchanged.

'The irony of Watkins Glen is that it is one of a number of outstanding tracks in America which is a country that doesn't have the history and heritage of Formula 1.'

EYEWITNESS

Linda Carlson, resident of New York State:

'I attended my first Grand Prix at Watkins Glen in October of 1968, having spent weeks beforehand convincing my parents it would make an interesting family outing. At the time the drive from our home was about three hours. My mother and seven-year-old sister were in it only for the fall foliage and I believe they spent most of the race sitting in the car, out of the cold. I stood, with my dad and two younger brothers, through the entire race, by the spectator fencing along the uphill section later known as the Esses – my first chance to see Grand Prix cars in action, in person, and I was hooked for life. I never missed another Grand Prix at

the Glen, right up to the last in 1980.

'In the years that followed I had the chance to walk the track on a number of occasions and, once, even bicycled around it with my husband, Gary, who, luckily came to share my enthusiasm for Grand Prix racing. This was usually accomplished in the spring on a day when the circuit was largely deserted. It was possible then to simply drive on to the grounds, even into the pits, although driving the track itself wasn't possible due to the barricades placed around it.

'We attended other races at various venues over the years but Watkins Glen held a special place for us and the autumn Grand Prix weekend was the highlight of our year. When we turned off of Route 414 to travel up Bronson Hill Road,

(Courtesy Linda Carlson)

The grandstand.

(Courtesy David Corbishley)

running along beside the western edge of the circuit, I'd strain for the first glimpse of that iconic blue Armco barrier snaking in and out of woods and fields. There was almost a sense of "coming home", and seeing the blue Armco meant we were finally there once again.

'At some point during the Grand Prix weekend, usually on Friday morning of the first practice session, I'd be standing on the pit roof letting the sights and sounds, the color and excitement wash over me. And then would come the sudden beautiful knowledge that I was, at that moment in time and space, *exactly* where I wanted to be. "Here and nowhere else." It was, for a girl who was toiling daily in an insurance firm's accounting office, a heady feeling.

'The Bog started out as a big muddy hole located outside the circuit between turns 10 and 11. Various vehicles were sent through the mud and those that failed were sometimes set on fire. At first, it seemed like a harmless sideshow to the race weekend, though it did become uglier over the few years it was in existence. This was brought to a head with the infamous "Greyhound bus of the Brazilian fans" incident in 1974, which brought about the end of the place. It's now a camping area.

'We usually didn't hang out in that area, especially at night when the activities probably seemed like great fun to anybody who was really drunk or stoned but could seem alarming if you were sober or even mildly inebriated. I do have a happy memory, though, of sitting around a campfire drinking cheap wine and listening to the distant roar of the bog crowd while the Goodyear blimp droned overhead displaying a colorful light show of advertisements in the night sky.

'From about 1973, I think, we started going to a section of the infield that the organisers happily called "Family Camping". In the beginning, at least, they tried to limit the campers to families and couples in an attempt (mostly successful) to keep the race-goers and party people separate.

'The first year they made a real effort to enforce the "no singles" rule. This posed a problem for a friend of ours who had driven his VW van from California to see the race. We got around it by having me walk outside the camping area to meet him at a designated time and

place. I climbed into the passenger seat and rode in with him as his "significant other", allowing him to camp next to us for the weekend.

'Watkins Glen carries such a sense of history about it. We still love the place. Some things at the circuit have been much improved since the Grand Prix days and it is, if anything, more beautiful than ever. We still enjoy going to the Glen at least several times a year particularly for the wonderful Historic and Vintage weekends in June and September.'

MILESTONES AND MEMORIES

1961 Jack Brabham (Cooper) took pole. Because Phil Hill had won the World Championship at Monza – the race before – Ferrari didn't go, so Hill, an American of course, was made Honorary Chief Marshal. Innes Ireland (Lotus) beat American Dan Gurney (Porsche) by 4.3 seconds. Just as important, the race made a profit and that guaranteed it would be back. Fastest lap: Brabham 105.9mph/170.4kph.

1962 The season developed into a struggle between Jim Clark in the Lotus and Graham Hill in the BRM. Hill had 37 points (36 counting) and Clark 21 (all counting). The Glen and South Africa remained. Clark, pole, led, was baulked by backmarkers, and that let Hill through. He led from 12 to 18 but Clark caught and passed him, winning by 9.2 seconds. Hill left with 43 points (39 counting) and Clark 30. He'd have to wait another year for the Championship. Fastest lap: Clark 110.4mph (-4.5)/177.7kph (+7.3).

1963 Clark came as Champion – he'd won it at Monza the race before. He was on the front row (Hill, BRM, pole) but had a flat battery and completed the opening lap last. By the end he was third: one of his best and least remembered drives. Graham Hill beat BRM team-mate Richie Ginther by 34.3 seconds. Fastest lap: Clark 111.1mph (+0.7)/178.9kph (+1.2).

1964 A three-way Championship between John Surtees (Ferrari), Hill (BRM), and Clark (Lotus). Clark, pole, led but had a fuel pump problem, Hill now leading. Surtees would remember: 'Graham began to consolidate first place … I knew that if I was to have a hope of winning, I would have to hang on in his slipstream for a big go on the last lap. As it happened, things didn't turn out this

way. Trying to stay with the BRM as we cut our way through traffic, I missed a gear and went sailing off the circuit on a long right-hander at the end of the back straight. By the time I recovered, Dan had slipped past into second place, but he retired with engine trouble shortly afterwards, with the result that I was able to trail home second behind the BRM.'[6] Hill beat Surtees by 30.5 seconds. Fastest lap: Clark 113.9mph (+2.8)/183.3kph (+4.6).

1965 Graham Hill arrived aiming for a hat-trick of victories, although his new BRM team-mate Jackie Stewart had just won Monza. Hill led all but three laps and Stewart dropped out when the throttle cable broke. Hill, pole, beat Dan Gurney (Brabham) by 12.5 seconds. Fastest lap: Hill 115.2mph (+1.3)/185.3kph (+2.0).

1966 Jack Brabham (Brabham) took pole and led but had an engine failure and Clark won it with a BRM engine. Jochen Rindt (Cooper) was classified second although he ran out of fuel and was deemed to be a lap down. Fastest lap: John Surtees (Cooper) 118.8mph (+3.6)/191.3kph (+6.0).

1967 Hill, pole, joined Clark at Lotus and they filled the front row, led every lap between them and finished 1-2. Clark beat Hill by 6.0 seconds. Fastest lap: Hill 125.5mph (+6.7)/201.9kph (+10.6).

1968 Another three-way Championship, now between Stewart (Matra), Denny Hulme (McLaren), and Hill (Lotus), but Mario Andretti in another Lotus took pole, the first time he'd driven in a Grand Prix meeting. All manner of technical problems slowed Andretti and Stewart led every lap, beating Hill by 24.7 seconds. Fastest lap: Stewart 127.0mph (+1.5)/204.3kph (+2.4).

1969 Although the Championship had been decided at Monza, Watkins Glen had turned such a profit in 1968 that the organisers offered a purse of $200,000 with the winner taking $50,000. They were astronomical sums then. Rindt (Lotus) took pole and won after a long duel with Stewart (Matra), who suffered an engine problem. Rindt beat Piers Courage (Brabham) by 46.9 seconds. Fastest lap: Rindt 128.7mph (+1.7)/207.1kph (+2.8).

1970 Rindt was killed at Monza and Jacky Ickx (Ferrari), pole, could overtake him to become Champion in the final three races, Canada, The Glen, and

The start, 1973. Ronnie Peterson (Lotus, pole) and Carlos Reutemann (Brabham) lead the way. (Courtesy Fred Lewis)

Arturio Merzario in the Ferrari, 1973. (Courtesy David Corbishley)

Mexico. Ickx won Canada but had a fuel feed problem at The Glen and drifted back. He recovered to be fourth, making Rindt the only posthumous Champion. Ickx was pleased. Emerson Fittipaldi (Lotus) beat Pedro Rodríguez (BRM) by 36.3 seconds. Fastest lap: Ickx 140.0mph (+3.3)/212.4kph (+5.3).

Speed increase 1961–70: 26.1mph/42.0kph.

The circuit was extended to 3.3 miles, making it in essence a sequence of loops with two 90° corners added. There were new pits, an enormous garage to store things, and better vantage points for spectators.

1971 François Cevert was far more than a Frenchman who charmed everyone he met. He was Stewart's anointed successor at Tyrrell, and although Stewart, pole, bestrode the season – he actually won the Championship in Austria in mid-August – and led the race his tyres overheated. Cevert had his first and only victory, beating Jo Siffert (BRM) by 40.0 seconds. Fastest lap: Ickx 117.5mph/189.1kph.

1972 Stewart supreme, pole, a five-second lead by lap two, leading every lap to beat Cevert by 37.4 seconds. Fastest lap: Stewart 119.6mph (+2.1)/ 192.5kph (+3.4).

1973 Stewart had won the Championship at Monza, Ronnie Peterson (Lotus) took pole at the Glen. In practice, however, Cevert's Tyrrell 'crashed violently in the uphill Esses, the car … split open by parting Armco rails', and Cevert died instantly.[7] In the race Peterson beat James Hunt (March)

by 00.6 of a second. Fastest lap: Hunt 119.6mph/192.5kph (no change).

1974 Carlos Reutemann (Brabham) took pole, the 250th Championship race, the final race of the season, and the Championship decider. Emerson Fittipaldi (McLaren) and Clay Regazzoni (Ferrari) had 52 points, Jody Scheckter (Tyrrell) 45. On lap 9 Austrian Helmut Koinigg's Surtees veered off and he suffered terrible, fatal injuries. Lauda (Ferrari) bunched the cars behind, hoping Regazzoni, in the midst of them, could get through – but Regazzoni had suspension problems and Fittipaldi drove prudently to the championship, fourth. Carlos Reutemann (Brabham) beat team-mate Carlos Pace by 10.7 seconds. Fastest lap: Pace 120.8mph (+1.2) /194.5kph (+2.0).

1975 Lauda, the third youngest

Champion when he won it at Monza, took pole and led all 59 laps to beat Fittipaldi (McLaren) by 4.9 seconds. Fastest lap: Fittipaldi 117.6mph (-3.2)/189.3kph (-5.2).

1976 Swirling mist and heavy, incessant rain destroyed the Saturday session so Hunt (McLaren) had pole from the Friday and won, beating Scheckter (Tyrrell) by 8.0 seconds – Hunt's rival Lauda third. It took the Championship to the final race, in Japan. Fastest lap: Hunt 118.2mph (+0.6)/190.2kph (+0.9).

1977 A wet race and Lauda (Ferrari) needed a single point to take the

The start in 1977 and James Hunt (McLaren) leads the pack away while Carlos Reutemann (Ferrari, 12) makes a run up the side. (Courtesy Bill Wagenblatt)

FACTS OF THE MATTER

2.300m/3.701km circuit

Year	Winner
1961	I. Ireland (Lotus)
1962	J. Clark (Lotus)
1963	G. Hill (BRM)
1964	G. Hill (BRM)
1965	G. Hill (BRM)
1966	J. Clark (Lotus)
1967	J. Clark (Lotus)
1968	J. Stewart (Matra)
1969	J. Rindt (Lotus)
1970	E. Fittipaldi (Lotus)
Fastest pole	J. Ickx (Ferrari) 1970 (131.3mph/211.3kph)
Fastest lap	J. Ickx (Ferrari) 1970 (140.0mph/212.4kph)

Revised, including The Anvil, 3.377m/5.435km circuit

Year	Winner
1971	F. Cevert (Tyrrell)
1972	J. Stewart (Tyrrell)
1973	R. Peterson (Lotus)
1974	C. Reutemann (Brabham)
1975	N. Lauda (Ferrari)
1976	J. Hunt (McLaren)
1977	J. Hunt (McLaren)
1978	C. Reutemann (Ferrari)
1979	G. Villeneuve (Ferrari)
1980	A. Jones (Williams)
Fastest pole	B. Giacomelli (Alfa Romeo) 1980 (130.3mph/209.7kph)
Fastest lap	A. Jones (Williams) 1980 (129.2mph/208.0kph)

Championship (with Canada and Japan to spare). Fourth place did him nicely. Hunt (McLaren), pole, beat Andretti (Lotus) by 2.0 seconds. Fastest lap: Peterson (Tyrrell) 108.7mph/174.9kph (no comparison).

1978 Andretti (Lotus), pole, had taken the Championship at Monza, but team-mate Ronnie Peterson died and Riccardo Patrese (Arrows) was widely blamed. Some leading drivers said they would not go to The Glen unless Patrese's entry was refused, which eventually it was. Reutemann (Ferrari) dominated the race after Andretti led the first two laps – he had an engine problem – and beat Alan Jones (Williams) by 19.7 seconds. Fastest lap: Jean-Pierre Jarier (Lotus) 122.1mph (+3.9)/196.5kph (+6.3).

1979 Jones (Williams) took pole. Heavy rain on the Friday and only eight drivers ventured out, two so briefly that they didn't record times. Gilles Villeneuve in the Ferrari did and, through the spray, gave a joyous, audacious, intoxicating performance lap after lap at the limit. His best time, 2m 01s was *ten seconds* faster than team-mate Scheckter (2m

The 1977 race was very wet. This is Brett Lunger in the McLaren on his way to tenth position. (Courtesy Bill Wagenblatt)

11s). Villeneuve led every lap (except a pit stop) to beat René Arnoux (Renault) by 48.7 seconds. Fastest lap: Nelson Piquet (Brabham) 121.5mph (-0.6)/195.5kph (-1.0).

1980 Bruno Giacomelli (Alfa Romeo) took pole. Jones (Williams) had taken the Championship in Canada, the race before, and now only qualified fifth. Those who thought Jones might decide to be uncompetitive did not know Jones. He took 32 laps to get into the lead (from Giacomelli) and didn't lose it, beating Reutemann (Williams) by 4.2 seconds. Fastest lap: Jones 129.2mph (+7.7)/208.0kph (+12.5).

Speed increase 1971–80: 11.7mph/18.9kph.

Footnotes

[1] www.grandprix.com/gpe/cir-074.html. [2] *Life at the Limit*, Watkins. [3] www.grandprix.com/gpe/cir-074.html. [4] Unusually (for a Grand Prix team) Brabham fielded three cars, for Reutemann, Wilson Fittipaldi, and Watson.

[5] American place names have a potency, almost a mysterious, quality about them – so potent they lend themselves to words and music in a way unthinkable in Britain (think of *Twenty Four Hours from Tulsa/I Left My Heart In San Francisco/New York, New York/Oklahoma!* etc against *Alice in Sunderland* and *Stars Fell on Stockton* by the Shadows and you get the idea). [6] *World Champion*, Surtees. [7] *The United States Grand Prix*, Nye.

The Americans weren't shy about making their feelings known. *(Courtesy Linda Carlson)*

Paul Newman, VIP guest and a man who knew what he was watching. *(Courtesy David Corbishley)*

THE RECORDS

THE TOTALS

Seasons	60 (to the end of 2009)
Races	820
	(including 11 at Indianapolis 500)
Venues	66
Host countries	28
Laps 1950–2009	54,431.6
	(including 2,138 at Indianapolis 500)
Distance (miles/km)	166,400.0m/267,738.0km
	(including 5,346.1m/8,601.9km at
	Indianapolis 500)

THE 28 COUNTRIES

Argentina	Great Britain	Singapore
Australia	Hungary	South Africa
Austria	Italy	Spain
Bahrain	Japan	Sweden
Belgium	Malaysia	Switzerland
Brazil	Mexico	Turkey
Canada	Monaco	United Arab
China	Morocco	Emirates
France	Netherlands	United States of
Germany	Portugal	America

THE 66 CIRCUITS

Circuit	Country	Races	Years
A1 Ring/ Österreichring	Austria	25	1970–3
Adelaide	Australia	11	1985–95
Aida/Ti	Japan	2	1994–5
Âin-Diab	Morocco	1	1958
Aintree	Great Britain	5	1955–62
Anderstorp	Sweden	6	1973–8
Avus	Germany	1	1959
Brands Hatch	Great Britain	14	1964–86
Bremgarten	Switzerland	5	1950–4
Buenos Aires	Argentina	20	1953–98
Bugatti au Mans	France	1	1967
Clermont-Ferrand	France	4	1965–72
Dallas	USA	1	1984
Detroit	USA	7	1982–8
Dijon-Prenois	France	6	1974–84
Donington Park	Great Britain	1	1993
East London	South Africa	3	1962–5
Estoril	Portugal	13	1984–96
Fuji	Japan	4	1976–2008
Hockenheim	Germany	31	1970–2008
Hungaroring	Hungary	24	1986–2009
Imola	Italy	27	1980–2006
Indianapolis	USA	19	1950–2007
Interlagos	Brazil	27	1973–2009
Istanbul	Turkey	5	2005–9
Jarama	Spain	9	1968–81
Jerez de la Frontera	Spain	7	1986–97
Kyalami	South Africa	20	1967–93
Las Vegas	USA	2	1981–2
Long Beach	USA	8	1976–83
Magny-Cours	France	18	1991–2008
Melbourne	Australia	14	1996–2009
Mexico City	Mexico	15	1963–92
Monsanto Park	Portugal	1	1959
Monte Carlo	Monaco	56	1950–2009
Montjuïc	Spain	4	1969–75
Montmeló	Spain	19	1991–2009
Montréal	Canada	30	1978–2008
Mont-Tremblant	Canada	2	1968–70
Monza	Italy	59	1950–2009
Mosport Park	Canada	8	1967–77
Nivelles-Baulers	Belgium	2	1972–4
Nürburgring	Germany	38	1951–2009
Paul Ricard	France	14	1971–90
Pedralbes	Spain	2	1951–4
Pescara	Italy	1	1957
Phoenix	USA	3	1989–91
Porto	Portugal	2	1958–60
Reims/Reims-Gueux	France	11	1950–66
Rio de Janeiro	Brazil	10	1978–89
Riverside	USA	1	1960
Rouen-les-Essarts	France	5	1952–68
Sakhir	Bahrain	6	2004–9
Sebring	USA	1	1959
Sepang	Malaysia	11	1999–2009
Shanghai	China	6	2004–9
Silverstone	Great Britain	43	1950–2009
Singapore	Singapore	2	2008–9
Spa-Francorchamps	Belgium	42	1950–2009
Suzuka	Japan	21	1987–2009
Valencia	Spain	2	2008–9
Watkins Glen	USA	20	1961–80
Yas Marina, Abu Dhabi	United Arab Emirates	1	2009
Zandvoort	Netherlands	30	1952–85
Zeltweg	Austria	1	1964
Zolder	Belgium	10	1973–84

CIRCUIT LENGTH

Longest	km	miles
Pescara 1957	25.579	15.894
Nürburgring 1967–76	22.835	14.189
Nürburgring 1951–66	22.810	14.173
Spa 1950–56	14.120	8.774
Spa 1958–70	14.100	8.761
Monza 1955–6, 1960–1	10.000	6.214
Sebring 1959	8.369	5.200
Reims 1953	8.347	5.187
Reims 1954–66	8.302	5.159
Avus 1959	8.300	5.157

Shortest	km	miles
Monte Carlo 1955–72	3.145	1.954
Monte Carlo 1950	3.180	1.976
Zeltweg 1964	3.200	1.988
Long Beach 1976–81	3.251	2.020
Long Beach 1983	3.275	2.035
Monte Carlo 1973–5	3.278	2.037
Dijon-Prenois 1974	3.289	2.044
Jarama 1981	3.312	2.058
Monte Carlo 1976–85	3.312	2.058
Monte Carlo 1986–96	3.328	2.068

MOST RACES BY COUNTRY

Italy	87 (a)	Hungary	24	
Germany	70 (b)	South Africa	23	
Great Britain	63 (c)	Argentina	20	
United States	62 (d)	Portugal	16	
France	59 (e)	Mexico	15	
Monaco	56	Malaysia	11	
Belgium	54	Bahrain	6	
Spain	43 (f)	China	6	
Canada	40	Sweden	6	
Brazil	37	Switzerland	5	
Netherlands	30	Turkey	5	
Japan	27 (g)	Singapore	2	
Austria	26	Morocco	1	
Australia	25	United Arab Emirates	1	(h)

Notes
(a) includes 1 Pescara and 26 San Marino GPs.
(b) includes 12 European and 2 Luxembourg GPs.
(c) includes 3 European GPs.
(d) includes 11 Indianapolis 500 races.
(e) includes 1 Swiss GP.
(f) includes 4 European GPs.
(g) includes 2 Pacific GPs.
(h) known as the Abu Dhabi Grand Prix.

The only countries to produce a race-winning driver and yet never host a Grand Prix are Colombia, Finland, Poland, and New Zealand. Interestingly, Finland, with a population of 5.3 million, has produced three World Champions (Keke Rosberg, Mika Häkkinen and Kimi Räikkönen), while France, with a population of 62 million, has produced one, Alain Prost.

MOST RACES

Monza	59	Jerez de la Frontera	7
Monte Carlo	56	Anderstorp	6
Silverstone	43	Dijon-Prenois	6
Spa-Francorchamps	42	Sakhir	6
Nürburgring	38	Shanghai	6
Hockenheim	31	Aintree	5
Montréal	30	Bremgarten	5
Zandvoort	30	Istanbul	5
Imola	27	Rouen-les-Essarts	5
Interlagos	27	Clermont-Ferrand	4
A1-Ring/Ö-Ring	25	Fuji	4
Hungaroring	24	Montjuïc	4
Suzuka	21	East London	3
Buenos Aires	20	Phoenix	3
Kyalami	20	Aida/Ti	2
Watkins Glen	20	Las Vegas	2
Indianapolis	19	Mont-Tremblant	2
Montmeló	19	Nivelles-Baulers	2
Magny-Cours	18	Pedralbes	2
Mexico City	15	Porto	2
Brands Hatch	14	Singapore	2
Melbourne	14	Valencia	2
Paul Ricard	14	Âin-Diab	1
Estoril	13	Avus	1
Adelaide	11	Bugatti au Mans	1
Reims	11	Dallas	1
Sepang	11	Donington Park	1
Rio de Janeiro	10	Monsanto Park	1
Zolder	10	Pescara	1
Jarama	9	Riverside	1
Long Beach	8	Sebring	1
Mosport Park	8	Yas Marina, Abu Dhabi	1
Detroit	7	Zeltweg	1

OPENING VENUE (most races at)

Buenos Aires	15	1953–80
Melbourne	13	1996–2009
Kyalami	8	1967–93
Rio de Janeiro	7	1983–9
Monte Carlo	5	1959–66

CLOSING VENUE (most races at)

Adelaide	11	1985–95
Watkins Glen	8	1961–80
Mexico City	7	1964–70
Monza	6	1950–7
Suzuka	6	1996–2003

CIRCUITS WHICH HAVE MOVED THEIR STARTLINE

Kyalami	Monte Carlo	Montréal
Silverstone	Spa-Francorchamps	Watkins Glen

RACE LENGTH
(duration)
Longest

German GP 1954	3h 45m 45.800s
German GP 1956	3h 38m 43.700s
German GP 1957	3h 30m 38.300s
German GP 1951	3h 23m 03.300s
French GP 1951	3h 22m 11.000s
Spanish GP 1954	3h 13m 52.100s
Monte Carlo GP 1950	3h 13m 18.700s
Monte Carlo GP 1957	3h 10m 12.800s
French GP 1957	3h 07m 46.400s
British GP 1955	3h 07m 21.200s

Shortest (all shortened races)

Australian GP 1991	24m 34.899s
Spanish GP 1957	42m 53.700s
Malaysian GP 2009	55m 30.622s
Austrian GP 1975	57m 56.690s
Monte Carlo GP 1984	1h 01m 07.740s
Italian GP 1978	1h 07m 04.540s
Belgian GP 2001	1h 08m 05.002s
Italian GP 2003	1h 14m 19.838s
Italian GP 2005	1h 14m 28.659s
Italian GP 1987	1h 14m 47.707s

The shortest full-distance race was Italy 2003 at 1h 14m 19.838s

RACE LENGTH
(distance)

Longest	km	miles
French GP 1951	601.832	373.961
Belgian GP 1951–6	508.320	315.855
Belgian GP 1960	507.600	315.408
French GP 1954–6	506.422	314.676
Spanish GP 1954	505.280	313.966
Italian GP 1950–4	504.000	313.171
French GP 1957	503.734	313.006
German GP 1954–7	501.820	311.816
French GP 1953	500.820	311.195
Italian GP 1957	500.250	310.841

Shortest	km	miles
Australian GP 1991	52.920	32.883
Monte Carlo GP 1984	102.672	63.797
Spanish GP 1975	109.939	68.313
Austrian GP 1975	171.419	106.515
Malaysian GP 2009	171.833	106.772
Monte Carlo GP 1997	208.692	129.675
Belgian GP 1981	230.148	143.007
Italian GP 1978	232.000	144.158
Brazilian GP 2003	232.656	144.566
Canadian GP 1997	238.734	148.342

Each of the 60 race tracks made their own, unique contribution to Grand Prix history. Paul Ricard did this fourteen times between 1971 and 1990. (LAT).

LAPS IN A RACE
Most

US GP 1963–5	110
US GP 1966–70	108
Monte Carlo GP 1957	105
Austrian GP 1964	105
British GP 1956	101
Argentinean GP 1957	100
Monte Carlo 1950–6, 1958–67	100
Dutch GP 1955	100
US GP 1961–2	100
Argentinean GP 1956	98

Least

German GP 1971	12
German GP 1968–9, 1972–6	14
Australian GP 1991	14
German GP 1958, 1961–7	15
German GP 1952–3	18
Italian GP (Pescara) 1957	18
German GP 1951	20
German GP 1954–7	22
Belgian GP 1958	24
Belgian GP 1966–70	28

LAPS RACED IN A SEASON

Most		Least	
2005	1,180	1950	391
2006	1,137	1951	415
1977	1,132	1952	447
1995	1,124	1956	468
2004	1,122	1955	472
2008	1,117	1961	490
2002	1,090	1957	499
2000	1,074	1954	522
2001	1,065	1953	536
2007	1,065	1959	536

Figures exclude Indianapolis.

CIRCUIT ADDRESSES

ARGENTINA
BUENOS AIRES
Address: Autódromo de la Ciudad de Buenos Aires, Av General Paz y Av General Coronel Roca,
C1439DWS,
Ciudad Autónoma de Buenos Aires,
Argentina.
Telephone: (0054) 4605 3333.
Website: www.autodromoba.com.ar

AUSTRALIA
ADELAIDE
Adelaide city centre.

MELBOURNE
Address: Australian Grand Prix Corporation, Grand Prix House,
220 Albert Road,
South Melbourne, Victoria 3205,
Australia.
Telephone: (0061) 3 9258 7100.
Fax (0061) 3 9682 0410.
Email: enquiries@grandprix.com.au
Website: www.grandprix.com.au

AUSTRIA
A1-RING (formerly Österreichring)
Address: A1-Ring,
8724 Speilberg,
Austria.
Telephone: (0043) 3577 7530.
Fax: (0043) 3577 753107.
Website: www.a1ring.at

ZELTWEG
4 miles (6km) from Knittlefeld.

BAHRAIN
SAKHIR
Address: Gate 255, Gulf of Bahrain Ave, Umm Jidar 1062, Sakhir,
Kingdom of Bahrain
(postal address: Bahrain International Circuit, PO Box 26381, Sakhir,
Kingdom of Bahrain).
Telephone: (00973) 17450000.
Fax: (00973) 17451111.
Website: www.bahraingp.com

BELGIUM
NIVELLES-BAULERS
20 miles (30km) south of Brussels.

SPA-FRANCORCHAMPS
Address: Route du Circuit, 38, B-4970 Francorchamps, Belgium.
Telephone: (0032) 87 22 44 66.
Fax: (0032) 87 22 445 55.
Website: www.spa-francorchamps.be

ZOLDER
Address: Circuit Zolder, vzw Terlamen/ Terlamen asbl, Terlaemen 30, B-3550 Heusden-Zolder,
Belgium.
Telephone: (0032) 11 85 88 88.
Fax: (0032) 11 85 88 95.
Website: www.zolder.glo.be

BRAZIL
INTERLAGOS
Address: Autodromo Carlos Pace, Avenida Teotonio Vilela 267, 04801-890 São Paulo, Brazil.
Telephone: (0055) 11 5666 8822.
Fax: (0055) 21 221 4531.
Website: www.gpbrasil.com

RIO DE JANEIRO
Address: Autodromo Nelson Piquet, Ave Embaixador Abelardo Bueno, Barra 22600, Rio de Janeiro, Brazil.
Telephone: (0055) 21 24412158.
Website: www.autodromodebrasilia.com. br

CANADA
MONT-TREMBLANT
Address: Circuit Mont-Tremblant, PO Box 2610, Station B, Mont-Tremblant, Quebec, J8E 1H5, Canada.
Telephone: (001) 819 425 6363.
Fax: (001) 819 425 1195.
Email: info@lecircuit.com

MONTRÉAL
Address: Circuit Gilles-Villeneuve, Bassin Olympique,
Ile Notre-Dame Montréal (Québec),
H3C 1A0, Canada.
(For tickets: 222 Circuit Gilles-Villeneuve, Parc Jean-Drapeau, Montréal (Québec), H3C 6AI, Canada.)
Telephone: (001) 514 392 4731. (For tickets: (001) 514 397 0007.)
Fax: (001) 514 397 9666.

MOSPORT PARK
Address: Regional Road 20 East, Bowmanville, ON L1C 3K6, Canada.
Telephone: (001) 800 866 1072.
Fax: (001) 905 983 9141.
Email: info@mosport.com

CHINA
SHANGHAI
Address: Shanghai International Circuit No. 2000, Yining Rd., Jiading District, Shanghai, China 201814.
Telephone: (0086) 21 6956 9980.
Fax: (0086) 21 6956 9996.

FRANCE
BUGATTI AU MANS
At the Le Mans circuit, Le Mans.

CLERMONT-FERRAND
Address: Rue Nicolas Joseph Cugnot, ZI Brezet, 63100 Clermont-Ferrand,
France.
Telephone: (0033) 473 981681.
Website: www.charade.fr

DIJON-PRENOIS
Address: Circuit Dijon-Prenois, 21370 Prenois, France.
Telephone: (0033) 3 80 35 32 22.
Fax: (0033) 3 80 35 33 22.
Website: www.circuit-dijon-prenois.com

MAGNY-COURS
Address: Circuit de Nevers, Magny-Cours Technopole, 58470 Magny-Cours, France.
Telephone: (0033) 03 86 21 80 80.
Website: www.magnycours.com

PAUL RICARD
Address: Circuit Paul Ricard HTTT, RDN8 2760, Route des Hauts du Camp, 83 330 Le Castellet, France.
Telephone: (0033) 0 494 983 666.
Email: circuit@circuitpaulricard.com

REIMS-GUEUX
4 miles (7km) west of Reims, northern France.

ROUEN-LES-ESSARTS
7 miles (12km) south-west of Rouen, northern France.

GERMANY

AVUS
West of Berlin in woodland.

HOCKENHEIM
Address: Hockenheim-Ring GmbH, Motodrom, 68766 Hockenheim, Germany.
Telephone: (0049) 06205 950 0.
Fax: (0049) 06205 950 299.
Website: www.hockenheimring.de

NÜRBURGRING
Address: Otto-Flimm-Straße, D–53520 Nürburg, Germany.
Telephone: (0049) 2691 30 2 0.
Fax: (0049) 2691 30 2 155.
Website: www.nuerburgring.de

GREAT BRITAIN

AINTREE
6 miles (9km) from Liverpool city centre.

BRANDS HATCH
Address: Brands Hatch Circuit, Fawkham, Longfield, Kent, DA3 8NG, United Kingdom.
Telephone: (0044) 01474 872331.
Fax: (0044) 01474 874766.
Website: www.motorsportvision.co.uk

DONINGTON
Address: Donington Park Grand Prix Circuit, Donington Park, Castle Donington, Derby, DE74 2RP, United Kingdom.
Telephone: (0044) 01332 810048.
Fax: (0044) 01332 850322.
Website: www.donington-park.co.uk

SILVERSTONE
Address: Silverstone Circuit, Towcester, Northamptonshire, NN12 8TN, United Kingdom.
Telephone: (0044) 0844 3728 200.
Fax: (0044) 3278 250.
Website: www.silverstone.co.uk

HUNGARY

HUNGARORING
Address: H-2146 Mogyoród Pf. 10, Budapest, Hungary.
Telephone: (0036) 28 444 444.
Fax: (0036) 28 441 860.
Email: office@hungaroring.hu
Website: www.hungaroring.hu

ITALY

IMOLA
Address: Formula Imola SpA, via F.lli Rosselli, 2 40026 Imola, Italy.
Telephone: (0039) 0542 65511.
Fax: (0039) 0542 30420.
Email: info@autodromoimola.it

MONZA
Address: Autodromo Nazionale Monza, via Vedano 5, 20052 Monza (MI), Italy.
Telephone (0039) 039 24821.
Fax: (00 39) 039 320324
Email: infoautodromo@monzanet.it

PESCARA
North-west of the town of Pescara, Adriatic Coast.

JAPAN

AIDA
Address: TI Circuit Aida, 1210 Takimiya, Aida Cho, Aida Gun, Okayama-Ken 701-26, Japan.
Website: www.okayama-international-circuit.jp

FUJI
Address: Fuji International Speedway Co Ltd, 694 Nakahinata Oyama-Cho Sunto-Gun Shizuoka-Ken, 410-1307, Japan.

SUZUKA
Address: Mobilityland Corporation Head Office, 7992 Ino-cho, Suzuka-shi, Mie Prefecture, 510-0295, Japan.
Telephone: (0081) 059 378 1111 (main line).
Fax: (0081) 593 70 3603.

MALAYSIA

SEPANG
Address: Sepang International Circuit Sdn Bhd, Jalan Pekeliling, 64000 KLIA, Selangor Darul Ehsan, Malaysia.
Telephone: (001) 603 8778 2300.
Fax: (001) 603 8783 1000.
Email: inquiries@sepangcircuit.com.my

MEXICO

MEXICO CITY
Address: Autódromo Hermanos Rodríguez, Av Rio Churubusco S/N, Puerta 5 Int Ciudad Deportiva, Col Granjas México, Delg Iztacalco, CP 08400, México, DF.
Telephone: (0052) 5764 84 99.
Fax: (0052) 5764 84 78.
Email: ventas@autodromohermanosrodriguez.com.mx

MONACO

MONTE CARLO
Address: Automobile Club de Monaco, BP 464-23, blvd Albert Ier, MC 98012 Monaco, Principality of Monaco.
Telephone: (00377) 93 15 26 00.
Fax: (00377) 93 25 80 08.
Website: www.acm.mc

MOROCCO

ÂIN-DIAB
Western outskirts of Casablanca.

NETHERLANDS

ZANDVOORT
Address: Circuit Park Zandvoort, Burgemeester van Alphenstraat 108, 2041 KP Zandvoort, Netherlands (postal address: Circuit Park Zandvoort, Postbus 132, 2040 AC Zandvoort, Netherlands).
Telephone: (0031) 23 57 40 740.
Fax: (0031) 23 57 40 741.
Email: info@circuit-zandvoort.nl
Website: www.circuit-zandvoort.nl

PORTUGAL

ESTORIL
Address: Circuito do Estoril, Av Alfredo César Torres, Apartado 49, 2646-901 Alcabideche, Portugal.
Telephone: (00 351) 21 460 95 00.
Fax: (00 351) 21 460 23 86.
Email: dep.comercial@circuito-estoril.pt

MONSANTO PARK
3 miles (5km) west of city centre.

PORTO
Western outskirts of the city.

SINGAPORE

SINGAPORE – Central Singapore.
Telephone (0065) 6738 6738
Email: info@singaporegp.sg

SOUTH AFRICA

EAST LONDON – Cape Province, on the outskirts of East London.

KYALAMI
Address: Kyalami Grand Prix Circuit, 1 Allendale Road, Kyalami, Midrand, South Africa (postal address: Kyalami Events and Exhibitions (Pty) Ltd, PO Box 30004, Kyalami 1684, South Africa).
Telephone: (0027) 11 466 2800.
Fax: (0027) 11 466 2628.
Email: denis@kyalamiracing.co.za or celeste@kyalamiracing.co.za

SPAIN

JARAMA
17 miles (28km) from Madrid.

JEREZ DE LA FRONTERA
Address: Ctra de Arcos,
Km 10 – Aptdo Correos 1709,
Jerez,
Spain.
Telephone: (0034) 956 151 100.
Fax: (0034) 956 151 105.

MONTJUÏC PARK
West of Barcelona city centre.

MONTMELÓ (Barcelona)
Address: Circuits de Catalunya SL,
Mas 'La Moreneta',
Apartat de Correus 27,
08160 Montmeló,
Barcelona,
Spain.
Telephone: (0034) 93 5719700.
Fax: (0034) 93 5722772.
Email: tickets@circuitcat.com

PEDRALBES
North-west of Barcelona city centre.

VALENCIA
Telephone: (0044) 121 661 4961 (main
booking line).
Email: sales@valenciagrandprix.org

SWEDEN

ANDERSTORP
50 miles (80km) south of Jönköping.

SWITZERLAND

BREMGARTEN
Near Berne.

TURKEY

ISTANBUL
Address: Göçbeyli Köyü Yolu, Istanbul
Park Circuit, 34959 Tuzla, Istanbul, Turkey.
Telephone: (0090) 216 677 1010.
Fax: (0090) 216 677 1039.

UNITED ARAB EMIRATES

ABU DHABI
Yas Island on the east coast of
Abu Dhabi.

UNITED STATES OF AMERICA

DALLAS
Dallas city centre.

DETROIT
Detroit city centre.

INDIANAPOLIS
Address: 4790 West 16th Street,
Speedway, IN 46222, USA.
Telephone: (001) 317 481 8500.
Website: www.
indianapolismotorspeedway.com

*Spa provided a unique corner, Eau Rouge,
which was a panorama all by itself.*
(Peter J. Fox)

LAS VEGAS
West side of the Las Vegas 'Strip'.

LONG BEACH
Address: Grand Prix Association of Long
Beach, 3000 Pacific Avenue, Long Beach,
CA 90806, USA.
Telephone: (001) 562 981 2600.
Fax: (001) 562 981 2616.
Email: info@gpalb.com

PHOENIX
West of city centre.

RIVERSIDE
60 miles (100km) east of Los Angeles.

SEBRING
Address: Sebring International Raceway,
113 Midway Drive, Sebring, Florida
33870, USA.
Telephone: (001) 863 655 1442/(001) 800
626 RACE.
Fax: (001) 863 655 1777.
Website: www.sebringraceway.com

WATKINS GLEN
18 miles (30km) from Elmira, New
York State.

RACES AND PLACES

Abu Dhabi Grand Prix
Abu Dhabi   2009

Argentine Grand Prix
Buenos Aires   1953–58, 1960,
1972–75, 1977–81,
1995–98

Australian Grand Prix
Adelaide   1985–95
Melbourne   1996–2009

Austrian Grand Prix
A1-Ring (formerly
Osterreichring)   1970–87, 1997–2003
Zeltweg   1964

Bahrain Grand Prix
Sakhir   2004–2009

Belgian Grand Prix
Nivelles-Baulers   1972, 1974
Spa-Francorchamps 1950–1956, 1958,
1960–68, 1970, 1983,
1985–2002, 2004,
2005, 2007–09
Zolder   1973, 1975–1982,
1984

Brazilian Grand Prix
Interlagos   1973–77, 1979, 1980,
1990–2009
Rio de Janeiro   1978, 1981–89

British Grand Prix
Aintree   1955, 1957, 1959,
1961, 1962
Brands Hatch   1964, 1966, 1968,
1970, 1972, 1974,
1976, 1978, 1980,
1982, 1984, 1986
Donington   1993
Silverstone   1950–54, 1956, 1958,
1960, 1963, 1965,
1967, 1969, 1971,
1973, 1975, 1977,
1979, 1981, 1983,
1985, 1987–2009

Caesars Palace Grand Prix
Las Vegas (USA)   1981, 1982

Dallas Grand Prix
Dallas (USA)   1984

Detroit Grand Prix
Detroit (USA)   1982, 1983–88

Canadian Grand Prix
Mont-Tremblant   1968, 1970
Montréal   1978–86, 1988–2008
Mosport Park   1967, 1969, 1971–74,
1976, 1977

Chinese Grand Prix
Shanghai   2004–09

Dutch Grand Prix
Zandvoort   1952, 1953, 1955,
1958–71, 1973–85

European Grand Prix
Brands Hatch
(Great Britain)   1983, 1985
Jerez de la Frontera
(Spain)   1994, 1997
Nürburgring
(Germany)   1984, 1995, 1996,
1999–2007
Valencia (Spain)   2008, 2009

French Grand Prix
Bugatti au Mans   1967
Clermont-Ferrand   1965, 1969, 1970,
1972
Dijon-Prenois   1974, 1977, 1979,
1981, 1984
Magny-Cours   1991–2008
Paul Ricard   1971, 1973, 1975,
1976, 1978, 1980,
1982, 1983, 1985–90
Reims-Guex   1950, 1951, 1953,
1954, 1956, 1958–61,
1963, 1966
Rouen-Les-Essarts   1952, 1957, 1962,
1964, 1968

German Grand Prix
Avus   1959
Hockenheim   1970, 1977–84, 1986–
2006, 2008
Nürburgring   1951–54, 1956–58,
1961–69, 1971–76,
1985, 2009

The way it was – Reims 1950, an ordinary road and a traditional pit board for Philippe Etancelin (Lago-Talbot). He finished fifth. (LAT)

Hungarian Grand Prix
Hungaroring	1986–2009

Italian Grand Prix
Imola	1980
Monza	1950–1979, 1981–2009

Japanese Grand Prix
Fuji	1976, 1977, 2007, 2008
Suzuka	1987–2006, 2009

Luxembourg Grand Prix
Nürburgring (Germany)	1997, 1998

Malaysian Grand Prix
Sepang	1999–2009

Mexican Grand Prix
Mexico City	1963–70, 1986–92

Monaco Grand Prix
Monte Carlo	1950, 1955–2009

Moroccan Grand Prix
Âin-Diab	1957

Pacific Grand Prix
Aida (Japan)	1994, 1995

Pescara Grand Prix
Pescara (Italy)	1957

Portuguese Grand Prix
Estoril	1984–96
Monsanto Park	1959
Porto	1958, 1960

San Marino Grand Prix
Imola	1981–2006

Singapore Grand Prix
Singapore	2008, 2009

South African Grand Prix
East London	1962, 1963, 1965
Kyalami	1967–1980, 1982–85, 1992, 1993

Spanish Grand Prix
Jarama	1968, 1970, 1972, 1974, 1976–79, 1981
Jerez de la Frontera	1986–90
Montjuïc Park	1969, 1971, 1973, 1975
Montmeló (Barcelona)	1991-2009
Pedralbes	1951, 1954

The way it is – Bahrain 2009, a tailor-made track, proper kerbing and a run-off area, which would have helped Jenson Button (Brawn) if he'd needed it. He didn't. (LAT)

Swedish Grand Prix
Anderstorp	1973–78

Swiss Grand Prix
Bremgarten	1950–54
Dijon-Prenois (France)	1982

Turkish Grand Prix
Istanbul	2005–09

United States Grand Prix*
Indianapolis	2000–07
Phoenix	1989–91
Riverside	1960
Sebring	1959
Watkins Glen	1961–80*

*1976–80 races also known as United States Grand Prix East to distinguish them from United States Grand Prix West held at Long Beach.

United States Grand Prix West
Long Beach	1976–83

BIBLIOGRAPHY

Andretti, Mario. *World Champion*, Hamlyn,1979.

Bagnall, Tony. *The Unfulfilled Dream*, tfm Publishing, 2004.

Ball, Adrian (editor). *My Greatest Race*, Granada Publishing, 1974.

Beaumont, Charles, and Nolan, William F. *Omnibus of Speed*, Stanley Paul, 1961.

Besqueut, Patrice. *Charade: 'The plus beau circuit du monde'*, Editions du Palmier, 2003.

Biot, Roger. *Rouen-les-Essarts 1950–1993*, Normandie, 2001.

Brabham, Jack. *When the Flag Drops*, William Kimber, 1971.

Caracciola, Rudolf. *A Racing Driver's World*, Cassell, 1962.

Chula, Prince. *Dick Seaman: Racing Motorist*, G.T. Foulis, 1946.

Clark, Jim. *At the Wheel*, Arthur Barker, 1964.

Delsaux, Jean-Paul. *Grote Prijzen 50 van België*, Grandes épreuves, 1993.

— and Wijckmans, Koes. *30 Jaar/Ans Zolder*, Penta Groep, 1993.

Deschenaux, Jacques. *Grand Prix Guide 1950–2004*, Charles Stewart & Company, 2005.

Desmond, Kevin. *The Man with Two Shadows*, Proteus Books, 1981.

Donaldson, Gerald. *The Grand Prix of Canada*, Avon Books of Canada, 1984.

— *Villeneuve*, MRP, 1989.

— *Grand Prix People*, MRP, 1990.

Fangio, Juan Manuel. *My Twenty Years of Racing*, Temple, 1961.

— *My Racing Life*, PSL, 1986.

Fittipaldi, Emerson, and Hayward, Elizabeth. *Flying on the Ground*, William Kimber, 1973.

Frostick, Michael, and Klemantaski, Louis. *Motor Racing Circuits of Europe*, B.T. Batsford, 1958.

Gauld, Graham. *Jim Clark: The Legend Lives On*, PSL, 1989.

Hamilton, Maurice. *British Grand Prix*, The Crowood Press, 1989.

Hart, Roger. *Postcards from Detroit*, David Bull Publishing, 2006.

Hawthorn, Mike. *Champion Year*, William Kimber, 1959.

— *Challenge Me the Race*, William Kimber, 1964.

Hayhoe, David, and Holland, David. *Grand Prix Data Book*, Haynes, 2006.

Higham, Peter. *The Guinness Guide to International Motor Racing*, Guinness, 1995.

— and Jones, Bruce. *World Motor Racing Circuits*, André Deutsch, 1999.

Hill, Graham. *Life at the Limit*, Kimber, 1969.

Hilton, Christopher. *1982*, Haynes, 2007.

Hodges, David. *The French Grand Prix*, Temple, 1967.

— *The Monaco Grand Prix*, Temple, 1964.

Hunt, James. *Against All Odds*, Hamlyn, 1977.

Izco, Javier del Arco de. *Montjuïc: 40 years of Motor Racing History at the Park Circuit*, RACC Club, 2000.

Jones, Alan. *Driving Ambition*, Stanley Paul, 1981.

Klemantaski, Louis, and Frostick, Michael. *Motor Racing Circuits of Europe*, B.T. Batsford, 1958.

Lang, Mike. *Grand Prix!* (three volumes), Haynes, 1981.

Lauda, Niki. *To Hell and Back*, Stanley Paul, 1985.

Mansell, Nigel. *My Autobiography*, Collins Willow, 1995.

Montagna, Paolo. *Monza: Una Grande Storia*, Giorgio Nada Editore, 2005.

Moss, Stirling. *A Turn at the Wheel*, William Kimber, 1961.

— *My Cars, My Career*, PSL, 1987.

Nixon, Chris. *Mon Ami Mate*, Transport Bookman Publications, 1991.

— *Racing the Silver Arrows*, Osprey, 1986.

Nye, Doug. *The United States Grand Prix*, B.T. Batsford, 1978.

— *Great Moments in Sport: Motor Racing*, Pelham Books, 1976.

Posthumus, C. *The German Grand Prix*, Temple, 1966.

Prost, Alain. *Life in the Fast Lane*, Stanley Paul, 1989.

Prüller, Heinz. *Jochen Rindt*, William Kimber, 1971.

Raffaelli, Fabio e Filippo. *Magia di Imola*, Inedita, 1996.

Rutherford, Douglas. *The Chequered Flag*, Collins, 1956.

Salvadori, Roy. *Racing Driver*, PSL, 1985.

Saward, Joe. *The World Atlas of Motor Racing*, Hamlyn, 1989.

Sinibaldi, Patrick. *Circuit de Reims*, E-T-A-I, 2006.

Small, Steve. *The Grand Prix Who's Who*, Guinness, 1996.

Stewart, Jackie. *World Champion*, Pelham, 1970.

— *Faster! A Racer's Diary*, Farrar, Straus and Giroux, 1972.

Surtees, John. *World Champion*, Hazleton Publishing, 1991.

Taruffi, Piero. *Works Driver*, Temple Press Books, 1964.

Watkins, Sid. *Life at the Limit*, Macmillan, 1996.

Williams, Richard. *The Last Road Race*, Weidenfeld, 2004.

Young, Robert. *Springbok Grand Prix*, Malcolm R. Kinsey, 1969.

SUID-AFRIKAANSE
GRAND PRIX
OF SOUTH AFRICA

Firestone
RACE-BRED FOR SAFETY AND MILEAGE

FIA FORMULA 1 WORLD CHAMPIONSHIP

GRANDE PRÊMIO DO BRASIL
RIO DE JANEIRO
24 - 25 - 26 MARÇO 1989

PROGRAMA OFICIAL
NCZ$ 3,00

F-1 WORLD CHAMPIONSHIP
IN JAPAN

OCTOBER 1976

F1

F-1世界選手権インジャパン
公式プログラム
22日(金)—公式予選
23日(土)—公式予選
24日(日)
12:00—マシン入場
13:30—一次走

FIA FORMULA 1 WORLD CHAMPIONSHIP

THE STATE FAIR OF TEXAS presents THE INAUGURAL
DALLAS · GRAND · PRIX · 1984
JULY 6 · 7 · 8

Detroit Grand Prix
June 4, 5, 6 1982
FIA Formula 1 World Championship
Official Program $3.00

F1
Formula 1
中国石化 F1
中国大奖赛
2005.10.14-15-16
上海

05
世紀記念版

1969
GRAND PRIX
OF THE
UNITED STATES
$1.00   WATKINS GLEN

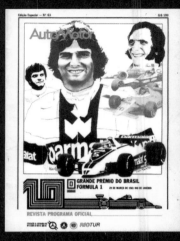

Edição Especial – Nº 63   GS 100

Autohoral

parma

GRANDE PRÊMIO DO BRASIL
FORMULA 1
29 DE MARÇO DE 1981 RIO DE JANEIRO

REVISTA PROGRAMA OFICIAL

F1
Formula 1
2007
FORMULA 1
PETROL OFISI TURKISH GRAND PRIX
ISTANBUL
24,25,26 AUGUST

LONG
BEACH
Mar. 30
1980

TOYOTA GRAND PRIX OF LONG BEACH

F1
Formula 1
PETRONAS MALAYSIAN
GRAND PRIX
KUALA-LUMPUR
15-16-17 OCTOBER 1999

MALAYSIA

29/30 MAI
34e GRAND PRIX
MONACO 76

Player's
GRAND PRIX
OF CANADA
FOR THE PLAYERS' AWARD

MOSPORT PARK
AUGUST 27, 1967
12 noon
OFFICIAL PROGRAMME 95c

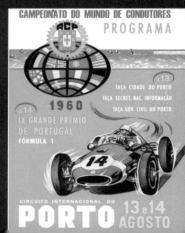

CAMPEONATO DO MUNDO DE CONDUTORES
PROGRAMA

a 13
TAÇA CIDADE DO PORTO
TAÇA SECRET. NAC. INFORMAÇÃO
a 14
TAÇA GOV. CIVIL DO PORTO

1960
IX GRANDE PRÉMIO
DE PORTUGAL
FÓRMULA 1

CIRCUITO INTERNACIONAL DO
PORTO
13 e 14
AGOSTO

GROSSER PREIS
VON DEUTSCHLAND
AvD

WELTMEISTERSCHAFTSLAUF
6. AUGUST 1967
NÜRBURGRING

AUTOMOBILCLUB VON DEUTSCHLAND
OFFIZIELLES PROGRAMM
DM 2,—

IV
British Grand Prix
Silverstone, Saturday 14th July 1951

ORGANIZED BY THE
Royal Automobile Club
Official Programme 2s.